Lecture Notes of the Institute
for Computer Sciences, Social-Informatics
and Telecommunicat 6

Chonggang Wang (Ed.)

Access Nets

Third International Conference
on Access Networks, AccessNets 2008
Las Vegas, NV, USA, October 15-17, 2008
Revised Papers

 Springer

Volume Editor

Chonggang Wang
NEC Laboratories America
4 Independence Way, Suite 200
Princeton, NJ 08540, USA
E-mail: drchongwang@gmail.com

Library of Congress Control Number: 2009934965

CR Subject Classification (1998): C.2, D.4.4, G.2.2, H.3.4, B.4.4

ISSN   1867-8211
ISBN-10   3-642-04647-9 Springer Berlin Heidelberg New York
ISBN-13   978-3-642-04647-6 Springer Berlin Heidelberg New York

© ICST Institute for Computer Science, Social Informatics and Telecommunications Engineering 2009
Printed in Germany

Typesetting: Camera-ready by author, data conversion by Scientific Publishing Services, Chennai, India
Printed on acid-free paper   SPIN: 12649587   06/3180   5 4 3 2 1 0

Preface

The annual International Conference on Access Networks (AccessNets) aims to provide a forum that brings together researchers and scientists from academia as well as managers and engineers from industry to meet and exchange ideas and recent work on all aspects of access networks. AccessNets 2008 was the third edition of this event, which was successfully held in Las Vegas, Nevada, USA, during October 15–17, 2008.

The conference consisted of two keynote addresses, five invited talks, seven technical sessions, and two panel sessions. Leonid Kazovsky from Stanford University and Kevin Schneider, Chief Technology Officer of ADTRAN, delivered their exciting keynote addresses on "Future Evolution of Broadband Access," and "Carrier Ethernet and the Evolving Access Networks," respectively. Maurice Gagnaire, Martin Reisslein, Martin Maier, Paolo Giacomazzi, and John M. Cioffi gave interesting invited talks on different research topics on access networks. The technical papers presented original and fundamental research advances in the area of access networks, while the panels focused on the interesting topics of "Fiber Assisted Wireless for Broadband Access Networks and Dynamic Spectrum Management (DSM) Successes."

These conference proceedings include all the technical papers that were presented at AccessNets 2008. We hope that it will become a useful reference for researchers and practitioners working in the area of access networks.

Jun Zheng
Pascal Lorenz

Organization

Steering Committee

Imrich Chlamtac (Chair)   Create-Net Research, Italy
Jun Zheng   University of Ottawa, Canada
Nirwan Ansari   New Jersey Institute of Technology, USA

General Chair

Hussein T. Mouftah   University of Ottawa, Canada

TPC Co-chairs

Jun Zheng   University of Ottawa, Canada
Pascal Lorenz   University of Haute Alsace, France

Workshop Co-chairs

Tarek S. El-Bawab   Jackson State University, USA
Ting Wang   NEC Laboratories America, Inc., USA

Panel Co-chairs

Alex Vukovic   Communications Research Center, Canada
Wenye Wang   North Carolina State University, USA

Industry Track Chair

Frank Effenberger   Huawei Technologies, USA

Publication Chair

Chonggang Wang   University of Kansas, USA

Publicity Co-chairs

Yuanqiu Luo   Huawei Technologies, USA
Joao M. Santos   Siemens Networks S.A., Portugal
Tarik Taleb   Tohoku University, Japan

Industry Sponsorship Chair

Kevin Xu   EMC Corporation

Financial Chair

Karen Decker   ICST

Conference Coordinator

Karen Decker   ICST

Local Arrangement Chair

Mei Yang   University of Nevada, USA

Technical Program Committee

Nirwan Ansari	New Jersey Institute of Technology, USA
Radim Bartos	University of New Hampshire, USA
Gee-Kung Chang	Georgia Institue of Technology, USA
Tibor Cinkler	Budapest University of Technology and Economics, Hungary
Zhiguo Ding	Imperial College London, UK
Paolo Giacomazzi	Politecnico di Milano, Italy
Maurice Gagnaire	ENST, France
Ibrahim Habib	City University of New York, USA
Anpeng Huang	Peking University, China
David Hunter	University of Essex, UK
Wojciech Kabacinski	Poznan University of Technology, Poland
Kenneth J. Kerpez	Telcordia Technologies, USA
Ken-Ichi Kitayama	Osaka University, Japan
Polychronis Koutsakis	McMaster University, Canada
Chang-Hee Lee	KAIST, Korea
Hellen-C LeLigou	National Technical University of Athens, Greece
Pascal Lorenz	University of Haute Alsace, France
Kejie Lu	University of Puerto Rico at Mayagüez, Puerto Rico
Yuanqiu Luo	Huawei Technologies, USA
Raj Jain	University of Washington in St. Louis, USA
Martin Maier	University of Quebec, Canada
Enzo Mingozzi	University of Pisa, Italy
John Mitchell	University College London, UK
Djafar K. Mynbaev	City University of New York, USA
Qiang Ni	Brunel University, UK

Table of Contents

Invited Papers

Full Papers

HOWRAN:
An Hybrid Optical Wireless Radio Access Network for WiMAX Antennas Backhauling

Maurice Gagnaire and Tony Youssef*

Telecom ParisTech (ENST), Institut Telecom,
46 rue Barrault, 75013 Paris, France
{maurice.gagnaire,tony.youssef}@telecom-paristech.fr

Abstract. In comparison to existing 3G or 3G+ wireless systems, fourth generation (4G), long-term evolution (LTE) or mobile Wimax are characterized by higher bit rates, highly fluctuant traffic matrices and higher antenna's density. Current backhauling techniques federating radio antennas are not suited to these new characteristics. Several investigations are carried out for the design of new generation radio access networks (NG-RAN) in charge of concentrating radio cellular traffic from the base stations to the core network. In this paper, we propose an original approach based on an Hybrid Optical Wireless Radio Access Network (HOWRAN) exploiting the benefits of radio-over-fiber technologies and of recent advances in the field of optical devices and systems. As an illustration, we apply the HOWRAN concept to the backhauling of fixed or mobile WiMAX base stations. The two main innovative aspects of HOWRAN are depicted: its hardware architecture and its control plane.

Keywords: New Generation RAN (NG-RAN), Radio-over-Fiber (RoF), SCM, reflective modulator, control plane, radio cell planning, WiMAX, AWG, VCSEL.

1 Introduction

In this paper, we propose another innovative RAN architecture that relies on Radio-over-Fiber (RoF) technology. The basic principle of RoF is to transport modulated millimeter radio frequencies via an optical carrier onto an optical fiber. In the context of broadband wireless communications, the main advantage of RoF is to enable a mutualization of the radio equipment traditionally installed close to each antenna by allowing their co-location at a remote site (for instance at Node-B in UMTS). In existing wireless systems (GSM, GPRS, UMTS), two local oscillators need to be installed at each BS, one for building the radio multiplex at an intermediate frequency (IF) and another one for shifting

---

* This work has been carried out in the context of the Work Package WP13 of the BONE European network of excellence. The HOWRAN architecture and control plane are under the process of a patent.

C. Wang (Ed.): AccessNets, LNICST 6, pp. 1–15, 2009.

this multiplex at the radio frequency (RF). Various modulation techniques can be adopted for RoF. The simplest one consists in using the internal modulation of a laser diode by means of an RF signal. In that case, it is possible to remove all the signaling and data processing equipment usually installed at the BSs to the RNC.

This paper is organized as follows. In Section 2, we recall the main characteristics of the WiMAX technology. We then describe in Section 3 the global HOWRAN architecture . A detailed analysis of the hardware architecture of the HOWRAN head-end node is presented in Section 4. The optical network units of an HOWRAN system are qualified of hybrid since they deal with radio-frequency and optical modulation/demodulation. The hardware architecture of an Hybrid Optical Network Unit (HONU) is depicted in Section 5. In Section 6, we discuss the rationale of the HOWRAN control plane. In Section 7, we outline through simple examples how practically an HOWRAN system can be used to facilitate Wimax cell planning.

2   WiMAX Basics

These recent years, several commercial implementations of fixed WiMAX (Worldwide Interoperability for Microwave Access) cellular systems (also known as the IEEE 802.16d standard) have been proposed by the carriers. As mentioned in our introduction, WiMAX is a non-line-of-site wireless (NLOS) system based on Orthogonal Frequency Division Mutiplexing Access (OFDMA). Figure 1 depicts the frequency bands reserved for either licensed or unlicensed WiMAX systems. Today, fixed WiMAX uses in Europe either the 3.5 GHz licensed band or the 5.8 GHz unlicensed band. According to the WiMAX Forum [8], the 2.5 GHz band is today proposed in many countries for fixed broadband wireless under licensed WiMAX. In the USA, the most recent FCC (Federal Communications Commission) rules specify a total available spectrum ΔF of 195 MHz including guard-bands between

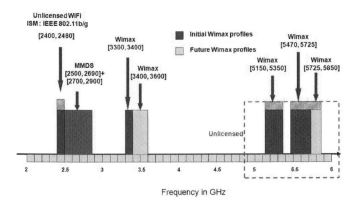

Fig. 1. Licensed and unlicensed WiMAX channels bandwidth

2.495 GHz and 2.690 GHz. Fixed two-way or broadcast communications are possible, in using either Time Division Duplexing (TDD) or Frequency Division Duplexing (FDD).

The design of HOWRAN systems takes into account some of the characteristics of future mobile WiMAX. Mobile WiMAX characteristics are specified in the 2005 revised version of the IEEE 802.16e standard. Although multiple channels bandwidths are considered for mobile WiMAX, a consensus between the vendors and the operators focuses on a 10 MHz bandwidth (BW). In terms of modulation, mobile WiMAX uses an extended version of OFDMA called Scalable OFDMA (SOFDMA). Similarly to Discrete Multitone modulation used in ADSL, fixed and mobile WiMAX uses OFDM. The main objective of OFDM consists in reducing the negative impact of propagation disparity (due to multipath phenomenon) by spreading data flows onto multiple narrowband channels called subcarriers. Due to their very limited bandwidth, these subcarriers are not subject to propagation disparity. In order to optimize the available BW, these subcarriers are orthogonal. The capacity in bit/s of each subcarrier is evaluated according to the quality of the radio channel in the considered frequency band. The Fast Fourier Transform (FFT) algorithm enables to assign the optimum capacity to each subcarrier in order to maximize the global data rate, either upstream or downstream. Both fixed and mobile WiMAX rely on three types of subcarriers: data subcarriers, pilot subcarriers (for operation and maintenance) and null subcarriers (used as guard bands). Data and pilot subcarriers are logically associated to form subchannels. A subchannel represents the capacity assigned to a given user. In practise, the subcarriers associated to the various subchannels are interleaved in the frequency domain. For each channel bandwidth (BW) specified for mobile WiMAX, various numbers of OFDM subcarriers referred as N_{FFT} can be used. Among the N_{FFT} subcarriers, $N_{data-DL}$ and $N_{data-UL}$ are used for downlink transmission from the BS to the mobile terminal and for uplink transmission from the mobile terminal to the BS respectively. The values of $N_{data-DL}$ and $N_{data-UL}$ are specified in the standard as maximum values for dowstream and upstream transmission isolately. In other terms, the sum of these two terms may be greater than N_{FFT}, each of them remaining lower than N_{FFT}. Another figure called N_{used} is specified in the standard. It is equal to the sum of the effective number of used data subcarriers N_{data}, the number of pilot subcarriers N_{pilot} and the Direct Current (DT) carriers used for hardware purposes. Finally, $N_{SubchDL}$ and $N_{SubchUL}$ correspond to the maximum number of subchannels (that is of users) that may share some of the $N_{data-DL}$ and of the $N_{data-UL}$ subcarriers respectively. Table 1 summarizes the typical values of N_{FFT}, N_{used}, $N_{data-DL}$, $N_{data-UL}$, $N_{SubchDL}$ and $N_{SubchUL}$ for different values of BW [6].

If one considers the transmission window ΔF of 195 MHz between 2.495 GHz and 2.690 GHz mentioned above, we have then the possibility to create up to 9 WiMAX channels each with a 20 MHz bandwidth. In OFDM, a test sequence enables to evaluate the quality of the radio channel in each subcarrier. For each subcarrier, the FFT algorithm determines the size of the QAM constellation

Table 1. Mobile WiMAX OFDMA parameters

BW	N_{FFT}	N_{used}	$N_{data-DL}$	$N_{data-UL}$	$N_{SubchDL}$	$N_{SubchUL}$
1.25 MHz	128	85	72	56	3	4
5 MHz	512	421	360	280	15	17
10 MHz	1024	841	720	560	30	35
20 MHz	2048	1681	1440	1120	60	70

enabling to maximize the global data rate on the air interface, either in the upstream or in the downstream direction. Once the WiMAX link has been initiated, the FFT algorithm computes on the fly on the basis of a common symbol duration and for each subchannel, a set of samples of the modulated signal. At each symbol duration, a cyclic prefix corresponding to redundant information is added to the set of the samples obtained over all the active subcarriers. The aim of this prefix is to reduce the impact of multipath effect on BER. According the the fluctuations of the air interface observed by each end-user, mobile WiMAX uses an adaptive modulation. The better the quality of the air interface, the higher the size of the adopted QAM constellation. In WiMAX, mainly three basic modulations are considered: QPSK, 16-QAM and 64-QAM. For each modulation, different coding rates may be used depending on the adopted Forward Error Correction (FEC) technique. FEC introduces redundant bits that consume some of the user data bits in the QAM constellations. The coding rate r corresponds then to the ratio of the number of data bits per symbol to the sum of the number of data bits per symbol and of redundant bits per symbol. The number of information bits per symbol is then equal to $r \log(M)/\log(2)$ where M stands for the number of bits per symbol. For instance, in the case of 64-QAM ($M=6$) with a coding rate $r = 3/4$, we have $r \log(M)/\log(2) = 4.5$ bits per symbol. In [7], the author determines the admissible Signal-to-Noise Ratio (SNR) in presence of Additive White Gaussian Noise (AWGN) assuming the usage of Reed-Solomon techniques and convolution codes to prevent erroneous bits. In this context, Table 2 extracted from [7] shows typical values of required SNR in order to guarantee a BER lower than 10^{-6}.

In OFDM, one defines a frame that groups a certain number of successive symbols with their associated additive cyclic prefixes. The WiMAX Forum sets the

Table 2. Example of SNR values for Mobile WiMAX

Modulation scheme	SNR
QPSK 1/2	5 dB
QPSK 3/4	8 dB
16-QAM 1/2	10.5 dB
16-QAM 3/4	14 dB
64-QAM 1/2	16 dB
64-QAM 2/3	18 dB
64-QAM 3/4	20 dB

duration T_{frame} of this periodical frame to 5 milliseconds. During T_{frame}, a total of N_{symbol} OFDM symbols are generated with among them $N_{data-symbol-DL}$ OFDM symbols corresponding to data symbols. In [9], a WiMAX cell capacity evaluation is carried on the basis of the above mentioned parameters. The downlink data rate Φ_{DL} observed at the physical layer per WiMAX carrier is given by:

$$\Phi_{DL} = \frac{N_{data-DL} \times N_{data-symbol-DL}}{T_{frame}} \times r \frac{\log(M)}{\log(2)} \qquad (1)$$

As an example, in the case of BW = 10 MHz (see Table 1), we have $N_{data-DL}$ = 720. If we consider a 64-QAM modulation with coding rate $r = 3/4$, knowing from [9] that in that case, $N_{data-symbol-DL}$ = 44, we obtain numerically Φ_{DL} = 28.51 Mbps. In the case of an uplink WiMAX carrier operating under the same conditions, we have to replace $N_{data-DL}$ by $N_{data-UL}$ = 560 and $N_{data-symbol-DL}$ by $N_{data-symbol-UL}$ = 42. We get Φ_{UL} = 21.17 Mbps. The WiMAX carrier range has been investigated in [7] under different types of modulation, error correction techniques and radio propagation models. Due to space limitation, we simply provide in Table 3 interesting figures in this matter that will also be useful for the remaining of our study.

Table 3. Typical ranges in meters of fixed WiMAX cells in urban areas

Up/Down	QPSK 1/2	QPSK 3/4	16-QAM 1/2	16-QAM 3/4	64-QAM 1/2	64-QAM 3/4
Downlink	1150	970	850	700	620	500
Uplink	770	720	660	610	550	480

We notice that the maximum cell size in urban areas is 770 meters. This corresponds to an antenna's density at least four times higher than in current systems. SOFDMA consists in searching in a cell the users that could communicate with the BS at the highest rate (64-QAM with 3/4 coding rate) under acceptable BER. Once the potential users have been served (they are probably located close the BS), another search is carried out for users that could communicate at a lower data rate (64-QAM with 2/3 coding rate). The operation is repeated recursively until the cell capacity has been fully utilized. As it will be outlined in Section 3, HOWRAN systems are particularly designed for urban areas rather than for rural areas.

3 Global HOWRAN Architecture

Figure 2 depicts the global configuration of an HOWRAN system in which four main sections can be distinguished: the head-end node, an Arrayed Waveguide Grating (AWG) router, several feeder WDM loops and several WiMAX BSs. The head-end node is in charge of supervising the behavior of the whole infrastructure. It can be assimilated to an Hybrid Optical Line Termination (HOLT) since it manages both radio and optical carriers. The main role of the head-end

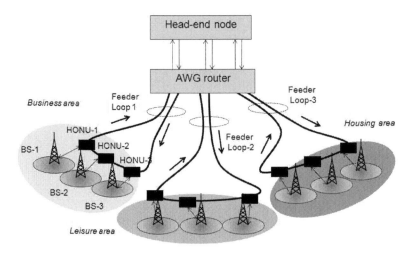

Fig. 2. The HOWRAN configuration

node is to generate continuous millimeter frequencies for upstream traffic and modulated millimeter frequencies for downstream traffic. Each of these radio frequencies modulate continuous tunable optical carriers by means of Sub-Carrier Modulation (SCM). The head-end node is in charge of the supervision of the whole HOWRAN system by means of an innovative control plane. This control plane aims to distribute dynamically upstream and downstream radio frequencies to the various WiMAX BSs of the system. An out-of-band optical channel λ^* is used to coordinate this supervision. The head-end node is interfaced with a low-cost Arrayed Waveguide Grating (AWG) router. The flexibility of such a router is mainly provided by the tunability of the continuous optical carriers. Let $\Delta_o = \{\lambda_1, \lambda_2 \dots \lambda_n\}$ be the pool of these n optical carriers. If N stands for the number of HONUs in the system, we assume that $n \leq N$. This means that, according to the maximum number of radio frequencies that can be transported by a same optical channel, a single optical channel has the capacity to feed a WiMAX BS under its maximum load.

The third section of an HOWRAN system is made of multiple WDM optical loops connected to the output ports of the AWG. As illustrated in the figure, the AWG is inserted into each loop via two distinct of its output ports. Once they have been routed to their dedicated loop, the downstream continuous optical carriers generated at the head-end node pass through successive Hybrid Optical Network Units (HONU) inserted in the lower part of each loop. The HONUs represent the fourth main section of an HOWRAN system. As described in the figure, a single WiMAX BS is connected to an HONU. In a first approach, we can assimilate an HONU to a Reconfigurable Optical Add-Drop Multiplexer (ROADM) in charge of extracting the right downstream optical channel, and from this optical channel, the right radio frequencies. In parallel, the out-of-band signaling channel λ^* is demodulated. In order to reduce the best as possible the cost of an HONU, no laser diodes is necessary for the upstream transmission of the radio channels, a Reflective Semiconductor Optical Amplifier (RSOA) being used for that purpose. In addition, no costly local oscillator is necessary at the HONUs. Indeed, all the radio frequencies used for both upstream and downstream transmissions are located at the head-end node thanks to RoF technique. The technical feasibility of such an hardware configuration has been demonstrated in [10]. In parallel, the signaling channel uses at each HONU a low-cost VCSELs (Vertical Cavity Surface Emitting Laser) instead of a laser diode. The way the RF frequencies are used at the HONUs is depicted in Section 5. As an illustration, we consider in Figure 2 three WDM loops corresponding to three different zones of a same urban area. These three zones cover a business area, a leisure area and a housing area respectively. Our motivation for such an architecture aims to a mutualization of the radio resources since the same population is supposed to move every day from one zone to another one depending on the hour of the day. In other terms, instead of serving these three areas in installing three times the same radio resources, we want to exploit the intelligence of the HOWRAN control plane to shift dynamically the same radio resources from one zone to another one.

4   Head-End Node Hardware Architecture

Figure 3 details the internal configuration of the head-end node. A pool of n continuous tunable lasers is used to transport radio frequencies to the BSs thanks to RoF technique. In HOWRAN systems, we have adopted the most simple RoF transmission technique based on intensity modulation at the sender and direct detection at the receiver. As it is illustrated, the tunable continuous laser sources may be eventually modulated by one or several radio frequency (RF) signals by means of SCM. These RF signals can themselves be pre-modulated or not by user data. In Figure 3, we have assumed an internal modulation of the laser sources. In practise, external modulation by means of Mach-Zender modulators should provide better performance but at a higher cost. A direct detection is used at the HONUs to get-back the transmitted RF signals which are then simply amplified by WiMAX BSs. It is recalled in [7] that intensity modulation coupled with direct detection is easy to implement. It can be used for multi-level modulation formats such as QAM or SCM. The set of the RF oscillators is divided into two subsets. A first subset $\Delta_{RF1} = \{f_1, f_2 \ldots f_m\}$ of pre-modulated RF signals is used for downstream radio traffic. A second subset $\Delta_{RF2} = \{f_{m+1}, f_{m+2} \ldots f_{2m}\}$ of continuous RF signals is used for upstream radio traffic. The HOWRAN control plane supervises via the control channel λ^* a matrix of $n \times 2m$ OADMs in order to activate RoF modulation of the optical carriers with the desired RF signals. Similarly to the RoFnet architecture introduced in 5, Optical Single Sideband (OSSB) modulation is preferred to Optical Double Sideband (ODSS) modulation because it is less sensitive to chromatic dispersion effects.

Due to space limitation, we do not describe in this paper the configuration of the HOWRAN head-end node receiver configuration.

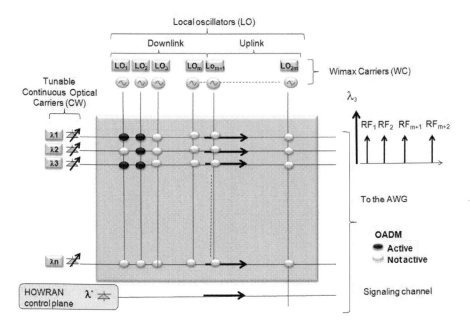

Fig. 3. Head-end node transmitter configuration

5   HONU Hardware Architecture

The internal architecture adopted for an HONU, let us say ONU-#k, is depicted in Figure 4. It is strongly inspired by the architecture proposed in [10] for the RoFnet network. The incoming section of the loop transports a subset Δ'_o of Δ_o optical channels and λ^*. After demultiplexing, λ^* is directed to a photo-detector. The signaling information transported on λ^* is analyzed in the electrical domain by the HONU control plane. For instance, the HONU is informed by the head-end node of the index i of the optical channel that must be extracted, the other optical channels by-passing this HONU. This extraction is carried out by means of a MEMS switching fabric. Once it has been isolated, channel λ_i is directed by means of an optical circulator to both an high bandwidth tunable photo-detector and to an RSOA.

Thanks to the high bandwidth tunable photo-detector, the two subsets Δ_{RF1} and Δ_{RF2} of RF signals are extracted. The m downstream modulated RF signals of Δ_{RF1} are amplified before being transmitted by BS-#k to the mobile users. The m continuous RF signals of Δ_{RF2} are used as local oscillators in order to convert the upstream radio channels coming from the antenna to intermediate frequencies (IF) within the electrical band of the RSOA (1.2 GHz). These m modulated signals at intermediate frequency are multiplexed. The resulting signal modulates the RSOA. The obtained optical signal centered on λ_i is Optically Double Sideband (ODSB) modulated. Figure 5 illustrates the shape of λ_i when it is inserted in the output multiplexer.

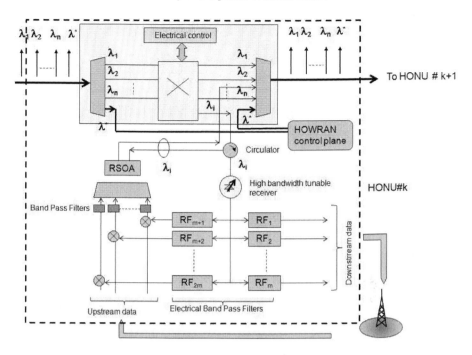

Fig. 4. HONU configuration

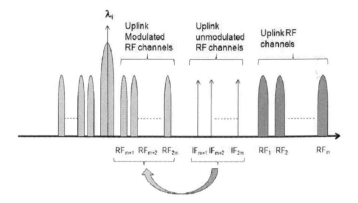

Fig. 5. Global signal on an optical loop

6   HOWRAN Control Plane

The aim of the HOWRAN contro plane is to dynamically assign radio carriers to the various WiMAX BSs spread out over the multiple loops according to the upstream/downstream traffic of the WiMAX cells. The main complexity and originality of this control plane concerns upstream traffic. Upstream traffic is viewed either as the global traffic generated within each cell, or the global traffic generated by the set of BSs belonging to a same loop. The HOWRAN control plane is then MAC agnostic since it does not see the packet level. Thus we assume that the standardized WiMAX MAC protocol is applied at layer 2. The HOWRAN control plane operates at two timescales: microscopic and macroscopic. At the microscopic timescale, one assumes that the number of optical carriers assigned to an optical loop is fixed, for instance w. Let us recall that at most N optical channels serve a same loop made of N HONUs ($w \leq N$). At this timescale, the control plane is in charge of reallocating the RF carriers belonging to the w subsets Δ_{RF1} to such or such BS belonging to the same loop. At the macroscopic timescale, if the utilization ratio of these radio frequencies becomes greater than a given threshold, the head-end node activates a wavelength reallocation procedure between the loops. For instance, one or several optical channels assigned to a loop with low loaded BSs are retrieved by the control plane to the benefit of the BSs suffering of starvation and belonging to another loop. In reference to Figure 2, let us consider that around 9am, the subscribers of a WiMAX operator leave their homes to go to work. Automatically, the HOWRAN control plane shifts progressively some of the radio resources focused on the housing area to the business area. The same type of operation should occur several times every day between the housing area, the business area and the leisure area. The rationale of the HOWRAN control plane is inspired from a similar tool we have proposed for Next-Generation WDM-PON access systems [13]. Due to space limitations, we cannot describe into details how this control plane is adapted to the cellular context. Let us simply say that the HOWRAN control plane is based on two bin-packing optimization algorithms, one being activated on the fly at the microscopic timescale, the other one being used at the macroscopic timescale.

7   Wimax Cell Planning with HOWRAN

Figure 6 illustrates an example of loop configuration adapted to the hexagonal WiMAX cell planning. According to Table 3, the smallest radius of a WiMAX cell equal to 480 meters is obtained under 64-QAM modulation with a 3/4 coding rate. In [11], the feasibility of a 10 Gbps OSSB modulation using SCM in the C-band has been demonstrated. In this study, the microwave frequencies used for SCM are distributed between 3.6 GHz and 10 GHz. According to the adopted sub-channel spacing, it is shown experimentally in this paper that the global required bandwidth around 1550 nm is 20 GHz. In reference to Section 2, we can notice that this 20 GHz bandwidth is largely greater than the 195 MHz bandwidth ΔF reserved around 2.5 GHz for WiMAX systems. Let us recall that up to 9 WiMAX carriers may be be included in ΔF. This corresponds to the maximum capacity of a WiMAX cell. We can conclude that there is no problem at all to transport in practice 9 WiMAX carriers modulated with the highest bit rate (64-QAM with 3/4 coding rate) on a same optical channel operating in the C-band. In practise, up to M BSs can be connected to a same loop and up to K loops (in our scenario, $K = 3$) can be connected to the AWG. In this case, the

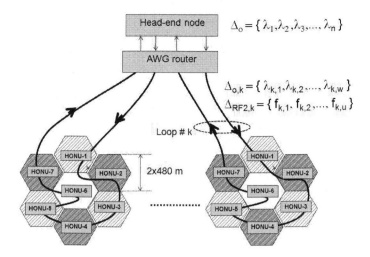

Fig. 6. Wimax frequency planning

number n of optical carriers available at the head-end is such as $n \leq K \times M$. These n optical carriers transport a maximum of $n \times 9$ WiMAX carriers. We can assume that, whatever the hour of the day, at least 10% of the population remains geographically in each loop. For instance, between 9am and 12am, 80% of the population are located in the business area whereas 10% are in the housing area and 10% are in the leisure area. The value of n must then be such as:

$$\left\lceil \frac{M}{10} \right\rceil \times 9 \times (K - 1) + \left\lceil \frac{8 \times M}{10} \right\rceil \times 9 \leq n \leq K \times M \qquad (2)$$

In [12],the problem of interference avoidance for frequency planning in cellular mobile WiMAX is investigated. In this paper, the concept of Partial Usage Subchannel (PUSC) is exploited. It enables a subscriber to use only fractions of the subchannels (see Section 2). Considering a decomposition of each hexagonal cell into three sectors of 120 degrees each, the basic idea is to enable the users close to the antenna to consume all the available subchannels. The users located at the periphery of the cell can only use a fraction of the available subchannels as it is illustrated in Figure 7.

To validate the basic operation of the HOWRAN control plane, let us consider the same type of scenario as the one considered in [14] which corresponds to realistic WiMAX deployment. We assume that 80% of the WiMAX subscribers use 64-QAM evenly split with a coding rate 3/4 or 2/3, 10% of the WiMAX subscribers use 16-QAM evenly split with a coding rate 3/4 or 1/2, and 10% of the WiMAX subscribers use QPSK evenly split with a coding rate 3/4 or 1/2. In using equation 1, we determine an average bit rate per WiMAX carrier of 17.76 Mbps. Thanks to PUSC, the minimum bandwidth allocation granularity corresponds to a single WiMAX subchannel. Knowing from Table 1 that for 10 MHz WiMAX, we have $N_{SubchUL} = 35$, this minimal granularity is then $17.76/35 = 0.507$ Mbps. In the remaining of this section, we illustrate the characteristic

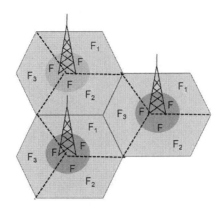

Fig. 7. Principle of Partial Usage Subchannel in WiMAX

instants at which the microscopic and the macroscopic behavior of the control plane are activated. For that purpose, we consider a very simple scenario with $K = 3$ and $M = 3$, the three cells of each loop forming the same pattern as in Figure 7.

As a reference scenario, Figure 8 depicts the successive activations of the WiMAX carriers provided by a single optical channel to a given cell. We assume the other cells of the same loop are inactive. When the offered traffic increases linearly with time, the number α of activated WiMAX carriers increases as a step function with 0.507 Mbps gaps. The HONU sends to the head-end an alarm via λ^* when α reaches a threshold α_{th} ($\alpha_{th} = 8$ in the figure) at instant t_0. The value of α_{th} is chosen such as, in the worst case, the signaling message may arrive at the head-end, may be interpreted, and the control plane may send to the HONU a confirmation signaling message specifying that an additional optical channel has been routed to the considered loop before α reaches 9.

Figure 9 illustrates an example of the macroscopic behavior of the control plane when the three BSs of the same loop are active. The offered load in each

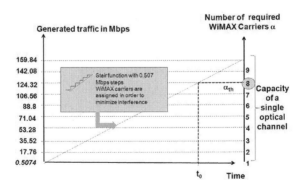

Fig. 8. Principle of WiMAX carrier's assignment

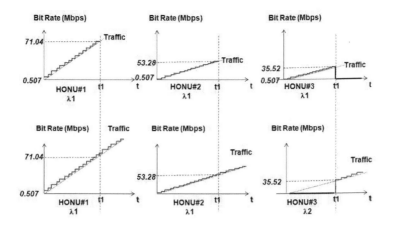

Fig. 9. Macroscopic behavior of the HOWRAN control plane: example 1

cell increases linearly. We have plotted the evolution of α proper to each HONU of the loop. When the three cells are under loaded, they use WiMAX carriers provided by a same optical carrier λ_1. One notices that at instant t_1, the global offered load (71.04 Mbps + 53.28 Mbps + 32.52 Mbps = 160 Mbps) reaches the maximum capacity that can be provided by 9 WiMAX carriers. In this case, by convention, the HONU with the lowest load sends an alarm to the head-end in order to require for another λ. This second λ is provided, if possible, from another loop. One notices that after t_1, HONU1 and HONU2 still operate on λ_1 whereas HONU3 starts to operate on λ_2. By simplification, we have not considered in this scenario an anticipation threshold that should be applied to HONU3 in the same spirit as the threshold mentioned in our previous example.

Figure 10 illustrates a second example of macroscopic behavior of the control plane. At instant t_0, let us assume that HONU1, HONU2 and HONU3 are served by the same optical channel λ_1. They use 4, 3 and 2 WiMAX carriers respectively. Each HONU increases its offered load progressively, like in the previous example.

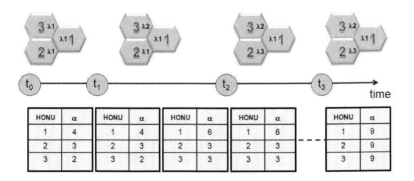

Fig. 10. Macroscopic behavior of the HOWRAN control plane: example 2

At instant t_1, one notices that the 9 WiMAX carriers of λ_1 are used. Via the signaling channel, the head-end assigns to HONU3 a new optical channel λ_2. At instant t_2, the 9 WiMAX carriers of λ_1 are consumed by HONU1 and HONU2. Via the signaling channel, the head-end assigns to HONU2 a new optical channel λ_3. The three cells are potentially saturated at instant t_3 when the 9 WiMAX carriers of λ_1, λ_2 and λ_3 are consumed. Again, by simplification, we have not considered in this scenario an anticipation threshold. Due to space limitation, we cannot describe the microscopic behavior of the control plane. It is mainly activated to solve the inter-cell interference problems.

8   Conclusion

In the paper, we have proposed an innovative RAN architecture well suited to fixed or mobile WiMAX cellular networks. The HOWRAN network originality covers two aspects: the physical topology and the control plane. Multiple advanced devices (MEMS, RSOA, AWG) and modulation techniques (SCM, RoF, OSSB) are judiciously exploited in order to facilitate a great flexibility in terms of frequency planning. To the best of our knowledge, the HOWRAN control plane is the first one that enables a mutualization of the radio resources in dense urban areas. Our coming studies are focused on the design of a simulator of an HOWRAN system from which realistic scenarios will be investigated.

References

1. Otsu, T., et al.: Network Architecture for Mobile Communications Systems beyond IMT-2000. IEEE Wireless Commun. 8(5), 31–37 (2001)
2. Ghosh, S., Basu, K., Das, S.K.: What a Mesh! An Architecture for Next-Generation Radio Access Networks. IEEE Network Magazine, 35–42 (September/October 2005)
3. Koonen, T., Ng'oma, A., Smulders, P.F.M., Boom, H.P.A., Tafur Monroy, I., Khoe, G.D.: In-House networks using Multimode Polymer Optical Fiberfor broadband wireless services. Photonic Network Communications 5(2), 177–187 (2003)
4. Park, Y.H., Okada, M., Komaki, S.: The Performance of Fiber-Radio Road Vehicle Communication System with Macro-Diversity. Wireless Personal Communications 14, 125–132 (2000)
5. Lannoo, B., Colle, D., Pickavet, M., Demeester, P.: Radio-over-Fiber-Based Solution to Provide Broadband Internet Access to Train Passengers. IEEE Communications Magazine, 56–62 (February 2007)
6. Lannoo, B., Verbrugge, S., Ooteghem, J.V., Quinart, B., Castteleyn, M., Colle, D., Pickavet, M., Demeester, P.: Business scenarios for a WiMAX deployment in Belgium. In: IEEE Mobile Wimax Conference, Orlando-FL, USA (2007)
7. Lannoo, B.: Study of access communications networks for heterogeneous environments. PhD Dissertation, University of Gent, Belgium (2008)
8. Wimax Forum. Considerations for Fixed Wireless Access in the 2.5 and 3.5 GHz Licensed Bands (June 2005)
9. Mobile WiMAX part 1: a technical overview and performance evalation, The WiMAX Forum (August 2006), http://www.wimaxforum.org/home/

10. Medeiros, M.C.R., Avo, R., Laurencio, P., Correia, N.S., Barradas, A., da Silva, H.J.A., Darwazeh, I., Mitchell, J.E., Monteiro, P.M.N.: Radio over Fiber Access Network Architecture Employing Reflective Semiconductor Optical Amplifiers. In: IEEE ICTON Conference (2007)
11. Hui, R., Zhu, B., Huang, R., Allen, C., Demarest, K., Richards, D.: 10-Gb/s SCM Fiber System using Optical SSB Modulation. IEEE Photonics Technology Letters 13(8) (August 2001)
12. Jias, H., Zhang, Z., Yu, G., Cheng, P., Li, S.: On the performance of IEEE 802.16 OFDMA system under different frequency reuse and subcarrirer permutation patterns. In: IEEE ICC Proceedings (August 2007)
13. Gagnaire, M., Koubaa, M.: A new control plane for Next-Generation WDM-PON access systems. In: IEEE Accessnets Proceedings, Ottawa-Canada (2007)
14. Wimax capacity White Paper, Chapter 7 "Capacity Scenarios", SR Telecom, Canada (August 2006)

The Audacity of Fiber-Wireless (FiWi) Networks

(Invited Paper)

Martin Maier[1], Navid Ghazisaidi[1], and Martin Reisslein[2]

[1] Institut National de la Recherche Scientifique (INRS)
800, Gauchetière West, suite 6900, Montréal, QC, H5A 1K6, Canada
{maier,navid}@emt.inrs.ca
[2] Department of Electrical Engineering, Arizona State University
P.O. Box 875706, Tempe, AZ 85287-5706, USA
reisslein@asu.edu

Abstract. A plethora of enabling optical and wireless technologies have been emerging that can be used to build future-proof bimodal fiber-wireless (FiWi) broadband access networks. After overviewing key enabling radio-over-fiber (RoF) and radio-and-fiber (R&F) technologies and briefly surveying the state of the art of FiWi networks, we introduce an Ethernet-based access-metro FiWi network, called SuperMAN, that integrates next-generation WiFi and WiMAX networks with WDM-enhanced EPON and RPR networks. Throughout the paper we pay close attention to the technical challenges and opportunities of FiWi networks, but also elaborate on their societal benefits and potential to shift the current research focus from optical-wireless networking to the exploitation of personal and in-home computing facilities to create new unforeseen services and applications as we are about to enter the Petabyte age.

Keywords: EPON, FiWi, FTTH, MAC, optical-wireless integration, path selection, QoS, R&F, RoF, RPR, WiFi, WiMAX, WMN.

1 Introduction

We are currently witnessing a strong worldwide push toward bringing optical fiber closer to individual homes and businesses, leading to fiber to the home/fiber to the premises (FTTH/FTTP) networks [1]. In FTTx networks, fiber is brought close or all the way to the end user, whereby x denotes the discontinuity between optical fiber and some other, either wired or wireless, transmission medium. For instance, cable operators typically deploy hybrid fiber coax (HFC) networks where fiber is used to build the feeder network while the distribution network is realized with coax cables. Another good example for wired fiber-copper access networks are hybrid fiber-twisted pair networks which are widely deployed by telephone companies to realize different variants of digital subscriber line (DSL) broadband access solutions.

C. Wang (Ed.): AccessNets, LNICST 6, pp. 16–35, 2009.

From a capacity point of view, one might seriously argue that there is no techno-economic need and justification to replace hybrid fiber-twisted pair based DSL networks with all-optical solutions, e.g., passive optical networks (PONs). According to [2], the so-called Copper-PON (CuPON) multidropping DSL architecture is able to provide 50 Gb/s of shared bandwidth in each direction on existing twisted pair of copper telephone lines through exploitation of all modes of crosstalk. Thus, CuPON is able to offer much higher data rates than state-of-the-art standardized access network solutions, e.g., IEEE 802.3ah Ethernet PON (EPON) and ITU-T G.984 Gigabit PON (GPON), without requiring any costly replacement of widely installed twisted pairs by fiber. Note, however, that the speed of CuPON is higher than that of current fiber PONs not because copper has a wider bandwidth than fiber, but because current fiber PONs do not use their extra bandwidth. In fact, optical fiber provides an unprecedented bandwidth potential that is far in excess of any other known transmission medium. A single strand of fiber offers a total bandwidth of 25 000 GHz. To put this potential into perspective, it is worthwhile to note that the total bandwidth of radio on the planet Earth is not more than 25 GHz [3]. Beside huge bandwidth, optical fiber has some further advantageous properties such as low attenuation, longevity, and low maintenance costs which will eventually render fiber the medium of choice in wired first/last mile access networks. This trend can be observed in most of today's greenfield deployments where fiber rather than copper cables are installed for broadband access. On the other hand, in brownfield deployments it is important that installation costs, which largely contribute to overall costs of access networks, be reduced. A promising example for cutting installation costs is NTT's do-it-yourself (DIY) installation of FTTH optical network units (ONUs) deploying a user-friendly hole-assisted fiber that exhibits negligible loss increase and sufficient reliability, even when it is bent at right angles, clinched, or knotted, and can be mass produced economically [4]. Another interesting enabling technology is the so-called plastic optical fiber (POF) which is well suited for simple wiring of low-cost optical home networks. POF provides consumers with user-friendly terminations, easy installation, and tolerance of dirty connections. Furthermore, POF's resistance to bending is comparable to that of twisted pair of copper telephone lines. An interesting application of POF-based networks is the concept of "Fiber to the Display" where POFs are directly connected to a large flat panel display to enable transmission rates of several Gb/s in support of telemedicine or the emerging digital cinema standard for next-generation cinema [5].

FTTH networks are expected to become the next major success story for optical communications systems [6]. Future FTTH networks will not only enable the support of a wide range of new and emerging services and applications but also unleash their economic potential and societal benefits by opening up the first/last mile bandwidth bottleneck between bandwidth-hungry end users and high-speed backbone networks [7]. In this paper, we assume that optical fiber paves all the way to and penetrates into the home of residential and business customers. Arguing that due to its unique properties optical fiber is likely to entirely replace copper wires in the near to mid term, we will elaborate on the final frontier of optical networks, namely, the convergence with their wireless counterparts. Optical and wireless technologies can be thought of as quite complementary and will expectedly coexist over the next decades. Future broadband access networks will be bimodal, capitalizing on the respective strengths of both technologies and smartly merging them in order to realize future-proof fiber-wireless (FiWi) networks that strengthen our information society while avoiding its digital divide. By combining the capacity of optical fiber networks with the ubiquity and mobility of wireless networks, FiWi networks form a powerful platform for the support and creation of emerging as well as future unforeseen applications and services, e.g., telepresence. FiWi networks hold great promise to change the way we live and work by replacing commuting with teleworking. This not only provides more time for professional and personal activities for corporate and our own personal benefit, but also helps reduce fuel consumption and protect the environment, issues that are becoming increasingly important in our lives.

The remainder of the paper is structured as follows. In Section 2, we set the stage by briefly reviewing radio-over-fiber (RoF) networks, a previously studied approach to integrate optical fiber networks and wireless networks, and explain their difference to so-called radio-and-fiber (R&F) networks. Section 3 elaborates on enabling technologies and the state of the art of FiWi networks. In Section 4, we introduce our proposal for future FiWi networks. Section 5 concludes the paper.

2   RoF vs. R&F Networks

RoF networks have been studied for many years as an approach to integrate optical fiber and wireless networks. In RoF networks, radiofrequencies (RFs) are carried over optical fiber links between a central station and multiple low-cost remote antenna units (RAUs) in support of a variety of wireless applications. For instance, a distributed antenna system connected to the base station of a microcellular radio system via optical fibers was proposed in [8]. To efficiently support time-varying traffic between the central station and its attached base stations, a centralized dynamic channel assignment method is applied at the central station of the proposed fiber optic microcellular radio system. To avoid having to equip each radio port in a fiber optic microcellular radio network with a laser and its associated circuit to control the laser parameters such as temperature, output power, and linearity, a cost-effective radio port architecture deploying remote modulation can be used [9].

Apart from realizing low-cost microcellular radio networks, optical fibers can also be used to support a wide variety of other radio signals. RoF networks are attractive since they provide transparency against modulation techniques and are able to support various digital formats and wireless standards in a cost-effective manner. It was experimentally demonstrated in [10] that RoF networks are well suited to simultaneously transmit wideband code division multiple access (WCDMA), IEEE 802.11a/g wireless local area network (WLAN), personal handyphone system (PHS), and global system for mobile communications (GSM) signals. Fig. 1 illustrates the method investigated in [10] for two different radio

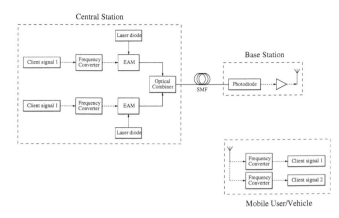

Fig. 1. Radio-over-SMF network downlink using EAMs for different radio client signals [10]

client signals transmitted by the central station on a single-mode fiber (SMF) downlink to a base station and onward to a mobile user or vehicle. At the central station, both radio client signals are first upconverted to a higher frequency by using a frequency converter. Then the two RF signals go into two different electroabsorption modulators (EAMs) and modulate the optical carrier wavelength emitted by two separate laser diodes. An optical combiner combines the two optical signals onto the SMF downlink. At the base station, a photodiode converts the incoming optical signal to the electrical domain and radiates the amplified signal through an antenna to a mobile user or vehicle which uses two separate frequency converters to retrieve the two different radio client signals.

While SMFs are typically found in outdoor optical networks, many buildings have preinstalled multimode fiber (MMF) cables. Cost-effective multimode fiber (MMF)-based networks can be realized by deploying low-cost vertical cavity surface emitting lasers (VCSELs). In [11], different kinds of MMF in conjunction with commercial off-the-shelf (COTS) components were experimentally tested to demonstrate the feasibility of indoor radio-over-MMF networks for the in-building coverage of second-generation (GSM) and third-generation cellular radio networks [universal mobile telecommunications system (UMTS)] as well as IEEE 802.11a/b/g WLAN and digital enhanced cordless telecommunication packet radio service (DECT PRS).

To realize future multiservice access networks, it is important to integrate RoF systems with existing optical access networks. In [12], a novel approach for simultaneous modulation and transmission of both RoF RF and FTTH baseband signals using a single external integrated modulator was experimentally demonstrated, as shown in Fig. 2. The external integrated modulator consists of three different Mach-Zehnder modulators (MZMs) 1, 2, and 3. MZM 1 and MZM 2 are embedded in the two arms of MZM 3. The RoF RF and FTTH baseband signals independently modulate the optical carrier generated by a common laser diode by using MZM 1 and MZM 2, respectively. Subsequently, the optical wireless RF and wired-line baseband signals are combined at MZM 3. After propagation over

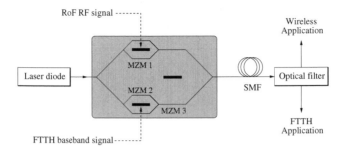

Fig. 2. Simultaneous modulation and transmission of FTTH baseband signal and RoF RF signal using an external integrated modulator consisting of three Mach-Zehnder modulators (MZMs) [12]

an SMF downlink, an optical filter (e.g., fiber grating) is used to separate the two signals and forward them to the wireless and FTTH application, respectively. It was experimentally demonstrated that a 1.25 Gb/s baseband signal and a 20-GHz 622 Mb/s RF signal can be simultaneously modulated and transmitted over 50 km standard SMF with acceptable performance penalties.

The aforementioned research projects successfully demonstrated the feasibility and maturity of low-cost multiservice RoF networks. Their focus was on the investigation of RoF transmission characteristics and modulation techniques, considering primarily physical layer related performance metrics, e.g., power penalty, error vector magnitude (EVM), and bit error rate (BER) measurements. It was shown that RoF networks can have an optical fiber range of up to 50 km. However, inserting an optical distribution system in wireless networks may have a major impact on the performance of medium access control (MAC) protocols [13]. The additional propagation delay may exceed certain timeouts of wireless MAC protocols, resulting in a deteriorated network performance. More precisely, MAC protocols based on centralized polling and scheduling, e.g., IEEE 802.16 WiMAX, are less affected by increased propagation delays due to their ability to take longer walk times between central station and wireless subscriber stations into account by means of interleaved polling and scheduling of upstream transmissions originating from different subscriber stations. However, in distributed MAC protocols, e.g., the widely deployed distributed coordination function (DCF) in IEEE 802.11a/b/g WLANs, the additional propagation delay between wireless stations and access point poses severe challenges. To see this, note that in WLANs a source station starts a timer after each frame transmission and waits for the acknowledgment (ACK) from the destination station. By default the ACK timeout value is set to 9 μs and 20 μs in 802.11a/g and 802.11b WLAN networks, respectively. If the source station does not receive the ACK before the ACK timeout it will resend the frame for a certain number of retransmission attempts. Clearly, one solution to compensate for the additional fiber propagation delay is to increase the ACK timeout. Note, however, that in DCF the ACK timeout must not exceed the DCF interframe space (DIFS), which prevents other stations from accessing the wireless medium and thus avoiding collision with the ACK frame (in IEEE 802.11 WLAN specifications DIFS is set to 50 μs). Due to the ACK timeout, optical fiber can deployed in WLAN-based RoF networks only up to a maximum length. For instance, it was shown in [14] that in a standard 802.11b WLAN network the fiber length must be less than 1948 m to ensure the proper operation of DCF. In addition, it was shown that there is a trade-off between fiber length and network throughput. As more fiber is deployed the network throughput decreases gradually.

The aforementioned limitations of WLAN-based RoF networks can be avoided in so-called radio-and-fiber (R&F) networks [15]. While RoF networks use optical fiber as an analog transmission medium between a central control station and one or more RAUs with the central station being in charge of controlling access to both optical and wireless media, in R&F networks access to the optical and wireless media is controlled separately from each other by using in general two different MAC protocols in the optical and wireless media, with protocol translation taking place at their interface. As a consequence, wireless MAC frames do not have to travel along the optical fiber to be processed at the central control station, but simply traverse their associated access point and remain in the WLAN. In WLAN-based R&F networks, access control is done locally inside the WLAN without involving any central control station, thus avoiding the negative impact of fiber propagation delay on the network throughput. R&F networks are well suited to build WLAN-based FiWi networks of extended coverage without imposing stringent limits on the size of the optical backhaul, as opposed to RoF networks that limit the length of deployed fibers to a couple of kilometers. Recall that this holds only for distributed MAC protocols such as DCF, but not for MAC protocols that deploy centralized polling and scheduling, e.g., WiMAX.

3   FiWi Networks

Both RoF and R&F technologies can be found in FiWi networks. In this section, we discuss enabling technologies in greater detail and elaborate on the state of the art of FiWi networks.

3.1   Enabling Technologies

RoF Technologies. Several RoF technologies have been emerging for the realization of low-cost FiWi networks. In the following, we briefly summarize some of the key enabling RoF technologies. For further details and a technically more profound discussion, we refer the interested reader to [16].

Optical RF Generation. To avoid the electronic bottleneck, the generation of RF signals is best done optically. The following novel optical RF generation techniques were experimentally studied and demonstrated in [16]:

  – FWM in HNL-DSF: Four-wave mixing (FWM) in a highly nonlinear dispersion-shifted fiber (HNL-DSF) can be used to realize simultaneous all-optical up-conversion of multiple wavelength channels by using optical carrier suppression (OCS) techniques. FWM is transparent to the bit rate and modulation format which may be different on each wavelength. Due to the ultrafast response of HNL-DSF, Terahertz optical RF generation is possible.

- XPM in HNL-DSF: Cross-phase modulation (XPM) in a nonlinear optical loop mirror (NOLM) in conjunction with straight pass in HNL-DSF enables the all-optical up-conversion of multiple wavelength channels without any interference- and saturation-effect limitation.
- XAM in EAM: All-optical wavelength up-conversion by means of cross-absorption modulation (XAM) in an electroabsorption modulator (EAM) has several advantages such as low power consumption, compact size, polarization insensitivity, and easy integration with other devices.
- External IM: External intensity modulation (IM) is another approach for optical RF generation, deploying one of three following modulation schemes: double-sideband (DSB), single-sideband (SSB), and OCS.
- External PM: Instead of external IM, external phase modulation (PM) can be used for optical RF generation.

According to [16], external intensity and phase modulation schemes are the most practical solutions for all-optical RF generation due to their low cost, simplicity, and long-distance transmission performance.

Remote Modulation. An interesting approach to build low-cost FiWi networks is the use of a single light source at the central office (CO) to generate a downlink wavelength that is reused at RAUs for upstream transmission by means of remote modulation, thereby avoiding the need for an additional light source at each RAU. The following remodulation schemes were experimentally studied in [16]:

- DPSK for Downstream/OOK for Upstream: PM is deployed to generate a differential phase-shift-keyed (DPSK) optical downstream signal. The DPSK is up-converted through OCS modulation. An optical splitter is used at each RAU to divide the arriving optical signal into two parts. One part is demodulated by a Mach-Zehnder interferometer and is subsequently detected by a photodetector. The other part is on-off-keyed (OOK) remodulated with upstream data using a Mach-Zehnder modulator and is sent to the CO.
- OCS for Downstream/Reuse for Upstream: At the CO, an optical carrier is split prior to optical RF generation by means of OCS and is then combined with the RF signal and sent downstream. Each RAU utilizes a fiber Bragg grating (FBG) to reflect the optical carrier while letting the RF signal pass to a photodetector. The reflected optical carrier is remodulated with upstream data and is then sent back to the CO.
- PM for Downstream/Directly Modulated SOA for Upstream: Similar to the aforementioned scheme, an optical carrier is combined with an RF signal, generated by means of PM, and sent downstream where an FBG is used at the RAU to reflect the optical carrier and pass the RF signal. The reflected optical carrier is amplified and directly modulated with upstream data using a semiconductor optical amplifier (SOA).

The use of a colorless (i.e., wavelength-independent) SOA as an amplifier and modulator for upstream transmission provides a promising low-cost RoF solution that is easy to maintain [16].

R&F Technologies. R&F-based FiWi access networks may deploy a number of enabling optical and wireless technologies.

Optical Technologies. Apart from PONs, the following optical technologies are expected to play an increasingly important role in the design of a flexible and cost-effective optical backhaul for FiWi networks [17].

- Tunable Lasers: Directly modulated external cavity lasers, multisection distributed feedback (DFB)/distributed Bragg reflector (DBR) lasers, and tunable VCSELs can be used as tunable lasers which render the network flexible and reconfigurable and help minimize production cost and reduce backup stock.
- Tunable Receivers: A tunable receiver can be realized by using a tunable optical filter and a broadband photodiode. Other more involved implementations exist (see [17]).
- Colorless ONUs: Reflective SOAs (RSOAs) can be used to build colorless ONUs that remotely modulate optical signals generated by centralized light sources.
- Burst-Mode Laser Drivers: Burst-mode transmitters are required for ONUs. They have to be equipped with laser drivers that provide fast burst on/off speed, sufficient power suppression during idle period, and stable, accurate power emission during burst transmission.
- Burst-Mode Receivers: Burst-mode receivers are required at the central optical line terminal (OLT) of a PON and must exhibit a high sensitivity, wide dynamic range, and fast time response to arriving bursts. Among others, design challenges for burst-mode receivers include dynamic sensitivity recovery, fast level recovery, and fast clock recovery.

Wireless Technologies. A plethora a broadband wireless access technologies exist [18]. Currently, the two most important ones for the implementation of the wireless part of FiWi networks are WiFi and WiMAX.

- WiFi: Due to the use of unlicensed frequency bands (2.4 GHz with 14 distinct channels) in IEEE 802.11b/g, providing up to 11/54 Mbps data rate, wireless LANs, also referred to as WiFi networks, have gained much attention. The initial IEEE 802.11 PHY layer includes: (*i*) Frequency Hopping Spread Spectrum (FHSS), (*ii*) Direct Sequence Spread Spectrum (DSSS), and (*iii*) Infrared (IR). IEEE 802.11b uses High-Rate DSSS (HR-DSSS), while IEEE 802.11g deploys Orthogonal Frequency Division Multiplexing (OFDM). The IEEE 802.11 MAC layer deploys the above mentioned DCF as a default access technique. In this contention based scheme, subscriber stations (STAs) associated with the Access Point (AP) use their air interfaces for sensing channel availability. If the channel is idle, the source STA sends its data to the destination STA through the associated AP. If more than one STA try to access the channel simultaneously a collision occurs. The standard uses the Carrier Sense Multiple Access/Collision Avoidance (CSMA/CA) mechanism to avoid collisions. Point Coordination Function (PCF) is another technique that may be used in the MAC layer. In PCF, the data transmission is arbitrated in two modes: (i) centralized mode, where the AP polls each STA in a round-robin fashion, and (ii) contention-based mode, which works similarly to DCF. In addition, the Request To Send (RTS)/Clear To Send (CTS) mechanism is applied to solve the hidden node problem.

– WiMAX: The initial IEEE 802.16 WiMAX standard was established in the frequency band of 10-66 GHz, providing up to 75 Mbps data rate line-of-sight (LOS) connections in both point-to-multipoint (PMP) and mesh modes. IEEE 802.16a provides non-LOS connections in the frequency band of 2-11 GHz (licensed and unlicensed). The WiMAX PHY layer uses WirelessMAN-OFDMA (Orthogonal Frequency Division Multiple Access) and transfers bidirectional data by means of Time Division Duplex (TDD) or Frequency Division Duplex (FDD). IEEE 802.16 is a connection-oriented standard, i.e., prior to transmitting data between Subscriber Stations (SSs) and Base Station (BS), connections must be established. Each connection is identified by a 16-bit Connection Identifier (CID). The MAC layer is responsible for assigning CIDs as well as allocating bandwidth between SSs. It consists of the following three sublayers: (i) Convergence Sub-layer (CS), whereby different higher-layer protocols are implemented in different CSs, e.g., ATM CS and packet CS are used for ATM and Ethernet networks, respectively; (ii) Common Part Sub-layer (CPS), which is responsible for bandwidth allocation and generating MAC Protocol Data Units (PDUs); and (iii) security sub-layer. In the PMP mode, the requested services of each SS are first registered during the initialization phase and subsequently the connections are established. If a given SS changes its services, additional connections can be established in the network. Each connection is associated with a Service Flow (SF). An SF is defined based on available scheduling services and includes a set of QoS parameters, an SF Identifier (SFID), and a CID. To implement wireless mesh networks (WMNs), two scheduling types are used: (i) centralized and (ii) distributed. In the centralized scheduling mode, such as the PMP, each Mesh-SS (MSS) sends its request to the Mesh-BS (MBS) that manages the network. In the distributed scheduling mode, each MSS distributes its scheduling information and one-hop neighbors among all its adjacent MSSs. A three-way handshake mechanism is deployed for bandwidth allocation. Coordinated (collision-free) and uncoordinated (non-collision-free) methods are used for distributed scheduling. The two different mesh scheduling methods can be applied together by subdividing the data part of the frame into two parts, one for centralized scheduling and another one for distributed scheduling.

3.2   State of the Art

Cellular networks used for fast moving users, e.g., train passengers, suffer from frequent hand-overs when hopping from one base station to another one. The frequent hand-overs cause numerous packet losses, resulting in a significantly decreased network throughput. An interesting approach to solve this problem for train passengers is the use of an RoF network installed along the rail tracks in combination with the so-called moving cell concept [19]. The proposed solution provides high-capacity wireless services to high-speed train passengers using a hierarchical approach that consists of a wireless link between the railway and the train on the one hand and a separate wireless link between the train and the users on the other hand. In each train carriage, one or more WLAN access points are used to provide Internet connection.

Fig. 3 depicts the moving cell based RoF network architecture for train passengers. Several RAUs are located along the rail tracks. An optical wavelength division multiplexing (WDM) ring interconnects the RAUs with the central station where all processing is performed. Each RAU deploys an optical add-drop multiplexer (OADM) fixed tuned to a separate wavelength channel. That is, each RAU is allocated a separate dedicated wavelength channel for transmission and reception to and from the central station. At the central station, a WDM laser generates the desired wavelengths in order to reach the corresponding RAUs. The generated wavelengths are optically switched and passed to an array of RF modulators, one for each RAU. The modulated wavelengths are multiplexed onto the optical fiber ring and received by each addressed RAU on its assigned wavelength. An RAU retrieves the RF signal and transmits it to the antennas of a passing train. In the upstream direction, the RAUs receive all RF signals and sends them to the central station for processing. By processing the received RF signals, the central station is able to keep track of the train location and identifying the RAU closest to the moving train.

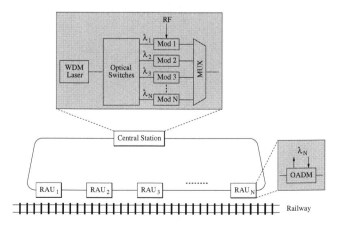

Fig. 3. Moving cell-based RoF network architecture for train passengers [19]

In conventional cellular radio networks, a hand-over would take place whenever the train crosses the cell boundary between two neighboring RAUs. To avoid hand-overs, the applied concept of moving cells lets a cell pattern move together with the passing train such that the train can communicate on the same RF frequencies during the whole connection without requiring hand-overs. The central station implements the moving cells by subsequently sending the RF frequencies used by the train to the next RAU following in the direction the train is moving. Based on the received upstream RF signals, the central station is able to track the location of the train and assign downstream RF signals to the corresponding RAU closest to the train such that the train and moving cells move along in a synchronous fashion.

Fig. 4 shows a two-level bidirectional path-protected ring R&F architecture for dense WDM/subcarrier multiplexing (SCM) broadband FiWi networks [20]. In this architecture, the CO interconnects remote nodes (RN) via a dual-fiber ring. Each RN cascades wireless access points (WAPs) through concentration nodes (CNs), where each WAP offers services to mobile client nodes (MCNs). For protection, the CO is equipped with two sets of devices (normal and standby). Each RN consists of a protection unit and a bidirectional wavelength add-drop multiplexer based on a multilayer dielectric interference filter. Each CN contains a protection unit. The WAP comprises an optical transceiver, a protection unit, up/down RF converters, and a sleeve antenna. Each WAP provides channel bandwidth of at least 5 MHz and covers up to 16 MCNs by means of frequency division multiplexing (FDM). Under normal operating conditions, the

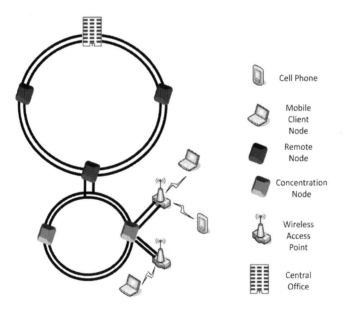

Fig. 4. Optical interconnected bidirectional fiber rings integrated with WiFi-based wireless access points [20]

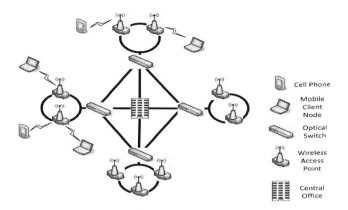

Fig. 5. Optical hybrid star-ring network integrated with WiFi-based wireless access points [21]

CO transmits downstream signals in the counter-clockwise direction via RNs and CNs to the WAPs. If a fiber cut occurs between two RNs or between two CNs, their associated controllers detect the failure by monitoring the received optical signal and then switch to the clockwise protection ring. If a failure happens at a WAP, the retransmitted signals are protection switched through other optical paths by throwing an optical switch inside the affected WAP. This architecture provides high reliability, flexibility, capacity, and self-healing properties.

Fig. 5 depicts an R&F-based hybrid FiWi network topology that combines optical star and ring networks [21]. Each fiber ring accommodates several WiFi-based WAPs and is connected to the CO and two neighboring fiber rings via optical switches. The optical switches have full wavelength conversion capability and interconnect the WAPs and CO by means of shared point-to-point light-paths. The network is periodically monitored during prespecified intervals. At the end of each interval, the lightpaths may be dynamically reconfigured in response to varying traffic demands. When traffic increases and the utilization of the established lightpaths is low, the load on the existing lightpaths is increased by means of load balancing. Otherwise, if the established lightpaths are heavily loaded, new lightpaths need to be set up, provided enough capacity is available on the fiber links. In the event of one or more link failures, the affected lightpaths are dynamically reconfigured using the redundant fiber paths of the architecture.

The FiWi network proposed in [22] consists of an optical WDM backhaul ring with multiple single-channel or multichannel PONs attached to it, as shown in Fig. 6. An OADM is used to connect the OLT of each PON to the WDM ring. Wireless gateways are used to realize an R&F network that bridges the PONs to a WiFi-based WMN. In the downstream direction, data packets are routed from the CO to the wireless gateways through the optical backhaul and are then forwarded to the MCNs by wireless mesh routers. In the upstream direction, wireless mesh routers forward data packets to one of the wireless gateways, where they are then transmitted to the CO on one of the wavelength channels of the optical backhaul WDM ring, as each PON operates on a separate dynamically

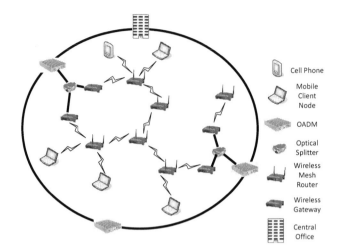

Fig. 6. Optical unidirectional WDM ring interconnecting multiple PONs integrated with a WiFi-based wireless mesh network [22]

allocated wavelength channel. Since the optical backhaul and WMN use different technologies, an interface is defined between each ONU and the corresponding wireless gateway in order to monitor the WMN and perform route computation taking the state of wireless links and average traffic rates into account. When the traffic demands surpass the available PON capacity, some of the time division multiplexing (TDM) PONs may be upgraded to WDM PONs. If some PONs are heavily loaded and others have less traffic, some heavy-loaded ONUs may be assigned to a lightly-loaded PON by tuning their optical transceivers to the wavelength assigned to the lightly-loaded PON. This architecture provides cost-effectiveness, bandwidth efficiency, wide coverage, high flexibility, and scalability. In addition, the reconfigurable TDM/WDM optical backhaul helps reduce network congestion and average packet latency by means of load balancing. Moreover, the dynamic allocation of radio resources enables cost-effective and simple hand-overs.

4   SuperMAN

As we have seen in the previous section, most previously reported FiWi networks used WiFi technologies for the wireless part. Only a few reported FiWi networks considered the deployment of WiMAX technologies. One notable example is the integration of single-channel TDM EPON and WiMAX networks. Several TDM EPON-WiMAX integration approaches were outlined and discussed in [23], ranging from independent to unified connection-oriented architectures. The integration of TDM EPON and WiMAX access networks seems to be interesting due to the similarity of the two technologies. Both EPON and WiMAX networks typically have a point-to-multipoint topology with a central control station (OLT in EPON, BS in WiMAX) performing dynamic bandwidth allocation by means of centralized polling and scheduling. These similarities give rise to interesting convergence problems whose optimization is expected to lead to an improved FiWi network performance.

In our proposed FiWi network, we take a different approach. Given the similarities of EPON and WiMAX, we argue that the two technologies are more likely to target the same network segment rather than being cascaded to cover different network segments. In other words, we expect that network operators will make a choice between EPON and WiMAX depending on a number of factors, e.g., right-of-way. Furthermore, recall from Section 1 that EPON networks will bring fiber close or all the way to end users. It seems somewhat impractical to deploy a metropolitan-reach wireless technology such as WiMAX for realizing wireless drop lines of rather short length to or inside offices and homes. Instead, using next-generation low-cost WiFi technologies in conjunction with WDM-enhanced EPON access networks while integrating WiMAX with optical metropolitan area network (MAN) technologies appears to be a more promising approach, giving rise to a novel FiWi network architecture which we call SuperMAN.

Fig. 7 depicts the network architecture of SuperMAN. It builds on our all-optically integrated Ethernet-based access-metro network, described at length in [24], extended by optical-wireless interfaces with next-generation WiFi and WiMAX networks. More specifically, the optical part of SuperMAN consists of an IEEE 802.17 Resilient Packet Ring (RPR) metro network that interconnects multiple WDM EPON access networks attached to a subset of RPR nodes. RPR is an optical dual-fiber bidirectional ring network that aims at combining Ethernet's statistical multiplexing gain, low equipment cost, and simplicity with SONET/SDH's carrier-class functionalities of high availability, reliability, and

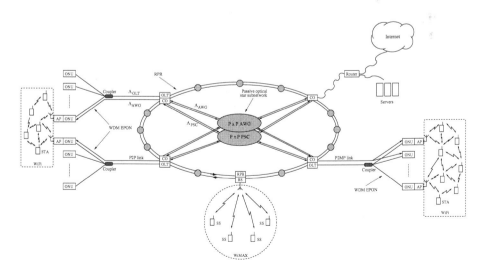

Fig. 7. SuperMAN architecture integrating next-generation WiFi technologies with WDM EPON and next-generation WiMAX technologies with RPR

profitable TDM (voice) support. In RPR, destination stripping is deployed to improve spatial reuse of bandwidth and thus increase the capacity of the network. Each of the attached WDM EPONs has a tree topology with the OLT at the root tree being collocated with one of the P COs. No particular WDM architecture is imposed on the ONUs, thus allowing the decision to be dictated by economics, state-of-the-art transceiver manufacturing technology, traffic demands, and service provider preferences. The recommended WDM extensions to the IEEE 802.3ah MultiPoint Control Protocol (MPCP), described in greater detail in [25], guarantee backward compatibility with legacy TDM EPONs and enable the OLT to schedule transmissions to and receptions from ONUs on any supported wavelength channel. The optical access-metro network lets low-cost PON technologies follow low-cost Ethernet technologies from access networks into metro networks by interconnecting the P collocated OLTs/COs with a passive optical star subnetwork whose hub consists of an athermal wavelength-routing $P \times P$ arrayed waveguide grating (AWG) in parallel with a wavelength-broadcasting $P \times P$ passive star coupler (PSC). It is important to note that in each WDM EPON two different sets of wavelengths, Λ_{OLT} and Λ_{AWG}, are used. The first wavelength set, Λ_{OLT}, is used for upstream and downstream transmissions between ONUs and respective OLT residing in the same WDM EPON. Whereas the second set, Λ_{AWG}, comprises wavelengths that optically bypass the collocated OLT/CO and allow ONUs residing in different WDM EPONs to communicate all-optically with each other in a single hop across the AWG of the star subnetwork, provided the ONUs are equipped with transceivers operating on these wavelengths. We finally note that similar to IEEE 802.3ah EPON, the optical part of SuperMAN is not restricted to any specific dynamic bandwidth allocation (DBA) algorithm. A plethora of DBA algorithms for WDM EPONs exist [26]. These DBA algorithms need to be adapted to SuperMAN. The aforementioned optical part of SuperMAN interfaces with next-generation WiFi and WiMAX networks. Both optical-wireless interfaces are described in greater detail in the following.

4.1 RPR/WiMAX Interface

As shown in Fig. 7, some of the RPR nodes may interface with WiMAX rather than EPON access networks. Fig. 8 depicts the optical-wireless interface between RPR and WiMAX networks in greater detail, where an integrated rate controller (IRC) is used to connect an RPR node to a WiMAX BS.

In RPR, packets undergo optical-electrical-optical (OEO) conversion at each ring node. An RPR node deploys in general two separate electrical transit queues, one primary transit queue (PTQ) and one secondary transit queue (STQ), for service differentiation. In addition, an electrical stage queue is used to store traffic ready to be sent by the RPR station. The RPR scheduler gives priority to in-transit ring traffic over station traffic such that in-transit packets are not lost due to buffer overflow. Furthermore, RPR deploys a distributed fairness control protocol that dynamically throttles traffic in order to achieve network-wide fairness while maintaining spatial reuse.

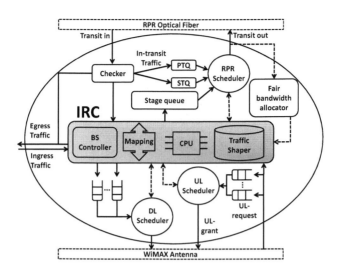

Fig. 8. Optical-wireless interface between RPR and WiMAX networks

The WiMAX BS deploys a downlink (DL) scheduler and an uplink (UL) scheduler, whereby the latter one processes UL requests from and sends UL grants to its attached SSs. In our ongoing work, we consider IEEE 802.16e and the emerging amendment IEEE 802.16m. The first one adds mobility support to conventional IEEE 802.16d WiMAX networks, while the latter one provides increases the data rate to 1 Gb/s.

The IRC in Fig. 8 plays a key role in our ongoing work on integrating RPR and WiMAX technologies. The IRC comprises a BS controller, traffic class mapping unit, CPU, and traffic shaper. It will be used to seamlessly integrate both technologies and jointly optimize the RPR scheduler and WiMAX DL and UL schedulers.

4.2   WDM EPON/Next-Generation WiFi Interface

Recall from Section 2 that WiFi-based RoF networks can sustain acceptable throughput performance only if the inserted fiber does not exceed a certain maximum length. Due to the fact that EPONs can have a reach of up to 20 km, the WDM EPON tree networks with WiFi extensions are realized as R&F networks, where each WiFi-based network operates independently of its attached WDM EPON tree network. In our ongoing work, we focus on the MAC enhancements of next-generation IEEE 802.11n WLANs and path selection algorithms for IEEE 802.11s WLAN mesh networks.

Next-generation WLANs will offer a throughput of at least 100 Mb/s measured at the MAC service access point (SAP). The IEEE standard 802.11n isn't expected to be approved until March 2009, but devices built to the current 802.11n draft will require only software upgrades to be compliant with the ratified standard. The draft provides both PHY and MAC enhancements. By using MIMO-OFDM and channel bonding, 802.11n WLANs offer raw data rates of about 600 Mb/s at the physical layer. To achieve a net MAC throughput of 100 Mb/s and higher, 802.11n WLANs allow wireless stations for the truncation of transmission opportunities (TXOPs), reverse direction (i.e., bidirectional TXOP), and use of a reduced interframe space (RIFS) to decrease the dead time between frames (a TXOP, specified in IEEE 802.11e, is a time interval during which a wireless station following a single channel access is allowed to send multiple data frames). The most important MAC enhancement of next-generation WLANs is frame aggregation. In 802.11n, the following two methods exist for frame aggregation: (i) aggregate MAC protocol data unit (A-MPDU), and (ii) aggregate MAC service data unit (A-MSDU). A-MPDU concatenates up to 64 MPDU subframes into a single physical layer SDU, provided all constituent MPDUs are destined to the same receiver. A-MSDU concatenates multiple MSDU subframes into a single MPDU, whereby all constituent MSDUs not only have to be destined to the same receiver but also must have the same traffic identifier (TID), i.e., the same QoS level. A-MPDU and A-MSDU can be used separately or jointly to increase the MAC throughput of next-generation WLANs.

As shown in Fig. 7, SuperMAN deploys a next-generation 802.11n WLAN mesh network. The emerging amendment IEEE 802.11s aims at specifying a wireless distribution system (WDS) among WLAN APs which can be used to realize municipal networks that provide public wireless access throughout cities, neighborhoods, and campuses. IEEE 802.11s introduces a new mesh frame format and radio-aware routing framework which uses the so-called Hybrid Wireless Mesh Protocol (HWMP) as default routing protocol. HWMP works on layer 2, uses MAC addresses for path selection, and contains both reactive and proactive routing components. In SuperMAN, proactive routing can be used to configure routing trees toward the collocated AP/ONU(s) that act as mesh portals bridging the WLAN mesh network to the optical (wired) WDM EPON access network. For intra-mesh communication between wireless stations, a given mesh portal (i.e., AP/ONU) may apply reactive routing by setting up a direct route between the involved wireless stations, thereby eliminating the need to send intra-mesh traffic through the mesh portal. It is important to note that the routing framework of IEEE 802.11s is extensible. Thus, other routing protocols and routing metrics can be deployed in order to optimize network performance according to given traffic demands and usage scenarios.

In our ongoing work, we study integrated hybrid path selection algorithms for SuperMAN that take both proactive and reactive components as well as different routing metric combinations into account. Particular attention will be paid to the design and performance evaluation of QoS-aware scheduling algorithms that ensure QoS continuity across the WDM EPON/next-generation WiFi interface and provide end-to-end QoS assurances across SuperMAN.

5 Conclusions

Hybrid optical-wireless FiWi networks form a powerful future-proof platform that provides a number of advantages. Introducing optical fiber into broadband wireless access networks helps relieve emerging bandwidth bottlenecks in today's wireless backhaul due to increasing traffic loads generated by new applications, e.g., iPhone. By simultaneously providing wired and wireless services over the same infrastructure, FiWi networks are able to consolidate (optical) wired and wireless access networks that are usually run independently of each other, thus potentially leading to major cost savings.

More interestingly, and certainly somewhat controversially, by paving all the way to and penetrating into homes and offices with high-capacity fiber and connecting wireless laptops and handhelds with high-throughput WiFi technologies to high-speed optical wired networks, SuperMAN, and FiWi networks in general, give access to the ever increasing processing and storage capabilities of memory and CPUs of widely used desktops, laptops, and other wireless handhelds, e.g., Wii. Note that nowadays desktop and laptop computers commonly operate at a clock rate of 1 GHz with a 32-bit wide backplane, resulting in an internal flow of 2-8 Gb/s with today's limited hard drive I/O, while future desktops and laptops are expected to reach 100 Gb/s by 2010 [7]. At present, these storage and processing capabilities are quite often utilized only in part. After bridging the notorious first/last mile bandwidth bottleneck, research focus might shift from bandwidth provisioning to the exploitation of distributed storage and processing capabilities available in widely used desktops and laptops, especially as we are about to enter the Petabyte age with sensors everywhere collecting massive amounts of data [27]. As an early example for this shift can be viewed the design of P2P on-line game architectures that have begun to increasingly receive attention, where players' computing resources are utilized to improve the latency and scalability of networked on-line games, whose groundbreaking technologies might also be used to realize the future 3D Internet. On the other hand, in-house computer facilities might be replaced with computer utilities as in-house generators were replaced with electrical utilities [28]. Indeed, utility-supplied computing, e.g., Google, will continue to have an increasing impact on society and replace personal computer facilities unless new services and applications are developed that capitalize on them. Toward this end, it is important that FiWi networks are built using low-cost, simple, open, and ubiquitous technologies which allow all end users to have broadband access and to create unforeseen services and applications that help stimulate innovation, generate revenue, and improve the quality of our every-day lives, while at the same time minimizing the associated technical, economical, societal, and personal risks.

References

1. Koonen, T.: Fiber to the Home/Fiber to the Premises: What, Where, and When. Proceedings of the IEEE 94(5), 911–934 (2006)
2. Cioffi, J.M., Jagannathan, S., Mohseni, M., Ginis, G.: CuPON: The Copper Alternative to PON 100 Gb/S DSL Networks. IEEE Communications Magazine 45(6), 132–139 (2007)
3. Green, P.E.: Optical Networking Update. IEEE Journal on Selected Areas in Communications 14(5), 764–779 (1996)

4. Shinohara, H.: Broadband Access in Japan: Rapidly Growing FTTH Market. IEEE Communications Magazine 43(9), 72–78 (2005)
5. Koike, Y., Ishigure, T.: High-Bandwidth Plastic Optical Fiber for Fiber to the Display. IEEE/OSA Journal of Lightwave Technology 24(12), 4541–4553 (2006)
6. Ramaswami, R.: Optical Networking Technologies: What Worked and What Didn't. IEEE Communications Magazine 44(9), 132–239 (2006)
7. Green, P.E.: Fiber To The Home—The New Empowerment. John Wiley & Sons, Inc., Chichester (2006)
8. Chu, T.-S., Gans, M.J.: Fiber Optic Microcellular Radio. IEEE Transactions on Vehicular Technology 40(3), 599–606 (1991)
9. Wu, J., Wu, J.-S., Tsao, H.-W.: A Fiber Distribution System for Microcellular Radio. IEEE Photonics Technology Letters 6(9), 1150–1152 (1994)
10. Tang, P.K., Ong, L.C., Alphones, A., Luo, B., Fujise, M.: PER and EVM Measurements of a Radio-Over-Fiber Network for Cellular and WLAN System Applications. IEEE/OSA Journal of Lightwave Technology 22(11), 2370–2376 (2004)
11. Lethien, C., Loyez, C., Vilcot, J.-P.: Potentials of Radio over Multimode Fiber Systems for the In-Buildings Coverage of Mobile and Wireless LAN Applications. IEEE Photonics Technology Letters 17(12), 2793–2795 (2005)
12. Lin, C.-T., Chen, J., Peng, P.-C., Peng, C.-F., Peng, W.-R., Chiou, B.-S., Chi, S.: Hybrid Optical Access Network Integrating Fiber-to-the-Home and Radio-Over-Fiber Systems. IEEE Photonics Technology Letters 19(8), 610–612 (2007)
13. Dang, B.L., Niemegeers, I.: Analysis of IEEE 802.11 in Radio over Fiber Home Networks. In: Proc. IEEE Conference on Local Computer Networks, pp. 744–747. IEEE Press, Sydney (2005)
14. Kalantarisabet, B., Mitchell, J.E.: MAC Constraints on the Distribution of 802.11 using Optical Fibre. In: Proc. European Conference on Wireless Technology, pp. 238–240. IEEE Press, Los Alamitos (2006)
15. Henry, P.S.: Integrated Optical/Wireless Alternatives for the Metropolitan Environment. IEEE Communications Society Webinar (2007)
16. Jia, Z., Yu, J., Ellinas, G., Chang, G.-K.: Key Enabling Technologies for Optical-Wireless Networks: Optical Millimeter-Wave Generation, Wavelength Reuse, and Architecture. IEEE/OSA Journal of Lightwave Technology 25(11), 3452–3471 (2007)
17. Kazovsky, L.G., Shaw, W.-T., Gutierrez, D., Cheng, N., Wong, S.-W.: Next-Generation Optical Access Networks. IEEE/OSA Journal of Lightwave Technology 25(11), 3428–3442 (2007)
18. Kuran, M.S., Tugcu, T.: A Survey on Emerging Broadband Wireless Access Technologies. Computer Networks 51(11), 3013–3046 (2007)
19. Lannoo, B., Colle, D., Pickavet, M., Demeester, P.: Radio-over-Fiber-Based Solution to Provide Broadband Internet Access to Train Passengers. IEEE Communications Magazine 45(2), 56–62 (2007)
20. Lin, W.-P., Kao, M.-S., Chi, S.: A Reliable Architecture for Broad-Band Fiber-Wireless Access Networks. IEEE Photonics Technology Letters 15(2), 344–346 (2003)
21. Bhandari, S., Park, E.K.: Hybrid Optical Wireless Networks. In: Proc. International Conference on Networking, International Conference on Systems, and International Conference on Mobile Communications and Learning Technologies, pp. 113–117. IEEE Press, Mauritius (2006)

22. Shaw, W.-T., Wong, S.-W., Cheng, N., Balasubramanian, K., Zhu, X., Maier, M., Kazovsky, L.G.: Hybrid Architecture and Integrated Routing in a Scalable Optical-Wireless Access Network. IEEE/OSA Journal of Lightwave Technology 25(11), 3443–3451 (2007)
23. Shen, G., Tucker, R.S., Chae, C.-J.: Fixed Mobile Convergence Architectures for Broadband Access: Integration of EPON and WiMAX. IEEE Communications Magazine 45(8), 44–50 (2007)
24. Maier, M., Herzog, M., Reisslein, M.: STARGATE: The Next Evolutionary Step Toward Unleashing the Potential of WDM EPONs. IEEE Communications Magazine 45(5), 50–56 (2007)
25. McGarry, M.P., Maier, M., Reisslein, M.: WDM Ethernet Passive Optical Networks. IEEE Communications Magazine 44(2), S18–S25 (2006)
26. McGarry, M.P., Reisslein, M., Maier, M.: Ethernet Passive Optical Network Architectures and Dynamic Bandwidth Allocation Algorithms. IEEE Communications Surveys and Tutorials (to appear)
27. The Petabyte Age. WIRED, p. 106 (July 2008)
28. Carr, N.: The Big Switch: Rewiring the World, from Edison to Google. W. W. Norton & Company, Inc. (2008)

When Are Online and Offline Excess Bandwidth Distribution Useful in EPONs?

(Invited Paper)

Jason R. Ferguson[1], Michael P. McGarry[2], and Martin Reisslein[3]

[1] ADTRAN, Phoenix, AZ, USA
jason.ferguson@adtran.com
[2] The University of Akron, Department of Electrical and Computer Eng.,
Akron, OH 44325, USA
mmcgarry@uakron.edu
[3] Arizona State University, Department of Electrical Engineering, Goldwater Center,
Tempe, AZ 85287-5706, USA
reisslein@asu.edu

Abstract. Excess bandwidth distribution techniques have recently been proposed to improve the dynamic bandwidth allocation in EPONs. We compare existing offline excess bandwidth distribution with conventional IPACT Limited in terms of packet delay performance. We identify the factors that result in packet delay reduction with excess bandwidth distribution compared to IPACT-Limited and discover that existing offline excess distribution mechanisms become unstable at moderate to high loads in long-range EPONs with large round trip propagation delays. We propose and evaluate a novel Online Excess Bandwidth Distribution (OEBD) mechanism to provide stable excess bandwidth distribution even at high loads in long-range EPONs.

Keywords: EPON, excess bandwidth distribution, IPACT Limited, packet delay.

1 Introduction

Excess bandwidth distribution for Ethernet Passive Optical Networks (EPONs) has originally been proposed in [1] as an improvement over the Limited allocation approach of Interleaved Polling with Adaptive Cycle Time (IPACT) [2,3], which we refer to as IPACT-Limited. IPACT-Limited is characterized by a maximum grant size G_i^{max} [Bytes], also frequently referred to as minimum guaranteed bandwidth, for each Optical Network Unit (ONU) i, $i = 1, \ldots, M$. Let R_i [Bytes] denote the size of the upstream transmission request from ONU i. If ONU i requests less than G_i^{max}, i.e., $R_i \leq G_i^{\mathrm{max}}$, then IPACT-Limited grants the full request, i.e., the size of the grant to ONU i is $G_i = R_i$. If the request exceeds G_i^{max}, i.e., $R_i > G_i^{\mathrm{max}}$, then IPACT-Limited grants an upstream transmission window for $G_i = G_i^{\mathrm{max}}$ Bytes.

C. Wang (Ed.): AccessNets, LNICST 6, pp. 36–45, 2009.

The intuitive reasoning behind excess bandwidth distribution is to declare the unused portions $(G_i^{\max} - G_i)$ as excess bandwidth and distribute the total excess bandwidth $\sum_{m=1}^{M} (G_i^{\max} - G_i)$ among the ONUs with $R_i > G_i^{\max}$. Thus, the basic tradeoff made with excess bandwidth distribution is to extend the cycle within which all ONUs are served once (to no more than approximately $\sum_{m=1}^{M} G_i^{\max}/C$, with C denoting the upstream transmission rate in Byte/sec) so that heavily loaded ONUs can transmit more than $G_i^{\max}$ in a cycle. In contrast, IPACT-Limited enforces shorter cycles by strictly limiting upstream transmissions to at most $G_i^{\max}$ in a cycle, resulting in heavily loaded ONUs having to use more cycles to clear backlogs.

To the best of our knowledge, IPACT with Limited allocation has not been, in detail, quantitatively compared with the various proposed excess bandwidth distribution mechanisms. That is, the outlined basic tradeoff between clearing traffic backlogs with more shorter cycles with IPACT-Limited versus fewer longer cycles with excess distribution techniques has not been quantitatively investigated to identify the factors leading to improvements with excess bandwidth distribution. Oftentimes, the excess bandwidth distribution research has focused on quantitatively comparing different excess bandwidth distribution techniques, against each other, as reviewed in Section 2.

In this paper, we conduct for the first time a detailed quantitative comparison between IPACT-Limited and excess bandwidth distribution techniques. We conduct extensive simulations to assess the packet delays. We identify the factors that influence the relative performance differences between IPACT-Limited and excess bandwidth distribution. We find that existing offline excess bandwidth distribution mechanisms achieve significant delay reductions compared to IPACT-Limited for traffic with large bursts in mid-range EPONs. However, we also find that the existing offline excess bandwidth distribution mechanisms suffer from instability problems in long-range EPONs, which are currently intensely studied [4,5,6]. We propose a novel Online Excess Bandwidth Distribution Mechanism (OEBD) to overcome the stability problems of existing offline excess bandwidth distribution mechanisms.

2   Related Work

Excess bandwidth distribution as part of the dynamic bandwidth allocation process in EPONs [7] has received significant interest in recent years. Following the seminal work [1], several refinements and a range of different mechanisms have been proposed for excess bandwidth distribution. The research in [8], for instance, significantly advanced excess bandwidth allocation by introducing a weighted excess division technique that enforces fair division of the total excess bandwidth among the overloaded ONUs requesting more than $G_i^{\max}$. Several studies explored further refinements of excess bandwidth distribution to incorporate features, such as differentiated services, see e.g., [9] and traffic prediction, see e.g., [10]. The excess bandwidth allocation refinement in [11] included some limited performance comparisons with IPACT-Limited. Our comparisons are fundamentally different from [11] in that we consider a wide range of scenarios, including a range of round-trip propagation delays, to identify the factors leading to improvements with excess bandwidth distribution over IPACT-Limited.

A modification to IPACT-Limited was explored in [12], whereby the excess bandwidth of a given ONU is immediately equally distributed among the other ONUs to increase their maximum grant limits. Our Online Excess Bandwidth Distribution (OEBD) is fundamentally different from the distribution technique in [12] in that it maintains an excess bandwidth credit pool for carrying excess bandwidth across cycles, as explained in Section 4, and supports unequal weight-based excess distribution.

More recently, some excess bandwidth distribution techniques originally proposed for single-channel EPONs have been investigated in the context of Wavelength Division Multiplexing (WDM) EPONs with several upstream transmission channels [13]. The performance evaluation in [13] includes comparisons of excess bandwidth distribution with some form of IPACT, namely the Single Table extension of IPACT to WDM [14]. Specifically, the Gated allocation of IPACT, where the grant is set equal to the ONU request, without any upper limit, was considered. Gated allocation can lead to unfairness because grant sizes are determined solely as a function of reported queue depth, which is obviously unfair. IPACT with Limited allocation, which we consider in this study, avoids this fairness problem by strictly limiting the size of a granted upstream transmission.

3   Comparison of IPACT-Limited and Offline Excess Bandwidth Distribution

We initially consider IPACT-Limited bandwidth allocation in conjunction with (a) the *offline* scheduling framework, where all ONU Reports must be received before allocating bandwidth, which idles the upstream channel for one round-trip time, (b) the ONU load status *hybrid* scheduling framework, where underloaded ONUs with $R_i \leq G_i^{\mathrm{max}}$ are immediately granted bandwidth, and overloaded ONUs with $R_i > G_i^{\mathrm{max}}$ are granted bandwidth once all ONU Reports have been received, and (c) the *online* scheduling framework, where all ONUs are immediately granted bandwidth.

Among the many different excess distribution schemes, we focus on the weighted excess division dynamic bandwidth allocation scheme from [8], which enforces fair distribution of the excess bandwidth by divided the excess according to the weights of the ONUs. We combine this with the Iterative excess allocation [8] which iteratively allocates excess bandwidth to ONUs in an effort to maximize the number of satisfied ONUs. By maximizing the number of satisfied ONUs, unused slot remainders are minimized. We refer to this combined excess bandwidth distribution scheme as *Iterative*. We consider this Iterative scheme in conjunction with (a) the *offline* scheduling framework, whereby all ONU Reports need to be received at the OLT before commencing the dynamic bandwidth allocation, as well as (b) the ONU load status *hybrid* scheduling framework (referred to as DWBA-2 in [13]), whereby underloaded ONUs receive their grant (online) immediately and the excess bandwidth distribution is executed for the over-loaded ONUs (offline), once all the Report messages have been received. Note that in both cases, the excess bandwidth distribution operates in offline fashion, in that the excess is allocated only after all ONU Reports for the present cycle have been received. We note that we do not consider DBA-3 from [13], which allocates overloaded ONUs (online) immediately the maximum grant size, and then additional *excess bandwidth in offline fashion*, because of its increased com-plexity, limited delay reductions, and increased wasted bandwidth, as evaluated in [13].

3.1 Simulation Set-Up

We developed an EPON simulation engine using the CSIM simulation library. We set the upstream transmission bit rate to $C = 1$ Gbps. We initially consider an EPON with $M = 16$ ONUs, each with a 10 MByte buffer. We consider round trip (RTT) propagation delays (ONU to OLT and back to ONU) for short-range ([8, 10]μs corresponding to OLT-to-ONU distances up to 1 km), mid-range ([13.36, 100]μs corresponding to OLT-to-ONU distances up to 10 km), long-range ([0.8, 1]ms corresponding to OLT-to-ONU distances up to 100 km), and extra long-range ([1.6, 2]ms corresponding to OLT-to-ONU distances up to 200 km) EPONs; for each range the different ONUs draw their RTT independently randomly from a uniform distribution over the respective intervals.

Each ONU independently generates self-similar traffic with a Hurst parameter of 0.75 [15] using 32 traffic sources. The burst size (number of data packets) and time between bursts were independently randomly drawn from Pareto distribu-tions. Following common packet size models, 60% of the packets have 64 Byte, 4% have 300 Byte, 11% have 580 Byte, and 25% have 1518 Byte. Each of the 32 sources of a given ONU has initially a maximum burst size of $B = 10$ MByte, which is achieved by truncating the Pareto distribution to produce a maximum burst size no greater than $B/1518$ Bytes = 6907 packets. Each ONU contributed equally to the overall traffic load.

For upstream transmission, each data packet is sent with a Preamble of 8 Bytes and an Inter-packet Gap of 12 Bytes (which count toward the upstream transmission grant). Gate and Report messages each have 64 Bytes and there is a $t_{\text{guard}} = 1$ μs guard time between upstream transmissions. For the IPACT-Limited and Hybrid-Iterative bandwidth allocation schemes, we initially set the maximum grant size to $G_{\text{max}} = G_i^{\text{max}} = 15,500$ Bytes for each ONU; the corre-sponding cycle time is $MG_{\text{max}}/C + Mt_{\text{guard}} = 2$ ms.

As primary performance metric we consider in this paper the packet queuing delay, defined as the time interval from the generation of a packet at an ONU to the instant the upstream transmission of the packet commences. We note that the total packet delay in the network would be obtained by adding the packet transmission delay and the one-way propagation delay to the packet queuing delay.

Table 1. Packet delay in ms as function of load in Mbps for different scheduling frameworks. Fixed Parameters: mid-range RTT, $M = 16$ ONUs, $B = 10$ MByte max. burst size, $G_{\max} = 15,500$ Byte.

Load	200	400	600	800
Offline-Limited	0.30	0.44	0.78	2.34
Offline-Iterative	0.21	0.31	0.55	1.47
Online-Limited	0.25	0.33	0.54	1.39
Hybrid-Iterative	0.20	0.28	0.45	1.10

3.2   Impact of Offline, Hybrid, and Online Scheduling

As expected, we observe from Table 1 that Online-Limited substantially reduces the delay compared to Offline-Limited since the extra round trip time (between the last ONU completing the upstream transmission of a cycle and the first ONU commencing the upstream transmission of the next cycle) is eliminated for *all* grants. (Hybrid-Limited, where only overloaded ONUs are scheduled in offline fashion, performed very similarly to Online-Limited.) With Hybrid-Iterative the extra round trip time is avoided only for the underloaded ONUs, resulting in a relatively smaller delay reduction compared to Offline-Iterative.

We further observe from Table 1 that for online/hybrid scheduling the difference between Limited and Iterative is relatively smaller than for offline scheduling. This is mainly because the cycles in Online-Limited are much shorter than in Offline-Limited reducing the impact of the larger number of cycles needed to work off large traffic bursts. At the same time, it is more likely that upstream transmissions from ONUs requesting less than $G_{\max}$ mask the shorter delay between the upstream transmissions working off a large burst from a given ONU.

To further examine the impact of the larger number of cycles, we simulated a hypothetical EPON with all transmission overhead directly associated with an upstream transmission (guard time as well as Report message transmission time) set to zero. For this hypothetical EPON with a load of 800 Mbps, Online-Limited achieves a delay of 1.01 ms compared to Hybrid-Iterative giving 0.94 ms, i.e., the gap has significantly narrowed compared to the 1.39 ms vs. 1.10 ms with all the overheads. This significant narrowing of the gap indicates that the delay difference between Online-Limited and Hybrid-Iterative is to a large degree due to the upstream transmission overheads (guard time, Report message transmission time), which are experienced more often when transmitting large bursts in more, but shorter cycles with Online-Iterative. Note in particular, that each cycle in a real EPON contains a guard time and a Report message transmission for each ONU, even if only one or a few ONUs have data to send. These delays can not be masked by the interleaved transmissions of several ONUs.

We proceed to examine Online-Limited and Hybrid-Iterative, the best performing approaches from this section, in more detail in the subsequent section.

Table 2. Packet delay in ms as function of load in Mbps for different maximum burst sizes B. Fixed Parameters: $M = 16$ ONUs, mid-range RTT.

Load	200	400	600	800
$B = 65\text{k}$, $G_{\max} = 15,500$ B, On.-Lim.	0.135	0.147	0.179	0.313
$B = 65\text{k}$, $G_{\max} = 15,500$ B, Hyb.-It.	0.135	0.147	0.179	0.309
$B = 4\text{M}$, $G_{\max} = 15,500$ B, On.-Lim.	0.206	0.271	0.421	0.974
$B = 4\text{M}$, $G_{\max} = 15,500$ B, Hyb.-It.	0.180	0.237	0.363	0.790
$B = 10\text{M}$, $G_{\max} = 31,125$ B, $M = 16$, On.-Lim.	0.213	0.289	0.473	1.16
$B = 10\text{M}$, $G_{\max} = 31,125$ B, $M = 16$, Hyb.-It.	0.199	0.271	0.440	1.06
$B = 10\text{M}$, $G_{\max} = 15,500$ B, $M = 32$, On.-Lim.	0.281	0.410	0.689	1.80
$B = 10\text{M}$, $G_{\max} = 15,500$ B, $M = 32$, Hyb.-It.	0.213	0.312	0.526	1.31

3.3 Impact of Burst Size B and Maximum Grant Size $G_{\max}$

We examine in Table 2 the impact of smaller burst sizes as well as larger maximum transmission grants. Recall that the results in Table 1 were obtained with a maximum burst size of 10 MBytes for each of the 32 traffic streams producing the load at a given ONU. We observe from Table 2 that reducing the maximum burst size to 4 MBytes and further to 65 kBytes reduces the delay difference between Online-Limited and Hybrid-Iterative, with both giving essentially the same delays for the 65 kByte maximum burst size. This is because smaller bursts require fewer cycles for transmission, both with Online-Limited and Hybrid-Iterative.

Further, we observe from Table 2 that a larger maximum grant size of $G_{\max} = 31,125$ Byte compared to the $G_{\max} = 15500$ Byte considered in Table 1 narrows the gap between Online-Limited and Hybrid-Iterative for the large $B = 10$ MByte maximum burst size. This is again mainly because of the fewer cycles required to work off bursts, which are this time due to the larger maximum grant size, and correspondingly longer cycle.

Finally, we observe from Table 2 that a larger number of ONUs makes the delay differences between Online-Limited and Hybrid-Iterative more pronounced. This is primarily due to the increased upstream transmission overheads (guard time and Report transmission time) which are incurred for each ONU once in each cycle.

3.4 Impact of Round Trip Time RTT and Maximum Grant Size $G_{\max}$

In this section we focus on the impact of the round trip time, in conjunction with the maximum grant size, on the relative delay performance of Online-Limited and Hybrid-Iterative. (Ignore for now the OEBD results in Table 3; these are discussed in the next section.) We first observe that for the short round trip time up to 10 μs, the delays for high loads are very similar to the delays for high loads for round trip times up to 100 μs in Table 2.

Importantly, we observe from Table 3 that Hybrid-Iterative exhibits a pronounced threshold behavior. For loads below a critical threshold, Hybrid-Iterative gives substantially smaller delays than Online-Limited. In fact, the

Table 3. Packet delay in ms as function of load in Mbps for different round trip times. Fixed Parameters: $M = 16$ ONUs, $B = 10$ MByte maximum burst size.

Load	200	400	600	800
$G_{\max} = 15,500$ Bytes, 2 ms cycle				
short RTT, Online-Limited	0.158	0.259	0.486	1.36
short RTT, Hybrid-Iterative	0.123	0.209	0.398	1.08
short RTT, OEBD	0.131	0.218	0.412	1.11
long RTT, Online-Limited	2.43	2.60	2.93	3.85
long RTT, Hybrid-Iterative	1.31	1.44	1.76	> 2 s
long RTT, OEBD	1.82	1.88	2.03	2.61
X-long RTT, Online-Limited	5.37	6.64	10.13	34.23
X-long RTT, Hybrid-Iterative	2.57	3.01	> 2 s	> 2 s
X-long RTT, OEBD	3.65	3.91	4.62	8.91
$G_{\max} = 31,125$ Bytes, 4 ms cycle				
long RTT, Online-Limited	1.66	1.70	1.81	2.30
long RTT, Hybrid-Iterative	1.25	1.33	1.51	2.11
long RTT, OEBD	1.68	1.73	1.87	2.43

delay differences become more pronounced with increased round trip time, with Hybrid-Iterative achieving delays less than half as large as Online-Limited for low loads and the extra long round trip time up to 2 ms. However, for loads above a critical load threshold, which decreases for increasing round trip time, Hybrid-Iterative becomes unstable and gives excessively large delays. On the other hand, Online-Limited robustly continues to provide low delays even at very high loads.

The explanation for this behavior is as follows. Consider an extreme scenario in Hybrid-Iterative where only one ONU has upstream traffic, namely a very large burst. Then, this overloaded ONU receives all the upstream transmission bandwidth in the cycles, namely $MG_{\max}$ per cycle (neglecting the grants for Report messages to the other ONUs). A given cycle consists of an upstream transmission of $MG_{\max}$ [Byte], lasting $MG_{\max}/C$ [s], plus one round trip time RTT for reporting the remaining size of the backlog and receiving the next grant. In addition, the cycle contains M guard times and the Report transmission times of the other $M-1$ ONU's Report messages (which we neglect in this approximate analysis). Thus, the maximum sustainable upstream transmission rate is approximately

$$\frac{MG_{\max}}{RTT + \frac{MG_{\max}}{C} + Mt_{\text{guard}}} = \frac{G_{\max}}{\frac{RTT}{M} + \frac{G_{\max}}{C} + t_{\text{guard}}}. \qquad (1)$$

We note that this threshold is approximate in that upstream transmissions from underloaded ONUs may mask some of the round trip time incurred due to offline excess bandwidth distribution, leading to a higher threshold in an actual EPON. On the other hand, the neglected overheads may slightly reduce the threshold for a actual EPON. For the specific realizations of the randomly drawn RTT which gave an average RTT of 0.871 ms for the long range EPON simulation and an average RTT of 1.74 ms for the extra long range EPON simulation, the approximate theoretical thresholds are 691.3 Mbps for the long range EPON and 530.5 Mbps for the extra long range EPON. Our simulations indicate that these theoretical approximation are very close to the actual thresholds found in simulations, which are around 690 Mbps for the long range and 513 Mbps for the extra long range scenario. For loads well below the derived threshold, Hybrid-Iterative is able to provide small delays and to fairly allocate excess bandwidth to overloaded ONUs in offline fashion. When the load grows well above the threshold, then waiting for the excess bandwidth distribution until all Report messages are received for a cycle, reduces the capacity so much to render the network effectively unstable.

In order to overcome the stability problems due to the offline excess bandwidth distribution in Hybrid-Iterative, we propose and examine a novel Online Excess Bandwidth Distribution (OEBD) approach in the next section.

4   Online Excess Bandwidth Distribution (OEBD)

In this section we introduce and evaluate online excess bandwidth distribution (OEBD) for an *online* scheduling framework that makes grant decisions based on a single report; extensions to online Just-in-Time (JIT) scheduling [16] are left for future work. Recall that we let R_i denote the bandwidth requested by the considered report from a given ONU i, $i = 1, \ldots, M$, whereby bandwidth is measured in units of Bytes of transmitted data (i.e., corresponds to an upstream transmission window in seconds times the upstream bandwidth in Byte/sec), and that we let $G_i^{\max}$ [Bytes] be a constant denoting the maximum bandwidth that can be allocated to ONU i in a grant. We let w_i, $0 \le w_i \le 1$, $\sum_{i=1}^{M} w_i = 1$ denote the weight of ONU i in a weighted fair excess division [8]. We define an excess bandwidth credit pool and let E_t [Bytes] denote the current total amount of bandwidth credits in the excess pool. In addition, we let δ, $0 \le \delta \le 1$, be a constant aging factor.

The OEBD bandwidth allocation proceeds as follows. If the considered ONU i is underloaded, i.e., requests less than the prescribed maximum allocation ($R_i \le G_i^{\max}$), then the bandwidth R_i is granted and the excess $G_i^{\max} - R_i$ is added to the excess bandwidth pool E_t. If the considered ONU is overloaded, i.e., requests more than its prescribed maximum allocation ($R_i > G_i^{\max}$), then the ONU is allocated its prescribed maximum $G_i^{\max}$ plus up to $w_i E_t$ excess bandwidth from the pool. With a controlled excess allocation technique, the allocation is capped at R_i, i.e., the ONU is allocated $\min\{G_i^{\max} + w_i E_t, R_i\}$. Accordingly, the excess pool is reduced by $\min\{G_i^{\max} + w_i E_t, R_i\}$. In addition, after every N grants, we "age" the pool, E_t, using the multiplicative constant δ.

4.1   Simulation Results

We conducted initial simulations to identify good settings for the parameters N and δ. We found that generally larger δ reduces the delays and set $\delta = 0.75$

for the results presented here. We have set $N = M$ to "age" the pool after a full grant cycle. A $\delta = 1$ may cause OEBD to degenerate in the long run to Gated bandwidth allocation. We observe from the OEBD results for $G_{\max}$ in Table 3 that OEBD gives delays that are generally between Online-Limited and Hybrid-Iterative, typically closer to the Hybrid-Iterative delays. Importantly, for the long-range and extra-long range scenarios with moderate to high load, for which Hybrid-Iterative becomes unstable, OEBD remains stable and consistently provides significantly lower delays than Online-Limited.

We also observe from Table 3 that for $G_{\max} = 31,125$ Bytes, OEBD gives delays slightly larger than Online-Limited.

5   Conclusion

We have examined the delay and fairness performance of conventional IPACT with Limited allocation and existing excess bandwidth allocation strategies, which allocate excess in an offline fashion. We discovered that offline excess bandwidth allocation significantly reduces the delay compared to IPACT-Limited for traffic with large bursts and EPONs with mid-range round-trip times. For traffic with small bursts or EPONs with short round-trip times, IPACT-Limited achieves delays almost as low as with offline excess bandwidth distribution.

Importantly, we found that for long-range EPONs with large round-trip times, offline excess bandwidth distribution exhibits a pronounced threshold behavior: For loads below a critical threshold, offline excess bandwidth distribution provides lower delays than IPACT-Limited. For loads above the threshold, offline excess bandwidth distribution becomes unstable, resulting in excessively large delays, whereas IPACT-Limited continues to achieve small delays.

We introduced Online Excess Bandwidth Distribution (OEBD) to overcome the stability problems of the existing offline excess bandwidth distribution mechanisms. We found that OEBD generally achieves delays between offline excess bandwidth distribution and IPACT-Limited below the stability limit of offline excess bandwidth distribution, and below IPACT-Limited for load levels above the stability limit.

There are numerous important avenues for future research on OEBD. One important direction is to further comprehensively study the parameter setting for OEBD to ensure robust, good performance across a wide range of scenarios. Another avenue is to examine the compatibility of OEBD with emerging dynamic bandwidth allocation strategies for long-range EPONs, such as multi-thread polling [6]. Furthermore, not only the delay performance, but also the fairness performance of OEBD requires careful evaluation.

References

1. Assi, C., Ye, Y., Dixit, S., Ali, M.: Dynamic bandwidth allocation for Quality-of-Service over Ethernet PONs. IEEE Journal on Selected Areas in Communications 21(9), 1467–1477 (2003)

2. Kramer, G., Mukherjee, B., Pesavento, G.: IPACT: A dynamic protocol for an Ethernet PON (EPON). IEEE Communications Magazine 40(2), 74–80 (2002)
3. Kramer, G., Mukherjee, B., Dixt, S., Y., Y., Hirth, R.: Supporting differentiated classes of service in ethernet passive optical networks. OSA Journal of Optical Networking 1(8), 280–298 (2002)
4. Shea, D., Mitchell, J.: A 10 Gb/s 1024-Way Split 100-km Long Reach Optical Access Network. IEEE/OSA Journal of Lightwave Technology 25(3), 685–693 (2007)
5. Talli, G., Townsend, P.: Hybrid DWDM-TDM Long-Reach PON for Next-Generation Optical Access. IEEE/OSA Journal of Lightwave Technology 24(7), 2827–2834 (2006)
6. Song, H., Banerjee, A., Kim, B.W.: B., M.: Multi-Thread Polling: A Dynamic Bandwidth Distribution Scheme in Long-Reach PON. In: Proceedings of IEEE Globecom, pp. 2450–2454 (November 2007)
7. Zheng, J., Mouftah, H.: Media access control for Ethernet passive optical networks: an overview. IEEE Communications Magazine 43(2), 145–150 (2005)
8. Bai, X., Shami, A., Assi, C.: On the fairness of dynamic bandwidth allocation schemes in Ethernet passive optical networks. Computer Communications 29(11), 2123–2135 (2006)
9. Zheng, J.: Efficient bandwidth allocation algorithm for Ethernet passive optical networks 153(3), 464–468 (2006)
10. Hwang, I.S., Shyu, Z., Ke, L.Y., Chang, C.C.: A Novel Early DBA Mechanism with Prediction-based Fair Excessive Bandwidth Reallocation Scheme in EPON. In: Proceedings of IEEE Int. Conference on Networking (ICN) (April 2007)
11. Choudhury, P., Saengudomlert, P.: Efficient Queue Based Dynamic Bandwidth Allocation Scheme for Ethernet PONs. In: Proceedings of IEEE Globecom, pp. 2183–2187 (November 2007)
12. Lee, S.-H., Lee, T.-J., Chung, M., Choo, H.: Adaptive window-tuning algorithm for efficient bandwidth allocation on EPON. In: Akyildiz, I.F., Sivakumar, R., Ekici, E., de Oliveira, J.C., McNair, J. (eds.) NETWORKING 2007. LNCS, vol. 4479, pp. 1217–1220. Springer, Heidelberg (2007)
13. Dhaini, A., Assi, C., Maier, M., Shami, A.: Dynamic Wavelength and Bandwidth Allocation in Hybrid TDM/WDM EPON Networks. IEEE/OSA Journal of Lightwave Technology 25(1), 277–286 (2007)
14. Kwong, K., Harle, D., Andonovic, I.: Dynamic bandwidth allocation algorithm for differentiated services over WDM EPONs. In: Proceedings of The Ninth IEEE International Conference on Communications Systems (ICCS), pp. 116–120 (September 2004)
15. Park, K., Willinger, W.: Self-Similar Network Traffic and Performance Evaluation. Wiley Interscience, Hoboken (2000)
16. McGarry, M., Reisslein, M., Colbourn, C., Maier, M., Aurzada, F., Scheutzow, M.: Just-in-Time Scheduling for Multichannel EPONs. IEEE/OSA Journal of Lightwave Technology 26(10), 1204–1216 (2008)

Cost-Performance Planning of Municipal Wireless Access Networks

Paolo Giacomazzi and Alessandro Poli

Dipartimento di Elettronica e Informazione, Politecnico di Milano
via Ponzio 34/5, 20133 Milano, Italy
{giacomaz,poli}@elet.polimi.it

Abstract. Planning Municipal Wireless Access Networks is a challenging task, since many optimization choices must be taken into account in large metropolitan areas and, in turn, the number of free variables is very large, on the order of several millions, if the position of wireless access points is to be optimized, as well as their connection to the backbone network. This paper formalizes the problem of choosing appropriate access points' locations and to connect the so built wireless access network to the backbone network. We provide an optimization algorithm able to find a solution with a fast heuristic approach, and apply it to a real-world scenario about a 51 km^2 area of Milano (Italy). The proposed heuristic solution is compared with the result of a simulated-annealing-based optimization algorithm and the result is that the cost of the solutions of the heuristic algorithm is larger than that of the optimal solution by a few percents.

Keywords: access networks, wireless, municipal, planning, optimization, cost, performance.

1 Introduction

Municipal Wireless Access Networks (MWAN) planning is a hot topic nowadays. In the world, about 500 projects have been started [1], and the municipalities' interest in the field is rapidly increasing, due to the significant and important services for citizens enabled by these infrastructures. A municipal wireless access network is a viable solution for municipalities to provide the community a broadband network with a relatively low deployment cost, if compared to wired networks [2]. The success of MWANs greatly varies from city to city. Cities where a well-planned risk sharing model between the private and the public sectors has been implemented, typically obtained greater success. Most current literature focuses on economic or social issues of municipal wireless networks. In [3], the role of municipalities as wireless broadband access providers is examined, also presenting current business models. [4] provides an high-level framework, for guiding communities that seek to implement a MWAN, composed of three steps: identification of goals, planning and implementation. [5] analyzes the motivation driving MWAN deployment in three U.S.A. major metropolitan areas, considering standards and technology evolution. A

C. Wang (Ed.): AccessNets, LNICST 6, pp. 46–61, 2009.

variety of technologies and options for wireless access networks is explored in [6], in addition to actual deployment examples. [7] is an attempt to study the feasibility of a MWAN in a specific context, exploring political issues and technological options; a coarse-grained estimation of costs is also reported. The topic of Municipal Wireless Access Networks planning is not faced thoroughly by current literature, mainly due to the extreme difficulty of the problem. This complex task requires the identification of access points' sites and the connection of the wireless access network to a backbone infrastructure. This paper formalizes the problem and provides an optimization algorithm that minimizes the total cost of the infrastructure to be deployed. A real case scenario about a 51 km^2-area of the city center of Milan is studied.

The paper is organized as follows. Section 2 presents the optimization problem which is modelled in Section 3. Section 4 describes the algorithm proposed to solve the optimization problem. Section 5 illustrates the optimization scenario, and empirical results are discussed in Section 6. Section 6 also provides a comparison between the proposed heuristic algorithm and a simulated annealing optimization algorithm. Conclusions are drawn in Section 7.

2 The Optimization Problem

The objective of the methodology presented in this paper is the outdoor coverage of a given metropolitan area with a wireless network at minimum cost. All chosen access points must be connected to a backbone network. In this section, technology requirements and technology resources are presented.

2.1 Technology Requirements

This section describes the formalization of the requirements of the municipal wireless network.

Metropolitan Area Map. The reference area conformation is described by the *metropolitan area map matrix* m_{ij}, identifying, for each latitude-longitude pair, the height in meters of the highest construction in the point, from a fixed reference altitude rh. The actual distance among consecutive indexes (rows or columns) in the matrix, measured in meters, is set by the constant l. As a consequence, in the concrete, each ij-point identifies an $l \times l$ area. The geographical coordinates of the m_{11} position should also be known, so that absolute geographical positions can be mathematically translated into points of the map matrix, and *vice versa*.

Coverage Requirement Map, Coverage Radius Map and Cluster Size Map. For each ij-point in the metropolitan area map, the *coverage requirement map* c_{ij}^{req} identifies whether an outdoor point must be covered by the wireless network ($c_{ij}^{req} = 1$) or not ($c_{ij}^{req} = 0$). A *coverage ratio requirement* parameter cr^{req} defines the minimum acceptable ratio of points actually covered by the wireless network to the total number of points that are required to be covered (i.e. $c_{ij}^{req} = 1$). cr^{req} value is typically near to 1.

Since different zones in the metropolitan area map have different environmental peculiarities, different population densities and users with different behavior, the resulting wireless network should be designed accordingly. Different requirements are taken into account by defining, as further input data, the *coverage radius map* r_{ij}, defining, for each point, the maximum distance, measured in meters on the latitude-longitude plane, from any access point to the points it is allowed and requested to cover, and the *cluster size map* s_{ij}, defining, for each point, the maximum size of a cluster of access points that should share one connection to the backbone network; cluster size greatly affect the wireless network available bandwidth. A *backhaul radius br*, in meters, defines the maximum distance between a pair of access points that can reciprocally communicate, and thus possibly form a wireless mesh *cluster*. Access points in the same cluster share a single connection to the backbone network.

2.2 Technology Resources

The technology requirements for the municipal wireless network can be satisfied by means of the infrastructural resources defined in the following.

Backbone Connection Technologies. A set of available *backbone connection technologies* is given as input. For each connection technology ct_k, the following parameter is specified:

1. Cost c of the connection, as a function of the link length. This cost also includes a fixed cost for the activation of the connection.

Backbone Interconnection Points. A set of all the available interconnection points b_j is considered. An interconnection point can be directly connected to the backbone network, or can require to be connected to another interconnection point. For each interconnection point, a set of properties is defined:

1. Latitude and longitude.
2. Interconnection point type bt_i.
3. Sets of backbone interconnection points that can be reached with the different connection technologies. For each interconnection point, the estimated link length is also known.

The backbone interconnection point type bt_i defines the following characteristics:

1. Maximum number of ingoing connections, for each connection technology ct_k.
2. Whether or not the interconnection point is directly connected to the backbone.
3. Whether or not the interconnection point can establish a connection to another interconnection point using the connection technology ct_k. This option is specified for all connection technologies.
4. Cost c of the interconnection point, as a function of the number of ingoing connections for each technology.
5. Additional cost for using each specific connection technology for the outgoing connection.

6. Estimated average cost of one ingoing connection tc to the interconnection point, for each technology. The heuristic methodology is driven by this cost, which, in turn, is strictly related to the actual cost function of the interconnection point.

Candidate Poles for Access Points. The planning methodology considers a set of all the poles p_j in the metropolitan area that can host a wireless access point. For each pole we know the geographical position and the reachable backbone interconnection points. Altogether, the following properties are available:

1. Latitude and longitude.
2. Sets of backbone interconnection points that the access point installed on the pole can reach with the different connection technologies. For each interconnection point, the estimated link length is also known.
3. Pole type pt_i.

The pole type pt_i defines the following characteristics:

1. Height from the fixed reference altitude rh.
2. Cost c for the use of the pole if it is chosen for hosting an access point. This cost also includes the AP equipment, arrangement, and installation costs.
3. Additional cost for using each specific connection technology.

3 The Optimization Model

3.1 Decision Variables

The following choices should be taken by the optimization methodology:

1. Whether or not a pole is used for hosting an access point. Since there is no need for discrimination in the model, a *pole* used for hosting an access point is also simply referred to as *access point*.
2. Every access point is assigned to a particular *cluster* of access points c_i.
3. For each cluster, one access point is chosen for being connected to the backbone network.
4. Whether or not a backbone interconnection point is used for receiving ingoing connections.
5. For each connected access point, one connection technology is used.
6. For each connected access point, one backbone interconnection point is reached with a *connection*.
7. For each used interconnection point not directly connected to the backbone network, one connection technology towards another interconnection point is used.
8. For each used interconnection point not directly connected to the backbone network, another backbone interconnection is reached with a connection.

Decision variables from 4 to 8 also implicitly define the number of *actually used ingoing connections* for each interconnection point, for all connection technologies.

3.2 Line of Sight and Coverage Evaluation

A three-dimensional point in the map is identified by its three coordinates (x,y,z), where z is the height in meters form the reference altitude rh, while x and y are the latitude and longitude coordinates. x and y can be easily translated into the ij-indexes of the metropolitan area map matrix m_{ij}.

In order to evaluate the mutual visibility of two 3D points, the 3D straight line between the points is projected on the (x,y) plane, and thus all crossed ij-positions in the area map matrix are identified. 3D points are said to be in *sight* when, for every ij-position, the height z of the straight line is above the area map m_{ij} quota, i.e. no obstacles are in between. To cope with rounding and approximation issues, this constraint is relaxed, allowing the existence of a limited overall length occupied by obstacles (obstacles are the points where m_{ij} is above the straight line quota).

For each ij-point in the metropolitan area map, the *coverage map* c_{ij} identifies how many access points are able to reach and cover the specific point. When no poles are used for hosting access points, c_{ij} is equal to zero for all coordinates. For each access point, the coverage area is identified, and then the corresponding c_{ij} values are set. An ij-point is said to be covered by an access point placed on a pole if and only if the 3D point at quota m_{ij} (i.e. it is on the ground) is in sight of the point placed on the top of the pole (its height can be computed by summing the height of the pole to the m_{hk} quota, where h and k are the indexes corresponding to the pole coordinates) and the distance between the two points in the (x,y) plane is no greater than the radius identified by the coverage radius map r_{hk}.

Given an initial state of the coverage map c_{ij}', the use of the additional pole p_c, placed in ij-position, for hosting an access point, causes the coverage map to change to c_{ij}''. The *relative coverage gain* cg for the access point p_c is the ratio of the number of hk-points required to be covered ($c_{hk}^{req} = 1$) and covered for the first time by p_c (such that $c_{hk}' = 0$ and $c_{hk}'' = 1$), to the number of all mn-points required to be covered ($c_{mn}^{req} = 1$) inside the coverage circle with radius r_{ij}.

3.3 Additional Constraints

In addition to the constraints implicitly derived from the decision variables specification, the following constraints must be enforced:

1. *Coverage ratio cr* should be above the required value cr^{req}. Coverage ratio is the ratio of points required to be covered ($c_{ij}^{req} = 1$) and actually covered by at least one access point (for which $c_{ij} \geq 1$), to the total number of points that are required to be covered (i.e. $c_{ij}^{req} = 1$).

2. All used backbone interconnection points must be either directly connected to the backbone network, or connected to a backbone interconnection point that is connected to the backbone (directly, or through a chain of interconnection points).
3. For each connection going from an access point (or an interconnection point) to an interconnection point, the use of the same connection technology on both sides is required.
4. For each used interconnection point, the sum of the ingoing connections, for each connection technology, must not exceed the maximum number defined by the interconnection point type.
5. For each cluster of access points c_a, the number of access points in the cluster must not exceed the requirement of maximum cluster size. The maximum cluster size for cluster c_a is the minimum of the s_{ij} values in all the ij-positions where an access point's pole in cluster c_a is located.
6. Each access point not connected to a backbone interconnection point in a cluster c_a must be in sight, and no farther than the backhaul radius br in the (x,y) plane, of an access point, in the same cluster c_a, connected to a backbone interconnection point (directly, or through a chain of access points in sight of the same cluster). A pair of access points is said to be in sight when the two 3D points placed on the top of the poles are in sight (see Section 3.2) and no farther than the backhaul radius br in the (x,y) plane.

3.4 Objective Function

The objective function to be minimized is the total cost of the municipal wireless network. The total cost can be computed by adding the following costs:

1. Sum over each used interconnection point of its cost (a function of the number of ingoing connections for each technology plus the additional cost for using each specific connection technology for the outgoing connection).
2. Sum over each used interconnection point not directly connected to the backbone of the connection cost.
3. Sum over each pole used for hosting an access point of its cost.
4. Sum over each pole used for hosting an access point connected to the backbone of the connection cost.

4 The Optimization Algorithm

Our heuristic methodology for the planning of a municipal wireless network comprises two phases: (a) wireless *coverage* of the designated area, (b) *connection* of access points *to the backbone* network. Both phases are independent from the other; nevertheless, the first phase, while exploring its solution space, also takes into account the impact of its choices over the objective function because of the second phase.

4.1 Wireless Coverage

The wireless coverage algorithm aims at finding a set of poles where to install access points, such that coverage requirements are satisfied. Access points must be grouped in clusters where the wireless mesh network communication is feasible. Even though the minimization of overlaps among the wireless coverage of different access points is not a requirement, the proposed algorithm also implicitly tries to minimize such zones (i.e. the points where $c_{ij} > 1$). The algorithm uses the following additional parameters:

1. A *pole preference ratio* value pr, for each pole type pt_i. This value is set to 1 for standard poles, while it is smaller than 1 for poles that should be preferred during the wireless coverage phase and greater than 1 for poles to be penalized. pr values should be empirically determined in such a way to minimize the total cost of the infrastructure, privileging the choice of poles whose use is cost-beneficial.
2. *Minimum coverage gain mcg* for an additional access point. This parameter forces the coverage procedure to avoid the use of access points whose additional contribution to the global coverage is slight. This value should be carefully chosen, since with high *mcg* values the coverage ratio constraint could not be satisfied.

The algorithm also uses the following additional variable:

1. *Used poles stack ps*, a stack used to keep track of previously chosen poles.

The algorithm follows these steps:

1. A pole p_c is randomly chosen among those placed in a point required to be covered (such that $c_{ij}^{req} = 1$) and not yet covered ($c_{ij} = 0$). Current cluster is chosen among already existing *not full* clusters; the cluster containing the nearest pole to p_c, and in sight with p_c, within a maximum distance $\left(2 \cdot r_{ij}\right) - \varepsilon$, is selected. If no clusters satisfy all requirements and if current cluster is not empty (i.e. at least one access point has been assigned to it), then create a new empty cluster. A cluster is said to be *full* if the number of access points in it is not smaller than the minimum s_{ij} value, evaluated among all the *ij*-positions of the access points in the cluster and the currently chosen access point p_c.
2. The chosen current pole p_c is used for hosting an access point. As a consequence, the coverage map c_{ij} is updated, according to the procedure described in Section 3.2.
3. A new cluster c_h is created (h is incremented by one) if current cluster is *full*.
4. Chosen pole p_c is assigned to current cluster c_h and pushed into the *ps* stack.
5. Being i and j the positions in the metropolitan area map of current pole p_c, next pole is chosen among those which are in sight with current pole p_c, not placed in

an already covered area, and within a maximum distance $\left(2 \cdot r_{ij}\right) - \varepsilon$ in the (x,y) plane, where r_{ij} is the coverage radius requested for the specific area, and ε is a short distance used to force a small overlap of the coverage circles, such that their union does not leave small uncovered pieces of land on road sides. The methodology supposes that, in all areas, the backhaul radius br is greater than $\left(2 \cdot r_{ij}\right) - \varepsilon$. Poles not reaching the minimum coverage gain (such that $cg < mcg$) are discarded and not taken into account. Identified candidate next poles are ranked by their decreasing distance from p_c divided by their preference ratio pr. The first pole is then assumed to be the following current pole p_c.

6. If not any pole has been identified by the previous step:

   a. If ps stack is not empty, next current pole p_c is identified by popping a pole from the ps stack. A new empty cluster is created. Then go to step 5.

   b. If ps stack is empty create a new empty cluster. Then go to step 1.

7. If coverage ratio is above the required threshold ($cr \geq cr^{req}$) then stop. Else go to step 2.

4.2 Connection to the Backbone Network

This phase goal is the identification, among the access points in a cluster, of the access point designated to be connected to an interconnection point, and the identification of the interconnection points to be used.

The algorithm uses the following additional parameters:

1. *Security fulfillment ratio threshold* ft for each connection technology ct_i. This ratio threshold (spanning from 0 to 1) is used to avoid, in the heuristic algorithm, states when a pole or an interconnection point can not reach any interconnection point with available ingoing connections. Its use will be better explained in the following.

2. *Average number of ingoing connections* $bt_i.acn\left(ct_j\right)$ for each backbone interconnection point type bt_i, for all its available connection technologies ct_j.

These parameters guide the cost estimation of the heuristic, and should be set with values reflecting the actual average number of ingoing connection for each interconnection point type. The estimation of these parameters can be performed by evaluating the solutions found by the whole heuristic algorithm.

The algorithm also uses the following additional variable:

1. *Average overall cost per termination* otc, for each backbone interconnection point, and for each connection technology ct_j, referring to the estimated overall cost for one ingoing connection. This cost includes all the costs for linking one ingoing connection till the backbone, and thus accounts for the entire path to the backbone network. In the following, we will refer to the average overall cost per

termination with technology ct_j for the backbone interconnection point b_i as $b_i.ct_j.otc$.

The algorithm operates as follows:

1. For all the interconnection points b_i directly connected to the backbone, for each connection technology ct_j, the average overall cost per termination otc is set as the average cost tc of one ingoing connection, defined by its type bt_k. At this stage, all backbone interconnection points are set as *not used* for receiving ingoing connections.

2. For all the interconnection points b_i not directly connected to the backbone and not already set as *used*, for each connection technology ct_j, all the available interconnection points that can be reached, that are either directly connected to the backbone or that have an outgoing connection already set, and such that the number of *actually used ingoing connections* is not above the maximum number of available ingoing connections multiplied by the *security fulfillment ratio threshold ft*, are explored. The minimum cost option is chosen and, consequently, destination interconnection point and related connection technology ct_j are set for current interconnection point. If not any option is found, the security fulfillment requirement is relaxed, and the evaluation is performed again. Costs are evaluated as the average overall cost per termination otc of one ingoing connection of the destination interconnection points, plus the cost $ct_j.c$ of the connections as function of link lengths. The cost of the chosen option is then divided by the average number of ingoing connections $bt_k.ct_j.acn$ and added to the average costs $ct_j.tc$, for all incoming connection technologies; the resulting value is stored as the average overall costs per termination $ct_j.otc$.

3. In the previous step, destination interconnection points and related connection technologies ct_j have been set for a part of all backbone interconnection points, and average overall costs per termination otc, for all connection technologies, have been computed. Now, for each backbone interconnection point, a larger set of reachable interconnection points, that are either directly connected to the backbone or that have an outgoing connection already set, is available. Step 2 is consequently iteratively executed until not any average overall cost per termination otc does change, i.e. the minimum cost path from any backbone interconnection point to the backbone has been identified.

4. Randomly choose a *cluster* of access points c_i not already connected to the backbone network. All the available interconnection points that can be reached with all the connection technologies available from cluster's access points, and that are either directly connected to the backbone or have an outgoing connection already set, and such that the number of *actually used ingoing connections* is not above the maximum number of available ingoing connections multiplied by the

security fulfillment ratio threshold ft , are explored. The minimum cost option is chosen and, consequently, destination interconnection point and related connection technology ct_j are set for corresponding access point and cluster; the access point and the cluster are then marked as connected to the backbone. If not any option is found, the security fulfillment requirement is relaxed, and the evaluation is performed again. Costs are evaluated as the average overall cost per termination *otc* of one ingoing connection of the destination interconnection points, plus the cost $ct_j.c$ of the connections as function of link lengths. Access point's destination interconnection point and, iteratively, all the interconnection points met along the path to the backbone network, are consequently set as *used*; concurrently, the number of *actually used ingoing connections* for all met interconnection points is updated; if the assignment caused a *security fulfillment threshold* to be passed for any backbone interconnection point, a smaller set of reachable interconnection points is now available. Step 2 (only) is consequently iteratively executed until not any average overall cost per termination *otc* does change.

5. If still exist at least one *cluster* of access points c_i not already connected to the backbone network then go to step 4.
   Else stop.

5 The Optimization Scenario

The algorithm described in Section 4 has been applied on a large area of the city of Milan. The area of interest is a rectangular 51 km^2 zone of the city center. Since the information about the height of the buildings is not extensively available, the *metropolitan area map matrix* only discriminates among points where a street or a building is there. The used *coverage requirement map* is such that all the streets and all the parks in the area are required to be covered by the wireless network. The map is shown in Fig. 1; the white points are the areas to be covered ($c_{ij}^{req} = 1$). A *coverage ratio requirement* parameter of 0.97 has been used in the performed optimizations.

The *cluster size map*, defining, for each point, the maximum size of a cluster of access points, has been set to 3 for all points. The *backhaul radius* has been safely considered equal to 200 m.

The available *backbone connection technologies* are two classes of *Optical Fiber*, respectively provided by a *Third Party* company or by the *Municipality of Milan*, *Power Line Communication* (PLC), and *Direct Connection* with a local area network link. A direct connection is a connection that can be reached by an access point with a local area link, for example when the access point is located on the same building as the interconnection point. The cost of the Third Party Optical Fiber is 7 €/m, while the Optical Fiber of the Municipality of Milan is provided for free. A Power Line Communication link has a fixed cost of 95 €, accounting for the PLC client installation, and a cost of 480 € every 150 m, if the total length of the link is above 150 m, and a signal repeater is required. A Direct Connection has a fixed cost of 500 €.

Fig. 1. Coverage requirement map of the considered zone, representing a 51 km² area of the city center of Milan

There are 4 types of backbone interconnection points:

1. *Third Party Cabinets* owned by a third party company, 8 in the considered area, directly connected to the backbone, not any reachable interconnection point, can terminate an unlimited number of Third Party Optical Fibers, and 3 PLC connections. The cost is given by the Router Chassis (8,864 € each) capable of hosting up to 6 2xEth 100base FX adapter modules (6,332 € each) able to terminate up 2 optical fibers, and by the PLC Head End (465 €), if required.

2. *CampusII Buildings* owned by the Municipality of Milan, 319 in the considered area, directly connected to the backbone, not any reachable interconnection point, can terminate an unlimited number of Third Party Optical Fibers, 3 PLC connections, and one Direct Connection. The cost is given by the Router Chassis (8,864 € each) capable of hosting up to 6 2xEth 100base FX adapter modules (6,332 € each) able to terminate up 2 optical fibers, and by the PLC Head End (465 €), if required.

3. *Municipal Traffic Control Facilities* sites owned by the Municipality of Milan, 582 in the considered area, directly connected to the backbone, not any reachable interconnection point, can terminate an unlimited number of Municipal Optical Fibers, and one Direct Connection. The cost is given by the Router Chassis (8,864

€ each) capable of hosting up to 6 2xEth 100base FX adapter modules (6,332 €
each) able to terminate up 2 optical fibers.

4. *Medium to Low-Voltage Electric Cabins* owned by the Local Electric Grid
   Company of Milan, one per electric cell, 778 in the considered area, not directly
   connected to the backbone, can reach any Third Party Cabinets and any CampusII
   building with Third Party Optical Fibers, can terminate 3 PLC connections. The
   cost is given by the Power Line Communication Head End (465 €), used to
   terminate no more than 3 connections. The number and the position of the Medium
   to Low-Voltage Electric Cabins, at current stage, are not exactly known, and have
   been estimated.

We consider 3 types of poles:

1. *Streetlamp poles* owned by the Local Electric Grid Company of Milan, 85,285 in
   the considered area, can reach any Third Party Cabinet and any CampusII building
   with Third Party Optical Fibers, or the nearest Medium to Low-Voltage Electric
   Cabin with PLC technology. The cost is given by the access point device and its
   installation (2,900 €) plus an additional pole adaptation cost (3,200 €) if using
   Third Party Optical Fibers as connection technology. The number and the position
   of streetlamp poles, at current stage, are not exactly known, and have been
   estimated.
2. *CampusII poles* placed on CampusII buildings, 319 in the considered area, owned
   by the Municipality of Milan, can reach the corresponding CampusII buildings
   with a Direct Connection. The cost is given by the access point device (1,900 €).
3. *Traffic Lights and CCTV poles* owned by the Municipality of Milan, 909 in the
   considered area, can reach any Municipal Traffic Control Facility with Municipal
   Optical Fibers, and the nearest Medium to Low-Voltage Electric Cabin with PLC
   technology; every Traffic Lights pole can also reach one specific Municipal Traffic
   Control Facility with a Direct Connection. The cost is given by the access point
   device and its installation (2,400 €).

The above described available technology resources are such that can be mixed
together only in ways that do not cause bottlenecks to appear, since the bandwidth
availability sufficiently increases along the paths from the Access Points to the
backbone network. This is an implicit requirement of the optimization problem that
must be ensured by appropriate input data.

6 Optimization Results

Optimizations have been performed by an ad-hoc software tool, called MUWI
(MUnicipal WIreless optimizer), implementing the algorithm presented in this paper.
Results are about the scenario described in Section 5, considering a set of different
values for the *coverage radius maps*, defining, for each point, the maximum distance
reached by an access point. The considered radiuses, the same for all the points in the
same map, range from 40 m to 90 m. Optimizations have been carried out in 5
different variations of the considered scenario:

1. Scenario **THIRD PARTY**: availability of *Third Party Cabinets* interconnection
   points, and *Streetlamp poles* only.

2. Scenario **CAMP+TC**: availability of *Third Party Cabinets, CampusII Buildings, Municipal Traffic Control Facilities* interconnection points, and *Streetlamp poles, CampusII poles* and *Traffic Lights and CCTV poles* only.
3. Scenario **TC+PLC**: availability of *Third Party Cabinets, Municipal Traffic Control Facilities, Medium to Low-Voltage Electric Cabins* interconnection points, and *Streetlamp poles* and *Traffic Lights and CCTV poles* only.
4. Scenario **CAMP+PLC**: availability of *Third Party Cabinets, CampusII Buildings, Medium to Low-Voltage Electric Cabins* interconnection points, and *Streetlamp poles* and *CampusII poles* only.
5. Scenario **CAMP+TC+PLC**: availability of *Third Party Cabinets, CampusII Buildings, Municipal Traffic Control Facilities, Medium to Low-Voltage Electric Cabins* interconnection points, and *Streetlamp poles, CampusII poles* and *Traffic Lights and CCTV poles* (the full scenario).

The execution of the algorithm for one optimization took about 3 hours on one CPU/core of a machine equipped with two Intel Xeon E5440 quad-core 2,83 GHz. The total costs of the municipal wireless infrastructures generated by the optimization algorithm are shown in Fig. 2.

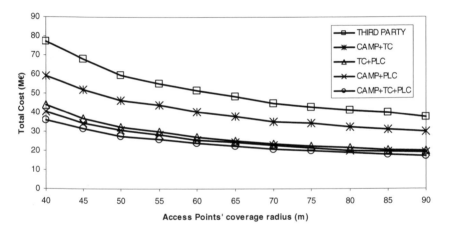

Fig. 2. Total cost of the municipal wireless network generated by the optimization algorithm in different scenario variations

Total cost doubles when coverage radius decreases from 90 m to 40 m, in all scenario variations. However, smaller radiuses allow offering higher bandwidth capacity per unit of area, depending on the specific wireless technology. The use of the third party company's infrastructures only, brings to the highest cost network, equal to 59.4 M€ with a coverage radius of 50 m. When preexisting municipality-owned infrastructures are taken into account (CAMP+TC scenario), a cost reduction of about 20% can be achieved in all coverage radius options. The Power Line Communication technology has the highest impact over the infrastructure cost; an additional 40% (CAMP+TC+PLC scenario compared to CAMP+TC scenario) can be gained by installing PLC Head End on designated Medium to Low-Voltage Electric Cabins and PLC Clients on well-chosen city poles.

The cost shares of the devices in three different scenario variations, using a coverage radius of 50 m, are reported in Fig. 3. The use of municipality-owned infrastructures (CAMP+TC and CAMP+TC+PLC scenarios) allows a cost reduction because of a lower use of Third Party Optical Fibers, from a 32% share to 7% and 5%. Access points cost is similar, in absolute value, in the three scenario variations. The use of the PLC technology, having an impact of 2% only on costs, allows an additional cost reduction mainly affecting APs arrangement, APs installation, router chassis, and router modules, because of a smaller amount of optical fibers to be connected to access points and to be terminated in routers.

The solution found for the full scenario (CAMP+TC+PLC), using a coverage radius of 50 m, has a total cost of 27.7M€ and uses 6949 poles/access points, 6261 of which are *Streetlamp poles*, 319 *CampusII poles*, and 369 *Traffic Lights and CCTV poles*. A total number of 2558 poles are infrastructured by means of the PLC technology.

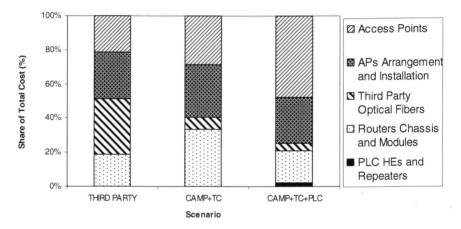

Fig. 3. Cost shares of the solutions obtained with a coverage radius of 50 m in three different scenario variations

6.1 Assessment through Simulated Annealing Optimization

The assessment of the heuristic algorithm proposed in Section 4 has been performed by means of comparisons with solutions found by a simulated annealing procedure. Simulated Annealing [8] is a probabilistic meta-algorithm for optimization problems, able to find good approximations of the global optimum in large search spaces. Simulated Annealing executes a random sequence of moves; every move is evaluated and is executed with a transition probability $P(\delta E, T)$, where δE is the variation of the objective function value caused by the move and T is the temperature of the system at a given moment.

In our implementation, if the move brings to a better solution, the move is always accepted (transition probability equal to 1), while it is $P(\delta E, T) = e^{\frac{-\delta E}{T}}$ if the move worsens the solution, according to the original formulation [8]. T decreases at every step until it reaches zero; we use exponential decreases with slow cooling ratios (0.99 or higher), and stop the Simulated Annealing algorithm when 1 million consecutive moves have not been accepted. The Simulated Annealing algorithm randomly chooses among a set of simple moves. A move transition probability is evaluated only if it brings to a feasible solution, i.e. no constraint is violated. Two groups of moves have been implemented: moves affecting the wireless coverage and moves affecting the connection to the backbone. Moves are described in the following.

Wireless Coverage Moves. This group of moves affects the selection of poles and, consequently, the wireless coverage.

1. *Remove AP*: remove an access point if it is not required for the communication among the access points in a cluster.
2. *Add Mesh AP*: add an access point to a pole and then add it to an already existing not full cluster in sight and no farther than the backhaul radius *br* .
3. *Add Infrastructured AP*: add an access point to a pole, add it to a new cluster, and then connect it to a random reachable interconnection point with free ingoing connections.

Backbone Connection Moves. This group of moves affects the connection to the backbone network.

1. *AP from IP to IP*: disconnect an access point connected to a backbone interconnection point and then connect it to a random reachable interconnection point with free ingoing connections. Update the set of used backbone interconnection points, if needed.
2. *AP from Mesh to IP*: remove an access point from a cluster, add it to a new cluster, and then connect it to a random reachable interconnection point with free ingoing connections. Update the set of used backbone interconnection points, if needed.
3. *AP from IP to Mesh*: disconnect an access point connected to a backbone interconnection point, and then merge its cluster's access points to an already existing not full cluster in sight and no farther than the backhaul radius *br* . Update the set of used backbone interconnection points, if needed.
4. *AP from Mesh to Mesh*: remove an access point from a cluster, and then add the access point to an already existing not full cluster in sight and no farther than the backhaul radius *br* .
5. *IP from IP to IP*: disconnect a backbone interconnection point connected to another backbone interconnection point and then connect it to a random reachable interconnection point with free ingoing connections. Update the set of used backbone interconnection points, if needed.

Simulated Annealing Results. Since the solution space of our optimization scenario is huge, the simulated annealing optimization would have required very slow cooling ratios and long time in order to converge towards a good approximation of the global optimum. As a consequence, our comparison has been performed on a smaller city area of 0.9 km^2 with reduced solution space. The reduction of the solution space required a decrease of the number of poles available for hosting access points (257 in the considered area).

The solution found by the optimization algorithm described in Section 4 has been used as starting solution for the Simulated Annealing algorithm. We tried a large set of different initial temperatures T and different cooling ratios. The minimum cost solution has been found with an initial temperature equal to 1,000 and a cooling ratio equal to 0.9999999. The cost of the best identified solution is 102,175 €, and execution took 275 minutes on our reference machine. This solution must be compared to the ones identified by the heuristic algorithm proposed in Section 4; the execution of 100 iterations of our heuristic algorithm with different random seeds required a total time of 20 minutes on our reference machine, and allowed to identify a solution with a cost equal to 105,625 €, i.e. about 3% more expensive than the solution found by the best parameterized Simulated Annealing algorithm.

7 Conclusions

We have proposed a new planning algorithm for Municipal Wireless Access Networks. The algorithm is based on a heuristic optimization procedure aiming at minimizing solutions cost. A heuristic approach has been followed because of the great complexity of the problem, which involves millions of decision variables when a large metropolitan area has to be taken into account all together. The algorithm has been implemented in a software tool and has been applied on a scenario about a 51 km^2 area of the city of Milan. Different scenario variations have been considered; results show that the reuse of preexisting municipality-owned infrastructures allows cost reduction in the order of 20%. An additional 40% cost reduction can be gained by the extensive use of the Power Line Communication technology.

The proposed heuristic algorithm has been assessed through Simulated Annealing optimization, and results show that our algorithm is able to provide solutions that are only about 3% far away from the approximation of the global optimum reached by Simulated Annealing algorithms.

References

1. MuniWireless, http://www.muniwireless.com
2. Gibbons, J., Ruth, S.: Municipal Wi-Fi: big wave or wipeout? IEEE Internet Computing 10(3), 66–71 (2006)
3. Tapia, A., Maitland, C., Stone, M.: Making IT work for municipalities: Building municipal wireless networks. Government Information Quarterly, Issues in Wireless Broadband 23(3-4), 359–380 (2006)
4. Mandviwalla, M., et al.: Municipal Broadband Wireless Networks. Communications of the ACM 51(2), 72–80 (2008)
5. Reinwand, C.C.: Municipal Broadband - The Evolution of Next Generation Wireless Networks. In: IEEE Radio and Wireless Symposium, pp. 273–276 (2007)
6. Sirbu, M., Lehr, W., Gillett, S.: Evolving wireless access technologies for municipal broadband. Government Information Quarterly, Issues in Wireless Broadband 23(3-4), 480–502 (2006)
7. Abelém, A.J.G., Stanton, M.A.: Alternatives for community metropolitan networks for the major cities of the Amazon region of Brazil: the case of Belem. In: 2nd International Conference on Broadband Networks, vol. 2, pp. 1492–1498 (2005)
8. Kirkpatrick, S., Gelatt, C.D., Vecchi, M.P.: Optimization by Simulated Annealing. Science 220(4598), 671–680 (1983)

Greener Copper with Dynamic Spectrum Management

(Invited Paper)

John Cioffi[1,2], Sumanth Jagannathan[1], W. Lee[1], H. Zou[1], A. Chowdhery[1], W. Rhee[2], G. Ginis[2], and P. Silverman[2]

[1] Stanford University, Stanford, CA 94305-9515 USA
cioffi@stanford.edu
[2] ASSIA, Inc., Redwood City, CA 94065-1317 USA
gginis@assia-inc.com

Abstract. This paper investigates the benefits of Dynamic Spectrum Management (DSM) in terms of reducing the power consumption and improving the data rates in digital-subscriber-line (DSL) networks. The proposed techniques at the three different DSM levels simultaneously also provide a significant improvement in the stability of DSLs. The proposed DSM methods are compared with other non-DSM solutions, which sacrifice power and/or data-rate in order to improve the stability, while also harming other DSLs through impolite power usage. Various examples are presented showing that the proposed DSM methods can avoid such unnecessary impoliteness, and that stability and politeness can be simultaneously achieved in a DSL network that is efficiently managed using DSM.

Keywords: DSM, spectrum balancing, power savings.

1 Introduction

Dynamic Spectrum Management (DSM) methods stabilize and increase Digital Subscriber Line (DSL) data rates through service-provider surveillance and management of various DSL physical-layer parameters. Correct use of DSM methods encourages "politeness" or power-control of DSL transmitters so that they radiate less crosstalk into other DSLs. This process of statistical noise reduction also lowers DSL transmit power. Since the power consumed by DSL modems is often dominated by circuits used for transmitting power, there is a consequent large secondary DSM benefit of reduced power consumption by DSL systems. This reduction in consumed power can be beneficial to DSL networks and is consistent with growing worldwide pressure for telecommunication networks to reduce their power consumption.

DSL management of many service providers often leads to a power increase because service providers may simply (but in retrospect, incorrectly) attempt to increase the margin on any observed unstable DSL. The margin is a controlled parameter dating to the earliest DSL standards' specifications. Specifically, the

C. Wang (Ed.): AccessNets, LNICST 6, pp. 62–77, 2009.

margin specifies how much larger (in dB) the line noise may rise before DSL performance (that is bit error rate) becomes unacceptable. A management system's increase of margin on an unstable DSL line means either or both of a power increase and a rate reduction, and is largely ineffective against the enormous intermittent noises that often lead to field-DSL instability[1]. This power increase may also induce a crosstalk increase, which is generally considered as impolite behavior. Section 2 discusses margin and the fallacy of its increase for unstable lines, and instead shows that DSM Level 1 methods of politeness, often called "tiered rate adaptation" (TRA), instead do stabilize the DSL and reduce average power consumption of DSLs simultaneously - DSM's first example of greening of the copper. DSM's power reductions can be very large when TRA is used correctly compared to any impolite management as Section 2 shows.

Section 3 advances to a frequency-dependent form of politeness known as spectrum balancing or DSM Level 2. A particular version of this politeness, known as "band-preference" in North American DSM standards documents [1], is shown to effect additional greening of the copper (that is, additional power savings), while caution is urged with respect to other impolite methods sometimes called "virtual noise," which are here shown to substantially increase power consumption if used. Thus, Section 3 illustrates a correct, polite, and low-power way of implementing DSM, further greening the copper.

Section 4 then explores the limits of DSM Level 3 (the highest DSM level in standards), also known as "vectoring," for further reduction of transmit power, which should ultimately lead to the smallest power consumption and thus, the best greening of the copper.

2   DSM Level 1: Dynamics and Politeness

DSL modems are dynamic by standard. The long-mandated DSL-standardized "bit-swapping" procedure [2] allows the transmitter and receiver to react simultaneously to changes in the line's noise by redistributing energy from regions of relatively high noise increase to those of noise decrease (or of relatively low noise increase). This capability to react to noise changes helps maintain an optimized information (or bit) distribution on the DSL through a hand-shaking procedure, where the DSL's transmitter and receiver use a control channel to reallocate information synchronously. This "bit-swapping" is the key difference between the multi-carrier DSL systems and the Orthogonal Frequency Division Multiplexing (OFDM) systems used successfully in wireless transmission, where the information distribution is not changed and there is no bit-swapping. DSL systems thus call the highly adaptive transmission format "Discrete Multi-Tone" or DMT to distinguish it from the non-swapping wireless OFDM systems. The dynamic bit-swapping capability improves line stability and reduces the number of retrains or restarts of DSL modems when used with effective DSM methods as in this section. While standards mandate bit-swapping, some DSLs are nevertheless non-compliant and

---

[1] Simply stated, the intermittent noise is so large that no practical value of margin is large enough to accommodate this transient noise.

require retraining upon significant noise changes. DSM can also help such systems through TRA, although not as much as bit-swapping systems.

This section begins with a discussion of DSL stability and intermittent noises, and then progresses to the appropriate polite and power-saving solutions that use DSM Level 1.

2.1 The DSL Environment and Stability

Instabilities limit today's DSL deployment range[2]. Such deployment range is typically well below the DSL range exhibited in carefully crafted and standardized lab/interoperability tests, which prior to the advent of DSM were thought to have tested "worst-case" conditions. Thus, range of field-deployed DSL is often much less on average than found in such "worst-case" testing unless DSM is correctly used. Instability is typically measured by retrain counts, packet-error counts, or combinations of both. If such measures are unacceptably high, the DSL is labeled "unstable." Statistically, both instability measures (retrains, packet errors) increase with loop length, but many short loops can have high instability caused by large intermittent noises. These large intermittent noises often easily exceed any DSL management system's "margin" against noise, thus often rendering a management system's margin increase ineffective.

Customer satisfaction, measured in complaint-call volume, number of dispatches ("truck rolls"), and/or customer turnover ("churn"), decreases with increasing instability. DSL service providers determine deployment range to maintain an acceptable level of customer satisfaction. Thus, deployment range is today almost always limited by such instability. Examples of such instability and its importance appear in references [1],[3]-[10]. The main causes are large intermittent noises that occur when the DSL is in operation, which are so large that bursts of errors or even modem retrains occur.

Video quality is strongly reduced by DSL instability, but data and voice-over-internet services also exhibit strong correlation between stability and customer satisfaction. Level 1 DSM has several effective mechanisms to stabilize DSLs and thereby to improve deployment range.

Level 1 DSM[3] [1] focuses largely upon the management of a single line. A Level 1 DSM system-controller collects DSL performance data from the DSL equipment's maintenance interface. The Level 1 Spectrum Management Center (SMC) then assesses DSL stability. The Level 1 DSM system may consequently re-profile[4] the DSL through the maintenance interface. Each DSL service provider can have their own DSM system - there is no central controller for

---

[2] "Range" means the curve of data rate versus line length. DSLs typically offer lower data rates on longer lines; however, DSM methods can statistically improve the average "range," thus raising the curve of data rate vs. length.

[3] Level 1 DSM is sometimes also called "Dynamic Line Management" or DLM, although not in standards.

[4] "Re-profiling" is a term commonly used to mean changing a file of DSM-control parameters imposed through the DSM-C interface. Such a file is sometimes called a profile, whence the term "re-profiling."

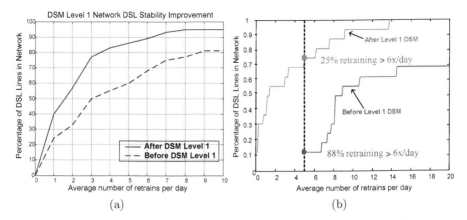

Fig. 1. Stability improvement with DSM Level 1 (a) bit-swapping DSLs (b) without bit-swapping

all service providers in DSM. However, spectrum management standards may impose some guidelines for polite management in various situations.

Figures 1(a) and 1(b) reflect the average stability experience of field data taken from several DSL service providers around the world on bit-swapping and non-bit-swapping equipment, respectively. Figure 1(a) illustrates the percentage of DSL customers on a typical network that have fewer retrains per day than the abscissa value (horizontal axis). The figure illustrates DSL stability before and after the use of DSM Level 1 management known as TRA (see Section 2.3). If 5 retrains per day is the threshold for unacceptable stability,the stable-DSL-customer improvement is roughly 25% in Fig. 1(a)). Experience shows that such a stability improvement typically extends actual deployment range by at least 20% (which could mean 30-50% more customers possible for a higher-speed DSL service).

Figure 1(b) illustrates the stability improvement without bit-swapping. All improvements here come through DSM Level 1 management that tries to leave sufficient tolerance in the DSL's programmed parameters to improve stability. A large stability improvement is possible with Level 1 DSM in Fig. 1(b) for non-swapping modems, but the total number of stable customers in Fig. 1(b) with no swapping is understandably smaller than with swapping in Fig. 1(a). For instance, at 5 retrains/day, the improvement in stability is almost 60% of the customers in the non-swapping composite networks of Fig. 1(b), increasing the number of stable customers to 75%. The bit-swapping system can increase this same point to almost 90% in Fig. 1(a). With or without swapping, the number of stable customers is not 100%, even after DSM Level 1 correction - but the customer-satisfaction gains are very large, rendering proper DSM-use a major initiative by most DSL service providers today. However, there are green and good methods to achieve such gains, and then some not-so-green methods to effect a smaller gain in stability. The next subsection reviews margin and its use/abuse.

2.2   Margins as Control Parameters

The DSL management parameter called "margin" measures the amount by which noise can increase before the DSL link performance is unacceptably degraded. Margin thus helps guard against unforeseen noise increases. Most DSL systems today use a default margin value of 6dB, which means the noise can increase in power by a factor of 4 before the DSL starts making appreciable errors. Management of an unstable line thus might increase margin, a process here called "automatic margin adaptation" or AMA. Typically, retraining the DSL with higher margin increases power and/or reduces data rate. It is impolite because the DSL will use maximum power levels if the margin is set sufficiently high. However, margin levels are often not sufficiently high to offset large transient noises or intermittent/impulse noise. Furthermore, such large noise only occurs for a fraction of the time. Thus, increasing the margin simply increases the power (and/or reduces the rate) all the time, while typically having little or no effect on a very intermittent noise. AMA is thus not power efficient. DSL modems have long used 3 margin parameters:

1. Target SNR margin (TSNRM)
2. Minimum SNR margin (MINSNRM)
3. Maximum SNR margin (MAXSNRM).

The target margin is used during training of the modem and is the margin used to counter a future noise-increase as stated above, typically 6 dB. The DSL modems continue to measure and update the margin of the link as the noise (and thus margin) changes. MINSNRM is a margin level (typically 0 dB) below which the DSL link will retrain. MAXSNRM is important and is the maximum margin allowed in bit-swapping. If the noise reduces, bit-swapping reduces power to keep the consequent margin below the MAXSNRM in standard-compliant modems. Setting the MAXSNRM adaptively is important in politeness, reducing transmitted power, emitted crosstalk, and also consumed power when intermittent noise is not present. Thus, wise Level 1 DSM might better set the MAXSNRM low than set the TSNRM high. The next subsection explores this effect with TRA.

2.3   Tiered Rate Adaptation (TRA)

TRA maintains a low TSNRM (typically 6 dB) even on unstable lines. The MAXSNRM is also kept relatively low, creating a low used power and a low emitted crosstalk when intermittent noise is not present. TRA tiers the allowed data-rate range with several (typically overlapping) ranges within which the modem is allowed to train as shown in Fig. 2(a).

Instead of increasing the TSNRM, TRA instead caps the data rate at a level for which instability has acceptably low probability of occurrence. It is thus polite because power is maintained at a low level when noise is normal (not increased). A minimum rate is also imposed (below which the DSL will retrain) such that a retrain during a very unlikely (but possible) large noise event will not cause

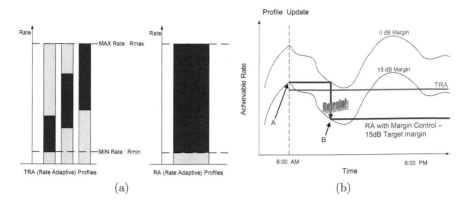

Fig. 2. Illustrations of (a) the tiered rate-ranges of TRA as opposed to the usual RA profile with a single, wide rate-range (b) The "stuck-at" low-rate problem of AMA (blue curve with retrain) and aversion of the problem by TRA

the modem to stay at a very low data rate[5]. AMA systems will retrain anyway upon a large such noise event, thus training at an even lower data rate because of the large margin, leading to a very poor eternally maintained low data rate. Figure 2(b) illustrates the "stuck-at-low-rate" problem of AMA.

Section 3 proceeds to show that there is a rate/reach loss, along with an increased power-usage for a target rate, from AMA because of the additional crosstalk it creates.

3   DSM Level 2: Frequency-Dependent Politeness

Level 2 DSM goes beyond TRA stabilization and considers the frequency-dependent effect that short lines' crosstalk may have on the longer victim lines. The first two subsections of this section look at spectrum balancing and its practical implementation using band-preference algorithms. The last subsection looks at a frequency-dependent extension of the non-DSM AMA known as "virtual noise," a pre-programmed large noise that the DSL is told to pretend to be always present, stripping it of dynamics and forcing a maximum power transmission, crosstalk, and power consumption. Several examples are provided to show the power savings of polite Level 2 DSM with respect to virtual-noise use.

3.1   Spectrum Balancing Concept

Spectrum balancing theory projects bounds on the best trade-offs between the data rates of different mutually crosstalking DSL customers. Because of crosstalk, those rates are not independent, so a region of trade-off can be plotted as shown in Fig. 3. Optimal Spectrum Balancing (OSB) [12] (with considerable complexity) computes this largest region. Gains in data rate are sometimes large when there are long-line DSLs as victims in the same binder with short-line users.

---

[5] Unless the customer intentionally resets the modem by power-cycling it.

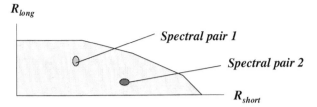

Fig. 3. A rate region for two users with asymmetric line length

The rate region contains all the possible pairs (generally U-tuples, where U is the number of users) that can be achieved by balancing the spectra of the different users. The data rate of one DSL customer can often depend upon the practices of another when the crosstalk between their lines is strong.

3.2 Band-Preference

Band-preference observes that shorter-line users (or more generally those with better channels) may often choose several different energy allocations to reduce crosstalk into other users. Often a short line's use of higher frequencies, largely above the lower frequency band that long lines can only typically use, can lead to much less crosstalk to long lines. These higher frequencies on one line may require somewhat more energy for transmission of a given data rate on that line, but through crosstalk reduction, the longer line uses much less power. The general trade-off is often very good for overall DSL data rates and power consumption. The practice of using only the higher frequencies above some management-specified cut-off frequency is known in DSM Level 2 as band-preference; that is, a preference applied to the use of higher frequencies.

This simple band-preference concept is easily managed in a distributed manner by letting each service provider's management system (SMC) decide if a line is strong (that is, will use band-preference on higher frequencies) or weak (the line needs to use all frequencies available to achieve its target minimum data rate). The strong lines then use a more polite form of bit-swapping that is described elsewhere [13][14][15]. The weak lines use normal swapping. Each line then does its best (still also retaining TRA) to minimize its own power consumption while also meeting the politeness and data-rate constraints. Figure 4 provides a representative example using band-preference, where this highly distributed (and thus usable in unbundled or bundled environments) method performs very close to the actual bounds of a theoretical optimum spectrum balanced system (that would require central control of all lines and their swapping) [15][16]. The proximity is so good that band-preference essentially allows optimal performance with very practical implementation by each DSL circuit of their own bit-swapping procedures.

3.3 Zap Your Neighbor First: Virtual Noise Power Increases

A non-DSM future proposal is Virtual Noise (VN) [17]. Management by VN mandates a DSL circuit to pretend that a pre-programmed large noise is always

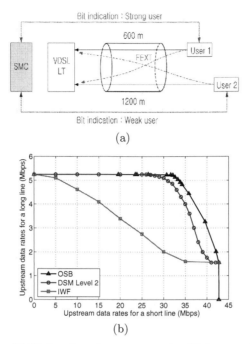

Fig. 4. (a)Upstream VDSL band-preference example. (b) Rate regions corresponding to Fig. 4(a) for the DSM Level 2, OSB, and iterative water-filling.

present as a threat to it. By pretending the noise is always present, and if the noise is the worst that can occur, then the DSL is always ready for this worst case. Effectively bit-swapping is disabled (unless the actual noise exceeds the programmed virtual-noise level). VN is similar to AMA, but is frequency-selective so that AMA's all-frequency abusive use of spectrum is narrowed to some frequencies in VN. Both VN and AMA essentially keep transmit power at the highest possible level. VN can also be more impolite than AMA since the amount of effective margin increase caused by the pretended programmed virtual noise can be larger than an AMA system's highest margin. Thus, the most abusive of AMA and VN actually depends on the management practice, but both attempt to address instability by reducing data rate and increasing power (and thus, crosstalk) without allowing dynamics of modems. Typically, VN proponents cite crosstalk transients as the reason for VN use. Crosstalk transients are caused by transition of a DSL from a dormant/off state to an "on" state. However, TRA is here shown to be a more appropriate remedy than these static and worst-case methods.

The non-DSM virtual noise presumes the use of a central control system for each service provider to determine and pre-program a large fake noise into each DSL's modems. A VN quandary thus occurs in an environment where each service provider subsequently sets their VN increasingly higher to protect against their competitors' most recent increase in crosstalk, leading each in turn to send at higher power levels. Thus, each user creates more crosstalk into their neighbors, leading to a loss in the data rates of all lines, and essentially larger

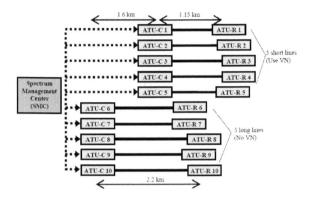

Fig. 5. Illustration of mixed-binder ADSL2+ lines. (RA = rate adaptive)

or maximum crosstalk between all lines. In an unbundled environment, there is no ability to set VN on different circuits with knowledge of the levels on other service providers' circuits. VN is thus a largely static operation of the DSL as if the large noise were always present (if the actual noise exceeds the virtual noise, then the DSL can adapt, but only in this case). All lines essentially prepare for the worst reaction of the others' possible VN (and thus power) settings.

The band-preference method of the previous subsection (a frequency-dependent DSM method) is usually implemented by classifying DSLs into two subsets, strong and weak. Power is set at maximum levels only when it must be so set because the largest noise is actually present. This subsection's simulations emulate all possible settings of virtual noise from none to all users using the largest-possible feared noise A level of 0 means that the virtual noise is less than or equal to the background noise and a level of 1 means all lines use a virtual noise that is equal to the sum of all others' crosstalk. Levels between 0 and 1 thus attempt to emulate various intermediate strategies. AMA is presumed to be equivalent to at least one of the possible choices for VN within the range considered, and is thus listed on the same curve as VN in the figures that follow. More detailed simulation settings can be found in [16].

A first example of mixed binder ADSL2+ is described in Fig. 5 and Table 1. Ten users are located roughly 1.15 km to 2-3 km from a central office or a remote terminal with a target rate of 10 Mbps for video service on those served from a service provider's fiber-fed RT (at 1.6 km) in the same binder. The lines emanating from the central office are all allowed to rate-adapt to the best service possible. One operator, serving lines 1-5, uses virtual noise. The other CO-based operator does not use VN. The 2nd service provider's lines are harmed by the VN use: Figure 6(a) shows the data rate loss of the 2nd service provider's lines with respect to TRA, and further, the larger loss with respect to band-preference.

Figure 6(b) shows the average power per line required to achieve [10, 10, 10, 10, 10, 5, 5, 5, 5, 5] (Mps), respectively. Figure 6(b) shows large power savings. More examples can be provided for a variety of situations and the losses can be

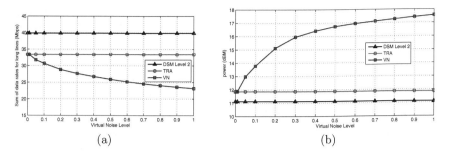

(a)   (b)

Fig. 6. (a) Sum of data rates on lines 6-10 for downstream ADSL2+ with DSM Level 2 Band-Preference, DSM Level 1 TRA, and Virtual-Noise/AMA. (b) Average power use for the configuration of Fig. 5.

Table 1. Line lengths and target rates of Fig. 5

User Index	1	2	3	4	5	6	7	8	9	10
CO/RT Location (km)	1.6	1.6	1.6	1.6	1.6	0	0	0	0	0
CPE Location (km)	2.75	3.0	3.2	3.2	3.0	1.8	1.8	2.3	2.0	2.2
Target Rate (Mbps)	10	10	10	10	10	RA	RA	RA	RA	RA

larger in more boundary situations. The example provided is mid-range in terms of losses to be expected.

A second situation occurs in Figures 7, 8(a) and 8(b) for upstream VDSL. Gains are larger because higher-speed DSLs use wider bandwidth and thus, experience larger amounts of crosstalk, and consequently, benefit even more from politeness. Figure 7 illustrates a line-length distribution for upstream VDSL. Many other line length distributions could be used without changing the conclusions. This particular set is reasonable. In these simulations, the operators for odd-numbered lines will use various strategies for VN, while the operator for the even numbered lines use DSM Level 1 or 2 without VN. The target data rates appear in Table 2.

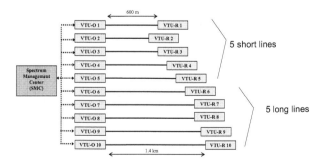

Fig. 7. Line-length distribution of 10 lines used in the upstream VDSL study of Level 1 and 2 DSM vs VN. (RA = rate adaptive). VN is used on odd-numbered lines in simulations.

72   J. Cioffi et al.

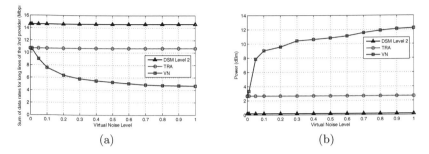

(a)   (b)

Fig. 8. (a) Upstream VDSL VN's loss of data rate by a 2nd service provider when a first provider uses VN. (b) Average power use for the configuration of Fig. 7.

Table 2. Line lengths and target rates of Fig. 7

User Index	1	2	3	4	5	6	7	8	9	10
CO/RT Location (km)	0	0	0	0	0	0	0	0	0	0
CPE Location (km)	0.6	0.52	0.58	0.76	0.98	1.1	1.2	1.2	1.25	1.4
Target Rate (Mbps)	13	10	8	6	2	RA	1.5	RA	1.5	RA

Figure 8(b) illustrates, in addition to any power savings, the effect of virtual noise on other customers by again sweeping a virtual noise level from 0, for no VN use, to 1. The sum of the 2nd operators' data rates for lines 6, 8, and 10 is plotted both with and without virtual noise.

A final example in Figures 9(a) and 9(b) illustrates a similar situation for 1.5 km ADSL2+ single loop with AM radio noise varying by as much as 10 dB in amplitude assuming that tones from 550KHz to 1.7MHz are affected by AM noise and that AM noise source could exist at every 10 KHz radio channel in this frequency band.

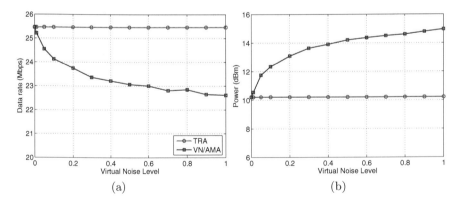

(a)   (b)

Fig. 9. (a) ADSL2+ data rates for variable level AM noise. (b) Average power use for variable level AM noise.

4 DSM Level 3: Vectored Power Reduction

Level 3 DSM attempts cancellation of crosstalk. If this is possible, then transmitted power levels can be further reduced. This section quantifies such potential power savings.

4.1 Noise Cancellation Basics

DSM Level 3 vectoring [18] can cancel nearly all upstream crosstalk and also downstream far-end crosstalk. Such "Vectored VDSL" data rates can increase substantially over non-vectored environments[6]. Specific to management interfaces, vectoring naturally introduces a concept of user/customer order or priority. Users with higher priority have the crosstalk from their neighbors pre-removed before making their decisions, and thus, get a higher data-rate increase. The assignment of decoding order can significantly impact the different users' data rates and the total power consumption of the users' transceivers. This section evaluates the magnitude of data rate gains (and/or power consumptions) under a specific type of management interface that effectively determines the appropriate order for the service providers subtended by a common Level 3 vectored VDSL DSLAM.

   Figure 10 illustrates the basic vector-cancelling situation: A common outside noise impinges upon two DSL lines, and the cancellation reconstructs the noise from line 2's receiver and subtracts it from line 1. In digitally-duplexed VDSL2, this cancellation can occur independently on every tone of the synchronized DMT line signals, thus simplifying implementation. Essentially, on any tone during every symbol period, line 2's data is detected in the presence of the noise, and the resultant noise-only signal is reconstructed from the decision and channel knowledge[7]. The consequent noise is then filtered to align its gain and phase with the noise on line 1 and then subtracted from line 1. Any far-end crosstalk (FEXT) from line 2 into line 1 can also be removed by filtering the decision-device output and subtracting that FEXT noise also. Line 1 then has lower noise prior to its detection and thus, can carry a higher data rate in the absence of the common external noise and FEXT[8]. Such common noise can be crosstalk from other lines out of the vectored group. This entire process applies equally with reversal of the terms "user 1" and "user 2," thus emphasizing the trade-off in decoding order on each tone. For 3 or more users, the concept readily generalizes

---

[6] A concatenation of Level 3 DSM and VDSL is sometimes called VDSL3 (which also could eventually be the name for the current G.vector effort within the ITU, which focuses on Level 3 DSM vectoring use in VDSL).

[7] Such reconstructed noise is the difference between the tone decision devices' input and output.

[8] It is well established now [19] that the diagonal dominance of common-vector-group FEXT allows a linear pre-decision filtering to remove this FEXT only. Thus, order for such diagonally dominated systems' FEXT is usually of little consequence. However, this is not true for the other common noises, nor is it true for shared line use as in Section 4.3.

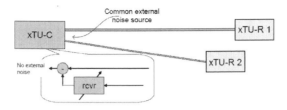

Fig. 10. Simple illustration of vectoring

with a highest priority (benefit) for the last user in the order, decreasing to the first user whose benefit is least.

4.2 Reducing Power by Cancelling Noise

Figure 11(a) illustrates the savings in power for a 3 Mbps upstream vectored VDSL vs. line length with simulation settings found in [20]. The power savings can be substantial for this case of 4 vectored VDSLs and 4 other VDSLs outside the vectored group. For such a system, with a good analog front-end design, the spatial correlation of the noises should approach 1 (that is, .99 is most realistic). Typically, when the number of vectored lines equals or exceeds the number of out-of-vector group lines, the spatial noise correlation is high. This effect can be made pronounced by using split-pair sensors in the analog front-end thus augmenting the number of dimensions used. Even with low spatial correlation, the savings is substantial. A factor of 10 or more savings essentially causes the transmitted power to be negligible. At this point, signal processing costs would limit further power reduction.

Figure 11(b) instead illustrates the power savings as a function of data rate, and of course the power increases as the data rate increases. However, the gap

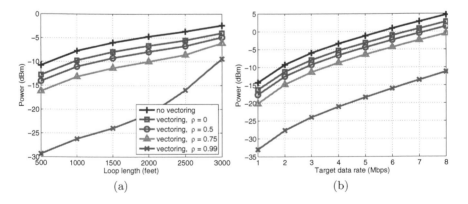

Fig. 11. (a) Power savings vs. loop length for 3 Mbps upstream vectored VDSL. (b) Power savings versus data rate for upstream vectored VDSL.

(savings) becomes relatively constant for these 1500ft lines. Again there are 4 vectored lines and 4 lines with FEXT from outside the vectored group. Additional configurations appear in [20][21].

4.3 CuPONs

CuPONs [22] copy the passive-optical-network (PON) architecture of shared line bandwidth for up to 2-4 customers, using the multiple-pair drops as shown in Fig. 12(a). Such multi-drop sharing allows much higher bandwidths - for instance, 4 line drops can have over 1 Gbps of symmetric bandwidth as first noted in [23]. 1 Gbps shared over 4 users is 250 Mbps each, while it is 500 Mbps symmetric for each of two users. Such data rates are very feasible at line lengths of 300 to 500 meters (1000-1500 feet). The CuPON makes use of all the copper and in particular, allows vectored receivers over the 4 bonded pairs. Then crosstalk from outside the vectored group can again be cancelled. The concept of order between the users sharing common lines is again important in CuPON.

The downstream problem is known in multi-user information theory as the broadcast channel. This channel requires a duality transformation [24] of the measured FEXT and noise correlation matrices to use the algorithm discussed in Section 4.2 directly. Also, the spatial correlation between noises needs to be reported for the (2 to 4) common pairs at each customer location. Technically, only the noise-whitened equivalent insertion loss (Xlog's) could be reported, but this would be an abuse of the definition of insertion loss as currently defined in standards. Thus, a separate reporting of the spatial noise correlation matrix would be desirable.

Figure 12(b) illustrates the further potential power reduction and rate increase using the CuPON architecture with respect to best power and rates for no vectoring and vectoring.

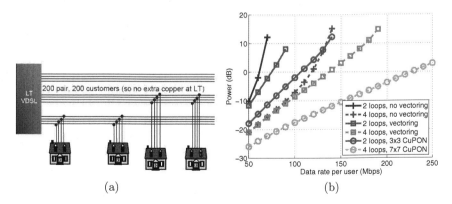

| (a) | (b) |

Fig. 12. (a) Basic CuPON access-network architecture. (b) Power savings with shared CuPON architecture versus data rate.

5   Conclusion

Dynamic Spectrum Management offers many successively larger mechanisms to reduce consumed power in DSL systems, as well as to improve data rates. Such power savings could be of serious consequence to large DSL deployments that routinely consume megawatts of power today. The consequent savings provide a way to make copper greener in an evolving and increasingly energy-efficient world.

References

1. Dynamic Spectrum Management Technical Report, ATIS Committee NIPP Pre-published document ATIS-PP-0600007 (2007)
2. Starr, T., Sorbara, M., Cioffi, J.M., Silverman, P.J.: DSL Advances. Prentice-Hall, Englewood Cliffs (2003)
3. Masson, J. L., France Telecom R&D: DSL access and advantages from DSM in France. In: IEEE Globecom Access, Washington, DC (2007)
4. Foster, K., BT Design UK: DSL & Dynamic Line Management. In: IEEE Globecom Access, Washington, DC (2007)
5. Starr, T.: AT&T: Experiences from Dynamic Spectrum Management. In: IEEE Globecom Access, Washington, DC (2007)
6. Cioffi, J.M.: Dynamic Spectrum Management (DSM): 3 Steps to Ubiquitous High-Speed DSL. In: IEEE Globecom Access, Washington, DC, ASSIA, Inc. (2007)
7. Kerpez, K.: Telcordia: Operationalizing DSM into DSL Test and Maintenance. In: IEEE Globecom Access, Washington, DC (2007)
8. Cioffi, J.M.: ASSIA, Inc.: Dynamic Spectrum Management (DSM): 3 Steps to Ubiquitous High-Speed DSL. In: IEC Broadband World Forum, Berlin (2007)
9. Polano, M.: Telecom Italia: xDSL stability and performance: current issues and future solutions. In: IEC Broadband World Forum, Berlin (2007)
10. Berndt, E.: Goals for the Future Access Network and Economic Aspects. In: IEC Broadband World Forum, Berlin (2007)
11. Cook, J.: BTexact UK: Simulation parameters for discussion in the NICC-DSL TG. NICC Contribution PNO-DSLTG/CP38 (04)2 (2004)
12. Cendrillon, R., Yu, W., Moonen, M., Verlinden, J., Bostoen, T.: Optimal Multiuser Spectrum Balancing for Digital Subscriber Lines. IEEE Trans. Commun. 54(5), 922–933 (2006)
13. Cioffi, J., Lee, W., Jagannathan, S., Ginis, G.: The Inherent Simplicity of Distributed Band Preference. ATIS Contribution NIPP-NAI-2007-129R2, Miami, FL (2007)
14. Jagannathan, S., Cioffi, J.M.: Distributed adaptive bit-loading for spectrum optimization in multi-user multicarrier systems. Elsevier Physical Communication 1(1), 40–59 (2008)
15. Lee, W., Kim, Y., Brady, M., Cioffi, J.: Distributed Band-Preference Dynamic Spectrum Management for Digital Subscriber Lines. Submitted to IEEE Trans. Commun.
16. Lee, W., Jagannathan, S., Cioffi, J., Ginis, G., Silverman, P.: Higher-Rate Level 2 DSM Power-Saving Examples. ATIS Contribution NIPP-NAI-2007-160R2, Vancouver, Canada (2007)
17. Verlinden, J., Bruyssel, D.V.: Virtual Noise Mechanism. ATIS Contribution NIPP-NAI-2005-049, San Francisco, CA (2005)

18. Ginis, G., Cioffi, J.M.: Vectored Transmission for Digital Subscriber Line Systems. IEEE J. Select. Areas Commun. 20(5), 1085–1104 (2002)
19. Cendrillon, R., Ginis, G., Bogaert, E.V., Moonen, M.: A Near-Optimal Linear Crosstalk Precoder for Downstream VDSL. IEEE Trans. Commun. 55(5), 860–863 (2007)
20. Lee, W., Chen, C., Jagannathan, S., Cioffi, J., Ginis, G., Silverman, P.: Power and Rate Management for Level 3 DSM Vectored DSLs. ATIS Contribution NIPP-NAI-2007-162R2, Vancouver, Canada (2007)
21. Cioffi, J., Jagannathan, S., Ginis, G., Brady, M.: DSM is for Unbundled DSL. ATIS Contribution NIPP-NAI-2006-087R1, Savannah, GA (2006)
22. Cioffi, J.M., Jagannathan, S., Mohseni, M., Ginis, G.: CuPON: The Copper Alternative to PON - 100 Gb/s DSL Networks. IEEE Commun. Mag. 45(6), 132–139 (2007)
23. Lee, B., Cioffi, J.M., Jagannathan, S., Mohseni, M.: Gigabit DSL. IEEE Trans. Commun. 9(55), 1689–1692 (2007)
24. Cioffi, J.M.: EE479 course reader, http://eeclass.stanford.edu/ee479

Performance Comparison of Orthogonal and Quasi-orthogonal Codes in Quasi-Synchronous Cellular CDMA Communication

Sujit Jos[1], Preetam Kumar[2], and Saswat Chakrabarti[2]

[1] Dept. of Electronics and Electrical Communication Engineering
[2] G. S. Sanayal School of Telecommunications
Indian Institute of Technology, Kharagpur
sujit@gssst.iitkgp.ernet.in, preetam@gssst.iitkgp.ernet.in,
saswat@ece.iitkgp.ernet.in

Abstract. Orthogonal and quasi-orthogonal codes are integral part of any DS-CDMA based cellular systems. Orthogonal codes are ideal for use in perfectly synchronous scenario like downlink cellular communication. Quasi-orthogonal codes are preferred over orthogonal codes in the uplink communication where perfect synchronization cannot be achieved. In this paper, we attempt to compare orthogonal and quasi-orthogonal codes in presence of timing synchronization error. This will give insight into the synchronization demands in DS-CDMA systems employing the two classes of sequences. The synchronization error considered is smaller than chip duration. Monte-Carlo simulations have been carried out to verify the analytical and numerical results.

1 Introduction

Direct Sequence Code Division multiple Access (DS-CDMA) is considered to be a promising technology for broadband deployment of next generation cellular networks. The performance of DS-CDMA system relies largely on the correlation properties of the codes employed for the spreading of the user signal [1]. Synchronous CDMA(S-CDMA) has been proposed in [2], whereby Multiple Access Interference (MAI) could be completely eliminated by the use of orthogonal spreading codes. Hence, orthogonal codes are the obvious choice when perfect synchronization is maintained. This perfect synchronization is difficult to implement in the uplink and the performance will degrade in the presence of access timing error. When the synchronization error present in the system is less than a chip period, the DS-CDMA system is usually referred to as Quasi-Synchronous CDMA or QS-CDMA system [3].

Behavior of orthogonal codes in quasi-synchronous environment has been well addressed in [4]-[6]. In QS-CDMA system, quasi-orthogonal codes provide superior performance compared to orthogonal codes. They are extensively employed in uplink communication where different users are misaligned in time. Hence, quasi-orthogonal sequences attract a great deal of attention in systems where synchronizations errors are inevitable. Performance analysis of quasi-orthogonal codes in QS-CDMA has been presented in [6]-[8]. But, a quantitative comparison between the two classes of codes has not been addressed sufficiently.

C. Wang (Ed.): AccessNets, LNICST 6, pp. 78–88, 2009.

In this work, orthogonal and quasi-orthogonal codes have been compared with respect to the maximum tolerable synchronization error that can be tolerated so that complete error-free despreading is guaranteed. BER analysis of QS-CDMA system is also presented in presence of timing synchronization error. The analysis for maximum tolerable synchronization error for Walsh Hadamard codes has been done in [4].

In the next section we will describe the system model of QS-CDMA with BPSK modulation. We compare orthogonal and quasi-orthogonal codes in section 3. In section 4, we present the BER analysis in presence of noise. Simulation results are presented in section 5. Finally we conclude the paper.

2   System Model for QS-CDMA with BPSK

The DS-CDMA system is modeled as in [4]. The system consists of K users simultaneously signaling over a common transmission channel. With BPSK transmission, the signal of k'th user can be written as

$$u_k(t) = A_k \sum_{l=-\infty}^{\infty} b_k^l s_k(t - lT_b), k = 0, \ldots, K-1 \tag{1}$$

with amplitude A_k, symbol duration T_b, $b_k^l \in \{-1, 1\}$ and spreading code $s_k(t)$, which is given by

$$s_k(t) = \sum_{j=0}^{N-1} s_k^j p_c(t - jT_c) \tag{2}$$

with $T_b = NT_c$ and $s_k^j = \pm 1$ the elements of the k'th codeword with chip duration T_c and length N. The function $p_c(t) = 1$ if $0 < t < T_c$, and $p_c(t) = 0$ otherwise. The received signal $r(t)$ is the summation of all K signals

$$r(t) = \sum_{k=0}^{K-1} u_k(t - \tau_k) \tag{3}$$

where $\tau_k \in [-T_c, T_c]$ is the time shift between the transmitted and the received signal of user k. Since noise is common to all systems, we have ignored the effect of AWGN in equation (3). Analysis in presence of noise will be resumed in section 4.

If a correlation receiver is used to detect the desired symbol b_i^n, the received signal $r(t)$ has to be multiplied with the desired user code $s_i(t)$ and integrated over the symbol duration.

$$b_i^{\sim n} = \frac{1}{T_b} \int_0^{T_b} s_i(t) r(t + nT_b) dt$$

$$= \frac{1}{T_b} \int_0^{T_b} s_i(t) \left[\sum_{k=0}^{K-1} A_k \sum_{l=-\infty}^{\infty} b_k^l s_k(t + (n-l)T_b - \tau_k) \right] dt \tag{4}$$

Due to the time shift τ_k between the spreading and despreading code of user k, the integration not only contains the cross correlation from b_k^n but also from $b_k^{n\pm1}$. This minor contribution can be neglected when $\tau_k < T_c$ [5]. Hence the received symbol is given as:

$$\tilde{b}_i^{\,n} = \frac{1}{T_b} \int_0^{T_b} s_i(t) \left[\sum_{k=0}^{K-1} A_k b_k^n s_k(t-\tau_k) \right] dt$$

$$= A_i b_i^n \varphi_{ii}(\tau_i) + \sum_{k=0,k\neq i}^{K-1} A_k b_k^n \varphi_{ik}(\tau_k) \tag{5}$$

Where,

$$\varphi_{ik}(\tau_k) = \frac{1}{NT_c} \int_0^{NT_c} s_i(t) s_k(t-\tau_k) dt \tag{6}$$

is the correlation between codeword $s_i(t)$ and codeword $s_k(t)$ delayed by τ_k. From (5), we observe that the amplitude of the desired user is degraded by the autocorrelation coefficient which is unity in the case of perfect synchronization. The nonunity autocorrelation coefficient results in reduced signal strength in the despreaded signal. Synchronization errors generally results in increased MAI because of the higher value of crosscorrelation compared to the zero phase crosscorrelation. The original user data symbol b_i^n can be deduced from the received signal as long as

$$A_i \varphi_{ii}(\tau_i) + \sum_{k=0,k\neq i}^{K-1} A_k \left(\frac{b_k^n}{b_i^n} \right) \varphi_{ik}(\tau_k) > 0 \tag{7}$$

Assuming all user amplitudes to be equal, i.e., $A_i = A_k$ for all k, we find the worst-case situation under which (7) is guaranteed to be fulfilled so that the reception is completely error-free. In the worst case scenario, (7) is transformed into

$$\varphi_{ii}(\tau_i) - \sum_{k=0,k\neq i}^{K-1} \left| \varphi_{ik}(\tau_k) \right| > 0 \tag{8}$$

It follows from (8) that whenever the autocorrelation value is larger than the sum of absolute crosscorrelation values, it is possible to recover the desired data stream b_n^i. Hence, the strict condition for error-free despreading requires that synchronization errors for all users are smaller than the maximum tolerable synchronization error ΔT, which would be derived subsequently. The autocorrelation function for i'th user may be expressed as

$$\varphi_{ii}(\tau_i) = \left(\frac{\varphi_{ii}(T_c) - \varphi_{ii}(0)}{T_c - 0} \right) \tau_i + \varphi_{ii}(0) \tag{9}$$

Similarly, the crosscorrelation function can be written as

$$\varphi_{ik}(\tau_k) = \frac{\varphi_{ik}(T_c)}{T_c}\tau_k + \varphi_{ik}(0), 0 \le \tau_k \le T_c \tag{10}$$

with $\varphi_{ik}(0) = 0$ for orthogonal code and $\varphi_{ik}(0) = -\dfrac{1}{N}$ for quasi-orthogonal codes. We first derive the expression for maximum tolerable synchronization error for orthogonal codes. Substitution of (9) and (10) into (8) gives

$$\frac{\varphi_{ii}(T_c)-1}{T_c}\tau_i + 1 - \frac{\displaystyle\sum_{k=0,k\neq i}^{K-1}\left|\varphi_{ik}(T_c)\right|}{T_c}\tau_k > 0, 0 \le \tau_i, \tau_k \le T_c \tag{11}$$

The maximum tolerable synchronization error ΔT can be incorporated into (11) with the following equality

$$\frac{\varphi_{ii}(T_c)-1}{T_c}\Delta T + 1 = \frac{\displaystyle\sum_{k=0,k\neq i}^{K-1}\left|\varphi_{ik}(T_c)\right|}{T_c}\Delta T \tag{12}$$

Equation (12) can be written as:

$$\Delta T = \frac{T_c}{\displaystyle\sum_{k=0,k\neq i}^{K-1}\left|\varphi_{ik}(T_c)\right| - \varphi_{ik}(T_c) + 1} \tag{13}$$

with ΔT upper bounded by T_c. The minimum of ΔT over all users gives the maximum tolerable synchronization error. Hence, the maximum tolerable synchronization error for orthogonal codes is obtained as

$$\Delta T = \min_i\left\{\frac{T_c}{\displaystyle\sum_{k=0,k\neq i}^{K-1}\left|\varphi_{ik}(T_c)\right| - \varphi_{ii}(T_c) + 1}\right\} \tag{14}$$

Now we proceed to obtain a similar expression for quasi-orthogonal codes. The autocorrelation function remains same as in the case of orthogonal codes. The crosscorrelation function with appropriate substitution in (10) is given by

$$\varphi_{ik}(\tau_k) = \frac{\varphi_{ik}(T_c)}{T_c}\tau_k - \frac{1}{N}, 0 \le \tau_k \le T_c \tag{15}$$

Substitution of (9) and (15) into (8) gives

$$\frac{\varphi_{ii}(T_c)-1}{T_c}\tau_i + 1 - \sum_{k=0,k\neq i}^{K-1}\left|\frac{\varphi_{ik}(T_c)\tau_k}{T_c} - \frac{1}{N}\right| > 0, 0 \le \tau_i, \tau_k \le T_c \tag{16}$$

With a small approximation, equation (16) can now be written as

$$\frac{\varphi_{ii}(T_c)-1}{T_c}\tau_i + 1 - \frac{\sum\limits_{k=0,k\neq i}^{K-1}\left|\varphi_{ik}(T_c)\right|\tau_k}{T_c} + \frac{1}{N} > 0 \tag{17}$$

Since $\left|\varphi_{ik}(T_c)\right| - \left|\varphi_{ik}(0)\right| \leq \left|\varphi_{ik}(T_c) - \varphi_{ik}(0)\right|$, the inequality of equation (17) still holds good. From (17), it follows that

$$\frac{\varphi_{ii}(T_c)-1}{T_c}\Delta T + 1 = \frac{\sum\limits_{k=0,k\neq i}^{K-1}\left|\varphi_{ik}(T_c)\right|}{T_c}\Delta T - \frac{1}{N} \tag{18}$$

which can be written as:

$$\Delta T = \frac{\left(1+\dfrac{1}{N}\right)T_c}{\sum\limits_{k=0,k\neq i}^{K-1}\left|\varphi_{ik}(T_c)\right| - \varphi_{ii}(T_c) + 1} \tag{19}$$

Taking minimum over all codewords, we have ΔT for quasi-orthogonal codes as

$$\Delta T = \min_i \left\{ \frac{\left(1+\dfrac{1}{N}\right)T_c}{\sum\limits_{k=0,k\neq i}^{K-1}\left|\varphi_{ik}(T_c)\right| - \varphi_{ii}(T_c) + 1} \right\} \tag{20}$$

3 Comparison between Orthogonal and Quasi-orthogonal Codes

An accurate comparison of the two types of codes is not possible since orthogonal codes have even length while quasi-orthogonal codes have odd length. But looking at equations (14) and (20), we can make an approximate comparison of the two classes of codes. From the two equations we can observe that quasi-orthogonal can tolerate a synchronization error which is $\left(1+\dfrac{1}{N}\right)$ times that tolerated by orthogonal sequences for a given code length N. Hence, this justifies the usage of quasi-orthogonal codes in the uplink communication from user to base station, where perfect synchronization cannot be maintained between different user signals.

The maximum tolerable synchronization error is numerically evaluated for some of the commonly employed orthogonal and quasi-orthogonal codes. The orthogonal codes considered are Walsh-Hadamard, Orthogonal Gold and Quadratic-Residue (QR) orthogonal codes, while m-sequences and balanced gold codes are considered for the evaluation of quasi-orthogonal codes. Both the quasi-orthogonal sequences have normalized crosscorrelation value of $-\frac{1}{N}$. The value of ΔT as a fraction of chip duration for different orthogonal codes are given Table 1. The spreading code length N is 8, 16, 32, 64 and 128. Table 2 shows the values of ΔT for quasi-orthogonal sequences. The spreading lengths considered are 7,15,31,63 and 127 respectively.

Table 1. Maximum Tolerable synchronizatrion error of orthogonal codes for different values of N

N	*Walsh Code*	*QR Code*	*Orthogonal Gold Code*
8	0.3333	0.3333	0.3333
16	0.2857	0.2857	0.2857
32	0.2353	0.2667	0.1739
64	0.2051	0.2581	0.1600
128	0.1798	0.2540	0.1019

Table 2. Maximum Tolerable synchronizatrion error of Quasi-orthogonal codes for different values of N

N	*m-sequence*	*Gold Code*
7	0.4000	0.4000
15	0.3636	0.3636
31	0.3478	0.1882
63	0.3404	0.1768
127	0.3368	0.1061

As seen from tables 1 and 2, quasi-orthogonal codes have better immunity towards synchronization error. Hence, quasi-orthogonal codes are often employed in uplink communication where perfect orthogonality cannot be maintained due to timing synchronization errors.

4 BER Analysis in Presence of Noise

In this section, we derive the BER expression for individual users in a QS-CDMA system when BPSK signaling is employed. In presence of noise, (7) is modified as

$$A_i \varphi_{ii}(\tau_i) + \sum_{k=0,k \neq i}^{K-1} A_k (\frac{b_k^n}{b_i^n}) \varphi_{ik}(\tau_k) + z > 0 \tag{21}$$

where,

$$z = \frac{1}{T_b} \int_0^{T_b} s_i(t)n(t)dt \tag{22}$$

and $n(t)$ is the additive white Gaussian noise process with two sided power spectral density $\frac{N_0}{2}$. An error is made in the detection process of b_i^n when I_i exceeds $A_i\varphi_{ii}(\tau_i)$. To determine the probability of error we need the distribution of MAI_i which depends on the crosscorrelation of the codewords. Since, we assume that data symbols are equiprobable, MAI_i approaches a Gaussian random variable as the number of interferers increases. Under the Gaussian approximation of MAI_i, we can model the interference noise I_i as Gaussian. With the Gaussian approximation the probability of error or BER of i'th user is given by

$$BER_i = \frac{1}{\sqrt{2\pi}\sigma} \int_{A_i\varphi_{ii}(\tau_i)}^{\infty} e^{-I_i^2/2\sigma^2} dI_i \tag{23}$$

Let

$$x = I_i/2\sigma \tag{24}$$

Equation (23) now takes the form

$$BER_i = \sqrt{2}\sigma \times \frac{1}{\sqrt{2\pi}\sigma} \int_{\frac{A_i\varphi_{ii}(\tau_i)}{\sqrt{2\sigma}}}^{\infty} e^{x^2} dx \tag{25}$$

$$= \frac{1}{2} erfc\left(\frac{A_i\varphi_{ii}(\tau_i)}{\sqrt{2\sigma}}\right) \tag{26}$$

$$= Q\left(\sqrt{\frac{A_i^2\varphi_{ii}^2(\tau_i)}{\sigma^2}}\right) \tag{27}$$

where

$$\sigma^2 = \sigma_z^2 + \sigma_{MAI_i}^2 \tag{28}$$

Here, $\sigma_z^2 = \frac{N_0}{2}$ and the variance of MAI, $\sigma_{MAI_i}^2$ can be calculated as

$$\sigma_{MAI_i}^2 = E\{MAI_i\}$$

$$= \sum_{k=0, k\neq i}^{K-1} A_k^2\varphi_{ik}^2(\tau_k) \tag{29}$$

From (27) and (29), we have the final equation for the BER of the i'th user as

$$BER_i = Q\left(\sqrt{\dfrac{A_i^2 \varphi_{ii}^2(\tau_i)}{\dfrac{N_0}{2} + \displaystyle\sum_{k=0,k\neq i}^{K-1} A_k^2 \varphi_{ik}^2(\tau_k)}}\right) \tag{30}$$

5 Simulation Results

Monte-Carlo simulations have been carried out to verify the analytical and numerical results presented in the previous sections. Fig. 1 shows the BER curves of 5th and 20th codeword of Walsh Hadamard codeset in presence of synchronization error of 0.3Tc when the number of users and the spreading length of the code is 64. The analytical curve is also shown to support the BER analysis presented in the earlier section. Gaussian approximation for MAI seems to be more valid for lower values of Eb/No.

Fig. 2 shows the BER performance of 1st codeword of balanced Gold code in presence of synchronization error of 0.3Tc when the number of users and the spreading length of the code is 63. Quasi-orthogonal spreading sequences like balanced gold codes and m-sequences which are generated from shift register sequences exhibit a greater degree of randomness. Hence, the Gaussian approximation for MAI becomes more valid for quasi-orthogonal sequences. This fact could be observed from figures 1 and 2.

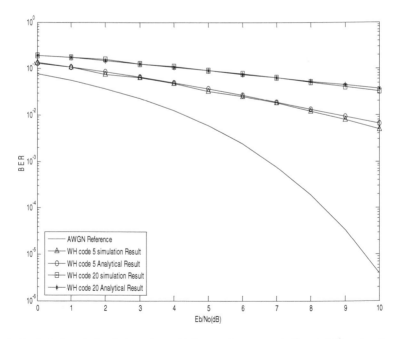

Fig. 1. Analytical and simulation plots of BER performance of 5th and 20th codes from WH matrix of order 64 at synchronization error of 0.3Tc when K=N=64

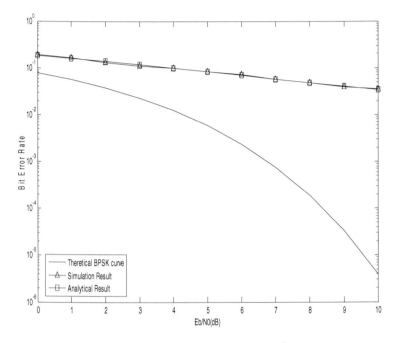

Fig. 2. Analytical and simulation plots of BER performance of 1st code from balanced gold set at synchronization error of 0.3Tc when K=N=63

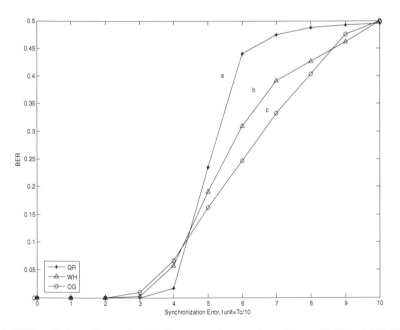

Fig. 3. BER variation with synchronization error when number of users, K=N and AWGN =0 for the following: a) QR Code; b) WH code and c) OG code

Fig. 3 shows the BER plots for the three orthogonal codes at different synchronization errors. As observed from the figure, QR codes have maximum tolerance to synchronization errors. The BER is very less till 0.4Tc for QR codes but it increases rapidly from this value and it gives higher BER as compared to WH and OG codes. In contrast orthogonal Gold codes provide very small BER till 0.3Tc and beyond this value, it generally gives less error. For Walsh Hadamard codes there is no despreading error till 0.2Tc, but it increases rapidly and gives error performance between QR and OG codes.

Fig. 4 shows the variation of BER of two quasi-orthogonal codes for different synchronization errors. It is observed from Fig 4 that the BER is very less for m-sequences till 0.4Tc and increases rapidly beyond this point while balanced gold codes give very less errors till 0.3Tc and moderate errors beyond this point. The precision in the plots is limited to 0.1Tc, hence finer insight is not obtained from the plots. These results seem to in agreement with the analytical expression for the maximum tolerable synchronization error for free despreading.

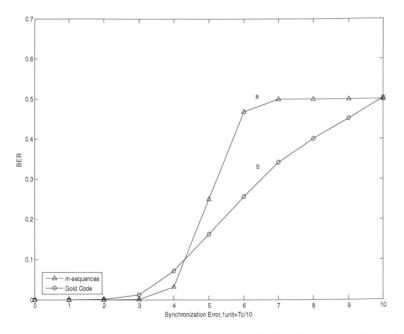

Fig. 4. BER versus timing synchronization error of a QS-CDMA system, with number of users, K=N=63 and AWGN =0 for the following quasi-orthogonal codes : a)m-sequence and b)Gold codes

6 Conclusion

Orthogonal and quasi-orthogonal codes have been compared in terms of the maximum tolerable synchronization error for error-free despreading. It has been shown that quasi-orthogonal codes are more immune to synchronization errors compared to their orthogonal counterparts. The orthogonal codes considered were Walsh-Hadamard, Orthogonal Gold and Quadratic-Residue(QR) codes, while m-sequences and balanced gold codes were considered for the performance evaluation. BER analysis in presence of noise has also been presented. Monte-Carlo simulation was carried out to verify the analytical and numerical results. Among the orthogonal codes considered, it is observed that QR orthogonal codes have better immunity towards synchronization errors as compared to Walsh Hadamard and Orthogonal Gold codes while m-sequences perform better in case of quasi-orthogonal codes.

References

1. Pursley, M.: Performance Evaluation for Phase-Coded Spread-Spectrum Multiple-Access Communication–Part I: System Analysis. IEEE Trans. Commn 25, 795–799 (1977)
2. Zhu, J., Nomura, T., Yamada, T.: Performance of Spread Spectrum Synchronous access Communication system by Orthogonal Sequences. IEICE Trans. Commn 68, 319–326 (1985)
3. Lin, X.D.: Optimal PN sequence design for quasi-synchronous CDMA communication systems. IEEE Trans. Commn 45, 221–226 (1997)
4. Houtum, W.J.V.: Quasi-synchronous code-division multiple access with high-order modulation. IEEE Trans. Commn. 49, 1240–1249 (2001)
5. Dasilva, V.M.V., Sousa, E.S.: Multicarrier Orthogonal CDMA signals for quasi-synchronous communication systems. IEEE JSAC 12, 842–852 (1994)
6. Khairy, M.M., Geraniotis, E.: Effect of time-jitter on CDMA networks with orthogonal and quasi-orthogonal sequences. In: Proceedings of Symposium on Computers and Communications, pp. 260–264 (1997)
7. Matolak, D.W., Manchiraju, D.: Evaluation of pseudorandom sequences for third generation spread spectrum systems. In: Proceedings of Southeastern Symposium on system theory 2003, pp. 288–290 (2003)
8. Sunay, M.O., McLane, P.J.: Sensitivity of a DS CDMA system with long PN sequences to synchronization errors. In: Proceedings of ICC 1995, pp. 1029–1035 (1995)

Supporting Session and Access Point Mobility in a Large Multi-provider Multi-vendor Municipal WiFi Network

Timo Ojala, Toni Hakanen, Ossi Salmi, Mikko Kenttälä, and Juha Tiensyrjä

MediaTeam Oulu, University of Oulu
P.O. Box 4500, 90014 University of Oulu, Finland
{firstname.lastname}@ee.oulu.fi

Abstract. We present a simple network design for a large multi-provider municipal WiFi network where the WiFi zones of multiple organizations are merged into a single IP subnet at a central layer 2 switch. The design provides built-in session mobility support for the WiFi clients using the network, without any additional software at the client. We also provide a simple design for mobile access points so that they belong to the same IP subnet. We analyze the session mobility of the over 12000 devices using our network in January 2008. We also provide a comparison of the usage of multi-mode mobile devices and WiFi laptops, and characterize the roaming performance of a standard WiFi laptop in our network.

Keywords: municipal, wireless, network design, mobility, roaming, handover.

1 Introduction

This paper addresses session and access point (AP) mobility in a large multi-provider multi-vendor municipal WiFi network provisioned primarily for the purpose of providing open and free wireless Internet access to the general public. With session mobility we refer to a WiFi user device using multiple APs during a continuous application session so that connections are maintained during transitions between APs. Thus, we wish to make a clear distinction to user mobility, which has been used to characterize usage of multiple access points by an individual user over many sessions [2]. With AP mobility we refer to an AP, installed for example in a bus, moving around, possibly among stationary APs. With multi-provider we refer to a municipal wireless network comprising of subnets provided by multiple independent organizations. With multi-vendor we refer to the network comprising of devices produced by multiple manufacturers.

Session mobility in a WiFi network is important from both the application point of view and the network design point of view. This is particularly true for a multi-provider network comprising of subnets provided by multiple independent organizations. If the user device roams between APs in different IP subnets so that the subnet prefix changes, then the IP address of the user device changes. Since the IP address determines the communication endpoints at the application layer, e.g. a 4-tuple TCP connection < source IP address, source port number, destination IP address, destination port number>, roaming and the subsequent change of the IP address

C. Wang (Ed.): AccessNets, LNICST 6, pp. 89–101, 2009.

results in the interruption of all existing TCP connections. So, in terms of session mobility, we want to make sure that the IP address of the user device does not change, even though the device roams from an AP of one organization to an AP of another organization during the session.

AP mobility is equally important, particularly if mobile AP's move around among fixed APs belonging to the same network. If a stationary user device can hear many APs of a network, the device can "ping pong" between different APs. In other words, a user device may associate and reassociate with several APs many times in succession, without moving an inch. This does destroy session mobility, if the APs in question reside in the same LAN for example. But the "ping pong" effect may become a problem if the user device is associated to an AP placed in a bus driving through a cluster of fixed APs, for typically the fixed and mobile APs have different backhaul networks (fixed vs wireless) with different IP address spaces. Again, we want to make sure that the IP address of the user device does not change, even though it roams from the mobile AP to a fixed AP or vice versa.

We present a simple network design for supporting session and AP mobility in a large multi-provider multi-vendor municipal wireless network. The WiFi zones of multiple organizations are merged into a single IP subnet at a central layer 2 switch, i.e. we effectively reduce the multi-provider network into a single-provider case in terms of IP addressing. Session mobility is based on the self-learning property of layer 2 switches, i.e. upon receiving frames from a mobile node the switches automatically learn the current location of the mobile node and build their forwarding tables accordingly. The design is user-friendly in the sense that session mobility is provided without any additional client application at the user device. This is partially motivated by the fact that a large proportion of the users of our municipal wireless network are one time users, visiting our city for business or leisure and happily using our network for Internet access. The design is suitable for a multi-vendor network, where we cannot and do not want to rely on proprietary vendor-specific solutions. However, as the experimental evaluation of the roaming performance will show, the design does not provide good support for highly mobile devices.

This paper is organized as follows. After briefly discussing related work we first provide an overview of our panOULU network [5]. Then we describe the network design and its simple built-in support for session and AP mobility. Our municipal network has been in everyday use for several years, hence we have a plenty of real life traces to work on. After presenting some general usage statistics of the network, we focus on estimating the amount of session mobility in our network. If there is very little session mobility, then there is very little motivation to provide specific support for it and vice versa. We also present quantitative performance characterization of our design in different roaming scenarios. We conclude with a discussion on the strengths and weaknesses of our design, which should prove useful in designing similar networks.

2 Related Work

2.1 Municipal WiFi Networks

In terms of the design of the wireless user access and backhaul, municipal WiFi networks have evolved from the basic ESS (Extended Service Set) topology towards mesh topology. In the former multiple single-radio APs connected to a wired distribution (backhaul) system provide wireless user access. In leading-edge mesh topologies multiple-radio APs typically provide user access in the 2.4 Ghz band using the 802.11b/g technology, while inter-AP backhaul links are implemented in the 5 GHz band using the 802.11a technology. One motivation is to reduce operational expenses in the long run, as the mesh topology allows cutting down the number of wired backhaul links, possibly down to just 10% of the traditional design. Our wireless network is a mixture of the two topologies.

In terms of combining multiple network providers' WiFi zones into a single access network, in our case each organization first aggregates its APs into a VLAN. These VLANs are then merged into a single aerially large layer 2 network and a single IP subnet. This is a very rare if not a unique design. Boingo acting as the service provider for multiple network providers is a good example of more traditional WiFi roaming. The opposite are commercial open access networks, where the goal is to connect multiple service providers into a single WiFi access network provided by some network operator. The best-known example of commercial open access networks is probably StockholmOpen.net [6]. Its core component is a DHCP relay, which first establishes the initial connection with the user device and then provides a list of ISPs to choose from. Once the user has selected the ISP, the DHCP relay redirects the connection to the selected ISP, which assigns IP address and other network settings to the user device.

Another type of multiple-provider networks include community networks such as SeattleWireless [7] or FreiFunk [8], where the members of the community agree on granting each other access to APs and forwarding traffic. If a mesh topology is used, then only a fraction of the APs need to have backhaul access.

2.2 Session Mobility

We can identify two principal levels of session mobility. On the first level we just maintain active sessions (connections) during transitions between APs, which is effectively a mobility management problem. On the second, more advanced level we provide session mobility with some level of QoS. It could for example refer to communication delays or packet loss, which are very relevant to real-time interactive applications such as VoIP. If no specific support is provided, even roaming between APs of the same technology (horizontal handover) and belonging to the same subnet can lead to packet loss and degraded quality of service. This is mainly due to the long latency in the network learning of the new location of a highly mobile node to route packets accordingly.

Interestingly, the original IEEE 802.11 specifications did not specify the intra AP communication protocol to inform the network about a client's roaming. This led to many proprietary vendor-specific implementations and interoperability concerns. Later, in 2003 the 802.11f IAPP (Inter-Access Point Protocol) protocol was published as a trial standard for this purpose. However, it did not gain popularity in the industry and consequently was withdrawn in 2006. The current standardization effort is 802.11r ("Fast Roaming/Fast BSS Transition"), which is scheduled to be published in 2008. In 802.11r the client can use the current AP as a conduit to other APs, which allows the client to establish security and QoS state information at a new AP before making a transition.

A number of mobility management technologies have been presented for higher layers of the protocol stack, for example Mobile IP [9] at the network layer, TCP-Migrate [10] at the transport layer, and SIP [11] at the application layer. Further, WiFi vendors have developed proprietary mobility managers for maintaining seamless connections for mobile nodes traversing between subnets. The common goal of the mobility management technologies and mobility managers is to provide location transparency for a mobile node. The main challenge in their deployment is that they require possibly costly changes to the network infrastructure and/or mobile node.

A number of studies on session or user mobility in WiFi networks have been conducted in the past. For example, in their analysis of the usage of a large campus network Henderson *et al.* [3] reported that 95.1% of users had a home location, and 50% of those users spent 98.7% of their time there. Balazinska and Castro [2] found in their study of a corporate wireless network that 50-80% of users fell into the occasionally and somewhat mobile categories. In our earlier study [4] based on a 14-months long monitoring of our network covering both the city and university campus, we found that on average 9% of the sessions in the city were mobile, while the corresponding figure on the campus was 5%. These studies and reported findings are not directly comparable as different things were measured in different contexts.

3   panOULU Network

3.1   General Description

panOULU is a municipal wireless network in the City of Oulu in Northern Finland. With about 130000 citizens Oulu is the sixth largest city in Finland. The Oulu region is well-known for its ICT competence and with about 14000 ICT jobs has by far the largest regional R&D expenditure per capita in Finland. Back in 1998 the Wired Magazine ranked Oulu as #3 'silicon valley' in the world, after the original Silicon Valley in California and Austin in Texas. The city's central administration is very much pro ICT and pro R&D, which has proven very valuable over the years, also for the panOULU network.

panOULU comprises of two basic types of subnets: campus networks of five public organizations and so-called panOULU subscriptions sold by three ISPs. The City of Oulu, University of Oulu, Oulu University of Applied Sciences, VTT Technical Research Centre of Finland, and Pulmonary Association Heli each have large premises around Oulu covered by WiFi networks. Each organization is responsible for the expenses and the management of its own campus network. panOULU subscription is an ISP product, and by purchasing it any organization can acquire panOULU coverage into its premises.

As of now the campus networks and panOULU subscriptions total 1050 APs. The APs come from multiple vendors (Cisco, Linksys, Strix, Buffalo) and have different types of backhaul links (Ethernet, xDSL, IEEE 802.11a, Flash-OFDM). From the user's point of view the APs appear as one large uniform network with SSID 'panoulu'. The APs provide both indoor and outdoor coverage in places deemed relevant for public access. The city center and its immediate surroundings are blanketed with a WiFi mesh network, but otherwise the coverage is provided in a hotspot manner. In some locations such as the city hospital providing public access is secondary and supplementary to actual production use of wireless access to patient databases.

In its coverage area the panOULU network provides open (no login, authentication or registration) and free (no payment) wireless internet access to the general public with a WiFi-equipped device. After associating to the network the device is granted a private IPv4 address created with NAT and allocated with DHCP, and a public IPv6 address. Public IPv4 addresses are also available upon request for R&D use. The first HTTP request of a particular device on a particular day is redirected to a splash page providing basic information about the network. Excluding the blocking of outgoing port 25 (SMTP), which is required by the Finnish legislation, there are no limitations or restrictions on the use of the network. Other services include SMTP server for sending email, help desk during office hours and panOULU Luotsi [12]. It is a mash up combining real-time AP-ID positioning of the user device and various information feeds into a location-based web service with map-based guidance.

3.2 Network Topology

A simplified version of the panOULU network topology is shown in Figure 1. Each organization contributing a WiFi zone depicted as a green cloud groups its APs into a VLAN. The VLANs are then aggregated at the central layer 2 switch #1 residing at the DNA server room. The WiFi clouds labeled DNA, Elisa and Netplaza correspond to the APs of the panOULU subscriptions (see Section 3.3) sold by the three respective telcos. OukaMESH is a 60 AP WiFi mesh network built with Strix System's OWS-2400 series APs. Other WiFi clouds are built with Cisco 1100/1200 series, Linksys WRT54GL and Buffalo WHR-G54S APs using the 'traditional' approach of hooking up each AP into the backbone with different types of wired backhaul (xDSL, Ethernet). The Mobile APs are explained in detail in Section 3.4.

The server farm providing the core services (e.g. DHCP, DNS, HTTP, SMTP) is located at the City of Oulu's server room. The server farm residing in the DNA server room includes a high performance probe for collecting packet headers from the central switch for monitoring purposes. The 100 Mbps Internet uplink is provided by Oulu University of Applied Sciences. The management of the server farms is currently sponsored and conducted by the City of Oulu, but will soon be purchased as a service from a company.

The straightforward "KISS" layer 2 design merges the organizations' WiFi zones into a single IP subnet. Among other things the design provides built-in session mobility support for the WiFi clients, which was one of the original design decisions of the panOULU network. Session mobility is based on the self-learning property of the layer 2 switches used to connect the APs into the backbone (not necessarily switches #1 and #2 shown in Figure 1). When a mobile node moves between APs in two different BSSs (Basic Service Sets), the layer 2 switch connecting the two BSSs will eventually receive a frame from the mobile node, thus automatically learning the new location of the mobile node and updating its forwarding table accordingly. However, as we will see in the experiments, this approach is not really optimal for highly mobile users.

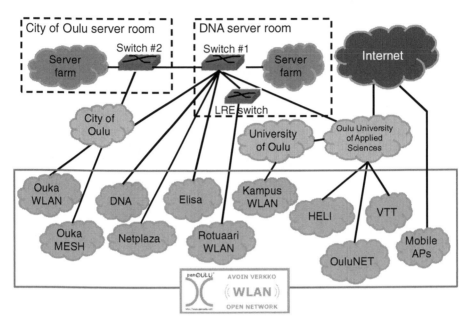

Fig. 1. Simplified topology of the panOULU network

3.3 panOULU Subscription

panOULU subscription is a panOULU compatible product offered by three ISPs. It includes both a regular business subscription with whatever services the customer wishes to purchase, and a panOULU hotspot providing open and free wireless Internet access at the customer's premises. The idea behind this bundling is that the customer does not have to purchase two separate services in order to provide a panOULU hotspot. panOULU subscription is a leasing package in the sense that the ISP own all hardware. Hence, the subscriber does not have to invest in WiFi APs or other devices, but pays for them in the monthly fee. The subscription also includes installation and maintenance.

Figure 2 illustrates the network topology of a panOULU subscription. It is implemented with one physical link (the red solid line from operator's point-of-presence to the customer's premises), typically an xDSL, atop which two VLANs are set up. The first VLAN is for the regular business subscription of the restaurant manager and its traffic is routed via the ISP's Internet uplink (green dashed line below). The other VLAN connects the WiFi AP(s) providing the panOULU hotspot in the restaurant into the panOULU's central switch. The traffic of the WiFi AP(s) is routed via the panOULU's Internet uplink (blue/yellow dashed line). We see that the AP installed inside the restaurant resides in the same layer 2 network as other panOULU APs.

The organizations having purchased a panOULU hotspot into their premises for the purpose of improving their customer service and image include Oulu Airport, Oulu Cathedral (!), Technopolis (one of Europe's largest technology center operators), a

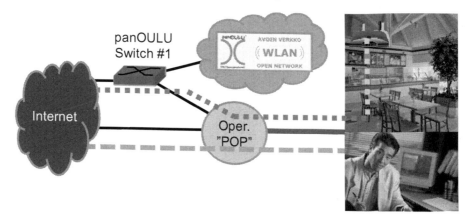

Fig. 2. Network topology of a panOULU subscription

large training and management institute, a large sports complex, a private hospital, the largest department store in the city, a large bank, many media and IT companies, and many cafes, pubs and restaurants. With the inception of the panOULU subscription we have managed to incorporate telco incentive in municipal wireless offering.

3.4 Mobile APs

The panOULU network has about 15 mobile APs, residing in buses, a ferry and a mobile library. The simple network topology of a mobile AP is illustrated in Figure 3. The Linksys WRT-54 GL AP placed in front of the bus is connected to a Flash-OFDM modem, which provides wireless backhaul over the @450 Wireless Broadband network of Digita [1].

The @450 network uses the 450 MHz band and the Flash-OFDM technology originally developed by Flarion. It provides theoretical maximum 5.3 Mbps downlink and 1.8 Mbps uplink data rates per sector. The @450 service can be purchased either with 1 Mbps or 512 kbps downlink data rate. The nominal radius of a @450 cell is 30 km, but with a high-gain directional antenna the range can be easily doubled outdoors. The @450 MHz network provides very good mobility support and about 50 ms RTT.

The @450 network has naturally its own IP address space different from that of the panOULU network. The WiFi clients of the mobile AP are provided with a regular panOULU IP address as follows. Upon startup the mobile AP creates a VPN tunnel through the @450 network to the panOULU core. A WiFi client associating with the mobile AP obtains an IP address from the panOULU DHCP server, just like with a regular stationary AP connected 'directly' to the panOULU network.

Hence, from the clients' point of view, the mobile AP is in the same IP subnet as stationary APs. Consequently, a client's possible "ping ponging" between a mobile AP in a bus and a nearby stationary AP would not have any effect on the IP address and on-going connections.

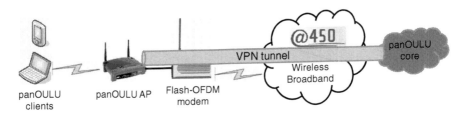

Fig. 3. Network topology of a mobile AP

We assessed the behavior of WiFi clients aboard panOULU buses by riding back and forth through the city center, which is the most probable place for the "ping pong" effect to take place. However, once the WiFi client has established a connection with the AP inside the bus, it never strayed to an outside stationary AP nearby the bus.

4 Session Mobility in panOULU Network

4.1 General Network Usage Statistics

In January 2008, 12118 unique WiFi devices used the panOULU network, totaling 279850 sessions and 12 million minutes of online time. A unique device is identified by its unique MAC address. A session is defined to start when the DHCP server acknowledges a client device's DCHP REQUEST with DHCP ACK. A session is deemed to end when the device does not respond to four consecutive *arping* calls made at 60 second intervals. The session is clocked to have ended at the time of the first unanswered *arping* call. Online time corresponds to the duration of the session. The devices are mostly PCs furnished with the Windows operating system. The proportion of Nokia manufactured multi-mode mobile handsets equipped with both cellular and WiFi radios has been growing steadily so that they make up 15-20% of all devices now.

As discussed earlier, one of the motivations behind panOULU network is to provide visitors coming to Oulu free and convenient Internet access. The graph in Figure 4 provides a weak estimate on the proportion of visiting users, based on identifying the devices that had not been seen in the network before during year 2007. We see that up to 40% of the devices using the network in a given month had not used the network before during year 2007. Of course, we have no way telling if these 'new' devices actually correspond to devices owned by visiting users, or if they are just new devices acquired by local panOULU users.

A somewhat more reliable estimate can be obtained by profiling individual devices based on their network usage patterns. For this purpose we define as a "heavy user" a device that uses the network at least 50% of the days in the analysis period, i.e. in a 30-day period a "heavy user" has used the network on 15 days minimum. As a "one time user" we regard a device that has used the network on at least four days during a period of at most one week in length. Devices not categorized as "heavy users" or "one time users" are regarded as "casual users". Using this categorization the 12118

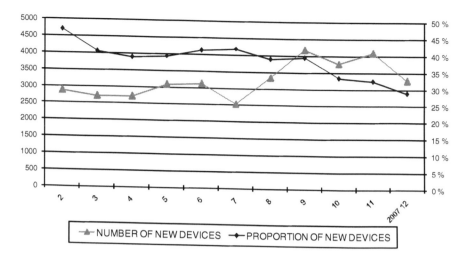

Fig. 4. Numbers and proportions of new devices in the panOULU network in 2007

devices seen in the network in January 2008 were classified as follows: 9.8% "heavy users", 70.0% "one time users" and 20.3% "casual users".

4.2 Session Mobility

We have studied session mobility, in order to obtain solid evidence on the need to provide mobility support. To quantify session mobility we define a session to be mobile, if during the session the WiFi device uses at least three APs so that at least two of them are 50 meters apart. Employing this definition only 5.1% of the 279850 sessions in January 2008 were mobile.

Another way at looking mobility is to analyze how many devices have a so-called "home AP", via which the majority of the network usage of this particular device takes place. A device is deemed to have a "home AP", if 0.7 x (homeAPsessions / totalsessions) + 0.3 x (homeAPonlinetime / totalonlinetime) ≥ 0.5. Using this criterion a whopping 91.5% of the 12118 devices had a "home AP".

We have studied in more detail the macro mobility of devices between administrative domains (providers), to obtain solid evidence on the need for IP mobility support such as the one provided by the layer 2 design of our multi-provider network. The most prominent place to study macro mobility is the city center where five of the eight providers in the panOULU consortium have at least one AP. We geographically limit our study by placing a circle of 750 m in radius at the city centre, taking into consideration all 409 APs residing within the circle. As a single-provider reference region we use the university campus, placing a circle of 450 m in radius at the university main hall, and taking into account the 278 APs within the circle.

Table 1 lists the key statistics for the two regions in January 2008. In addition to mobility we also include other statistics allowing other comparisons between the two different usage environments. A provider crossing refers to the event where a device roams from an AP of a particular network provider to an AP of another network provider during a session.

Table 1. Comparison of network usage at the city center and the university campus

Statistic	City center	University campus
APs	409	278
Devices	6031	2646
• Nokia multi-mode	929 (15.4%)	386 (17.5%)
• "Home AP"	5653 (93.7%)	2314 (87.5%)
• "Heavy user"	579 (9.6%)	159 (6.0%)
• "One time user"	4516 (74.9%)	1829 (69.1%)
• "Casual user"	936 (15.5%)	658 (24.9%)
Sessions	128480	44396
• Mobile	10376 (8.1%)	2205 (5.0%)
• Provider crossing	4465 (3.5%; 43.0%)	-

Table 2. Comparison of network usage between multi-mode mobile devices and other devices

Statistic	Nokia multi-mode devices	Other devices
Devices	929	5102
• "Home AP"	864 (93.0%)	4789 (93.9%)
• "Heavy user"	8 (0.9%)	571 (11.2%)
• "One time user"	862 (92.8%)	3654 (71.6%)
• "Casual user"	59 (6.4%)	877 (17.2%)
Sessions	4990	123940
• Mobile	518 (10.4%)	9858 (8.0%)
• Provider crossing	236 (4.7%; 45.6%)	4229 (3.4%; 42.9%)
• Per device	5.4	24.3
• Average duration (mins)	64	1001
• Median duration (mins)	6	37

We see that in the city center 4465 sessions, 3.5% of all 128480 sessions and 43.0% of the 10376 mobile sessions, involve a provider crossing. It is difficult to judge if these 4465 sessions justify the current layer 2 design, partially motivated by our desire to provide easy support for session mobility.

Although the amount of session mobility appears small at this point, we expect it to increase as multi-mode mobile devices become more popular. A PC is not really intended to be used in a mobile manner. Table 2 provides a compact comparison of the usage statistics of Nokia made multi-mode devices and other devices (largely PCs) within the same 750 m circle at the city center in January 2008.

We see that the multi-mode devices have a clearly smaller number of sessions per device (5.4 vs 24.3), and their median duration is much shorter (6 vs 37 minutes) as expected. The fact that many residents at the city centre have their PCs constantly connected to the network skews the averages. Multi-mode devices have a slightly larger proportion of mobile sessions (10.4% vs 8.0%), but the difference is not significant. The usage of multi-mode devices is much more active on the university campus than in the city center with 9.7 sessions per device of much longer duration (average 154 min, median 28 min).

4.3 Roaming Performance

So, our network contains a simple built-in mobility support for WiFi devices. We conclude the experimental part by characterizing the roaming performance in our network with two simple experiments. With roaming we refer to the WiFi device roaming from a particular AP to another AP. We are particularly interested in the performance at the application layer, how long the application processes are "offline" and what is the expected packet loss.

The client device used in both experiments was a Lenovo X60S laptop with Ubuntu OS and an integrated Intel PRO/Wireless 3945ABG WiFi card. During the experiments the laptop was moved spatially at walking space to force roaming. The experiments were executed in different locations to study roaming in varying radio conditions and between different pairs of APs, from a Cisco 1200 series AP to another Cisco 1200 series AP, from a Strix OWS-2400 series mesh AP to a Cisco 1200 series AP and vice versa. The beacon rate of each AP was set to 100 ms. During the experiments the network was being normally used by arbitrary other clients, which may have had an impact on our results.

In the first experiment we measured the throughput of a TCP connection between the WiFi laptop and a server using the *iperf* TCP/UDP bandwidth measurement tool [13]. This experiment serves two purposes, firstly verifying session mobility, i.e. the TCP connection survives the roaming, and secondly quantifying the "offline" time of the TCP connection during roaming. The *iperf* tool was configured to use 128 KB TCP windows and to measure TCP throughput over 0.5 s intervals. While the TCP throughput was typically in the 1-5 Mbps range during successful data transfer, immediately after handover between two APs the connection was "offline" (throughput 0 bps) for a lengthy period ranging from 8 s to sometimes even over 20 s. This long latency is due to problems in packet routing. When the laptop moves between APs in two different BSSs, the layer 2 switch connecting the two BSSs is not informed. Eventually, it will learn of the new location of the laptop, when it receives a frame from the laptop. However, this self-learning property of the switches is not designed to support highly mobile users who want to maintain TCP connections while moving between APs in different BSSs.

In the second experiment a client process in the WiFi laptop generated every 20 ms a 160-byte payload containing a timestamp and a running sequence number and the payload was encapsulated into an UDP packet. This type of traffic would be very typical for a VoIP call, for example. The client process sent the packet into an UDP socket for immediate transmission to a server process, which stored all arriving packets. By analyzing the gaps in the arriving packet sequence we could quantify the "offline" time the client process experienced due to roaming. Typical minimum "offline" time of the client process during a roaming was 2.6 seconds corresponding to about 130 lost packets. The maximum "offline" time measured several times was staggering 5.6 seconds with 280 lost packets! In this case the latency is due to the upper layers of the protocol stack, as layer 2 handover takes clearly less than 100 ms.

The experiments show what kind of roaming delays a client process running on a standard off-the-shelf WiFi laptop can expect to experience in our network, when no special measures are taken to speed up the handover.

5 Discussion

We presented a simple layer 2 network design for merging the WiFi zones of multiple organizations into a large multi-provider municipal WiFi network that in terms of IP addressing appears as a single IP subnet. We also provided a simple design for mobile APs so that they are part of the same IP subnet. The design provides built-in session mobility support for the WiFi clients using the network, without any specific support either in the network or in the client. The latter requirement is partially motivated by the fact that a large proportion of the users of our network are one time visitors. We cannot expect them to install any particular client software just for the sake of having session mobility in our network.

We analyzed the session mobility of the over 12000 devices using our network in January 2008. The proportion of mobile sessions is below 10%. About 40% of the mobile sessions at the city center involved a "provider crossing", where our layer 2 design comes handy in terms of keeping the connections alive. We also provided a brief comparison of the usage statistics of multi-mode mobile devices and WiFi laptops. Finally, we characterized the roaming performance of a standard WiFi laptop in our network with two simple experiments.

We believe that our "KISS" layer 2 network design can serve as a good model for similar municipal multi-provider WiFi networks. The design effectively reduces a multi-provider network into a single-provider case, which requires the providers to agree on common IP addressing. This could impose severe limitations in terms of AAA (Authentication, Authorization and Accounting). However, since we currently do not authenticate users nor charge them for the network usage, AAA is not really an issue for us.

The most intense debate we have had has focused on the geographically large panOULU VLAN of the City of Oulu, which spans pretty much every public office and service point. The large VLAN is suspect to large amounts of broadcast traffic and broadcast storms. We have measured the broadcast traffic at the central switch to average about 37 kbps over 24-hour periods. We have had two major broadcast storms in the city's panOULU VLAN due to a faulty OS in newly acquired AP's. The software bug in the OS resulted in an incoming IGMP packet being reflected into all outgoing ports. Consequently, a single IGMP packet was replicated into millions in a blink of an eye, forcing a temporary shutdown of the VLAN.

In the near future we will expand the WiFi coverage to key locations in nearby ten townships. We are also currently building a Mobile WiMAX network around the City of Oulu, to be part of the open and free wireless access provided by the panOULU network.

Acknowledgments. The authors wish to thank the members of the panOULU consortium for their support.

References

1. @450 Wireless Broadband network, `http://www.450laajakaista.fi/`
2. Balazinska, M., Castro, P.: Characterizing mobility and network usage in a corporate wireless local-area network. In: The First International Conference on Mobile Systems, Applications, and Services, pp. 303–316 (2003)
3. Henderson, T., Kotz, B., Abyzov, I.: The changing usage of a mature campus-wide wireless network. In: Tenth Annual International Conference on Mobile Computing and Networking, pp. 187–201 (2004)
4. Ojala, T., Hakanen, T., Mäkinen, T., Rivinoja, V.: Usage analysis of a large public wireless LAN. In: 2005 International Conference on Wireless Networks, Communications and Mobile Computing, pp. 66–667 (2005)
5. panOULU network, `http://www.panoulu.net/`
6. Pelletta, E., Lilieblad, F., Hedenfalk, M., Pehrson, B.: The design and implementation of an operator neutral open wireless access network at the Kista IT-University. In: 12th IEEE Workshop on Local and Metropolitan Area Networks, pp. 149–150 (2002)
7. SeattleWireless, `http://seattlewireless.net/`
8. FreiFunk, `http://freifunk.net`
9. Perkins, C.: Mobile IP: Design Principles and Practices. Addison-Wesley, USA (1998)
10. Snoeren, A.C., Balakrishnan, H.: An end-to-end approach to host mobility. In: 6th ACM/IEEE International Conference on Mobile Computing and Networking, pp. 155–166 (2000)
11. Rosenberg, J., Schulzrinne, H., Camarillo, G., Johnston, A., Peterson, J., Sparks, R., Handley, M., Schooler, E.: SIP: Session Initiation Protocol, RFC 3261 (2002)
12. panOULU Luotsi, `http://luotsi.panoulu.net`
13. Iperf, `http://sourceforge.net/projects/iperf`

A Fast MAC-Layer Handover for an IEEE 802.16e-Based WMAN

Sayan K. Ray[1], Krzysztof Pawlikowski[1], and Harsha Sirisena[2]

[1] Dept. of Computer Science and Software Engineering,
skr29@student, krys.pawlikowski@canterbury.ac.nz
[2] Dept. of Electrical and Computer Engineering,
harsha.sirisena@canterbury.ac.nz
University of Canterbury, Christchurch, New Zealand

Abstract. We propose a modification of the IEEE 802.16e hard handover (HHO) procedure, which significantly reduces the handover latency constraint of the original HHO procedure in IEEE 802.16e networks. It allows a better handling of the delay-sensitive traffic by avoiding unnecessary time-consuming scanning and synchronization activity as well as simplifies the network re-entry procedure. With the help of the backhaul network, it reduces the number of control messages in the original handover policy, making the handover latency acceptable also for real-time streaming traffic. Preliminary performance evaluation studies show that the modified handover procedure is able to reduce the total handover latency by about 50%.

Keywords: IEEE 802.16e, hard handover, ranging, backhaul network.

1 Introduction

The IEEE 802.16 (WiMAX) technology, both in its IEEE 802.16d [1] and IEEE 802.16e [2] versions, is regarded as a very promising candidate for next-generation WMANs, as it successfully addresses the requirements of higher data rate and efficient spectral efficiency for provisioning full-fledged mobile broadband access [3]. Mobility related research in IEEE 802.16e is mostly focused on the two main areas of concern: location management and handover. This paper deals with the latter and aims at minimizing the overall handover latency experienced by 802.16e supported Mobile Stations (MSs) when they are crossing cell boundaries. The IEEE 802.16e standard supports three types of handover. While Hard Handover (HHO) is the default and the most common scheme, Fast Base Station Switching (FBSS) and Macro-Diversity Handover (MDHO) are two other optional procedures. This paper will concentrate on performance issues related to the HHO procedure only. The entire HHO process in the IEEE 802.16e can be divided into the Network Topology Acquisition Phase (NTAP) and the Actual Handover Phase (AHOP), which consist of such sub-phases as scanning and synchronization, ranging and association, handover decision and initialization, authorization and registration.

C. Wang (Ed.): AccessNets, LNICST 6, pp. 102–117, 2009.

During the NTAP, the MS performs scanning and downlink synchronization activities with the neighbouring Base Stations (BSs), to select one of them as the Target BS (TBS) for the handover activity. During AHOP, the MS releases its connection with the current Serving BS (SBS) and performs synchronization and registration procedures with the selected TBS for completing the handover process. However, both NTAP and AHOP in their standard versions suffer from many ambiguities. During NTAP, unwanted handover delays and resource wastages may be introduced due to excessive (though not blind) scanning, synchronization and ranging activities. The AHOP suffers from drawbacks related to long inter-handover gap, owing to prolonged ranging and network re-entry activities. While Connection Disruption Time (CDT) in the range of 200 ms is generally acceptable for real-time streaming media traffic [4], the CDT of the IEEE 802.16e HHO handover exceeds this limit [5].

This paper reports results of research aimed at reduction of the overall handover latency along with the CDT. A fast handover procedure is obtained by merging and redesigning some steps of the original procedure. This modified BS-initialised, backhaul-assisted, fast and smooth HHO scheme not only simplifies the overall IEEE 802.16e handover procedure but also minimises wastage of network resources. The current SBS predicts the potential TBS based on the MS's direction of motion, the current load of Neighbouring BSs (NBSs), their locations with respect to the SBS and the estimated time needed by the MS for travelling from one cell to another [6]. The MS then performs fast ranging activities directly with the TBS, i.e. with the potential next SBS. The results of the ranging process are buffered until the AHOP, in which the stored results facilitate the resumption of fast downlink (DL) and uplink (UL) transmissions, avoiding execution of further synchronisation and ranging handshaking activities. Prolonged network authentication and authorisation phases are also avoided with the help of prior message passing over the backhaul network, which links BSs with routers. The scheme has been evaluated in simulation studies, which clearly show that it outperforms the standard IEEE 802.16e handover procedure, both in terms of overall handover latency and utilization of channel resources.

The rest of this paper is organised as follows. The IEEE 802.16e HHO procedure and the related research are discussed in Section 2. Section 3 details our new scheme and Section 4 describes our simulation studies and the obtained numerical results. This is followed by Conclusions in Section 5.

2   IEEE 802.16e HHO Scenario

A handover occurs when an MS moves through a cellular boundary to a cell served by another BS. In the IEEE 802.16e, the handover process is triggered when the strength of signal between the MS and its SBS drops below a certain threshold level. The handover is executed in the following two phases.

2.1   Network Topology Acquisition Phase

During the NTAP, the MS and SBS, with the help of the backhaul network, jointly gather information about the underlying network topology before the actual handover decision is made; see Figure 1(a)[6]. Using MOB_NBR-ADV (Mobile_Neighbour-Advertisement) message, the SBS periodically broadcasts information about the state of the neighbouring BSs, making preparation for potential handover activity. The MS scans the advertised BSs within specific time frames to select suitable candidate BSs for the handover. The scanning is followed by contention/non-contention ranging and optional association activities through which the MS gathers further information about the PHY channels related with the selected BSs.

2.2 Actual Handover Phase

During AHOP (Figure 1(b)), once a particular TBS is selected from the list of the candidate BSs, the MS informs the current SBS about the beginning of the HO activity by sending a MOB_HO-IND (Mobile_Handover-Indication) message. It is at this point that the MS terminates its connection with the current SBS. Appropriate synchronisation and ranging activities take place once again to resume DL/UL re-transmissions. Next, the lengthy authorization and registration process of the MS with the TBS follows. It marks the onset of the network re-entry phase of this MS, after which it becomes fully functional with the new SBS.

IEEE 802.16e is not free from drawbacks related with relatively large handover delays and resource wastages. During NTAP, prolonged scanning and ranging related activities are the primary hindrances for satisfying delay-sensitive real-time applications. Recent 802.16e HHO-related research has focused mostly on attempts of reduction of the disruptive effects of these constraints. The schemes proposed in [6] and [7] suggest prediction of TBSs before the scanning and ranging activities. While [6] discusses a procedure for fast and hybrid BS-oriented selection of TBSs on the basis of such factors as coverage, MSs mobility direction and load of NBSs, [7] predicts TBSs on the basis of the required bandwidth and QoS. In both cases, scanning and ranging related activities are reduced, being limited only to the predicted TBSs. However, these schemes do not lower the overall handover delay significantly. Adaptive Channel Scanning Algorithm (ACSA) introduced in [8] focuses on minimizing the disruptive effects of channel scanning activities in case of different types of traffic.

Similar to NTAP, AHOP also suffers from lengthy CDT. This is because an MS undergoing handover should complete the network re-entry procedures with the TBS for resuming normal connectivity. Apart from the ranging process, the MS needs also to undergo security related authentication, authorization and registration processes, to successfully resume its IP connectivity with the new SBS. As mentioned before, the total CDT in case of an 802.16e HHO exceeds 200 ms, which makes the packet transmission delay perceivable to users in case of such real-time delay-sensitive applications like video streaming or voice-over IP. Considerable research has been focused on reducing the CDT, thus making the 802.16e HHO scheme suitable for real-time traffic. For example, in the case of delay-sensitive real-time applications, [9] and [5] propose to resume DL and UL transmissions prior to completion of the authorization and registration

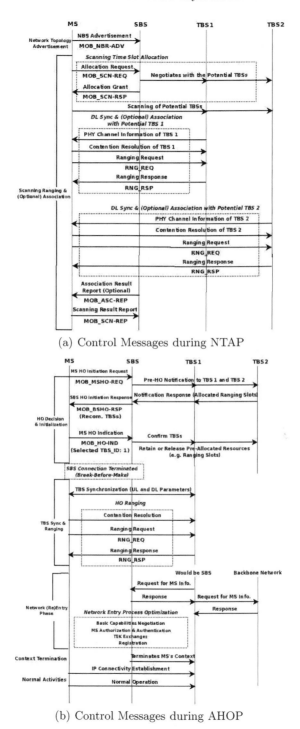

(a) Control Messages during NTAP

(b) Control Messages during AHOP

Fig. 1. Control Messages during the 802.16e HHO Procedure

procedures. However, a possibility of unsuccessful authorization and registration while switching domains is not considered. An 802.16e cross-layer HHO scheme, in which the MAC layer CDT- related delays are reduced with support from Layer 3, is proposed in [10]. In that scheme, some of the messages exchanged between the MS and the TBS during the network re-entry phase can be relayed with the help of the SBS, to make the entire procedure shorter. However, there is still room for further reduction of the overall 802.16e HHO latency.

3   Proposed Scheme

In this section, we propose a new HHO scheme, which does not suffer from the drawbacks of the standard version. We will show that by merging and re-designing some steps of the standard version, one can significantly improve performance of that HHO. In particular, we reduce delays caused by HHO-related MAC layer messages during the scanning, ranging and authorization phases, with the help of the backhaul network. In the current work, the SBS is tasked with the bulk of the handover-related decision-making responsibilities. The proposed HHO procedure is described in the following subsections.

3.1   Handover Initiation

As in [6], we assume that an MS keeps track of its movement trajectory. However, we assume additionally that all MSs apply the mobility prediction scheme proposed in [11], in which a hexagonal cell structure is divided into three zones: the No Handover (No-HO) Zone, the Low Handover (Lo-HO) Zone and the High Handover (High-HO) Zone, as shown in Figure 2 [11]. The No-HO zone marks zero handover probability, while Lo-HO and High-HO zones mark medium to very high handover probabilities. This division subsequently reduces the actual area of tracking of MS's random movement during a potential handover activity. We assume that while in the Lo-HO zone an MS may receive mild beacons from neighbouring cells, the communicating signal from the current SBS is still strong enough (though not as strong as in the No-HO zone), so the chance that an MS in the Lo-HO zone performs a handover is small.

As per the IEEE 802.16e standard, an MS initiates handover activity at the time instant when it perceives that the communication signal strength has dropped below a certain threshold L_0. However, the handover activity can take a considerable time before the MS can actually resume communication with the new SBS. Long delays associated with handovers are unsuitable for real-time traffic handling as it may cause packet losses and call disruptions. To combat this, in our scheme an MS initiates a handover activity if the strength of a signal drops to L_{Max}, where $L_{Max} > L_0$. It is also assumed that a potential handover activity has to be finished before the strength of a given signal drops to L_{Min}, where $L_{Min} < L_0$ [12]. Otherwise, a call disruption would become highly probable. This probability of a call disruption at the time instant when the signals strength drops to L_{Min} is much larger than at L_0, which is much larger at L_{Max}.

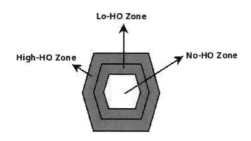

Fig. 2. Zone-wise Division of a Cell

Thus, in the time interval when the signal strength is between L_0 and L_{Max}, the MS is in a safe region, where delay-sensitive traffic is unlikely to suffer a disruption. On the other hand, the time interval when the signal strength is between L_{Min} and L_0 represents a high-risk zone. To minimize the likelihood of call disruptions, we propose that the NTAP of the handover is completed within the safe zone and the AHOP within the high-risk zone.

3.2 TBS Selection and Insinuation

Step 1: TBS Prediction - The MS initiates a handover activity by sending a MOB_HO-REP (Mobile_Handover-Report) message [6] to the current SBS. On receiving the message, the SBS creates a list of potential TBSs by taking into account the MSs movement direction, load factor of NBSs, the areas of coverage of NBSs and the estimated time interval needed by the MS to travel from one cell to another. Details of the procedure are the same as in [6]. The topmost BS from the list is chosen as the TBS.

Step 2: Pre-HO Notification -After predicting the suitability of a particular BS as the TBS, the SBS uses the backhaul network for sending a pre-handover backhaul network notification (BH_NW-NOTF1) message (Figure 3(a)) addressed to the TBS with the MS ID, the required bandwidth, frequency, QoS and CQICH (Channel Quality Indication Channel) [1] parameters, which the SBS knows from its communication with the MS.

Step 3: TBS Selection - On receiving this pre-notification message, the TBS assumes that a handover activity with the particular MS might occur soon. Provided it has the required resources, it replies to the SBS with a BH_NW-RSP (pre-handover backhaul network response) message containing such information as its ID, DCD, UCD, and other frequency-related information. The TBS also allocates dedicated ranging slots (fast ranging IE) in advance, anticipating a potential ranging activity. However, if this TBS fails to provide the required resources (it might get overloaded in the meantime), it will send an error report in the response. In that case, the SBS would try another candidate for TBS from the list of potential TBSs [6].

Step 4: Authorization Information Exchange -Successful selection of the TBS quickly prompts the SBS to channelize all network re-authentication related

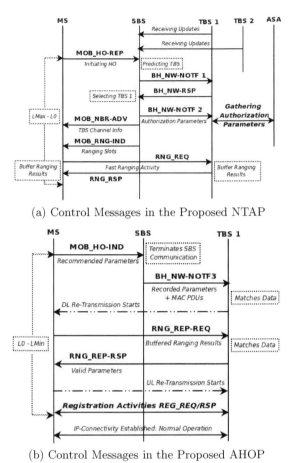

(a) Control Messages in the Proposed NTAP

(b) Control Messages in the Proposed AHOP

Fig. 3. Control Messages in the Proposed HHO Procedure

information relevant for the particular MS to the TBS, which would help to achieve a more optimised network re-entry phase [13]. A BH_NW-NOTF2 message containing relevant connection IDs (CIDs), encryption keys and associated parameters, MS's digital certificate, MAC address and other relevant information is used for this purpose. During NTAP, the TBS also connects with the ASA server, to get more authorization related information for the particular MS [13].

Step 5: MOB_NBR-ADV Message Now, the SBS forwards all the TBS channel related information to the MS through the MOB_NBR-ADV message, indicating the availability of that TBS for handover. This allows the MS to get DL synchronised directly and be ready to perform ranging activities with the TBS, bypassing the time consuming scanning procedures.

Step 6: Fast Ranging Interval Allocation - Anticipating probable ranging activities, the SBS allocates a time slot for the MS to perform fast ranging with the TBS. In this context, we propose a fast ranging interval allocation message, MOB_RNG-IND (Mobile_Ranging-Indication), specified in Table 1.

Table 1. MOB_RNG-IND Message Format

Syntax	Size	Notes
MOB_RNG-IND_Message_format( ) {	-	-
Management Message Type=X	8 bits	-
Ranging duration	8 bits	In units of frames
Report Mode	2 bits	Periodic Report
Initial Frame	4 bits	-
Data Interleaving Interval	8 bits	Duration in frames
Iteration	8 bits	-
Recommended_TBS_Index	8 bits	Selected TBSs=1
Recommended TBS_ID	48 bits	48 bit BS ID of the selected TBS
Fast_Ranging_IE( ) {	-	-
Subcode	4 bits	FRNG=0x01
Length	4 bits	Length=8
Offset	12 bits	TBD
Reserved	4 bits	-
}	-	-
Rendezvous Time	8 bits	In units of frames
TLV Encoded Information	Var	-
}	-	-

3.3   Fast Ranging Activity

***Step 7: Fast Ranging Activity* -** The SBS, acting as a relay agent between the TBS and the MS, forwards the allocated ranging slots to the MS in the MOB_RNG-IND message so that the MS can undergo a fast ranging activity with the TBS using conventional RNG_REQ (Ranging_Request) and RNG_RSP (Ranging_Response) messages. This shortens handover delay and saves resources considerably, as the MS does not have to contend for ranging slots. The RNG_RSP message also contains the primary management CID [1] that the MS uses to send further MAC management messages to the TBS during the AHOP. As per our current scheme, both the MS and the TBS buffer the ranging result-related parameters to be used during future ranging activities. A timer maintained for that purpose remains valid until the underlying channel condition changes considerably.

3.4   HO Indication and DL Retransmissions

***Step 8: HO Indication* -** On accomplishment of the ranging procedure, the MS immediately indicates the handover activity to the SBS by sending the MOB_HO-IND message (Figure 3(b)). As per our scheme, the message also contains the assigned CIDs, TBS ID, the recorded UCD, DCD, and other PHY frequency-related parameters from the NTAP. At this point, the MS also releases its connection with the current SBS.

***Step 9: Channelization of MAC PDUs* -** Unlike the conventional 802.16e handover procedure, in which the SBS retains the MS MAC PDUs up to a certain instant of time, in our scheme, on receiving the handover indication message, the SBS quickly communicates a handover BH_NW-NOTF3 message to the backbone network indicating its disassociation from the MS. It also forwards the MAC PDUs of the MS to the TBS, having encapsulated them in this message. This actually reduces chance of packets buffered by the SBS being lost. The message sent via the backhaul network also contains the MS's recorded parameters indicated in Step 8, along with other MAC state related parameters [13]. Thus, the backhaul network channelizes any further traffic meant for that MS directly to the TBS, where it is buffered until DL transmission resumes.

Step 10: DL Retransmission - On receiving the notification message via the backhaul network, the TBS matches the transmitted and the buffered data and can immediately start the DL retransmissions using the CIDs assigned during the NTAP.

According to our scheme, the interval between the time when the TBS generates the DL synchronisation parameters during the NTAP and the beginning of processing of BH_NW-NOTF2 message by this TBS lasts about 70 ms. Depending on the underlying hardware used, these parameters can remain valid for as long as 600 ms [1]. Moreover, since the time interval between termination of MS-SBS communication and TBS receiving the channelized MS MAC PDUs over the high-speed IP backhaul network is very short (few ms), intermediate packet loss is practically negligible. The uplink retransmission can only resume once the MS-TBS jointly comes to an agreement regarding the validity of the buffered result from the previous pre-coordinated ranging activity during the NTAP. In contrast to the schemes proposed in [5] and [9], ranging in our proposal is performed during NTAP rather than during AHOP, in order to reduce the overall CDT.

3.5   UL Retransmissions and Registration

Step 11: Request for Ranging Data Matching - Using the allocated CIDs, the MS sends such relevant data to the TBS as the TBS ID, resultant service level prediction and ranging purpose indication parameters, along with the HMAC / CMAC tuple (message authentication codes) [2] buffered during the previous ranging activity. It is done by using a new MAC management message, RNG_REP-REQ (Ranging_Report-Request), specified in Table 2.

Table 2. RNG_REP-REQ Message Format

Syntax	Size	Notes
RNG_REP-REQ_Message_format( ) {	-	-
Management Message Type = Y	-	-
TBS ID	48 bits	Selected TBS
MAC Address	8 bits	MS MAC Address
Ranging Purpose Indication	4 bits	Bit#0=1
Service Level Prediction	4 bits	Encoding=2
HMAC/CMAC tuple	-	-

Step 12: UL Retransmission - Next, the TBS matches the transmitted parameters with those already stored, and communicates the outcome in the RNG_REP-RSP (Ranging_Report-Response) message. A flag value is maintained for this and, provided the buffered ranging parameter-related timer is still valid, the value in the RNG_REP-RSP is equal to 1, implying a successful resumption of UL traffic. Otherwise it is 0. Through a valid response, the TBS also indicates the successful completion of all authorization related activities. On the other hand, if the response is 0 then this TBS allocates new fast ranging IEs [2] for a probable repeat ranging option. In our scheme, the interval between the previous RNG_RSP message and the time when the TBS receives the RNG_REP-REQ message is about 50 ms. So, according to [1] and [13], chances of values fluctuating significantly within such a short interval is very small. Thus, for a positive response message, UL transmission resumes immediately with the TBS.

Step 13: Registration Activities - Registration activities follow next with the TBS communicating the updated CIDs to the MS.

The total handover procedure is accomplished before the signal strength drops down to L_{Min} i.e. before a call disruption might occur. In order to prevent undesirable ping-pong activities the actual handover occurs only after the signal strength drops below the 802.16e threshold value L_0, i.e if the MS finds itself the High-HO zone. To identify such activities, the TBS maintains a timer right from the time instant when it receives the forwarded MAC PDUs from the SBS until the successful resumption of the UL traffic (the timer tracks round-trip delays along with sufficient processing times). For a failed UL retransmission, the TBS sends back all the MAC PDUs to the previous SBS, interpreting it as a ping-pong activity.

4   Simulation Scenario

The performance of our new scheme was evaluated in a moderately populated centralised architecture [14] consisting of 6 different BSs deployed in a multicell environment operating with different radio frequencies (2.4 GHZ–2.45 GHZ). Among these, one BS is the SBS. The latencies in the different phases of handover were studied using the IEEE 802.16e OFDMA model implemented in the Qualnet 4.0 simulator [15]. Table 3 lists the simulation parameters assumed according to the WiMAX forum specifications [16]. The BSs are connected to an ASN-GW (Access Service Network Gateway) via wired point-to-point links. Figure 4 shows the simulated topology with total of 25 nodes spread randomly over a terrain of 1500 m x 1500 m. BS 4 is the current SBS and BSs 5, 10, 13, 17 and 21 are the NBSs. Node 25 is the ASN-GW, while the remaining nodes are the MSs. For simplicity, we have considered that within a cell, each BS serves three different randomly placed MSs, and all the BSs are under the same administrative domain. Within each cell, all the MSs simultaneously communicate with their respective BSs. On the other hand, BSs also communicate amongst themselves through the

Table 3. The Assumed Key Simulation Parameters

Parameters	Value
Number of BSs	6
Number of MSs	18
Bandwidth	10 MHz
Cellular Layout	Hexagonal
Terrain size	1500 m x 1500 m
FFT size	1024
No. of subchannels	30
Channel Frequencies	2.40 - 2.45 GHz
Transmission Power	20 dBm
MAC Propagation Delay	1 μs
Environment Temperature (K)	290
Noise Factor (K)	10
Antenna Height	1.5 m
BSs Propagation Limit	-111.0 dBm
L_{Max}, L_0, L_{Min}	-76, -78, -80 dBm
QPSK Encoding Rate	0.5
BS Link Propagation Delay	1 ms
Frame length	5 ms
MS speed	60 km/h

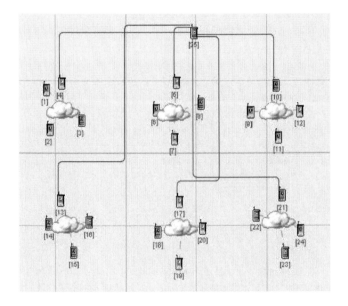

Fig. 4. Simulation Topology Consistig of Six BSs

backhaul network. We assume that the single round-trip delay plus the message-processing time over the backhaul network is not larger than 20 ms [2],[17]. We have modelled a single MS, initially under SBS 4, moving randomly between the different BSs and performing different numbers of handovers in each replication. A random waypoint mobility model [18] was used to modelling movements of MS. For simplicity of the performance analysis, we have considered only the data recorded during the first six handover activities in each replication. All graphs depict results based on multiple replications. The maximum relative statistical error is 3% at the 0.95 confidence level.

We have considered the following time-related parameters in order to analyse the performance of our proposed scheme:

- ΔT_{Ini}: Mean duration of handover initiation time interval before the on-set of the scanning phase.
- ΔT_{Scan}: Mean time required for an MS to complete scanning the different BSs. It depends on the number of BSs to be scanned.
- ΔT_{DL_Sync}: Mean DL synchronisation time.
- ΔT_{UL_Sync}: Mean UL synchronisation time.
- ΔT_{Cont_Rang}: Mean contention-oriented ranging time required. It was assumed that at least two ranging iterations occur before a successful ranging operation is accomplished.
- ΔT_{Fast_Rang}: Mean time required for a fast ranging opportunity with dedicated ranging slots.
- ΔT_{Cap_Neg}: Mean time required for performing capabilities negotiation.
- ΔT_{Re_Auth}: Mean time required for a successful re-authorization procedure through authorization hand-shaking framework during network re-entry [2].
- ΔT_{Reg}: Mean time required for accomplishing a successful registration policy during network re-entry.
- ΔT_{Back_Proc}: Round-trip delay and message processing time in backhaul network equal 20 ms [2],[17].

4.1   NTAP HO Latency Analysis

Our scheme can reduce the overall NTAP-related handover latency to as much as 50%. Note that handover latency in the conventional IEEE 802.16e NTAP is

$$\Delta T_{Ini} + \Delta T_{Scan} + \Delta T_{DL\_Sync} + \Delta T_{UL\_Sync} + \Delta T_{Cont\_Rang} \qquad (1)$$

On the other hand, latency in our NTAP equals

$$\Delta T_{Ini} + \Delta T_{Fast\_Rang} + \Delta T_{Back\_Proc} \qquad (2)$$

Figures 5(a) and 5(b), respectively, show the reductions in the overall handover latency and NTAP latency for individual BSs using our proposal. Depending on the load factor of different BSs, the latency for the conventional NTAP scenario can be over 0.7 seconds [6], whereas, the maximum NTAP latency in our scheme is about half of that.

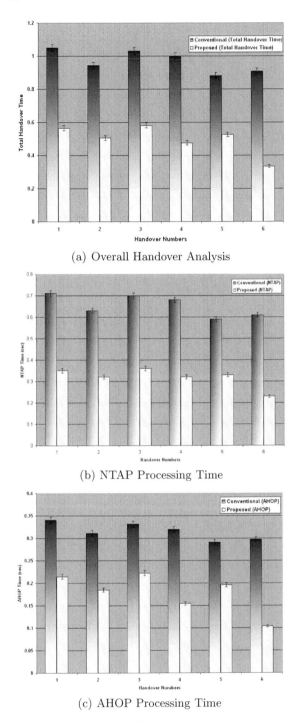

(a) Overall Handover Analysis

(b) NTAP Processing Time

(c) AHOP Processing Time

Fig. 5.

4.2   AHOP HO Latency Analysis and CDT Analysis

Handover latency during the AHOP in the conventional IEEE 802.16e equals:

$$\Delta T_{DL\_Sync} + \Delta T_{UL\_Sync} + \Delta T_{Cont\_Rang} + \Delta T_{Cap\_Neg} + \Delta T_{Re\_Auth} + \Delta T_{Reg} \quad (3)$$

whereas the best case AHOP latency in our scheme equals:

$$\Delta T_{Reg} + \Delta T_{Back\_Proc} \quad (4)$$

and in the worst case scenario:

$$\Delta T_{Fast\_Rang} + \Delta T_{Reg} + \Delta T_{Back\_Proc} \quad (5)$$

As discussed in Section 3, DL retransmission can readily depend on the previously recorded data once the processing of the BH_NW-NOTF2 message is done, skipping the time-consuming DL synchronisation procedure. The same is valid for UL retransmission, which can resume immediately with the RNG_REP-RSP message, avoiding the time-consuming authorization procedure. Simulation results shown in Figure 5(c) indicate that the proposed scheme is capable of reducing the overall AHOP-related handover delays by up to 65%, in the best-case scenario.

Figure 6 indicates that, in the best-case scenario, our framework can reduce the conventional downlink service retransmission interval by up to 89% and the up link service retransmission interval to a maximum of 82%, with the average UL improvement range varying from 66% to 78%. Compared to the large CDT of over 200 ms in the conventional scheme, which is due to a series of lengthy network re-entry activities performed by an MS during each handover before it can resume normal activities, our scheme proves to be more efficient in handling delay-sensitive high-speed real-time traffic. Time-consuming ranging and re-authorization activities are omitted during the AHOP. This also results in significant reduction of the inter-handover packet loss and non-consecutive data flow.

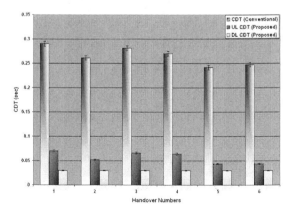

Fig. 6. Comparison of CDT in the Conventional and Proposed HO Procedures

There is scope for extending the current work to cross-layer scenarios, to see how the proposed scheme can cope with the network layer handover latencies. Further analysis of performance of our scheme in case of heavily loaded cells and different mobility models is planned in the near future.

5   Conclusion

In this paper, we have proposed a fast and seamless handover framework for IEEE 802.16e systems assisted by the backhaul network. The conventional 802.16e handover procedure impairs the service level processes for real-time delay-sensitive application, owing to high latency constraints resulting from time-consuming scanning and synchronisation activities along with a prolonged network re-entry phase. Our scheme has shown that, with the help of new handover messages and tunneling certain important information between the SBS and TBS over the backhaul network, the overall handover latency as well as the CDT of the 802.16e HHO procedure can be significantly improved, making it a realistic choice for delay-sensitive applications.

References

1. IEEE 802.16-2004: IEEE Standard for Local and Metropolitan Area Networks-Part 16: Air Interface for Fixed Broadband Wireless Access Systems (2004)
2. IEEE 802.16e-2005: IEEE Standard for Local and Metropolitan Area Networks-Part 16: Air Interface for Fixed and Mobile Broadband Wireless Access Systems (2006)
3. Li, B., Qin, Y., Low, C.P., Gwee, C.L.: A Survey on Mobile WiMAX. IEEE Comms. Mag., 70–75 (December 2007)
4. Banerjee, N., Basu, K., Das, S.K.: Handoff Delay Analysis in SIP-based Mobility Management in Wireless Networks. In: Int. Parallel and Distributed Processing Symp., pp. 224–231 (2003)
5. Jiao, W., Jiang, P., Ma, Y.: Fast handover Scheme for Real-Time Applications in Mobile WiMAX. In: IEEE Int. Conference on Communications, Glasgow, pp. 6038–6042 (2007)
6. Ray, S.K., Mandal, A., Pawlikowski, K., Sirisena, H.: Hybrid Predictive Base Station (HPBS) Selection Procedure in IEEE 802.16e-Based WMAN. In: Australasian Telecommunication Networks and Applications Conference, Christchurch, pp. 93–98 (2007)
7. Choi, H., Jeong, J., Choo, H.: CTBS: Cost-Effective Target BS Selection Scheme in IEEE 802.16e Networks. In: Australasian Telecommunication Networks and Applications Conference, Christchurch, pp. 99–103 (2007)
8. Rouil, R., Golmie, N.: Adaptive Channel Scanning for IEEE 802.16e. In: IEEE Military Communications Conference, Washington DC, pp. 1–6 (2006)
9. Choi, S., Hwang, G.-H., Kwon, T., Lim, A.-R., Cho, D.-H.: Fast handover Scheme for Real-Time Downlink Services in IEEE 802.16e BWA System. In: IEEE Vehicular Technology Conference, Stockholm, pp. 2028–2032 (Spring 2005)
10. Chen, L., Cai, X., Sofia, R., Huang, Z.: A Cross-layer fast Handover Scheme for Mobile WiMAX. In: IEEE Vehicular Technology Conference, Baltimore, pp. 1578–1582 (Fall 2007)

11. Chellappa, R., Jennings, A., Shenoy, N.: A Comparative Study of Mobility Prediction in Fixed Wireless Networks and Mobile Ad Hoc Networks. In: IEEE Int. Conference on Communications, Anchorage-Alaska, vol. 2, pp. 891–895 (2003)
12. Liao, Y., Gao, L.: Practical Schemes for Smooth MAC Layer Handoff in 802.11 Wireless Networks. In: IEEE International Symposium on a World of Wireless, Mobile and Multimedia Networks, Buffalo-New York, pp. 180–190 (2006)
13. Hoymann, C., Grauer, M.: WiMAX Mobility Support. In: ITG Conference on Measurement, Modeling and Evaluation of Computer and Communication Systems, Nurnberg, pp. 85–90 (2006)
14. Das, S., Klein, T., Rajkumar, A., Rangarajan, S., Turner, M., Viswanathan, H.: System Aspects and Handover Management for IEEE 802.16e. Bell Labs Technical J. 1, 123–142 (2006)
15. Scalable Network Technologies, `http://www.scalable-networks.com`
16. WiMAX Forum Mobile System Profile. Release 1.0 Approved System Specification, WiMAX Forum Working Group
17. Leung, K.K., Mukherjee, S., Rittenhouse, G.E.: Mobility Support for IEEE 802.16d Wireless Networks. In: IEEE Wireless and Communications and Networking Conference, New Orleans, pp. 1446–1452 (2005)
18. Camp, T., Boleng, J., Davies, V.: A Survey of Mobility Models for Ad Hoc Network Research. J. WCMC 5, 483–502 (2002)

A Conflict-Free Low-Jitter Guaranteed-Rate MAC Protocol for Base-Station Communications in Wireless Mesh Networks

T.H. Szymanski

Bell Canada Chair in Data Communications
Dept. ECE, McMaster University, Hamilton, ON Canada

Abstract. A scheduling algorithm and MAC protocol which provides low-jitter guaranteed-rate (GR) communications between base-stations (BS) in a Wireless Mesh Network (WMN) is proposed. The protocol can provision long-term multimedia services such as VOIP, IPTV, or Video-on-Demand. The time-axis is partitioned into scheduling frames with F time-slots each. A directional antennae scheme is used to provide each directed link with a fixed transmission rate. A protocol such as IntServ is used to provision resources along an end-to-end path of BSs for GR sessions. The Guaranteed Rates between the BSs are then specified in a doubly stochastic traffic rate matrix, which is recursively decomposed to yield a low-jitter GR frame transmission schedule. In the resulting schedule, the end-to-end delay and jitter are small and bounded, and the cell loss rate due to primary scheduling conflicts is zero. For dual-channel WMNs, the MAC protocol can achieve 100% utilization, as well as near-minimal queueing delays and near minimal delay jitter. The scheduling time complexity is $O(NFlogNF)$, where N is the number of BSs. Extensive simulation results are presented.

Keywords: scheduling, multihop, mesh, networks, low jitter, quality of service.

1 Introduction

Emerging multihop *Wireless Mesh Networks* (WMNs) represent a key opportunity to deploy wireless broadband services in a relatively inexpensive manner [1][2]. A multihop WMN consists of a collection of geographically-fixed wireless mesh routers and gateways, called Base-Stations (BSs), which provide wireless access to the global Internet network, as shown in Fig. 1 [1]. A WMN can provide broadband access to both fixed residential users and to mobile users. This paper presents a collision-free low-jitter guaranteed-rate (GR) scheduling algorithm and MAC protocol for inter-BS communication in an infra-structure-based WMN. The protocol supports the efficient delivery of multimedia services such as VOIP, IPTV, and Video-on-Demand (VOD).

WMNs can utilize the emerging IEEE 802.16 WiMAX network standard [3]. The WiMAX physical layer provides data rates between 32 and 130 Mbps, given appropriate physical link parameters, including the available channel spectrum, modulation scheme, signal constellation and distance. The standard exploits OFDM technology to enable a

C. Wang (Ed.): AccessNets, LNICST 6, pp. 118–137, 2009.

high utilization of the available spectrum between any pair of nodes. A multi-hop WMN using WiMAX technology can potentially offer both high access rates while spanning distances of tens of kilometers.

Each BS manages a physical region called a *wireless cell*, which contains multiple *Stationary Subscriber Stations* (SSs) and multiple *Mobile Subscriber Stations* (MSs), as shown in Fig. 1a. The SSs communicate with the BS for access to the global Internet. A multi-hop WMN can be described as a graph, where BSs are represented by vertices, and where radio links between BSs are represented by directed links, as shown in Fig. 1b. The communications within a WMN can be viewed at two levels; (1) the communications within a cell between the BS and the SSs and occasionally between the SSs, and (2) the communications between BSs and the gateway BS.

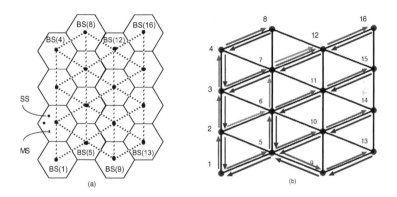

Fig. 1. (a) Hexagonal WMN. (b) Graph Model

This paper addresses the scheduling and MAC protocol between BSs. Assume an infrastructure-based multi-hop WMN, where the physical locations of the BSs are fixed. All BSs have smart antennae arrays and can implement beamforming algorithms on the IO channels, as in [2]. Beamforming antennas will allow for increased transmission rates between selected neighbors and lower interference among non-selected neighbors, which will increase the capacity of a multi-hop WMN. In Fig 1, all link performances are affected by the weather, and they can be optimized periodically by recomputing the physical link parameters, such that each directed link achieves the required data rate and SNR ratio. A similar model was proposed in [2].

The multi-hop nature of WMNs leads to several technical challenges. Capacity and scalability are critical requirements for WMNs. To increase capacity, wireless routers can exploit multiple wireless transceivers, exploiting multiple orthogonal radio channels. However, the design of routing and scheduling algorithms for such networks is challenging. According to [4], '*scheduling link transmissions in a wireless network so as to optimize one or more performance objectives has been the topic of much interest over the past several decades*'. According to a recent survey article [1], '*These advanced wireless radio technologies all require a revolutionary design in higher-level protocols, especially MAC and routing protocols*'. Currently, there are no scheduling algorithms /MAC protocols for single or multi-channel WMNs which have low computational complexity, whichachieve 100% throughput and which achieve near-minimal queueing delays, near-minimal delay jitter and near-optimal QoS.

Tassiulas and Ephremides [5,6,7] first considered the problems of routing and scheduling in multihop networks and other *constrained queueing systems*. The BSs typically exploit *time division duplexing* (TDD). The time-axis consists of many physical time-slots, and a BS with a single radio transceiver can either transmit or receive during one time slot. Two types of conflicts can occur [2,5,6,7]. A *primary* conflict occurs when the number of active directed links incident to one BS exceeds the number of radio transceivers available at that BS. To avoid primary conflicts, the MAC protocol must ensure that the number of active directed links per BS in every time-slot does not exceed the number of radio transceivers. A *secondary* conflict occurs when the signal power from remote nodes interferes with the signal power of the intended receiver. To mitigate secondary conflicts, smart antenna arrays and power adjusting algorithms can be used [2].

The design of interference-free schedulers for mesh networks is a hard problem [2]. References [8,9] establish that the problem of finding schedules with optimal throughput under a general multi-hop WMN interference model is NP-hard. They also establish the difficulty of scheduling and state: '*we assume the packet transmissions at the individual nodes can be finely controlled and carefully scheduled by an omniscient and omnipotent central entity, which is unrealistic*'. Many recent papers propose a joint-layer design methodology, which considers multiple layers simultaneously, ie, the physical layer, the network routing layer, and the MAC layer [6,12-17]. Parameters from each layer are thereby exposed and can be used to express an optimization problem over many layers, which can then be solved. Reference [13] decouples the routing and scheduling problems and presents polynomial time approximation algorithms for routing and scheduling, the latter relying upon graph coloring. The approach taken in this paper decouples the physical, routing and the scheduling/MAC layer optimizations. The goal of the physical layer is to provide directed links with a fixed data-rate. The goal of the routing layer is to route the end-to-end traffic flows such that no capacity constraints are violated. The goal of the scheduling algorithm and MAC layer is to allocate access to the shared wireless medium in a throughput-optimal manner, while simultaneously striving for near-perfect QoS.

In this paper, we propose a low-jitter guaranteed-rate scheduling algorithm and MAC protocol for conflict-free communications between BSs in a WMN. A resource reservation algorithm such as IntServ or DiffServ is used to reserve resources (ie buffer space and bandwidth) along an end-to-end path of BSs, for long-term multimedia flows. The bandwidth demands between all BSs in the WMN are then be specified in a doubly stochastic *NxN* traffic rate matrix, where N is the number of BSs. This traffic rate matrix is decomposed to yield a low-jitter frame transmission schedule, using a recursive fair stochastic matrix decomposition algorithm presented in [33,34,35]. This algorithm will yield a sequence of partial or full permutations which form a *frame transmission schedule*. For dual-channel WMNs, the frame transmission schedule can achieve 100% throughput and directly yields a conflict-free set of transmitting BSs denoted $T(j)$ and a set of receiving BSs denoted $R(j)$ for each time-slot j in the frame, where $1 \leq j \leq F$. For single-channel WMNs, some post-processing of the permutations is required to achieve a conflict-free schedule.

In the resulting schedule, all primary conflicts are avoided, all guaranteed-rate traffic demands are met, and the delay jitter between any cells in a traffic flow is small and bounded by $K*IIDT$ time-slots for fixed constant K, where an $IIDT$ denotes the ideal number of time-slots between successive cells in a provisioned flow. Given the small jitter bound, several important properties can be shown to hold [39]: (a) the expected number of cells belonging to one GR multimedia flow which are queued in any BS is near-minimal and bounded, and is typically < 2 cells per flow, (b) the expected end-to-end delay of a flow along a path of BSs with H-hops is near-minimal and bounded, and is typically $< 2H*IIDT$ time-slots, (c) the cell drop rate due to scheduling conflicts is zero, and (d) all network-introduced delay-jitter can be removed using a playback queue with a depth of $O(K)$ cells. For dual channel WMNs with doubly stochastic traffic rate matrices, in addition to achieving near-minimal queuing delays and near-minimal jitter for provisioned multimedia traffic flows, the proposed scheduling algorithm and MAC protocol are *throughput-optimal*, ie they can achieve 100% of the allowable throughput, given an admissible routing of flows.

In our WMN model, bursty multimedia traffic such as IPTV will be transmitted over an end-to-end path with a provisioned GR. Large video-frames are partitioned into fixed-size cells, which are inserted into the WMN at the maximum provisioned rate, which will introduce an application-specific queuing delay and delay jitter for video frames at the source node (which is external to the network), as in [18,19]. This application-specific delay jitter is external to the network and can be filtered out using application-specific playback buffers at the end-users. However, all network-introduced delay jitter can be provably removed from consideration. To the best of our knowledge, this is the only known throughput-optimal scheduling algorithm and MAC protocol which yields bounded queue sizes and bounded queueing delays within general WMNs with doubly-stochastic traffic rate matrices, and which can remove all network-introduced delay jitter.

Section 2 describes constrained queueing systems, scheduling in WMNs, scheduling in Input-Queued (IQ) crossbar switches, and the WiMax technology. Section 3 describes the transformation from a scheduling problem in IQ switches to a scheduling problem in WMNs, presents the methodology to specify the traffic rate matrix between BSs in a WMN, and describes the proposed algorithm to solve the scheduling problem. Section 4 describes a typical hexagonal WMN and illustrates experimental results. Section 5 contains concluding results.

2   Problem Formulations

2.1   Constrained Queueing Systems

Tassiulas and Ephremides developed the concept of a *constrained queueing system*, a network of queues where the servers in a constrained set cannot provide service simultaneously [5,6,7]. This model can describe multihop wireless networks, database systems, parallel processing systems, and IQ switches. The *stability region* was defined as the set of flow traffic rate vectors which yield a stable system. They established that given an admissible traffic flow rate vector, a *dynamic scheduling algorithm* which solves a *Maximum Weight Matching (MWM)* problem on a bipartite graph for each time-slot will yield a stable system. The *MWM* will define a *transmission set* for each time-slot, ie a set of simultaneously enabled servers which do not violate the interdependency constraints. They also established that the *MWM* algorithm is a *throughput-optimal* solution, when the edge weights reflect the queue lengths in the system, such that the *MWM* scheduling maximizes throughput and minimizes the backlog of traffic in each time-slot.

The problem of determining whether a flow traffic rate vector is admissible in a multi-hop WMN is NP-hard, since it entails 2 phases: (1) the routing phase, ie determining whether the flows can be routed such that no resource is overloaded, and (2) the scheduling phase, the scheduling of cells for transmission for each multiclass queue, once the flows have been routed. The routing problem is known to be NP-hard in the general case. For a multi-hop interference model with secondary interference, scheduling in a WMN is NP-hard [8,9], while under a 1-hop interference model with primary interference, a throughput-optimal solution can be found in polynomial time using the dynamic *MWM* scheduling [5]. Tassiulas recognized that the solution of a *MWM* algorithm for each time-slot of a WMN may not be practical. He also presented a randomized iterative algorithm with linear time complexity for achieving stability and optimal throughput in the capacity region [6].

It is now well known that use of dynamic scheduling algorithm relying on computation of a *MWM* in each time-slot will achieve 100% throughput [4,5,21], but it will also result in queue sizes approaching several thousand cells [21,22,23]. In [22], a dynamically tunable control algorithm was proposed to improve the performance of existing (sub-optimal) dynamic WMN scheduling algorithms. The time allocated for any heuristic scheduling algorithm is tunable, such that more time can be used to obtain a better solution. Simulations presented in [22] indicate that typical existing algorithms lead to queue sizes of between 2,000 and 18,000 cells for loads approaching 92 percent of capacity, and that their tunable algorithm yields queue sizes of 100-800 cells for loads approaching 92 percent of capacity. However, their algorithm becomes unstable for larger loads, and the queue sizes approach infinity.

Reference [4] defined a k-hop interference model for WMNs, and it was shown that for a given k a throughput-optimal dynamic scheduler needs to solve a *MWM* problem given the k-hop interference constraints in each time-slot, consistent with the work of Tassiulus [5]. They formulate the scheduling problem as an optimization problem. For $k=1$, they also propose a greedy *Maximal Matching* (*MM*) scheduling algorithm which provably achieves 50% of the optimal throughput in the capacity region. The importance of the *MWM* problem to dynamic scheduling is thus well established.

Referring to the WMN in Fig. 1b, BS(1) is the gateway BS which has access to the wired Internet. A WMN can be represented as a directed Graph $G=\{V,L\}$, where $V=\{1,2,...,N\}$ is the set of labels for all the BSs and where $L=\{1,2,...,|L|\}$ is the set of labels for all the directed links [2]. Define the topology matrix E where $E \in R^{N \times L}$ as

$$E(n,l) = \begin{cases} 1 & \text{if BS(n) is the transmitter of link l} \\ -1 & \text{if BS(n) is the receiver of link l} \\ 0 & \text{otherwise} \end{cases}$$

Extending the formalism in [2], let $I(n)$ denote the set of incoming links to BS(n), and let $O(n)$ denote the set of outgoing links from BS(n). Define the 0-1 incidence matrix I as

$$I(l,n,t) = \begin{cases} 1 & \text{if link l is active at time-slot t and is incident to/} \\ & \text{from node n} \\ 0 & \text{otherwise} \end{cases}$$

In a single-channel WMN, primary conflicts are avoided when the following condition is met:

$$\sum_{u \in O(n), v \in I(n)} I(u,n,t) \cdot I(v,n,t) = 0, \quad n = 1,2,\ldots,N, \ t = 1,2,\ldots F$$

In a multi-channel WMN where each BS has R radio transceivers and can transmit or receive on up to R orthogonal channels during one time-slot, primary conflicts are avoided when the following condition is met:

$$\sum_{u \in O(n), v \in I(n)} I(u,n,t) + I(v,n,t) \le R, n = 1,\ldots,N, \ t = 1,\ldots F$$

In our infra-structure based WMN model, secondary conflicts can be mitigated by optimizing the physical link parameters (beamforming antennae weights, modulation scheme, signal constellation, and transmission power) once the WMN topology has been fixed. When an ISP is deploying the WMN, the physical positioning of the base-stations is a variable that the network administrators can adjust to eliminate or reduce secondary conflicts. Once the positions are fixed, the antennae weights can be optimized to achieve a constant datarate over every directed link.

Define a transmission set $TS(t)$ as a subset of directed links which is free of primary and secondary conflicts during a given time-slot t. Any subset $T'(t) \in TS(t)$ is also a valid transmission set. A *maximal* transmission set is defined as one which is not a subset of any other transmission set [2,5]. The goal of this paper is to describe a scheduling algorithm which finds maximal transmission sets for each time-slot such that throughput is optimized, and which simultaneously achieves near-perfect QoS for every statically provisioned traffic flow in the WMN.

2.2 Scheduling in IQ Crossbar Switches

An input-queued (IQ) crossbar switch is shown in Fig 2a, and an output-queued (OQ) crossbar switch is shown in Fig 2b. An IQ switch is one example of the *constrained queueing systems* proposed by Tassiulas and Ephremides [5]. An NxM IQ crossbar switch has N input and M output ports, for which a traffic rate matrix can be specified. Each input port j $0 \le j < N$ has M Virtual Output Queues (VOQs), one for each output port k, $0 \le k < M$. The GR traffic requirements for an $N \times N$ crossbar switch can specified in a doubly substochastic or stochastic traffic rate matrix Λ:

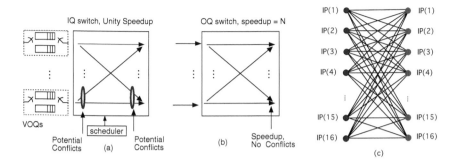

Fig. 2. (a) IQ crossbar switch. (b) OQ crossbar switch. (c) Bipartite graph model.

$$\Lambda = \begin{pmatrix} \lambda_{0,0} & \lambda_{0,1} & \cdots & \lambda_{0,N-1} \\ \lambda_{1,0} & \lambda_{1,1} & \cdots & \lambda_{1,N-1} \\ \cdots & & & \cdots \\ \lambda_{N-1,0} & \lambda_{N-1,1} & \cdots & \lambda_{N-1,N-1} \end{pmatrix}, \quad \begin{array}{l} \sum_{i=0}^{N-1} \lambda_{i,j} \leq 1, \\[2mm] \sum_{j=0}^{N-1} \lambda_{i,j} \leq 1 \end{array}$$

Each element $\lambda_{j,k}$ represents the fraction of the transmission line rate reserved for guaranteed traffic between IO pair (j,k), equivalently $VOQ(j,k)$. The transmission of cells through the IQ switch is governed by the *frame transmission schedule*. In a schedule with F time-slots per frame, the minimum amount of reservable bandwidth is one time-slot reservation per frame on a recurring basis, which guarantees the fraction $1/F$ of the line rate. Define a new quantized traffic rate matrix R where each rate is represented as an integer number of time-slot reservations per frame:

$$R = \begin{pmatrix} R_{0,0} & R_{0,1} & \cdots & R_{0,N-1} \\ R_{1,0} & R_{1,1} & \cdots & R_{1,N-1} \\ \cdots & & & \cdots \\ R_{N-1,0} & R_{N-1,1} & \cdots & R_{N-1,N-1} \end{pmatrix}, \quad \begin{array}{l} \sum_{i=0}^{N-1} R_{i,j} \leq F, \\[2mm] \sum_{j=0}^{N-1} R_{i,j} \leq F \end{array}$$

One challenge when scheduling IQ crossbar switches [20,21,23-35] is resolving the conflicts which occur at the input and output ports. A conflict-free permutation which maps the input ports onto the output ports must be found for each time-slot. The problem of scheduling transmissions in IQ switches so as to optimize one or more performance objectives has been the topic of much interest over the past five decades. A related problem on time-slot-assignments was first considered by Slepian and Duguid, Benes and Clos in the 1950s [20]. See [34] for a brief history of the IQ switch scheduling problem.

It has been established that a dynamic scheduling algorithm for IQ crossbar switches which formulates and solves a **MWM** problem in each time-slot can achieve stability and 100% throughput [21], consistent with the conclusions of Tassiulas and Ephremides on generalized constrained queueing systems [5]. Simulations of many dynamic scheduling algorithms based upon **MWM** are presented in [22,23]. The number of queued cells in the steady-state will grow to several thousand cells as loads approach 100%. Not only is the complexity of *MWM* too excessive for practical use, the delay and jitter are very large such that QoS cannot be guaranteed. One approach to achieve better QoS in constrained queueing systems such as IQ switches is formulate the *MWM* problem to be solved in each time-slot such that the edge weights reflect the '*lag*' of an IQ switch, relative to an OQ switch with near ideal QoS [23]. The QoS of this scheduler is indeed better, but the computational complexity of the *MWM* is still a problem and the steady-state queue sizes, while bounded, can still reach several thousand cells at high loads [23]. As a result, there has been a considerable renewed interest into finding scheduling algorithms for IQ switches which are throughput optimal and which have low jitter and guaranteed QoS performances. Many recent algorithms rely upon stochastic matrix decompositions [24,26-30].

The problem of finding a perfect zero-jitter schedule for IQ switches with bounded speedup has been shown to be NP-hard [26,27]. Those authors present a polynomial time scheduler based upon *Greedy Low Jitter Decomposition* which achieves reasonably low jitter for loads near 80%, while requiring a worst-case speedup of $O(logN)$.

A stochastic matrix decomposition algorithm which attempts to bound the jitter in IQ switches was proposed in [24]. A traffic rate matrix is quantized and decomposed into a convex set of permutation matrices and weights, which are then scheduled. With speedup $S=1+sN$ between 1... 2, the maximum '*Service Lag*' over all *IO* pairs is bounded by $O((N/4)(S/(S-1)))$ time-slots. The speedup affects the QoS provided by the switch. According to [24]: "*with a fairly large class of schedulers a maximum service lag of $O(N^2)$ is unavoidable for input queued switches. To our knowledge, no scheduler which overcomes this $O(N^2)$ has been developed so far. For many rate matrices, it is not always possible to find certain points in time for which the service lag is small over all I-O pairs simultaneously*". For a speedup approaching 2 the service lag does not exceed approximately $N/2$ time-slots, whereas is can go as large as $O(N^2)$ time-slots when no speedup is allowed.

A greedy stochastic matrix decomposition algorithm was also proposed in [30]. The algorithm cannot guarantee 100% throughput or short-term fairness. The authors establish a jitter bound, but their bound grows as the IQ switch size N increases. The authors identify an open problem: "*to determine the minimum speedup required to provide hard guarantees, and whether such guarantees are possible at all*". The problem of finding low-jitter schedulers with low speedup requirements is difficult.

A low-jitter scheduling algorithm based on recursive fair stochastic matrix decomposition was introduced in [33,34,35]. The algorithm is throughput-optimal, ie it can achieve 100% throughput and will also bound the delay jitter on every competing traffic flow to a small number of *IIDTs*, while requiring unity speedup. Proofs establishing very low delay and jitter are presented in [34]. A custom network simulator with over 20,000 lines of code was developed to gather detailed jitter statistics, to complement the theory. An exposition of very low jitter in a linear chain of IP routers is presented in [37]. An exposition of very low jitter in a multi-hop Fat-Tree mesh network with 256 simultaneous competing traffic flows is presented in [38]. Mathematical bounds on the end-to-end queuing delay and jitter are established in [39]. In this paper, this low-jitter algorithm will be adapted to the problem of scheduling traffic in a WMN, bounds on the delay and jitter are stated and detailed simulation results are presented.

2.3 The WiMAX Technology

The WiMAX standard defines 3 operation modes; (i) point-to-multipoint (PMP), (ii) centralized mesh mode (CMM), and (iii) distributed mesh mode (DMM) [3]. A WiMAX WMN system consists of BSs (Mesh Base Stations - MBS) that are connected to the wired IP network and which manage communications between the SSs in a wireless cell. In the PMP and CMM modes, the time axis is divided into scheduling frames, each consisting of several time-slots.

WiMax allows for both centralized and distributed scheduling [3]. In the centralized scheme the transmission schedules for all SSs within a cell are made by the centralized gateway BS. The scheduling information is distributed to the other SSs within a wireless cell using the 'Mesh Centralized Scheduling' (MCS) control messages on the control channel. Statistics on the traffic loading can be sent from the SSs back to the gateway BS using the same MCS control messages. Therefore, a BS can act as the centralized scheduler which can precompute transmission schedules of all the SSs within the cell. We assume a similar model in a multi-hop WMN: the gateway BS can act as the centralize scheduler which can precompute transmission schedules for all other inter-BS communications within the WMN.

WiMax supports several service categories: (i) The Unsolicited Grant Service (UGS) which can be used for real-time constant-rate services, (ii) the real-time polling service (ttPS) suitable for IPTV multi-casting [3], (iii) the non-real-time polling service (nrtPS) suitable for video-on-demand (VOD) [3], and (iv) the best-effort service (BE). In this paper, all long-term multimedia traffic, such as VOIP, IPTV and VOD can be handled. The frame transmission schedules can be used to provide GR service in the UGS class for all these traffic types, or the schedule can be used to reserve bandwidth for a preferred polling order, to minimize cell jitter and queue sizes within base-stations, when the rtPS and nrtPS service classes are used.

In the WiMax standard, a TDD frame may have durations of 0.5, 1 or 2 milliseconds in the PMP mode, or 2.5, 4, 5, 8, 10, 12.5 or 20 milliseconds in the mesh mode. Typically, the physical parameters controlling the data-rate for each SS can be recomputed for each frame. In all physical layer transmissions, data bits are randomized for robustness, forward error correction is employed, and the modulation schemes, the signal constellations and the power transmission levels can be optimized. The modulation scheme and constellations include binary phase-shift keying (BPSK), quadrature phase shift keying (QFSK), and 16, 64 or 256-quadrature amplitude modulation (QAM). [3]

3   Transformation of IQ Switch Scheduling to WMN Scheduling

We describe the transformation for the IQ switch scheduling problem to the WMN scheduling problem. An NxN IQ switch has N input ports and N output ports. Each input port has N VOQs, and the IQ switch has N^2 VOQs. The switch also has N^2

internal links from the N^2 VOQs to the N output ports. An IQ switch has 2 sets of constraints, denoted $c1$ and $c2$. Constraint ($c1$) requires that each set of N VOQs belonging to an input port transmits at most 1 cell per time-slot. Constraint ($c2$) requires that from each set of N VOQs associated with an output port, only 1 VOQ can be active per time-slot, so that each output port receives at most 1 cell per time-slot.

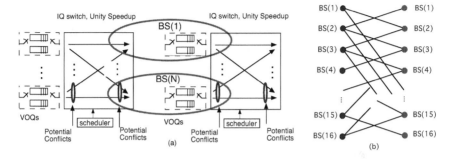

Fig. 3. (a) Transformation, IQ Switch to WMN. (b) Bipartite graph model.

The transformation from an IQ switch with N ports to a WMN with N Base-Stations is illustrated in Fig. 3. Fig. 3a illustrates a single IQ switch where the N external output links labeled $1..N$ are fed back into the N input ports $1.. N$ of the same switch (two IQ switches are drawn for simplicity). Each Base-Station j in the WMN equals the union of the output port j of the IQ switch, plus the N VOQs at input port j of the IQ switch, as shown in Fig 3a. The N^2 internal links of the IQ switch become the (up to) N^2 wireless links in the WMN, and each BS can be modeled as an Output-Queued (OQ) switch. The constraint ($c1$) of the IQ switch requires that each BS transmits at most 1 cell per time-slot. The constraint ($c2$) of the IQ switch requires that each BS receives at most 1 cell per time-slot. Effectively, the input (output) constraints on the IQ switch become the output (input) constraints on the WMN, respectively.

The traffic requirements to be met by an IQ switch can be specified in a doubly stochastic traffic rate matrix as established in section 2.2, and this matrix can be represented by a weighted bipartite graph. By the above transformation, the traffic requirements to be met by a WMN must also be specified by a doubly stochastic traffic rate matrix and weighted bipartite graph. The hexagonal WMN of Fig. 1 with N base-Stations can be represented as a bipartite graph, as shown in Fig 3b. Each BS has ≤ 6 incoming links and ≤ 6 outgoing links.

A frame-based low-jitter GR scheduling algorithm for IQ switches based on recursive fair stochastic matrix decomposition was proposed in [33,34,35]. A doubly substochastic or stochastic traffic rate matrix is first quantized to have integer values, and then is recursively decomposed in a relatively fair manner. Let $P(M,F)$ denote the problem of scheduling an admissible quantized traffic rate matrix M into a transmission frame of length F time-slots. The problem $P(M,F)$ is recursively decomposed into 2 problems $P(M1,F/2)$ and $P(M2,F/2)$, such that matrices $M1+M2=M$, where $M1$ and $M2$ are admissible traffic rate matrices, and for all j and k where $0 \leq j < N$ and $0 \leq k < N$, $M1(j,k) \leq M2(j,k) + c$ and $M2(j,k) \leq M1(j,k) + c$ for constant $c=1$ or 2, depending upon assumptions. One step in an example decomposition for an 4x4 switch operating at 99.2% load with unity speedup is shown below:

$$\begin{bmatrix} 106 & 222 & 326 & 345 \\ 177 & 216 & 303 & 326 \\ 459 & 232 & 183 & 147 \\ 282 & 352 & 211 & 178 \end{bmatrix} = \begin{bmatrix} 53 & 111 & 163 & 172 \\ 88 & 108 & 152 & 163 \\ 230 & 116 & 91 & 74 \\ 141 & 176 & 105 & 89 \end{bmatrix} + \begin{bmatrix} 53 & 111 & 163 & 173 \\ 89 & 108 & 151 & 163 \\ 229 & 116 & 92 & 73 \\ 141 & 176 & 106 & 89 \end{bmatrix}$$

The low-jitter GR scheduling algorithm proposed in [33,34,35] for IQ crossbar switches bounds the service lead and service lag of each VOQ to $K \cdot IIDT$ time-slots for constant K, where $IIDT$ represents the '*Ideal Inter-Departure Time*' for cells belonging to a VOQ. The bound applies to all VOQs in an IQ switch simultaneously. Furthermore, it can be shown that the bound applies to all cells in an end-to-end GR flow, provided that cells are selected for service within each VOQ along the end-to-end path according to a GPS scheduling algorithm. This algorithm will be applied to scheduling in WMNs. We now define several terms for the scheduling problem in WMN. These definitions are adapted from [33,34].

Definition: A "*Frame transmission schedule*" of length F is a sequence of partial or full permutation matrices (or vectors) which define the transmission sets and reception sets for a WMN, for F time-slots within a frame. Each transmission set identifies up to N conflict-free matchings of Base-Stations for service in the time-slot. The frame transmission schedule for a WMN with N BSs can be represented as an FxN matrix, where in each time-slot t for $1 \leq t \leq F$ up to N BSs are identified for transmission and reception. Given directed links with a capacity of L, the frame length F is determined by the desired minimum quota of reservable bandwidth, which equals L/F. To set the minimum quota of reservable bandwidth to $\leq 1\%$ of L, set $F \geq 100$, *ie F = 128*.

Definition: A GR 'flow' in a WMN specifies the guaranteed traffic-rate between one origin BS and one destination BS. This traffic flow must be routed along an end-to-end path of BSs, in which buffer space is reserved in the queues of each BS and in which bandwidth is reserved in each inter-BS radio link in the path.

Definition: A "*Flow transmission schedule*" of length F is a sequence of vectors which define which flow to be serviced in each Base-Station, in the F time-slots within a frame, given a 'frame transmission schedule' which identifies the BSs to be serviced. The flow transmission schedule for a WMN with N BSs can be represented as an FxN matrix, where in each time-slot t for $1 \leq t \leq F$ a set of up to N flows is identified for service.

A flow transmission schedule can be computed from the frame transmission schedule; When a Base-Station receives service, select the flow to be serviced using the GPS algorithm. Based upon a flow transmission schedule, the following properties can be stated. Unfortunately, space constrains prevent the presentation of all results here and the proofs are established in [39].

Definition: At a given BS, the *"Inter-Departure Time"* (*IDT*) of a scheduled cell in a GR flow is defined as follows: Let the scheduled service time of cell c in flow f at the given BS be denoted $s(f,c)$. The *IDT* of cell c is defined as $s(f,c)-s(f,c-1)$ for $c \geq 2$.

Definition: At a given BS, the *"Ideal Inter-Departure Time"* (*IIDT*) of scheduled cells in a GR flow f with quantized guaranteed traffic rate of $\phi(f)$ time-slot reservations per frame, given a frame of length F, a link datarate L in bytes/sec and fixed-sized cells of C bits, is given by: $IIDT(f) = F/\phi(f)$ time-slots, each of duration (C/L) sec.

Definition: At a given BS, the *'Received Service"* of a GR flow f with guaranteed rate $\phi(f)$ time-slot reservations per frame, at time-slot t within a frame schedule of length F, denoted $S_f(0,t)$, equals the number of matches in the frame transmission schedule in time slots $1...t$, where $t \leq F$, in which flow f is serviced.

Definition: At a given BS, the *"Service Lag"* of scheduled cell c of GR flow f, within a frame transmission schedule of length F, denoted $LAG_f(t)$, equals the scheduled service time of the cell minus the ideal service time of the cell, ie $LAG_f(t) = s(f,cf) - c \cdot IIDT$. Intuitively, a positive Service Lag represents how many time-slots behind service the flow has fallen, relative to an ideal service schedule. A negative Service Lag is called a Service Lead, and represents how many time-slots ahead of service the flow has fallen.

The following four theorems are established in [39]. They assume each traffic flow is admitted into a network subject to shaping, and has a maximum service Lead/lag of K *IIDT*. Each BS is scheduled according to the proposed algorithm, with a maximum service lead/lag of K *IIDT* times-slots. The traffic rate matrix is doubly stochastic.

Theorem 1: Given a queue which receives a GR service of C cells per frame with a maximum Service Lead/Lag of $K \cdot IIDT$ time-slots, given an arriving traffic flow with a maximum Service Lead/Lag of $K \cdot IIDT$ time-slots, and given an initial queue state with $\leq O(K)$ cells, then the number of cells in the queue is upper bounded by $O(K)$ cells.

Theorem 2: When all queues in all intermediate nodes have reached steady-state, the maximum end-to-end queuing delay of a GR flow traversing H Base-Stations is $O(KH \cdot IIDT)$ time-slots.

Theorem 3: In the steady-state, a traffic flow f which leaves a Base-Station along an end-to-end path in a WMN will exhibit a maximum service lead/lag of $O(K \cdot IIDT)$ time-slots, ie the service lead/lag of a flow is not cumulative when traversing multiple Base-Stations. Equivalently, the delay jitter is not cumulative.

Theorem 4: A traffic flow which traverses H Base-Stations along an end-to-end path can be delivered to the end-user with *zero network-introduced delay jitter*, when a playback buffer of size $O(K)$ cells is employed.

3.1 Routing in a WMN

In order to specify the doubly stochastic traffic rate matrix to be decomposed, a set of GR flows to be provisioned in the WMN must be specified, and these flows must be routed through the WMN such that no constraints are violated. This section summarizes a typical routing problem formulation and describes how the traffic rate matrix is computed from the routing information.

Let F be the set of all traffic flows, denoted as (source,destination) pairs. Each flow f has a stationary unidirectional traffic rate r_f from the source to the destination nodes. Let P_f be set of all directed paths from the source to the destination nodes, available to carry the traffic required by flow f. Let p denote an individual path within the set P_f. Let x_p be the traffic rate in bits/second assigned along a path p. Let $\bar{x}$ be the rate vector of all path flows $\left\{ x_p \mid f \in F, p \in P_f \right\}$. For an *admissible routing*, the rate vector must satisfy the two constraints: (a) for every flow f, the sum of the traffic rates over all paths in P_f must equal the specified traffic rate for the flow f, and (b) the traffic rate along any path must equal or exceed 0 (ie negative traffic rates are not allowed).

In our WMN model, assume every Base-Station i has a constraint on the sum of the incoming and outgoing traffic it can carry, which is denoted $C(i)$:

$$\sum_{(i,j)\in p,\, p\in P_f,\, f\in F} x_p + \sum_{(j,i)\in p,\, p\in P_f,\, f\in F} x_p \leq C(i)$$

The first summation is the sum of all traffic leaving node i (for fixed i), over all edges (i,j), over all paths and flows. The second summation is the sum of all traffic entering node i, over all edges (j,i) for fixed i, over all paths and flows.

Given a set of paths available for each flow to be provisioned, a constrained optimization problem which minimizes the *unrouted traffic* in the WMN can be stated as follows:

$$\text{minimize} \sum_{f\in F} r_f - \sum_{f\in F}\sum_{p\in P_f} x_p$$

$$\text{subject to} \quad \sum_{p\in P_f} x_p = r_f \quad \text{for all } f \in F$$

$$x_p \geq 0 \quad \text{for all } p \in P_f, \quad f \in F$$

$$\lambda_i \leq C_i \quad \text{for all } i \in V$$

where $\lambda_i = \displaystyle\sum_{(i,j)\in p,\, p\in P_f,\, f\in F} x_p + \sum_{(j,i)\in p,\, p\in P_f,\, f\in F} x_p$.

This problem can be solved in polynomial time using a linear programming approach. As observed by Tassiulas [5], determining an optimal routing has considerably more difficult. In the above optimization problem, the set of paths for each flow is fixed. However in an optimal formulation there are exponentially many paths and combinations of paths to be considered [5]. Fortunately, there are many polynomial time heuristic algorithms for determining good routings in general networks and WMNs. In this paper, we have decoupled the routing and scheduling problems, and we assume that an acceptable routing has been achieved. We focus on the scheduling problem.

Once an admissible routing for the GR traffic has been found, the traffic rate matrix for the WMN can be computed as follows:

$$for\ f \in F$$
$$for\ p \in P_f$$
$$for\ (u,v) \in p$$
$$M(u,v) = M(u,v) + r_f$$

Once the traffic rate matrix is specified, it can be decomposed as described in [33,34], and the resulting frame transmission schedule yields the scheduling information for the WMN.

3.2 The Dual-Channel WMN

Each BS contains 2 radio transceivers which can simultaneously send and receive over 2 orthogonal channels. Therefore, the frame transmission schedule computed by the algorithm can be used directly to specify the conflict-free transmission sets of BSs in each time-slot. Link utilizations as high as 100 % for GR traffic can be achieved.

3.3 The Single-Channel WMN

Each BS contains 1 radio transceiver which can only receive or transmit during any one physical time-slot. Therefore, the frame transmission schedule computed by the algorithm cannot be used directly to specify the transmission sets in each time-slots.

To avoid primary conflicts, each permutation in the frame transmission schedule must be partitioned into multiple (J) sets of transmitting BSs denoted $T(1..J)$ and J sets of receiving BSs denoted $R(1..J)$. Each BS can appear at most once as a source in one set T and at most once as a receiver in another set R. The following algorithm will partition a permutation into 3 conflict-free sets. Therefore, to find a frame-transmission schedule of length $F=2048$ time-slots, we may construct a traffic rate matrix for a smaller frame $F'=512$, and then expand each of the 512 permutations, to yield 1536 permutations, which will be partially utilized. For single-channel WMNs, each full permutation specifies at least 2 time-slots with N active BSs each to be realized. The partitioning algorithm specifies 3 time-slots with $2N$ active BSs. Therefore, the maximum loading of GR traffic each single-channel BS is therefore 67%. The remaining 33% of the bandwidth can be used for BE traffic, which can be scheduled using the usual polling schemes.

```
Partition_Permutation(P)
T(1..3) = NULL;  R(1..3) = NULL;
for j=1:N {
    for k = 1:3 {
        u = j, v = P(j)
        if ( v∩T(k) = NULL ) and
            u ∩ R(k) = NULL )) {
            T(k) = T(k)∪u ;
```

$$R(k) = R(k) \cup v \,;$$
$$break; \quad \} \} \}$$

4   A WMN Example

4.1   A Communication Tree in a 16 Node WMN

In Fig. 2, 16 wireless cells are arranged in a conventional hexagonal mesh. This example is selected since the large number of directed edges will be difficult to schedule without conflicts. BS(1) at the lower left is the gateway BS with access to the wired IP network. Assume each directed link has bandwidth 128 Mbps, ie the physical link parameters are precomputed to ensure that each directed link can support a bandwidth of 128 Mbps. Since the BS locations are fixed and the physical environment (weather) is relatively static, these physical link parameters can be precomputed once and will only need to be updated when the physical environment (ie weather) changes.

Consider a downward communication tree with a root at BS(1) which delivers traffic to each BS (2..16). This tree is statically routed in the WMN, as shown by the blue arrows in Fig. 1b. Typically, trees are routed according to various optimization criteria, ie the tree may be a chosen to be minimum weight spanning tree rooted at BS(1). In this paper, the focus is the low-jitter GR scheduling algorithm and MAC protocol. Assume any traffic flows can be routed into the WMN according to any optimization criteria selected by the network administrator, as described in section 3. The proposed scheduling algorithm and MAC protocol will apply given any admissible routed communication pattern with a doubly stochastic traffic rate matrix.

An upward communication tree leading from each BS (2..16) and ending at BS(1) is also statically routed into the WMN in Fig. 1b. In Fig. 1b, the upward tree (ie red) follows the same topology as the downward tree, although this is not essential. In the tree in Fig 1b, we assume each BS adds 3 Mbps of bandwidth demand to the upward and downward tree. The embedding of any multicast trees into the WMN results in the specification of a traffic rate matrix for the WMN, which reflects the resulting loads on all the wireless links due to the multicast trees.

We assume additional point-to-point traffic between selected BSs is added, as represented by the green line in Fig 1b. In this example, the point-to-point traffic is generated between pairs of Base-Stations, to saturate every BS, ie every BS is essentially 100% saturated with traffic. This point-to-point traffic results in the specification of a second traffic rate matrix, which reflects the resulting loads on all the wireless links due to the point-to-point traffic.

The final traffic rate matrix is given by the sum of the multicast tree traffic rate matrix and the point-to-point traffic rate matrix described above. The resulting traffic rate matrix must be doubly substochastic or stochastic. This resulting matrix can then be decomposed to yield a set of F permutations or partial permutations, each of size N, as described in section 3. Each permutation specifies a set of up to N transmitting BSs, and a set of up to N receiving BSs per time-slot.

4.2 Experimental Results

Fig. 4a illustrates the observed normalized service lead/lag for every GR flow in the WMN of Fig. 1b, based upon the decomposition of the *16x16* traffic rate matrix derived in section 4.1, with *F=2048,* assuming the dual-channel WMN. The ideal service is represented by the bold diagonal line in Fig. 4a. Each single red line denotes the normalized service times observed for one GR flow which traverses its end-to-end path through the WMN. The individual red service lines for GR flows are indistinguishable, due to the large number of flows plotted on the same graph. However, the observed service closely tracks the ideal service. In Fig. 4a, the dashed green lines above and below the main diagonal correspond to service leads/lags of *3 IIDT* time-slots. The *X*-axis denotes the cell arrival time, expressed in terms of the IIDT for every flow *f*. The *Y*-axis denotes the cell number. The minimum and maximum Service Lead/Lags are visible from this graph. According to Fig. 4a, the observed Service Lead/Lags are within $K \cdot IIDT$ time-slots, as established in [33,34].

Fig. 4b plots the experimentally observed IDT PDF for cells leaving any BS, based upon the dual-channel WMN network model. According to theorem 3, all cells leaving a BS will exhibit a service lead/lag $\leq O(K \cdot IIDT)$ time-slots. Fig. 4b illustrates this property experimentally, ie the delay jitter remains bounded.

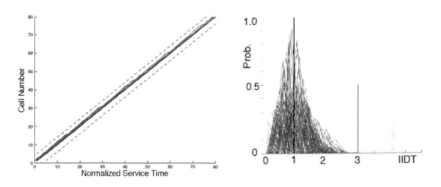

Fig. 4. (a) Service Lead/Lag over all Base-Stations. (b) IDT PDF over all Base-Stations.

The average and maximum number of cells per flow queued in every BS was also recorded by the network simulator. On average, every GR flow buffers less than 1 cell in each BS, indicating that each cell typically receives service within 1 *IIDT*, so that queuing is near-minimal. The maximum number of queued cells per flow in each BS is ≤ 6 cells, in this simulation, consistent with theorem 1. The simulator also verified that no cells were ever dropped for any GR flow.

The MAC protocol and scheduling algorithm applies to any arbitrary WMN topology with any number of BSs. The scheduling experiment has been repeated for WMNs with varying sizes and with varying topologies, with up to *1K* Base-Stations. The results are consistent with the theory established in [33,34,39] and with Fig. 4, ie the end-to-end delay and jitter are near-minimal and bounded. Additional results for other topologies are presented in [37,38].

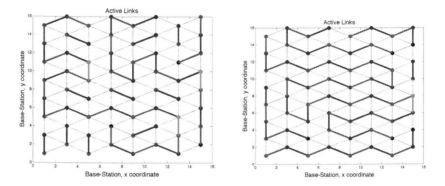

Fig. 5. Active links, 64 node WMN, 2 time-slots

Fig. 5 illustrates 2 typical transmission and reception sets, for a multi-channel hexagonal WMN with 64 nodes, arranged in an 8x8 mesh. Each BS has 2 transceivers and can simultaneously receive and transmit with 2 directed neighbors. A communication tree routed at BS(1) which provides each BS with a fixed rate of non-broadcast traffic was embedded into the WMN, as shown in Fig 1b. Additional point-to-point traffic between BSs was added, to saturate every wireless link. The resulting 64x64 traffic rate matrix was decomposed to yield a frame transmission schedule. A transmitting BS is denoted by a bold colored circle with a bold line to the receiver. In each time-slot, a greedy graph coloring algorithm is used to assign frequencies to the radio channels. Three frequencies are used in Fig. 5, while for these particular time-slots only 2 colors are necessary. In a general planar graph corresponding to hexagonal WMN, 3 colors are sufficient to color the graph.

4.3 Scalability

The proposed scheduling algorithm finds a solution for multihop WMNs which achieves 100% throughput and bounds the queue sizes per flow, end-to-end queuing delay and delay jitter to very small amounts, with computational time $O(NFlogNF)$, where N is the number of Base-Stations, and F is the number of time-slots per scheduling frame. The runtime complexity is the same as that of the well-known Fast-Fourier Transform (FFT) algorithm with NF points. The author estimates that the proposed algorithm runs in about $1/5^{th}$ the time of a comparable size FFT problem. A serial version of the proposed algorithm will solve the multi-hop WMN scheduling problem for reasonable N (8..128) with reasonable frame sizes F (*1K-4K* time-slots per frame) in milliseconds, faster than the WiMAX frame rate (typically 1-10 milliseconds). A parallel version of the proposed scheduler will solve larger scheduling problems much faster. Therefore, the algorithm is scalable to very large WMNs. The proposed scheduling algorithm was first proposed for use in packet-switched Internet routers in [34], which have considerably more demanding time constraints.

5 Conclusions

A collision-free low-jitter guaranteed-rate scheduling algorithm and MAC protocol for WMNs was presented. Within the WMN, fixed-size cells move between the BSs. IP packets are disassembled at the ingress BS, delivered through the WMN and reassembled once at the egress BS. It was shown that the scheduling problem in IQ switches can be transformed into a scheduling problem for WMNs. Therefore, the low-jitter GR scheduling algorithm for IQ switches presented in [33,34,35] can be used to find conflict-free low-jitter GR transmission sets in a WMN. Extensive simulations of hundreds of simultaneous competing GR traffic flows traversing many randomly generated WMNs were performed. In the single-channel WMN, admissible GR multimedia traffic can be provisioned and scheduled to achieve up to 67% of the system capacity. The remaining 33% of capacity can be used for Best-Effort traffic. In dual-channel WMNs with doubly stochastic traffic rate matrices, admissible GR multimedia traffic can be provisioned to achieve up to 100% of system capacity. For all provisioned GR flows, the number of cells per flow queued in each BS is near-minimal and bounded, and was experimentally observed to be between 1 and 2 cells per flow on average. The end-to-end delay for a flow along a path with H hops is also near-minimal and bounded, and was experimentally observed to be less than $2H \cdot IIDT$ time-slots. The end-to-end jitter for a flow along a path with H hops is also near-minimal and bounded, and was experimentally observed to be less than $O(K \cdot IIDT)$ time-slots. The cell loss rate due to primary scheduling conflicts is zero. These experimental results are consistent with the theoretical bounds reported in [34,39].

References

[1] Akyildiz, I.F., Wang, X.: A Survey on Wireless Mesh Networks. IEEE Radio Communications, S23–S30 (2005)
[2] Cao, M., Wang, X., Kim, S.K., Madihian, M.: Multi-Hop Wireless Backhaul Networks: A Cross-Layer Design Paradigm. IEEE JSAC 25(4), 738–748 (2007)
[3] Xergias, S., Passas, N., Salkintzis, A.K.: Centralized Resource Allocation for Multimedia Traffic in IEEE 802.16 Mesh Networks. Proc. IEEE 96(1), 54–63 (2008)
[4] Sharma, G., Mazumda, R.R., Shroff, N.B.: On the Complexity of Scheduling in Wireless Networks. In: IEEE Mobicom 2006 (2006)
[5] Tassiulas, L., Ephremides, A.: Stability Properties of Constrained Queueing Systems and Scheduling Policies for Maximum Throughput in Multihop Radio Networks. IEEE Trans. Automatic Control 37(12), 1936–1948 (1992)
[6] Tassiulas, L.: Linear Complexity algorithms for maximum throughput in radio networks and input queued switches. IEEE, Los Alamitos (1998)
[7] Tassiulas, L., Ephremides, A.: Joint optimal routing and scheduling in packet radio networks. IEEE Trans. Inform. Theory 38, 165–169 (1992)
[8] Jain, K., Padhye, J., Padmanabhan, V., Qiu, L.: Impact on Interference on multi-hop wireless networks performance. In: ACM Mobicom 2003 (2003)
[9] Jain, K., Padhye, J., Padmanabhan, V., Qiu, L.: Impact of Interference on Multi-Hop Wireless Network Performance. Wireless Networks 11, 471–487 (2005)

[10] Chou, C.T., Qadir, J., Lim, J.G.: Advances and Challenges with Data Broadcasting in Wireless Mesh Networks. IEEE Comm. Magazine, 78–122 (2007)

[11] Sharma, G., Shroff, N.B., Mazumdar, R.R.: Maximum Weighted Matching with Interference Constraints. In: IEEE Int. Conf. Pervasive Computing and Comm. Workshop (2006)

[12] Madan, R., Cui, S., Lall, S., Goldsmith, A.J.: Cross-layer design for lifetime maximization in interference-limited wireless sensor networks. In: IEEE Infocom (2005)

[13] Kodlialam, M., Nandagopal, T.: Characterizing Achievable rates in multi-hop wireless mesh networks: the joint routing and scheduling problem. In: ACM Mobicom 2003, San Diego, California (2003)

[14] Cruz, R.L., Santhaman, A.V.: Optimal routing, link scheduling and power control in multi-hop wireless networks. In: Proc. IEEE Infocom, vol. 1, pp. 702–711 (2005)

[15] Xiao, L., Johansoon, M., Boyd, S.P.: Simultaneous routing and resource allocation via dual decomposition. IEEE Trans. Comm. 52(7), 1136–1144 (2004)

[16] Elliot, T., Ephremides, A.: Joint scheduling and power control for wireless ad hoc networks. IEEE Trans. Wireless Comm. 1, 74–85 (2004)

[17] Sharma, G., Shroff, N.B., Mazumdar, R.R.: Joint Congestion Control and Distributed Scheduling for Throughput Guarantees in Wireless Networks. In: IEEE Infocom, pp. 2072–2080 (2007)

[18] Parekh, A.K., Gallager, R.G.: A Generalized Processor Sharing Approach to Flow Control in Integrated Service Networks: the Single Node Case. IEEE/ACM Trans. Networking 1, 344–357 (1993)

[19] Parekh, A.K., Gallager, R.G.: A Generalized Processor Sharing Approach to Flow Control in Integrated Service Networks: the Multiple Node Case. IEEE/ACM Trans. Networking 2(2), 137–150 (1994)

[20] Jajszczyk, A.: Nonblocking, Repackable and Rearrangeable Clos Networks: Fifty Years of the Theory Evolution. IEEE Comm. Magazine, 28–33 (2003)

[21] McKeown, N., Mekkittikul, A., Anantharam, V., Walrand, J.: Achieving 100% Throughput in an Input Queued Switch. Trans. Comm. 47(8), 1260–1267 (1999)

[22] Lotfinezhad, M., Liang, B., Sousa, E.S.: Dynamic Control of Tunable Sub-optimal Algorithms for Scheduling of Time-varying Wireless Networks. In: IEEE iWQoS Conf., Enschede, Netherlands, pp. 153–163 (2008)

[23] Gourgy, A., Szymanski, T.H., Down, D.: On Tracking the Behaviour of an Output Queued Switch using an Input Queued Switch. IEEE Trans. Networking (submitted)

[24] Koksal, C.E., Gallager, R.G., Rohrs, C.E.: Rate Quantization and Service Quality over Single Crossbar Switches. In: IEEE Infocom (2004)

[25] Gopya, P., Vin, H.M.: Generalized Guaranteed Rate Scheduling Algorithms: A Framework. IEE/ACM Trans. Networking 5(4), 561–571 (1997)

[26] Keslassy, I., Kodialam, M., Lakshamn, T.V., Stiliadis, D.: On Guaranteed Smooth Scheduling for Input-Queued Switches. IEEE/ACM Trans. Networking 13(6) (2005)

[27] Kodialam, M.S., Lakshman, T.V., Stilladis, D.: Scheduling of Guaranteed-bandwidth low-jitter traffic in input-buffered switches. US Patent Application #20030227901

[28] Chen, W.J., Chang, C.-S., Huang, H.-Y.: Birkhoff-von Neumann Input Buffered Crossbar Switches. IEEE Trans. Comm. 49(7), 1145–1147 (2001)

[29] Chang, C.-S., Chen, W.J., Huang, H.-Y.: On Service Guarantees for Input Buffered Crossbar Switches: A Capacity Decomposition Approach by Birkhoff and von Neuman. In: IEEE iWQoS 1999, pp. 79–86 (1999)

[30] Mohanty, S.R., Bhuyan, L.N.: Guaranteed Smooth Switch Scheduling with Low Complexity. In: IEEE Globecom, pp. 626–630 (2005)

[31] Sun, W., Shin, K.G.: End-to-End Delay Bounds for Traffic Aggregates Under Guaranteed-Rate Scheduling Algorithms. IEEE/ACM Trans. Networking 11(3), 1188–1201 (2005)

[32] Giaccone, P., Leonardi, E., Shat, D.: Throughput Region of Finite-Buffered Networks. IEEE Trans. PDS 11(12), 251–263 (2007)

[33] Szymanski, T.H.: QoS Switch Scheduling using Recursive Fair Stochastic Matrix Decomposition. In: IEEE Int. Conf. HPSR, pp. 417–424 (2006)

[34] Szymanski, T.H.: A Low-Jitter Guaranteed-Rate Scheduling Algorithm for Packet-Switched IP Routers, accepted (with revision). IEEE Trans. on Comm. (2008)

[35] Szymanski, T.H.: Method and Apparatus to Schedule Packets through a Crossbar Switch with Delay Guarantees, US Patent Application (2006)

[36] Szymanski, T.H.: Method and Apparatus to Schedule Packets through a Wireless Mesh Network with Near Minimal Delay and Jitter, US Provisional Patent App. (2008)

[37] Szymanski, T.H., Gilbert, D.: Delivery of Guaranteed Rate Internet Traffic with Very Low Delay Jitter. In: IEEE Pacific Rim Conf. on Comm. Comp. and Signal Processing, Canada, pp. 450–455 (2007).

[38] Szymanski, T.H., Gilbert, D.: Low-Jitter Guaranteed-Rate Communications for Cluster Computing Systems. Pacific Rim Special Issue. Int. Journal of Computer Networks and Distributed Systems (to appear) (2008)

[39] Szymanski, T.H.: Bounds on End-to-End Delay and Jitter in Input-Buffered and Internally Buffered IP Networks (submitted) (2008)

Coexistence of Collocated IEEE 802.11 and Bluetooth Technologies in 2.4 GHz ISM Band

Ariton E. Xhafa, Xiaolin Lu, and Donald P. Shaver

Texas Instruments, Inc.
12500 TI Boulevard
Dallas, TX 75243
USA
{axhafa,xlu,shaver}@ti.com

Abstract. In this paper, we investigate coexistence of collocated 802.11 and Bluetooth technologies in 2.4 GHz industrial, scientific, and medical (ISM) band. To that end, we show a time division multiplexing approach suffers from the "avalanche effect". We then provide remedies to avoid this effect and improve the performance of the overall network. For example, it is shown that a simple request-to-send (RTS) / clear-to-send (CTS) frame handshake in WLAN can avoid "avalanche effect" and improve the performance of overall network.

Keywords: medium access control, coexistence, wireless networks.

1 Introduction

We are witnessing a tremendous growth in wireless technologies. Different wireless technologies are now integrated in a single handheld device, allowing mobile users to access different networks simultaneously. Coexistence of these collocated technologies in the same device is an important problem that needs to be addressed in order to ensure smooth mobile user access to different networks. In this paper, we focus on the coexistence issues of collocated IEEE 802.11 and Bluetooth technologies. These technologies operate in 2.4 GHz band, with Bluetooth hoping in 79 MHz of the ISM band while 802.11 requiring 16 MHz or 22 MHz band (depending on whether 802.11b or 802.11g is used). Therefore, interference between these technologies greatly impacts the performance of both networks.

Most of the research/work has been focused on coexistence of these technologies when they are not collocated in the same device [1]-[9]. In [1], the authors propose two coexistence mechanism between 802.11 and Bluetooth that are based on scheduling techniques and result in interference mitigation between the two technologies. An improvement on the throughput for both 802.11 and Bluetooth has been shown at the expense of a small additional delay for data transfer. In [2] experimental results for the interference between IEEE 802.11b and Bluetooth technologies are presented; however, no remedies have been provided to mitigate the interference between these two technologies. Howitt in [3] present an analysis on the coexistence of WLAN and Bluetooth in UL band and derives

C. Wang (Ed.): AccessNets, LNICST 6, pp. 138–145, 2009.

a closed form expression for the collision probability in terms of the network and radio propagation parameters. However, in [6], the authors, for the first time, investigate the coexistence problem between 802.11 and Bluetooth technologies that are collocated in the same device and propose time-division multiplexing (TDM) coexistence solution. They analyse the performance of both technologies with and without the proposed coexistence solution.

In our paper, we investigate the coexistence between 802.11 and Bluetooth technologies collocated in the same device. Different from the work in [6], we show that TDM approach suffers from the "avalanche effect" (to be described in Section 1). We provide simple solutions to mitigate this undesired effect and further improve the performance of the overall network.

The remainder of the paper is organized as follows. In Section 1 we describe existing problem with TDM approach. Simulation setup is described in Section 2, while results follow in Section 3. Finally, we briefly discuss the impact of these results in Section 4 and we conclude our findings in Section 5.

In handheld devices where the Bluetooth and 802.11 radios are collocated, the interference problem becomes more severe due to the coupling and the distance between the radios, while for non-collocated case, this is less severe due to high-attenuation [6]. To mitigate this problem for the collocated technologies, in [6] the authors propose a time-division multiplexing (TDM) solution, where time is shared between the two technologies.

While TDM seems an attractive approach, it does suffer from the "avalanche effect", which greatly reduces the performance of both technologies. To explain the effect, consider the following scenario. Let assume that the network consists of an access point (AP), serving different stations (STAs) among which there is a combo STA (C-STA) that contains 802.11 and Bluetooth technologies collocated, as well as a Bluetooth slave device (see Figure 1, where AP is denoted as AP-STA0, and C-STA is STA1-Master). Note that we will use AP and C-STA throughout the paper, by implying AP-STA0 and STA1-Master.

According to the TDM scheme, the Bluetooth and 802.11 technologies in the C-STA will take turn in accessing the medium, thus transmit/receive operations. However, if AP has traffic to send to the C-STA, after n unsuccessfull transmitted packets it reduces the operational rate (physical data rate) to a lower value. Under this scenario, the time that it will take the same packet to be transmitted over the air will increase as the operational rate decreases. Therefore, the chances of the transmitted packet "colliding" with Bluetooth transmission/reception operation increases. Hence, the operational rate further decreases and the process continues till the AP transmission rate (to the C-STA) reaches the minimum operational rate. This is called the "avalanche effect", where the reduction in the operational rate increases the collision probability between 802.11 and Bluetooth operations and the increase in collision probability further decreases the operational rate. The operational rate during the "avalanche effect" is depicted in Figure 2. To be fair to the authors in [6], the "avalanche effect" is more observable when the network consists of many STAs served by the AP, while in their study, the authors concentrated on a single AP, single C-STA, and a Bluetooth device.

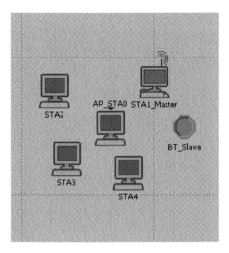

Fig. 1. Network under investigation

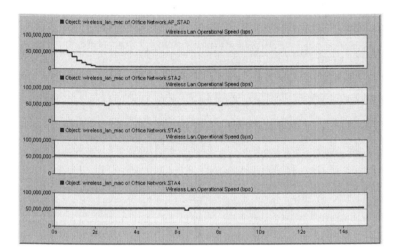

Fig. 2. Rate adaptation in the network under investigation

Next we describe the scenario and the simulation setup for "avalanche effect" investigation.

2   Simulation Setup

To investigate the impact of the "avalanche effect" on the performance of WLAN and Bluetooth networks as well as some of the proposed remedies for avoiding it, we consider the network depicted in Figure 1. In addition, we assume that the maximum data transmission rate in WLAN is 54 Mbps (belonging to 802.11g), while Bluetooth uses synchronous connection oriented (SCO) and asynchronous connection oriented (ACL) logical transports [9]. We also assume that Bluetooth carries voice traffic using HV3 packets, which carries 3.75 msec of speech at 64 kbps. Therefore, an HV3 packet is sent every 6 slots, where each slot consists of a 625 microsec duration [9]. While we could consider other logical transports for Bluetooth, as well as different packets, for illustration purposes, we focus on SCO and HV3 packets, which are the most common ones.

To evaluate the performance of the network, we use OPNET^{TM} simulations. We modified the code to implement rate adaption algorithm, which is based on the number of un-successfull/successfull transmission to decrease/increase the transmission rates. In addition, we enabled request-to-send (RTS) / clear-to-send (CTS) handshake between the AP and the C-STA. Thus, everytime that the AP gains access to the medium and has a data packet to transmit to C-STA, it starts with an RTS/CTS handshake. We also implement periodic/scheduled powersave negotiation between the C-STA and the AP, where the C-STA goes into powersave mode when Bluetooth transmit/receive operation is ongoing, and awakes when Bluetooth transmit/receive operation is off. The last two approaches can be used to avoid the un-necessary rate reductions. For example, when RTS/CTS handhshake is used, the C-STA does not reply to the AP with CTS if the remaining time duration from the end of CTS transmission frame is not sufficient to complete the data packet-ACK communication between the AP and the C-STA. Therefore, the AP assumes that there is a collision and hence, there is no drop in the operational rate. When periodic powersaving approach is used, the AP is aware of the time when C-STA is awake, therefore, data packet is sent only during this time and ensuring that the time required for data packet-ACK is smaller than the time remaining before the C-STA enters the powersave mode.

Next we report results obtained via our network simulations and discuss our findings.

3   Results

When Bluetooth is not present, for a 54 Mbps and saturated traffic load, the throughput is about 27 Mbps [10]. For Bluetooth HV3 traffic, the throughput is 64 Kbps. When both technologies are collocated on the same device, if HV3 traffic is given priority and it is protected, then WLAN throughput is expected to drop by about 33%. This is due to the fact that HV3 traffic occupies two 625 microsec slots for transmit/receive operation every 6 time slots. To better observe the impact of "avalanche effect" in WLAN/Bluetooth coexistence, we consider the network as in Figure 1 and traffic flows as depicted in Table 1. In our simulations we give priority to HV3 traffic and protect its transmission.

Figure 3 shows the performance of Bluetooth under the following:

☐ When rate adaption is not used; i.e., the AP does not decrease/increase the operational rate with the combo STA regardless of whether transmitted packets are successfull or not.

☐ With rate adaptation, where the AP decreases/increases the operational rate if the transmitted packets are un-successfull/successfull.

□ RTS/CTS handshake and rate adaptation, where the AP starts with an RTS/CTS handshake with the C-STA before transmitting and data packet.

□ Periodic powersave with rate adaptation, where the C-STA negotiates a periodic powersave time interval with the AP based on the Bluetooth transmit/receive cycles.

It is clear that rate adaption (RA) results in lower throughput for Bluetooth due to the fact that it increases the time that WLAN packet transmitted from the AP occupies over the air. Since the operational rate decreases and reaches its minimum operational value, the collisions between Bluetooth and WLAN transmission increases; hence, the Bluetooth throughput decreases. When RTS/CTS handshake, the collision probability decreases and Bluetooth performance is even better than that when RA is not used. This can be explained with the fact that RTS/CTS mechanism may not fully utilize the medium; e.g., CTS is not received and all the STAs in the WLAN network have to wait for a CTS timeout before they can start competing for the medium again. Periodic powersave approach results in slightly better Bluetooth performance and could be explained with the fact that better utilization during Bluetooth off period "pushes" the back-off times (for WLAN STAs) in the Bluetooth transmit/receive operations. To

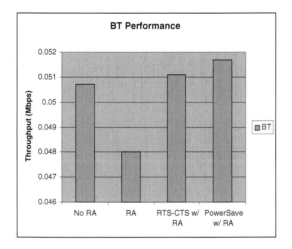

Fig. 3. Bluetooth performance for different approaches

Table 1. Traffic flows for the scenario depicted in Figure 1

Traffic flows	Offered Load	Traffic Type	PER	Max. Delay
AP-STA0->STA1	10 Mbps	Email attach.	N/A	Non-QoS
Blt-Master (STA1)->Blt-Slave	64 Kbps	HV3	5%	2.5 msec
STA2-> AP-STA0	30 Mbps	FTP	N/A	Non-QoS
STA4-> AP-STA0	2 Mbps	Stream. Video	10^{-4}	0.2 sec
STA3-> AP-STA0	0.096 Mbps	VoIP	5%	0.03 sec

achieve better Bluetooth throughput, one can incorporate adaptive frequency hoping (AFH) approach, where Bluetooth hops in the frequencies that do not overlap with WLAN channel. In our study, however, we do not consider AFH.

Figure 4 shows the performance of WLAN for different approaches as mentioned earlier. Again, it is clear that RTS/CTS and periodic powersave approach achieve a throughput of almost 3 times better than that of RA alone.

Figure 5 shows the performance of WLAN QoS flows for different approaches as mentioned earlier. It is clear that the throughput achieved for these flows meet QoS requirements for all approaches.

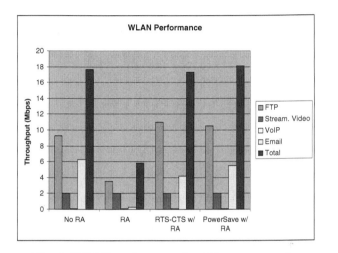

Fig. 4. WLAN performance for different approaches

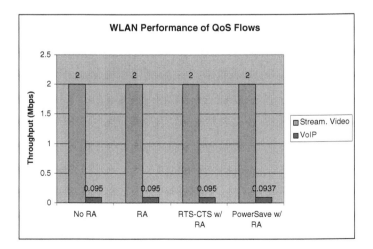

Fig. 5. WLAN QoS flows performance for different approaches

4   Discussions

We presented the "avalanche effect" as well as solutions that can avoid this undesirable effect. It is shown that the performance of the overall network improves when the proposed solutions are used.

It is worth mentioning here that one could consider scenarios that make use of different logical transports for Bluetooth as well as different packet types. Nevertheless, from the proposed solutions, RTS/CTS handshake will be more robust to different scenarios for the simple reason that periodic/scheduled powersave approach is valid if the traffic in Bluetooth technology has a known pattern.

Furthermore, out of band interference between WLAN and Bluetooth technologies were not considered; rather, only if the transmission/reception bands were overlapping, the interference was measured at each of the technologies.

As it is, the use of RTS/CTS and/or periodic/scheduled powersave mechanism would require changes in the AP/STA behavior, since current products do not associate these two approaches to coexistence. The need to have many different wireless technologies integrated in the same device is forcing standards and/or consortiums to design with coexistence issues in mind.

5   Conclusions

In this paper, we presented and discussed issues related to the collocated IEEE 802.11 and Bluetooth technologies coexistence in 2.4 GHz ISM band. Our results show that simple modifications to the AP/STA behavior in WLAN networks can mitigate the "avalanche effect" and improve the performance of both networks.

References

1. Chieaserini, C.F., Rao, R.R.: Performance of IEEE 802.11 WLANs in Bluetooth environment. In: Proceedings of IEEE Wireless Communications and Networking Conference, IL, September 2000, vol. 1, pp. 94–99 (2000)
2. Punnoose, R.J., Tseng, R.S., Stancil, D.: Experimental results for interference between Bluetooth and IEEE 802.11b DSSS systems. In: IEEE Vehicular Technology Conference, Atlantic City, NJ, October 2001, vol. 1, pp. 67–71 (2001)
3. Howitt, I.: WLAN and WPAN Coexistence in UL Band. IEEE Trans. Vehicular Technology 50(4), 1114–1124 (2001)
4. IEEE Std. 802.15.2, Coexistence of wireless personal area networks with other wireless devices operating in unlicensed frequency bands (August 2003)
5. Golmie, N., Chevrollier, N., Rebala, O.: Bluetooth and WLAN Coexistence: Challenges and Solutions. IEEE Wireless Communications Magazine, 22–29 (December 2003)
6. Ophir, L., Bitran, Y., Sherman, I.: WI-FI (IEEE 802.11) and Bluetooth Coexistence: Issues and Solutions. In: IEEE International Symposium on Personal Indoor and Mobile Radio Communications, September 5-8, vol. 2, pp. 847–852 (2004)
7. Friedman, O., Tsfati, Y., Katz, R., Tal, N., Eliezer, O.: Coexistence performance enhancement techniques for DRP based WLAN/WPAN and cellular radios collocated in a mobile device. In: IEEE 24th Convention of Electrical and Electronics Engineers in Israel, November 2006, pp. 82–86 (2006)

8. IEEE 802.11g - Wireless LAN Media Access Control (MAC) and Physical Layer (PHY) Specifications: Further Higher Data Rate Extension in the 2.4 GHz Band, IEEE (2003)
9. Bluetooth SIG, Specification of Bluetooth System, Version 2.0+EDR (November 2004)
10. Xhafa, A.E., Batra, A., Zaks, A.: On the Coexistence of Overlapping BSSs in WLANs. In: IEEE Vehicular Technology Conference (VTC-Fall-2007), September 30-October 3, pp. 189–193 (2007)

Enabling Broadband as Commodity within Access Networks: A QoS Recipe

Enrique Areizaga[1], Andreas Foglar[2], Antonio J. Elizondo[3],
and Frank Geilhardt[4]

[1] Robotiker-tecnalia. E-48170, Zamudio (Bizkaia) Spain
enrique@robotiker.es
http://www.robotiker.com
[2] Infineon Technologies. 81726 Munich, Germany
andreas.foglar@infineon.com
[3] Telefonica I+D. Emilio Vargas, 6, Madrid, Spain
ajea@tid.es
[4] T-Systems. Goslarer Ufer 35, 10589 Berlin, Germany
frank.geilhardt@t-systems.com

Abstract. This paper describes the QoS features that will transform the access networks landscape in order to bring "Broadband" as a commodity while setting up the pillars of the "Future Media Internet". Quality of Experience is obviously key for emerging and future services. Broadcasting services will first need to equal the QoE of their counterparts in the Open-air market (for IP-TV examples would be artifact-free, no picture freezing, fast zapping times) and offer new features often using interactivity (Time-shifted TV, access to more content, 3DTV with feeling of presence). The huge variety of communications alternatives will lead to different requirements per customer, whose needs will also be dependent on parameters like where the connection is made, the time of the day/day of the week/period of the year or even his/her mood. Today's networks, designed for providing just Broadband connectivity, will not be enough to satisfy customer's needs and will necessarily support the introduction of new and innovative services. The Networks of the future should learn from the way the users are communicating, what services they are using, where, when, and how, and adapt accordingly.

Keywords: Broadband, QoS, QoE, access networks, resource managers, SLA.

1 Introduction

Quality of Service (QoS) is a key feature in multi-service multi-provider access networks to provide appropriate quality of user experience for the services offered. Approaches that rely on an end-to-end QoS signaling per individual flow (such as IntServ - Integrated Services) have not been deployed widely because of their complexity. Priority based scheduling of traffic per hop or node (e.g. DiffServ - Differentiated Services) is less complex but works best in an

C. Wang (Ed.): AccessNets, LNICST 6, pp. 146–161, 2009.

over-dimensioned core network. MUSE [1] therefore elaborated a resource management architecture aided by a simple policy control framework to result in a pragmatic and scalable QoS architecture. [3],[4],[5],[7].

2   The Challenge of Introducing QoS in IP Networks

The current best-effort approach used in IP networks implies not differentiating traffic irrespective of what kind of application has generated it or where the source or the destination points are located. In the best-effort approach, the normal practice is to provide more capacity, when possible, so that there is a reasonable quality of experience using the network. However, this practice leads to an increasing loss of control of both the nature of traffic the network is carrying and the relative importance that it has for the users. QoS should be introduced in access networks, so that requirements of traffic of different nature can be fulfilled by the same network without wasting resources. QoS in IP networks is a problem which can, in principle, be solved in a variety of ways. However there is still no consensus on the best way to tackle the QoS problem. Some solutions (e.g. IPoATM - IP e ATM, IntServ, MPLS TE, ...) are rather complex to be cost-effectively deployed in current access and aggregation networks, as they require radical and non-gradual changes both in network equipment and their control and management whereas others (e.g. DiffServ) may seem too simple or insecure to be useful. Part of the problem seems to be in trying to replicate the traditional carrier class quality. Another difficulty is the multi-service nature of IP networks, hence imposing a broad set of different requirements on the network. However, the main reason for not deploying complex QoS oriented architectures in actual networks is the inherent difficulty for the network operator to appropriately configure and manage them, especially when addressing the residential mass market. That is, one of the main reasons for lack of success of previous proposals is that they did not have a clear business orientation.

3   Pragmatism and Simplicity as the Main Design Principles

There is a need for a pragmatic and simple way to provide services with at least some degree of QoS. Pragmatism is needed to design a solution scalable enough to address the residential market and flexible enough to address the corporate one. By focusing on the needs of triple play offerings, it is possible to design a simple and cost-effective way to provide sufficient QoS for the mass market. QoS will be a way to add value to services that are offered by the network operator and thereby differentiate them from similar services offered over the Internet. The proposed solution should have a wider applicability than just triple-play, in order to adapt to the corporate market needs, although it may not meet the requirements of any conceivable service. Furthermore, triple play services demand a high amount of bandwidth that will require big investments from the

Telecom Operators side. These investments need to be financed. One option is to get the funds from the pockets of its users, but there are signs that they are quite reluctant to pay any more money just for plain connectivity services (i.e. Internet access). However, if the operators are able to differentiate their connectivity resources, they can better sell them to connectivity customers no matter if they are service providers, packagers [8], enterprise users or residential users with specific requirements. Therefore, the key issue is to setup a solution where operators are able to segregate their networks in connectivity resources with specific QoS that can be offered on-demand to "connectivity resource" consumers. This business model can lead to different architecture scenarios where the user, the service provider, the packager (service broker) or all of them simultaneously request resources with QoS for certain applications. Being pragmatic, it is also convenient to take into account the current situation of the broadband access networks already deployed as a starting point. Today's DSL broadband access architectures (based on TR-101 architecture) [9] consist of aggregating connectivity for mass-market Broadband Access in which all traffic goes to a single aggregation point, the Broadband Remote Access Server (BRAS). In fact TR-101 slightly extends this model, to allow for a second BRAS or Broadband Network Gateway (BNG), which is specifically included to allow video content to be sourced from a separate location. The QoS control is however centered on the BRAS. Bandwidth control is limited to the downstream direction, and is based on the concept of hierarchical scheduling.

4   End-to-End QoS Solution

Starting point for QoS implementation was the so-called preferred QoS implementation of MUSE phase 1. This solution has been described extensively in [10], so that here only the key features are summarized. Four QoS classes were defined which differentiate by their timing behavior (see figure 2). More precisely, to be compliant with MUSE/PLANETS QoS classes, a node must comply with the respective maximum jitter, packet loss and burst size values listed in Table 1. The QoS solution can be realized over existing ATM access networks, but more conveniently in course of the introduction of IP based access networks. The per-hop behavior of Table 1 can be requested in respective tenders. It is easy to realize in typical IP DSLAM, home gateway and aggregating Ethernet switches.

The novelty of this QoS classes is the specification of discrete jitter values. Other approaches such as DiffServ (RFC2474) only agreed on relative per-hop

Table 1. QoS Class per-hop Behavior

QoS Class	Max. Jitter	Max. Loss rate	Max.burst size
Low latency (LL)	1ms	10^{-11}	200 byte
Real Time (RT)	30ms	10^{-11}	1500 byte
Elastic (EL)	900 ms	10^{-7} (hi part) ≤ 1 (lo part)	9000 byte
Best Effort (BE)	-	≤ 1 (lo part)	-

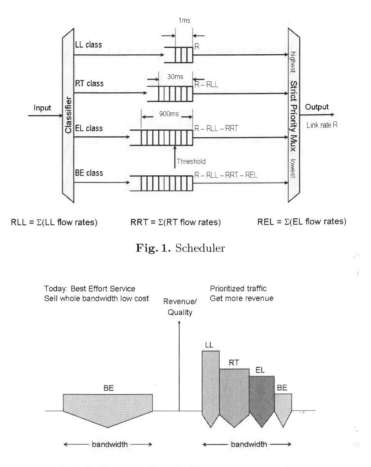

Fig. 1. Scheduler

Fig. 2. Operator benefit/Customer perception

behavior. From the discrete values, end-to-end delay values can be calculated. For this purpose a maximum of 10 nodes has been assumed. As an example, a subscriber with 2Mb/s upstream and 10Mb/s downstream has a maximum delay of about 100ms over 1000km distance RT service, while LL service over 100km has a mean delay of 3ms. These figures show that RT class is well suited for telephony, while the LL class is reserved for very demanding applications such as distributed computing or client-server applications. Another benefit of the discrete jitter values is the possibility to calculate queue sizes for the scheduler shown in Figure 1. In this figure RLL, RRT and REL denote the sum of reserved rates for the respective QoS class. Thanks to the per-flow reservation these rates are known and the minimum size needed to support the jitter values can be calculated. The PLANETS web site [2] lists the queue sizes depending on the load. For example an output port serving a link with 90 % load needs 23.6kB for the LL queue, 177kB for the RT queue and 677kB for the EL queue.

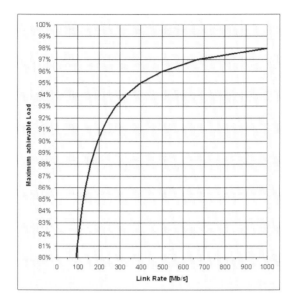

Fig. 3. Maximum Bandwidth Reservation

Queue length calculation assumed statistical arrival of maximum size packets using $M/D/1$ model [12]. In this model queue sizes go to infinity when load approaches 100 %, independent on the rate. The maximum allowed jitter puts an upper bound to the size of the queues, so that the maximum achievable load is limited. This load limit applies to reserved rate only, as it must be guaranteed at any time. Figure 3 gives the maximum rate which can be reserved on a link. The used rate is always up to 100 % due to the low priority part of the EL class and BE traffic which can go beyond the guaranteed rate. In Figure 3 it can be seen that below 100Mb/s link usage rapidly drops to unacceptably low values. For these link rates the number of independent packet sources is too low to allow a statistical treatment. Hence a deterministic approach is followed with worst case assumption that all sources send packets simultaneously. This limits the number of sources, but allows bandwidth reservation up to 100 %. The deterministic approach is used for example for DSL lines. The previous statistical treatment would remain appropriate for Gbps links higher in the Network architecture.

5   Realising QoS in the Access Network

With the introduction of a control plane, today's basic Internet access will be enhanced by on-demand broadband connections with selectable QoS. The new network element to support selectable QoS is the Multi-service Edge router (Border Gateway). It acts like a large firewall. Connection setup is equivalent to the opening of a pinhole. In particular a pinhole is defined by the subscriber's (residential gateway) IP address and a destination UDP port. The Multi-service Edge router is connected to a Multimedia Overlay Network which supports QoS. The Multi-service Edge router receives signaling from the Signaling Proxy, but not the Access Node. Terminating signaling on the Access Node is deprecated by network operators, as it leads to higher costs for the respective SW packages, their maintenance and a lot of control traffic. On the other hand, how to reserve bandwidth in the access network without signaling? Over-provisioning can not be the solution, as the 1st Mile is the most significant bottleneck. The solution chosen has been described by Toelle et al. [12]. It uses permanently configured Service Connections (SC) as transport pipes for application flows between Residential Gateway and Multi-service Edge router or Edge Node. A SC is characterized by QoS class and bandwidth. The bandwidth is reserved over the whole Aggregation Network. Examples for application flows are the voice packet stream of an IP phone or the data packet flows generated by a browser running on a PC. Each subscriber has at least one BE class SC to the Edge Node. It provides the basic Internet access as it is offered today. By definition a BE SC uses the unused bandwidth by the rest of the classes, not requiring bandwidth reservation. Any number of application flows can share a BE SC. In addition the subscriber can have up to three SC to the Multi-service Edge router, one for each class. In the example of Figure 4 two SC with RT and EL class are configured between a Residential Gateway and a Multi-service Edge router. Obviously the guaranteed rates of the flows must fit into the SC bandwidth. In addition, the maximum number of flows sharing a SC is limited by the maximum allowed jitter for the respective QoS class according to the deterministic approach mentioned above. Bandwidth and jitter limit are independent. The smaller of both determines the possible number of flows. The acceptance procedure can be done by the Multi-service Edge router if a subscriber is connected to one Multi-service Edge router only. In case of more than one Multi-service Edge router only the subscriber (i.e. the Residential Gateway) knows about all flows. This option is for further study. The Edge Node is not relevant as it receives BE flows only. Finally, note that the commercial exploitation of SC could be via additional flat rates.

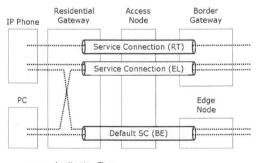

Fig. 4. QoS pipes

6 Realising QoS in the First Mile

In order to efficiently manage the available resources and fully utilize the DSL link capacity, a Copper Plant Manager (CPM) is needed [13]. The CPM tool processes key standardized DSL performance parameters such as Attainable Rate, Actual Rate, Actual Delay, Errored Seconds, and Unavailable Seconds. These parameters are not only monitored, but also statistically processed to support key performance indicators to be interpreted in an appropriate manner to inform the system about actual and/or average behavior of the lines, trends in performance parameters and live changes due to unexpected situations which could lead to service degradation. For example, Attainable Rate when compared with Actual Rate shows the headroom for rate increase in case of more demanding services while Actual Delay, Errored Seconds and Unavailable Seconds determine to a great extent the Quality-of-Service and the Quality-of-Experience (perceived quality by the end user of a given service) that can be expected in a given DSL link. All these parameters are taken into account by the CPM tool. In this way, the Network Management System (NMS) can use this information when determining the policies to enforce for a given service in order to fulfill the Service Level Specifications (SLS) or Service Level Objectives (SLO) defining the required QoS parameters on system level (node, link level).

The SLS is part of the service level agreement (SLA) that represents a formal negotiated agreement between the end-user and service/content providers on a common understanding of the service including service quality, priorities, responsibilities, and guarantee. The SLS, as technical interpretation of the SLA, specifies the end-to-end requirements on the network (nodes, links) to transport the service with the negotiated QoS. The most relevant SLS parameters for typical triple-play services via DSL are listed in Table 2. The resource manager within the NMS plays a central role in mapping the SLS into policies that break

Table 2. Most relevant SLS parameters for Triple Play services QoS and performance monitoring

Service	Parameter	Description
Best-Effort Internet	Peak Info. Rate (PIR)	No guaranteed rate, the rate is restricted with PIR
	Peak Burst Size (PBS)	Maximum number bits that can be transported at PIR
Guaranteed Data Serv.	Committed Info. Rate (CIR)	Guaranteed mean rate, mostly in combination with PIR/PBS maximum restrictions
	Committed Burst Size (CBS)	Maximum number of bits that can be transported guaranteed at CIR
Voice Serv.	Maximum Delay (MD)	Maximum delay caused by processing delay, shaping, queuing
	Delay Variation (DV), jitter	Packet delay variation, filling level in queues
Video Serv.	Packet drop rate (PDR)	Rate of lost packets on the link

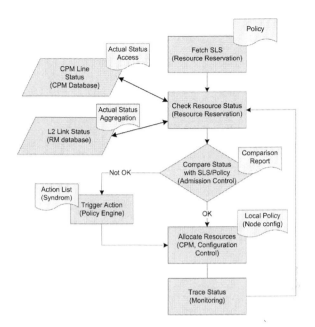

Fig. 5. Simplified CPM - NMS interaction workflow

down to local policies on the network nodes in different parts of the end-to-end service delivery workflow, as described in Figure 5.

7 Validation

The concept has been successfully verified in a lab trial at T-Systems in Berlin by means of a demonstrator (see Figure 6). This demonstrator implements the entire Multi-service Edge router data plane functionality and part of the control plane using prototypes based on Network Processor subsystems. At call setup the subsystem automatically initiates ARP requests at both aggregation network side and multimedia overlay network side, supporting up to 512 phone calls. For QoS measurements Triple Play scenarios have been set up with video streaming, phone calls and packet generators for background traffic. Zero packet loss has been proven for guaranteed traffic, even in the presence of abundant best effort traffic, as expected.

The concepts explained in previous sections as well as the Service Connnec-tions (SC) shown in Figure 4 were validated. This PlaNets demonstrator con-vered the Home Network and Access Aggregation Network including the First Mile. The First Mile was based on VDSL2 links over telco copper cable. The demonstrator supports IPv4 as well as IPv6. Four Home Networks have been re-alised in Berlin with typical terminal equipment (e.g. TVs, PCs, videophones). Two IPv6 Home Networks had access to the 'Public Network' via Home Gateway provided by partner Stollmann. In addition two IPv4 Home Networks were con-nected to the VDSL2 modems via Ethernet CPE switch. The prototype Access

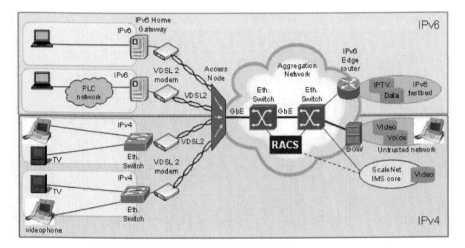

Fig. 6. Demonstrator Network

Node from Robotiker provided 4 VDSL2 lines and two electrical Gigabit Ethernet uplinks. It supported IP forwarding as defined in MUSE [1] and Layer-2 switching as well. The Access Node is connected to the Linux PC based Access Aggregation Network that consists of two aggregation layers. Several Edge Nodes are connected to the Aggregation Network. An IPv6 Edge Router offers access to IPv6 testbed providing IPv6 based Internet Access and video streaming. A cooperation with the German national project ScaleNet (Fixed, Mobile and Wireless IP-optimised convergent Next Generation Access Networks) provides an IMS overlay that enables an IMS controlled RACS implementation. The Border Gateway from Alcatel-Lucent provides conversational services with SIP controlled mechanisms and a trusted boundary to the packet network with NA(P)T traversal support for improved security.

Network Quality testing
Traditional performance tests focus on a per-port basis, addressing the evaluation of the performance of each port such as the maximum throughput, the packet loss and the average latency of the network device. To evaluate the QoS functionality some additional aspects must be considered. Flow-based measuring: Usually different applications are multiplexed onto a single device port, combining different QoS traffic classes. In order to evaluate the QoS feasibility of a network the tests had to address individual traffic flows. A flow-based measuring is the foundation of the QoS testing. The measuring equipment had to be able to provide flow-based measuring procedures.

QoS can be characterized by a set of network performance metrics including:

- End-to-End Throughput
- End-to-End Delay
- Frame Loss rate
- Delay variation or jitter

- Max. burst size
- Packet sequence the ability of the network to deliver packets in the proper sequence
- Service availability the ability to gain access to the network
- Connection availability the ability of the network to complete the required connections (i.e., TCP) with the requested performance characteristics

Perceived QoS testing
The perceived QoS is the quality of a service or application as experienced by an end-user. Recently it has become fashionable to use the term Quality of Experience (QoE) to denote perceived QoS.

Network Quality Measurement
Objective: Measuring the QoS handling of the network for IP flows with different priority in downstream direction.

Test set-up (see Figure 7)

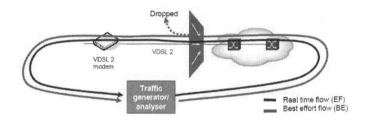

Fig. 7. Test setup for measuring downstream network quality

Procedure:

- Generate two IP flows with different priority (Real time and Best Effort)
  - Set-up a Layer-3 (IP) end-to-end Real time QoS class stream (downstream) using a Traffic Generator
  - Set-up an additional Best Effort traffic stream that fills the whole capacity of the link.
- Increase the traffic load (e.g. from 10 % to 100 % of the link capacity in steps of 10 %)
- Analyze end-to-end Throughput, end-to-end delay, end-to-end Packet loss rate, end-to- end Jitter, and packet sequence of the Real time stream with and without congestion situation using a Traffic Analyzer

Figure 8 and 9 show the QoS handling of the network for two IP flows with different priorities (Real time and Best Effort). The chart on the left-hand side shows the frame loss ratio in case of disabled QoS mechanism. The chart on the right-hand side shows the behaviour with enabled QoS mechanisms in downstream direction. Both charts show a congestion situation for a traffic load of 60 Mbps (maximum VDSL throughput). But with enabled QoS only the frames of the Best Effort flow are dropped and the frames of the Real Time flow are

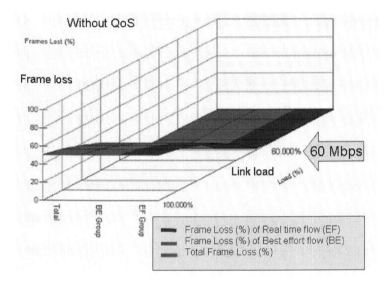

Fig. 8. Measuring the QoS handling of the network (without QoS)

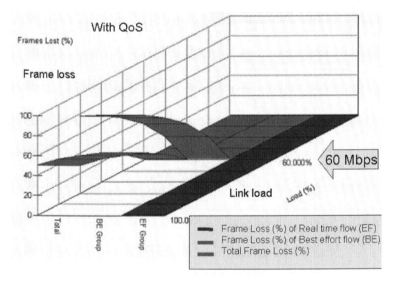

Fig. 9. Measuring the QoS handling of the network (with QoS)

forwarded with priority. Figure 10 shows the average Latency (μs) for Real Time and Best Effort flows with a frame size of 512 Bytes in case of congestion. 60 % link load is equivalent to 60 Mbps.

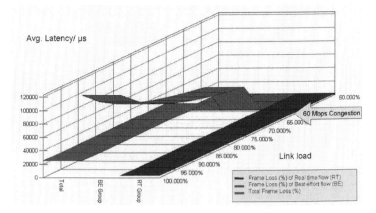

Fig. 10. Avg. Latency (μs) for Real time and Best Effort flows in case of congestion

The following table (Figure 11) shows the average Latency (ms) for Real Time and Best Effort flows with a frame size of 512 Bytes in case of congestion.

Link load in % of 100 Mbps	55 %	60 %	65 %	70 %	75 %	80 %	85 %	90 %	95 %
Best effort (ms)	1.68	1.74	48.32	53.26	58.73	65.49	74.00	85.03	100.44
Real tilme (ms)	1.62	1.67	2.34	2.35	2.42	2.50	2.53	2.53	2.53

Fig. 11. Average Latency (ms) for Real Time and Best Effort flows with a frame size of 512 Bytes in case of congestion

Perceived Voice quality end-to-end testing
The aim of the test described in this section was to determine the perceived QoS of a VoIP call between a SIDE A and a SIDE B including the end-to-end test network as depicted in Figure 12.

Procedure: In order to determine the conversational quality of a voice link a Voice Quality Tester was used. The test suite consisted of the following four steps:

1. One-way listening, speech quality in both directions with inside video-signal-transmission (video-telephony switched on) Measurement conditions
   – VQT Release 4.300
   – Voice Phone Adapter

- Method PESQ
- 10 samples
- Direction A → B and B → A
- IP VideoPhone Innomedia

2. One-way listening, speech quality in both directions without inside video-signal-transmission (video-telephony switched off) Measurement conditions are the same as for step 1.
3. One-way interaction, delay in both directions with inside video-signal-transmission (video-telephony switched on)
4. One-way interaction, delay in both directions without inside video-signal-transmission (video-telephony switched off)

In addition a traffic generator was used to generate background traffic in the network for a more realistic scenario.

The MOS-LQ (Mean Opinion Score-Listening Quality) -values between 3,8 and 4,0 represent a good voice-quality. The directional difference of the values is caused by the different videophones. In both directions the measured delay time does not influence the inter activity of the conversation. The delay is marginal

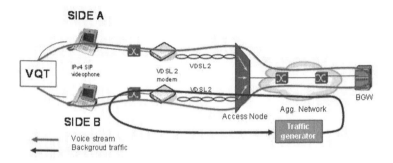

Fig. 12. Test set-up to determine the perceived QoS of a VoIP call

Direction	MOS-LQ (Average)	
	with video-signal	without video-signal
A -> B	3,82	3,80
B -> A	4,03	4,04

Direction	Delay			
	with video-signal		without video-signal	
	minimum delay	maximum delay	minimum delay	maximum delay
A -> B	130 ms	132 ms	121 ms	122 ms
B -> A	101 ms	105 ms	92 ms	93 ms

Fig. 13. Perceived Voice quality end-to-end testing

influenced by the video signal transmission. But the difference is small compared to the whole delay (< 10 ms). The video signal does not influence the voice-quality.

Perceived QoS for IPv6 web browsing

The aim of the test described in this section was to determine the perceived QoS of a web browsing session. Procedure: Determine the WEB _MOS as described in [6]. The test starts by starting the browser on an IPv6 PC and then typing a URL. After this URL is typed and the "enter" button or "go" button is pressed, two stopwatches are started: the first stopwatch measures T1 and the second measures T2. The latter time can be related to the text "done" appearing on the status bar of the browser. If there is interactivity with the web page, the same is done for the second page, measuring T3 and T4. In the test the second page is obtained by clicking a link on the webpage which was loaded before. This procedure is repeated ten times to be able to deal with variations in these times due to variability in network behaviour.

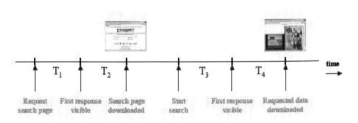

Fig. 14. Timing of a webpage downloading

The next step is to calculate the average values of T1...T4 which will be denoted as $\overline{T1}...\overline{T4}$. Then, the weighted session time (WST) needs to be determined, which is defined in equation 1

$$WST = 0.47 * \overline{T1} + 0.60 * \overline{T2} + 0.71 * \overline{T3} + 2.22 * \overline{T4} \qquad (1)$$

Finally the perceived QoS for the web browsing session is calculated:

$$WEB\_MOS = 4.38 - 1.30 * ln(WST) \qquad (2)$$

Results: The measurement method using a stop watch is quite difficult to handle because of all the short times below 800ms. It was decided to use the network protocol analyzer "Ethereal" to measure the different times described above. What means that the time between receiving an http packet and displaying the content on the monitor is not considered, leading to better results for MOS values than using the stop watch method. T1 is the time between the first "GET" of the client PC and the first received http packet with content from the server. T2 is the remaining time until the last http packet with content from the server is

160   E. Areizaga et al.

Table 3. Definition of MOS scale, based on Opinion Scores

MOS	Quality	Impairment
5	Excellent	Imperceptible
4	Good	Perceptable, not annoying
3	Fair	Slightly annoying
2	Poor	Annoying
1	Bad	Very annoying

web page	T1 (s)	T2 (s)	T3 (s)	T4 (s)	WST	WEB_MOS
www.ripe.net	0.0477	0.7918	0.0688	0.5461	1.7587	**3.65**
www.deepspace6.net	0.0981	0.5446	0.0958	0.47	1.4843	**3.87**

Fig. 15. WEB _MOS

received. For T3 and T4 this measurement was repeated after clicking a link on the originally page. The test was carried out with two different web pages.

For the page "www.deepspace6.net" the header icon was requested and received after 2s. This leaded to a $\overline{T2}$ value of around 2.5s and thus to a WEB _MOS of only 3.1. In the table above an adjusted value is used.

Furthermore some additional details according to the test setup:

– Client PC with MS Windows Vista Home Edition; Intel Core 2 Duo E6400 @2.13GHz; 2048 MB RAM
– Cookies and browser cache deleted before each test step
– Each test step starts from an empty page

The subjective QoE of web browsing is pretty good for the PlaNetS [2] network. The objective measurement according to the test method described above results in nearly good quality for the tested web pages. For the entire test case "QoS for web browsing" it is important to have in mind that a lot of different parameters have an impact on the objective measurement (especially PC and web server performance). The WEB _MOS value can strongly differ between different web pages.

8 Conclusion

The QoS concept presented in this paper is an innovative pragmatic and scalable QoS solution by a resource management system guarded by a flexible Policy Control Framework. With low implementation effort, fully traffic engineered network resources can be guaranteed on demand and real-time on a call-by-call basis. QoS together with QoE will be the "enablers" of the multi-provider multi-service concept within the Next Generation Networks (NGN) Access Network architecture. The implementation work presented in this paper shows a validated solution to achieve quality-based multimedia delivery over DSL broadband access networks.

Acknowledgment

The authors would like to acknowledge the contributions from all the Infineon, T-System, Telefonica, Ericsson, Lund University and Robotiker-tecnalia employees whose efforts made, directly or indirectly, the project possible. We acknowledge the financial support received from the European Commission IST 6th Framework and from the National Public Authorities , through the IST - MUSE and the Eureka - Medea+ PLANETS projects respectively, which partially enabled this work.

References

1. FP6 project MUSE (Multi Service Access Everywhere), http://www.ist-muse.eu
2. Eureka Medea+ project PLANETS (Platforms for Networked Service delivery), http://www.medea-planets.eu/QoSsolution.php
3. MUSE Deliverable D A2.2Network Architecture and Functional Specifications for the Multi-Service Access and Edge (January 2005), http://www.ist-muse.eu
4. MUSE Deliverable D A2.4 Network Architecture and Functional Specification for the Multi-Provider Access and Edge (December 2005), http://www.ist-muse.eu
5. MUSE Deliverable D TF1.2 Overview of QoS Principles in Access Networks (January 2005), http://www.ist-muse.eu
6. MUSE Deliverable D TF4.4 Test Suite, for Full-Service End-to-End Analysis of Access Solutions (July 2007), http://www.ist-muse.eu
7. MUSE Deliverable D TF1.6 Access Network Architecture III (November 2006), http://www.ist-muse.eu
8. MUSE White Paper MUSE Business Model in BB Access (April 2007), http://www.ist-muse.eu
9. Technical Report DSL Forum TR-101 Migration to Ethernet Based DSL Aggregation (April 2006)
10. Foglar, A.: A QoS solution exploiting the MUSE QoS concept. In: Proceedings of the 11th European Conference on Networks and Optical Communications NOC 2006, Berlin, Germany, pp. 223–230 (July 2006) ISBN: 3-923613-40
11. Kleinrock, L.: Queuing Systems, vol. 1. John Wiley and Sons, Chichester (1975)
12. Toelle, D., Areizaga, E., Sauer, C., Liss, C., Banniza, T., Jacob, E., Geilhardt, F.: NGN Platforms for Networked Service Delivery. In: Toelle, D., Areizaga, E., Sauer, C., Liss, C., Banniza, T., Jacob, E., Geilhardt, F. (eds.) Proceedings of IEEE Broadband Converged Networks (BCN 2007), Munich, Germany (May 2007)
13. Pinilla, I., Areizaga, E., Rius i Riu, J., Berg, M., Trojer, E., Olsson, J.: Quality multimedia distribution through resource management and performance monitoring over DSL networks. In: Proceedings of IEEE International Symposium on Broadband Multimedia Systems and Broadcasting, Las Vegas, USA, March-April (2008)

A Simulator of Periodically Switching Channels for Power Line Communications

Taro Hayasaki, Daisuke Umehara, Satoshi Denno, and Masahiro Morikura

Graduate School of Informatics, Kyoto University
Yoshida-honmachi Sakyo-ku, Kyoto 606-8501, Japan
Tel.: +81–75–753–5960; Fax: +81–75–753–5349
{taro,umehara,denno,morikura}@imc.cce.i.kyoto-u.ac.jp

Abstract. An indoor power line is one of the most attractive media for in-home networks. However, there are many technical problems for achieving in-home power line communication (PLC) with high rate and high reliability. One of such problem is the degradation in the performance of the in-home PLC caused by periodically time-varying channel responses, particularly when connecting the switching power supply equipment. We present a measurement method for power line channel responses and reveal the switching of the channel responses synchronized with power-frequency voltage when connecting switching power supply equipment in sending or receiving outlets. In this paper, we term them periodically switching channel responses. The performance of PLC adapters is seriously affected by the periodically switching channel responses. Therefore, we provide a modeling of the periodically switching channel responses by using finite impulse response (FIR) filters with a shared channel memory and construct a simulator for in-home power line channels including the periodically switching channel responses in order to evaluate the various communication systems through the power line. We present the validity of the proposed simulator through the performance evaluation of OFDM/64QAM over periodically switching channels with additive white Gaussian noise. Furthermore, we evaluate the influence of the periodically switching channel responses on the communication quality of a time-invariant modulation scheme by using the proposed simulator.

Keywords: power line communication, periodically switching channel response, switching power supply, OFDM, simulator.

1 Introduction

An indoor power line is a promising communication medium for constructing in-home networks. In particular, the broadband in-home power line communication (PLC) is receiving increasing attention lately. There are a large number of power outlets for supplying electrical power in any room. Therefore, new wiring for constructing an in-home PLC network is not required, and we can immediately access the PLC network by plugging them into power outlets.

However, users might experience unexpected troubles while communicating with one another in the house by using the indoor power line. Such troubles would be caused

C. Wang (Ed.): AccessNets, LNICST 6, pp. 162–175, 2009.

by the significant signal attenuation through power distribution boards, colored and impulsive noises generated from electrical appliances, the impedance mismatching due to the absence of electrical termination across the frequency band for in-home PLC, and the time-varying channel responses synchronized to twice the electrical power frequency. The technical problems encountered in in-home PLC have been reported in several studies papers: the multipath effect caused by impedance mismatching [1, 2], cyclostationary and impulsive noises [2, 3, 4, 5], and periodically time-varying channel response [6, 7].

Almost all in-home broadband PLC systems make use of the orthogonal frequency division multiplexing (OFDM) since OFDM systems can establish coexistence with the existing radio communication systems via subcarrier masking. Besides, the cyclic prefix of the OFDM could sufficiently mitigate the frequency selective effect caused by the multipath effect since the delay spreads for in-home PLC would not exceeds the length of the cyclic prefix.

Katayama et al. reported the cyclostationary noise that is synchronized to twice the electrical power frequency [3]. Further, Cañete et al. showed the periodically time-varying channel response that is synchronized to twice the electrical power frequency [7], and Sancha et al. presented a channel simulator that could emulate time fluctuations in channel response [6]. Katar et al. asserted that the cyclostationary noise would have a much greater impact on the performance of in-home PLC systems than on the periodically time-varying channel response, and proposed an optimal length of MAC frame and a countermeasure against the beacon loss for cyclo stationary noise in in-home PLC [8, 9].

However, we observed more intensive time fluctuation in the channel responses than in cyclostationary noise when connecting switching power supply equipment [10]. At this time, two or more channel responses switch during one half of a power cycle. In this paper, we term them periodically switching channel responses. These responses severely impair the performance of PLC adapters [10]. Therefore, countermeasures against these periodically switching channel responses are required constructing an in-home PLC network.

In this study, we show a measurement method for power line channel responses and present the periodically switching channel responses when connecting some switching power supply equipment. We provide a modeling of the periodically switching channel responses using finite impulse response (FIR) filters with a shared channel memory and construct a simulator that can emulate the periodically switching channel responses for in-home power line channels. Furthermore, we present the validity of the proposed simulator by evaluating the performance of OFDM/64QAM over the periodically switching channels with additive white Gaussian noise. In addition, by using the proposed simulator we evaluate the influence of the periodically switching channel responses on the communication quality of a time-invariant modulation scheme by using the proposed simulator.

The remaining part of the paper is organized as follows. Section 2 presents a measurement method for power line channel responses and analyzes the measurements by a time-frequency analysis. Section 3 shows a modeling of the periodically switching channel responses and estimates the parameters for the description of a power line channel. Section 4 proposes a simulator for in-home power line channels that can emulate the periodically channel responses and show the validity of the proposed simulator. Section 5 investigates the influence of the periodically switching channel responses to the communication quality by using the proposed simulator. Section 6 presents the conclusion of this study.

2 Measurement of Periodically Switching Channel

This section describes a method for obtaining time-varying channel frequency responses by a time-frequency analysis. Figure 1 illustrates the measurement system for time-varying channels synchronized with a commercial power supply.

In this study, we measure the fundamental power line topology with a single branch. Electrical power is supplied to this power line through a noise cut transformer. A cellphone charger is connected to the receiving outlet, and thereby, power-line channels become time-varying synchronized with the commercial power supply when the cell phone is charged.

We design a multicarrier signal that has a flat power spectrum density in the frequency range from 2 to 30 MHz and low peak-to-average power ratio (PAPR). This signal is based on the HomePlug AV specification [11], where its sampling frequency F_s is 75 MS/s, sampling time $T_s = 1/F_s$ is 13.3 ns, and fast Fourier transform (FFT) size N is 3072. The subcarriers are numbered in order from lowest frequency to highest frequency. The number of subcarriers corresponding to 2 MHz is represented as $k_f(= 82)$, and those corresponding to 30 MHz as $k_e(= 1228)$. The total number of subcarriers $N_s = k_e - k_f + 1$ is 1147. The Z-transform of this signal is given by

$$P(z) = \sum_{i=0}^{N-1} p_i z^{-i}, \tag{1}$$

$$p_i = \mathrm{Re}\left[\sqrt{\frac{2EZ_0}{N_s}} \sum_{k=k_f}^{k_e} \exp\left(\mathrm{j}\left(2\pi\frac{ki}{N} + \theta_k\right)\right)\right], \tag{2}$$

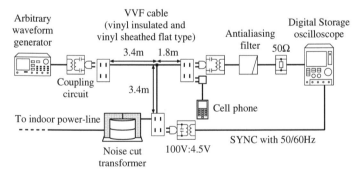

Fig. 1. A measurement system for time-varying channels synchronized with commercial power supply

where E is the energy of this signal, and Z_0 is the impedance of the arbitrary waveform generator (AWG). In order to overcome the effect of quantization noise, we optimize the phase θ_k of each subcarrier to minimize the variance of instantaneous power

$$\frac{1}{N} \sum_{i=0}^{N-1} \left(p_i^2 - \frac{1}{N} \sum_{j=0}^{N-1} p_j^2 \right)^2. \tag{3}$$

The designed signal is continuously transmitted from the AWG to the power line through a coupling circuit. The transmitted signal is received by a digital storage oscilloscope from the power line through the coupling circuit and an anti-aliasing filter. The digital oscilloscope is triggered by an attenuated power-frequency voltage. The coupling circuit comprises a high-pass filter and a balun for eliminating the effect of commercial power supply on the experimental equipment, and the anti-aliasing filter is a low-pass filter for removing aliasing. The digital oscilloscope records the digitized signal comprising a direct wave and some delayed waves because the power line has only one branch and some impedance-mismatched terminals.

The Z-transform of the transmitted signal is given by

$$S(z) = \sum_{\ell=0}^{\infty} \sum_{i=0}^{N-1} p_i z^{-i-N\ell} = \sum_{\ell=0}^{\infty} P(z) z^{-N\ell}, \tag{4}$$

and the Z-transform of the received signal is given by

$$R(z) = \sum_{\ell=0}^{\infty} H_\ell(z) P(z) z^{-N\ell} + N(z), \tag{5}$$

$$H_\ell(z) = \sum_{j=0}^{D-1} h_{\ell,j} z^{-j}, \tag{6}$$

where $H_\ell(z)$ represents the impulse response for the ℓ-th signal $P(z)$, $N(z)$ indicates the additive power line noise, and DT_s represents the maximum multipath delay (we assume $D < N$). The noise $N(z)$ can be approximated to zero because we exploit the noise cut transformer. The ℓ-th received signal $R_\ell(z)$ is given by

$$R_\ell(z) = \sum_{m=N}^{N+D-2} \sum_{j=m-N+1}^{D-1} h_{\ell-1,j} p_{m-j} z^{N-m} + \sum_{m=0}^{N-1} \sum_{j=0}^{D-1} h_{\ell,j} p_{m-j} z^{-m}. \tag{7}$$

Further, when $H_\ell(z)$ is equal to $H_{\ell-1}(z)$, $R_\ell(z)$ is expressed as

$$\begin{aligned} R_\ell(z) &= \sum_{m=0}^{D-2} \sum_{j=m+1}^{D-1} h_{\ell,j} p_{m+N-j} z^{-m} + \sum_{m=0}^{N-1} \sum_{j=0}^{D-1} h_{\ell,j} p_{m-j} z^{-m} \\ &= \sum_{m=0}^{N+D-2} \sum_{j=0}^{D-1} h_{\ell,j} p_{m-j} z^{-m} = H_\ell(z) P(z), \end{aligned} \tag{8}$$

where $z^{-m} \equiv z^{-m-iN}$ for any integers m and i. Therefore, the frequency response is given by

$$H(t,f)|_{t=\ell T} = H_\ell\left(\exp\left(j\frac{2\pi f}{F_s}\right)\right) = \frac{R_\ell\left(\exp\left(j\frac{2\pi f}{F_s}\right)\right)}{P\left(\exp\left(j\frac{2\pi f}{F_s}\right)\right)}, \tag{9}$$

where T is the duration of the designed multicarrier signal, and it is equal to NT_s.

Figure 2 illustrates the time-frequency analysis of the power line channel during two power cycles. The origin at the horizontal axis indicates an increasing in the

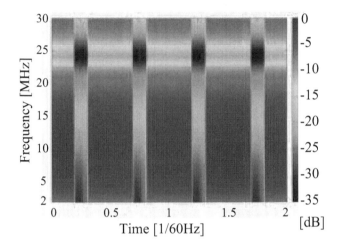

Fig. 2. Periodically switching channel responses

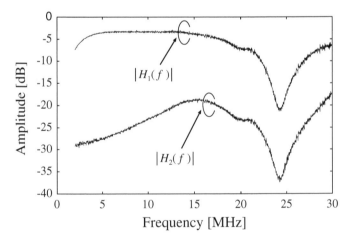

Fig. 3. Amplitude spectra of two channel responses

zero-crossover point of the commercial power supply. This figure shows that while charging a cell phone, the power line channel could be classified into almost two states and the duration of the state with higher loss is related to the timing when the instantaneous voltage of power supply comes near the peak. Let us indicate the state with lower loss as state 1 and that with higher loss as state 2, and their corresponding frequency responses as $H_1(f)$ and $H_2(f)$, respectively. Figure 3 illustrates the amplitude spectra of the channel responses of the two states. Although both the channel responses seem to be correlated, they are actually different, and hence, modeling of the responses required.

3 Modeling of Periodically Switching Channel

Indoor power line channels will be connected to several electrical appliances. Hence, the PLC signals reflect on the branches and terminals. As a result, the power line channels become multipath. The modeling of static channel responses for the power line channels is based on the following multipath model [1]

$$H(f) = \sum_{i=0}^{L-1} g_i e^{-(a_0 + a_1 f^k)d_i} e^{-j2\pi f(\tau_i - \tau_0)}, \tag{10}$$

with

$$\tau_i = \frac{d_i \sqrt{\varepsilon_r}}{c} = \frac{d_i}{v_p}, \tag{11}$$

where the parameters in the expressions are listed in Table 1.

Table 1. Parameters of the frequency response

L	total number of the dominant paths
g_i	weighting factor for i-th path
a_0	attenuation constant at constant term (> 0)
a_1	attenuation constant at term of f^k (> 0)
k	exponent of the attenuation factor (between 0.2 and 1)
τ_i	delay of i-th path $(\tau_0 < \tau_1 < \cdots < \tau_{L-1})$
d_i	length of i-th path
ε_r	dielectric constant
c	speed of light in vacuum $(3.0 \times 10^8 \mathrm{m/s})$
v_p	phase velocity

However, this model does not include the short-term variation of the channel responses. Considering the variation caused by the two channel states, the frequency response can be represented as

$$H(t, f) = \begin{cases} H_1(f), & \text{if } |v_{AC}(t)| \leq V_{th}, \\ H_2(f), & \text{if } |v_{AC}(t)| > V_{th}, \end{cases} \tag{12}$$

for power supply voltage $v_{AC}(t)$, where V_{th} represents the threshold of instantaneous voltage switching from one state to another state.

We assume that the frequency responses $H_1(f)$ and $H_2(f)$ can be represented by the above mentioned model. For $m = 0$ and 1, let us represent $H_m(f)$ as

$$H_m(f) = \sum_{i=0}^{L-1} g_i^{(m)} e^{-(a_0^{(m)} + a_1^{(m)} f^{k^{(m)}})} e^{-j2\pi f(\tau_i^{(m)} - \tau_0^{(m)})} . \qquad (13)$$

Let $h_m(t)$ represent the impulse response of the frequency response $H_m(f)$, and $h_j^{(m)} = h_m(jT_s)$ for $j = 0, 1, \cdots, D-1$. The Z-transform of $h_m(t)$ is denoted by $H_m(z)$, and we can obtain

$$H_m(z) \Big|_{z=\exp(j\frac{2\pi f}{F_s})} = H_m(f). \qquad (14)$$

We estimate the model parameters of $H_m(z)$, which are shown in Table 1, from the measurement data for a given number of paths L by a quasi-Newton method. Let us consider the measurement value $H_m(kF_s/N)$ at frequency kF_s/N for $k_f \le k < k_e$. We can obtain the estimated frequency response $\hat{H}_m(f)$ to minimize the mean square error (MSE)

$$\sum_{k=k_f}^{k_e} \left| \hat{H}_m\left(\frac{kF_s}{N}\right) - H_m\left(\frac{kF_s}{N}\right) \right|^2 . \qquad (15)$$

We are required to select an approximate number of paths L. If L is large, the estimated frequency response will sufficiently fit the exact frequency response, however, a long computational time is consumed. On the other hand, if L is small, the approximation of the estimated frequency response to the exact frequency response will lack precision. Figure 4 illustrates the MSE between the estimated and measured frequency responses for a given number of paths.

From Fig. 4, we assign the number of paths as 8. Let $\hat{H}_m(f)$ be the frequency response obtained by fitting the model parameters to the measured frequency response $H_m(f)$, and $\hat{H}(t, f)$ be the estimated periodically switching channel responses consisting of $\hat{H}_1(f), \hat{H}_2(f)$, and V_{th}.

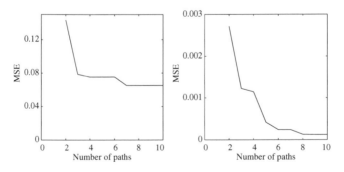

Fig. 4. MSE of the estimated frequency response for a given number of paths

4 Channel Simulator

It is effective to construct a channel simulator that emulates the power line channel for developing the PLC systems. Therefore, we propose a simulator using the parameters estimated in Section 3 and two FIR filters with shared channel memory. The two FIR filters are switched according to V_{th}. Figure 5 shows the block diagram of the simulator for periodically switching channels.

To evaluate the validity of this simulator, we first compare the amplitude and the phase of $\hat{H}_m(f)$ of the simulator with those of $H_m(f)$.

Figures 6 and 7 illustrate the amplitude and phase of $H_m(f)$ and $\hat{H}_m(f)$, and Table 2 shows the model parameters for $\hat{H}_1(f)$ and $\hat{H}_2(f)$. These figures show that the amplitude of $\hat{H}_m(f)$ is sufficiently approximated to that of $H_m(f)$, whereas the phase

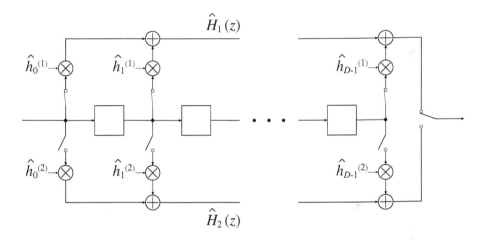

Fig. 5. The block diagram of the simulator for periodically switching channels

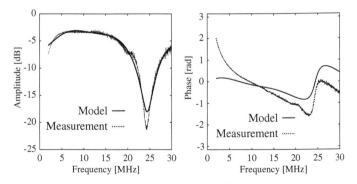

Fig. 6. The spectra of the estimated frequency response $\hat{H}_1(f)$ and the measured frequency response $H_1(f)$

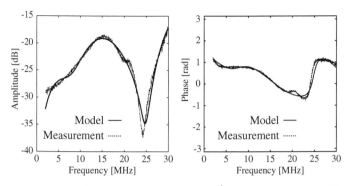

Fig. 7. The spectra of the estimated frequency response $\hat{H}_2(f)$ and the measured frequency response $H_2(f)$

Table 2. Model parameters for the estimated frequency responses $\hat{H}_1(f)$ and $\hat{H}_2(f)$

	$\hat{H}_1(f)$	$\hat{H}_2(f)$
L	8	8
g_i	1.00, 0.277, −0.0712, −1.00 −0.0792, 0.561, −0.784, 0	0.0660, −0.0341, 0.266, −0.328 0.434, −0.401, 0.156, −0.123
a_0	4.33×10^{-13}	5.20×10^{-11}
a_1	4.60×10^{-3}	1.59×10^{-7}
k	0.205	0.599
d_i	5.20, 8.80, 12.0, 12.4, 15.6, 16.0, 18.8, 19.2	
v_p	1.73×10^8	1.73×10^8

of $\hat{H}_m(f)$ may not be sufficiently approximated to that of $H_m(f)$. Therefore it is necessary to consider the effect on the communication system by using the difference between the phase of $\hat{H}_m(f)$ and $H_m(f)$.

We evaluate the simulator by using a typical modulation scheme for the in-home PLC. We utilize the OFDM and the quadrature amplitude modulation (QAM) as a subcarrier modulation, which is adopted in HomePlug AV [11] and UPA [12]. Figure 8 illustrates the block diagram of the in-home PLC system, and Table 3 lists the simulation parameters.

Table 3. Simulation parameters

sampling frequency	75 MHz
number of FFT points	3072
number of subcarriers	1147 (2–30 MHz)
number of cyclic prefix	417
subcarrier modulation	4, 16, 64QAM
average noise power	−42.6 dBm

The transfer function shown in Fig. 8 indicates the measured periodically switching channel response $H(t, f)$ or the estimated periodically switching channel response $\hat{H}(t, f)$. We compare the bit error rate (BER) of the measured channel response $H(t, f)$ with that of the estimated channel response $\hat{H}(t, f)$. In the simulation, a random binary sequence is mapped to the QAM symbol sequence. The QAM symbol sequence is modulated by OFDM. The resultant OFDM/QAM signal is inputted to the periodically switching channels. The change the frequency response is obtained by switching the two frequency responses when measuring the frequency response changes. The white Gaussian noise is added to the signal outputted from the channel, and the received signal is equalized with respect to each subcarrier and demodulated. In general, the evaluation of modulation schemes would be done by BER versus received signal-to-noise ratio (SNR). However, BER versus received SNR is not suitable for the evaluation of

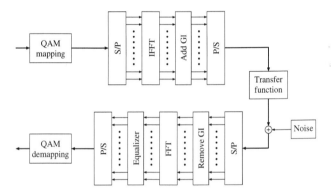

Fig. 8. The block diagram of the in-home PLC system with the proposed channel simulator

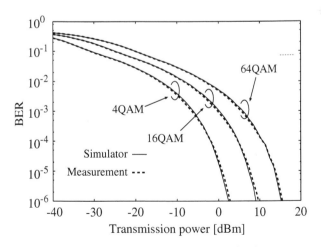

Fig. 9. BER performances for the measured channel response $H(t, f)$ and the estimated channel response $\hat{H}(t, f)$ by using the proposed channel simulator

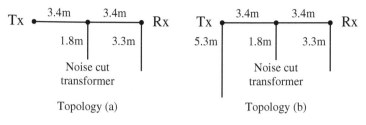

Fig. 10. Topologies

different channel responses. Hence, in this study, we add the white Gaussian noise, which includes the noise power obtained by measuring the power line noise, and evaluate the BER versus the transmission power. We measure the noise on the power line connected some desktop computers in our laboratory. For a bandwidth of 28 MHz, the average noise power measured is -42.6 dBm, and the one-side power spectral density N_0 is -117.0 dBm/Hz. Figure 9 illustrates the comparison between the BER and the transmission power using the measured and estimated channel responses.

This figure shows that the BER for the estimated channel response is almost equal to that for the measured channel responses regardless of the phase difference, as can be seen in Fig. 6. This is because the OFDM with guard interval mitigates the phase difference. Therefore, it would be appropriate to simulate OFDM communication systems with the power line channels with periodically varying frequency responses by using the proposed channel simulator.

Further, we apply two additional topologies (a) and (b), as shown in Fig. 10, to our proposed channel simulators. Figures 11 and 12 illustrate the spectra of the estimated frequency response $\hat{H}_1(f)$ and the measured frequency response $H_1(f)$ of topology (a). As well, Fig. 13 and 14 illustrate the spectra of the estimated frequency response $\hat{H}_1(f)$ and the measured frequency response $H_1(f)$ of topology (b). The estimated spectra of topologies (a) and (b) match excellently with the measured spectra of topologies (a) and (b), respectively. Therefore, we conclude that our proposed simulators could describe a lot of actual power line channels.

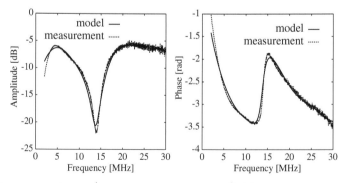

Fig. 11. The spectra of the estimated frequency response $\hat{H}_1(f)$ and the measured frequency response $H_1(f)$ of topology (a)

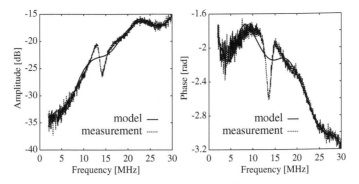

Fig. 12. The spectra of the estimated frequency response $\hat{H}_2(f)$ and the measured frequency response $H_2(f)$ of topology (a)

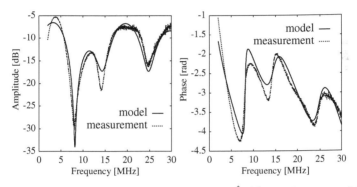

Fig. 13. The spectra of the estimated frequency response $\hat{H}_1(f)$ and the measured frequency response $H_1(f)$ of topology (b)

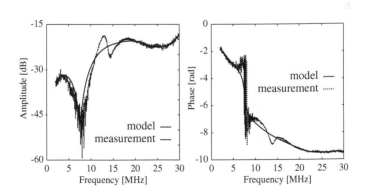

Fig. 14. The spectra of the estimated frequency response $\hat{H}_2(f)$ and the measured frequency response $H_2(f)$ of topology (b)

5   Effect of Incorrect Channel Estimation

There might exist short-term variations in the channel response of in-home PLCs. In the case where the channel is estimated to be time-invariant but the actual channel is a periodically switching channel synchronized with the power frequency voltage, equalization in the receiver would be erroneous, resulting in a drastic increase in the BER. By using the channel simulator (Section 4), we can examine the influence of the channel responses on the communication quality. We evaluate the BER performance when equalized by $\hat{H}_1(f)$ in the entire interval, when equalized by $\hat{H}_2(f)$ in the entire interval, and when equalized by $\hat{H}_1(f)$ and $\hat{H}_2(f)$ in each state correctly. We perform the simulation in these cases and show a comparison between the BER and the transmission power in Fig. 15.

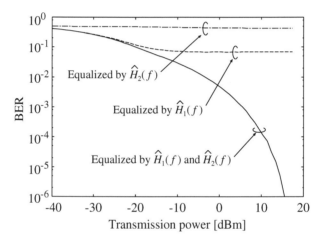

Fig. 15. Evaluating time-varying channel

When the periodically switching channel is estimated to be time-invariant, bit errors would randomly occur for an incorrect equalization. Assuming that the BER can be approximated to zero for a correct equalization, we can obtain

$$\text{BER}_{\text{eq1}} = 0.5 \times \frac{T_2}{T_1 + T_2} = 6.63 \times 10^{-2}, \tag{16}$$

$$\text{BER}_{\text{eq2}} = 0.5 \times \frac{T_1}{T_1 + T_2} = 4.34 \times 10^{-1}, \tag{17}$$

where T_1 and T_2 denote the time interval of state 1 and state 2, respectively. BER_{eq1} denotes the BER when equalized by $\hat{H}_1(f)$ over the entire interval, and BER_{eq2} denotes the BER when equalized by $\hat{H}_1(f)$ over the entire interval. Figure 15 shows that the BER can be approximated to these values as the transmission power is large. Hence, in the case where the periodically switching channel is estimated as a time-invariant channel, we can roughly estimate the BER if the time intervals of both the two states are known. The simulation results show that the BER in the periodically switching channels increases if the time-varying channel response is not estimated in every state and the equalization would be incorrect.

6 Conclusion

In this study, we showed a measurement method of periodically switching channels that are observed in power line channels. By using the frequency responses obtained by the analysis, we proposed a modeling of the periodically switching channels. We constructed a simulation system for examining the effect of periodically switching channels and evaluated the validity of the proposed simulator. Furthermore, we showed the effect of estimating periodically switching channels as a time-invariant channel. As a result, we could simply evaluate the performance of time-invariant equalization schemes by using the switching intervals of the periodically switching channels.

References

1. Zimmermann, M., Dostert, K.: A multipath model for the powerline channel. IEEE Transactions on Communications 50(4), 553–559 (2002)
2. Open PLC European Research Alliance (OPERA), http://www.ist-opera.org/
3. Katayama, M., Yamazato, T., Okada, H.: A mathematical model of noise in narrowband power line communication systems. IEEE Journal on Selected Areas in Communications 24(7), 1267–1276 (2006)
4. Zimmermann, M., Dostert, K.: Analysis and modeling of impulsive noise in broad-band power-line communications. IEEE Transactions on Electromagnetics Compatibility 44(1), 249–258 (2002)
5. Umehara, D., Hirata, S., Denno, S., Morihiro, Y.: Modeling of impulse noise for indoor broadband power line communications. In: International Symposium on Information Theory and Its Applications 2006, pp. 195–200 (2006)
6. Sancha, S., Cañete, F.J., Díez, L., Entrambasaguas, J.T.: A channel simulator for indoor power-line communications. In: IEEE International Symposium on Power-Line Communications and Its Applications 2007, pp. 104–109 (2007)
7. Cañete, F.J., Cortés, J.A., Díez, L., Entrambasaguas, J.T.: Analysis of the cyclic short-term variation of indoor power line channels. IEEE Journal on Selected Areas in Communications 24(7), 1327–1338 (2006)
8. Katar, S., Mashburn, B., Afkhamie, K., Newman, R.: Channel adaptation based on cyclostationary noise characteristics in PLC systems. In: IEEE International Symposium on Power-Line Communications and Its Applications 2006, pp. 16–21 (2006)
9. Katar, S., Krishnam, M., Mashburn, B., Afkhamie, K., Newman, R., Latchman, H.: Beacon schedule persistence to mitigate beacon loss in HomePlug AV networks. In: IEEE International Symposium on Power-Line Communications and Its Applications 2006, pp. 184–188 (2006)
10. Umehara, D., Hayasaki, T., Denno, S., Morikura, M.: The influence of time-varying channels synchronized with commercial power supply on PLC equipments. In: IEEE International Symposium on Power-Line Communications and Its Applications 2008, pp. 30–35 (2008)
11. HomePlug Powerline Alliance (HPA), http://www.homeplug.org/
12. Universal Powerline Association (UPA), http://www.upaplc.org/

Placement of Base Stations in Broadband Power Line Communications Access Networks by Means of Multi-criteria Optimization

Abdelfatteh Haidine and Ralf Lehnert

Chair for Telecommunications
Dresden University of Technology
Dresden, Germany
haidine@ifn.et.tu-dresden.de

Abstract. Broadband Power Line Communications (B-PLC) technology is an alternative for broadband access networks, allowing bit rates up to currently 200Mbps. This technique uses the wiring of the low-voltage grid in order to offer to the users the telecommunications services, such as Internet, VoIP, VoD, etc. The B-PLC design process is sub-divided into two parts: the *Generalized Base Station Placement* (GBSP) problem and the *PLC Channel Allocation Problem* (P-CAP). This paper focuses on GBSP that is modeled as multi-criteria combinatorial optimization problem. Based on our published mathematical modeling, this paper supplies more numerical experiments for the evaluation of Multi-Objective Evolutionary Algorithms (MOEAs) in solving GBSP. Their performance is compared with the single-objective optimization.

Keywords: network costs, uplink delay, Broadband Power-Line Communications (B-PLC), access network planning, generalized base station placement, multi-criteria optimization.

1 Introduction

The Internet is becoming more dominated by complex applications such as video (video-on-demand, video-broadcast or streaming) and the audio streaming, etc. These applications consume large portions of bandwidth and demand high a quality of service. This forces network operators to seek for new promising access alternatives, which try to realize an optimal trade-off between network costs and high bit rates. One of such alternatives is the Broadband Power Line Communications (B-PLC). This technology uses a frequency band [3-30 MHz] of the already existing power cables of the Low-Voltage Network (LVN) to build a B-PLC Access Network (B-PLC AN). Through this resources reuse, huge savings in the investment costs are possible. Recent advances in the development of the PLC system hardware have reached bit rates up to 200Mbps; [1]. This has pushed B-PLC on the way of standardization, which is organized in the framework of the Open PLC European Research Alliance (OPERA) Project [2], or HOMEPLUG Powerline Alliance in North America; [3].

C. Wang (Ed.): AccessNets, LNICST 6, pp. 176–191, 2009.

In the field trials where the network size is very small, the planning tasks are done with simple empirical rules. However, since the PLC technology is starting to spread in different countries and application fields become larger, deep investigations of the planning process become necessary. First investigations concerning the design of the B-PLC AN have been done in [4]. In [4], the B-PLC planning problem is subdivided into two main parts: the Generalized Base Station Placement (GBSP) problem and PLC Channel Allocation Problem (P-CAP). However, these have been simplified by avoiding the usage of PLC repeaters, which has a big influence on the problem complexity. In this paper, we analyze and solve the GBSP by considering the use of repeaters. For solving the GBSP problem, two objectives have to be achieved: minimization of network costs and delay. These are conflicting objectives, because the optimization of one of them leads to the penalization of the other. Therefore, the GBSP is a Multi-criteria (or multi-objective) Optimization Problem (or MOP), which can be solved by two different approaches. The classical approach consists in scaling the different objectives into one general objective in a linear way by the means of weighting factors. Then, this general objective is solved by any one of the known algorithms of the combinatorial Single-Objective Optimization (SOO). Recent class of algorithms has been developed, called Multi-Objective (or Criteria) Optimization Algorithm (MOA), to optimize the different objective without scaling them. Firstly, we evaluate the performance of the MOO and then we compare it with the SOO. This paper is based on our previous work from [5], where detailed theoretical analysis of GBSP with initial results can be found. In this paper, we avoid this detailed mathematics, in order to focus more on the analysis and the evaluation of the numerical results for the evaluation of MOO and SOO algorithm and their comparison; and their impacts from the network planner/operator point of view.

The remaining of the paper is organized as follows: The process of building a broadband access network on the low-voltage grid is described in the next section. Overview on the optimization approaches is given in the third section. Exact definition of the GBSP is given and its optimization objectives are modeled in the fourth section. In the fifth section, numerical experiments and results are discussed.

2 Building Broadband Access over Low-Voltage Grid

The B-PLC AN is realized by placing a Base Station (BS), which plays the role of a bridge between telecommunications backbone network and the low-voltage network. The end user device uses a PLC modem to communicate with the BS. Because the PLC systems have a limited coverage, one or several repeaters can be sued to reach user (or users) above this distance. A general structure of a B-PLC AN and its environment is shown in Figure 1. In the practice, one or several BSs have to be installed in the LVN to serve all the users. Therefore, the LVN must have potential locations, where BSs could be installed. Generally, the BSs are installed in the transformer station and the street cabinets. This makes the LVN structure important information for the B-PLC network planner. Because of that the different LVN structures have been investigated and modeled in [6]. These investigations are based on the European LVN (especially the German) with underground wiring. North America, Asia and Oceania have another structure of LVN, which makes the GBSP easily solvable, as shown in Figure 2. For this case, a practical solution consists in using B-PLC in low-voltage network for serving the last meters towards the subscribers and in the Medium-Voltage (MV) network to cover the last mile. The information signal is injected/extracted by the MV Head End (or BS) in/from the Metropolitan Area Network of the city.

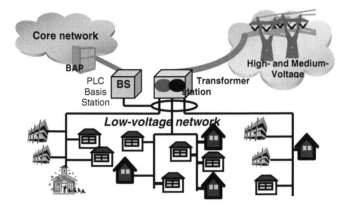

Fig, 1. Structure of Broadband Power Line Communications (B-PLC) access networks over an underground infrastructure; example of Europe

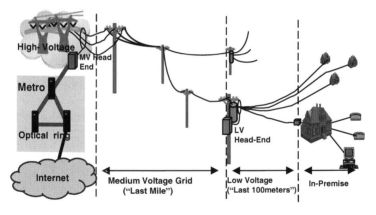

Fig. 2. Example of broadband access networks over aerial infrastructure (North America)

The first task of B-PLC AN design is the placement of the BSs. An optimal placement consists in defining the optimal number of the needed BSs and to place them in the optimal locations in the LVN. A second planning subtask consists in defining which users have to be served by which BS. This is strongly affected by the distance between user and BS. Because the LVN wirings were not designed to use their high frequencies, the distortions affecting PLC signals are too strong. This makes the BS coverage (L_{max}) very short, typically about the 300m. Therefore, if a user is apart from BS by more than L_{max}, one or several PLC repeaters have to be used. After that, each BS has to be connected with the backbone network. We assume that in the LVN environment different possible access points to the WAN are available, which we refer to them as Backbone network Access Points (BAPs). A BAP can be for example an optical line termination. The problem to solve in this phase is to determine over which BAP each BS can access the backbone network. These sub-tasks defined above can be classified under a general problem, called *Generalized Bas Station Placement* (GBSP) problem. This is of same class than problem of base station placement in wireless networks, which is NP-hard. The solution of GBSP builds a *PLC site*, which contains a set of PLC cells. A PLC Cell is built by: a BS j, its sub-set of allocated users $U^{(j)}_S$, its repeaters and its BAP $W^{(j)}_{BAP}$.

3 Optimization Paradigms

Usually network planning related optimization problems are modeled as one objective function (mostly the costs), which has to be minimized in presence of constraints. Such problems are said to be single-objective optimization problems. The GBSP is modeled in this work as Multi-Objective Optimization Problem (MOP). A MOP consists in optimizing simultaneously a vector of objectives under certain constraints, and has the general form in Eq.1. Generally all or some of those objectives are conflicting, where the optimization of one results in deterioration of other(s).

$$minimize \qquad \mathbf{z} = \mathbf{f}(\mathbf{x}) = [\, f_1(\mathbf{x}), f_2(\mathbf{x}), ..., f_k(\mathbf{x})\,] \qquad (1)$$

The classical method for solving the MOO problems consists in aggregating the different objectives into a single general objective function, which is then optimized by the means of the traditional SOO algorithms. This method is called "*scaling method*" that achieves the conversion by forming a linear combination of the objectives using weights or scaling factors w_k's, with $\sum w_k = 1$. Another classical approach takes into consideration only one objective for the optimization, where the remaining ones are converted into constraints. Another solving paradigm for MOPs is gaining an increasing interest, both in engineering as well as in academic fields. This is the Multi-objective Optimization (MOO), which is known also as Multi-Criteria Optimization (MCO), where the different objectives are optimized quasi-independently. Most of the research in MOO is oriented towards the Metaheuristics. These have three main advantages: *i)* find good (but not necessarily the best) solution; *ii)* require acceptable computation time; and *iii)* have a generic form that makes them adaptable to any engineering optimization problem.

In this work, the evolutionary algorithms have been chosen for the application, in its both variants (SOO and MOO). This choice has been motivated by two facts. Firsts, these metaheuristics have been widely and successfully used in different engineering fields. Especially, these algorithms are the mostly used in different telecommunications fields, as stated in [7] and [8], where more than 450 references are listed. Seconds, the evolutionary algorithm is the most investigated and developed variant in the multi-objective optimization; [9]. A metaheuristic MOA is an algorithm that samples the solution space, in a random-controlled way. These samples are evaluated separately and compared in all optimization dimensions. With this comparison, the dominated (i.e. the worst in all dimensions, like S_2 in Figure 3 (*left*))

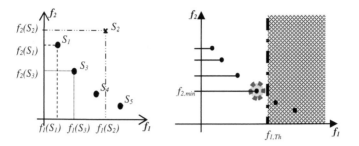

Fig. 3. Example of Pareto front or approximation set for a minimization problem (left, for a MOP: minimize **f**=*[f1,f2]*) and the front reduction (right)

solutions are eliminated and only the non-dominated (i.e. relative good) ones are kept. These will build a *Pareto front* or *Approximation Set*, which is referred as **A**={S_1,S_3,S_4,S_5}. Further examples and details can be found in [10] [11].

SOO supplies exactly one optimal solution to the considered problem, while the MOO supplies a set of trade-off solutions. Therefore, they can not be directly compared. Because of that, the approximation set (or front) is reduced to one solution. Firstly, a threshold for one objective dimension is set (like in Figure 3 *(right)*). This threshold is set by the best solution of SOO. The sub-space above this threshold is considered as unfeasible. Among the remaining solutions of the MOO, we choose the solution with the minimum value according to the other objective dimension. This solution is then considered as the best MOO solution. Then the comparison of SOO and MOO is done according to this second dimension. Practical examples are given in the section with numerical results.

4 Definition and Modeling of GBSP Problem

4.1 Problem Description

Generally, the GBSP is a combinatorial optimization problem that can be summarized as follows:

Given: LVN topology; set of available BAPs (W_S); BAP-BS cost matrix (M_{BS-BAP}); users traffic demand; PLC element costs (BS and TDR); and an access scheme to the medium;

Tasks: Place an optimal number of BSs; allocate each user; place repeaters where needed; and connect BSs to backbone over the BAPs;

Objectives: **minimize** costs, **minimize** delay;

Constrained by: in-sight constraints; system coverage (BS and repeaters); and BAP capacities.

4.2 Network Costs

The total GBSP costs include the BSs, TDRs and BS-BAP costs. Generally, the costs of BSs and TDRs contain the hardware as well as the installation costs. The potential locations for placing these PLC network elements (namely the transformer stations and the street cabinets) are very hostile for communications devices, because of their characteristics. Among such hostile characteristics are: the temperature that varies between -10C° and 70C°, the weak ventilation, humidity <95%, very dusty, risk of flooding, etc. Because of the complexity of modeling the installation costs, only the hardware costs are taken into consideration in this work. Example of BS placements are given in Figure 4, where BS is placed in an on-the-ground transformer station – example form Europe- and another BS (i.e. head end) placed on a pole near to the aerial transformer; example from Asia. Detailed mathematical formulation of the costs minimization as function of network decision variables and all the optimization constraints can be found in [5]. Among the main constraints, we have:

i) The in-sight condition, represented by the variable $\hat{y}_{ij}$, guarantees the free sight between user i and his BS j. A user and BS are said to be in-sight if they are not separated by any other BS. This variable is equal to one if the in-sight constrained is fulfilled, as it is the case between user 1 (*u1*) and BSs j and k in Figure 5. Otherwise it is zero; which is the case of user u1 and BS m. This constraint is very important, because if there is another BS between the user and his BS, to which he is allocated, the communication between them is impossible. Each BS transmits only its signal, while it sees other BS signals as noise, which is filtered out. The in-sight constraint is also valid in case of BS-TDRs and TDR-user;

ii) Because of the reachability limitation, the distances (BS and its adjacent TDR), (BS and its adjacent user), (TDR and its adjacent TDR) and (TDR and its adjacent user) must remain below the distance limit (L_{max});

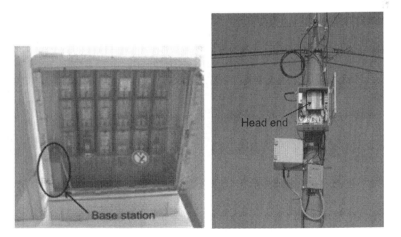

Fig. 4. Example of practical placement of base station (i.e. head end) in on-the-ground transformer station (left – Source: Drewag, Dresden, Germany) and on a pole near to the aerial transformer; example form Asia (right - Source: Kepco, Jeju Island, South Korea)

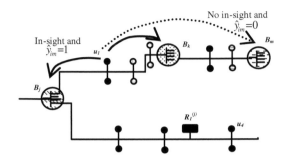

Fig. 5. Example of in-sight constraint between PLC subscriber and BS

In this paper, we consider that B-PLC systems (BS and TDR) coverage (L_{max}) is a constant. However, this is not true in the practice. In fact, the system coverage is influenced by several parameters at the same time; such as the medium size, number of connected users, their activities, the age of the cable, etc. For example, if the transmitted signal crosses a street cabinet, which contains generally different coupling of the outgoing segments. This results in considerable lost of signal energy. On the other hand, if a higher number of households is connected to the, then line impedance is higher. Furthermore, these households connect different household appliances, which generate stronger noise over this medium segment; [12]. The consideration of all those factors in one model for the channel model to compute the system coverage in each line segment makes the problem too complex. However, in future works the coverage has to be taken as function of most important parameters affecting the attenuation, such as cable characteristics (length, type, impedance, number of connected households, etc.), multi-path effect, number/types of coupling inside the street cabinets, used frequency, etc.

4.3 Downlink and Uplink Delay in B-PLC Access Networks

The packet delay in the b-PLC AN represents the time required by the packet to arrive from it source (BS or user) to its destination (user or BS). Here we differentiate two-types of delay; the downlink (from BS to end user – referred as $\boldsymbol{D_{BS2e}}$) and the uplink delay (from user to BS - $\boldsymbol{D_{e2BS}}$). In the downlink, the BS gets the packet from the backbone (or metro network) and broadcast it over the access network; as illustrated in the queuing system in Figure 6. The service time is the time needed by the packet to arrive to the ser destination, and represents the propagation/transmission time over all network segments between the BS and the targeted user. The uplink delay is more complex, because each user willing to send a packet to the BS hat to get the right to access the medium. The power line is used by several users at the same time, because of that it is pointed out as shared medium and a Medium Access Control (MAC) mechanism is needed, in order to guarantee a good utilization of the medium.

In this paper, we focus only the uplink delay that is also called *End-user-to-BS* Delay (D_{e2BS}). For the computation of the delay, the B-PLC cell is assumed as an *M/G/1*-queuing system. Such system assumes that users (or user packets) arrive in memory-less fashion with rate λ. The service X is assumed to be memory-less random

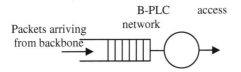

Fig. 6. Queuing model for the B-PLC AN downlink

variable $(X_1, X_2, ..., X_i, ...)$ with an arbitrary distribution. The total delay affecting user packets in such system contains a waiting time in the queue, plus a service time. The mean value of the total delay can be written as; [13]:

$$E\{D_{Total}\} = E\{X\} + \frac{\lambda \cdot E\{X^2\}}{2(1-\rho)} \qquad (2)$$

With $E\{X\} = 1/\mu$ is the average service time, $E\{X^2\} = \sum_i p(X_i)X_i^2$ is the second moment of service time, and $\rho = \lambda/\mu$. Thus, the next step consists in calculating the first and the second moment of the service time by firstly modeling the service time in the uplink.

The service time of a packet of user i contains two components. Firstly, this waits in the queue until it arrives to the front of the queue. Even if it is in the front of the queue, this packet can not be automatically served, because it must wait until the station gets the right to access the medium by the means of a polling message. This delay is called polling waiting time that a user packet must wait in the queue ($D_i^{(poll)}$). Seconds, when the packet has the right to access the medium, then a transmission time ($D_{(i \rightarrow j)}^{(Tx)}$) is needed so that the packet goes from the user i to the BS j. In this case, the service time has the form:

$$D_{(i \rightarrow j)}^{(Serv)} = D_i^{(poll)} + D_{(i \rightarrow j)}^{(Tx)} \qquad (3)$$

Transmission Delay: A PLC repeater extends the coverage of BS, which reduces the network costs, because the BS is more expensive than repeater. However, its utilization results in some drawbacks, such increase of delay and/or reduction of the available bit rate. Because the BS and its repeaters use the same medium, their transmissions must be multiplexed, either in time, or in frequency, or in time and frequency. Based on some technical and costs considerations, the Time Division-based Repeaters (TDR) are considered as the best solution. Therefore, only TDRs are considered in this work. In a network using TDRs, the time is organized in Time Slots (TS). Any packet transmission must occur at the beginning of a TS and the packet arrives to its destination in this same TS. An example of the effect of the TDRs is shown in Figure 7, where a data packet has to be sent from BS to user #3. At a 1st time TS, data packet is sent by the BS and will be received by repeater #1 (R1). At the 2nd TS, R1 sends the packet further to arrive to R2. At the beginning of the 3rd TS, R2 sends further the packet to R3. At 4th TS, R3 sends the packet further. The

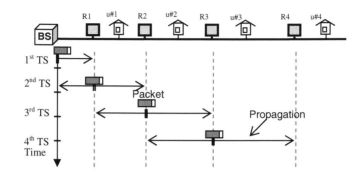

Fig. 7. Effect of time division repeaters in the B-PLC access networks

transmission time of packet from/to user i is a function of the number of TDRs separating this user from his BS j ($R_{(j \to i)}$), and can be written in the following form:

$$D_{(i \to j)}^{(Tx)} = (1 + R_{(j \to i)}).T_{TS} \qquad (4)$$

MAC-related Delay: Because several energy users share the same wiring, the PLC medium is called *"shared medium"*, and the BS should also realize the Medium Access Control (MAC) tasks. Different MAC mechanisms have been investigated to be implemented for PLC systems; [14]. In this work, we consider a master-salve mechanism that is used in some commercialized PLC systems. This works according a *Round Robin Polling* scheme, where the BS polls its users in a cyclic deterministic way. When the packet of user i arrives to the front of the queue, the access right (i.e. polling message) can be at any one of the $|U^{(j)}{}_s|$ user stations of the cell. Because the polling message is sent to stations in a deterministic cyclic way without priorities, then the probability that the polling message is at station i' is equal for all stations. This probability is $p_{i'}^{(poll)} = 1/|U_s^{(j)}|$. If we assume that the BS polls its users in a cyclic way in the following succession $\{u\#1, u\#2, ..., u\#|U^{(j)}{}_s|\}$, then the BS has to poll the subset of users $\overline{U}_{(i' \to i)}^{(j)} = \{u\#i', u\#(i'+1), ..., u\#(i-1)\}$ before to arrive to poll the user i. The time $D_{(j \to i' \to i)}^{(poll)}$ represents the time required to poll each user $i'' \in \overline{U}_{(i' \to i)}^{(j)}$ and to receive back a message of *"no-data-to-send"* from this user. This message is sent by the user, when he has no data to send. After that, a delay $(R_{(j \to i)} + 1).T_{TS}$ is required by the BS to transmit the polling message to user i. In this case, the mean value of the polling waiting time for user i becomes as follows:

$$(5)$$

$$E\{D_i^{(poll)}\} = \sum_{i' \in U_s^{(j)}} p_{i'}^{(poll)} . D_{(j \to i' \to i)}^{(poll)}$$

$$= \frac{1}{|U_s^{(j)}| - 1} \sum_{\substack{i' \in U_s^{(j)} \\ i' \neq i}} \left(\sum_{i'' \in \overline{U}_{(i' \to i)}^{(poll)}} 2.(R_{(j \to i'')} + 1).T_{TS} \right) + (R_{(j \to i)} + 1).T_{TS}$$

Combining (4) and (5) in (3), it becomes:

$$E\{D_{j,UL}^{(Serv)}\} = \frac{1}{|U_S^{(j)}|} \sum_{i \in U_S^{(j)}} \left(E\{D_i^{(poll)}\} + D_{(i \to j)}^{(Tx)}\right) \tag{6}$$

$$= \frac{1}{|U_S^{(j)}|} \sum_{i \in U_S^{(j)}} \left(\frac{1}{|U_S^{(j)}|-1} \cdot \sum_{\substack{i' \in U_S^{(j)} \\ i' \neq i}} \left(\sum_{i'' \in \bar{U}_{(i' \to i)}^{(poll)}} 2.(R_{(j \to i'')}+1).T_{TS} \right) \\ + 2.(R_{(j \to i)}+1).T_{TS} \right)$$

The mean value of the uplink delay in cell j becomes as follows (more details can be found in [5]):

$$E\{D_{e2BS}^{(j)}\} = E\{D_{(j,UL)}^{(Serv)}\} + \frac{|U_S^{(j)}|.\lambda^{(UL)}.E\left\{\left(D_{(j,UL)}^{(Serv)}\right)^2\right\}}{2\left(1 - |U_S^{(j)}|.\lambda^{(UL)}.E\left\{D_{(j,UL)}^{(Serv)}\right\}\right)} \tag{7}$$

A PLC site is constituted by several cells. Therefore, to model the delay in the site, either the average delay over all cells is taken or the maximum one. In later case, the mean uplink delay in the site can be written as:

$$minimize \qquad f_{Delay} = E\{D_{e2BS}^{(Site)}\} = \max_{j \in P_S^{(BS)}} \left(E\{D_{e2BS}^{(j)}\}\right) \tag{8}$$

The GBSP problem can be then formulated as a multi-objective optimization problem in the following standard form:

$$minimize \qquad \mathbf{f}_{GBSP} = \left[f_{Costs}, f_{Delay}\right] \tag{9}$$

5   Experiments and Numerical Results

5.1   Parameters Setting

Generally the performances of any algorithm are depending on several factors, like the characteristics of the planning problem that are generally referred as instance size. This is represented in this work by the LVN structure and its environment. In order to check how hard the algorithm performances can be affected by the problem (i.e. LVN) characteristics, two problem instances with different sizes (a small and a large network) are used for the generation of numerical results. Two main characteristics of the instances can be seen as basic parameters, namely the users' density and the LVN size. Therefore, the small instance has short distances and a lower number of users (7 potential locations for BSs placement and 45 users, as shown by the solution samples depicted in Figure 8). The large network instance has 14 potential BS locations and 934 users. For the realization of the B-PLC access network in the practice, there are different PLC systems that are available, where each offers a kind of tradeoff between the costs and the system performances. Generally, the recent systems still have relative high prices, but they are offering better characteristics. Different characteristics are interdependent, such as the total bit rate, the time slot duration and the number of channels. Because of that, two possible B-PLC systems are used as reference for the planning of B-PLC in this work, which characteristics are listed in Table 1. Time slot duration must be equal or larger than the time needed to transmit one packet with maximum length. In B-PLC the Ethernet packets are used to transmit the data, with a maximum length of 1500Bytes.

Table 1. Characteristics of two different used B-PLC systems

--	Bit rate	TDR cost	BS cost	T_{TS}	Coverage
System#1	30Mbps	100cu	300cu	0.5ms	500m
System#2	15Mbps	50cu	150cu	1ms	500m

From numerous possible Multi-Objective Evolutionary Algorithms (MOEAs), two versions of Non-dominated Sorting Genetic Algorithm (NSGA and NSGA-II) and Strength Pareto Evolutionary Algorithms (SPEA) have been selected. These are called Pareto-based MOEA and are more powerful than the other ones, according to their performances in solving other engineering MOO problems; [10] [11]. A solution violating one or more constraints is applied to some repair mechanisms. If in spite of the repair the solution is still violating a constraint, then it will be discarded and another one is generated. The evolutionary search uses the following parameter: 100 generations, population of 100 individuals, crossover probability $p_c=1$ and mutation probability $p_m=0.01$.

5.2 Pareto-Based Multi-objective Evolutionary Algorithm Solving the GBSP

Different possible quality indicators (i.e. performance metrics) of multi-objective algorithms can be used for the performance evaluation; [11]. However, in this section we focus only on two metrics; namely *front cardinality* (or approximation set cardinality) and *the coverage of two sets*. Concerning the front cardinality, this does not play a big role in the comparison in case of GBSP. The numerical results show similar cardinality in case of all three MOEAs for all problem instances, which average varies between 5 and 7 solutions. This very low cardinality seems to be normal, because of the high number of optimization constraints (i.e. boundary conditions). During the simulation also the infeasible solutions belonging to the front have also saved separated of the feasible ones. An infeasible solution is a solution that violates at least one solution in spite of the use of some repair mechanisms. Their number was very large in the case of the large network instance. In this case, only the coverage of two sets is used to compare the algorithms. The results related to this metric are given in Tables 2 and 3 for the small and the large network; respectively. This metric measures the percentage of solutions in front A_1 that are dominated by at least one solution from front A_2. It shows how good is the solutions convergence towards the optimal front in comparison to solutions of the other front.

A first remark that can be made concerns the clear variation of the values of this metric in case of small and large network instances. For example, $C(A_{NSGA}, A_{NSGA-II})=0.43$ in case of small network with system#1, while $C(A_{NSGA}, A_{NSGA-II})=0.03$ in

Table 2. Coverage of two sets for evaluation of different MOEAs for small network

	NSGA	NSGA-II	SPEA
Small network – System#1			
	NSGA	NSGA-II	SPEA
NSGA	#	0.43±0.05	0.23±0.04
NSGA-II	0.37±0.05	#	0.14±0.03
SPEA	0.51±0.104	0.68±0.05	#
Small network – System#2			
	NSGA	NSGA-II	SPEA
NSGA	#	0.46±0.06	0.26±0.04
NSGA-II	0.31±0.05	#	0.14±0.04
SPEA	0.52±0.05	0.68±0.05	#

Table 3. Coverage of two sets for evaluation of different MOEAs for large network

	NSGA	NSGA-II	SPEA
Large network – System#1			
	NSGA	NSGA-II	SPEA
NSGA	#	0.03±0.04	0.05±0.08
NSGA-II	0.68±0.22	#	0.41±0.37
SPEA	0.59±0.26	0.23±0.21	#
Large network – System#2			
	NSGA	NSGA-II	SPEA
NSGA	#	0.3±0.14	0.14±0.1
NSGA-II	0.31±0.14	#	0.19±0.12
SPEA	0.42±0.15	0.43±0.14	#

case of large network with system#1. This considerable changes in this relative behavior can be explained by the exponentially increase of the search space, which requires longer computation time to allow the algorithms to converge. In this experiment, the small number of generation (100 generations) has been used in case of both instance sizes. In case of small network, NSGA and NSGA-II show similar relative performances. This means, that the mechanisms introduced by NSGA-II to conserve the population diversity do not make a major difference. This could be explained by the very low number of the feasible solutions; and therefore, the very low number of solutions in the partial fronts. In this case, the solutions are not crowded in narrow regions of the objective space. This explains why the NSGA-II which mechanisms are based on the crowded-distances measurements does not show higher performances in comparison to its original version (i.e. NSGA). However, the advantage of NSGA-II became clearer in the case of large network. Furthermore, the use of elitism by this variant allows preserving the good solutions found in the early generations. In fact, in larger problem the MOEA needs longer time for the convergence, and it is possible that the good solutions found at the beginning of the search get lost, because the genetic operators (esp. crossover) can destroy them. The SPEA, which solution samples from the front of one run are shown in Figure 8, shows better performances than both NSGA variants.

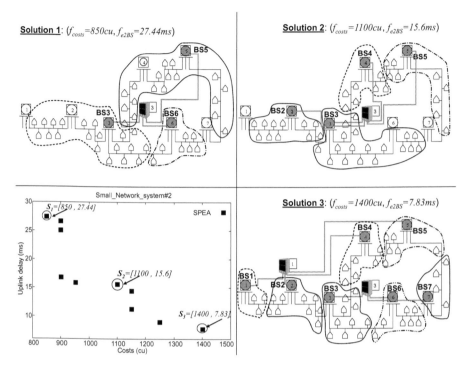

Fig. 8. Example of SPEA solutions for GBSP -small network and system#2

5.3 Comparison of Single- and Multi-objective Optimization

A single-objective optimization algorithm supplies a unique solution as output, while a multi-objective optimization algorithm supplies a set (or front) of optimal solutions. Because of that, such front has to be reduced into one solution, in order to make any comparison between SOO and MOO possible. The front reduction is done by fixing a threshold to one objective. The surface above this threshold is considered as infeasible in the objective space. In the remaining feasible part, we choose the solution that realizes the best value according to the second objective. In the GBSP, we define a delay threshold (D_{Thr}). This threshold is the best value realized by the SOO. The numerical results for the SOO and MOEAs comparison are given in Tables 4 and 5 for small and large network; respectively. In case of small network using system#1, the delay threshold is 5.8ms. This delay is realized by the SOO by the means of 2051cu, while the SPEA realizes it with less costs; namely 2001cu. The other MOEAs algorithms can also realize a delay under this threshold with lower costs that SOO; namely 2006cu and 2009cu for NSGA-II and NSGA; respectively. However, this advantage of MOO toward the SOO is not so large, since it disappears in the case where the small network is designed with system#2. In this case, the costs form the different optimization approaches are closer. A remark can be done concerning the stability of the algorithms convergence. The results show very small confidence intervals of the costs values achieved by MOEAs in comparison to the SOO. However, this characteristic is deteriorated for all MOEAs in the experiments with

Table 4. Comparison of SOO and MOO costs for given delay threshold DThr – Small network

Algorithm	System#1		System#2	
	D_{Thr}(ms)	Costs(cu)	D_{Thr}(ms)	Costs(cu)
SOO	5.8	2050.98±40.58	12.5	1137.47±28.88
NSGA	5.8	2009.33±7.35	12.5	1154.33±2.39
NSGA-II	5.8	2006.33±5.95	12.5	1151.33±0.0
SPEA	5.8	2001.33±0.0	12.5	1151.33±0.0

Table 5. Comparison of SOO and MOO costs for delay threshold D_{Thr}– case of large network

Algorithm	System#1		System#2	
	D_{Thr}(ms)	Costs(cu)	D_{Thr}(ms)	Costs(cu)
SOO	175	6275.27±86.29	323	4092.08±297.36
NSGA	175	8718.64±823.25	323	4401.11±273.02
NSGA-II	175	8290.65±380.7	323	4383.78±191.2
SPEA	175	8790.69±978.3	323	4308.91±256.82

large network, especially when using system#1. The large network instance does not only cause an instable behavior of MOEAs convergence, but also a bad convergence, as this is reflected by the numerical results. For example, SOO supplies solution for the large problem with system#1 and threshold of 175ms by costs of 6275cu, while the SPEA solution costs are of 8790cu for a same delay. A cause of this behavior can be the convergence time that is longer in case of MOO.

A general advantage of the MOO lies in the diversity of the output. In fact, if the network planner would like to have different possible solutions for his problem, and then to decide which one to keep according either to delay or costs or both, then MOO is advantageous. If the network planner lets the SOO runs several times, then he will mostly get two or three completely different solutions. But this is possible with the MOO in one run. As an example, Figure 9 is given, where the solutions resulting form 10 different SOO runs and solutions from one SPEA run are plotted in the objective space. In case of system#1, the 10 runs of SOO supply only 4 different solutions, in the time where one SPEA run reaches 8 different solutions. Furthermore, the front of MOO covers all the solutions found by SOO in different runs. Similar is the remark concerning the network using system#2, where 4 and 10 different solutions are found by 10 SOO runs and one SPEA run; respectively. Also in this case, the SOO results are covered by the unique SPEA run. Another advantage of the MOO is that it allows to find a solution for extreme cases. For example, if the network has to be designed to transport a service that constraints hardly the delay, then MOO is the best approach to solve this problem. The problem of SOO to deal with such scenario lies in the fact that it is generally hard to model correctly the preference in the optimization weighting factors (i.e. w_i's), which are used for objectives scaling. The MOO supplies front of solutions that can be used to design B-PLC AN for any scenario (independently of service desired to transport). Such front will allow choosing the solution that is adequate for any faced scenario. This option is not possible with SOO,

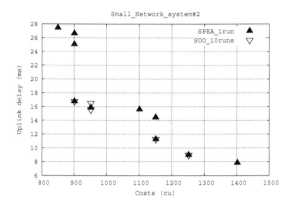

Fig. 9. Comparison of solutions from 10 SOO runs and 1 MOO run in objective space

as it is stated in Figure 9, where the MOO reaches the shortest delay. This effect is clear also in larger networks.

6   Conclusions

The Generalized Base Station Placement (GBSP) problem consists of the following: *a)* finding the optimal locations where an optimal number of BSs has to be placed; *b)* allocating in an optimal way a number of PLC subscribers to each BS; *c)* placing time division PLC repeaters where this is necessary; and *d)* to connect each placed BS to the backbone network over an available Backbone network Access Point (BAP). This optimization problem is a Multi-objective Optimization Problem (MOP) because different conflicting objectives have to be optimized at the same time. The main GBSP optimization objectives that have been considered are the network costs, network delay (in uplink and downlink). For the solution of the mathematically formulated MOP, two optimization paradigms have been used: the single objective optimization (SOO) where the MOP is converted into a single-objective problem and the Multi-objective Optimization where the objective are optimized separated from each other. In the numerical experiments two problem instances have been used (small and large low-voltage networks) with two possible B-PLC systems (system#1 and system#2), which differ in the costs and performances. The used optimization algorithms, for both SOO and MOO, are based on the evolutionary search.

The MOO can perform better than the SOO; however, it must have enough computation time to be able to converge as it was the case with the small network instance. In large problem instance, the SOO supplies the best results, because it needs short time for the convergence. However, The MOO has the major advantage to offer wider choice to the decision making. In this way, the network planner gets a deeper sight into the optimization process. In fact, the use of MOO allows the network planner to find solution even for hardly constrained objectives. For example, the MOO found in each run network solutions where the uplink delay is less than 5ms, while this case is rare if the SOO is used.

References

1. Design of System on Silicon (DS2): DSS900X: Power Line Communication Chipsets for Broadband Access Applications. DSS9002 Products Datasheet, http://www.ds2.es
2. Open PLC European Research Alliance (OPERA) Project: Initial paper on the Project and Plans. Deliverable D84 (January 2004), http://www.ist-opera.org/
3. HOMEPLUG Powerline Alliance, http://www.homeplug.org/
4. Haidine, A., Mellado, I., Lehnert, R.: PANDeMOO: Powerline communications Access Network Designer based on Multi-Objective Optimisation. In: 9th International Symposium on Power-Line Communications and its Applications, Vancouver (2005)
5. Haidine, A.: Solving the Generalized Base Station Placement Problem in the Planning of Broadband Power Line Communications Access Networks. In: Proceeding of IEEE Inter. Sym. on Powerline Communications and Its Applications, South Korea, April 2-5 (2008)
6. Haidine, A., Hrasnica, H., Lehnert, R.: Analysis and Modelling of Low-Voltage Networks for Planning of Powerline Communications Access Networks. In: Proceeding of 8th International Symposium on Power-Line Communications and its Applications, Zaragossa (2004)
7. Kampstra, P.: Evolutionary Computing in Telecommunications: A likely EC Success Story. Master Thesis at the Free University of Amsterdam, Holland (2005)
8. Kampstra, P., van der Mei, R.D., Eiben, A.E.: Evolutionary Computing in Telecommunication Network Design: A Survey (2006), http://www.math.vu.nl/~mei/publications.php
9. Ehrgott, M., Gandibleux, X.: Approximative Solution Methods for Multiobjective Combinatorial Optimization Problems. Spanish Journal on the Operation Research (Sociedad de Estadistica e Investigacion Operativa Top) 12(1), 1–90 (2004)
10. Deb, K.: A Fast and Elitist Multiobjective genetic Algorithm: NSGA-II. IEEE Transactions on Evolutionary Computation 6(2) (2002)
11. Zitzler, E.: Evolutionary Algorithms for Multiobjective Optimization: Methods and Applications. PhD Thesis, Swiss Federal Institute of technology (ETH), Switzerland (1999)
12. Zimmermann, M., Dostert, K.: The Low Voltage Distribution Network as Last Mile Access Network - Signal Propagation and Noise Scenario in the HF-Range. AEÜ International Journal of Electronics and Communications 54(1), 13–22 (2000)
13. Kleinrock, L.: Queuing Systems. Theory, vol. 1. J. Wiley, New York (1975)
14. Hrasnica, H.: Medium Access Control Protocols for Powerline Communications networks. PhD Thesis, Technische Universität Dresden, Germany (2004)

Modeling of Channel Allocation in Broadband Powerline Communications Access Networks as a Multi-Criteria Optimization Problem

Abdelfatteh Haidine and Ralf Lehnert

Chair for Telecommunications
Dresden University of Technology, 01062 Dresden, Germany
haidine@ifn.et.tu-dresden.de

Abstract. The planning process of the Broadband Powerline communications access networks contains two main problem parts: the *Generalized Base Station Placement* (GBSP) problem and the *PLC Channel Allocation Problem* (P-CAP). The GBSP is investigated/solved in our previous works. In this paper, we focus on the P-CAP. The task of the P-CAP consists in allocating a sub-set of channels from an available set of PLC channels to each base station in the B-PLC site. Two optimization objectives are considered for the solution of this problem; namely the maximization of the resource reuse and the minimization of the generated interferences in the site. These objectives are conflicting, since the optimization of one of them results in the deterioration of the other. Therefore, this problem is modeled as a Multi-objective (or multi-criteria) Optimization Problem (MOP). Three variants of Pareto-based multi-objective algorithms, using evolutionary search, are used to solve it. Their performances are evaluated on four problem instances.

Keywords: Channel allocation, broadband powerline communications, access network planning, multi-criteria optimization, evolutionary algorithms.

1 Introduction

Broadband PowerLine Communications (B-PLC) access network uses low-voltage supply networks as a transmission medium to provide high data rates to the end-users. Current B-PLC systems are reaching a raw bit rate of 200Mbps, which allows the realization of a large platform of services. The B-PLC presents an alternative solution for the realization of broadband access networks. Because of the high costs and the liberalization of the telecommunications market, the access area is very important for new network providers, who are trying to overcome their position, which is disadvantageous, compared to incumbent network providers. The direct access to the customers can be realized by building new networks or by use of existing infrastructure; e.g. CATV (Cable TV) or electrical power supply infrastructure. Installing new networks can realize high bit rates; such Passive Optical Network (PON) with up to Gbps, but it is economically not yet feasible. Another alternative is wireless solutions, in form of WiMAX, even if this reaches a maximum shared bit

C. Wang (Ed.): AccessNets, LNICST 6, pp. 192–207, 2009.

rate of 70Mbps. PLC access networks use the low-voltage networks to connect a number of subscribers within a geographically small area (~ few hundred meters), covering the "last meters" communications areas, and represent a cost-effective solution. This is achieved by installing a base station (BS, called also Head-End -HE), which builds a kind of bridge between the telecommunications world (i.e. backbone network) and low-voltage network; as depicted in Figure 1.

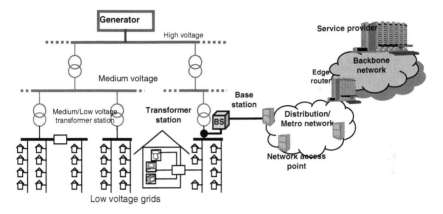

Fig. 1. Typical structure of a Broadband Powerline Communications (B-PLC) access networks

The power supply networks are not designed for communications and they do not present a favorable transmission medium. Therefore, the PLC transmission channel is characterized by a strong attenuation, changing impedance and fading, as well as a strong influence of noise caused by various devices usually connected to the supply networks. This could require the installation of PLC repeaters to allow the extension of the system coverage/reachability. Additionally, PLC networks providing higher data rates have to operate in a frequency spectrum up to 30 MHz, which is also used by other radio services. Therefore, the regulatory bodies specify very strong limits regarding the electro-magnetic emission from PLC networks to the environment. As consequence, an optimal use of the resources (i.e. the available frequencies) is decisive in the design and the management of this access network. This paper investigates the resources (channels) allocation to the different installed bases stations in the low-voltage grid. The goal of these investigations is the maximization of the resource reuse in the network; however, this maximization must not lead to (high level) interferences. In this paper, the PLC Channel Allocation Problem (P-CAP) is modeled as a Multi-criteria Optimization Problem (MOP). This problem is described, mathematically formulated and solved by evolutionary search-based metaheuristics.

The paper is organized as follows: An overview on the design of the B-PLC access network is given in the next section. Also the design of B-PCL and wireless network is done here. In the third section, the P-CAP is described in more details, its input information is analyzed and the optimization objectives are mathematically formulated. Short overview on the optimization algorithmic is given in the fourth section. Section five is reserved for the experiments and the evaluation of the results.

2 Planning Process of B-PLC Access Networks

2.1 Design of B-PLC Sites

The realization of Broadband Power Line Communications (B-PLC) access network consists of placing an element called Base Station (BS), which allows the connection of the Low-Voltage Network (LVN) and the backbone network. This BS uses a part of the power line spectrum to communicate with the PLC modem of the end-user. The planning process of the B-PLC access networks can be subdivided into two main problems; [1]. The first one is called *Generalized Base Station Placement* (GBSP) Problem, where an optimum number of base stations have to be installed to serve all the PLC subscribers. Each BS gets allocated a subset of users. If a user is located above a certain coverage distance from his BS, one or several PLC repeaters will be used. Adequate locations have to be determined, where such repeaters can be installed. The installed base stations have to be connected to the backbone/metro network over some network access points. Such access points can be for example an Optical Line Termination (OLT) or a Passive Optical Network (PON) node that could be available in the neighbourhood of the low-voltage grid. Solutions for these tasks must be realized with minimum network costs and a good quality of service. The PLC systems considered in this paper are assumed to use Orthogonal Frequency Division Multiplexing (OFDM) modulation, which has been chosen as a standard within the OPERA consortium [2]. In OFDM systems, the spectrum is subdivided into small frequency bands called subcarriers. If two base stations, which are too close to each other, use the same subcarrier, then interferences between them will occur. Therefore, a kind of subcarrier (i.e. frequency) allocation has to be realized, so that each BS gets enough frequencies to serve its users, but without interfering with its neighbours. To simplify the problem, we assume that a subset of the available subcarriers is virtually bundled to build an entity called *PLC channel*, with capacity $K_{Ch}=64kbps$, as illustrated in Figure 2. In this case, the problem of allocating frequencies to BSs can be called *PLC Channel Allocation Problem* (P-CAP). This problem is analysed in this paper and solutions are proposed and evaluated. The P-CAP has similarities with CAP in mobile networks. Therefore, similar analysis could be used to model the P-CAP. Such similarities may lead to the assumption that P-CAP is also a NP-hard optimization problem like wireless CAP; [3].

The different subtasks of the design of the broadband powerline communications access networks can be organized under two main subproblems; a GBSP and a P-CAP.

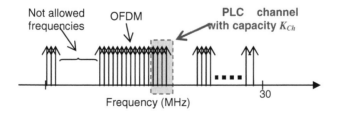

Fig. 2. Organization of powerline spectrum utilization

The entity built by the quintet: BS j, its user sub-set $|U^{(j)}{}_S|$, its set of repeaters, its WAP and the channel sub-set $F^{(j)}{}_S$ builds a *PLC cell*. A set of PLC cells of a LVN builds a *PLC site*, as shown in Figure 3 using a German LVN.

2.2 Comparison with Wireless Networks

As already mentioned above, the design process of B-PLC access networks has a strong similarity to the design of wireless networks. However, the B-PLC design has the following characteristics:

Complex cells and neighbourhood structures: PLC uses a physical medium that is having a certain wiring topology, and not like the wireless network that is using the free space. Because of that, a PLC cell j can have two types of neighbourhoods (or neighbours), which are called *in-line* and *in-space neighbourhood*. Thus, if a cell j' is belonging to in-space neighbourhood $\mathcal{N}^{(j)}_{in-space}$ of cell j, this means that one or more segments building the wiring of cell j' are located too near to a line segment belonging to cell j. This is the case of cell 7 and cell 2 in Figure 4. If cell j' is belonging to the in-line neighbourhood $\mathcal{N}^{(j)}_{in-line}$ of cell j, then these cells have one or more common line segments; like cells 3 and 2 in Figure 4. Therefore, the standard wireless model, where a cell is represented as a hexagon having at maximum six neighbouring cells is not valid here. A *neighbourhood matrix* $(M_{\mathcal{N}})$ is used to define the neighbourhood of cells in PLC site. An element $\eta_{jj'}$ of this matrix is one if the cells j and j' are neighbours; and zero otherwise. General qualitative comparison between wireless cells/site and B-PLC cells/site is illustrated in Figure 3;

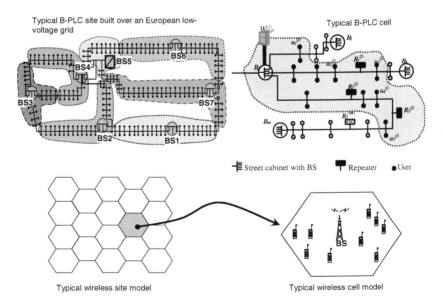

Fig. 3. Analogy between B-PLC sites/cells and wireless sites/cells

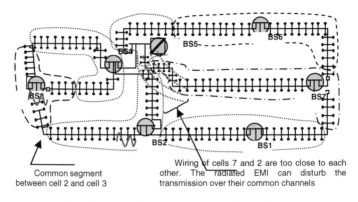

Common segment
between cell 2 and cell 3

Wiring of cells 7 and 2 are too close to each other. The radiated EMI can disturb the transmission over their common channels

Fig. 4. Types of interferences in a B-PLC site

Two types of interferences: A PLC cell *j* can have two types of neighbours (in-line and in-space ones); therefore, there are two types of interferences in PLC site. On one hand, the in-space interferences that are Electro-Magnetic Interferences (EMI) and are similar to those encountered in wireless sites. On the other hand, there are the in-line interferences that are conducted interferences. These occur between cells that are in-line neighbours. Interference occurrence is illustrated in Figure 4;

Use of wired medium requires recovery mechanism: the B-PLC uses an existing wired topology, which limits the number of potential locations, where networks elements could be placed. Also each BS and its users must be in-sight; [1]. Furthermore, a physical medium is a subject of failures (e.g. cuts in the line). In this case, recovery mechanisms are needed to overcome this problem;

Use of repeaters: because of the usage of PLC repeaters, for extending BS coverage, the BS and its repeaters have to be multiplexed either in time or in frequency domain or both. In all cases, the effective bit rate of a cell *j* is lower than the row bit rate offered by the allocated channels. Thus, quality of service (delay, bit rate, etc.) can be different from a user to another according to his distance from BS.

3   Analysis of PLC Channel Allocation Problem

3.1   Problem Definition

For solving a P-CAP for a given B-PLC problem instance, some information about the GBSP solution is necessary. It is necessary to know the number of installed BSs (i.e. cells) in the site (referred by $|B_S|$), the number of users allocated to each BS and the characteristic of the traffic generated by them, and the neighbourhood matrix (M_N). This allows knowing the neighbourhood of each cell and the calculation of the elements of the interference distance matrix (M_{ID}). An element $\delta_{jj'}$ of this matrix defines the minimum channel distance separation between the channels allocated to cell *j* and those allocated to cell *j'*, such that no interferences occur. A P-CAP solution without interferences is a solution where the distances between the channels of cells are equal or larger than the values specified by M_{ID}. Due to some possible technical or regulatory restrictions, some channels may not be available in some PLC environments. Such channels are said to be *locally blocked*, and build the set $F^{(j)}_{block}$, which has to be specified for every cell j, in order to be avoided during the allocation.

$$\mathbf{M}_{CA} = \begin{pmatrix} a_{1,1} & \cdots & a_{1,f} & \cdots & a_{1,|F_S|} \\ \vdots & \ddots & & & \vdots \\ a_{j,1} & & a_{j,f} & & a_{j,|F_S|} \\ \vdots & & & \ddots & \vdots \\ a_{|B_S|,1} & \cdots & a_{|B_S|,f} & \cdots & a_{|B_S|,|F_S|} \end{pmatrix} \quad \text{such that } a_{jf} = \begin{cases} 1; & if \ j \ uses \ f \\ 0; & otherwise \end{cases} \quad (1)$$

The task of any P-CAP solver is to allocate to each cell j a subset $F^{(j)}_{alloc}$ from the set of the PLC system channels F_S. Each cell should get enough capacity to serve its users adequately. A P-CAP solution can be expressed in the form of a ($|B_S|\times|F_S|$) matrix is called *channel allocation matrix* (M_{CA}) as represented in (1). This matrix is built by the *allocation decision variables* a_{jf}, which values must be optimally chosen from set {0;1}. The problem investigated here is Fixed P-CAP and not dynamic, since each cell gets a fix channel subset.

Generally, the different mathematical models that are met in wireless CAP could be applied for P-CAP. Examples of such models are: *the maximum service* proposed in [4], *minimum block* in [5], *minimum order* (MO-FAP) in [6], *minimum span* (MS-FAP) in [6], and *minimum interferences* (MI-FAP) in [7], etc. In this work, maximum service (referred here as maximum resource reuse and synonym to *maximum network throughput per cell*) and minimum interferences are considered. They are two conflicting objectives, and this makes the P-CAP a MOO problem.

The P-CAP can generally be defined as an optimization problem by the following:

Given: Neighbour matrix M_N; interference distance matrix M_{ID}; set of available PLC channels (F_S); traffic demand; set of locally blocked channels for each cell j ($F^{(j)}_{blocked}$);

Tasks: Allocate to each cell j sub-set of channel $F^{(j)}_{alloc}$;

Objectives: maximize resource reuse, minimize interferences

3.2 Traffic Demand in B-PLC Sites

Each BS j serves a set of users $U^{(j)}$s. Each user i generates a traffic demand $A_i^{(j;UL)}$ in uplink (UL) and a traffic $A_i^{(j;DL)}$ in downlink (DL) direction, with:

$$A_i^{(j,UL)} = \frac{\lambda_i^{(j,UL)} / \mu_i^{(j,UL)}}{K_{Ch}} \quad \text{and} \quad A_i^{(j,UL)} = \frac{\lambda_i^{(j,UL)} / \mu_i^{(j,UL)}}{K_{Ch}}$$

with $\lambda_i^{(j,UL)}$ and $\lambda_i^{(j,UL)}$ are the mean inter-arrival rate of the data packets of user i in UL and DL; respectively. The arrival processes are assumed to be a Poisson process. The average packet length of this user in UL and DL are $1/\mu_i^{(j,UL)}$ and $1/\mu_i^{(j,DL)}$; respectively. The constant K_{Ch} is the channel capacity. Let us assume $\lambda_i^{(j,UL)} = \lambda_{UL}$, $1/\mu_i^{(j,UL)} = 1/\mu_{UL}$, $\lambda_i^{(j,DL)} = \lambda_{DL}$ and $1/\mu_i^{(j,DL)} = 1/\mu_{DL}$ for all users i and all cells j. Thus, the total traffic demand in cell j has the following form:

$$A_{Total}^{(j)} = \left|U_S^{(j)}\right| \cdot \left(\frac{\lambda_{UL}/\mu_{UL}}{K_{Ch}} + \frac{\lambda_{DL}/\mu_{DL}}{K_{Ch}}\right) = \left|U_S^{(j)}\right| \cdot A_{User} \tag{2}$$

Thus, the number of channels needed by BS j is $F_{demand}^{(j)}$ that can be formulated by, where "$\lceil . \rceil$" is the rounding operator:

$$F_{demand}^{(j)} = \left\lceil A_{Total}^{(j)} \right\rceil = \left\lceil \left|U_S^{(j)}\right| \cdot A_{User} \right\rceil \tag{3}$$

3.3 Resource Reuse and Network Throughput

The main goal of the P-CAP is to allocate from the available channels as much as possible to each cell. This means to maximize the value the elements a_{jf} of the channel allocation matrix (M_{CA}), and this can be formulated as follows:

$$maximize \quad f_{RR} = \frac{1}{|B_S|}\sum_{j \in B_S} \frac{\left|F_{alloc}^{(j)}\right|}{F_{demand}^{(j)}} \tag{4}$$

Such that:
$$\left|F_{alloc}^{(j)}\right| = \sum_{f \in F_S} a_{j,f} \qquad\qquad \forall j \in B_S \tag{5}$$

$$a_{j,f} \in \{0;1\} \qquad\qquad \forall j \in B_S; \forall f \in F_S \tag{6}$$

$$a_{j,f} = 0 \qquad\qquad \forall j \in B_S; \forall f \in F_S \wedge f \in F_{block}^{(j)} \tag{7}$$

The resource reuse measure (f_{RR}) supplies a normalized metric, which simplies the theoretical analysis. However, network operators could be interested in having a practical measure of network performance, such as network throughput. In our previous investigations, we considered the *Cell Throughput* ρ_{Cell} as practical metric; [8]. This was derived from f_{RR} and represents the average capacity (or bit rates) of the cells. The maximization of the network throughput has the same constraints.

3.4 Modelling of Interferences in B-PLC Sites

The interference between two different cells of the site is called *co-site interferences* in wireless networks. In such a network, the co-site interferences can be treated in different ways. On one hand, the co-site interference is considered as a hard constraint. This means, any candidate solution that generates any co-site interference (i.e. the distance $\delta_{jj'}$ is not respected at least once) is considered as infeasible solution rejected. This approach has been used in [9] [10]. On the other hand, in [11] co-site interferences occurrence is accepted; however, they must be as low as possible. This means, the distance $\delta_{jj'}$ can be not always fulfilled. In this case, the interference minimization in CAP becomes similar to the *Constraint Satisfaction Problem* (CSP). In CSP, if no solution exists that satisfies all constraints, the solver tries to find a solution that minimizes the number of constraints violations, or to minimize some function(s) of the costs incurred to the violated constraints. This is used in this work.

In B-PLC network, two types of co-site interferences that require frequency separation can occur:

In-line interferences: These occur in the case illustrated in Figure 4, where the disturbance source and the victim are in-line neighbours. The coupling path is in this case the power line segment that is common between the cells;

In-space interferences: the source and the victim are in-space neighbours, and the coupling path is the space separating their cables. In this case, the signal from a cell j generates an electromagnetic field (seen by a cell j' as radiated disturbance). Such example is illustrated in Figure 4. This means that some of the cells wires are geographically very close to each others, so that interfering signal is strong enough to disturb the original signal. The extreme case of in-space neighbouring is the case where one or more segments from both cells are in the same bundle or duct.

For simplification reasons, the in-space interferences are not considered. Therefore, a frequency separation is needed between the channels of two cells, only if those cells are in-line neighbours. Therefore, the elements $\delta_{jj'}$ can be defined as follows, where $\Delta F_{in\text{-}line}$ is a constant:

$$\delta_{jj'} = \begin{cases} \Delta F_{in\text{-}line}; & \text{if} \quad j' \in \aleph_j^{(in\text{-}line)} \\ 0; & \text{otherwise} \end{cases} \tag{8}$$

The objective of P-CAP optimization is the minimization of interferences by minimizing number of interference distance violations. This is formulated as follows:

$$\text{minimize} \quad f_I = \sum_{j \in B_S} \sum_{j' \in \aleph_j^{(in\text{-}line)}} \sum_{g \in F_S^{(j)}} \sum_{g' \in F_S^{(j')}} \kappa_{gg'}^{(jj')} \tag{9}$$

Such that: $\kappa_{gg'}^{jj'} = \begin{cases} I_{in\text{-}line}^{(Interf)}; & \text{if} \quad |g - g'| < \delta_{jj'}; \\ 0; & \text{otherwise} \end{cases} \quad \forall j, j' \in B_S; \forall g \in F_S^{(j)}; \forall g' \in F_S^{(j')} \tag{10}$

Finally, the P-CAP can be formulated as a MOP as follows:

$$\text{minimize} \quad \mathbf{f}_{P\text{-}CAP} = \left[-f_{RR}, f_I \right] \tag{11}$$

such that: (4), (5), (6), (7), (9) and (10).

4   Optimization Approaches and Used Metaheuristics

The classical method for solving the MOP problems consists in aggregating the different objectives into a single general objective function, which is then optimized by the means of the traditional Single-Objective Optimization (SOO) algorithms. This method is called "scaling method" that combines linearly the objectives using weighting factors w_i's, $\Sigma w_k = 1$. In the last years, the Multi-Objective Optimization (MOO) (called also Multi-Criteria Optimization -MCO) approach has been intensively investigated, in order to optimize the conflicting objectives quasi-independently. Different MOO Algorithms (MOA) have been developed, in order to solve the MOPs without using the conversion into SOO. A MOA explores the solution space by eliminating dominated (i.e. the worst) solutions and keeping

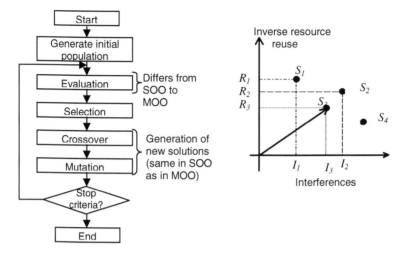

Fig. 5. General flowchart of evolutionary search-based algorithm (*left*) and principles of the multi-criteria optimization in case of minimization of both objectives (*right*)

non-dominated (i.e. the relative good) ones to build the so-called *Approximation Set A* (called also *Front* or *Pareto Front A*). An example of the solutions comparison in a two-dimensional optimization space is depicted in Figure 5. In this example, two objectives are minimized: the interferences and the inverse of resource reuse (i.e. maximization of reuse). The comparison of solutions S_1 and S_2 shows that the first one is better than the second, because $I_1 < I_2$ and $R_1 < R_2$. In this case, S_1 dominates S_2; therefore, S_2 is seen as bad (i.e. dominated) solution and has to be eliminated. The comparison of S1 and S3 shows that S1 is better than S3 in the interference dimension ($I_1 < I_3$), but worst in the other dimension ($R_1 > R_3$). In this case, S_1 and S_3 are called to be indifferent, also non-dominated. At the end of the algorithm iterations, the non-dominated solutions build the approximation set. In the example, the approximation set is built by S_1, S_3 and S_4, i.e. $A = \{ S_1, S_3, S_4 \}$.

In these investigations, Metaheuristics have been used, because they deliver good (but not always the best) solution to the problem in relative short computation time, in comparison to exact algorithms. The class of Metaheuristics is very large. From this class, the metaheuristics using the evolutionary search have been selected, because of their successful application in different engineering application, especially in network planning. In the numerical experiments, the SOO uses the genetic algorithm; [12]. For MOO both versions of Non-dominated Sorting Genetic Algorithm (NSGA and NSGA-II) ([13]) and Strength Pareto Evolutionary Algorithms (SPEA) ([14]) are applied. The evolutionary search consists in sampling the search space in a controlled random way. To realize this search, an initial population (i.e. set of solutions/individuals) is randomly generated. Iteratively, this population is evaluated and some solutions (generally the fittest/best) to generate new individuals/solutions until a break criteria is filled. The new solutions are generated using by means of crossover and mutation operations, according the flowchart shown in Figure 5; [12].

These genetic operators have a decisive effect on the algorithms performances, as we will see in the section of numerical results.

5   Numerical Experiments and Results Analysis

5.1   Problem Instances and System Characteristics

The experiment results have to be realized for different problem instances, in order to evaluate the optimization algorithm in different levels of problem complexity, such different number of cells, different number of users per cells, etc. For the generation of the problem instances for P-Cap, a low-voltage network with 14 locations for the BS/repeaters placement and 943 users. Through the solution of the generalized bases stations placement problem with different heuristics, two solution of B-PLC have been selected as instances. On one hand, a B-PLC site is constituted by 9 cells, which use the PLC system#1 in one case and a system#2 in the other case. These systems are also used to build the other remaining two P-CAP instances, which site contains 12 cells. This results in four P-CAP instances; as presented in Figure 6.

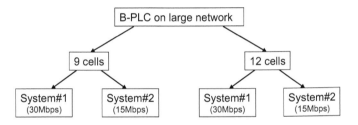

Fig. 6. Problem instances used in the numerical experiments

The four P-CAP instances are modeled by the neighborhoods matrices and the number of users per each cell. Users' distribution in cells is shown in Tables 1 and 2. Two PLC systems are considered, so that system#2 has $|F_s|=235$ (which characterizes a system with 15Mbps) and system#1 with $|F_s|=469$ (equivalent to 30Mbps).

For the interference calculation, we take $I^{in-line}_{interf}=1$ (i.e. no penalization function, only constraints violations counting), $\delta_{jj'}=1$. The users traffic demand is characterized by $A_{User}=3$, which represents an average of 128kbps in the downlink and 64kbps for the uplink. The statistical results are generated from 21 experiment runs.

Table 1. Number of users per cell inside the 9 cell-based site

BS	1	2	3	4	5	6	7
$|U^{(j)}_s|$	137	137	99	70	None	None	173
BS	8	9	10	11	12	13	14
$|U^{(j)}_s|$	None	156	90	None	None	42	30

Table 2. Number of users per cell in case of 12cell-based site

BS	1	2	3	4	5	6	7
$|U^{(j)}_s|$	105	80	62	149	None	47	54
BS	**8**	**9**	**10**	**11**	**12**	**13**	**14**
$|U^{(j)}_s|$	None	109	88	58	30	68	84

5.2 Solution Encoding and Evolutionary Operators

The encoding of P-CAP solution is realized by the means of a binary matrix that builds a solution (or an individual) in the form of an allocation matrix. The columns are corresponding to the available PLC channels, while the rows are corresponding to the installed BSs. The bit in the j-th row and f-th column corresponds to the element a_{jf} of the allocation matrix. This is equal to 1 if the channel f is allocated to the cell j in the considered solution (i.e. individual). Otherwise, this bit is a zero. There are different ways to realize the crossover of two matrices or individuals. In this paper, four schemes are considered and evaluated. These crossover schemes are illustrated in Figure 7. The first crossover scheme is referred to as 1-Point Simple Crossover (1-PSC) (Figure 7-a, 1st row-left). In this scheme, the parent solutions are cut vertically at one and the same point for all rows (i.e. cells). The same is realized also in the 2-Point Simple Crossover (2-PSC) (Figure 7-b, 1st row-right). But in this scheme the matrix is cut in two different points by 2-PSC instead of only one point like 1-PSC. The third crossover operator is called 1-Point Multiple Crossover (1-PMC) (Figure 7-c, 2nd row-left). In this case, each row of the matrix is cut exactly at one point, but this point differs from a row (i.e. cell) to another. Each row can be also cut at two different locations and in this case we have 2-Point Multiple Crossover (2-PMC) (Figure 7-d, 2nd row-right). All the four crossover schemes are tested later and compared by the numerical results, in order to choose the efficient one for the generation of the final numerical results that will be used for the evaluation of the algorithms performance. The mutation operator can be built also in different ways. Among the possible schemes, two variants have been selected for test and evaluation in this section; namely the 1-Bit Mutation (1-BM) and the 1-Cell Bit Mutation (1-CBM), as represented in Figure 8-*left*. In the 1-BM, exactly one bit is chosen randomly in the whole matrix and its values is switched by a given probability (mutation probability $-p_m$). In the 1-CBM, one bit is randomly selected from each matrix row (i.e. cell) and its value is switched by a given mutation probability.

5.3 Parameters Setting

The genetic operators (crossover and mutation) are decisive factors for the evolutionary algorithm performance. Because of that, ten simulation runs have been executed, in order to check the effect of the different operators' realizations on the evolutionary search. More intention has been given to the effect of those schemes in the multi-objective optimization paradigms. For such initial experiments, the following parameters have been used: 100 generations, 100 individuals in the

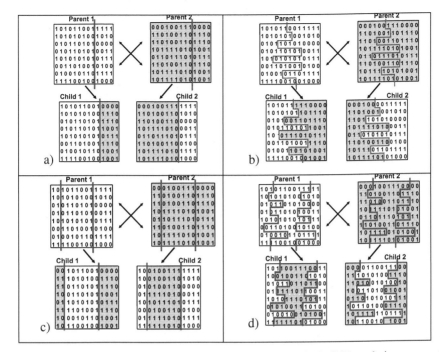

Fig. 7. Different schemes of crossover operator that can be used for P-CAP evolutionary search

Fig. 8. Mutation operators for the evolutionary search

population, crossover probability is 1 and mutation probability is 0.1 using 1-Bit Mutation for crossover schemes testing. All the runs have issued similar results. A sample of the resulted approximation sets is shown in Figure 9 for crossover. For the crossover, the 2-PMC supplies better front, which converges better (i.e. faster) than the other three schemes; for of all three MOEAs. Such behavior is expected, because this scheme allows the realization of larger springs in the search space. A large spring is represented in large difference between parents' solutions and their children. The difference considered here is in the representation (i.e. coding) space. These wide springs are the main characteristics of the global search, such as the evolutionary search or any other population search-based algorithm. In other words, the 2-PMC crossover scheme allows the population to keep a higher diversity. Such diversity prevents the search form getting trapped in local optima. A possible drawback of very high diversity in the population could result in a bad convergence, because in such case the search becomes more oriented toward exploration of the search space, but with a bad exploitation (i.e. learning process).

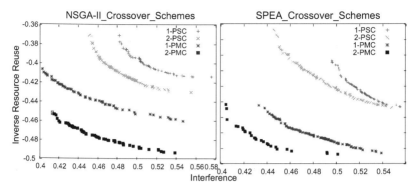

Fig. 9. Approximation sets of diff. crossover schemes using NSGA-II (*left*) and SPEA (*right*)

Similar remarks and argumentation are valid also for the mutation operators. The 1-CBM mutation method has shown a clear dominance in comparison to the 1-BM method. For the final numerical experiments, the number of generations has been set to 300 generations, while the population size is 150 individuals. With higher number of iterations, the drawback of the 2-MPC scheme becomes clearer, in comparison to the 1-PSC for the case of SPEA and NSGA-II. The very high diversity lets the individuals be spread out in the objective space and only a few individuals remain not dominated. This is reflected by the low cardinality of the approximation set. A very high diversity becomes destructive for the convergence of the population. The scheme with 1-PSC allows a progressive convergence of population individuals. This leads to dense non-dominated set. Furthermore, a slower convergence (or small springs) allows a balanced convergence. This means, that the non-dominated solutions are almost equally distributed over the front spread in both optimization objective dimensions. The relative behavior of 2-PMC and 1-PSC in this case is similar to the relative behavior of genetic algorithms (which is a global search) and the simulated annealing (which is local search) in the SOO. In fact, the GA converges early and more quickly than the SA. But if the optimization algorithm has enough time for the convergence (i.e. higher number of iterations), then the SA will converge later, but to better solution than GA, which early convergence leads to less good solution. However, 2-MPC has been kept for numerical experiments, in spite of this drawback, because 2-MPC could be strongly preferred for its higher resource reuse.

From the discussion above and from different test runs, the following parameters are set for the numerical experiments: Number of generations: 300; Population size: 150; Crossover probability: 1; Mutation probability: 0.1; Crossover method: 2-PMC; and Mutation method: 1-CBM.

5.4 Evaluation of Pareto-Based MOEAs

The evaluation of the MOEAs in the P-CAP is based on the coverage of two sets. This metric measures the percentage of solutions in front A_1 that are dominated by at least one solution from front A_2. It shows how good is the solutions convergence towards the optimal front in comparison to solutions of the other front. The coverage of two sets shows also a constant dominance behavior between the algorithms over all four

Table 3. Coverage of two sets for MOEAs in case of 9cells-based site

9 Cells-based site – System#1			
	NSGA	NSGA-II	SPEA
NSGA	#	0.07±0.01	0.55±0.19
NSGA-II	0.84±0.11	#	0.93±0.06
SPEA	0.33±0.15	0.04±0.06	#
9 Cells-based site – System#2			
	NSGA	NSGA-II	SPEA
NSGA	#	0.09±0.14	0.61±0.21
NSGA-II	0.88±0.1	#	0.9±0.14
SPEA	0.28±0.25	0.05±0.08	#

Table 4. Coverage of two sets for MOEAs in case of 12cells-based site

12 Cells-based site – System#1			
	NSGA	NSGA-II	SPEA
NSGA	#	0.06±0.06	0.38±0.26
NSGA-II	0.9±0.06	#	0.72±0.27
SPEA	0.54±0.25	0.14±0.13	#
12 Cells-based site – System#2			
	NSGA	NSGA-II	SPEA
NSGA	#	0.15±0.12	0.54±0.18
NSGA-II	0.71±0.14	#	0.8±0.08
SPEA	0.38±0.24	0.11±0.09	#

considered P-CAP instances. It can be generally concluded from the coverage of two sets shown in Tables 3 and 4 that NSGA-II outperforms the SPEA, while the SPEA is dominating the NSGA. For example, in case of 9 Cells with System#1 instance, the SPEA dominates about 86\% of all NSGA solutions, while only 8% of them are dominated. The NSGA is also outperformed by its extension (i.e. NSGA-II). In the same instance example, the NSGA-II dominates about 90% of NSGA solutions, while only 5% of its solutions are dominated. The difference in the coverage of two sets metric between NSGA and NSGA-II is clear in P-CAP, as can be observed in Figure 10. A reason of the relative low convergence is the possible losses of the good

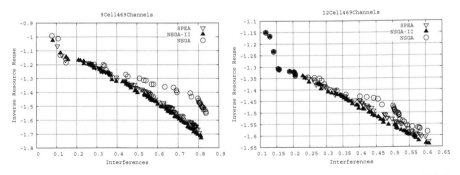

Fig. 10. Samples of approximation sets achieved by the Pareto-based MOEAs in case of 9Cell- and 12Cells-based B-PLC sites using system#1

solutions found during the search, either through the destruction through genetic operators (crossover and mutation) or through the randomness in the selection procedure. The destruction of the good solutions by the crossover operators is more probable with 2-PMC mechanism, because it introduces strong changes on the resulting offsprings compared to their parents. Such destructive effect is less present in other crossover schemes, especially with 1-PSC. This problem is avoided by NSGA-II and SPEA by using the elitism.

During the parameter setting for the numerical experiments, a big influence of the used crossover scheme was observed, as discussed previously. The results discussed above have been realized with 2-PMC crossover scheme. Results with 1-PSC have been also realized and a part of them is given in the appendices for two problem instances only. Three observations have been made concerning the MOEAs results: *(i)* the very large cardinalities of the approximation sets (for all three variants); *(ii)* this higher number of solutions performs finer numerical results for the coverage of two sets metric (with very small confidence intervals). This exactitude comes also from the fact of the stability on the convergence, where the MOEA explores the whole Pareto fronts, on the contrary to the 2-PMC MOEAs that converge to a narrow part of the front; and *(iii)* the NSGA-II shows also in this scenario with 1-PSC best performances, followed by SPEA and then NSGA (on the contrary to the 2-PMC where NSGA has light advantage compared to SPEA).

6 Conclusions

This paper deals with the design of Broadband Power Line Communications access networks, with focus on the PLC Channel Allocation Problem (P-CAP). In the P-CAP, each installed BS (or cell) has to get allocated a subset from the set of the available B-PLC channels. This problem is a Multi-objective Optimization Problem (MOP), where the resource reuse has to be maximized, while the interferences have to be kept as minimal as possible. The interferences in a B-PLC have been categorized into two main classes; the in-line and the in-space interferences. In the application section only the in-line interferences have been considered, while the in-space interference that are more complex to model have been avoided.

For the solution of the P-CAP, two optimization paradigms have been used: the single objective optimization (SOO) where the MOP is converted into a single-objective problem and the Multi-objective Optimization (MOO), where the objectives are optimized quasi-independently from each other. In the numerical experiments two problem instance sizes have been used (9 cell- and 12 cell-based sites) with two possible B-PLC systems (system#1 and system#2), which differ in the costs and performances. Four crossover schemes have been proposed and tested. Among those schemes, the two-point multi-crossover (2-PMC) has shown the best convergence. The comparison of MOEA variants with each other is sometimes not fine, because of the large realized confidence intervals. Main cause of this effect is relative low cardinality of approximation sets. This is clear in P-CAP with 2-PMC crossover. However, P-CAP using 1-PSC supplies precise results. In spite of this, it can be seen that the NSGA-II is more successful for P-CAP followed by NSGA and then SPEA.

References

1. Haidine, A., Mellado, I., Lehnert, R.: PANDeMOO: Powerline communications access network designer based on multi-objective optimisation. In: 9th ISPLC, VC, Canada (2005)
2. Open PLC European Research Alliance (OPERA), http://www.ist-opera.org/
3. Hale, W.K.: Frequency assignment: theory and applications. Proceeding of the IEEE 68(12), 1497–1514 (1980)
4. Maniezzo, V., Carbonaro, A.: An ANTS Heuristic for the Frequency Assignment Problem. Future Generation Computer Systems 16, 927–935 (2000)
5. Koster, A.: Frequency Assignment - Models and Algorithms. Dissertation at University of Maastricht, Netherlands (1999)
6. Aardal, K., et al.: Models and Solution Techniques for Frequency Assignment Problems. Konrad-Zuse-Zentrum für Informationstechnik Berlin –Report 01-40 (2001)
7. Schulz, M.: Solving Frequency Assignment Problems with Constraint Programming. Diploma thesis at Institute for Mathematics, Berlin University of Technology (February 2003)
8. Haidine, A., Lehnert, R.: Analysis of the Channel Allocation Problem in Broadband Power Line Communications Access Networks. In: 11th IEEE ISPLC, Pisa, Italy (2007)
9. Eisenblätter, A.: Frequency Assignment in GSM Networks: Models, Heuristics, and Lower Bounds. Dissertation at Berlin University of technology, Berlin (2001)
10. Beckmann, D.: Algorithmen zur Planung und Optimierung moderner Kommunikationsnetze. PhD at Hamburg-Harburg University of Technology (2003)
11. Maniezzo, V., Montemanni, R.: An exact algorithm for the min-interference frequency assignment problem. Research Report WP-CO0003, University of Bologna, Italy (2000)
12. Goldberg, D.E.: Genetic algorithms in search, optimization, and machine learning. Addison Wesley, Reading (1989)
13. Deb, K.: A Fast and Elitist Multiobjective genetic Algorithm: NSGA-II. IEEE Trans. on Evolutionary Comput. 6(2) (2002)
14. Zitzler, E.: Evolutionary Algorithms for Multiobjective Optimization: Methods and Applications. PhD Thesis, Swiss Federal Institute of Technology (1999)

Topology Design of Hierarchical Hybrid Fiber-VDSL Access Networks with Enhanced Discrete Binary PSO

Rong Zhao[1,2], Yi Zhang[1], and Ralf Lehnert[1]

[1] Technische Universität Dresden, Chair for Telecommunications,
01062 Dresden, Germany
{rong.zhao,ralf.lehnert}@tu-dresden.de
[2] Detecon International GmbH, Oberkasseler Straße 2,
53227 Bonn, Germany

Abstract. As one of the most efficient access solutions, VDSL technology is becoming a highlight in the next generation network. This paper addresses the topology design of hierarchical Hybrid Fiber-VDSL Access Networks (HFVAN) as a NP-hard problem. An efficient strategy with general binary models is proposed to find a cost-effective and high-reliable network with heuristic algorithms in a short time. An enhanced Discrete Binary Particle Swarm Optimization (DBPSO) is developed and successfully implemented for this network planning problem, both for clustering and positioning. In terms of numerical results, the performance of the enhanced DBPSO is compared with some previous approaches.

Keywords: Hybrid Fiber-VDSL Access Network, network architecture, network survivability, network planning and optimization, Discrete Binary Particle Swarm Optimization.

1 Introduction

In the last decade DSL Access Network has become one of the most efficient access technologies to provide a high bandwidth for SOHO subscribers. As the milestone for DSL technology, the DSL specification VDSL2 (ITU-T, G.993.2) enables network operators to provide up to 200 Mbps bandwidth over twisted pair. This increase has a huge impact on global connectivity coupled with multifarious applications, such as IPTV in HDTV quality.

Similar to a PSTN access network, the Hybrid Fiber-VDSL access network (HFVAN) is divided into two parts: the distribution network between Central Office(CO) and Street Cabinets (SCs), and the *Last 100 Meters* network. The *Last 100 Meters* network is the part between SCs and the subscribers, where the VDSL technology is implemented to realize a high transmission speed of subscribers over twisted pair. This work focuses on the planning and optimization of the distribution network in HFVANs, i.e. finding out a low-cost hierarchical structure with suitable positions for the intermediate layer and optimal

C. Wang (Ed.): AccessNets, LNICST 6, pp. 208–223, 2009.

connections of all network nodes subject to delay and network reliability with node-biconnectivity. The hierarchical HFVAN design is NP-hard [1][2][3].

Some prior approaches addressed the topological design for hierarchical backbone networks by [4][5][6][7] and access networks by [8][9][10][11]. Generally, network structures are illustrated by hierarchical star-star, tree-star, or mesh-star topology. Most of these optimization problems are NP-hard. Due to their complexity, different methodologies are investigated, such as Linear Programming, Simulated Annealing, Tabu Search, Genetic Algorithms, Ant Colony Optimization, etc. Some algorithms have been investigated for HFV access network planning problems in [1][2][3].

Particle Swarm Optimization (PSO) is a metaheuristics, which is inspired by the observation of the behaviors of birds and fishes. This optimization method introduced by Kennedy and Eberhart in 1995, has shown an excellent performance in many applications. PSO was designed for the optimization of continuous optimization problems, in particular to some mathematical problems [12][13][14][15]. In the last years more real-world problems have been studied with PSO [16], such as constrained optimization problems [17] and the neighbor selection in Peer-to-Peer Networks [18]. Moreover, PSO-algorithms have been extended to cover multifarious discrete optimization problems [19][20][21][22]. However, only few approaches to hierarchical topology design problems with Discrete Binary PSO (DBPSO) were published in the last years. PSO with a Non-binary Model (NBM) was studied for HFVAN topology design problems, but its performance was not stable enough due to the complex encoding process [2]. This work adopts DBPSO and proposes an enhanced update function for the topology design of hierarchical HFVANs.

This paper is organized as follows: section 2 describes the hierarchical structure of HFVANs and makes a problem statement for their planning. Section 3 presents the complete strategy to fulfill the hierarchical topology design of HFVANs and binary models for its network topology. Section 4 introduces Discrete Binary Particle Swarm Optimization and proposes the enhanced DBPSO for the HFVAN topology design. Consequently, some optimization results from DBPSO will be analyzed and compared with Simulated Annealing (SA), Tabu Search (TS), Genetic Algorithms (GA), Ant Colony Optimization (ACO) and PSO with NBM in Section 5. Finally the conclusion and further work will be presented.

2   Problem Statement

2.1   Hybrid Fiber-VDSL Access Networks

In Fig.1 the Central Office (CO), Street Cabinets (SCs) and end users compose a hierarchical infrastructure of a HFVAN. Its two main parts are the distribution network (CO-SCs) and the *Last 100 meters* network (SCs-VDSL end users), which are interconnected by the optical fiber and the existing twisted pair, respectively. This work focuses on planning and optimization of the distribution network due to the fixed connection within the *Last 100 Meters* area. To reduce the investment costs and improve network reliability, the hierarchical structure

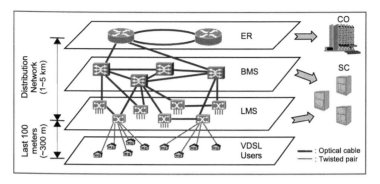

Fig. 1. Hierarchical structure of hybrid fiber-VDSL access networks

(middle layer with meshing) in the distribution network has been proposed subject to constraints of network elements, such as Edge Router (ER), Branch Micro Switch (BMS) and Leaf Micro Switch (LMS). Keeping up the infrastructure of the PSTN access network, the HFVAN respectively installs ER into CO and BMS or LMS into SC, as shown in Fig.1. All VDSL subscribers are connected with a star topology to a LMS located in the SC.

The top layer of this network is the Edge Router which provides the interface between the distribution network and the backbone network. As assumed, only one ER will be placed in this layer. Some BMSs compose the intermediate layer of this network. The third layer of the network consists of a number of LMSs, accessing to residential and SOHO subscribers. In consideration of the network availability and reliability, a LMS must have at least two paths to reach the ER, i.e. each LMS at the low layer must have two uplinks either to BMSs in the high layer or to be joined with other LMSs. The hierarchical network topology of HFVANs should fulfill the requirements of both edge-biconnectivity and node biconnectivity.

2.2   Objective Function and Constraints

The major planning problem in this work is to build up the intermediate BMS-layer of the hierarchical network. More precisely, it is to determine the corresponding number of BMSs, the position of each BMS and to find out the optimal links within the network nodes, subject to minimal costs and some constraints. The objective function (costs function) Z_{net} is formulated by:

$$Z_{net} = \sum_i x_i^{bms} C_{bms} + \sum_i \sum_j x_{ij} c(l_{ij}) + N_{lms} C_{lms} \qquad (1)$$

where N_{lms} is the number of LMSs, C_{bms} and C_{bms} are the costs of each LMS and BMS, l_{ij} is the edge length between node i and j ($i, j \in 1..N_{lms}$), x_i^{bms} and x_{ij} are binary variables (if a node or link is selected, then 1; otherwise 0). $c(l_{ij})$ is the cost of link ij that is assumed to be a linear function of the link length l_{ij}:

$$c(l_{ij}) = C_l l_{ij} + c_{ij}^k \qquad (2)$$

where C_l is the cost unit of the fiber. c_{ij}^k is the fixed cost for different link types within ER, BMSs and LMSs, i.e. $k=1$ for link ER-BMS, $k=2$ for link BMS-BMS, $k=3$ for link BMS-LMS. As we assume that the number and costs of LMSs and ER are fixed, therefore these costs can be ignored in the objective function.

The constraints for the planning of HFVANs are made up of *physical constraints*, *flow constraints*, maximal *delay*, and *reliability*. *Physical constraints* are related to topology, location and selection of BMSs in the HFVAN. The maximal and minimal uplink/downlink ports are limited for node degrees. Considering the characteristics of HFVANs, the network can be modeled with M/M/1 system to derive the *end-to-end delay* [1]. To deal with single link failures, a minimum connectivity of the topology should be satisfied to guarantee the network reliability. In this work edge- and node-biconnectivity for single node failures is considered.

3   Analysis of HFV Access Network Topology Design

3.1   Strategy

A complete strategy of the HFVAN topology design with heuristic algorithms is proposed in [3].

```
Initialization (network structure, algorithms parameters)
while stop_criterion=false do
    Generation of new network structures:
        Positioning of BMSs;
        Clustering of LMSs with BMSs;
    Reparation of links (BMS-LMS, LMS-LMS);
    Multi-constrained MST (ER-BMS layer);
    Augmentation (ER-BMS layer);
    Costs evaluation (total network costs);
endwhile
Output the best solution found so far.
```

Fig. 2. Strategy of the HFVAN topology design

Fig.2 presents an iterative procedure of planning the HFVAN structure with heuristic algorithms. The whole optimization process updates network structures dynamically by generating new neighbors. Firstly, the initial network structure is randomly generated, but it is ensured to be valid using some repair functions. As described in section 2, HFVANs are built with a hierarchical topology. The middle layer of BMSs, i.e. the positions and numbers of BMSs, are unknown. After positioning of BMSs and clustering of LMSs, the connections between BMSs and LMSs can be determined. With local repair functions the redundant or invalid links will be removed, a few improved links will be added, respectively. In this case a Minimum Spanning Tree (MST) is an efficient solution to build up a fundamental structure of the BMS-layer. However, multi-constraints, such as node degree, delay, capacity, make the MST problem more complex. This problem is called Multi-Constrained Minimum Spanning Tree (MCMST). Based on MCMST and Augmentation, a bi-connected, cost-effective, and degree/capacity/delay-valid network structure with three layers will be achieved. Costs evaluation will estimate network costs including the costs of LMSs, BMSs and the selected links within them. The stop criterion is assumed as a certain iteration subject to the visited solutions.

Optimization algorithms, such as DBPSO, will have significant effects on this network planning procedure, particularly for the generation of new neighbors (Positioning of BMSs and Clustering of LMSs) and Costs evaluation. In a sense other functions in the loop are necessary for HFVAN topology design, but have little influence on heuristic optimization algorithms studied. The optimal solutions found so far have less than 2% difference to reference global optima. It verifies the proposed strategy to be suitable for this design problem.

3.2 Binary Modeling

Besides the Linear 0-1 Integer Programming, the binary modeling can be applied to optimization problems with heuristic algorithms, such as Simulated Annealing, Tabu Search, Genetic Algorithms, etc. Similarly, the network topology of a HFVAN can be modeled as a particle with a group of binary individuals. Hereby, two scenarios are proposed in Fig.3. *Full Particle Modeling*(FPM) is used for DBPSO to fulfill both Positioning and Linking of BMSs, and Clustering of LMSs, including all binary codes. All changes of binary codes are dependent on DBPSO. *Partial Particle Modeling*(PPM) is adopted to present DBPSO influencing only the Positioning and Linking of BMSs, i.e. BMSs, ER-BMS, BMS-BMS in the first terms. As assumed, the links between ER and LMS are not allowed due to the high cost. In the current approach there is only one ER. Hence, the first binary code for ER should be 1.

As shown above for *Full Particle Modeling*, the overall particle length with N_{lms} SC (LMS) and 1 CO (ER) consists of different individuals numbers:

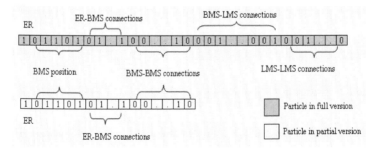

Fig. 3. Full Particle Modeling and Partial Particle Modeling for HFVANs

- first entry for ER;
- N_{lms} entries for potential BMSs' positions;
- N_{lms} entries for the connections between ER and BMSs;
- $N_{lms}(N_{lms} - 1)/2$ entries for the connections within BMSs;
- N_{lms}^2 entries for the connections between BMSs and LMSs;
- $N_{lms}(N_{lms} - 1)/2$ entries for the connections within LMSs;

where 1 means the presence of nodes or edges in the network solution, 0 means the absence of nodes or edges. If the first code of ER is ignored, the particle length of *Full Particle Modeling* (FPM) is described as:

$$L_{FPM} = (2N_{lms} + 1)N_{lms} \qquad (3)$$

Comparatively, the particle length of *Partial Particle Modeling* (PPM) is:

$$L_{PPM} = N_{lms}(N_{lms} + 3)/2 \qquad (4)$$

The length of PPM is obviously less than FPM, where a deterministic method will fulfill the connection within LMSs and BMSs. If N_{lms} is large enough, then L_{FPM} is approximated to $4L_{PPM}$. With the deterministic method the PPM could make optimization results locally optimal, but the computation time can be significantly reduced. In the previous study a non-binary model was proposed for continuous PSO [2].

4   Discrete Binary Particle Swarm Optimization

4.1   Introduction

As a swarm intelligent computation technique, PSO has its roots in the simulation of a simplified social system such as bird flocking, fish schooling, and swarm theory in particular. Different from GA and some other Evolutionary Computational (EC) algorithms, each individual in PSO searches for the optimum under the spirit of *Cooperation*.

A general strategy of PSO is described in Fig.4, which is suitable for all continuous and discrete PSO algorithms. The main procedure of PSO is fulfilled by the

```
Initialization (position, velocity, PSO parameters)
while stop_criterion=false do
    Schedule_Activities
        Evaluate positions (calculate solutions);
        Find global optimum and personal optimum;
        Update velocity and position;
    end Schedule_Activities
endwhile
Output the optimal solution.
```

Fig. 4. Pseudo code of Particle Swarm Optimization

Schedule-Activities: calculate solutions, find the current best value of all particles and the personal best value of each particle, update the velocity and position.

The intensification of an optimization process with PSO is fulfilled by keeping or strengthening a useful particle, i.e. the particle with the best value found so far. It can accelerate the convergence of the search processes. Inversely, the personal optimum and the random change can improve the diversification of PSO to avoid the local optimum.

4.2   Formulation and Notation

The standard PSO which operates in a continuous search space is suited to handle real valued optimization problems. But many optimization problems are set in a discrete search space. The algorithm tends to fall apart if a particle is flying to either zero and one. A discrete binary version of the PSO was introduced by Kennedy and Eberhart [19], using the concept of velocity as a probability that a bit takes on 0 or 1. The original update functions for the velocity and the position of particles in DBPSO are described as:

$$v_n(k+1) = v_n(k) + c_1 r_1 (p_{best,n} - x_n(k)) + c_2 r_2 (g_{best} - x_n(k)) \qquad (5)$$

$$x_n(k+1) = \begin{cases} 0 & sign(v_n(k+1)) \leq r_3 \\ 1 & sign(v_n(k+1)) > r_3 \end{cases} \qquad (6)$$

$$sign(\alpha) = 1/(1 + e^{-\alpha}) \qquad (7)$$

where
c_1 and c_2 are the acceleration factors with constant and positive values;
V_{max} is the maximum of the velocity;
N_p is the number of particles;
n is the n-th particle in the swarm, $n \in [1, N_p]$;
k is the iteration number;
$v_n(k)$ is the velocity of the particle n, $|v_n(k)| \leq V_{max}$;
$x_n(k)$ is the position of particle n, binary variable;
$p_{best,n}$ is the best position of particle n;
g_{best} is the best position for all particles;
r_1, r_2, r_3 are uniformly distributed number between 0 and 1.

4.3   Enhanced DBPSO

Obviously, the acceleration factors c_1 and c_2 are two important parameters influencing the performance of DBPSO. c_1 can strengthen the effect of $p_{best,n}$, c_2 emphasizes the effect of g_{best}, respectively. They control each optimization step, in which a particle will move to either the best personal position $p_{best,n}$ or the best global position g_{best}. A suitable setting of two parameters can lead particles to reach the balance between *Cognition* and *Social* behaviors well [13]. Anyway, the independence of c_1 and c_2 makes it difficult to apply DBPSO for real-world problems.

Generally, V_{max} in DBPSO is taken as a complementary factor to limit the further exploration rate. The velocity should be limited to V_{max}. A high V_{max} in the continuous-valued version increases the range explored by a particle. Conversely, a smaller V_{max} leads to a higher mutation rate [19]. However, numerical results in this work show that V_{max} plays an important role in the HFVAN topology design by updating the velocity and position. An inefficient setting of V_{max} could disturb the performance of DBPSO. Some numerical results will be shown later.

To avoid this negative effect, an enhanced update function is proposed, where V_{max} is taken into account. However, adding a new parameter into the update function could make it more difficult to obtain a suitable configuration for all control parameters. To reduce the complexity, we will combine a few control parameters in the current update function of DBPSO.

In the DBPSO $|r_1(p_{best,n} - x_n(k))|$ and $|r_2(g_{best} - x_n(k))|$ are less than 1. Actually, the main change of $v_n(k+1)$ strongly depends on the ratio of c_1 and c_2 besides the prior state $v_n(k)$. We assume $c_1 + c_2 = V_{max}$. Then the ratio $\gamma = c_2/c_1$ is defined to describe the effects of $p_{best,n}$ and g_{best}. Therefore, a new update DBPSO function is proposed as:

$$v_n(k+1) = v_n(k) + V_{max}\frac{1}{1+\gamma}r_1(p_{best,n} - x_n(k)) + V_{max}\frac{\gamma}{1+\gamma}r_2(g_{best} - x_n(k))$$

$$(8)$$

where the old control parameters c_1, c_2, V_{max} are replaced by γ and V_{max}. The further characteristics of γ and the performance of the enhanced update function will be discussed later in terms of numerical results.

4.4   Application

Tab.1 provides a mapping from DBPSO to HFVAN topology design problems. Other parameters have been explained in *Formulation and Notation*.

5   Results and Analysis

5.1   Optimization Environment

1) Test bed: three typical networks are studied.

- Network I: 13 Street Cabinets (SCs) and 1 Central Office (CO), where CO is located at the boundary of the network;
- Network II: 40 SC and 1 CO , the position of CO is similar to that in Network I;
- Network III: 87 SC and 1 CO, where CO is located in the middle of the network.

Table 1. Mapping of DBPSO in HFVANs topology design

DBPSO	Application
Particle n	n-th network topology
Code i in particle n	i-th node (or edge) in n-th network topology
Modification of particles	Generation of new topologies
Position $x_{n,i}(k) = 0$ or 1	State of i-th node (or edge) in n-th topology (1:selected, 0:unselected)
Velocity $v_{n,i}(k) = 0$ or 1	State change of i-th node (or edge) in n-th topology
Personal best position $p_{best,n,i} = 0$ or 1	State of i-th node (or edge) in the local best n-th topology
Global best position $g_{best,i} = 0$ or 1	State of i-th node (or edge) in the global best network topology
Objective function	Cost function
Goal	Find the optimal network topology

2) Hardware and software: in this approach several heuristic algorithms have been implemented in the standard platform of a planning tool for HFVAN designs in C++. Generally, each parameter or scenario has been tested at least 20 times (runs). *CPLEX* is used to obtain a global or near-global optimum as reference results. The test environment is made up of two parts:

- Heuristic algorithms in C++ are tested at the *HPC* of TU Dresden: *Linux Networx PC-Farm Deimos, CPU: AMD Opteron dual Core 2.6GHz, RAM: 2 GB*;
- *CPLEX* works with a computer: *CPU: Intel(R) Xeon(TM) 3.20GHz, RAM: 4 GB*.

5.2   Results and Comparison

1) Original DBPSO vs. enhanced DBPSO: in the original DBPSO, V_{max} is usually used as a constraint for the update of the velocity. Actually, it plays a relevant role in the optimization process with DBPSO. However, this effect is a negative factor to disturb the performance of DBPSO in HFV access network designs. Fig.5a, Fig.6a and Fig.7a show the relationship between V_{max} and c_2 for Full Particle Modeling (FPM) for Network I/II/III, where c_1=1. Each test point in the figures presents the mean value of optimal costs from at least 20 runs. These results explicitly verify that different V_{max} leads to different results. This effect makes the selection of c_1 and c_2 more complex for the HFV access network topology design. Due to bad solutions, the results of V_{max} ($V_{max} < 5$ for Network I/II, $V_{max} < 10$ for Network III) are not depicted in Fig.5a, Fig.6a and Fig.7a. Hence, they are disregarded for the comparison.

To avoid this negative influence of V_{max}, the enhanced DBPSO is implemented. Fig.5b, Fig.6b and Fig.7b present the optimization results from V_{max}

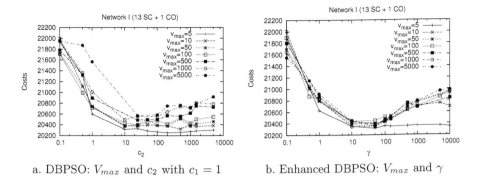

a. DBPSO: V_{max} and c_2 with $c_1 = 1$ b. Enhanced DBPSO: V_{max} and γ

Fig. 5. Comparison of DBPSO and Enhanced DBPSO with the Full Particle Modeling for Network I (5 particles)

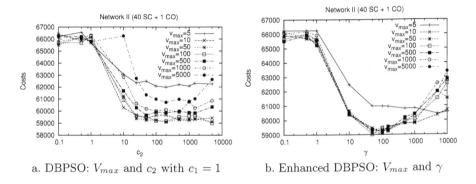

a. DBPSO: V_{max} and c_2 with $c_1 = 1$ b. Enhanced DBPSO: V_{max} and γ

Fig. 6. Comparison of DBPSO and Enhanced DBPSO with the Full Particle Modeling for Network II (10 particles)

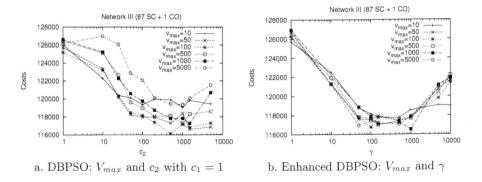

a. DBPSO: V_{max} and c_2 with $c_1 = 1$ b. Enhanced DBPSO: V_{max} and γ

Fig. 7. Comparison of DBPSO and Enhanced DBPSO with the Full Particle Modeling for Network III (10 particles)

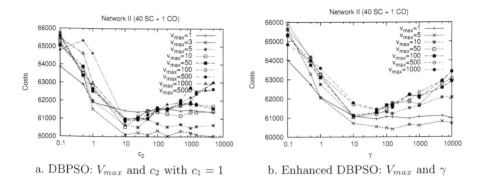

a. DBPSO: V_{max} and c_2 with $c_1 = 1$ b. Enhanced DBPSO: V_{max} and γ

Fig. 8. Comparison of DBPSO and Enhanced DBPSO with the Partial Particle Modeling for Network II (10 particles)

and γ for Network I/II/III with FPM, which are almost independent on V_{max} as γ in $[10, 500]$. Then V_{max} works only as the constraint for the velocity. We do not need to consider it, while studying other parameters, such as the number of particles and iterations. These results identify the advantage of the enhanced DBPSO with γ, which can efficiently work for DBPSO with Full Particle Modeling. A special case appears for Network I and II with $V_{max}=5$ in Fig.5b and Fig.6b, where V_{max} has no significant influence in these two scenarios with FPM.

The optimization results from DBPSO and enhanced DBPSO with Partial Particle Modeling (PPM) for Network II are depicted in Fig.8. Similar results from PPM for Network I/III are ignored here. However, the improvement of the enhanced DBPSO can not be explicitly seen for Partial Particle Modeling. It stands to reason that only a part of codes are updated by DBPSO with PPM, other binary codes are decided by a few deterministic algorithms. Therefore, the results from DBPSO with PPM for Network I/III are not discussed in this paper.

2) Particle number and visited solutions: if the number of the optimization iterations is fixed, more particles (i.e. visited solutions) at each iteration improve the optimization. Conversely, the optimization time could be increased. Hence, a suitable number of particles is meaningful for the performance of DBPSO. Fig.9 presents the optimization process with different numbers of particles and FPM/PPM for Network II, where the maximal number of solutions is limited. For Network II with FPM or PPM five particles provide the best costs. However, the number of particles depends on the optimization problem. For the HFVAN topology design a higher particle number does not mean that better optimal solutions can be easily found. It stands to reason that more particles could improve the diversification of DBPSO and reduce the intensification. The balance of intensification and diversification of DBSPO has to be obtained subject to empirical results in this work. Hence, the suitable number of particles has to be selected to adapt different real-world problems.

3) Partial Binary Modeling vs. Full Binary Modeling: in terms of Fig.9, DBPSO with FPM has better performance than DBPSO with PPM, because DBPSO with PPM realizing Clustering of LMSs easily leads to trap into local optima. Fig.10

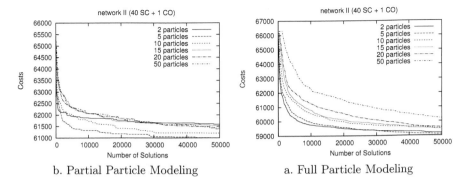

b. Partial Particle Modeling   a. Full Particle Modeling

Fig. 9. Comparison of the number of particles with limited solutions ($\gamma = 50$, $V_{max} = 50$)

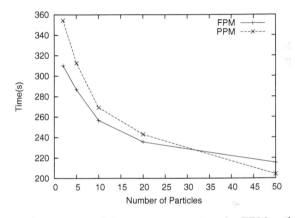

Fig. 10. Comparison of the optimization time for FPM and PPM

compares the optimization time of DBPSO with FPM and PPM. For low numbers of particles the optimization time by DBPSO with FPM is shorter than that by DBPSO with PPM. It stands to reason that a considerable part of the optimization time depends on the repair of the LMSs-BMSs clustering. As mentioned, DBPSO with PPM uses a deterministic method to realize the clustering of LMSs. As assumed, γ is 50, which makes g_{best} more important. During the update of the velocity, other particle are moving to the current best particle. More precisely for HFVAN topology design problems, other network topologies will be changed similar to the best network topology. The best network topology must be a valid solution. Hence, other particles have higher probability to become a valid solution and does not need many reparation for DBPSO with FPM. It can reduce the optimization time. Anyway, the higher number of particles has stronger diversification. By updating the velocity other particles (network topologies) change dynamically, which requires more reparation processes and explicitly increases the optimization time. Therefore, the number of particles and the optimization time should be taken into account simultaneously.

220   R. Zhao, Y. Zhang, and R. Lehnert

4) Comparison with SA, TS, GA, ACO and PSO with NBM: the number of solutions visited is limited to compare different algorithms. In many papers the comparison of some algorithms is based on the iteration or generation of an optimization process. However, the iteration (i.e. generation) has different meaning or definition for these algorithms. In principle an iteration of trajectory-based search (e.g. SA and TS) means that one valid neighbor or one valid neighboring solution is found. But for population-based search one generation means that the population including a group of valid solutions are changed at the same time. Then the visited solutions by population-based search (e.g. GA, ACO, PSO) at an iteration is much more than those by trajectory-based search at one iteration. The total optimization time depends on the number of solutions and the time needed by each solution. Based on experimental results, the mean time to find one valid solution is similar. Therefore, the limited number of solutions visited is defined to efficiently compare different algorithms in this work.

Tab.2 shows optimization results with maximal solutions 25000/50000/50000 for Network I/II/III. More precisely, SA takes 50/100/100 steps without any change of the temperature as the inner loop and 500 iterations as the outer loop, respectively; TS iteratively finds 5/25/25 neighbors (i.e. solutions) as the

Table 2. Comparison of SA, TS, GA, ACO, PSO with NBM, enhanced DBPSO for HFV Access Network Topology Design

Algorithm	Network	Best	Rel. Dif.	Average	Rel. Dif.	Time(s)
SA	I	20284.0	0.69%	20497.5	1.75%	6.9
	II	59345.1	5.70%	59967.1	6.81%	319.3
	III	113026.0	4.86%	114473.0	6.20%	7963.0
TS	I	20284.0	0.69%	**20284.0**	**0.69%**	3.3
	II	58934.3	4.97%	59229.0	5.49%	335.1
	III	112643.0	4.50%	113634.0	5.426%	9127.2
GA	I	20284.0	0.69%	20375.5	1.15%	2.7
	II	58830.0	4.79%	59492.0	5.97%	119.4
	III	112471.0	4.35%	**113440.0**	**5.25%**	4741.2
ACO	I	20209.9	0.32%	20307.1	0.80%	6.1
	II	58353.9	3.93%	**58918.7**	**4.94%**	192.4
	III	113376	5.18%	114302	6.04%	696.6
PSO	I	20269.3	0.62%	20495.4	1.74%	6.23
	II	58462	4.13%	59777.3	6.48%	331.23
	III	112982	4.82%	115305	6.98%	6728.8
DBPSO	I	**20194.4**	**0.24%**	20372.1	1.13%	7.3
	II	**58031**	**3.36%**	59103.5	5.27%	268
	III	**111426**	**3.38%**	116145	7.75%	5359.3

Candidate List for 2000 steps; GA with Partial Chromosome Modeling generates 50/100/100 new children (i.e. solutions) at each generation, the total generation is 500; ACO fulfills 50/100/100 times Ant-based Clustering to obtain an optimal solution for BMS-LMS layer, where the total generation of Ant-based Positioning is 500 generations; PSO with NBM uses 25/50/50 particles to illustrate solutions for 1000 iterations; DBPSO uses 5/10/10 particles with 5000 iterations to find the required number of solutions.

The relative cost difference to reference optima (Rel.Dif.) can explicitly represent the performance of an algorithm besides the time difference. Reference optima are obtained by *CPLEX*: 20144.1 with 92.96s, 56142.4 with 14938.62s, 107785.8 with 326480.64s for Network I/II/III.

Different optimization results are shown in Tab.2, where the enhanced DBPSO can find the best optima for Network I/II/III and provide excellent average results for Network I/II. The average results of Network III are not satisfying. By reason of the strong diversification and the binary modeling, DBPSO can effectively explore the unvisited space to catch new better solutions. However, it can have negative influence on the search process of DBPSO. For instance, some good solutions have been found, which could be improved by a further search. But the dynamic update of DBPSO could miss these efficient positions. Therefore, the DBPSO can find an excellent solution for the topology design of HFVANs, but the unstable performance could lead the optimization process into local optima. Anyway, the enhanced DBPSO works better than PSO with a non-binary model in Tab.2.

6   Conclusion

This paper presents a strategy for the topology design of hierarchical hybrid fiber-VDSL access networks with heuristic algorithms. Two binary models have been studied for DBPSO. An enhanced update function is proposed to improve the performance and simplify the application of DBPSO. Based on numerical results, the enhanced DBPSO performs better than the original DBPSO in consideration of the maximal velocity. Furthermore, this algorithm can be efficiently used for HFVAN topology design problems, particularly for small or medium-sized networks. It could be helpful for other research in this field.

However, DBPSO strongly depends on the length of particles and initial network topologies. More test networks are required to study them continuously. As a further work, the update function of $x_n(k+1)$ could be studied by another function to avoid the premature convergence. The stability for large scale networks should be studied continuously.

References

1. Zhao, R., Goetze, S., Lehnert, R.: A Visual Planning Tool for Hybrid Fiber-VDSL Access Networks with Heuristic Algorithms. In: The 5th International Workshop on Design of Reliable Communication Networks (DRCN 2005), Island of Ischia (Naples), Italy, pp. 541–548 (2005)

2. Zhao, R., Dai, Q., Lehnert, R.: Planing of Hybrid Fiber-VDSL Access Networks Using Particle Swarm Optimization. In: WTC/ISS (World Telecommunications Congress/International Switching Symposium) and ISSLS (International Symposium on Services and Local Access), Budapest, Hungary (2006)
3. Zhao, R., Liu, H.J., Lehnert, R.: Topology Design of Hierarchical Hybrid Fiber-VDSL Access Networks with ACO. In: The Fourth Advanced International Conference on Telecommunications (AICT2008), Athens, Greece, June 8-13, 2008, pp. 232–237 (2008)
4. Gavish, B.: Topological design of Telecommunication Networks-the Overall Design Problem. European Journal of Operations Research 58(2), 149–172 (1992)
5. Bley, A., Koch, T., Wessaely, R.: Large-scale hierarchical networks: How to compute an optimal architecture? In: Proceeding of Networks 2004, Vienna, Austria, pp. 13–16 (2004)
6. Pioro, M., Medhi, D.: Routing, Flow, and Capacity Design in Communication and Computer Networks. Elsevier Inc., America (2004)
7. Tsenov, A.: Simulated Annealing and Genetic Algorithm in Telecommunications Network Planning. International Journal of Computational Intelligence 2(1), 240–245 (2005)
8. Gavish, B.: Topological design of Telecommunication Networks-local Access Design Methods. Annals of Operations Research 33(1), 17–71 (1991)
9. Godor, I., Magyar, G.: Cost-optimal Topology Planning of Hierarchical Access Network. Computers & Operations Research 32, 59–86 (2005)
10. Chamberland, S., Sanso, B., Marcotte, O.: Topological Design of Two-Level Telecommunication Networks with Modular Switches. Operations Research 48(5), 745–760 (2000)
11. Girard, A., Sanso, B., Dadjo, L.: A Tabu Search Algorithm for Access Network Design. Annals of Operations Research 106(1–4), 229–262 (2001)
12. Eberhart, R.C., Kennedy, J.: A New Optimizer Using Particle Swarm Theory. In: Pro. of the Sixth International Symposium on Micro Machine and Human Science, Nagoya, Japan, pp. 39–43. IEEE Service Centre, Piscataway (1995)
13. Shi, Y.H., Eberhart, R.C.: A Modified Particle Swarm Optimizer. In: IEEE International Conference on Evolutionary Computation, Anchorage, Alaska, May 4-9 (1998)
14. Eberhart, R.C., Shi, Y.: Particle Swarm Optimization: Developments, Applications and Resources. In: IEEE Proc. of Congress on Evolutionary Computation (CEC 2001), IEEE Service Centre, Seoul Korea (2001)
15. Hu, Y., Eberhart, R.C., Shi, Y.: Engineering Optimization with Particle Swarm. In: Proceeding of IEEE Swarm Intelligence Symposium 2003, pp. 53–57 (2003)
16. Hu, X.H., Shi, Y., Eberhart, R.: Recent Advances in Particle Swarm. In: IEEE Proc. of Congress on Evolutionary Computation (CEC 2004), June 19-23, 2004, pp. 90–97 (2004)
17. Parsopoulos, K.E., Vrahatis, M.N.: Particle Swarm Optimization for Constrained Optimization Problems, Intelligent technologies-theory and applications: new trends in intelligent technologies. Frontiers in Artificial Intelligence and Applications, vol. 76, pp. 214–220. IOS Press, Amsterdam (2002)
18. Sun, S.C., Abraham, A., Zhang, G.Y., Liu, H.B.: A Particle Swarm Optimization Algorithm for Neighbor Selection in Peer-to-Peer Networks. In: CISIM 2007, June 28-30 (2007)
19. Kennedy, J., Eberhart, R.: A Discrete Bindary Version of the Particle Swarm Algorithm. In: Proc. 1997 Conference Systems, Man, Cybernetics, Piscataway, NJ, USA (1997)

20. Chandrasekaran, S., Ponnambalam, S.G., Suresh, R.K., Vijayakumar, N.: A Hybrid Discrete Particle Swarm Optimization Algorithm to Solve Flow Shop Scheduling Problems. In: IEEE Conference on Cybernetics and Intelligent Systems, June 2006, pp. 1–6 (2006)
21. Chen, M., Wang, Z.W.: An Approach for Web Services Composition Based on QoS and Discrete Particle Swarm Optimization. In: Eighth ACIS International Conference on Sotftware Engineering, Artificial Intelligence, Networking, and Parallel/Distributed Computing, July 30 - August 1, 2007, vol. 2, pp. 37–41 (2007)
22. Zhang, C.S., Sun, J.G., Wang, Y., Yang, Q.Y.: An Improved Discrete Particle Swarm Optimization Algorithm for TSP. In: IEEE/WIC/ACM International Conferences on Web Intelligence and Intelligent Agent Technology Workshops, No. 5-12, pp. 35–38 (2007)

Near-Optimal Multi-user Greedy Bit-Loading
for Digital Subscriber Lines

Alastair McKinley and Alan Marshall

Queens University Belfast, Belfast BT7 1NN, Northern Ireland
amckinley03@qub.ac.uk

Abstract. This work presents a new algorithm for Dynamic Spectrum Management (DSM) in Digital Subscriber Lines. Previous approaches have achieved high performance by attempting to directly solve or approximate the multiuser spectrum optimisation problem. These methods suffer from a high or intractable computational complexity for even a moderate number of DSL lines. A new method is proposed which is a heuristic extension of the single user greedy algorithm applied to the multi-user case. The new algorithm incorporates a novel cost function that penalises crosstalk as well as considering the *usefulness* of a tone. Previous work has proved the performance of the new algorithm in simple 2-user scenarios. In this work we present new results which demonstrate the performance of the algorithm in larger DSL bundles. Simulation results are presented and it is shown that the new method achieves results within a few percent of the optimal solution for these scenarios.

Keywords: Digital Subscriber Lines, Dynamic Spectrum Management, greedy bit-loading.

1 Introduction

Crosstalk is a major limiting factor in xDSL systems. In fact, crosstalk noise is the dominant noise source in DSL. Recently, new techniques which fall under the category of Dynamic Spectrum Management (DSM) have been proposed which seek to mitigate the effects of crosstalk. Although it is possible in theory to almost eliminate crosstalk [1], this is often impractical due to local loop unbundling, as signal level co-ordination is required between co-located modems. Where crosstalk cancellation is not possible, other techniques have focused on new bit-loading algorithms which are multiuser aware [2] [3] [4] [5] [6] [7] [8]. Rather than eliminate crosstalk, these techniques seek to reduce the effect of crosstalk, improving the performance of a binder group.

All of the aforementioned techniques require some form of centralised calculation, with varying computational demands depending on the particular algorithm. In particular the Optimal Spectrum Balancing algorithm (OSB) [2] and Iterative Spectrum Balancing [5] (ISB) require a significant amount of time to produce a solution for a large number of lines. The new algorithm presented here attempts to solve the spectrum balancing problem using a different approach to these methods.

C. Wang (Ed.): AccessNets, LNICST 6, pp. 224–239, 2009.

The rest of the paper is laid out as follows. Section 2 of this paper describes the system model used for simulation. Section 3 outlines the multi-user spectrum balancing problem and related work in this area. Section 4 gives a synopsis of the multi-user greedy algorithm [4], on which the method presented here is based. Section 5 presents the new algorithm "Near-Optimal Multi-User Greedy Bit-Loading" and details the enhancements made to the algorithm in [4] to arrive at the new method. Section 6 contains the new contribution of this work, demonstrating the performance of the new algorithm described here for a number of larger DSL bundles.

2   System Model

The system model adopted in this paper is an xDSL system based on DMT modulation, with N users and K tones per user. For simplicity, it is assumed that NEXT is eliminated by frequency division duplexing (FDD) and transmission is considered in the downstream direction only. Crosstalk noise is purely from FEXT coupling and occurs on a tone by tone basis.

The Signal-Noise Ratio for user n on tone k is computed as follows:

$$SNR_n(k) = \frac{p_n(k)|h_{nn}(k)|^2}{\sum_{j\neq n} p_j(k)|h_{jn}(k)|^2 + \sigma_n^2(k)} \tag{1}$$

Where $p_n(k)$ is the transmit power spectral density (PSD) of user k on tone n. The term $|h_{nn}(k)|^2$ represents the direct channel power transfer function of the DSL line for user n on tone k. The term $|h_{jn}(k)|^2$ represents the crosstalk power transfer function (FEXT in this case) of user j into user n on tone k. The crosstalk gains are calculated according to standard models [9]. $\sigma_n^2(k)$ is the received background noise power for user n on tone k. It includes thermal noise plus background noise from other systems (e.g. ISDN, HDSL).

It is assumed that each modem has a maximum bit-loading of $b_{max} = 15$. It is further assumed that modems can only support integer bit-loading, which is the case in current implementations. The achievable bit-loading on tone k for user n is given by

$$b_n(k) = \log_2\left(1 + \frac{SNR_n(k)}{\Gamma}\right) \tag{2}$$

where Γ is the 'SNR-gap' which is a function of the line code and target BER [10].

3   The Spectrum Balancing Problem

The spectrum balancing problem is expressed in a number of different ways, depending on rate and power constraints. They are generally categorised into Rate Adaptive (RA) and Fixed Margin (FM) methods [10]. Rate adaptive algorithms attempt to maximise user's bit rates under power budget constraints.

Fixed Margin algorithms minimise the power required to transmit a target bit rate at a fixed performance margin.

In a multi-user channel, the spectrum balancing problem can be stated as follows:

$$max\ R_1\ s.t.\ R_n \geq R_n^{target}$$

$$s.t.\ \sum_{k=1}^{K} p_n(k) \leq P_n^{budget} \tag{3}$$

Equation (3) states that the rate of line 1 is to be maximised, subject to all other lines meeting or exceeding their rate targets and that all lines are within their respective power budgets.

3.1   Related Work

Many DSM algorithms have been proposed which address the multi-user spectrum balancing problem. Iterative Waterfilling (IW) [11] is a DSM technique which is distributed, whereby each modem calculates its own power spectral densities. Optimal Spectrum Balancing (OSB) [2] is a centralised DSM algorithm, where the power spectral densities are calculated centrally by a Spectrum Management Centre (SMC). In OSB, the spectrum balancing problem is reformulated using a dual-decomposition, transforming the power constrained optimisation problem into an unconstrained optimisation of the langrangian sub-problem. OSB provides better performance than IW at the cost of increased co-ordination and a higher computational complexity. The inner loop of the algorithm is an exhaustive search over all bit loading combinations on a particular tone. As such, the running time of OSB is exponential in the number of users N. Practically this means that OSB is intractable for more than 5-6 DSL lines. Iterative Spectrum Balancing (ISB) [5] [12] is a sub-optimal approach based on OSB, which reduces the computational complexity of the inner loop of ISB to $O(N^2)$ at the cost of the optimality of the solution. The exhaustive search of the inner loop is replaced by an iterative search on each individual line which converges to at least a local optimum solution, and often to the global optimum for a tone. The SCALE [3] algorithm takes a different approach, attempting to maximise the per tone lagrangian through an iterative convex relaxation procedure. SCALE has been shown to achieve close to optimal performance in networks with a moderate number of DSL lines and has a complexity similar to ISB [13].

Band-Preference techniques [6] [7] are a relatively new idea which follow from the results of SCALE. The main idea in Band-Preference is that each modem executes a "scaled water-filling" algorithm on a preset number of bands within its own spectrum. An SMC calculates the scaling factors for each band on each modem and communicates these results to the individual modems. Increasing the number of bands increases the performance of the algorithm. With unity band sizes, the result converges to the optimum solution [7]. An advantage of Band-Preference Algorithms is the possibility of using hooks in currently available standards (ADSL2,VDSL) to implement them.

4   Multi-User Greedy Bit Loading

The core of the new algorithm presented here is based upon the multiuser greedy algorithm [4], and is a heuristic extension of the single user greedy loading algorithm [14]. The single user greedy algorithm is a conceptually simple algorithm, where each line loads one bit on to the tone on which it will cost the least power to do so, until the line's power budget is fully utilised. In effect this is the discrete version of the classic waterfilling algorithm. This idea is extended to its multi-user counterpart in [4]. The entire binder group is considered as a whole and bits are added incrementally to the channel and line with the lowest energy cost. The cost metric is defined as the power required to add one bit to a particular line/tone and the sum of the power increases required on all other lines on that tone in order to bring those lines back within the performance margin given the increased crosstalk. We will denote this term Δp. The objective of the multi-user greedy algorithm is to minimise the total power required to transmit a total rate-sum. This algorithm does not consider fairness between users, or guarantee a minimum data rate for each user.

In order to calculate the cost metric, the power vector to support a particular bit vector must be calculated. The achievable bit-loading on line n tone k is as follows:

$$b_n(k) = \log_2\left(1 + \frac{p_n(k)|h_{nn}(k)|^2}{\Gamma\left(\sigma_n^2(k) + \sum_{j\neq n} p_j(k)|h_{jn}(k)|^2\right)}\right) \tag{4}$$

Re-arranging the formula (4) letting $f(b_n(k)) = \Gamma(2^{b_n(k)} - 1)$ we obtain:

$$p_n(k) - f(b_n(k)) \sum_{j\neq n} p_j(k)\frac{|h_{jn}(k)|^2}{|h_{nn}(k)|^2} = f(b_n(k))\frac{\sigma_n^2(k)}{|h_{nn}(k)|^2} \tag{5}$$

For a particular tone k, equation (5) is an N-dimensional linear system of equations, where N is the number of lines. This can be written in matrix form:

$$A(k)P(k) = B(k) \tag{6}$$

where

$$A(k)_{ij} = \begin{cases} 1, & \text{for } i = j \\ \frac{-f(b_i(k))|h_{ji}|^2}{|h_{ii}|^2}, & \text{for } i \neq j \end{cases} \tag{7}$$

$$P(k) = [p_1(k) \ldots p_i(k) \ldots p_N(k)]^T \tag{8}$$

$$B(k) = \left[\frac{f(b_1(k))\sigma_1^2}{|h_{11}|^2} \cdots \frac{f(b_i(k))\sigma_i^2}{|h_{ii}|^2} \cdots \frac{f(b_N(k))\sigma_N^2}{|h_{NN}|^2}\right]^T \tag{9}$$

This can be solved for $P(k)$ via direct inversion or by LU/QR decomposition. $P(k)$ is a vector which contains the power value required on each line to support

---

Algorithm 1. The Original Multi-User Greedy Loading Algorithm

---

1: **function** $main$
2:    $init()$
3:    **repeat**
4:       $n, k = \text{argmin } C[n][k]$ ▷ user n, tone k
5:       increment $b_n(k)$
6:       **if** $P_n > P_n^{budget}$ $\forall n$ **then**
7:          decrement $b_n(k)$
8:             $F[n][k] = 1$ ▷ Set tone as full
9:       **end if**
10:      **if** $b_n(k) == maxbits$ **then**
11:         $F[n][k] = 1$ ▷ Set tone as full
12:      **end if**
13:      **if** $R_n == R_n^{target}$ **then**
14:         $F[n][\forall k] = 1$ ▷ Set user n tones full
15:      **end if**
16:      $C[n][k] = cost\_function(n, k)$ ▷ $\forall n, k$
17:   **until** all tones full
18: **end function**

19: **function** $init$
20:    **for all** n, k **do**
21:       $F[n][k] = 0$ ▷ Matrix of flags set to 0
22:       $C[n][k] = cost\_function(n, k)$
23:    **end for**
24: **end function**

25: **function** $cost\_function(n, k)$
26:    $\hat{b}(k) = b(k) + e(n)$
27:    $\hat{P}(k) = A(k)^{-1}\hat{B}(k)$
28:    $cost = \displaystyle\sum_{n=1}^{N} \left(\hat{p_n}(k) - p_n(k) \right)$
29:    **return** $cost$
30: **end function**

---

a vector of bits $b(k)$ on tone k. (Note $B(k)$ is a function of $b(k)$). Also, the solution can only be computed in this way if it is assumed that each tone is independent, i.e. no adjacent channel interference.

Knowing the structure of equation (6), we can formulate the multi-user greedy algorithm shown in algorithm 1. In algorithm 1, F is an $N \times K$ matrix of flags which is initialised to 0 and set to 1 when a tone on a particular user is declared full. Also, C is an $N \times K$ matrix containing the cost to add one bit to a tone k on user n. The vector $e(n)$ is a zero vector of length N with element n set to 1. As previously discussed, the cost is the sum of the total extra power required on all lines when a bit is added to user n tone k.

4.1 Performance

The original multi-user greedy algorithm does not consider fairness between users or guarantee a minimum data rate for any user. Due to this fact, it performs poorly in some scenarios, such as the near-far scenario shown in figure 1. In this network configuration, there is a large amount of crosstalk from the "strong" line, i.e. the shorter RT-fed line into the "weak" line, i.e. the longer CO-fed line. Crosstalk from the RT line dominates the noise spectrum of the CO line, greatly reducing its potential performance. Crosstalk avoidance through some DSM technique can vastly improve performance in this scenario. Figure 2 compares the downstream power spectral density for the two line scenario shown in figure 1 using the multi-user greedy algorithm and the optimal spectrum balancing algorithm [2]. The RT line rate target is set to 4Mbps. In this scenario, the multi-user greedy algorithm achieves a rate of 1.084Mbps on the CO line. In contrast, the OSB algorithm achieves a rate of 3.484Mbps on the CO line. It is clear that the multi-user greedy algorithm does not perform well in this scenario. The following section will outline some changes to the multi-user greedy algorithm which dramatically improves its performance.

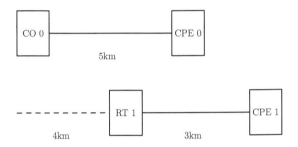

Fig. 1. A two user DSL network which exhibits the near-far effect

5 Near-Optimal Multi-user Greedy Bit-Loading

A simple observation from figure 2 is that in the optimal solution, the RT line only uses its higher frequency tones. This is because, to achieve a higher bit-rate on the CO line, the RT line will yield to the CO line at low frequencies, as the RT line is short enough that it can use its higher frequencies for data transmission. In the case of the multi-user greedy algorithm, we note that the cost function is based on the lowest incremental power to add a bit to a particular tone. When the cost matrix is first initialised, each tone contains zero bits. Therefore, when a bit is added to a tone, it will incur no extra cost due to generated crosstalk. This means that the highest gain channels will always be chosen first, which in the case of figure 1 will be the lowest frequency tones on the RT line. In doing so, the multi-user greedy algorithm will immediately choose the wrong tones for loading as compared to the optimal solution. It is now postulated that a new cost function which accounts for crosstalk effects in a different way may achieve better results.

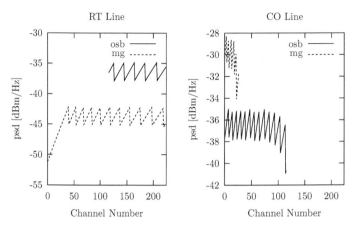

Fig. 2. PSD of RT line at CO line with OSB and multi-user greedy algorithms

5.1   A New Cost Function

The new cost function is fundamentally based on the same cost function as the original multi-user greedy algorithm, i.e. the incremental power cost to add one bit to a particular line and tone Δp. This is because this metric has some inherently good properties. Firstly, it generally chooses the tones with the highest gains and, secondly, it also chooses tones that do not cause large power increases on other lines due to crosstalk.

In addition to Δp, two new terms are included. The first is a crosstalk penalty term denoted by $w_n\beta$. The second is a factor $\gamma_n(k)$ which measures the relative "usefullness" of a tone relative to all other tones on that line. This is used to adjust the crosstalk penalty depending on how important that tone is on a particular line. The $w_n\beta$ term is an "inter-line" cost adjustment and the $\gamma_n(k)$ is an "intra-line" cost adjustment. The penalty term is summed over all victim tones (a victim tone is a tone which incurs crosstalk due to loading bits on line n) when calculating the cost for a tone.

Crosstalk Penalty Term. The crosstalk penalty term is calculated in the following manner. When calculating the cost for a particular tone k on line n, use the current bit value $b_n(k)$ and assume that the other lines on tone k are set to a reference PSD. In the simulations shown here -40 dBm/Hz was used. Given these initial parameters, calculate the vector of bits on tone k, b_k. Now increment the value of $b_n(k)$ and recalculate the vector b_k. From the two vectors calculated, a penalty term for each victim tone can be constructed as follows:

$$penalty = w_n \times \overbrace{(\underset{b_k(k)}{(b_k(j))} - \underset{b_n(k)+1}{b_k(j)})}^{\beta = \text{"lost bits"}}$$

$$\text{for } j = 1 \ldots N \; j \neq n$$

(10)

The term w_n in equation (10) is a weight which determines how much a crosstalking line is penalised due to its own generated crosstalk. Adjusting this value will determine the bit rates on each line. The second term in equation (10) is marked "lost bits", as it effectively is the number of bits lost on line j tone k after adding an extra bit on line n tone k. In this way a major pitfall of the original multi-user greedy algorithm is avoided, as crosstalking lines are penalised even if victim lines do not yet contain any bits.

Relative Usefullness Adjustment. The crosstalk penalty term is further adjusted by a factor which determines how useful a tone k on line j is relative to the rest of its tones. The rationale for this is that intuitively, if a line is crosstalking heavily into another line's strongest tones, it should be more heavily penalised for adding extra bits. Conversely, if a crosstalking line is heavily crosstalking into a "weak" line's worst tones, then the penalty should be less as the "weak" line will not use these tones in any case. To calculate $\gamma_n(k)$ for each line n and tone k we first assume zero FEXT into the line and calculate the total bits attainable on each tone k given a reference PSD (-40dBm/Hz) and also the average number of bits attainable on line n. The total number of bits attainable of line n tone k is given by $b_n(k)^{ref}$ and the average bits on line n by $\bar{b_n}$. This adjustment is calculated for each line n and tone k as follows:

$$\gamma_n(k) = \frac{b_n(k)^{ref}}{\bar{b_n}} \qquad (11)$$

$$\text{for } k = 1 \ldots K, n = 1 \ldots N$$

Cost Matrix Re-Initialisation. Another adjustment made to the multi-user greedy algorithm is the re-initialisation of the cost matrix C during loading. When a line n reaches its rate target R_n^{target} or its power budget P_n^{budget}, there is no longer any need to penalise a neighbouring line for crosstalking into that line. A *user_frozen* flag is set for each line that has finished loading bits. This is used in the cost function calculation to determine whether to penalise a crosstalking line or not. Although additional crosstalk into a line which has reached its power budget may cause the line to break its power constraint, this will be caught in the main loop of the algorithm, causing its flag in the matrix F to be set to 1. This re-initialisation ensures that no lines are unfairly penalised for crosstalking into lines that either cannot load any more bits due to reaching their power budget, or will not load any more bits because they have reached their rate target.

The revised cost function is shown in algorithm 2.

5.2   Algorithm Complexity

Although the algorithm here is slightly more complex than the multi-user greedy algorithm, tests showed that results for 50 line bundles could be achieved in a reasonable time (on the order of minutes) on standard PC hardware running non-optimised code. For the 8 line simulations presented in the results section, the running time was on the order of seconds. It was noted that most of the execution

---

Algorithm 2. Revised Cost Function

1: **function** $cost\_function(n, k)$
2:     $b\hat{(}k) = b(k) + e(n)$
3:     $P\hat{(}k) = A(k)^{-1} B\hat{(}k)$
4:     $\Delta p = \sum\limits_{n=1}^{N} \left(p_n\hat{(}k) - p_n(k) \right)$
5:     $p_m(k) = -40 dBm/Hz$ for $m = 1 \ldots N, m \neq n$

6:     Calculate $b(k)\big|_{p(k), b_n(k)}$
7:     Calculate $b(k)\big|_{p(k), b_n(k)+1}$

8:     **for** $m = 1 \ldots M, m \neq n$ **do**
9:         **if** $(!user\_frozen[m])$ **then**
10:            $\beta_m = b_m(k)\big|_{p(k), b_n(k)} - b_m(k)\big|_{p(k), b_n(k)+1}$
11:            $penalty+ = w_n \beta_m \gamma_m(k)$
12:        **end if**
13:    **end for**
14:    $cost = \Delta p \times penalty$
15:    **return** $cost$
16: **end function**

---

time of the algorithm was taken up by the PSD vector calculation of equation (6). As this step requires the inversion of a matrix, it requires $O(N^3)$ operations. A significant optimisation of this step is outlined in [4]. The cost function requires an evaluation of $P(k)$ given $b(k)$ and subsequently an evaluation of $P(k)$ given $b(k) + e(n)$. As the addition of $e(n)$ only makes a small rank update to $A(k)$, the calculation of successive inverses of $A(k)$ can be optimised using the matrix inversion lemma[1]. This reduces the complexity of calculating successive inverses of $A(k)$ to $O(N^2)$ operations. This optimisation was not implemented in the simulations here and it is expected that it would produce a significant decrease in execution time. There is also another possible optimisation presented in [15] where multiple bits are added at once to reduce the need for cost matrix updates without performance degradation. This optimisation was not used in the simulations presented here, but should also bring a significant performance increase.

6   Simulation Results

In this section the new algorithm is tested in two different scenarios by simulation. All DSL line diameters are assumed to be 0.5mm (24-AWG). The coding gain is set at 3dB and the noise margin at 6dB. The gap Γ is set to 9.8dB in all scenarios and a power budget of 110mW is assumed on each line. All lines are using DMT ADSL and transmission is in the downstream direction. The crosstalk damping terms w_n are chosen to meet the rate targets for each scenario.

---

[1] $(A + bc^T)^{-1} = A^{-1} - \left(\frac{1}{1 + c^T A^{-1} b} \right)(A^{-1} b)(c^T A^{-1})$.

Previous work [16] considered the performance of the new algorithm in 2-user network scenarios. The results presented here expand on previous results and in particular demonstrate the suitability of the new algorithm to larger bundles.

6.1   2-User Near Far Scenario

The first scenario is the near far scenario shown in figure 1. For this scenario, only self-FEXT is considered. The rate target for the RT line was set at 4.1Mbps. Figure 3 shows the resulting PSD graph against channel number beside the optimal solution obtained by the OSB algorithm. The corresponding bit-rates for this scenario are shown in table 1. In this case, the new algorithm actually achieves the same result as the optimal solution given by the OSB algorithm.

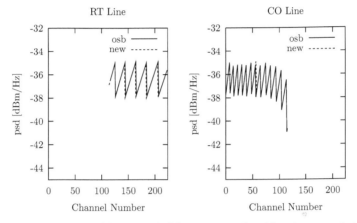

Fig. 3. PSD of RT line and CO line with OSB and new algorithm for scenario in figure 1

Table 1. Bit rates for OSB, Multi-User Greedy and new algorithm for the scenario in figure 1

	OSB	New Algorithm	Multi-User Greedy
CO Line	3.484Mbps	3.484Mbps	1.052Mbps
RT Line	4.1Mbps	4.1Mbps	4.1Mbps

6.2   8-User Central Office Scenario

In this scenario, eight DSL users are connected to a DSLAM in the Central Office. Four of the eight users lines are 3 kilometres in length, whilst the other four are 2 kilometres in length. The scenario is illustrated in figure 4. For this scenario, alien crosstalk is included as given by model A in [17]. The Iterative Spectrum Balancing algorithm (ISB) is used as a comparison to the new algorithm presented here, as OSB is intractable for 8 lines. Iterative Spectrum balancing has be shown to achieve near optimal results with a significant reduction in complexity relative to OSB. OSB with branch and bound [18] is tractable for an 8 line scenario, however due to time constraints it was not implemented here.

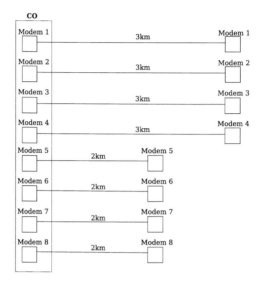

Fig. 4. An 8-User Scenario with all modems co-located at the Central Office

Table 2. Data rates for scenario in figure 4 comparing ISB to the new algorithm

	ISB	New Algorithm
User 1	2.912 Mbps	2.892 Mbps
User 2	2.932 Mbps	2.9 Mbps
User 3	2.912 Mbps	2.896 Mbps
User 4	2.904 Mbps	2.896 Mbps
User 5	4.172 Mbps	4.164 Mbps
User 6	4.172 Mbps	4.164 Mbps
User 7	4.148 Mbps	4.164 Mbps
User 8	4.168 Mbps	4.164 Mbps

The results are shown in table 2. The performance of the new algorithm is shown to to approach the performance of the ISB algorithm very closely. The average drop in data rate for each user is just 0.34% in comparison to ISB. In figure 5 the resulting PSDs are shown for one of the 3km lines and one of the 2km lines for both ISB the new greedy algorithm.

6.3   8-User Mixed Deployment Scenario

This scenario consists of an eight user network, with two remote terminals located 500 metres and 3 kilometres from the central office respectively. This is illustrated in figure 6. Once again, the ISB algorithm is used for comparison and alien crosstalk is included as in the eight user central office scenario. The results are shown in table 3. It can be seen that the results given by the new algorithm closely approach the performance of ISB. In this case, the average drop in data

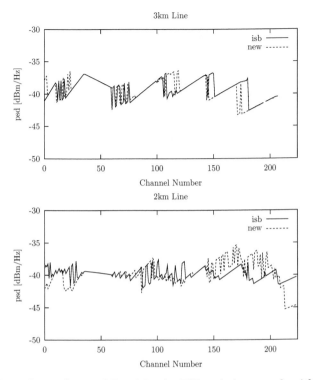

Fig. 5. Resulting Power Spectral Densities for ISB and the new algorithm for a 3km line and 2km line in scenario 4

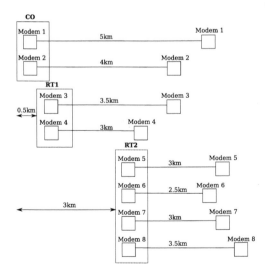

Fig. 6. An 8-User Scenario with two remote terminals

Table 3. Data rates for mixed deployment scenario in figure 6 comparing ISB to the new algorithm

	ISB	New Algorithm
User 1	0.240 Mbps	0.238 Mbps
User 2	0.772 Mbps	0.772 Mbps
User 3	1.528 Mbps	1.520 Mbps
User 4	2.600 Mbps	2.600 Mbps
User 5	0.744 Mbps	0.744 Mbps
User 6	1.064 Mbps	1.060 Mbps
User 7	0.744 Mbps	0.744 Mbps
User 8	0.528 Mbps	0.524 Mbps

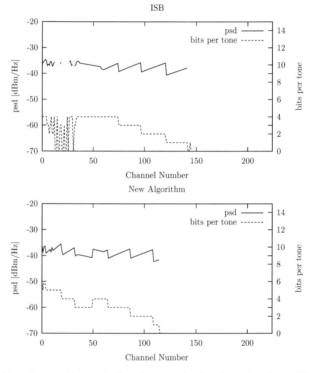

Fig. 7. Resulting Power Spectral Densities and bit allocation for ISB and the new algorithm for user 3 for the scenario in figure 6

rate for each user is 0.31%. The resulting PSD and bits per tone graphs for user 3 are shown in figure 7.

6.4   Discussion of Results

It is noted from figure 7 that the PSD graph of the new algorithm is more continuous than that of ISB. This is also true for the PSD graphs of the other 6 users

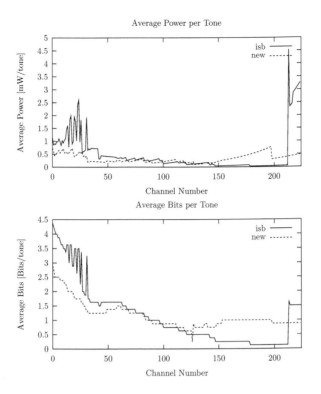

Fig. 8. Average Power and Average Bits per Tone for both ISB and new algorithm for scenario in figure 6

not shown here. This is further illustrated in figure 8 which shows the average power and average bits per tone for all lines in the scenario in figure 6 on each tone. It is clear from figure 8 that the PSD and hence the bit allocation of each user is flatter over all channels. It is speculated that this may make the algorithm particularly suitable for calculating the scaling factors in Band-Preference algorithms [7] [6]. In Band-Preference algorithms each modem executes a "scaled waterfilling" algorithm on each of its sub bands. This results in a relatively flat PSD on each of the sub bands. This has the effect of approximating a spectrum balancing solution given by, OSB, ISB or SCALE for example. With reference to figure 7 it relatively easy to see that the spectrum of the new algorithm could be better approximated with just two bands (one flat band at low frequencies and off at higher frequencies) than the ISB solution.

Furthermore, it appears that the new algorithm is able to leverage greater capacity at the higher frequency tones compared to ISB, and consequently requires less average power at lower frequencies. In practice it is expected that this will result in reduced adjacent channel interference compared to ISB.

7   Conclusion

New results for the algorithm developed in [16] have been presented. These demonstrate that the algorithm performs close to the optimum solution in three very different DSL bundle scenarios. The complexity is low enough to achieve results within a realistic time for a large number of DSL lines without significant optimisation.

Future work will attempt to formalise the calculation of the crosstalk damping weights w_n, investigate further complexity reductions and assess the suitability of the algorithm in relation to Band-Preference techniques.

Acknowledgment

The authors would like to thank DEL N.I. and Asidua Ltd. for their funding and support.

References

1. Ginis, G., Cioffi, J.: Vectored transmission for digital subscriber line systems. IEEE Journal on Selected Areas in Communications 20(5), 1085–1104 (2002)
2. Cendrillon, R., Moonen, M., Verlinden, J., Bostoen, T., Yu, W.: Optimal multiuser spectrum management for digital subscriber lines. In: IEEE International Conference on Communications, vol. 1, pp. 1–5 (2004)
3. Papandriopoulos, J., Evans, J.: Low-complexity distributed algorithms for spectrum balancing in multi-user dsl networks. In: IEEE International Conference on Communications, ICC 2006, June 2006, vol. 7, pp. 3270–3275 (2006)
4. Lee, J., Sonalkar, R., Cioffi, J.: Multiuser bit loading for multicarrier systems. IEEE Transactions on Communications 54(7), 1170–1174 (2006)
5. Cendrillon, R., Moonen, M.: Iterative spectrum balancing for digital subscriber lines. In: 2005 IEEE International Conference on Communications, ICC 2005, May 16-20, vol. 3, pp. 1937–1941 (2005)
6. Lee, W., Kim, Y., Brady, M.H., Cioffi, J.M.: Band-preference dynamic spectrum management in a dsl environment. In: Global Telecommunications Conference, GLOBECOM 2006, pp. 1–5. IEEE, Los Alamitos (2006)
7. Papandriopoulos, J., Evans, J.S.: Band preference design algorithms for improved iterative water-filling. In: Global Telecommunications Conference, GLOBECOM 2007, November 26-30, pp. 2899–2903. IEEE, Los Alamitos (2007)
8. Statovci, D., Nordstrom, T., Nilsson, R.: The normalized-rate iterative algorithm: A practical dynamic spectrum management method for dsl. Eurasip Journal on Applied Signal Processing 2006, 17 (2006)
9. Baldemair, R., Horvat, M., Nordstrom, T.: Proposed method of crosstalk calculations in a distributed environment. ETSI ETC TM6 Plenary Meeting (2003)
10. Starr, T., Cioffi, J.M., Silverman, P.J.: Understanding Digital Subscriber Line Technology. Prentice-Hall, Englewood Cliffs (1999)
11. Yu, W., Ginis, G., Cioffi, J.: Distributed multiuser power control for digital subscriber lines. IEEE Journal on Selected Areas in Communications 20(5), 1105–1115 (2002)

12. Lui, R., Yu, W.: Low-complexity near-optimal spectrum balancing for digital sub-scriber lines. In: IEEE International Conference on Communications, ICC 2005, May 16-20, vol. 3, pp. 1947–1951 (2005)
13. Cioffi, J.M.: Chapter 15 ee479 course notes - multiuser digital transmission systems, http://www.stanford.edu/class/ee479/
14. Campello, J.: Practical bit loading for dmt. In: IEEE International Conference on Communications, ICC 1999, vol. 2, pp. 801–805 (1999)
15. Akujuobi, C., Shen, J., Sadiku, M.: A new parallel greedy bit-loading algorithm with fairness for multiple users in a dmt system. IEEE Transactions on Communications 54(8), 1374–1380 (2006)
16. McKinley, A., Marshall, A.: A new penalty based algorithm for multi-user spectrum balancing in xdsl networks (submitted for inclusion in Networks 2008, Budapest, Hungary)
17. Oksman, V., Cioffi, J.: Noise models for vdsl performance validation (1999) ANSI-77E7.4/99.438R2
18. Tsiaflakis, P., Vangorp, J., Moonen, M., Verlinden, J.: A low complexity branch and bound approach to optimal spectrum balancing for digital subscriber lines. In: GLOBECOM - IEEE Global Telecommunications Conference, p. 4150666 (2007)

Case for Dynamic Reconfigurability in Access Networks

Rajeev Roy and Wim van Etten

Telecommunication Engineering, University of Twente,
P.O. Box 217, 7500AE Enschede, The Netherlands
{r.roy,w.c.vanetten}@ewi.utwente.nl

Abstract. The paper discusses the merits of having a reconfigurable access network. The network is viewed as a stack of logical PONs in which bandwidth can be redistributed on an inter-PON scale. The redistribution allows for optimal distribution of bandwidth to the end user.

Keywords: EPON; WDM PON; dynamic reconfiguration; OLT; ONU; access networks.

1 Introduction

The BBPhotonics (BBP) project under the consortium of Freeband projects looks into the design of an extended access network. The network is a reconfigurable and resilient multi-wavelength photonic access network. The network is expected to cater to multiple communities which are geographically spaced out. The paper discusses the salient features of the network and presents a case to have reconfigurability in access networks. Section 2 introduces the network design and presents the network as a conceptual stack of quasi independent PONs. Section 3 presents a study into typical bandwidth requirements foreseen in the access in the near future. Section 4 presents two network profiles which are used to discuss the merits of a reconfigurable network. Section 5 describes performance metrics of providing bandwidth to the user by means of a static network configuration and then comparing it with the dynamic network configuration presented.

2 Network Architecture

Fig. 1 illustrates the network schematically. The Head End (HE) houses a multiple of Optical Line Termination (OLT) Units. The HE is connected to Remote Nodes (RNs) through a diverse fiber link which is resistant to up-to a single fault in the HE-RN connectivity. The RNs then connect to Customer Premises Equipment (CPEs) which house the Optical Network Units (ONUs). The OLTs used are Commercial Off the Shelf (COTS) devices with modified optics to transmit on ITU-T gridded wavelengths in the C-Band. The ONUs used are COTS devices with modified optics to receive transmission in this band. The HE also transmits gridded Continuous Wave (CW) lasers which are modulated by a CPE based Reflective Semiconductor Optical Amplifier (RSOA) and used for upstream communication [1]. The RNs house

C. Wang (Ed.): AccessNets, LNICST 6, pp. 240–250, 2009.

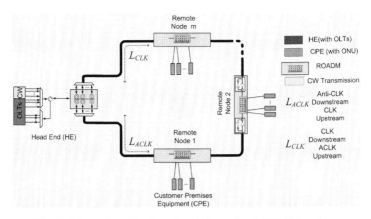

Fig. 1. Schematic of the Broadband Photonics (BBP) Network

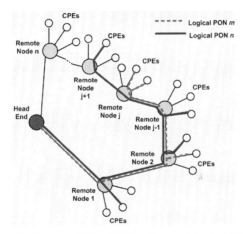

Fig. 2. Logical Connection between HE and CPEs. Two such logical PONs are illustrated.

micro-ring resonator based reconfigurable optical add/drop multiplexers (ROADMs) which are used to add/drop wavelength pairs towards the CPEs [2,3].

The logical network topology retains a tree architecture with redundancy in connectivity between the HE and the RN locations. Fig. 2 illustrates the logical connectivity between the HE and a set of CPEs connected to a set of diverse RNs. Each OLT operates on a unique wavelength add/drop pair. The RNs can be configured to add/drop any selected wavelength pair towards any ONU. The ONUs are wavelength agnostic and associate with the particular OLT operating on that wavelength pair.

Each OLT and the associated ONUs thus form a logical PON. A multiple of such logical PONs can be supported depending on the number of wavelength pairs that are supported by the network. The individual logical PONs can operate in their native format independent of the WDM overlay. The BBP network uses EPON as the underlying TDM PON specification. The concept however is flexible enough to let a mix in such operations both in terms of types of native PON operation like a mix of EPON and GPON or of speeds of operation like 1G EPON and the upcoming 10G EPON. Within the scope of each type of PON operation an optimal distribution of ONUs can be ensured to maximize the availability of bandwidth to the end user [4].

3   User Profiles and Bandwidth Requirement

The emergence of bandwidth intensive applications has driven the need for more bandwidth to the end user and hence in the access networks to a new high. In this section we estimate the bandwidth requirement of typical residential households in the near future.

3.1   User Categories

Studies of typical user profiles are available for the United Kingdom [5]. The study provides an estimation of bandwidth requirements in UK in the short and medium term (2008-2012). The study is used as a base to consider different kinds of user categories for this paper. Table 1 lists the different kinds of user categories considered.

Table 1. User Categories

Category	Description
A	Single adult, retired
B	Two adults, retired
C1	Single male, working
C2	Single female, working
D1	Two adults, empty nesters
D2	Two adults, working
E	Two adults with children
F	Single parent

3.2   Application Definitions

Triple play is the buzzword when it comes to defining applications for the access network. This refers to voice, video and data. An increasing blurring of the demarcation between them and the tendency to move towards a more converged network [6]. Table 2 lists typical applications that are considered for use by the end consumers in an access network [5, 7]. The nominal bandwidth requirement for future applications can be speculative however some applications like remote monitoring of health, remote premises monitoring and data back up seem to be uses in use in access networks.

3.3   User Application Profiles

The user bandwidth demand during the day will vary depending on the application usage. The peaking of traffic requirements for typical network exchanges is around 18:00 to 21:00 hours [8,9]. The typical applications considered to be used in this study by the different user categories in this period of interest are listed in Table 3. It should be noted that the applications listed are indicative of which applications can be expected in the "busy hour" from different category of users. Multiple instantiations

Table 2. Applications and Bandwidth requriements

Type	Application	Downstream Bandwidth (Mb/s)	Upstream Bandwidth (Mb/s)
Voice	PSTN quality call	0.032	0.032
	CD quality call	0.128	0.128
	DAB/CD quality audio streaming	0.192	
	High quality digital audio streaming	6.000	
	High quality digital audio fast download (at twice real time)	12.000	
Video	CIF quality web conferencing	0.320	0.320
	SDTV quality web conferencing	0.380	0.380
	SDTV video streaming (MPEG 4)	2.000	
	HDTV video streaming (MPEG 4)	9.000	
	HDTV download (at twice real time)	18.000	
Data	General web browsing and email download and upload	2.000	2.000
	File down/up load (10 MB in 30 s)	2.667	2.667
	File down/up load (50 MB in 30 s)	13.333	13.333
	Peer to Peer down/upload (60 MB in 30 min)	0.267	0.267
	Remote backup of data (400 GB in 30 days)		1.250
Others	Remote monitoring of health		0.00027
	Remote premises monitoring (5 channel SDTV quality CCTV)		0.69
	Online Gaming	2.000	2.000

Note: Video category calls include audio content in bandwidth calculations.

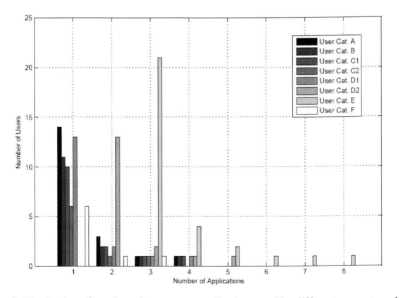

Fig. 3. Distribution of number of concurrent applications used by different user categories

of applications can be used in households with more than one person. The study presumes a generalized Pareto distribution (shape parameter =2 and scale parameter = 1) to estimate the application usage by different user categories in the period of interest. Fig.3 illustrates the number of users in the different categories and the number of applications used concurrently.

Table 3. User Category and applications used in period of interest

User Cat.	Applications	Concurrent Applications in Period of Interest							
		1	2	3	4	5	6	7	8
A	HDTV video streaming	■							
	DAB/CD quality audio strm.								
	SDTV quality web conf.								
	PSTN quality call								
B	HDTV video streaming	■							
	General web brows. & email								
	SDTV quality web conf.				■				
C1	HDTV video streaming	■							
	File dn/upload (50 MB in 30 s)								
	HQ digital audio streaming$								
	Online Gaming								
C2	HDTV video streaming	■							
	HQ digital audio streaming								
	General web brows. & email								
D1	HDTV video streaming	■	▲	▲	▲				
	General web brows. & email			■	▲				
D2	HDTV video streaming		▲	▲	▲	▲			
	File dn/upload (50 MB in 30 s)			■	■	■			
	General web brows. & email				■	▲			
E	HDTV video streaming			▲	▲	▲	▲	▲	▲
	SDTV video streaming			■	■	▲	▲	▲	▲
	File dn/upload (50 MB in 30 s)			■	■			▲	▲
	HQ digital audio streaming						■		
	DAB/CD quality audio strm.								
F	HDTV video streaming	■	▲	▲					
	SDTV quality web conf.		■						

Note: ■ One instance ; ▲ Two Instances

4 Network Configurations

We consider an access network in which 128 end users have to be served by a single fiber plant deployment. The users are assumed to be distributed over four distinct geographical regions with 32 users in each region. Two network profiles are considered; Network Profile 1 has uniform user category distributions while Network Profile 2 has a skewed distribution with clustering of high and low bandwidth users. Fig. 4 illustrates the user distribution the two network profiles. Fig. 5 illustrates bandwidth demand from the users in the two network profiles based on the typical application usage in the period of interest.

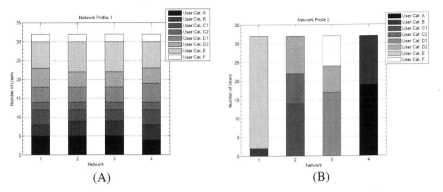

Fig. 4. Network Profiles: (A) Network Profile 1; (B) Network Profile 2

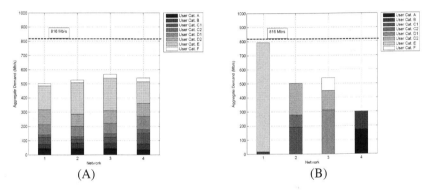

Fig. 5. Bandwidth demand in: (A) Network Profile 1 and (B) Network Profile 2

5 Static versus Dynamic Network Configuration

5.1 Static Configuration

In this network configuration we consider four PON deployments with each supporting 32 users. The IEEE Ethernet Passive Optical Network (EPON) [10] specification is considered for providing traffic in the access network. The typical throughput that can be achieved with EPON, for 32 end users in the downstream is 816.05 Mb/s [11]. The Network profile 1 would have a typical network usage of 65.5 %.Network profile 2 on the other hand shows a marked skew in the loading pattern with the 4th network group being least loaded at around 37 % while the 1st network group is loaded to around 97 %. Since the four groups are presumed to be in four distinct geographical locations, each with its own PON deployment it would not be possible to re-allocate the free capacity in other network groups to a more loaded Network group.

5.2 Sensitivity Analysis

User Category E is a typical household with multiple residents using multiple bandwidth intensive applications. A hypothetical scenario is presented by changing the distribution in the number of applications used by Category E users. Fig. 6 illustrates the change in profile of number of applications used by User Category E in four different scenarios. The distribution for the four different scenarios is created by changing the scale parameter of the generalised Pareto distribution from 1 to 4. We consider Network group 1 in Network Profile 2 to quantify the performance degradation in terms of the best download time for 50 MB files when the network is static. It is assumed that the non real time traffic such as for file down/upload is reduced to free bandwidth for streaming applications. The best download time for a 50 MB file increases from 30 s to about 80 s in the fourth scenario as illustrated in Fig. 7A. Fig. 7B illustrates additional HDTV. channels that can be supported in this configuration as a function of download time for a 50 MB file in each of the four

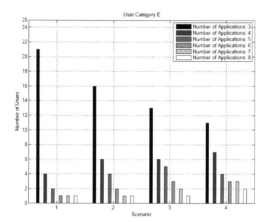

Fig. 6. Changing profile of User Category E

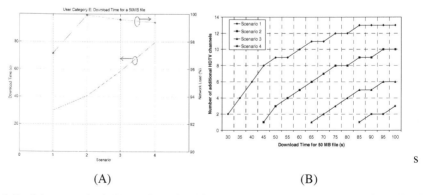

(A)   (B)

Fig. 7. Evolving scenarios in Network Profile 2 for User Cat. E; (A) Download time for a 50 MB file. (B) Number of HDTV channels available as a function of download time for a 50MB file.

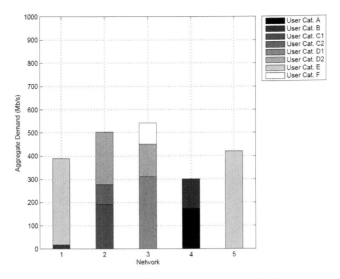

Fig. 8. Bandwidth demand in Network Profile 2 with 5 PON deployments

scenarios. The metrics of an agreeable download time is beyond the scope of this paper but it is clear that in the given profile the network cannot support an increased demand from users. In a static configuration the network provider would need to commission an additional PON deployment to provide acceptable performance for customers in Network group 1. Fig. 8 illustrates the bandwidth demand for Scenario 4 in Network Profile 2 with two PON deployments for Network group 1 (now marked as 1 and 5). These network groups are now less heavily loaded than earlier but come at an additional cost of another PON deployment and an underutilized network capacity.

5.3 Dynamic Network Configuration

A dynamic configuration should allow for reallocation of unused bandwidth from other Network groups which have less load. The BBP network is visualized as a conceptual stack of quasi independent logical PONs. In such a network it would be possible to balance out the aggregate demand over all the Network groups.

A logical PON is supported with a unique wavelength pair. The number of logical PONs that are supported depend on the number of such wavelength pairs that can be used in the network. The RNs which house the ROADM can drop any selected wavelength add/drop towards the ONUs. Since the ONUs are wavelength agnostic, they associate with any OLT which is operating on the particular wavelength pair. If the wavelength add/drop is changed to another pair, the ONUs will be associated with the corresponding OLT operating on that wavelength pair. The nominal bandwidth available to the ONU depends on the number of ONUs supported by any one logical PON. If the number of ONUs increases, the nominal bandwidth available decreases and if the number of ONUs is decreased, the nominal bandwidth available increases. Fig. 9 illustrates the concept with just two colours; the "Red" and the "Blue" logical PONs with a total of 5 ONUs. The network is depicted as a conceptual two stage

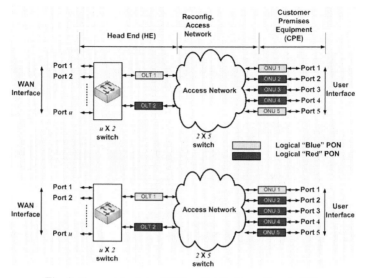

Fig. 9. Concept for inter PON re-distribution of bandwidth

cross connect, the first stage is a Gigabit Ethernet (GbE) switch (u x 2) which can switch traffic towards/from the OLTs towards the WAN while the reconfigurable network is considered as a second stage switch (2 x 5) which can switch traffic towards/from any of the ONUs to any of the OLTs. The number of ONUs supported in the "Red PON" is increased from three to four. The nominal bandwidth for the ONU in the "Red PON" now decreases while that for the single ONU in the "Blue PON" increases.

5.4 Inter-PON Bandwidth Re-allocation

The reconfiguration of the network and the consequent re-allocation of ONUs to do network load balancing can be viewed as dynamic bandwidth re-allocation on an inter PON scale. To do this a Linear programming (LP) based formulation has been proposed [4]. The technique considers optimizing the bandwidth distribution to the end user subject to constraints. The triggering of any network reconfiguration will be a planned response to user requirements and it should be possible to minimize any traffic disruptions. It is also visualized that the reconfiguration will be done on a time scale in the order of tens of minutes in which the change appears quasi static to the intra PON dynamics.

Using LP based techniques the OLT-ONU association is calculated for Network group 1 in Network Profile 2 as the demand evolves from scenario 1 to scenario 4. A detailed representation of reallocation of the ONUs of Network group 1 is illustrated in Fig. 10. The OLTs are colour coded to represent operation on four different wavelength pairs. The ONU association to the OLTs is indicated by the colour of the box in the four scenarios. In the initial state (scenario 1) all ONUs are associated with OLT1. As the network load increases, ONUs are re-allocated to OLT2. In this example the additional capacity required for network group 1 can be met with free

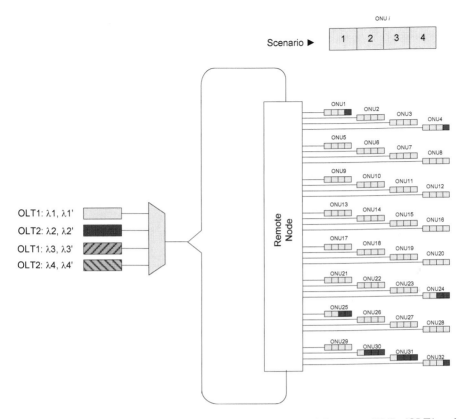

Fig. 10. Illustration of ONUs in Network group 1 being served from two OLTs (OLT1 and OLT2) over four scenarios

bandwidth from one of the other OLTs (here all the additional bandwidth requirements are met from OLT2).

6 Conclusions

A use case has been proposed to illustrate the cause for a dynamically re-configurable network in the access domain. The network allows for operation of existing PON protocols in the native format while introducing a WDM overlay over it. The concept of dynamic reconfiguration drives on the concept of being able to adapt the network configuration to make use of available resources which might otherwise not be possible. Variation in bandwidth demands can take place depending on the user profiles and user application usage profile. While the paper illustrates the concept of using a dynamically reconfigurable network in a residential setting, the concept can be extended to cases where there is a mix in residential and business customers where the diurnal variation amongst different user types will be even greater. The network concept also allows for using a single fiber plant deployment of multiple technologies of PON operations like EPON and GPON and allows for a logical upgrade path to higher speeds of operation for selected customers who might need them. The network further offers scalability in which the aggregate capacity of the network can be increased in a phased manner.

Acknowledgements

The work is funded by the Dutch Ministry of Economic Affairs through the BSIK Freeband Broadband Photonics project under contract BSIK 03025. The authors would like in particular to thank Mr. Gert Manhoudt of AimSys BV for his inputs.

References

1. Urban, P., et al.: 1.25-10 Gbit/s Reconfigurable Access Network Architecture. In: Proc. ICTON, pp. 293–296 (2007)
2. Geuzebroek, D.H., Klein, E.J., Kelderman, H., Bornholdt, C., Driessen, A.: 40 Gb/s Reconfigurable Optical Add-Drop Multiplexer based on Microring Resonators. In: Proc. ECOC, pp. 983–986 (2005)
3. Klein, E., et al.: Densely integrated microring resonator based photonic devices for use in access networks. Optics Express 15, 10345–10355 (2007)
4. Roy, R., Manhoudt, G., van Etten, W.: Bandwidth re-distribution techniques for extended EPON based multi-wavelength Networks. In: Proc. ICTON, vol. 4, pp. 80–83 (2007)
5. Predicting UK Future Residential Bandwidth Requirements, Broadband Stakeholder Group (2006), http://www.broadbanduk.org
6. Ulm, J., Weeks, B.: Next Play Evolution: Beyond Triple Play & Quad Play. In: IEEE International Symposium on Consumer Electronics, ISCE 2007, June 20-23, pp. 1–6 (2007)
7. Harrop, W., Armitage, G.: Quantifying the Broadband Access Bandwidth Demands of Typical Home Users. In: Proc. ATNAC (2006)
8. Amsterdam Internet Exchange, http://www.ams-ix.net
9. Munich Internet Exchange, http://www.inxs.de
10. IEEE 802.3-2005, Part1-Part5, Carrier sense multiple access with collision detection (CSMA/CD) access method and physical layer specifications, Clause 56-57 and 67, IEEE Standard
11. Kramer, G.: Ethernet Passive Optical Networks. McGraw-Hill, New York (2005)
12. Lin, C.: Broadband Optical Access Networks and Fiber to the Home-Systems Technologies and Deployment Strategies. Wile

Fragmentation in a Novel Implementation of Slotted GPON Segmentation and Reassembly

Yixuan Qin[1], Martin Reed[1], Zheng Lu[1], David Hunter[1],
Albert Rafel[2], and Justin Kang[2]

[1] Department of Computing and Electronic Systems, University of Essex,
Wivenhoe Park, Colchester, Essex CO4 3SQ, UK
{yqin,mjreed,zlu,dkhunter}@essex.ac.uk
[2] BT, Adastral Park, Ipswich, IP5 3RE, UK
{albert.2.rafel,justin.kang}@bt.com

Abstract. Gigabit passive optical network (GPON) is likely to play an important role in future access networks and the current challenge is to increase the existing GPON bit-rate to 10 Gb/s to provide next generation access (NGA). However, implementing this in a cost-effective manner is difficult and an important research topic. One of the difficulties in implementation for the electronic part of high-speed GPON is the fragmentation feature as it requires multiple pipeline paths. This paper proposes a novel segmentation and reassembly (SAR) scheme, which simplifies the implementation of fragmentation in that it employs fewer FPGA resources and allows a faster hardware clock rate. Analysis confirms that the scheme does not suffer from reduced efficiency in a variety of conditions. It is also backward compatible and suitable for current 1.25 Gb/s and 2.5 Gb/s GPONs. The novel SAR is verified by both a hardware GPON emulator and a software OPNET simulation.

Keywords: GPON, FPGA, SAR, fragmentation, pipeline, parallelism, emulator.

1 Introduction

Gigabit passive optical network (GPON) is one of the prevailing Optical Access Network technologies, with large-scale deployment being expected soon. A few GPON trial networks are being carried out in the Asia-Pacific region, Europe and North America. GPON uses a point-to-multipoint network architecture and provides a single network topology to provide data, voice and video services with QoS by means of transmission containers (TCONTs) and dynamic bandwidth allocation (DBA).

GPON can support legacy TDM services as well as the growing demands of bandwidth-hungry applications such as high definition television over IP. It is also considered as a candidate for implementing the next generation access (NGA) network which is broadly agreed will supply 10 Gbit/s downstream and the same or lower rate upstream. The technical challenges which must be overcome to implement 10 Gbit/s have been addressed [1,2]. In addition to supplying

C. Wang (Ed.): AccessNets, LNICST 6, pp. 251–263, 2009.

reliable and high quality access network service, cost-effective implementation is a big challenge faced by industry. The need for short time-to-market is a key driving force for today's manufacturers, enabling development cost reduction which would yield immediate returns. This paper will address a novel GPON segmentation and reassembly (SAR) method which will, without undesirable trade-offs, simplify implementation permitting higher hardware clock rates, minimize hardware resource usage and ease the development cycle . This should lead to a shorter time-to-market and make implementation more cost-effective, which are critical factors when implementing NGA. This novel GPON SAR has been verified by simulation using OPNET and demonstrated in a GPON emulator which was developed using a field programmable gate array (FPGA) using Handel-C (a proprietary hardware programming language provided by Agility Ltd). It is worth mentioning that this novel SAR method only applies to GPON rather than for example, EPON which does not need the SAR but with lower link utilization.

Pipelining and *parallelism* are commonly used techniques in hardware implementation to improve the efficiency and hardware running speed and are heavily used in the GPON implementations and the emulator described here. How the proposed SAR affects this heavily used *pipelining* and *parallelism* is addressed in the following section. The remainder of this paper is organized as follows. Section 2 describes the architecture of the FPGA-based GPON emulator. Section 3 describes the implementation of parallelism and pipelining. Section 4 addresses the issues of the current GPON SAR. Section 5 describes the novel GPON SAR which makes the implementation of pipelining and parallelism addressed in Section 3 much more efficient and easier; it also compares the new SAR based GPON implementation in terms of FPGA resource usage, timing constraints and design effort. Section 6 describes its advantages by comparing the system efficiency results from OPNET (an event based commercial simulator) by investigating the influence of different network traffic distributions, traffic loads, and GPON line speeds. Section 7 draws the conclusions.

2   FPGA Based GPON Emulator

Two MEMEC FPGA development boards featuring the high speed, high density Xilinx VirtexII Pro FF1152 FPGA are used to emulate the GPON shown in Figure 1. One is used as an OLT and another is used as an ONU. Both boards connect to Ethernet clients which act as the data, voice and video sources and sinks. The ONU generates upstream traffic with different interleave and different frame sizes in order to emulate a whole set of ONUs. The remaining upstream traffic will be contributed by an Ethernet client which is connected to the ONU. This emulator runs at a clock rate of 31.25 MHz and supports 1.25 Gb/s along with 40 bits data width (the generic width of RocketIO – a commercial high speed transceiver built inside the FPGA). Video streaming is demonstrated using this emulator. The OLT uses "hardcoded" grants (no DBA or status reporting) with a token buffer limiting the bit rate to each ONU to 64 Mb/s, emulating

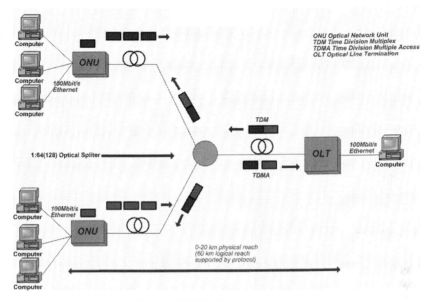

Fig. 1. GPON Emulator Setup

the limitation of competing ONUs (but allowing some peak beyond a 64-way typical maximum split). The emulator features full fragmentation support which is necessary for high-speed network transport. However, this desirable feature might become quite difficult to implement when aiming for very high speeds (over 1 Gb/s), making it very much more difficult to implement within the NGA (10 Gb/s). This GPON emulator demonstrates a novel SAR which we will show maintains high efficiency but is much more cost-effective.

3 Parallelism and Pipelines in the GPON Emulator

3.1 Common Method to Achieve Better Performance and Higher Throughput

Parallelism and pipelining are common methods which are widely used in FPGA design in order to achieve better performance and higher throughput. Hardware parallelism has significant advantages over loosely coupled software parallelism. Software parallelism relies upon a sequential set of statements that can be loosely aligned through operating system parallelism constructs and, unless the number of microprocessor cores is very large, only allows a limited level of parallelism. However hardware parallelism allows a large number of operations to be carried out in a tightly synchronous fashion with advantages in the number of operation that can truly be carried out at the same time and without the difficulties in aligning the operations compared to the software parallelism.

Pipelining allows operations to be performed on a fast data throughput in a manageable fashion. Data is stored in the pipeline so that it can be processed in parallel. This allows operations that take more than one clock cycle to be performed in a synchronous fashion one clock cycle at a time while the data moves through the pipeline. This requires an operation to be transformed from a straightforward software algorithm (as it is usually described and tested) into an implementation suitable for performing in a pipelined fashion.

While it is essential that both parallelism and pipelining are employed effectively in hardware implementations, they also cause a significant design complexity that increases the time-to-market. Furthermore, complex parallelism and pipelining consume more fabric resource and power. One example of the design penalty introduced by intensive parallelism and pipelining is that a far more complex fragmentation function is needed to align the parallel pipelines. Another example is the greater area used when implementing a high clock rate and high throughput that necessitates increasing the amount of pipelining used.

Thus it is crucial for NGA to retain parallelism and pipelining but implement the full functionality cost-effectively. Firstly, parallelism and pipelining within the GPON emulator, which widely employs the methods discussed above, are demonstrated in the following subsection. Then in Section 5 the improved implementation using the proposed SAR is discussed and compared with other options.

3.2   Common Techniques of Parallelism and Pipelining as used in the GPON Emulator

Instruction level parallelization and task level parallelization are used in the GPON Emulator. The former is based on space and lowest level parallelization, while the latter is based on logic where tasks communicate with one other through a channel or a first in first out (FIFO). Loop level pipelines which will initialize a new loop iteration before the current loop terminates and iterative modulo scheduling [3] are deployed intensively. In more detail, the pipeline has four clock cycles of delay, so that when the segregator prepares "current" data which needs to be sent, the RocketIO is actually sending the "past" data which

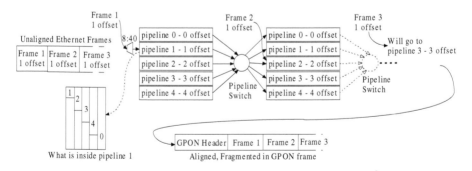

Fig. 2. Figure showing a simplified view of the use of pipelining and parallelism in GPON implementations. Pipeline needed to reduce the clock speed in the FPGA. Parallelism is needed in many parts, here the paralleled pipelines needed to align the output to one of five possible byte alignments is shown.

has already been delayed inside the pipeline. From the other side, when the RocketIO sends the "current" data, the segregator must calculate and prepare the "future" data which will be sent four clock cycles later. Figure 2 shows how Ethernet frames are encapsulated into GPON frame and also shows the parallelism and pipelining deployed.

4 Issues Facing Current GPON SAR Implementations

One of the contributions of this paper is the demonstration of a fully functional GPON emulator which can deal with different packet offsets while implementing fragmentation as specified by the GPON standards (G.984.3). This was required to compare with the proposed SAR scheme. The implementation of the standards compliant design demonstrated the substantial work required which may well be a major cost for commercial development, moreover, intensive pipelines and parallelism will cause area and power to impact more on the trade-off between area, power and clock rate. Finally this complexity creates difficulty in implementing a high-speed I/O system to support a 10Gb/s data stream while meeting the real-time constraints on the design.

In this work, the difficulties of implementing NGA are demonstrated and most importantly the major barrier is found in the development procedure. Depending on actual requirements, there are two major issues in the SAR procedure which affect the implementation of parallelism and pipelining, namely *offset* and *fragmentation*.

The first issue (offset) is caused by differing byte offsets of consecutively received data when compared to the hardware data width as used in the serial to parallel conversion and subsequent pipeline. When an Ethernet frame which is considered to represent arriving client data, the segregator will allocate a time slot according to the length of each data field. If the allocated time slot is aligned with the data bus width, then the time slot offset will be always zero, otherwise it will be any one of x as shown in Equation 1. w_d is the data width in bits.

$$x = \begin{cases} \frac{w_d}{8} - 1 & \text{if unaligned} \\ 0 & \text{otherwise} \end{cases} \tag{1}$$

The second issue (fragmentation) is caused by the demands of network efficiency, i.e. one cannot just waste the remaining space within the frame and wait until next frame rather than fragmenting. Therefore fragmentation is a desirable feature for high speed networks. In order to accommodate frames arriving in different time slots with varying length, the GPON implementation needs to have x replicated pipelines. In the case of the emulator $x = 5$ because the data bus width in the RocketIO is five bytes. Furthermore, the implementation must take into account the merging of data from the five pipelines between any two segments. Note that each pipeline is a complete logic implementation which will run indefinitely. To demonstrate the complexity involved, the Figure 3a shows the finite state machine (FSM) of a time slot. As one can see, transitions exist from each state to each one of the five states (including itself – a fully meshed net). Each state corresponds

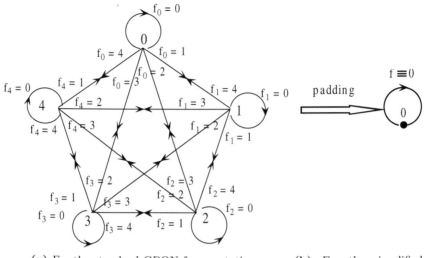

(a) For the standard GPON fragmentation

(b) For the simplified state with the proposed implementation

Fig. 3. Time slot offset FSM, each node represents the current state i, $f_i = j$ represents moving to a new offset j

to one pipeline; whenever new data arrives, a new offset needs to be calculated based upon the current one (the relation is shown in Figure 3). Consequently, the FPGA resource used expands dramatically; timing between logic gates becomes quite difficult to meet which is a barrier to the 10 Gb/s NGA.

5   Novel GPON SAR

The novel SAR reduces the five replicated pipelines to only one which implies one united time slot offset. The Figure 3b is the FSM for the new SAR. The middle part shows the key operation – padding applied to client data before being segregated into GEM payload.

Under the new SAR scheme, the length of the client data is monitored, and the segregator will always align (via padding) the Ethernet frame with the data bus width, consequently only one pipeline is needed to accommodate any length of Ethernet frame without slippage among different time slot offsets. This will reduce the number of large-width comparators which cause considerable delay in the FPGA fabric. Also it still implements fragmentation which makes the proposed SAR as efficient as the standard GPON [4], but greatly reduces the time-to-market and development cost. Moreover it reduces the FPGA resources required to fulfill the same function.

The novel and standard SAR implementation when Place-and-Routed using Xilinx ISE and the key performance attributes of the design are shown in Table 1. The flip flops and look up table (LUT) used are reduced by almost 80%. The

Table 1. GPON SAR Comparison

Standard GPON SAR		NEW GPON SAR	
Logic Utilization	*Used*	*Logic Utilization*	*Used*
Slice Flip Flops	5515	Slice Flip Flops	1205
4 input LUTs	17977	4 input LUTs	4009
Timing Constraints	*Achieved*	*Timing Constraints*	*Achieved*
Shortest Clock Cycle	31.89ns	Shortest Clock Cycle	7.923ns
Design Working hours	*Used*	*Design Working hours*	*Used*
Hours x Person	> 1000hp	Hours x Person	< 300hp

timing achieved improves four times; as known in practice, when the timing constraint approaches the limit, to improve it even by 1 ns is very difficult. However the new SAR improves it by 24 ns. This approach is unlike many solutions which trade off area for better clock speed. (e.g. pipeline stages can be inserted in order to increase the clock rate because reducing the number of independent operations in one clock cycle increases the achievable speed). Thus, this is a good solution which uses a much smaller area and has a much faster clock speed while keeping the same functionality. Consequently the power consumed should reduce too (however this is outside the scope of this paper). The most important benefit is the significant reduction in development time (estimated to be of the order of a 70% reduction using the proposed SAR), this is a key driver for manufacturers to deploy this technology widely in practice. All these benefits make the improved GPON a strong candidate for 10 Gb/s NGA.

The same benefits apply to the receiver part because reassembly does not have to take into account the different time slot offsets to maintain five duplicate pipelines; it just treats any unequal length Ethernet frames equally and will only need to have one unique pipeline to reassemble data. The user network interface (UNI) will filter out the time slot information and recover the received data according to the time slot information, then transmit it to clients.

One might argue that if the fragmentation function were omitted, then there would be no need to calculate the data offset; the offset would always be 0 as well, simplifying the SAR. Also one might argue that the offset alignment (padding) will lead to poor efficiency. The following sections will show that fragmentation is an important feature which improves efficiency considerably, and padding only affects efficiency to a small, quite acceptable, extent.

6   Efficiency Advantages Verified by OPNET Simulation Results

There has been considerable debate about what statistical distribution is most suitable when modeling network traffic. The Poission process was widely used when modeling traffic characteristics [5], then researchers argued that network traffic is self-similar [6]. Currently there is again a body of opinion arguing

Table 2. Simulation Scenarios

Traffic Load = 0.7		
	Traffic Distribution	
GPON Capacity	Poission	Self similar
1.25Gbps	Efficiency *v.s.* Packet size	Efficiency *v.s.* Packet size
2.5Gbps	Efficiency *v.s.* Packet size	Efficiency *v.s.* Packet size
10Gbps	Efficiency *v.s.* Packet size	Efficiency *v.s.* Packet size
Packet size = 1370 byte		
	Traffic Distribution	
GPON Capacity	Poission	Self similar
1.25Gbps	Efficiency *v.s.* Traffic load	Efficiency *v.s.* Traffic load
2.5Gbps	Efficiency *v.s.* Traffic load	Efficiency *v.s.* Traffic load
10Gbps	Efficiency *v.s.* Traffic load	Efficiency *v.s.* Traffic load

that network traffic obeys the exponential distribution when many self-similar traffic streams aggregate together [7]. Debating Internet traffic models is not the purpose of this paper, however. Regardless of this question, the proposed GPON SAR is shown to have superior performance with various of traffic type. The simulation scenarios are shown in Table 2.

The network is assumed in normal usage to have a load of 0.7. The GPON generic overhead factor of 0.06 is not considered, only the proposed SAR efficiency is taken into account to make its influence clear. The packet size obeys an exponential distribution. The mean packet size varies from 100 to 1500 bytes with step size of 200 bytes. The Hurst Parameter of the packet size is 0.7, and the Fractal Onset Time Scale is 1.0 for a self-similar distribution. In order to verify the scalability of the novel SAR for the NGA, the GPON capacity is simulated from 1.25 Gb/s up to 10 Gb/s. Assuming that the GPON employing the standard SAR (fragmentation but no padding) has efficiency of unity, the efficiency of the GPON using the new SAR (fragmentation with padding) is studied against packet size and load via simulation. Also the other two possible options, i.e. "no fragmentation and no padding", and "no fragmentation but with padding", are simulated as well in order to make a comparison. Finally, real Internet trace files [8] are used as source data to verify the correctness of the aforementioned simulation. In this paper the bandwidth efficiency E is defined as follows:

$$E = \begin{cases} \frac{lt_e}{lt_e} \equiv 1 & \text{if (fragment with padding, standard)} \\ \frac{lt_e}{lt_e+pt} & \text{if (fragment with padding, proposed)} \\ \frac{lt_e}{lt_e+nf_w} & \text{if (without fragment without padding)} \\ \frac{lt_e}{lt_e+pt+nf_w} & \text{if (padding without fragment)} \end{cases} \quad (2)$$

lt_e is the total length of an Ethernet frame, pt is the total length of the padding, nf_w is the total wasted time slots in bits due to non-fragmentation. The results shown in Figure 4 correspond to the scenarios shown in the upper part of Table 2 and show no matter what type of traffic the efficiency against packet size with different types of traffic (Poisson and self-similar) and with different GPON capacities (1.25 Gb/s, 2.5 Gb/s and 10 Gb/s). The proposed GPON SAR which is depicted by the curves with circles, dots and diamonds respectively (fragment with padding) always increases while package size increases no matter what traffic type and what GPON capacity is employed. The lowest efficiency of the proposed solution is 0.97 and it approaches unity as the packet size increases. If fragmentation is omitted as mentioned at the end of Section 5, with no padding (the curves with squares, crosses and triangle-downs respectively, non fragment non padding), the whole trend is of dropping efficiency. Obviously with no fragmentation but with padding (depicted by the curves with times, asterisks and triangle-ups respectively) efficiency is lowest. The proposed SAR solution out-performs the other two options when the packet size is greater than 200 bytes. In Figure 4 (a), when the packet size is less than 200 bytes, the curves with circles, dots and diamonds (non fragment non padding) are higher than the one we proposed (fragment with padding) namely the curve with squares, crosses

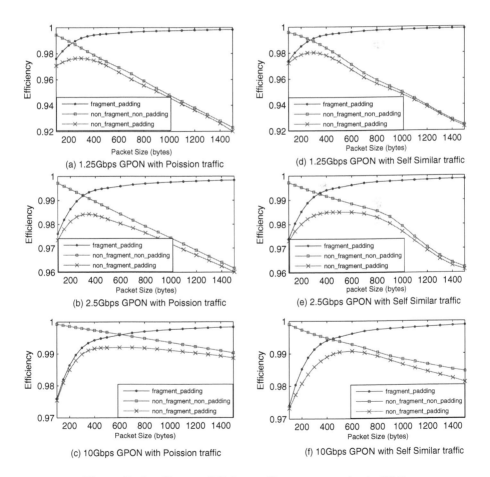

Fig. 4. Packet Size v.s. Efficiency. Choose average load of 0.7.

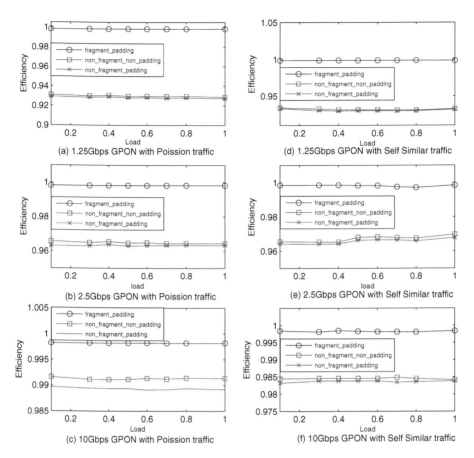

Fig. 5. Load v.s. Efficiency. Choose average packet size of 1370 byes.

and triangle-downs. That is because when the packet size is small, the number of padded bytes is comparable to the original length, hence *padding* dominates the influence of efficiency. When packet size increases, in this case bigger than 200 bytes, the fragmentation dominates and affects efficiency to a greater extent. When each Ethernet frame size is small, then one GPON frame contains more Ethernet frames and is padded more often. When the Ethernet frame size is sufficiently large, the number of Ethernet frame in a GPON frame becomes smaller, then they have a lower probability of being padded and the last part will waste time slots if there is no fragmentation applied. Also the crossing point of the curve with circles can be found with the curve with squares – this moves to the right part of the x-axis when the GPON capacity increases. This is because when GPON capacity increases, the GPON frame size increases linearly (19440 bytes for 1.25 Gb/s, 38880 bytes for 2.5 Gb/s and 155520 bytes for 10 Gb/s), then the padding effect will increasingly dominate.

The graphs in Figure 7, corresponding to the lower part of Table 2, show the efficiency against traffic load with different types of traffic (Poission and

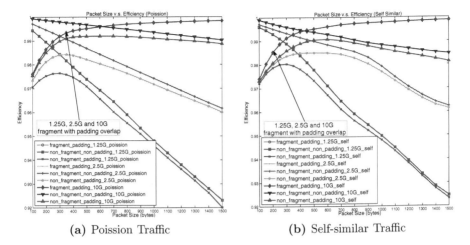

(a) Poission Traffic   (b) Self-similar Traffic

Fig. 6. Packet Size v.s. Efficiency. Assume 0.7 load of the full capacity.

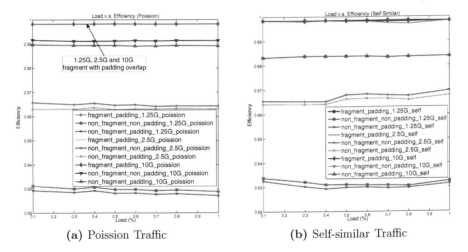

(a) Poission Traffic   (b) Self-similar Traffic

Fig. 7. Load v.s. Efficiency. Assume 0.7 load of the full capacity. Choose average packet size of 1370 bytes.

self-similar) with different GPON capacities (1.25 Gb/s, 2.5 Gb/s and 10 Gb/s), from which the proposed GPON SAR (the curve with circles, dots and diamonds respectively, fragment with padding) always performs better than the other two options (more than 0.995) and the efficiency is not affected by the load variation no matter what the traffic distribution and GPON capacity are. As listed in Table 2, the packet size has an exponential distribution with mean size the same as the video streaming data size, i.e. 1370 bytes. The numerical relationship of the three curves corresponds to the one in Figure 6 when the packet size is 1370 bytes. From this it can be found that the efficiency is mainly dependent on packet size rather than the traffic load, traffic distribution and GPON capacity. Figure 6 and 7 also compare the influence of GPON capacity; all the curves move to the top part of the y-axis when GPON capacity increases. All the values can be verified with reference to Figure 4 and 5. Because of the very high efficiency of the proposed SAR, the three curves (1.25 Gb/s, 2.5 Gb/s and 10 Gb/s) almost coincide (approaching the standard efficiency of unity). Finally, the results are verified by using an Internet trace file as the source [8]; the results are shown in Table 3 which are all very close to the other simulation curves.

Table 3. Simulation Results on Internet Trace

GPON Capacity	Efficiency		
Gb/s	Fragment with Padding	No Fragment No Padding	Padding without Fragment
1.25	0.978140084	0.996378372	0.976086154
2.5	0.978149578	0.996614944	0.976207582
10	0.978153429	0.996893023	0.976520454

7   Conclusions

From the co-verification of a hardware GPON emulator and a software OPNET simulation, the proposed GPON SAR dramatically simplifies implementation compared to that proposed in the GPON standard. In particular it should be noted that it occupies almost 80% less FPGA resource, achieves a hardware clock rate which is four times faster and in the experience of the authors reduces development time by 70%. Thus this scheme is a practical candidate for 10 Gb/s NGA. Using simulation it was demonstrated that the proposed SAR retains the important fragmentation feature with almost the same efficiency as standard GPON. It is robust to different traffic distributions, packet sizes and traffic loads, and is suitable for GPONs with different speeds between 1.25 Gb/s and 10 Gb/s.

References

1. Nesset, D., Davey, R., Shea, D., Kirkpatrick, P., Shang, S., Lobel, M., Christensen, B.: 10 Gbit/s bidirectional transmission in 1024-way split, 110 km reach, PON system using commercial transceiver modules, super FEC and EDC. In: ECOC 2005, September 2005, pp. 25–29 (2005)
2. Kimura, S., Nogawa, M., Nishimura, K., Yoshida, T., Kumozaki, K., Nishihara, S., Ohtomo, Y.: A 10Gb/s CMOS-Burst-Mode Clock and Data Recovery IC for a WDM/TDM-PON Access Network. Tech. Rep. (November 2004)
3. Lam, M.: Software pipelining: An effective scheduling technique for VLIW machines. In: Proceedings of ACM SIGPLAN Conference on Programming Language Design and Implementation, pp. 318–328 (1988)

4. I.-T. Recommendation, G.984.3: Transmission convergence layer specification, 2006, with amendment (2006)
5. Heffes, H., Lucantoni, D.: A Markov Modulated Characterization of Packetized Voice and Data Traffic and Related Statistical Multiplexer Performance. IEEE Journal on Selected Areas in Communications 4(6), 856–868 (1986)
6. Leland, W.E., Taqqu, M.S., Willinger, W., Wilson, D.V.: On the self-similar nature of Ethernet traffic (extended version). IEEE/ACM Trans. Netw. 2(1), 1–15 (1994)
7. Cao, J., Cleveland, W., Lin, D., Sun, D.: Internet traffic tends toward Poisson and independent as the load increases. Nonlinear Estimation and Classification (2002)
8. Four million-packet traces of LAN and WAN traffic seen on an Ethernet. The Internet Traffic Archieve sited at the Lawrence Berkeley National Laboratory, http://ita.ee.lbl.gov/html/contrib/BC.html

TCP Performance over Gigabit-Capable Passive Optical Networks

Julio Orozco[1] and David Ros[2]

[1] Orange Labs, 2 avenue Pierre Marzin, 22307 Lannion Cedex, France
julio.orozco@orange-ftgroup.com
[2] Institut TELECOM / TELECOM Bretagne, Rue de la Châtaigneraie, CS 17607,
35576 Cesson Sévigné cedex, France
David.Ros@telecom-bretagne.eu

Abstract. The deployment of optical access networks is considered by many as the sole solution able to cope with the ever-increasing bandwidth needs of data and media applications. Gigabit-capable Passive Optical Networks (GPON) are being adopted by many operators worldwide as their preferred fiber-to-the-home network architecture. In such systems, the Medium Access Control (MAC) layer is a key aspect of their operation and performance.

TCP is the transport protocol of choice of most popular applications. However, TCP performance is known to be sensitive to the behavior of MAC-layer mechanisms. Thus, it is important to assess the impact that the GPON MAC layer may have on TCP. Motivated by this, in this paper we present a preliminary study of TCP performance issues that may arise in GPON networks. Based on a simple system model, the interaction of some GPON MAC features with TCP is explored both analytically and by simulation.

Keywords: TCP, network asymmetry, Passive Optical Networks, GPON.

1 Introduction

A Passive Optical Network (PON) is a type of shared Fiber-To-The-Home (FTTH) network architecture, in which a single fiber is used to connect several users by means of passive splitters. As depicted in Fig. 1, a PON consists of an OLT (Optical Line Terminal) located at the provider's central office and multiple ONTs (Optical Network Terminations) installed inside the customers' premises. The OLT is connected to the ONTs by means of the passive Optical Distribution Network (ODN) composed of fibers and splitters, forming a point-to-multipoint configuration. Current technologies use two wavelengths for data transmission in the same fiber, one for the downstream and the other for upstream. The downstream operates in a broadcast-and-select TDM manner, whereas TDMA is used in the upstream.

Currently, two major PON standards are being deployed, ITU-T's Gigabit-capable PON (GPON) [1], and the IEEE 802.3ah Ethernet PON (EPON). In this paper we focus on the GPON, currently in deployment by major carriers in

C. Wang (Ed.): AccessNets, LNICST 6, pp. 264–279, 2009.

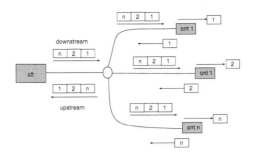

Fig. 1. Passive Optical Network

the US and Europe due to its advantages in terms of bit rates and transport of legacy services [2]. A typical GPON configuration defines an asymmetric capacity of 2.5 Gbit/s in the downstream, 1.25 Gbit/s on the upstream and a split ratio of 32 (i.e., 32 users/ONTs).

The Medium Access Control (MAC) is a key aspect in GPON operation and performance. In what follows, we briefly review the main features of this MAC, specially the Dynamic Bandwidth Allocation (DBA) feature. Recall that ONTs use a single wavelength for upstream transmission. Thus, individual transmissions must be time-scheduled in order to avoid contention. Due to the fact that a simple, fixed allocation is efficient only if all users are active, the standard includes mechanisms for dynamic bandwidth allocation, so that a better resource utilization can be achieved under different, dynamic usage and traffic patterns. Bandwidth allocation is controlled by the OLT, which performs scheduling and communicates the resulting allocation to ONTs periodically.

In GPON, bandwidth can be allocated with a very fine granularity thanks to an abstraction called *Traffic Container* (T-CONT). Indeed, the OLT allocates bandwidth not to ONTs or classes of service, but to individual T-CONTs. The system can ideally handle up to 4096 T-CONTs, each belonging to one of five bandwidth-allocation types and identifed by a number called *alloc id*.

The GPON operates in a cyclic fashion so as to carry TDM traffic. Downstream, a constant 125 μs frame is used. Each frame includes (among other control information) an allocation map which informs on the slots granted to each *alloc id*. Upstream, a reference frame of 125 μs is used. However, this is not an absolute value, since a round of allocations can span through multiple upstream frames. GPON uses the Generic Encapsulation Method (GEM), which allows for the transport, segmentation and reassembly of Ethernet frames and legacy traffic (ATM or TDM).

1.1   TCP and Asymmetry Issues

TCP is the transport protocol used by most Internet applications, including download-based video and rich data applications. The closed-loop nature of TCP becomes an issue with some networking technologies. The TCP source uses the acknowledgment feedback to regulate the transfer rate. When the flow of acknowledgments in the reverse direction is somehow imperfect or variable, the performance in the forward direction can be significantly degraded. This imperfection or variability is thoroughly discussed in RFC 3449 [3], where it is generically called *asymmetry*.

Several access technologies present asymmetric characteristics of different types. RFC 3449 distinguishes two direct types of asymmetry. The first one is plain bandwidth asymmetry, in which the capacities in the forward and reverse directions are different (like in ADSL). The other type of direct asymmetry is due to MAC layers in shared, hub-and-spoke access networks (packet radio, cable, satellite) where upstream transmission experiences higher overhead and latency. Additional asymmetry effects come from bidirectional traffic and the differences in loss rates between the forward and reverse directions. Usually, a GPON system has an inherent *bandwidth asymmetry*. However, due to the characteristics of the link layer there may also exist a *MAC-layer asymmetry*.

1.2   Related Work

To the best of our knowledge, TCP performance over PON networks has been the subject of few papers [4,5,6], and these have all focused on IEEE EPON systems. TCP has also been studied in access networks whose MAC bears some relation with GPON (like the use of TDMA, or the presence of bandwidth asymmetry). See e.g. [7] for an evaluation of TCP over the DOCSIS cable MAC, and [8] for the case of satellite networks. The general asymmetry issues treated in [3] (like the effect of delayed ACKs) are valid to some extent in each context, but the specific TCP behavior and performance issues depend on each type of network.

Prior GPON MAC and DBA performance studies have focused on the local PON system in the upstream direction using open-loop traffic sources [2,9]. However, many key applications are based on TCP, and their quality of service depends on the end-to-end, closed-loop performance. This subject needs to be studied now that large GPON deployments are under way, and both system vendors and operators tend to focus primarily on the optical-layer transmission capacity.

1.3   Goal and Structure of the Paper

This paper presents a preliminary study of the impact of GPON on TCP performance. By means of both a simple mathematical model and simulation, we assess the impact of the GPON MAC layer on TCP. The main focus is on the following aspects: (a) the TDMA operation of the uplink and the fragmentation of Ethernet frames; (b) Dynamic Bandwidth Allocation over the uplink; (c) Bidirectional traffic. The scenarios under study, though very simple, allow us to highlight some interesting effects of the workings of the MAC-level mechanisms.

The rest of the paper is organized as follows. A simple mathematical model of the effect of TDMA and fragmentation on TCP is described in Section 2. Simulation results are shown in Section 3. Lastly, Section 4 concludes the paper.

2   Model

Consider a simple scenario as follows. Without loss of generality, we will focus on a single ONT, connected to a GPON system as depicted in Fig. 1. For the optical link between the ONT and the OLT, let C_u and C_d denote the "raw" bandwidth (i.e., including GEM overhead) in the uplink and downlink, respectively. This link has a (symmetrical) one-way delay of d_o seconds.

Let r_d be the allocated bandwidth in the downstream direction, and r_u the rate allocation in the upstream direction. Both r_d and r_u include the GEM framing overhead. GEM encapsulation adds a header of constant size h. For the uplink, we will consider fixed-length TDMA frames of duration τ_u. Regarding the downlink, for the sake of simplicity we shall assume that there is *no* TDM framing; a GEM packet (i.e., an Ethernet frame with the added GEM header) will be sent to the ONT as soon as it is ready for transmission at the OLT, without waiting for a time slot, and without fragmentation. Note that it is straightforward to extend the model below to explicitly consider the downlink TDM framing.

Recall that GPON supports fragmentation of the transported Ethernet frames. The number of fragments needed to carry a given Ethernet frame will depend on the maximum *net* amount b_u of data that a single TDMA frame can transport, for a given ONT; such amount is given by:

$$b_u = r_u \tau_u - h \ . \tag{1}$$

Of course, allocated bandwidths and frame durations must be such that: $r_u \tau_u - h > 0$. Given our previous assumption on the downlink, there will be no fragmentation of downstream packets.

Let s_d be the (average) size of Ethernet frames sent in the downstream direction. Likewise, let s_u denote the (average) size of upstream Ethernet frames. Then, the minimum number of fragments N_u required for sending a frame of size s_u is given by:

$$N_u = \left\lceil \frac{s_u}{b_u} \right\rceil \geq 1 \ . \tag{2}$$

The number of *full-sized* fragments (i.e., fragments of size b_u) corresponding to an upstream packet of size s_u is:

$$n_u = \left\lfloor \frac{s_u}{b_u} \right\rfloor \geq 0 \ . \tag{3}$$

In other words, an Ethernet frame of size s_u could completely fill n_u TDMA bursts (each carrying $r_u \tau_u$ of GEM-level data), and a minimum of $N_u \geq n_u$ bursts would be needed to carry such a frame.

2.1   Packet Transmission Times

In GPON, the TDM/TDMA framing of data packets (i.e., Ethernet frames), together with the eventual fragmentation and "packing" of several GEM packets in a single burst, may have an impact on the time it takes to send a packet over the optical link, as well as on the spacing of packets over time. Packets of the same size may experience different sending times, depending on their transmission start and end times with respect to the framing. Moreover, in the case there is a backlog of packets ready to be sent, the transmission of a packet may not start immediately after the previous one, but it may be delayed until the next TDM/TDMA frame.

To better visualize the effect of the GPON link layer, consider the three different cases that may arise, illustrated in Fig. 2. Assume a packet i is ready to

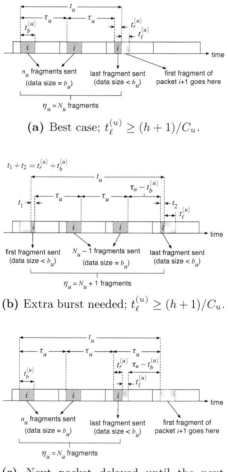

(a) Best case; $t_\ell^{(u)} \geq (h+1)/C_u$.

(b) Extra burst needed; $t_\ell^{(u)} \geq (h+1)/C_u$.

(c) Next packet delayed until the next burst; $t_\ell^{(u)} < (h+1)/C_u$.

Fig. 2. Effective transmission time for sending a packet upstream

be sent at the ONT, and there is a backlog of packets $i+1, i+2 \ldots$ to be transmitted upstream. Assume further that there is no actual bandwidth contention between ONTs, in the sense that every ONT can send a burst of size $r_u \tau_u$ in *every* TDMA frame.

We will denote by t_u the time interval between the transmission start times of two consecutive, backlogged upstream packets. Note that t_u can be regarded as an *effective* packet transmission time, in the sense that t_u includes any eventual delay due to the TDMA framing[1].

Let us examine first the case of Fig. 2a, in which the number of packet-i fragments sent (denoted as η_u) is *exactly* N_u. The first fragment of i completely fills an upstream burst of duration[2]:

$$t_b^{(u)} = r_u \tau_u / C_u . \tag{4}$$

Each fragment (including its GEM encapsulation) is sent at the uplink rate of C_u. Since $N_u \geq 1$, several TDMA frames may be needed to send a packet of size s_u. If $N_u = n_u$, all N_u frames carry a fragment of maximum size b_u. On the other hand, if $N_u = n_u + 1$ the last frame will carry the remaining $s_u - n_u b_u$ units of data, plus the GEM header of length h. This last GEM packet takes $t_r^{(u)}$ time units to be transmitted, where:

$$t_r^{(u)} = \frac{s_u - (N_u - 1) \cdot b_u + h}{C_u} . \tag{5}$$

Finally, the time $t_\ell^{(u)}$ that remains at the end of the last burst is long enough to hold a fragment, carrying at least one byte of data, of the next queued packet $(i+1)$. Hence, transmission of $i+1$ may start in the same burst as the last fragment of i. That is, assuming units of bytes and bytes/s: $t_\ell^{(u)} \geq (h+1)/C_u$.

Putting all this together, we can express the time t_u in the best case as:

$$t_u = n_u \tau_u + (N_u - n_u) \cdot t_r^{(u)} . \tag{6}$$

Note this formula covers both $N_u = n_u$ and $N_u = n_u + 1$ cases. It also includes the particular case in which one Ethernet frame is sent in a single GEM packet (i.e., a frame of size $< b_u$, so that $n_u = 0$ and $N_u = 1$), and the transmission of the next packet starts in the same burst.

In a worse case, it may happen that an extra upstream burst is required to send the whole packet—i.e., the number of transmitted fragments is $\eta_u = N_u + 1$ because the "excess" amount of data $s_u - n_u b_u$ (which is $< b_u$) ends up being sent in two GEM packets instead of a single one. This is illustrated in Fig. 2b, in which the first burst can only hold a "small" fragment of packet i (i.e., carrying less than b_u of data); hence, an extra GEM packet has to be sent in the end,

---

[1] In the case where there is no backlog, packets may of course be more spaced over time; t_u is thus a lower bound on the inter-arrival times of packets at the uplink.

[2] Without loss of generality, we do not consider here the physical- and MAC-layer overhead in GTC frames, which is assumed to be accounted for in the value of r_u.

incurring in an extra overhead of h. This adds a time length of $\tau_u - t_b^{(u)} + t_h^{(u)}$ to the actual transmission time, so that, in this case:

$$t_u = N_u \tau_u + t_r^{(u)} + t_h^{(u)} - t_b^{(u)}, \tag{7}$$

with $t_h^{(u)} = h/C_u$, and $t_r^{(u)}$, $t_b^{(u)}$ given by (5) and (4), respectively. Since $t_\ell^{(u)} \geq (h+1)/C_u$, transmission of packet $i+1$ can start in the same burst.

Finally, consider the case shown in Fig. 2c. The number of sent fragments is $\eta_u = N_u$, but the time $t_\ell^{(u)}$ available at the end of the last burst is too small to hold a fragment of the next packet; that is, $t_\ell^{(u)} < (h+1)/C_u$. In this case, an interval of $\tau_u - t_b^{(u)} + t_\ell^{(u)}$ time units is added to the actual transmission time of packet i, so finally we have:

$$t_u = (n_u + 1) \cdot \tau_u + (N_u - n_u) \cdot t_r^{(u)} + t_\ell^{(u)} - t_b^{(u)}. \tag{8}$$

2.2   Special Case: Small Packets

When Ethernet frames are "small enough", we may have: $N_u = 1$, $n_u = 0$ for a wide range of system parameter values. Generally speaking, this happens whenever $s_u < b_u$; in particular, this may often be the case when frames carry TCP pure ACK segments—i.e., segments carrying no data, only ACK information. In such a case, expressions (6)-(8) reduce respectively to:

$$t_u = \begin{cases} t_r^{(u)}, & \text{if } \eta_u = 1 \text{ and } t_\ell^{(u)} \geq \frac{h+1}{C_u} \\ \tau_u + t_r^{(u)} + t_h^{(u)} - t_b^{(u)}, & \text{if } \eta_u = 2 \\ \tau_u + t_r^{(u)} + t_\ell^{(u)} - t_b^{(u)}, & \text{if } \eta_u = 1 \text{ and } t_\ell^{(u)} < \frac{h+1}{C_u} \end{cases}$$

As we will see, given the common numerical values of C_u and other system parameters, it is safe to assume that $t_\ell^{(u)} \approx t_h^{(u)} \ll \tau_u$ in the latter case. Therefore, for the sake of simplicity we may treat the last two cases as a single one, so:

$$t_u = \begin{cases} t_r^{(u)}, & \text{if } \eta_u = 1 \text{ and } t_\ell^{(u)} \geq \frac{h+1}{C_u} & (9) \\ \tau_u + t_r^{(u)} + t_h^{(u)} - t_b^{(u)}, & \text{otherwise} & (10) \end{cases}$$

From (9) and (10) we see that, for a given packet size s_u, the absolute difference in effective transmission times of two consecutive small packets can be as large as $\tau_u + t_h^{(u)} - t_b^{(u)}$. With typical parameter values, this difference is $\approx \tau_u$, which may be much greater than the best-case time $t_r^{(u)}$. Fig. 3 illustrates this phenomenon, for the following settings: $C_u = 1.24$ Gbit/s, $C_d = 2.48$ Gbit/s, $r_u = 2$ Mbit/s, $r_d = 100$ Mbit/s, $h = 5$ bytes, $s_u = 78$ bytes.

As we can see in the figure, when $N_u = 1$, $n_u = 0$ (i.e., to the right of the dashed vertical line), the difference in effective transmission times between the worst and best cases is large. It is easy to see from (6)-(8) that, as soon as $N_u > 1$, the difference in the values of t_u for consecutive packets is still on the order of τ_u. Nevertheless, this difference is no longer large relative to the best-case time given by (6).

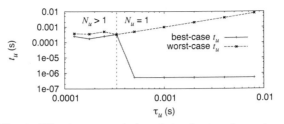

Fig. 3. Effective transmission times: best and worst cases

2.3 ACK Compression

TCP ACK compression effects [3] are characteristic of bandwidth-asymmetric networks. In the case of GPON, bandwidth asymmetry may of course arise depending on the allocated uplink and downlink rates r_u and r_d. Nonetheless, the potentially large "jitter" in the values of t_u may induce strong ACK compression *even in the absence of (normalized) bandwidth asymmetry and of reverse traffic*.

To illustrate this, consider a download-only scenario in which there is a single long-lived TCP flow, with data flowing downstream. For the sake of simplicity, we shall take fixed-size data packets, of length s_{data}. TCP pure ACK packets are of (fixed) size $s_{\text{ack}} \ll s_{\text{data}}$. We will consider that the receiver uses standard delayed ACKs, so that $\delta = 2$ data packets have to be received before an ACK is sent. Let us assume that network parameters are such that there is *no* bandwidth asymmetry, that is, the *normalized bandwidth ratio* κ [3]:

$$\kappa = \frac{1}{\delta} \cdot \frac{s_{\text{ack}} + h}{r_u} \cdot \frac{r_d}{s_{\text{data}} + h} \tag{11}$$

is such that: $\kappa < 1$; besides, $N_u = 1$ and $n_u = 0$, i.e., ACKs are "small" with respect to the burst size, so (9)-(10) hold. Further, the TCP sender's window is supposed large enough to ensure a steady flow of ACKs from the TCP receiver. That is, the sender is in principle able to "fill the pipe" by sending at a rate r_d.

Since the sender is not slowed down by bandwidth asymmetry effects, ACKs may arrive at the ONT at a rate $\lambda_{\text{ack}} = r_d/(\delta \cdot (s_{\text{data}} + h))$ ACKs per unit time. If, for some packet i (a TCP ACK), the effective transmission time t_u corresponds to the worst case (10), a total of B_{ack} ACKs will arrive at the ONT queue during this interval t_u, with:

$$B_{\text{ack}} = \lambda_{\text{ack}} t_u = \lambda_{\text{ack}} \cdot \left(\tau_u \cdot (1 - r_u/C_u) + t_r^{(u)} + t_h^{(u)} \right). \tag{12}$$

In order for this backlog to be cleared, during the next burst (lasting $t_b^{(u)}$ time units) the ONT has to send at least B_{ack} Ethernet frames of size s_{ack}, that is: $B_{\text{ack}} < t_b^{(u)} C_u/(s_{\text{ack}} + h)$. From (11) and (12), we see this condition is equivalent to: $\kappa < \tau_u/\left(\tau_u + t_r^{(u)} + t_h^{(u)} - t_b^{(u)} \right) \approx 1$. Hence, the ONT queue will oscillate between empty periods and periods where a (potentially large) number of ACKs get queued. As we will see in Section 3.1, the release of a burst of ACKs in a single TDMA frame may result in increased burstiness at the TCP sender.

Note from (12) that, for a fixed r_u, B_{ack} increases with increasing τ_u; on the other hand, for the values of r_u/C_u we will consider, the impact of the allocated uplink rate on B_{ack} should be negligible.

When there is bandwidth asymmetry (i.e., when $\kappa > 1$), a "permanent" backlog may form at the ONT due to the asymmetry, but such backlog may also oscillate due to the fluctuations in t_u. Such oscillations will be salient when $n_u = 0$ (so $N_u = 1$), since in that case several ACKs may be released in a single uplink burst of duration $t_b^{(u)}$ at the line rate C_u. The amount of ACKs ΔB_{ack} that can be sent during such a burst is approximately:

$$\Delta B_{\text{ack}} = \frac{t_b^{(u)} C_u}{s_{\text{ack}} + h} = \frac{r_u \tau_u}{s_{\text{ack}} + h}, \tag{13}$$

hence, longer TDMA frames should result in larger queue oscillations.

3   Simulation Results

In this section we will present some simulation results that support the analysis in Section 2. A simulation model of GPON was implemented in OPNET Modeler. The model allows to simulate with a fair level of detail the MAC layer of the optical access network, in particular: GEM encapsulation, fragmentation of Ethernet frames, and Time Division Multiple Access. Our model enables to explore different aspects related to Dynamic Bandwidth Allocation in a generic fashion, since the specific algorithms are vendor-proprietary. We consider a single explicit traffic container per ONT. The rate allocations can be fixed or variable (which allows for the representation of different types of T-CONTs like best-effort or assured), and can span through a configurable number of TDMA frames.

Fig. 4 shows the general simulation scenario and topology used. Though simplistic, such scenario allows to verify the occurrence of some phenomena predicted by the model in Section 2. The one-way delay between the router R2 and the end host H0 is 100 ms; all other propagation delays are negligible with respect to this value. Unless stated otherwise, buffer sizes in both routers, as well as in the OLT, are "infinite", so that no packet loss occurs in them; ONT buffers can contain up to 1000 maximum-sized Ethernet frames.

3.1   Download-Only Case: Fixed Bandwidth Allocation

In this scenario, host H0 acts as a server, and host H1 downloads a large file (of size 100 MB) from H0. The TCP connection is opened by H1 at time $t = 60$ s.

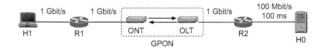

Fig. 4. Simulation scenario and topology

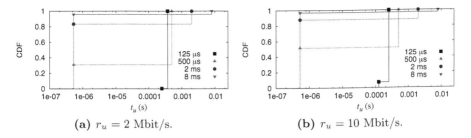

(a) $r_u = 2$ Mbit/s.   (b) $r_u = 10$ Mbit/s.

Fig. 5. CDF of the effective upstream transmission times t_u

The TCP sender at the server advertises a constant receiver window $rwnd$ of 2.5 MB; such a large value was chosen so as to ensure that the sender would in principle be able to fill its downstream pipe of bandwidth r_d (the bandwidth-delay product of the path between H0 to H1 is ≈ 2.5 MB).

The allocated upstream rate r_u remains constant during the simulation. We considered the common, realistic case of $r_u = 10$ Mbit/s, and also three lower rates: 1 Mbit/s, 2 Mbit/s and 5 Mbit/s. Remark that κ, as given by (11), is > 1 for $r_u = 1$ and 2 Mbit/s, but < 1 for $r_u = 5$ and 10 Mbit/s. In order to assess the impact of TDMA frame duration, we considered a wide range of values of τ_u, including a few extreme cases (i.e., very long frames) which are not necessarily realistic, but which allow to "push" the system in order to better highlight some potential issues. Values of τ_u are multiples of the basic frame length of 125 μs.

Values for other network parameters were fixed as follows: $C_u = 1.24$ Gbit/s, $C_d = 2.48$ Gbit/s, $r_d = 100$ Mbit/s, $h = 5$ bytes, $s_u = 78$ bytes, $s_d = 1518$ bytes.

Fig. 5 shows the distribution of the effective upstream transmission times t_u, for two different values of r_u and four different frame lengths τ_u (125 μs, 500 μs, 2 ms and 8 ms). As seen from the CDFs, the proportion of ACKs for which $t_u \approx \tau_u$ (i.e., "long" effective transmission times, during which the ONT queue fills up) gets lower with increasing τ_u; however, according to (12) the backlog B_{ack} of ACKs that builds up during such long transmission times should increase with increasing τ_u, leading to larger queue oscillations. This can be verified in Fig. 6a, which corresponds to the bandwidth-symmetric case ($\kappa < 1$). The value of B_{ack} predicted by (12) is shown for the two longest frame durations.

In the bandwidth-asymmetric case ($r_u = 2$ Mbit/s), shown in Fig. 6b, we can observe: (a) the persistent ACK backlog in the ONT queue; (b) the oscillations in this queue due to the large fluctuations in t_u, for long TDMA frames. The amplitude of the queue fluctuations for the 2-ms and 8-ms frames fits well with the value of ΔB_{ack} given by (13), as expected (≈ 6 and 24 packets, respectively).

ACK compression due purely to MAC-layer effects can be seen in Fig. 7, for a bandwidth-symmetric setting. Remark that, with respect to the $\tau_u = 500$ μs case, the burstiness of the sender increases sharply with a frame of 2 ms: bursts of $B_{ack} \approx 8$ ACKs arrive at H0 every 2 ms, so the sender generates bursts of $\approx \delta B_{ack} = 16$ data packets every 2 ms.

Download times (i.e., the time it takes to receive the full 100 MB file at H1) are shown in Fig. 8, for a wide range of TDMA frame durations. As expected,

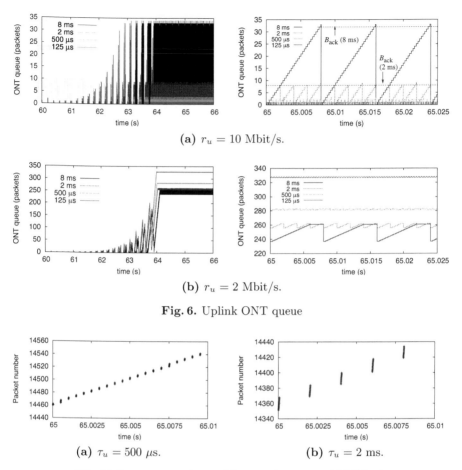

(a) $r_u = 10$ Mbit/s.

(b) $r_u = 2$ Mbit/s.

Fig. 6. Uplink ONT queue

(a) $\tau_u = 500$ μs.

(b) $\tau_u = 2$ ms.

Fig. 7. Sequence numbers of data packets; $r_u = 10$ Mbits/s

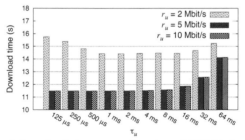

Fig. 8. Total download times as a function of TDMA frame duration

in the two bandwidth-symmetric cases (i.e., when $\kappa < 1$) the uplink rate has no sensible effect on the transfer time, whereas such time increases noticeably when the return path is "slow". Note that, in the $\kappa > 1$ case, download times increase when τ_u gets smaller. This is due to several factors. First, for $\tau_u = 125$

and 250 μs, we have $N_u > 1$, so the GEM overhead for every ACK gets larger in proportion. Second, as seen in Fig. 6b, the backlog at the ONT increases with decreasing τ_u, and so the mean RTT experienced by the flow (not shown for space reasons) grows; hence, the mean throughput gets lower and thus the transfer time increases. In all cases, when τ_u gets very large, its contribution to delay becomes non-negligible, so the download performance degrades.

3.2   Impact of DBA

In order to assess the effect of DBA, we performed a similar evaluation as that in Section 3.1 (i.e., a download-only scenario), but using a model of allocated bandwidth as follows[3]. The OLT grants the ONT a new rate allocation in a periodic fashion, every T_{DBA} seconds, with T_{DBA} an integer multiple of τ_u. The allocation values (in bytes) are drawn from an exponential distribution of mean a; outcomes from the distribution are truncated at a maximum value $a_{\max}$. An allocation of β bytes, valid for $N_f = T_{\mathrm{DBA}}/\tau_u$ frames, corresponds to the amount of data that can be sent in *one* TDMA frame lasting τ_u time units; hence, the "short-term" allocated rate (i.e., during an interval of T_{DBA} time units) would be $8\beta/\tau_u$ bit/s, and the mean allocated upstream rate $E(r_u)$ is $8a/\tau_u$ bit/s.

The TDMA frame duration was fixed at $\tau_u = 500$ μs. We used three different values of T_{DBA}: 500 μs, 2 ms and 8 ms, i.e., allocations may span $N_f = 1$, 4 or 16 TDMA frames. Values of a and $a_{\max}$ were chosen as follows: $a_{\max} = 6250$ bytes (so the short-term upstream rate may go up to a maximum of 100 Mbit/s); $a = 125$ and 625 bytes, corresponding respectively to $E(r_u) = 2$ and 10 Mbit/s.

Fig. 10a shows the ONT queue for the $E(r_u) = 10$ Mbits/s average rate allocation, for the three values of N_f. Remark that the fluctuations in allocated rate may induce strong ACK queue fluctuations—hence, a bursty behavior at the TCP sender. This is an expected result: since the allocations may fall to very low values, a fairly large backlog may build up at a given time, then be quickly released when a large allocation is granted—compare this with the fixed $r_u = 10$ Mbit/s case in Fig. 6a, for the $\tau_u = 500$ μs frame. Note that, the higher the value of N_f (i.e., the longer the allocations last), the higher both the "peaks" *and* the mean queue tend to be; thus, the TCP sender may be much more bursty, as seen in Fig. 9.

In the $E(r_u) = 2$ Mbit/s case, depicted in Fig. 10b, we see that the ONT queue tends to oscillate around a mean value of ≈ 260 packets, irrespective of the allocation cycle N_f. Again, the queue fluctuations are due to the varying allocations. Longer allocation cycles result in larger oscillations. However, the *mean* queue size, which depends essentially on the bandwidth asymmetry, remains stable.

---

[3] We do *not* claim that this model would correspond to actual bandwidth allocations among competing flows and ONTs, since we are not trying to describe explicitly a particular polling and scheduling mechanism, nor a specific traffic load. Rather, such a model is used simply to capture, in a straightforward manner, the fact that allocations may fluctuate widely over time, around a pre-defined mean value. In practice, this could be implemented as e.g. a Hybrid-type T-CONT.

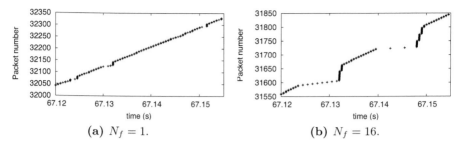

Fig. 9. Sequence numbers of data packets; $E(r_u) = 10$ Mbit/s

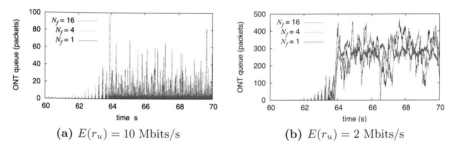

Fig. 10. Uplink ONT queue, when DBA is used

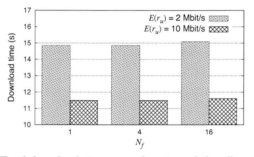

Fig. 11. Total download times as a function of the allocation cycle

Given that the kind of allocation mechanism modeled ensures a long-term, average rate, mean download times should remain close to those observed in the case of Section 3.1. This can be verified by comparing the values for $\tau_u = 500$ μs in Fig. 8 with the average values in Fig. 11, computed from 30 independent simulation runs (95%-confidence intervals, not shown in the plot, are all < 0.25 s).

3.3 Simultaneous Downloading and Uploading

In the previous sections we dealt with unidirectional content transfer in the downstream, so that the sole traffic in the upstream was the ACK flow. In the case of bidirectional, long-lived data transfers, traffic in each direction is a mix of data and ACK packets. On the average, the proportion of data and ACK packets can be approximated as $\frac{\delta}{1+\delta}$ and $\frac{1}{1+\delta}$, respectively. Therefore, the mean packet size in both directions will be: $s_u = s_d = \frac{s_{ack}}{1+\delta} + \frac{\delta \cdot s_{data}}{1+\delta}$, in which case the normalized bandwidth ratio becomes: $\kappa' = r_d/r_u > \kappa$; usually, this will mean $\kappa' > 1$, so there will be bandwidth asymmetry.

Here, we explore the case of bidirectional user traffic, adding a file transfer from H1 to H0 in the simulation model. A 25 MB upload starts after the download with a time offset uniformly distributed between 0 and 5 s. The same fixed allocations as in Section 3.1 were used. For each scenario, 30 independent simulation runs were done, and we measured the transfer times in both directions.

The plot in Fig. 12a shows the average transfer times with 95% confidence intervals, for $r_u = 2$ and 10 Mbit/s. In Fig. 12b we compare the download times obtained in the pure download case (shown previously in Fig. 8) to the mean download times in the bidirectional scenario. There are two salient aspects in these results. First, the download performance is heavily affected by the data

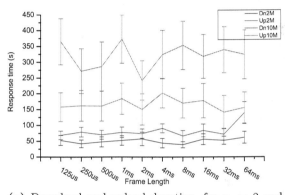

(a) Download and upload duration, for $r_u = 2$ and $r_u = 10$ Mbit/s.

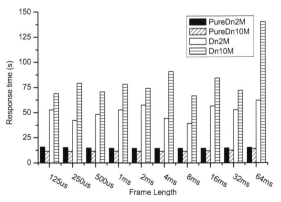

(b) Download times: pure download vs. bidirectional data traffic.

Fig. 12. Transfer times

traffic in the upstream direction, as expected. Second, remark the large variability in transfer times, as shown by the confidence intervals.

As seen in Fig. 12b, download times increase by an average factor of 3.4 for $r_u = 2$ Mbit/s and of 6.8 for $r_u = 10$ Mbit/s. This suggests that download performance degrades with *increasing* upstream rate. A possible explanation is that the higher allocated capacity allows the upstream TCP source to increase its transmission rate faster. Hence, the queue is filled by packets from the upstream data flow at a faster rate, leaving less "transmission opportunities per unit time" for sending ACK packets, and in general impairing the upstream ACK flow.

4   Conclusions and Perspectives

This paper has presented a preliminary assessment of the impact that the MAC layer of GPON systems may have on the performance of the TCP protocol. In particular, we have studied the effect of TDMA operation and fragmentation on quality metrics like transfer times. Also, we have looked at performance issues like TCP sender burstiness that may have an influence on packet loss, when more realistic settings (congestion along the end-to-end path, traffic from competing users, etc.) are considered. These preliminary findings require further analysis, and are of interest because of the potential service provisioning issues.

So far, we have focused on a simple scenario with a single ONT, abstracting the effect of competing traffic and contention between ONTs. As future work, we wish to consider multiple, competing ONTs, in order to evaluate aspects like the fairness among ONTs and the efficiency of resource utilization of the GPON as a system. Besides, more realistic network conditions, like more complex traffic patterns and congestion in different points of the end-to-end path, should be considered. Another subject of interest is the study of the case in which $r_u = r_d$, i.e., when any asymmetry effects would be due solely to the MAC layer. Finally, the behavior of high-speed TCP versions (which compete more aggressively for bandwidth) in the context of GPON is also worth investigating. Also, it would be interesting to compare the performance of TCP flows over GPON and EPON, under similar conditions.

References

1. ITU-T: Recommendation G.984.3: Gigabit-Capable Passive Optical Networks (G-PON): Transmission Convergence Layer Specification (2003)
2. Angelopoulos, J., Leligou, H.C., Argyriou, T., Zontos, S., Ringoot, E., Van Caenegem, T.: Efficient transport of packets with QoS in an FSAN-aligned GPON. IEEE Communications Magazine 42, 92–98 (2004)
3. Balakrishnan, H., Padmanabhan, V.N., Fairhurst, G., Sooriyabandara, M.: TCP performance implications of network path asymmetry. Best Current Practice RFC 3449, IETF (2002)
4. Chang, K.C., Liao, W.: On the throughput and fairness performance of TCP over Ethernet passive optical networks. IEEE Journal on Selected Areas in Communications 24, 3–12 (2006)

5. Chang, K.C., Liao, W.: TCP fairness in Ethernet over passive optical networks (EPON). In: Proceedings of IEEE CCNC, Las Vegas, pp. 740–744 (2006)
6. Ohara, K., Miyazaki, N., Tanaka, K., Edagawa, N.: Fairness of downstream TCP throughput among diversely located ONUs in a GE-PON system. In: Proceedings of the Optical Fiber Communication Conference (OFC) (2006)
7. Martin, J.: The impact of the DOCSIS 1.1/2.0 MAC protocol on TCP. In: Proceedings of IEEE CCNC, Las Vegas, pp. 302–306 (2005)
8. Papadimitriou, P., Tsaoussidis, V.: On TCP performance over asymmetric satellite links with real-time constraints. Computer Communications 30, 1451–1465 (2007)
9. Payoux, F., Niger, P., Vu-Brugier, G.: Modeling and simulation of Dynamic Bandwidth Allocation function for GPON and Next Generation PON. In: Proceedings of OPNETWORK 2007, Washington D.C (2007)

A Fast Channel Switching Method in EPON System for IPTV Service

Yaling Nie* and Hideya Yoshiuchi

Hitachi (China) Research & Development Corporation
301, Tower C Raycom infotech Park, 2 Kexueyuan Nanlu, Hai Dian District, Beijing
100190 China
{ylnie,hyoshiuchi}@hitachi.cn

Abstract. This paper presents a fast channel switching method in Ethernet Passive Optical Network (EPON) system for IPTV service. Fast channel switching is one of the important features of successful IPTV systems. Users surely prefer IPTV systems with small channel switching time rather than a longer one. Thus a channel switching control module and a channel/permission list in EPON system's ONU or OLT is designed. When EPON system receives channel switching message from IPTV end user, the channel switching control module will catch the message and search the channel list and permission list maintained in EPON system, then got the matching parameter of EPON for the new channel. The new channel's data transmission will be enabled by directly updating the optical filter of the ONU that end user connected. By using this method in EPON system, it provides a solution for dealing with channel switching delays in IPTV service.

Keywords: EPON, IPTV, QoE, Channel switching.

1 Introduction

Broadband services in Internet like IPTV, video phone, on line gaming and so on, have become the most important services for both carriers and end users. IPTV service [1], as one of the most important triple play services run over broadband network, will change the end user's entertainment style from cable TV to TV over Internet, from broadcast TV to inter-active TV enjoyment.

EPON system [2], standardized in IEEE, can provide up to 1Gbps bandwidth to end user. As one of the solutions for broadband access network, it is recognized one of the final solutions for 'last 1 mile access'.

Figure 1 is a typical system of IPTV service running over broadband IP network with EPON access network. In this system, there are IP core network and EPON access network. In the EPON access network; the Optical Line Terminal (OLT) and the Optical Network Unit (ONU) connected by fibers are the main components. The IPTV services are provided from ISP's IPTV servers to the end users through the

---

* Corresponding author.

C. Wang (Ed.): AccessNets, LNICST 6, pp. 280–288, 2009.

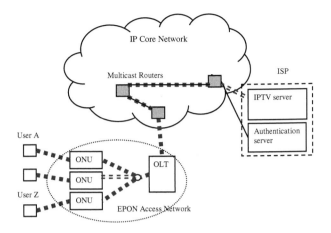

Fig. 1. IPTV/EPON system

whole network. The dotted blue lines in figure 1 are video packets route. The IPTV server connects with multicast routers in the IP core network. The video packets are sent though this core network to the access network (EPON) by multicast packets. In EPON, the packets are broadcast from the OLT to the ONUs in MAC layer with the specific address of the Logical Link Identifier (LLID).

Channel switching time is one of the key features that determine the Quality of Experience (QoE [3]) of IPTV service for end user. In the traditional cable TV system, it is around 100ms [4]. The end user almost can hardly notice the short period of interruption while they switch from one channel to another channel because of the nature of human eyes. So how to assure a small enough channel switching time in IPTV services?

In this paper, a fast channel switching method in EPON for IPTV service is presented. Chapter two includes the mathematical analysis for the factors that impact the channel switching time. Chapter three includes the detail description of the presented method. Chapter four includes the test system and the test result analysis. And the last chapter provides a final conclusion.

2   Problem Analysis

In figure 2 below, the channel switching event is divided into several sub-events in sequence. Thus the total channel switching time can be divided to several parts accordingly.

In figure 2, Event 0 is the user pushes button on remote controller, it needs time T0. Event 1 is the STB processing and sending IGMP leave message for old channel and IGMP join message for new channel. It needs time T1. Event 2 is IGMP processing in ONU. It needs time T2. Event 3 is IGMP processing in OLT. It needs time T3. Event 4 is IGMP processing in edge IPTV server. It needs time T4. Event 5 is IGMP processing in remote IPTV server. It needs time T5. Event 6 is first I frame

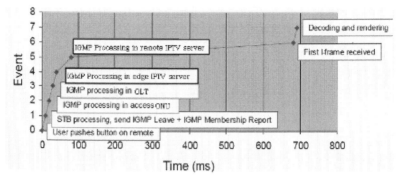

Fig. 2. Channel switching time

received. It needs time T6, Event 7 is decoding and rendering. It needs time T7. The channel switching time should be the summation of T1 to T7:

$$T_{ChannelSwitching} = T0 + T1 + Ti + T7$$

From T1 to T7, each has different feature and impact to the total channel switching time. In IPTV service, since both video data packets and control messages are transported over IP packet. And the TCP/IP system is a kind of "best effort" system. Even the core networks assure some level of QoS since they are engineered; Time for sending and receiving message is affected much by the IP network traffic status. Thus it can not assure key features for the time sensitive applications.

T5 is the longest delay parameter in all time parameters, because it will be affected by the traffic status of the core network.

IGMP (Internet Group Management Protocol) or MLD (Multicast Listener Discovery) leave/join delay (T1 to T5) has a direct impact on channel switching delay. As the analysis in paper 'Validating IPTV Service Quality under Realistic Triple Play Network Conditions' [5] said, acceptable channel switching delay is generally considered to be approximately 1 second total, end-to-end. A channel switching time of 100~200 ms is considered by viewers to be instantaneous. To keep overall channel switching delay within one second, the target multicast leave/join delay of each network component needs to be within the 10-200 ms range. Thus T1 to T5 should be within 10-200 ms range.

Increasing number of subscribers will make a strong impact to both network traffic and the channel switching time. As the analysis in paper 'Channel Change Performance Testing' [6] found, after increasing the subscribers number and hence the load on the multicast network, it increased the subscriber's perceived Join/Leave latencies by 70% and 65% respectively.

To solve or avoid the three problems above, a fast channel switching method in EPON is presented in this paper. EPON system can control multicast traffic for end users in access network. The downlink traffic is broadcasted from OLT to all end terminals (ONU), the ONU uses a filter to select and transport the corresponding traffic to the end user.

By doing channel switching control in EPON, it will reduce or avoid the impact of core network's traffic status. Processing IGMP message will also reduce the impact of IGMP message delay. This method collects information of all subscribers for cooperation but not make compete in subscribers, thus it decreases the impact of increasing of subscribers to network traffic and channel switching time.

3 The Fast Channel Switching Method

In the fast channel switching method in EPON system, a channel switching control module and a channel list module (in ONU or OLT) is designed. In case of authentication to different ISPs, a permission snooping module and a permission list are also designed.

The channel list is maintained and updated by using IGMP snooping function. The permission list is maintained and updated by the permission snooping function. The Permission snooping module communicates with the ISP's authentication servers to get authentication information.

When EPON system catches the message for channel switching from end user, the channel switching control module will search the channel list maintained in EPON system, and got the matching parameters for the new channel. The new channel's data transmission will be enabled by directly updating the optical filter of the ONU that the end user connected.

3.1 The Fast IPTV Channel Switching Processing Procedure

With one user is watching one channel at a time, for thousands or even millions of users in the same access network, there are more than one channel's traffic available to end users. These entire video traffic uses multicast inside the network. For example, when User A is watching channel 1, User X in the same access network might watch channel 2 at the same time. So when the end user A wants to switch from channel 1 to channel 2, the traffic of channel 2 to User X can be sent to User A by multicast control in the access network. EPON system controls this in MAC layer with a faster response and processing speed by updating the optical filter.

As shown in figure 3, the channel switching processing is:

1) EPON system catches the user's IGMP 'JOIN' request for switching to a new channel. Then in GMP EPON frame, there are fields of new channel's group address and the "TYPE" field indicating of joining a new group: 2. such parameters will be checked and recorded for next step.

2) Channel switching control module checks the channel list with the index of group address.

3) If there is a record in its channel list (the access network has the traffic already), go to next step. If no records in the channel list, go to step 6.

4) Get Logical Link Identifier (LLID [7]) of the new channel from channel list.

5) Update the LLID filter of the ONU with the new channel's LLID number. So that the new channel's traffic can go through the ONU's filter to the end user.

6) Forward the IGMP request to IGMP servers (IGMP router, IPTV servers) to finish message procedure with ISP.

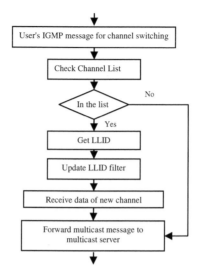

Fig. 3. Message flow of the IPTV channel switching

In some cases, it is the Contact Volume Editor that checks all the pdfs. In such cases, the authors are not involved in the checking phase.

3.2 Generating and Maintaining Channel List

1) Receives user's IGMP request for channel starting.
2) Then IGMP snooping module will check the MAC frame rom the IGMP message part, there are fields of new channel's group address and the "JOIN" field for channel starting.
3) gets the "group address" for the channel.
4) checks PHY data with the "group address" for LLID.

Then the first two fields of channel list have been generated as table 1 below:

Table 1. Channel List

Multicast Group Address	LLID
225.1.1.21	24
225.1.1.22	56
225.1.1.23	43

In case of authentication are needed. There are fields of authentication in the channel list.

1) Receives user's authentication message for channel starting.
2) analyzing the authentication message.
3) gets the authentication info.

Then the two fields of channel list authentication can be generated as table 2 below:

Table 2. Channel List

Multicast Group Address	LLID	Permission	ISP
225.1.1.21	24	Yes	X
225.1.1.22	36	Yes	Y
225.1.1.23	43	No	Z

The channels in EPON system usually changed dynamically according to end user's watching status. So the channel list should be updated dynamically or timely when the channel status changed.

3.3 Layered Implementations in ONU and OLT

This method can be implemented in OLT side or ONU side independently. Or it can be implemented in ONU and OLT at the same time as a kind of layered structure. For different implementation ways, the benefits are different.

When it is implemented in ONU only, it is an efficient implementation way, because ONU is the nearest node to end user. Thus it can make quicker response to its end user.

When it is implemented in OLT only, it is a secure way, because the OLT is located in carrier side and are managed by carriers, not by end user. And The OLT can have a channel list made by all the ONU it connected, the OLT can have larger channel list than ONU.

3.4 Message Sequences for Two Channel Switching Cases

There are two cases for end user about channel switching. One is to start a new channel when the TV is opened. The other is change a channel during watching a TV channel.

1) Start a new channel A

As shown in figure 4, it is the sequence of this method for end user to start a channel. The ONU uses the channel list method to control the channel list. User A sends F1 to Multicast sever to start for channel A. User A sends F2 to authentication server to start for channel A. User A sends F3 to IPTV server to start for channel A. The ONU catches F1 and checks the channel list. Then it updates the LLID filter for the new channel A. The end user receives data of channel A. Then before the end user receives "ACK" messages "F4", "F5", "F6", the channel starting has been finished. It saved time.

2) Switch to channel B from A

The ONU use the channel list method to control the channel list. User A is now watching Channel A. Then User A sends F1 to Multicast sever to switch to channel B. User A sends F2 to authentication server to switch to channel B. User A sends F3 to IPTV server to switch to channel B. The ONU finds F1 and checks the channel list. Then it updates the LLID filter for the new channel B. The end user receives data of channel B. Then before the end user receives "ACK" messages "F4", "F5", "F6", the channel switching has been finished. Then it saved time.

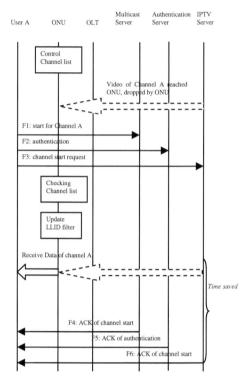

Fig. 4. Start a new channel

4 Test Bed

We implemented this method in a network structure as shown in figure 5 below. We tested the impacts about the channel switching method.

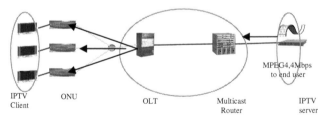

Fig. 5. Test bed

In figure 5, the method is implemented inside IPTV client. The IPTV server sends IPTV videos to 3 IPTV clients. In order to compare, IPTV client 1 has function of fast channel switching. IPTV Client 2 and IPTV Client 3 do not have the function of fast channel switching.

After testing the channel switching of three IPTV clients, we found the total time for channel switching are obviously different. IPTV client 1 that has the fast channel switching method has the shortest channel switching time.

To find out our method's benefit for IGMP message in channel switching time, we also test the system numerically. We measured the channel switching time in end user side especially for IGMP message.

When the end user made channel switching, IGMP 'JOIN 'message will be sent from the end user's terminal to the network. We record the starting time from the IGMP 'JOIN' message. The end time is from the first coming UDP multicast packet of the new channel.

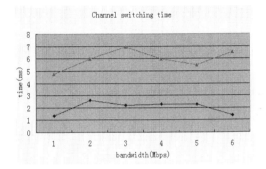

Fig. 6. Test result. The under blue line is result of the end user with the fast channel switching method. The upper pink line is the result of the end user without the fast channel switching method. For impact of IGMP delay, this presented method has a strong advantage.

It is critical to select the test tools and methodologies with the ability to test IPTV in the larger context of triple play networks to verify IPTV QoE under increasing scale, dynamic subscriber behavior, and amidst other voice and data services. Since quality can be inconsistent across the subscriber base, it's important to evaluate IPTV QoE on a per-subscriber basis. Our test is on such kind of structure to measure the behavior of subscriber.

5   Conclusion

In this paper, a fast channel switching method in EPON system for IPTV service is presented. Mathematical analysis for factors that impact channel switching time is discussed. The test system and test result show this method has strong impact on processing IGMP message. So that it can provide fast channel switching solution in EPON system.

References

1. Liu, duo, MII, standardization of ITU-T FG IPTV, 10.20 (2006)
2. IEEE STD 802.3ah-2004, Ethernet in the First Mile

3. http://imec.be/wwwinter/mediacenter/en/SR2005/html/142224.html
4. Yu, qing, multicast in IPTV system, magazine of science of telecommunication, 12.10 (2006)
5. Tara Van Unen, Agilent, Validating IPTV Service Quality under Realistic Triple Play Network Conditions, IP Television (2007)
6. IXIA, IPTV - Channel Change Performance Testing (2007)
7. Wei, Z.: The implementation of LLID multicast in EPON, Optical Communication, 3 (2005)

WDM Dynamic Bandwidth Allocation Schemes for Ethernet PONs

Kae Hsiang Kwong, Hammad Yaqoob, Craig Michie, and Ivan Andonovic

University of Strathclyde
Department of Electronic and Electrical Engineering
Royal College Building
204 George Street
Glasgow G1 1XW
United Kingdom
{kkhsiang,d.harle,i.andonovic}@eee.strath.ac.uk

Abstract. WDM based dynamic bandwidth allocation schemes are proposed as potential future-proof upgrade solutions for access PON systems. The schemes represent cost-efficient ways to exploit the virtually unlimited bandwidth afforded by passive optical architectures whilst remaining fully compatible with the IEEE Ethernet standard for the first mile (EFM 802.3ah).

Keywords: Ethernet, passive optical network (PON), wavelength division multiplexing, MPCP, MAC, polling, dynamic bandwidth allocation.

1 Introduction

Network operators are facing significant challenges in trying to satisfy the growing customer demand for new broadband services. Due to the economics, large scale deployment of optical technologies has not occurred yet in the access layer. However recent evidence indicates that point-to-multipoint passive optical network (PON) architectures implemented using only passive components along the optical transmission paths, are considered a viable solution for the most cost-sensitive network segment.

The deployment of PON can take various forms, such as fibre-to-the-home (FTTH), fibre-to-the-building (FTTB), or fibre-to-the-kerb (FTTK). Regardless of these various physical implementations, the fundamental operating principles for all the above systems are consistent. An optical line terminal (OLT) is located at the local central office, and optical network units (ONU) are either placed at the customer's premise, building, or kerb side depending on the degree of fibre penetration. The PON architectures utilise one wavelength channel each for upstream and downstream directions, and the medium access controls (MAC) are based on polling mechanisms or cyclic rotation. The MACs described in [1-6] arbitrate the access from ONUs to ensure that no collisions occur in the fibre trunk.

However both polling and cyclic rotation based MACs have an inherent problem in which the cycle time (or polling cycle) increases linearly as the number of attached

C. Wang (Ed.): AccessNets, LNICST 6, pp. 289–297, 2009.
© ICST Institute for Computer Sciences, Social-Informatics and Telecommunications Engineering 2009

ONUs are scaled up as shown in [7] and [8]. The longer cycle time (or polling cycle) means that an ONU will have to wait longer before the next transmission window to arrive thus contributing to an increased delay and poor QoS.

In this paper, two new wavelength division multiplexing (WDM) based dynamic bandwidth allocation schemes are proposed where a number of wavelength channels are established for communicating in both upstream and downstream directions. The WDM MACs are capable of supporting a large number of ONUs (64 or more) where bandwidth is dynamically allocated according to the load of individual ONUs.

2 WDM PON

One of the solutions that can be easily adopted in PONs to overcome increasing demand is to apply WDM techniques where the connection bandwidth can be multiplied by establishing new transmission channels at other wavelengths. This approach requires new terminal devices at both ends of the system to support simultaneous wavelength transmissions. Nevertheless the cost for this upgrade plan is still comparatively small compared to the cost required to lay new fibres [9,10].

Fig. 1 illustrates a WDM PON system where two upstream and two downstream wavelengths are employed. Each wavelength is operating at a line rate of 1Gbit/s; therefore a total bandwidth of 2Gbit/s is available for each direction. In the downstream direction, different services can utilise any of the downstream channels for transmission, the signal being fanned out to every ONU by the optical splitter. In the upstream direction, the ONU is scheduled to transmit packets by the OLT. Signals from ONUs are merged into a shared section of fibre via a combiner. To ensure that no collision or overlapping of signals from different ONUs occurs in the upstream channels, a WDM medium access control is required.

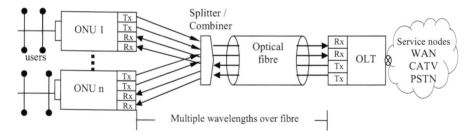

Fig. 1. WDM PON system

3 Control Message

IEEE 802.3ah EFM has defined two control messages - GATE and REPORT - to be used with the multi-point control protocol (MPCP) operation of Ethernet PONs [11]. The GATE message is used by the OLT to inform ONUs of transmissions, and the REPORT message is released by ONUs at the end of each transmission to notify the

OLT about its queue status which is then used as an input by the OLT for bandwidth allocation purposes.

To achieve collision-free transmission on all upstream channels, the GATE message has to be delivered to the ONU in advance so that the recipient ONU can start its transmission precisely at the time stated in the message. Thus the first bit of the ONU transmission arrives at the OLT just after the last bit of the previous ONU transmission (plus a guard time).

The GATE message is scheduled according to:

$$G[x]^{[i+1]} \leq T[x]^{[i]} + \frac{r^{[i]}}{2} + \frac{W[x]^{[i]}}{R_u} + B - r^{[i+1]} . \tag{1}$$

where,

$G[x]^{[i+1]}$	– Time when the next GATE message to i+1th ONU is transmitted on any of the downstream channel;
$T[x]^{[i]}$	– Time when the ith ONU start its transmission on upstream channel x;
$r^{[i]}$	– Round-trip time for the ith ONU;
$W[x]^{[i]}$	– Transmission windows size for ith ONU (including transmission of REPORT message) on channel x;
R_u	– Transmission speed (bit rate);
B	– Guard time (in μs);

Equation (1) defines when a GATE message should be delivered to schedule the next ONU for transmission. In general, the OLT should transmit the GATE message for i+1th ONU at time $G[x]^{[i+1]}$ or before but not later. This guarantees that all upstream channels avoid collision and only a minimum guard time exists between ONUs transmissions thus achieving high throughput.

4 WDM IPACT

The first WDM MAC proposed is referred to as WDM IPACT, a direct extension from the single channel IPACT scheme (i.e. single wavelength) described in [1-3]. Fig. 2(a) and Fig. 2(b) illustrates the ONU and OLT modules respectively of a 2-channel WDM IPACT in which two wavelength channels are established in both upstream and downstream directions.

Since there are multiple upstream channels, the ONUs and OLT are required to be equipped with transceivers that can operate at different wavelengths simultaneously. For the 2-channel case, each ONU is equipped with two pairs of transceivers, each configured to operate on one of the downstream channels constantly receiving signal broadcasts from the OLT. Each transmitter can be individually configured to operate on one of the upstream channels. Two independent physical queues are located inside the ONU storing incoming packets from end-users and each of the queues is attached

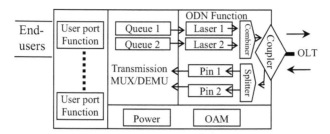

(a) The ONU Logical Structure

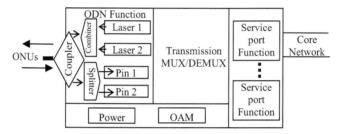

(b) The OLT Logical structure

Fig. 2.

to a transmitter. When a packet arrives at the ONU, it is forwarded to one of the queues according to a distribution mechanism. Each queue is scheduled for transmission independently by the OLT; thus queue 1 of all ONUs will be scheduled in turn for transmission over the first upstream channel and queue 2 will share the bandwidth of the second upstream channel.

Two polling tables are used in the OLT to record bandwidth requests made by ONUs. The polling tables hold information on identity (NID), round-trip time (RTT), and request bytes (V). The transmission starting time and transmission window length of each ONU is calculated and assigned by the OLT according to the information passed on by the ONU during the previous transmission. The OLT utilises polling table 1 to schedule ONUs to transmit packets stored in queue 1 on upstream channel 1, and polling table 2 for allocating bandwidth to ONUs to transmit packets stored in queue 2 on upstream channel 2.

The length of transmission window allocated to each individual ONU is assigned by the OLT and can be a predefined (fixed) or a variable value based on some algorithm that use the request from each ONU as an input for the allocation. In this paper, the Fixed, Limited, and Gated assignment schemes from [1-3] are used. In the Fixed assignment scheme, the OLT will allocate each ONU a fixed length of transmission window (W_{MAX}). In the Limited assignment scheme, the OLT will allocate an ONU the amount of bandwidth it has previously requested if the request is smaller than the upper bound limitation (W_{MAX}); otherwise W_{MAX} is assigned. In the Gated assignment scheme, the ONU will be granted a transmission window of the size it has requested regardless. The largest possible window size will be equal to the maximum length of the ONU's queue.

5 WDM IPACT-ST

The second WDM MAC discussed in this paper is referred to as WDM IPACT with single polling table (WDM IPACT-ST). The ONU and OLT modules in this MAC are similar to those in the WDM IPACT described above, except that a tuneable laser replaces the multiple fixed transmitters within the ONU. A single queue is attached to the tuneable laser instead of the multiple queue structure.

Transmission windows are assigned to ONUs in a round robin fashion allowing them to transmit on the first available upstream channel. Only one polling table is used to perform the scheduling process and bandwidth allocation to ONUs transmitting on the upstream channels. To apply this MAC, the OLT has to know which upstream channel will turn idle first.

The OLT keeps track of all upstream channels by calculating their next idle time. Since the OLT knows the round trip time (RTT) of all ONUs and the transmission window size (WS) assigned to ONUs for transmission on upstream channels (this information is recorded in the polling table), it can predict exactly when a particular upstream channel becomes idle by:

$$T_{idle[x]} = T[x] + \frac{W[x]}{R_u} + \frac{r}{2}. \qquad (2)$$

$T_{idle[x]}$ is the time when upstream channel x becomes idle and available for the next transmission. $T[x]$ is the time when the previous ONU starts transmission on upstream channel x. $W[x]$ is the transmission window size that was assigned to the previous ONU on upstream channel x. R_u is the transmission bit rate between the ONU and the OLT. And r (round trip time) is amount of time required by a bit to travel from the OLT to ONU and return.

Based on (2), the OLT knows exactly when a transmission will be finished on all upstream channels soon after it releases the GATE messages to the ONUs. Therefore, with knowledge of the next idle time, the OLT can schedule an ONU to transmit on the upstream channel that has the smallest value of $t_{idle[x]}$. Again, the Fixed, Gated, and Limited assignment schemes can be used by the OLT to determine the length of transmission window allocated to each ONU.

6 Simulations

In the simulation, all ONUs support identical traffic loads. The line rate of the distribution section from the ONU to an individual end-user is assumed to be 100Mbit/s. The line rate of each wavelength channel operating in the section between the OLT and the ONUs is 1Gbit/s. The guard time between ONU transmissions is fixed at 5μs. The queue size of each ONU is 10Mbytes, and W_{MAX} is set to 15000 bytes.

Fig. 3 summarises the simulation results for the single channel IPACT system [1-3] as a function of the number of ONUs. As the number of connected ONUs increases, the IPACT system quickly reaches saturation e.g. when the ONU number increases to 64, the IPACT system will become unstable even when the ONU is only providing a load of 20Mbit/s.

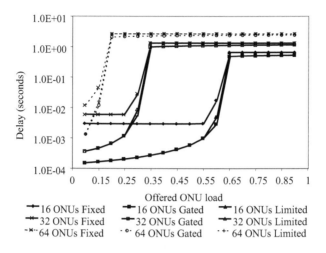

Fig. 3. Average packet delay for single channel IPACT

Fig. 4 plots the simulation results for a 2-channel WDM IPACT system, together with a 2-channel WDM IPACT-ST system. In these simulations, the OLT is connected to 24 ONUs, and each ONU is connected to a group of end-users via 100Mbit/s Ethernet.

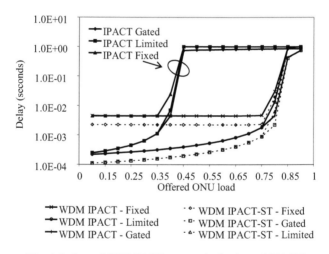

Fig. 4. 2-channel WDM PON versus single channel IPACT

Both WDM IPACT and WDM IPACT-ST perform better than the single channel IPACT. In the WDM system the saturation point has been deferred to 0.85 overall offered ONU load (OOL), compared to 0.45 in the single channel case.

Fig. 5 shows the simulation result for a 3-channel WDM PON system where the OLT is connected to 32 ONUs. In this configuration, the maximum traffic aggregation from all ONUs can reach 3200Mbit/s and the single channel IPACT

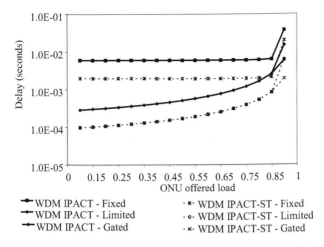

Fig. 5. 3-channel WDM IPACT versus 3-channel WDM IPACT-ST

system saturates even when each ONU is providing 35Mbit/s of traffic (Fig. 3). The results show that the WDM upgrade solutions proposed here has successfully resolved the bandwidth demand problem caused by the increase in ONU terminals.

In general, the performance of WDM IPACT-ST is 50-70% better than the WDM IPACT as a consequence of its shorter cycle time.

7   Differentiated Services WDM IPACT-ST

The principle of differentiated services (DiffServ) [12] is based on class discrimination where packets from end-users are categorised into a number of priority groups. Network resources are then distributed among these groups with varied proportions so that higher priority groups are always allocated more resources than the lower priority groups.

The WDM IPACT-ST is chosen to integrate with DiffServ as it has a far superior performance than the WDM IPACT. To support differentiated services over WDM IPACT-ST, the ONU is installed with an array of physical queues where each queue is used to store a particular class of traffic. When a packet arrives at the ONU, it will be first categorized into one of the priority groups according to its content and then placed into one of the queues accordingly.

In this paper, the Limited assignment scheme is used as an example to illustrate how the differentiated services can be integrated into WDM IPACT-ST. In the simulation, five different priority groups are defined (P1, P2,..., P5). Packets arriving at the ONU will be classified and placed into one of the five physical queues (Q1, Q2,..., Q5). Weighted Fair Queueing (WFQ) is used in the ONU to reserve bandwidth for these five priority groups. Through WFQ, each priority groups can reserve different weighted proportions in the next transmission window. For example, the ONU can reserve up to 35%, 30% 20% 10% and 5% of W_{MAX} to Q1, Q2, Q3, Q4, and Q5 respectively. Therefore, when the next GATE message arrives, the ONU can

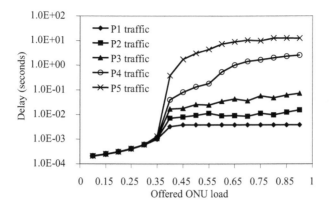

Fig. 6. Average delay of 3-channel DiffServ WDM IPACT-ST (64 ONUs)

transmit packet from priority queues (Q1,..., Q5) up to the amount it previously reserved. Fig. 5 shows the average delay for the DiffServ WDM IPACT-ST in which 3 wavelength channels are utilised in each direction, and 64 ONUs are connected to the OLT.

In the simulation, each ONU is said to support two E1 line emulations allowing a total of 64 PSTN phone calls simultaneously. E1 emulation packets are defined as the highest priority traffic (P1). The rest of the offered load is composed of P2, P3, P4 and P5 traffic with a ratio of 1:2:3:4. P2 and P3 traffic are said to be premium and normal business users; P4 and P5 are premium and normal home users. P1 traffic is constant bit rate, the rest of the traffic is generated by using self-similar traffic sources.

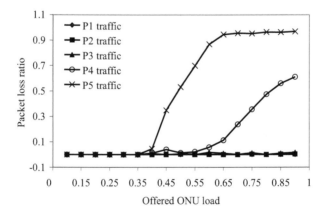

Fig. 7. Packet loss ratio of 3-channel DiffServ WDM IPACT-ST (64 ONUs)

8 Conclusions

Two WDM dynamic bandwidth allocation schemes are proposed here as potential future-proof upgrade solutions for PON systems. When facing increasing bandwidth demand caused by new customer subscriptions or new revenue generating services, the network operator's preferred solution are techniques that elegantly increase the level of usage of the deployed architectures. In the case of PONs, although the proposed MACs require the installation of new transceiver pairs in both the ONU and the OLT, the costs of this upgrade strategy is still comparatively small when compared to laying new OLT-ONU trees.

The proposed WDM MACs resolves the bandwidth bottleneck problem by introducing new upstream channels. As shown in the simulation results, the performance of the WDM PON improves dramatically when compared to the single channel case.

References

[1] Kramer, G., Mukherjee, B., Pesavento, G.: Interleaved Polling with Adaptive Cycle Time (IPACT): a dynamic bandwidth distribution scheme in an optical access network. Photonic Network Communications 4, 89–107 (2002)

[2] Kramer, G., Mukherjee, B., Pesavento, G.: IPACT: a dynamic protocol for an Ethernet PON (EPON). IEEE Communications Magazine 40, 74–80 (2002)

[3] Kramer, G., Mukherjee, B., Dixit, S., Ye, Y., Hirth, R.: Supporting differentiated classes of service in Ethernet passive optical networks. OSA Journal of Optical Networking 1, 280–298 (2002)

[4] Choi, S., Huh, J.: Dynamic bandwidth allocation algorithm for multimedia services over Ethernet PONs. ETRI Journal 24, 465–468 (2002)

[5] Ma, M., Zhu, Y., Cheng, T.H.: A bandwidth guaranteed polling MAC protocol for Ethernet passive optical networks. In: Proc. IEEE INFOCOM, San Francisco, pp. 22–31 (2003)

[6] Assi, C.M., Ye, Y., Dixit, S., Ali, M.A.: Dynamic bandwidth allocation for quality-of-service over Ethernet PONs. IEEE Journal on Selected Areas in Communications 21, 1467–1477 (2003)

[7] Son, K., Ryu, H., Chong, S., Yoo, T.: Dynamic bandwidth allocation schemes to improve utilization under non-uniform traffic in Ethernet passive optical networks. In: 2004 IEEE International Conference on Communication, vol. 3, pp. 1766–1770 (2004)

[8] Kwong, K.H., Harle, D., Andonovic, I.: WDM PONs: Next Step for the First Mile. In: The Second International Conference on the Performance Modelling and Evaluation of Heterogeneous Networks (2004)

[9] Ei-Sayed, M., Jaffe, J.: A view of telecommunications network evolution. IEEE Communications Magazine 40, 74–81 (2002)

[10] Huang, C.C., et al.: Bringing core and edge network for residential subscribers. IEEE Communications Magazine 40 (2002)

[11] IEEE 802.3ah task force home page, http://www.ieee802.org/3/efm

[12] Blake, S., Black, D., Carlson, M., Davies, E., Wang, Z., Weiss, W.: An Architecture for Differentiated Services, IETF, RFC 2475 (1998)

VoIP Performance with
Aggressive AMC and SINR Feedback
for WiMAX Downlink

Xiangning Fan[1] and Zhu Dengkui[2]

[1] Institute of RF-&-OE-ICs, School of Information Science and Engineering,
Southeast University, Nanjing, 210096, China
[2] National Mobile Communications Research Laboratory,
Southeast University, Nanjing, 210096, China
xnfan@seu.edu.cn

Abstract. WiMAX system is based on OFDMA, and it is very suitable for VoIP traffic. At the same time, aggressive AMC and frame bundling are two important techniques to improve the performance of VoIP, and so they are applied to WiMAX system in this paper. The simulation results show that when the system is in short of bandwidth, these two techniques indeed reduce the PER and delay jitter of the VoIP users, and also enhance the spectrum efficiency.

Keywords: WiMAX, VoIP, Aggressive AMC, Bundling.

1 Introduction

IEEE802.16e is put forward based on IEEE802.16d, and is modified to support the mobility of users. For the time being, WiBro (Wireless Broadband Service) in Korea and the rapidly growing WiMAX (World Interoperability for Microwave Access) are main commercial systems based on OFDM (Orthogonal Frequency Multiplexing Modulation). While VoIP (Voice over Internet Protocol) is important for future wireless mobile networks and there are many papers which have evaluated VoIP performance for 3GPP 1xEV-DO revision A mobile cellular system [1,2]. However, little evaluation has been made for WiMAX system. In this paper, both aggressive AMC (Adaptive Modulation and Coding) technique and voice frame bundling technique are applied to VoIP traffic in WiMAX system, and the analysis and simulations are given.

The organization of this paper is as follows: In Section 2, the system model of WiMAX downlink and the VoIP traffic model are given. In Section 3, voice frame bundling and aggressive AMC are discussed. Simulation conditions are summarized in Section 4. And in Section 5, the performance simulation results are presented and analyzed. Section 6 concludes the paper.

C. Wang (Ed.): AccessNets, LNICST 6, pp. 298–311, 2009.

2 System Model

2.1 WiMAX Downlink Frame Structure

For the PMP (Point to Multi-Point) structure based WiMAX system, the resource information allocated to SS (Subscriber Station) in the DL (DownLink) and UL (UpLink) are broadcasted through MAP message by BS (Base Station). In each TDD (Time Division Duplex) DL frame structure of WiMAX system (see Fig. 1), the first OFDM symbol is the preamble, which is used for timing, frequency synchronization and channel estimation. Following the preamble is FCH (Frame Control Header) and two MAP messages:UL-MAP and DL-MAP. DL-MAP is composed of DL-MAP-IE, which informs SS the property of data such as the position in frame, size, and modulation and coding scheme etc. After receiving the DL-MAP, SS decodes the message and learns from this decoded message the corresponding properties, and thus SS could correctly receive the data transmitted by BS 3. In WiMAX system, data belong to different SSs but using the same modulation and coding scheme are filled together into a same burst.

   In the DL frame, sub-carriers in OFDM symbols are arranged as permutation of PUSC (Partial Usage Sub-Carriers), thus the slots in DL frame is $N_{slot} = (N_{sym} - 1)/2 * N_{sch}$, where N_{sym} and N_{sch} are the number of OFDM symbols and sub-channels in DL frame respectively. As compared to normal MAP message, compressed MAP message is also used for smaller size message in WiMAX.

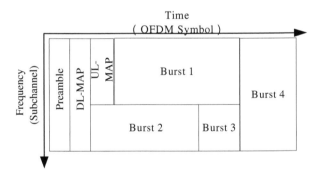

Fig. 1. DL Frame structure in WiMAX

2.2 VoIP Traffic Model in WiMAX

Typical phone talk is composed of active talking or talk spurt (ON) period and silence spurt (OFF) period. In the EVRC (Enhanced Variable Rate Codec) model [4], VoIP traffic arrivals at one of the four rates in each 20ms interval. Table 1 presents the value of the four data rates and their corresponding proportion. The state transfer of data transmission obeys Markov model as shown in Fig. 2.

Table 1. Parameters of VoIP traffic rate in WiMAX

Item	Parameter
Voice Active Factor	0.4
Full Rate （R-1）	29%
Half rate （R-1/2）	4%
Quarter Rate （R-1/4）	7%
Eighth Rate （R-1/8）	60%

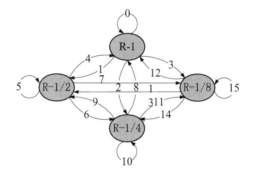

Fig. 2. Markov model of state transfer of VoIP data rate in WiMAX

Various protocol headers (such as RTP, UDP, and IP headers) are added to the data output from voice codec to form a voice frame, and then the frame is sent to the MAC (Medium Access Control) layer of BS. In the VoIP frame (packet), the packet size of the protocol is 40Bytes, and after header compressing, it reduces to 2Bytes. Therefore, the average rate of VoIP traffic in MAC is 5.71kb/s, and the average frame (packet) size is 98bits for WiMAX downlink frame.

3   VoIP with Aggressive AMC and SINR Feedback in WiMAX

3.1 Bundling of Voice Frame (Packet)

As we know, VoIP traffic arrives in periods, and the data size is relatively small. If protocol header compression is used, the largest size of VoIP packet is 203 bits and the average is 98 bits for the EVRC VoIP model. In WiMAX system, VoIP has the highest priority, so almost each packet is scheduled timely and forms a single PDU (Protocol Data Unit). PDU in WiMAX system contains a MAC header and CRC (cyclic redundancy check), and their size is 48 bits and 32 bits respectively (see Fig. 3). If we consider the average size of VoIP packets, the proportion of overhead in a VoIP PDU is: （48+32） /(48+32+98)=45%. So, quite a part of the bandwidth is used to transmit overhead which is useless for SSs, and therefore, the frequency efficiency is lowered. In order to increase the proportion of voice data in a VoIP PDU and make use of the bandwidth more efficiently, multiple VoIP frames (packets) should be bundled to form a super VoIP frame (packet) in the CS (convergence sub-layer) layer of WiMAX, and this technique is usually called bundling of VoIP frame (packet) (see Fig. 4) [5,6].

802.16 MAC header	VoIP data packet	CRC

Fig. 3. PDU data packet in WiMAX system

802.16 MAC header	VoIP data packet1	VoIP data packet2	VoIP data packet3	CRC

Fig. 4. Bundling VoIP packets in WiMAX system

Suppose that K VoIP packets form a super packet. Then, its average overhead ratio OHR_K can be expressed as follows:

$$OHR_K = \frac{L_{MacHead} + L_{CRC}}{L_{MacHead} + L_{CRC} + K*L_{Packet}} = \frac{80}{80 + K*L_{Packet}} \tag{1}$$

where, $L_{MacHead}$ is the MAC header size, L_{CRC} is the size of CRC in PDU, L_{Packet} is the average VoIP packet size (i.e., 98 bits in this paper). Suppose the average bandwidth (Bw) usage rate is R_1 when no bundling is used, then R_K of K VoIP packets bundling should satisfy:

$$R_1 \geq R_K \geq R_1(1 - OHR_1)/(1 - OHR_K) \tag{2}$$

According to (1) and (2), as the number K increases, i.e., as more packets are bundled together to form a super packet, the proportion of the overhead decreases gradually, and the average bandwidth efficiency is boosted consequently. However, one problem comes forth at the same time: the delay of the super VoIP packet also becomes larger. As the voice packets is generated each 20ms in the voice codec, if two packets are bundled, the first packet in the super VoIP packet has already been delayed 20ms when it enters the MAC of BS. So for K VoIP packets bundling, the first packet in the super VoIP packet will be delayed $20(K-1)$ ms, thus little time will be left for MAC scheduler because VoIP traffic is strictly time constrained. As a result, in order to guarantee the QoS (Quality of Service) of end to end delay for each VoIP packet in a super VoIP packet, delay sensitive MAC scheduling algorithm must be used.

3.2 Feedback of SINR

WiMAX is a system using multiple carriers. Data of each SS are modulated on multiple sub-carriers. At the receiver, the ith SS first calculates SINR (signal to interference and noise ratio) of each sub-carrier, then, the SS maps all of the SINR to an effective value $SINR_i(t)$ using EESM (Exponential Effective SNR Mapping) [7, 8]. The effective value $SINR_i(t)$ is filtered through a smooth filter and finally the average effective SINR $\overline{SINR_i(t)}$ can be gotten as following:

$$\overline{SINR_i(t)} = (1-\alpha)\overline{SINR_i(t-1)} + \alpha SINR_i(t) \tag{3}$$

where $1/32 \leq \alpha \leq 1$. $\overline{SINR_i(t)}$ is feed back to BS through CQICH (Channel Quality Identity Channel) in period, and BS uses this information as an input parameter to perform AMC and scheduling.

3.3 Aggressive AMC

For VoIP user in WiMAX system, the aggressive AMC [9] is implemented as follows: BS first gets the average effective SINR ($\overline{SINR_i(t)}$) from the CQICH, and then it adds an aggressive factor β ($\beta > 0$) to the $\overline{SINR_i(t)}$, i.e., :

$$SINR_i(t)_{AMC} = \overline{SINR_i(t)} + \beta \tag{4}$$

where $SINR_i(t)_{AMC}$ is used to perform AMC in the following way. BS first looks up the BLER-SINR (Block Error Ratio-SINR) curve, and then accordingly determines the highest data rate MCS (modulation and code scheme) that this $SINR_i(t)_{AMC}$ could support with the constraint of BLER satisfying less than 1%. And the highest MCS is selected as the MCS of the user.

Because of the aggressive factor β, the MCS of VoIP user may be a little higher than what should be for the user's channel condition. However, if we select the β elaborately, system spectral efficiency could be enhanced, while HARQ (Hybrid Automatic Repeat-Request) retransmission will not largely occur for the wrongly received data at the first transmission.

3.4 Scheduling Algorithm

Ref. [10] presents an M-LWDF (modified largest weighted delay first) scheduling algorithm to calculate the priority of SS, for any $\gamma_i > 0$, the formula of priority is:

$$s = \arg\max_i \left\{ \gamma_i D_i(t) W_i(t) \right\} \tag{5}$$

where γ_i is a parameter represents traffic priority. Ref. [10] has proved that the scheduling algorithm is throughput optimal, and it gives an optimal choice of γ_i. For only VoIP traffic is considered in this paper, so γ_i is neglected. $D_i(t)$ represents the maximum data transmitting rate of ith SS; $W_i(t)$ is the delay of data belonged to i^{th} SS in BS MAC buffer. Generally, $D_i(t)$ and $W_i(t)$ are normalized in practical system, and because only VoIP traffic is considered here, for each service flow, (5) could be rewritten as follows:

$$\text{Priority}(i) = \frac{D(i)}{\overline{D_i(t)}} \frac{W_i(t)}{T_i} \tag{6}$$

where, $\overline{D_i(t)}$ is the average data rate of ith SS, T_i is the maximum delay SS could endure which is thought to be the maximum delay of VoIP MAC. Because the maximum data rate of SS is closely correlative to its channel condition, we use $\frac{SINR(i)}{\overline{SINR_i(t)}}$ to replace $\frac{D(i)}{\overline{D_i(t)}}$ and finally get:

$$\text{Pr}iority(i) = \frac{SINR_i(t)}{\overline{SINR_i(t)}} \frac{W_i(t)}{T_i} \tag{7}$$

This algorithm tries to get a balance between the delay performance of data and the bandwidth spectral efficiency. It can maximize the bandwidth spectral efficiency when it satisfies the delay requirements of user's VoIP data. Therefore, it is a proper choice for real time VoIP traffic.

4 Simulation Configurations

4.1 Simulation Parameters

In this paper, three layered 19 cells 57sectors cellular model is used to simulate practical WiMAX wireless network. Each SS is uniformly located in the whole simulation area. Each SS in the center 3 sectors is static only, and such assumption doesn't affect the final results [11]. Because 1:1 frequency reusing scheme is used, so each SS is interfered by all other cells. Other basic simulation parameters are listed in Table 2.

4.2 Simulation Statistics

Statistic variables used in our simulation include PER (Packet Error Rate), average delay, average delay jitter, and bandwidth (Bw) usage rate.

When counting PER, error packets include: (1) the packet dropped in the BS MAC buffer because its maximum delay expires; and (2) the packet not being received rightly after maximum HARQ retransmission.

VoIP delay is the time between VoIP packets entering the convergence sub-layer, and it is rightly received by SS [8].

Bandwidth usage rate is the ratio of bandwidth used in fact with that allocated.

Table 2. Simulation parameters

Item	Parameter	Item	Parameter
Cell radius	866m	smooth factor (α)	0.25
BS transmission power	43dBm	HARQ mode	Chase combing
Path loss model	Costa231	ACK feedback delay	4frames
System bandwidth	10MHz	Maximum HARQ retransmission	3
Frequency reuse factor	1:1	Channel model	ITU PedA ITU Veh B & Veh A
Sub-carrier permutation mode	PUSC	Modulation scheme	QPSK, 16QAM, 64QAM
Symbols in DL frame	24	Channel code	Convolutional turbo code (CTC)
CQICH feedback period	3frames	Code rate	1/2, 2/3, 3/4, 5/6

5 Results and Analysis

5.1 Performance of Frame Bundling for VoIP in WiMAX

Fig. 5 to Fig. 8 respectively shows the performance of PER, average delay, average jitter, and average bandwidth usage ratio with different bundling number K. At a certain K value, three cases are evaluated:

(1) Bw is enough (120 users each sector);
(2) Bw is proper (135 users each sector);
(3) Bw is deficient (150 users each sector).

Fig. 5 shows the PER performance with different bundling number K and bandwidth (or user number). When Bw is enough, i.e., 120 users in each sector, the PER of no bundling is lower than that of bundling policy being used. But the case changes as the user number increases and Bw becomes deficient. For 135 users in each sector case (i.e., Bw is proper), when the maximum delay is set as 110ms, the PER of 2 VoIP packets bundling is close to that of no bundling. As for 150 users in each sector case (i.e., Bw is deficient), when the maximum delay is set as more than 90ms, the PER performances of bundling 2 or 3 VoIP packets become better than that of no bundling being used. The reason is that when Bw is not enough and bundling is not used, more Bw is occupied by overhead, and as a result, some packets are dropped for expiring the maximum delay, and PER increases rapidly as compared with that of bundling used.

In contrast, if bundling is used, overhead is reduced and more Bw is used for data transmission which improve the PER performance when Bw is not enough. In this case, even if the user number increases, the Bw usage rate is smaller than 1. The main reasons of PER increasing in this case are: (1) as PDU size is bigger for bundling being used, the probability of errors increase; and (2) as the bundling adds a fixed delay to VoIP packet, the HARQ retransmission time of a super VoIP packet is reduced with the strict delay constrain, which increases the probability of those packets being wrongly received.

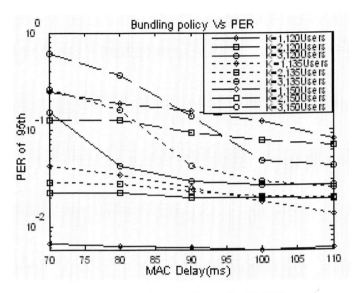

Fig. 5. SS number, bundling policy Vs PER

Fig. 6 shows the average delay performance with different bundling number K and bandwidth (or user number). When bundling K VoIP packets is used, Fig. 6 shows that the delay of super VoIP packet is always longer than that of no bundling being used. This is intuition because the first packet in each super VoIP packet has been delayed ($20(K-1)$ ms) when it enters the MAC layer of BS. But the delay gap between no bundling and with bundling gradually decreases as the user number in

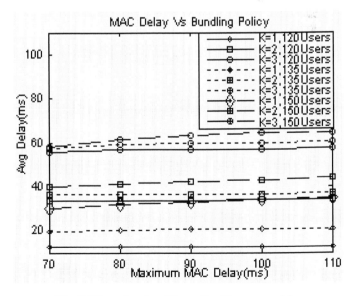

Fig. 6. SS number, bundling policy Vs average delay

each sector increases, and it indicates that super VoIP packets stay with a relatively short time in MAC layer.

Fig. 7 shows the average jitter performance with different bundling number K and bandwidth (or user number). When the user in each sector is 120 (i.e., Bw is enough), the jitter of no bundling is obviously smaller than that of bundling being used. However, as the user number increases to 135 (i.e., Bw is proper), the jitter of bundling 2 packets becomes smaller than that of no bundling used, and when the user number further increases to 150 (i.e., Bw is deficient), the jitters of bundling 2 and 3 packets are both smaller than that of no bundling used.

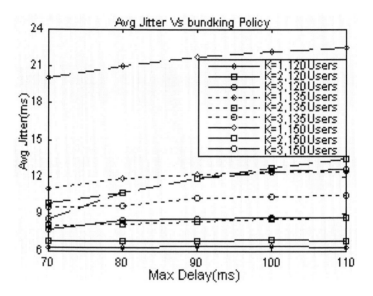

Fig. 7. SS number, bundling policy Vs average jitter

Fig. 8 shows the average Bw usage rate performance with different bundling number K and bandwidth (or user number). The average Bw usage rate of no bundling, 2 packets bundling and 3 packets bundling are $OHR_1 = 45\%$, $OHR_2 = 29\%$, and $OHR_3 = 21\%$ respectively. According to the simulation results (see Fig. 8), when the number of users in each sector is 120 (i.e., Bw is enough), Bw usage rate are $R_1 = 89\%$, $R_2 = 68\%$ and $R_3 = 60\%$ for no bundling, 2 packets bundling and 3 packets bundling respectively. When the number of users in each sector increases to be 135 (i.e., Bw is proper), Bw usage rate are improved to be $R_1 = 99\%, R_2 = 71\%$ and $R_3 = 79\%$ for no bundling, 2 packets bundling and 3 packets bundling respectively. And when the number of users in each sector is 150 (i.e., Bw is deficient), Bw usage rate are further improved to be $R_1 = 1, R_2 = 92\%$ and $R_3 = 83\%$ accordingly for no bundling, 2 packets bundling and 3 packets bundling respectively.

From the above results, bundling 2 packets is reasonable for predicting the Bw usage rate, and the simulation results also justify that VoIP packet bundling could save much Bw.

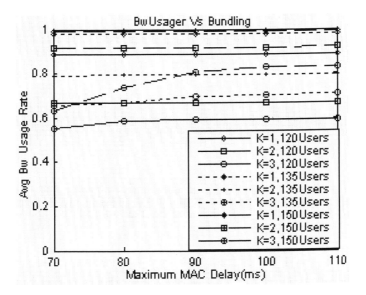

Fig. 8. SS number, bundling policy Vs average Bw usage rate

From the above simulation results and analysis, we can conclude that the bundling of VoIP packets not only lowers the PER and average jitter, but also saves much Bw and enhances the Bw spectral efficiency. The only shortage of frame (packet) bundling is that it may cause relatively longer delay. Combing all the above considerations and analysis, bundling 2 VoIP packets is a proper choice for VoIP traffic in WiMAX.

5.2   Performance of Aggressive AMC for VoIP in WiMAX

Fig. 9 to Fig. 12 respectively shows the performance of PER of 95% users, average delay, average jitter, and average spectral efficiency with different aggressive factor β and maximum delay constraint.

Fig. 9 indicates when the aggressive factor β increases from 0dB to 3dB, the PER decreases at first and begins to increase after coming to a minimum. Average delay (see Fig. 10), and average jitter (see Fig. 11) show similar variety trends while the average spectral efficiency shows a reverse trend (see Fig. 12).

As the maximum delay becomes larger, the reduction of PER of aggressive AMC becomes smaller. The reason is that if maximum delay constraint is relatively small, the majority of the error packets are those that are dropped because of maximum delay expiration. The SINR threshold of neighbour MCS is usually about 2-3dB, so if aggressive AMC is used and proper β (0.5dB) is selected, most users will keep their

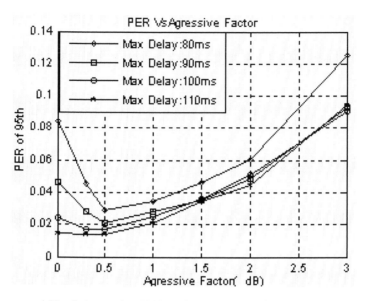

Fig. 9. Aggressive AMC performance: PER of 95% users

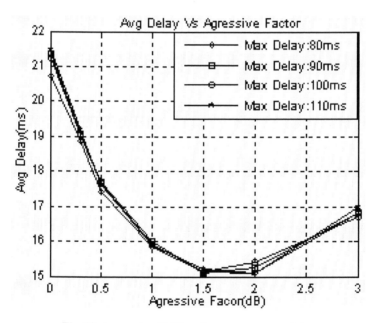

Fig. 10. Aggressive AMC performance: average delay

MCS unchanged while only those whose SINR are already close to the next higher SINR threshold will chosen a higher MCS, and they will use little bandwidth than when aggressive AMC is not used. As a result, the VoIP packets of all users could be scheduled in a relatively shorter time and little of the packets will be dropped, and

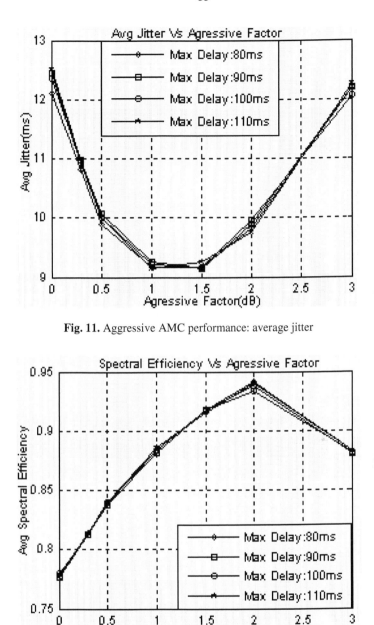

Fig. 11. Aggressive AMC performance: average jitter

Fig. 12. Aggressive AMC performance: average spectral efficiency

thus the system spectral efficiency is enhanced. At the same time, their SINR are close to next higher threshold, so the transmit error probability is low when a higher MCS is selected and its number is smaller than that of dropped because of maximum delay expiration when aggressive is not used. However, when a larger maximum delay constraint is selected, aggressive AMC brings a few benefits. So, the main factors which restrict the system performance are users' channel conditions and their corresponding MCS.

If a too large β (3dB for example) is selected, the system performance becomes bad. The PER increases for majority of users selects a higher MCS which couldn't be supported at its channel condition and much HARQ retransmission is need. As a result, packet delay and jitter increase, bandwidth resource is wasted, and spectral efficiency decreases.

Furthermore, when β increases to the point where PER comes to the minimum, the average delay and jitter still decrease, which indicates that we may get the best delay and jitter performance at the cost of a relatively higher PER.

According the above analysis, a proper selected aggressive factor is important to VoIP traffic in WiMAX system.

6 Conclusions

This paper mainly studies and analyses how the two techniques of frame (packet) bundling and aggressive AMC effect the performance of VoIP in the downlink of WiMAX system. The simulation results indicates that if these techniques are used properly, the performance of VoIP could be enhanced to a certain degree. The results show that when the system is in short of bandwidth, these two techniques indeed reduce the PER and delay jitter of the VoIP users, and also enhance the spectrum efficiency.

Acknowledgments. This paper is supported by the National High Technology Research and Development Program of China (863 Program) No.2007AA01Z2A7.

References

1. 3GPP (3rd Generation Partnership Project) TS 25 Series: Technical Specification Group Radio Access Network (2006)
2. 3GPP Technical Report (TR) 25.848: Physical Layer Aspects of UTRA High Speed Downlink Packet Access (Release (2000)
3. IEEE Standard for Local and metropolitan area networks Part 16: Air Interface for Fixed and mobile Broadband Wireless Access Systems Amendment 2: Physical and Medium Access Control Layers for Combined Fixed and Mobile Operation in Licensed Bands. IEEE Press, Los Alamitos (December 2005), http://ieee802.org/16
4. TIA/EIA/IS-127: Enhanced Variable Rate Codec, Speech Service Option 3 for Wideband Spread Spectrum Dgital Systems (1996)
5. Zheng, H., Rittenhouse, G.: Providing VoIP Service in UMTS-HSDPA with Frame Aggregation. In: IEEE ICASSP, March 2005, vol. 2, pp. 1157–1160 (2005)
6. Zheng, H., Rittenhouse, G., Recchione, M.: The Performance of Voice over IP over 3G Downlink Shared Packet Channels under Different Delay Budgets. In: IEEE VTC2003-Fall, October 2003, vol. 4, pp. 2501–2505 (2003)

7. Motorola: EESM Link Error Prediction for EUTRA System Evaluation. 3GPP TSG RAN WG1 #42, R1-050718 (2005)
8. Liu, H., et al.: EESM Based Link Error Prediction for Adaptive MIMO OFDM System. In: IEEE VTC2007-Spring, pp. 559–563 (April 2007)
9. Talukdar, A., et al.: Agressive Modulation/Coding Schedule for Maximum System Througput in a Multi-Carrier System. In: IEEE Int. Conf. Commun., vol. 3, pp. 1823–1828 (2002)
10. Kumaran, M., et al.: Providing Quality of Service Over a Shared Wireless Link. IEEE Comm. Mag. 39, 150–154 (2001)
11. Srinivasan, R., Zhuang, J., Jalloul, L.: Draft IEEE 802.16m Evaluation Methodology. IEEE 802.16 Broadband Wireless Access Working Group (August 2007)

Performance of Adaptive Sub-carrier and Bit Allocation Algorithms for Multi-user OFDM Wireless Systems

Xiangning Fan[1] and Chu Jintao[2]

[1] Institute of RF-&-OE-ICs, School of Information Science and Engineering,
Southeast University, Nanjing, 210096, China
[2] National Mobile Communications Research Laboratory,
Southeast University, Nanjing, 210096, China
xnfan@seu.edu.cn

Abstract. Multi-user orthogonal frequency division multiplexing (OFDM) with adaptive sub-carrier and bit allocation are considered in this paper. Assuming having the knowledge of the instantaneous users' channel gains, three typical dynamic sub-carrier and bit allocation algorithms are analyzed and compared. The goal of each algorithm is to minimize the total transmit power with the user's data rate constraint. Then, based on the comparison, an improvement method is proposed for Zhang algorithm. Finally, performance comparisons between adaptive schemes and static ones are given. The results prove that the performances of adaptive algorithms are much better than that of the traditional fixed sub-carrier allocation method.

Keywords: OFDM, OFDMA, bit loading, sub-carrier allocation, multi-user.

1 Introduction

Orthogonal Frequency Division Multiplexing (OFDM) is a parallel high-speed data transmission scheme, in which the transmission bandwidth is divided into a number of parallel orthogonal narrowband sub-channels (known as sub-carriers). Its purpose is to convert a frequency-selective fading channel into several flat-fading sub-channels. Data symbols are transmitted in parallel on each sub-carrier with low symbol rates. As a result, inter-symbol interference (ISI) caused by the multi-path in frequency selective fading channel is reduced. So, OFDM has been adopted for many high data rate systems such as digital audio broadcasting (DAB), digital video broadcasting-terrestrial (DVB-T), broadband radio access networks (BRAN), and asymmetric digital sub-carrier lines (ADSL). Recently, OFDM has also been considered for future use in fourth generation mobile communication systems. For OFDM systems, when different sub-carriers experience different channel gains, adaptive bit loading is needed to improve the spectrum efficiency [1-4].

C. Wang (Ed.): AccessNets, LNICST 6, pp. 312–322, 2009.
© ICST Institute for Computer Sciences, Social-Informatics and Telecommunications Engineering 2009

Multi-user OFDM system is a system that extends OFDM to multiple access environments, which allowing more than one user to transmit data over an OFDM symbol. Therefore, a problem of allocating sub-carriers for different users arises. One solution for this problem is to use fixed resource allocation schemes, such as time division multiple access (TDMA) and frequency multiple access (FDMA). But these static resource allocation schemes, simply dividing sub-channels in time or frequency, are not optimal. Another approach is OFDMA in which adaptive sub-carrier allocation combining with bit loading are performed according to the multi-users' channel information.

This paper will focus on the analysis and comparison of several typical sub-carrier and bit allocation algorithms for multi-user OFDM systems. The organization of this paper is as follows: In Section 2, system model and formulation of optimal problem are given. In Section 3, three typical adaptive sub-carrier and bit allocation algorithms are discussed and compared. In Section 4, the simulation comparisons of performance among dynamic allocation algorithms and traditional static scheme are presented. Section 5 concludes the paper.

2   System Model

The system model of adaptive multi-user OFDM is shown in Fig. 1. Assume that the system has N sub-carriers and K users. The kth user has data rate R_k bits/OFDM symbol. The transmitter gets all the K users' channel information through channel estimation. Assume that the information of channel characteristics is available at the transmitter. Using this channel information, the sub-carrier allocation and bit loading algorithms are applied to assign the sub-carriers and determine the number of data bits on each sub-carrier. The information of sub-carrier and bit allocation needed by demodulation at the receiver is assumed to be transmitted through a dedicated control channel.

Let $c_{k,n}$ denote the number of bits allocated to the nth sub-carrier for the kth user. And $c_{k,n}$ take value from $D = \{0,1,2,3,\cdots,M\}$. Where, M denotes the maximum number of bits transmitted on one sub-carrier during an OFDM symbol interval, and 0 means the sub-channel is so bad that it can not be used to transmit data bits. Define the magnitude of channel gain of the nth sub-carrier of kth user be $\alpha_{k,n}$, and assume that the single-sided noise power spectral density level N_0 is equal to unity. Let $f_k(c)$ denote the required receive power in sub-carrier for reliable reception of c bits which satisfies a certain BER requirement for user k. The function $f_k(c)$ should meet the requirement: a) $f_k(0) = 0$, which means no power is needed when no bit is transmitted; and b) $f_k(c)$ is a convex, which means that the required additional power to transmit an additional bit increases with the number c. As we know, all MQAM, MPSK modulation schemes satisfy these conditions.

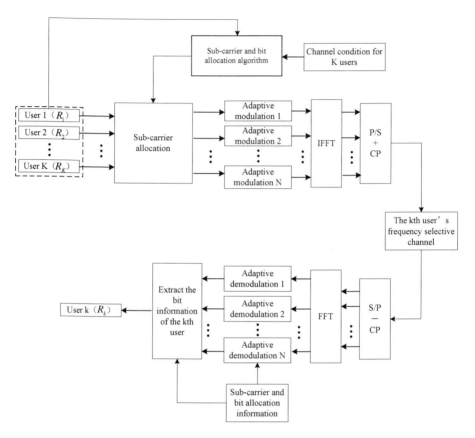

Fig. 1. Adaptive multi-user OFDM system model

Therefore, the transmitted power on sub-carrier n for user k is

$$P_{k,n} = \frac{f_k(c_{k,n})}{\alpha_{k,n}^2} \tag{1}$$

The total transmitted power for the system is

$$P_T = \sum_{n=1}^{N}\sum_{k=1}^{K} P_{k,n} = \sum_{n=1}^{N}\sum_{k=1}^{K} \frac{f_k(c_{k,n})}{\alpha_{k,n}^2} \tag{2}$$

The margin adaptive (MA) optimization problem can then be formulated as:

$$P_T^* = \min \sum_{n=1}^{N}\sum_{k=1}^{K} P_{k,n} = \min \sum_{n=1}^{N}\sum_{k=1}^{K} \frac{f_k(c_{k,n})}{\alpha_{k,n}^2} \tag{3}$$

and the minimization is subjected to the constraints:

$$1) \quad \text{For all } k \in \{1, \cdots, K\} \quad R_k = \sum_{n=1}^{N} c_{k,n} \tag{4}$$

$$2) \text{ For all } n \in \{1, \cdots, N\} \text{ , if } c_{k',n} \neq 0, \text{ then } c_{k,n} = 0, \ \forall k' \neq k \tag{5}$$

3 Algorithm Comparisons

3.1 Bit Allocation Algorithms for Single User

Before we solve the multi-user allocation problem, we first introduce bit loading algorithm for single user system, which will be applied in multi-user sub-carrier and bit allocation algorithm.

In single user environment, the margin adaptive optimization problem can be written as

$$P_T^* = \min \sum_{n=1}^{N} \frac{f(c_n)}{\alpha_n^{2}} \tag{6}$$

and the minimization is subjected to the constraint:

$$R_T = \sum_{n=1}^{N} c_n \tag{7}$$

A classical solution of this problem is greedy approach, which can be described as follows:

Step 1: Initialization. For all n, let $c_n = 0$, assume the modulation step length is Δc, then, compute the additional transmitted power $\Delta P_n = [f(\Delta c) - f(0)]/\alpha_n^{2}$

Step 2: Bit Allocation Iterations. Find the **minimum** ΔP_n, $\hat{n} = \arg \min_n \Delta P_n$, and add Δc bits on sub-carrier $\hat{n}$, $c_{\hat{n}} = c_{\hat{n}} + \Delta c$, then update the required additional transmitted power on sub-carrier $\hat{n}$, $\Delta P_{\hat{n}} = [f(c_{\hat{n}} + \Delta c) - f(c_{\hat{n}})]/\alpha_{\hat{n}}^{2}$

Step 3: Repeat. Repeat step 2) $R_T/\Delta c$ **times**, and $\{c_n\}_{n=1}^{N}$ is the final bit allocation solution.

3.2 Adaptive Sub-carrier and Bit Allocation Algorithms for Multi-users

In multi-user environment, as users can not share the same sub-carrier, allocating bits to a sub-carrier will prevent other users from using that sub-carrier. This makes the bit loading algorithm for single user could not be used directly for multi-users.

A number of papers have researched the sub-carrier and bit allocation algorithms for multi-user OFDM system. In [5], sub-carrier and bit allocation are done dynamically through the use of nonlinear optimization with integer variables. But an extremely computationally complex iteration is required to find the two Lagrangian multipliers which are used in the nonlinear optimization. So it may not be applied to practical system with high data rate transmission, and so we will not discuss this kind of algorithm further later in this paper.

In [6,7], C. Y. Wong et al present a method for real-time application to realize the sub-carrier and bit allocation, which separates the sub-carrier allocation from bit loading. After sub-carrier allocation is finished, bit loading is executed subsequently. As a result, the complexity declines. This scheme needs to convert all the user's data rate to user's sub-carrier demand, however, sometimes there may not all be matched. We denote this algorithm as **CYW algorithm** for brief in this paper.

In [8], a joint power and sub-carrier allocation scheme is proposed by E. Bakhtiari et al. This scheme can ensure each user's least sub-carrier demand. It executes in two steps: 1) In the first step, a simple solution is used to implement the initial sub-carrier allocation, which makes each user satisfy its lowest sub-carrier requirement. 2) An iterative improvement is then used to refine the solution. The iteration will stop when the reduction in total power is smaller than a threshold. We denote this algorithm as **EB algorithm** for brief in this paper.

And in [9], Guodong Zhang gives a new sub-carrier and bit allocation scheme. This scheme firstly assumes that all the sub-carriers can be used by all users, and bit loading algorithm is done for all the users. Then conflicting sub-carriers (shared by more than one user) are arbitrated to the user, which yields the lowest total reassignment power increase. Next, bits of other users are reassigned according to the reallocating solution and the conflicting sub-carrier list is updated. Then, repeat the arbitrating process of the conflicting sub-carriers until there are no conflicting sub-carriers. We call this algorithm as **Zhang algorithm**.

The flowchart of Zhang algorithm is shown in Fig. 2.

When dealing with the conflicting sub-carriers, **Zhang algorithm** arbitrates the conflicting sub-carriers to the user who brings the least increase of total transmit power. Viewed from another angle, it is equivalent to arbitrate the conflicting sub-carriers to the user who mostly needs to increase the transmit power if the conflicting sub-carriers are not given to the user. As a result, the computing complexity can be reduced to a certain amount.

However, there is a defect when actually using **Zhang algorithm**. If some user's magnitude of sub-channel gain is so small as compared to those of other users, most sub-carriers may be assigned to this user to minimize the total transmit power. Consequently, this user may occupy so many sub-carriers that other users have few sub-carriers, even fewer than the least sub-carriers requirement. **Zhang algorithm** will fail to carry on if this problem happens. So we improve this algorithm by adjusting the maximum sub-carriers that one user can occupy.

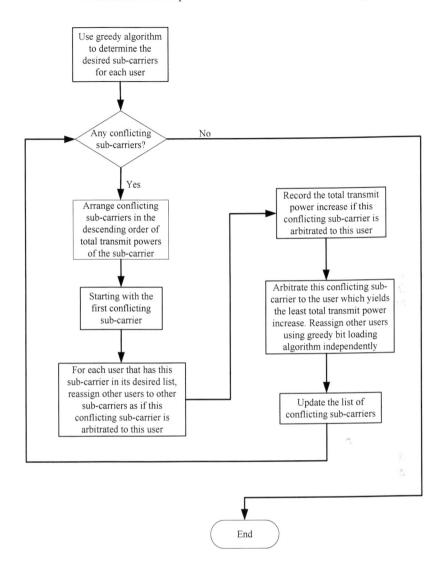

Fig. 2. The flowchart of **Zhang algorithm**

After adjusting, the maximum sub-carrier requirement of kth user is

$$Th_k = \frac{T_k + N_{av}}{2}, \quad k \in \{1, 2, \cdots, K\} \tag{8}$$

where T_k is the maximum sub-carrier requirement of kth user before adjusting, and $N_{av} = N/K$ is the average sub-carrier requirement of each user. So, T_k can be written as

$$T_k = N - \sum_{i=1, i \neq k}^{K} L_i, \quad k \in \{1, 2, \cdots, K\} \tag{9}$$

where L_k is the least sub-carrier requirement of user k, which can be defined as

$$L_k = ceil\left(\frac{R_k}{M}\right) \tag{10}$$

where, the function $ceil(\bullet)$ is rounded towards the nearest positive infinity. R_k and M have been defined in Section 2, being the data rate of user k and maximum available modulating level respectively. Some performance loss will happen after such adjustment to **Zhang algorithm**.

4 Simulation Results

Firstly, some assumptions are given here:

1) During an OFDM symbol, the channel fading is constant.
2) The channel estimation and synchronization are perfect.
3) The transmitter and receiver both know the channel information, and sub-carrier and bit allocation information.

And the simulation parameters are shown in Table 1.

For comparison purpose, some static sub-carrier allocation algorithms are briefly described here.

OFDM-FDMA with local sub-carrier allocation. Each user is allocated to a pre-determined sub-carrier group, which is composed of consecutive sub-carriers. Bit loading algorithm can be used to allocate bit of each user to sub-carriers. We call this algorithm as **Local OFDM-FDMA algorithm** in this paper.

Table 1. Simulation Parameters

Item	Parameters
Channel model	ITU VA
Number of users	4
Carrier frequency	2 GHz
Mobile speed of users	25 km/h
Doppler-shift	46.3 Hz
System bandwidth	5 MHz
Data rate of users	512 bit/OFDM symbol
Length of OFDM symbol	102.4 μs
Length of CP	25.6 μs
Sub-carrier requirements in **CYW algorithm**	128
Given BER	10^{-4}
Available modulation mode	No transmit, QPSK, 16QAM, 64QAM
Modulation mode in static allocation algorithms	16QAM

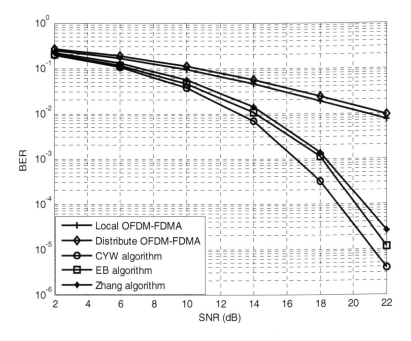

Fig. 3. Performance comparison for best user

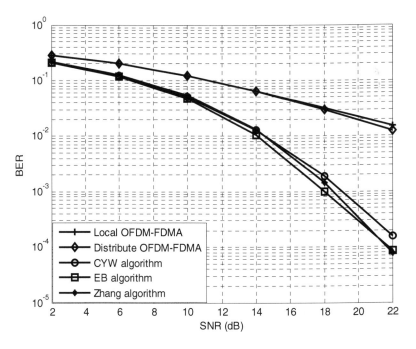

Fig. 4. Performance comparison for worst user

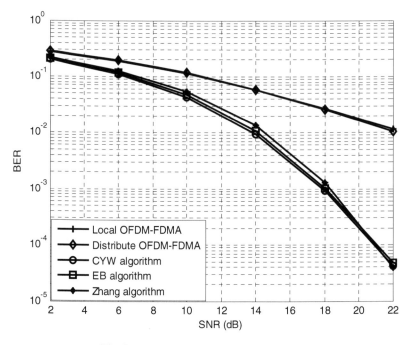

Fig. 5. Performance comparison for average user

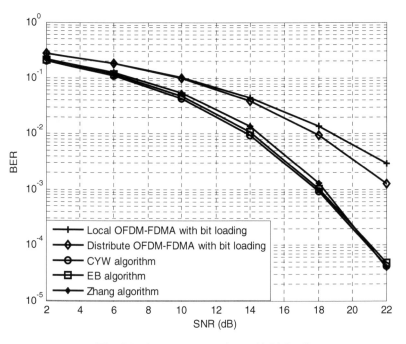

Fig. 6. Performance comparison with bit loading

OFDM-FDMA with distribute sub-carrier allocation. Each user is allocated to a pre-determined sub-carrier group, which is composed of comb sub-carriers. Bit loading algorithm can be used to allocate bit of each user to sub-carriers. We call this algorithm as **Distribute OFDM-FDMA algorithm** in this paper.

Simulation results are shown in Fig. 3, Fig. 4, and Fig. 5, which give the performance comparison of different algorithms for best user, worst user and average user cases respectively.

From these three simulation figures, we can conclude that the performance of OFDMA system with adaptive sub-carrier and bit allocation algorithms is much better than that of static OFDM-FDMA system. And for best user's performance, **CYW algorithm** is better than the other two adaptive algorithms. But **EB algorithm** and **Zhang algorithm**s' performances among their users are more stable than **CYW algorithm**. These three algorithms have similar performance for average user.

For further comparison, bit loading is applied to the static OFDM-FDMA systems. Fig. 6 presents the comparison results. Although after adding bit loading algorithm, static OFDM-FDMA systems get a large performance improvement, adaptive allocation algorithms still display an absolute superiority.

5   Conclusions

This paper discusses the principle of adaptive sub-carrier and bit allocation algorithms for multi-user OFDM systems. Three typical adaptive algorithms are analyzed and compared. The results show that these three adaptive algorithms have similar performance on average, and OFDMA systems with adaptive sub-carrier and bit allocation algorithms can get better BER performance than those of the static systems. Furthermore, among these three adaptive algorithms, **CYW algorithm** can get better performance in best users case, but **EB algorithm** and **Zhang algorithm** are superior in performance stability. Certainly, we have to pay more computing complexity and more time delay when we use these adaptive algorithms as compared with using a static system.

Acknowledgments. This paper is supported by the National High Technology Research and Development Program of China (863 Program) No.2007AA01Z2A7.

References

1. Hughes-Hartogs, D.: Ensemble Modem Structure for Imperfect Transmission Media. U. S. Patents No. 4-679-22 (July 1987); 4-731-816 (March 1988); and 4-833-796 (May 1989)
2. Chow, P.S., Cioffi, J.M., Bingham, A.C.: A Practical Discrete Multitone Transceiver Loading Algorithm for Data Transmission over Spectrally Shaped Channels. IEEE Trans. on Comm. 43(4), 773–775 (1995)
3. Fischer, R.F.H., Huber, J.B.: A New Loading Algorithm for Discrete Multitone Transmission. IEEE Proc. Globecom 42(11), 724–728 (1996)
4. SHRCWC R1-051133.: DFT-S-GMC_GMC based SC-FDMA for 3GPP LTE uplink. San Diego, USA. 3GPP (2005)

5. Grüheild, R., Bolinth, E., Rohling, H.: A Blockwise Loading Algorithm for the Adaptive Modulation Technique in OFDM Systems. In: IEEE Vehicular Technology Conference, pp. 948–951 (October 2001)
6. Wong, C.Y., Cheng, R.S., Letaief, K.B., Murch, R.D.: Multiuser OFDM with Adaptive Subcarrier, Bit and Power Allocation. IEEE Journal on Selected Areas of Comm. 17(10), 1747–1758 (1999)
7. Wong, C.Y., Tsui, C.Y., Cheng, R.S., Letaief, K.B.: A Real-time Sub-carrier Allocation Scheme for Multiple Access Downlink OFDM Transmission. In: IEEE VTC 1999, pp. 1124–1128 (September 1999)
8. Ehsan, B., Babak, H.K.: A New Joint Power and Subcarrier Allocation Scheme for Multiuser OFDM Systems. In: IEEE PIMRC 2003, pp. 1959–1963 (2003)
9. Zhang, G.: Subcarrier and Bit Allocation for Real-time Services in Multiuser OFDM Systems. In: IEEE ICC, pp. 2985–2989 (June 2004)

Proportional Increase Multiplicative Decrease (PIMD) Wireless Scheduler: An Efficient Scheduler for IEEE 802.11e HCF

Arshad Hussain and Shaban Qaiser

Department of Telecommunication and Computer Engineering,
National University of Computer & Emerging Sciences
Lahore, Pakistan
{arshad.hussain,shaban.qaiser}@nu.edu.pk

Abstract. In this paper, we propose a new wireless scheduling algorithm for the IEEE 802.11e HCF. The algorithm grants the mobile stations variable time for the upstream data flow in proportion to the queue size of the transmission buffer. At the same time, it retrieves half of the extra time allocated in previous cycle from those flows whose requirement has stopped. Hence, the system achieves stability by preventing the ping-pong phenomena. The algorithm is computationally simple, and as compared to the other algorithms, it gives bounded delays and jitter to the real-time applications under heavy load conditions.

1 Introduction

Wireless local area networks (WLANs) have provided an edge over wired networks in ease of installation, increased bandwidth and decreased prices. They hold the promise of providing unprecedented mobility, flexibility and scalability. The need for mobile computing has launched a successful market for WLAN promising to replace most of the wired LAN infrastructures in the near future, allowing users to roam inside a building or a university without interrupting their communication sessions and avoiding the use of cables.

The advancement in digital technology has also led to an increased demand in multimedia applications such as video conferencing, video on demand, voice chat, and other time-bounded data transfer activities over the networks. However, wireless networks also exhibit higher bit-error rates and fluctuating dynamic bandwidth. Hence, these applications necessitate that both wired and wireless networks provide such services. It makes the quality of service (QoS) provisions a critical issue. QoS is the capability of a network to provide resource assurance and service differentiation during the connection. Currently, IEEE 802.11 WLAN standard is being deployed widely and rapidly for its simplicity and robustness against failures. However, the widespread use of multimedia networking applications has created the need for WLANs to support real time services with stringent QoS requirements. The development of IEEE 802.11e can be considered as an effort in this direction. It is a new standard which defines QoS at MAC level of WLAN.

C. Wang (Ed.): AccessNets, LNICST 6, pp. 323–332, 2009.

Currently, various models are being developed in order to provide QoS to real time applications in WLANs. The core architecture of QoS models comprises efficient real-time scheduler and call admission control (CAC) mechanism. They are deployed in the centralized station called QoS access point (QAP) when WLAN is operating in infrastructure mode. The scheduler provides transmission opportunities to mobile stations so that their time-critical QoS requirements can be fulfilled. The QoS received by different applications running on mobile nodes depends on the efficient working of the scheduler, while CAC ensures that the scheduler is not overloaded, statically or statistically. Our research effort is aimed at developing a dynamic scheduling mechanism for IEEE 802.11e MAC. The motivation for this work comes from the fact that IEEE 802.11e specifies a sample scheduler in its standard, yet it leaves the door open for the development of more efficient scheduling mechanisms. The paper has been divided in the following sections. In section 2, we give a brief introduction of QoS, IEEE 802.11e, and the work done so far in developing wireless schedulers for QoS-WLAN. In section 3, we propose PIMD wireless scheduler and discuss its characteristics followed by its simulation comparison with most recognized FHCF scheduler [14] in section 4. In the last section, we conclude our work and give direction for further enhancement.

2 Background and Literature Survey of Wireless Scheduler

2.1 QoS and Wireless Scheduling

Broadband networks provide QoS differentiation and guaranteed services for heterogeneous classes of traffic with different QoS requirements, e.g., throughput, bit error rates, delay, jitter, packet loss rate etc. QoS support is dictated by the service models such as IntServ [1] for per-flow-based guaranteed QoS performance by pre-allocation of resources or DiffServ [2] for class-based QoS support. By using the QoS service primitives, the application provides the QoS-network with traffic specifications (TSPEC) that makes the network adapt to the traffic in an optimized manner. Since the most precious resource in wireless networks is the bandwidth, an efficient and optimized utilization of the bandwidth results in greater channel utilization and higher throughput. As the mobile host moves, channel parameters like the available bandwidth and bit error rate change dynamically due to the intrinsic nature of the wireless medium. An efficient wireless scheduling algorithm aims at minimizing the unproductive transmissions on erroneous links, and at the same time, maximize the effective service delivered and the utilization of the wireless channels. The challenges faced in designing schedulers for wireless networks have been described in [3], [4]. A good centralized scheduling algorithm should be designed so that minimal numbers of scheduling-related control messages are required to be sent from the mobile hosts in order to conserve limited battery power. The scheduling algorithm should be computationally efficient so that it can be executed at high speed to schedule real-time multimedia traffic with stringent timing requirements. Development of scheduling mechanisms for real-time applications is an active area of research. Its basic architecture has been modeled mathematically and characteristics of good schedulers have been defined in [6]. Also, many wireless schedulers have been compared with each other in terms of channel utilization, delay bound, fairness, and complexity in survey reports [3], [4], [6]

2.2 Wireless Schedulers for IEEE 802.11e WLAN

IEEE 802.11e standard [5] defines a MAC enhancement to provide QoS in WLANs. The basic service set (QBSS) consists of a QAP and mobile stations (QSTAs). QAP is usually a centrally located, fixed station with additional responsibilities of managing the WLAN in infrastructure mode. All QSTAs in the QBSS associate themselves with the QAP in order to communicate with the outside world. IEEE 802.11e introduces hybrid coordination function (HCF), which determines when a QSTA is permitted to transmit and receive MAC service data units (MSDU). HCF works by using two channel access mechanisms; enhanced distributed channel access (EDCA) and HCF controlled channel access (HCCA). The EDCA is a contention based channel access method which is used for prioritized QoS (DiffServ) during contention period (CP). The HCCA is used for parameterized QoS (IntServ) during both contention period (CP) and contention free period (CFP). HCCA is a polling based access mechanism in which the medium access is governed by the QAP when the network is set up in infrastructure mode. The HCF gets control of the channel after every *SI*. It can transmit downstream data by allocating TXOP to QAP or poll the QSTAs by giving TXOPs to their admitted traffic streams (TSs). A polled QSTA can transmit multiple MAC frames in a single TXOP provided it does not violate the TXOP limit. A traffic stream (TS) requiring certain parameterized QoS guarantees is described by a set of traffic specifications (TSPEC) which includes nominal MSDU size (L), maximum MSDU size (M), minimum service interval (SI_{min}), maximum service interval (SI_{max}), mean application data rates (ρ), maximum burst size, and peak data rate. The QSTA requests QAP for initialization of individual TSs (uplink, downlink or bi-directional). The call admission control (CAC) unit at QAP decides whether to include it in the polling list or not. Once TS has been admitted, it is the responsibility of QAP to poll the TS, based on its TSPEC. The QAP uses a centralized deadline scheduler to decide which TS to poll and when to poll it. It computes the duration of TXOP that is to be granted to the TSs and polices and shapes the amount of traffic to provide fairness among TSs. HCCA allows better channel utilization while maintaining low jitter and latency for high priority QoS streams.

The IEEE 802.11e standard has given a sample scheduler [5, Annex K]. It uses mandatory TSPEC and allocates constant TXOP for each traffic stream. The scheduler works for constant bit rate (CBR) applications but it doesn't incorporate variations in actual transmission rate, application data rate and packet size. Therefore, the transmission of variable bit rate (VBR) and traffic with occasional long bursts can lead to significant transmission delays, increased average queue length and packet drops. Grilo's scheduler [7] allocates variable TXOPs and polls STAs in variable time and service intervals. The variable TXOP is made available by using token bucket, and earliest due date (EDD) is used to select the flow from the subset of eligible flows. The Grilo Scheduler is more flexible and attains better performance with respect to delay constraints at the cost of increased complexity. Allocating variable TXOPs makes it more suitable for VBR applications. The Extended Grilo Scheduler incorporates the queue size and TXOP duration requested field, and traffic requirements in Grilo algorithm for the computation of next TXOP.

The fair HCF (FHCF) scheduler [8] uses the queue size of upstream TS sent by a non-QAP QSTA at the end of its TXOP finish time to predict its TXOP for the next *SI*. It also predicts the ideal queue size for the TS at the start of the next *SI* using TSPEC. This difference is used to compute the TXOP for the next *SI*. The computation also takes into account the moving average of the absolute difference of the predictions in the previous *SI*'s in form of adding a correction term in the next TXOP. The FHCF scheme supports variable application data rates and /or packet sizes. The stochastic nature of VBR and bursty traffic is taken care of by averaging the previous errors in queue size estimation. FHCF admits more flows in HCCA as compared to others, and it achieves a higher degree of fairness among various multimedia flows while supporting bandwidth and delay requirements for a wide range of network loads. However, it is biased towards increasing TXOPs for TSs and it is computationally very expensive.

There are many other schedulers which have been proposed for IEEE 802.11e. Grag et al. [9], [10] have proposed a simple scheduler for IEEE 802.11e based on the queue lengths and priority of the traffic streams at the STAs. Perfectly Periodic Scheduling [11] for 802.11e home networks as an efficient way to reduce the access waiting time based on probability usage. Feedback based dynamic scheduler (FBDS) [12] is a queue based algorithm in which the HC assigns TXOPs to each TSs such that each queue is drained during the next controlled access period (CAP). It employs a discrete time linear feedback model and proper disturbance model for predicting queue size at the non-AP QSTAs. It is an efficient scheduler as it achieves the desired delay asymptotically but its complexity is very high and it admits fewer flows. The stability of the feedback system is also a crucial issue.

3 Proportional Increase Multiplicative Decrease (PIMD) Wireless Scheduler for IEEE 802.11e

In this section, we propose a simple scheduler at QAP which dynamically allocates the TXOP based on actual data which is being generated by the application at the mobile nodes. In this scheme, the QAP polls all STAs with admitted TSs in one CAP, and uses the mandatory TSPEC to compute the initial TXOP for individual TSs. If the polled flow has transmitted the queue size of its non-transmitted data in the buffer at the end of polled TXOP, PIMD scheduler increases the TXOP of a flow dynamically in proportion to queue size in the next service interval. Once the data has been drained, the scheduler reduces the extra TXOP exponentially in subsequent *SI*'s in order to keep the system stable.

3.1 Initialization of PIMD

When a stream requests initialization, it also transmits QoS requirement parameter set $(\rho, L, SI_{max}, M, R)$ to the QAP in TSPEC. QAP uses the sample scheduler to allocate initial TXOPs to all flows by computing the schedule service interval (*SI*) for one CAP, and the TXOP (T_i) for all stations within *SI* using the following formulae;

$$SI \le \min_{i} \left\{ SI_{max,i} \right\} \tag{1}$$

$$T_i(1) = \max \left[\frac{\rho_i \times SI}{R_i}, \frac{M}{R_i} \right] + O \tag{2}$$

where O is physical layer overhead.

3.2 The PIMD Algorithm

During any service interval repetition (n=1, 2, 3...), if QAP receives a non-zero queue size $q_i(n)$ from a flow in its last upstream polled frame, the scheduler allocates additional TXOP to the flow in the next SI. We denote the extra TXOP by $\delta_i(n)$. The unallocated portion of the SI is divided among all such flows proportionally at the end of SI (proportional increase). However, if due to the additional allocation, the flow's buffer gets empty, $\delta_i(n)$ is not reduced to zero in the next SI; it is decreased by half (multiplicative decrease).

In order to model the algorithm, we define Ω as the set of all admitted flows. Let $D_{PI}(n)$, $D_{MD}(n)$, and $D_{NC}(n)$ be the three disjoint subset of Ω defined for SI(n) as below;

$$D_{PI}(n) = \{ \forall i : q_i(n) > 0 \}. \tag{3}$$
$$D_{MD}(n) = \{ \forall i : \delta_i(n-1) \ne 0, q_i(n) = 0 \}.$$
$$D_{NC}(n) = \{ \forall i : \delta_i(n-1) = 0, q_i(n) = 0 \}.$$

It is easy to see that

$$\Omega = D_{PI}(n) \cup D_{MD}(n) \cup D_{NC}(n). \tag{4}$$

Hence, $D_{PI}(n)$, $D_{MD}(n)$ and $D_{NC}(n)$ form partitions of Ω. It may be noted that number of flows in these partitions may vary at every repetition of SI(n). The TXOP $T_i(n+1)$ is allocated to every admitted flow in the following steps.

Step I (Multiplicative Decrease)

$$\delta_i(n+1) = \begin{cases} \delta_i(n)/2, & \forall i \in D_{MD}(n) \\ 0, & \forall i \in D_{NC}(n) \end{cases} \tag{5}$$

$$T_i(n+1) = T_i(n) + \delta_i(n+1).$$

Step II (Proportional Increase)

$$SI_{free}(n+1) = SI - \sum_{j \in D_{PI}(n)} T_j(n) - \sum_{j \in \Omega - D_{PI}(n)} T_j(n+1) \tag{6}$$

$$\delta_i(n+1) = SI_{free}(n+1) * q_i(n) / \sum_{j \in D_{PI}(n)} q_j(n), \qquad \forall i \in D_{PI}(n)$$

$$T_i(n+1) = T_i(n) + \delta(n+1).$$

3.3 Discussion

The PIMD scheduler provides long-term fairness and its computational complexity is extremely low. However, in implementing PIMD algorithm, the multiplicative decrease (MD) always precedes proportional increase (PI). This way, the extra bandwidth accumulated due to non-requirement of certain TSs during MD step is fairly allocated among the TSs with non-zero queue sizes.

4 Experimental Result

The PIMD algorithm has been tested by simulating it on the Network Simulator-2 (NS2) platform [13]. NS2 is an open-source public domain simulation tool that runs on Linux, and it is used for simulating local and wide area networks. FHCF 802.11e implementation by Pierre Ansel, Qiang Ni and Thierry Turletti has been used as the base of PIMD algorithm implementation in NS2 [14].

The algorithms have been tested for three types of traffic flows, namely, high priority audio (ON-OFF keying), medium priority VBR (H.261), and relatively low priority CBR (MPEG 4). The audio flows are implemented by an exponentially distributed traffic source generator with 400ms on time and 600ms off time. The traffic files provided by [8] have been used for VBR where the data rate varies between 170 Kbps to 240 Kbps in extreme cases. CBR traffic was generated with inter-arrival time of packets of 2ms. These traffic flows are mapped onto the traffic streams (TS) of a station. The basic traffic characteristics and the MAC parameters used in running TSs over IEEE 802.11e have been summarized in the Table 1.

The PIMD algorithm has been tested for two scenarios. In the first scenario, it was tested only for VBR traffic on 2 Mbps channel with HCCA capturing the 90% of the duration. In the second scenario, we have tested it by scheduling three different types of traffic, with only one type of traffic flow running on one station. The channel bandwidth in 2nd scenario was set to 36Mbps and HCCA duration was 98%, so purely HCCA is tested. In both scenarios, the numbers of stations were increased from 2 to 7 for each type of flow which equivalently amounts to 26—92% increase in load. The HCCA load calculation also included the overhead for each packet to be transmitted. The performance of PIMD has been compared with FHCF in terms of mean delay and jitter as the load was increased.

Table 1. Traffic Flows and MAC Parameters

Traffic Type	Mean data rate (kbps)	Mean MSDU size (bytes)	EDCA			HCCA
			CW_{min}	CW_{max}	Priority	SI_{max} (ms)
Audio	64	160	7	15	6	50
VBR	200	660	15	31	5	100
CBR	3200	800	15	31	4	100
ALL	EDCA Long Retry Limit= 4, EDCA Short Retry Limit=7					

4.1 Test Scenario 1: Only VBR Traffic

In the first scenario, both PIMD and FHCF were tested for variable bit rate (VBR) traffic only, and the results have been plotted in Fig. 1. Under light load, performance of both schedulers was similar. However, under heavy load, PIMD outperformed FHCF by a wide margin. For example, at the load of 6 stations, the delay in FHCF was beyond tolerable range (201 ms) where as in PIMD, it was within acceptable bound (74 ms), i.e., one-third of FHCF (Fig. 1a). The delay measurement for both schedulers at the load of stations load was unacceptable; yet, the delay in the case of

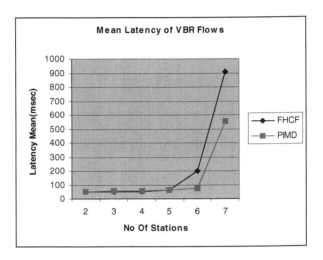

(a) Delay

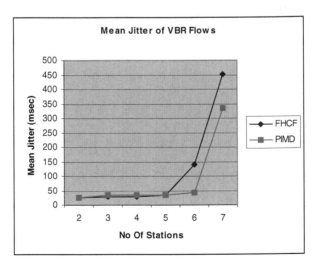

(b) Jitter

Fig. 1. PIMD vs. FHCF for Scenario I (a) Delay, (b) Jitter

PIMD was half as compared to that due to FHCF. A similar trend has been observed in jitter (Fig. 1b).

4.2 Test Scenario 2: Simultaneous Audio, VBR, and CBR Traffic

In this scenario the scheduling algorithms were tested for isolated traffic. Three types of isolated traffic were simulated (audio, variable bit rate and constant bit rate) with each of the traffic flow running on a separate node independently. Few nodes had only audio traffic running over them, while few had VBR traffic and other had only

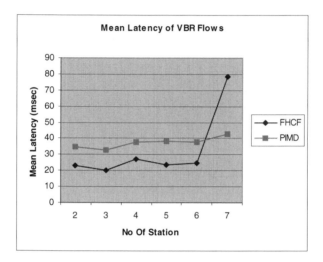

(a) Delay

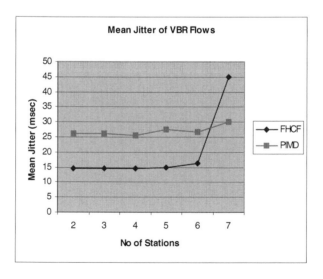

(b) Jitter

Fig. 2. PIMD vs. FHCF for VBR in Scenario 2. (a) Delay, (b) Jitter.

CBR traffic on them. At a given time, the number of all three types of flows is same. The load is increased by adding one flow of each type. The performance results of the all types of traffic have been plotted.

The simulation results of delay for audio and CBR flows show similar performs of both schedulers (Table II). There difference for a given load is insignificant. The simulation results for jitter were identical and within bounded range (13-17 ms), and hence the data have not been tabulated. In case of the VBR traffic, the delay and jitter using FHCF is lower than PIMD when the load is light. However, the delay and jitter in PIMD remains stable as the load increases, where as FHCF suffers from exceptionally long delay and jitter which makes this algorithm inoperable for real-time services. Hence, the performance of PIMD is much superior to FHCF under heavy load (Fig. 2), and, it can be effectively utilized for mixed traffic of constant and variable bit rate traffic streams.

Table 2. PIMD vs. FHCF in Scenario 2: Delay

No. of Stations	Audio (ms)		CBR (ms)	
	FHCF	PIMD	*FHCF*	*PIMD*
2	25.5	24.9	21.8	23.1
3	25.1	25.0	21.7	22.7
4	23.3	24.0	22.3	22.9
5	25.4	25.0	22.2	23.5
6	24.8	24.0	21.9	24.3
7	24.7	23.5	24.9	21.9

5 Conclusion

In this paper, we have proposed a computationally simple wireless scheduler for IEEE 802.11e, namely, PIMD wireless scheduler. The scheduler allocates the extra bandwidth in response to the amount of data left in the mobile stations' buffer at the end of allotted transmission opportunity. It has been demonstrated to be stable under heavy load as compared to the other wireless schedulers and it doesn't lower the performance of CBR traffic while allocating dynamic bandwidth for the VBR and bursty traffic. We have proposed an error-free model. The performance of the scheduler under error-prone environment and along with active EDCA has to be analyzed. Work is in progress in the direction of the adding lead-lag model in the scheduler and efficient CAC.

Acknowledgment. This research has partly been sponsored by the Pakistan Telecommunication Cooperation R&D fund under grant R&DF/A-23/2004-05. The first author wants to thank the efforts of his graduate student Mr. Najeeb ul Hassan for his help in editing this paper.

References

1. Wroclawski, J.: The use of RSVP with IETF integrated services. RFC2210 (September 1997)
2. Blake, S., et al.: An architecture for differentiated services. RFC2475 (August 1998)

3. Cao, Y., Li, V.O.K.: Scheduling Algorithms in Broad-Band Wireless Networks. The Proceedings of the IEEE 89(1) (January 2001)
4. Fattah, H., Leung, C.: An Overview of Scheduling Algorithms in Wireless Multimedia Networks. IEEE Wireless Communications (October 2002)
5. IEEE Std 802.11e, Wireless Medium Access Control (MAC) and Physical Layer (PHY) Specifications, Amendment 8: Medium Access Control (MAC) Enhancements for Quality of Service (QoS) (November 2005)
6. Nandagopal, T., Lu, S., Bharghavan, V.: A Unified Architecture for the Design and Evaluation of Wireless Fair Queuing Algorithms. In: ACM MOBICOM, pp. 132–142 (August 1999)
7. Grilo, A., Macedo, M., Nunes, M.: A Scheduling Algorithm for QoS Support in IEEE 802.11E Networks. IEEE Wireless Communications, 36–43 (June 2003)
8. Ansel, P., Ni, Q., Turletti, T.: An Efficient Scheduling Scheme for IEEE 802.11e. In: Proceedings of WiOpt, Cambridge, UK (March 2004)
9. Garg, P., Doshi, R., Malek, M., Greene, R., Cheng, M.: Achieving Higher Throughput and QoS in 802.11 Wireless LANs. In: IEEE International Performance Computing and Communications Conference (IPCCC 2003), Phoenix, Arizona (April 2003),
    http://nondot.org/~radoshi/cs444n/
10. Garg, P., Doshi, R., Greene, R., Baker, M., Malek, M., Chang, M.: Using IEEE 802.11e MAC for QoS over Wireless. In: IEEE International Performance Computing and Communications Conference (IPCCC 2003)
11. Dhanakoti, N., Gopalan, S., Vidya, S.: Perfectly Periodic Scheduling for Fault Avoidance in IEEE 802.11e in the Context of Home Networks. ISSRE (2003)
12. Annese, A., Boggia, G., Camarda, P., Grieco, L.A., Mascolo, S.: Providing Delay Guarantees in IEEE 802.11e Networks. In: the 59th IEEE Semi-annual Vehicular Technology Conference, VTC (Spring 2004)
13. Network Simulator Document, http://www.isi.edu/nsnam/ns/
14. Ansel, P., Ni, Q., Turletti, T.: FHCF: A Fair Scheduling Scheme for 802.11e WLAN, INRIA Research Report No 4883 (July 2003),
    http://www-sop.inria.fr/planete/qni/fhcf

Appropriate Templates for Broadband Access in Non-developed and Developing Countries

Morteza Haddadzadeh

Iran Telecommunication Research Center (ITRC)
End of North Kargar Ave.
Tehran, Iran
m-haddad@itrc.ac.ir

Abstract. Choosing the best access technology for delivering broadband services, is an important and complex step in moving toward NGN, specially in non-developed and developing countries. This paper, proposes a simple classification of users due to their communicational needs, and recommends the most appropriate access method for each class of users, considering network infrastructure in non-developed and developing countries, and capabilities and shortcomings of current technologies.

Keywords: Broadband access, DSL, NGN.

1 Introduction

Moving toward NGN is a "must", but "how to do it" is a "big question". However, development of broadband access is accepted as the first step in this way.

In non-developed and developing countries, with various economic problems and moderate communication needs, selecting an optimum solution for broadband access with lowest cost, is vitally important for operators.

By analyzing communicational infrastructure of these countries and knowing current access technologies and weighing their pros and cons, general templates can be proposed for different cases.

Here only two essential parameters have been used for proposing general templates for broadband access; "distance from CO" and "required bandwidth". In the final design steps, the influence of other parameters like "line quality", "crosstalk", "delay" and "jitter" on quality of services must be evaluated and initial proposed templates be modified if necessary.

2 User Classification

Classification is a common way for reducing the items and simplifying the problems.

In the communications world, users have different needs and access methods have different capabilities. On the other hand, users are located in different physical situations and also access methods have different weaknesses in reaching them.

C. Wang (Ed.): AccessNets, LNICST 6, pp. 333–340, 2009.

Network users have been classified according to different criteria, but bandwidth requirement is the most suitable criterion for choosing network access solutions.

Bandwidth requirement and its increase rate is mainly a function of interaction of technology, economy and social evolutions and may be different for various groups of users. To achieve a good estimation for required bandwidth in different user groups, a proper evaluation of technical, economical and social situation and current requests must be done and also global increase trend in user bandwidth requests be considered, otherwise the implemented network may have a short lifetime and investments in planning and implementation phases may not yield a handsome return.

As the main goal of this paper is simplifying the process of selecting the best access methods by recommending appropriate templates, user classification methods aren't treated deeply. All users are simply classified in four groups: A, B, C, and D. Typical services that each group needs have been determined and a suitable bandwidth has been assigned to it.

Although global request for bandwidth shows a tremendous growth (For some group of users a 50 fold growth has been estimated for a 5 to 10 year period [1]), in non-developed and developing countries, this request and its increase rate is much less than global index. So the recommended bandwidth for each group of users is less than global standards due to economic and cultural restrictions.

Class A- Include homes, shops, restaurants, small offices (with less than 10 employees), and so on, with capabilities like e-mail, file transfer, web surfing, games and low quality video communications.

We assume a maximum of 10Mb/s bandwidth for access to the network for this group of users.

Class B- Include schools, big shops and restaurants, hotels, banks, local offices, production centers, big professional centers (like legal offices) and small companies with 10 to 50 employees. These users, in addition to common services, need high-quality video communications, access to multimedia databases and reliable and high-speed data exchange.

A bandwidth of 10Mb/s to 50Mb/s is suitable for this group of users.

Class C- Include very big shops, big hotels, big governmental and industrial centers and enterprises with 50 to 250 employees which normally need high-speed private connections that a great many users share it. In addition to above-mentioned services, VLAN is one of the most important needs of this group.

A bandwidth of 50Mb/s to 200Mb/s has been assumed for this group of users.

Class D- Include universities, hospitals, big industrial centers and enterprises with more than 250 employees. This group needs a private network, due to its high communicational exchanges. This private network provides most of services and the major need is a reliable high-speed communication link.

A bandwidth of 200Mb/s to 1Gb/s is assumed for this group of users.

3 Recommended Access Methods

In many non-developed and developing countries in Africa, Asia-Pacific, South America, and Middle East, the copper twisted pair is still the dominant media for access to voice and data services.

Due to economical restrictions, considerable investments on this vast infrastructure couldn't be ignored in near future. On the other hand, wireless access solutions aren't well-known and cheap enough. So, xDSL or hybrid fiber-copper methods are the best and most cost-effective solutions for broadband access in these countries.

All-fiber method can be used for special user groups and as the final goal for NGN access in long-term plan.

Wireline can offer clearly higher data rates than wireless solutions. Fig.1 tracks the bit rate evolution. The wireline user data rate is some 30 times that of wireless, with both on a similar evolutionary trajectory. [2]

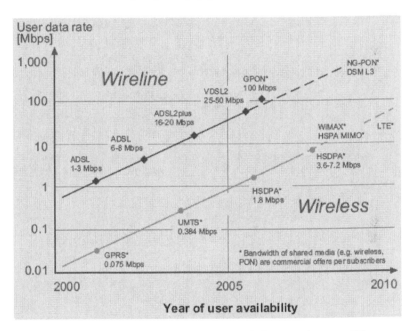

Fig. 1. The development of wireline and wireless user data rates [2]

Incumbent wireline operators leverage legacy copper assets to offer broadband services with DSL. In view of constantly growing end-user bandwidth demand, fiber must be brought closer to the subscriber. FTTC and FTTB are the fiber deployments of choice. The next step up is FTTH, where fiber runs right to the subscriber's home. Bandwidth-hungry applications like high-definition TV and corporate connectivity will drive the demand for wireline network deployments. [2]

CLASS "A"

FTTExch or FTTC with the aid of popular versions of ADSL can be used for this group of users, considering bandwidth requirements and distance from CO. Fig.2

shows the relationship between distance and bit rate in different versions of ADSL. As we see, the most improvements in new versions are made in short distances and performance in long distances is the same.

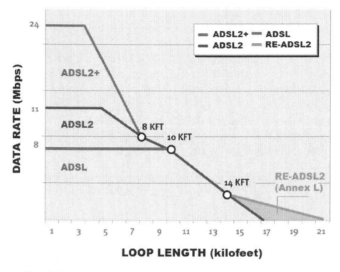

Fig. 2. Downstream capacity in different versions of ADSL [3]

In Fig.3, the local loop range that normally is less than 5km is divided to four intervals and the maximum ADSL bit rate for downstream and upstream has been determined for each one.

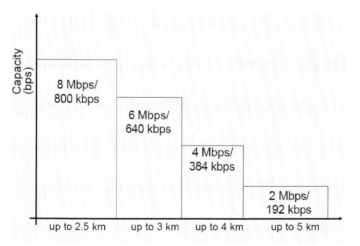

Fig. 3. ADSL capacity in different intervals [4]

With the aid of these figures, the criterion of choosing the appropriate method can be summarized as Fig.4, as a function of "distance from CO" and "requested bite rate".

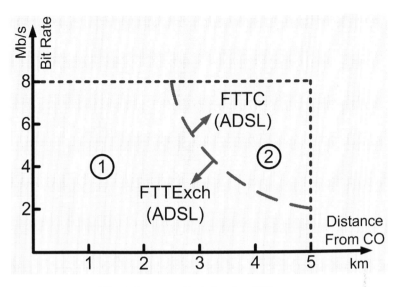

Fig. 4. Access methods for class "A" users

This diagram which only considers the users located in 5km radius is provided for this group of users, with emphasis on using cheap and common ADSL technology over available copper wires.

As we see, all users requesting less than 2Mb/s and a part of users requesting more than 2Mb/s in short distances can be served by FTTExch method and common ADSL technology (zone 1). Other users of this group in zone 2 need FTTC method.

For example for serving a user with 5km distance from CO and requesting 8Mb/s, the fiber must be neared at least 2.5km to user, in a FTTC architecture (Fig.5).

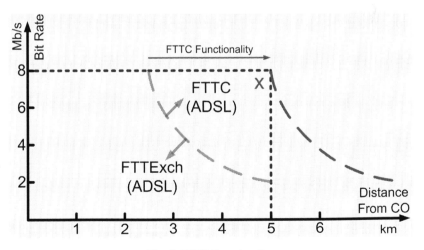

Fig. 5. FTTC Functionality

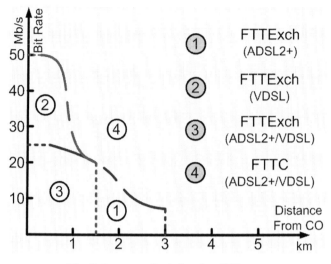

Fig. 6. Access methods for class "B" users

CLASS "B"

In this case, one of the FTTExch or FTTC methods with ADSL2+ or VDSL is recommended. Fig.6 shows the way of choosing the appropriate method, considering two parameters; "distance from CO" and "requested bite rate". The borders of zones are indeed the characteristic curves for ADSL2+ and VDSL technologies.

For users requesting symmetric bandwidth, SHDSL also is a possible choice.

As we see, all users located in zone 1 to 3 can be directly served from CO by copper wires, but zone 4 users need hybrid copper-fiber methods due to long distance or high bit rate request.

According to Fig.7, implementation cost for both copper and fiber networks is reducing, but the difference is reducing too, and it is anticipated that the costs will be the same in 2010 [3].

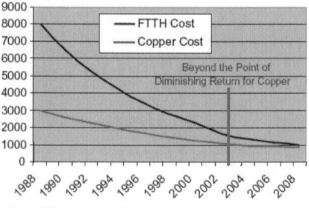

Source: OFS & Industry Studies & Estimates

Fig. 7. Implementation cost for FTTH and copper [5]

In the other word in that time, implementing a new copper access network will not be cost-effective, considering its bandwidth limitations. So for green fields, different types of TDM-PON will be suitable choices.

CLASS "C"
Among different types of DSL, only VDSL can provide more than 50Mb/s bit rate (Fig.8).

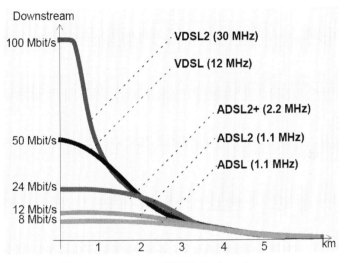

Fig. 8. The potency of VDSL in short distances

Fig.9 shows the way of choosing the appropriate method for this group of users. According to this diagram, VDSL versions can be used in FTTExch and FTTC configurations in zones 1 and 2.

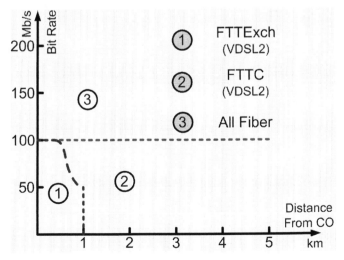

Fig. 9. Access methods for class "C" users

Users requesting more than 100Mb/s bandwidth exclusively need all-fiber solutions (zone 3). In all-fiber solutions, different types of TDM-PON technologies can be used which provide various bandwidths depending on number of splits. For more bandwidth requests, using active optical networks (and WDM-PON in near future) is inevitable.

CLASS "D"
This group needs all-fiber access and until WDM-PON technology generalization, only active fiber networks or direct fiber can answer bandwidth requirements of this group of users. As the total number of this group is few and the users in each center are voluminous, the cost of fiber cabling is tolerable for operators.

4 Conclusion

Broadband access generalization is the first step in moving toward NGN. Proposed templates in this paper can be used as a base for a general recommendation about implementation of novel broadband access technologies in most non-developed and developing countries.

In order to finalize these proposals, the influence of other parameters on real deliverable bandwidth like loop quality, crosstalk and user concentration must be considered.

On the other hand, service requirements in each group must be fully determined and quality characteristics of these services like delay, jitter and PLR must be noticed in final proposed architectures.

References

1. User and Service requirements, BROADWAN Deliverable D6 (May 2004)
2. Broadband Access for all – A brief technology guide, Nokia Siemens Networks (2007)
3. ADSL2 and ADSL2+: The New ADSL Standard White Paper, Revision 3, Aware Inc. (2005)
4. Hess, F.: Broadband Access Networks (Winter Semester 2002/2003)
5. Agarwal, A.: Broadband: A Case for Optical Fiber. Sterlite Optical Technologies Ltd., 13th Convergence India 2005 New Delhi, India (March 2005)

A Unified Framework of the Performance Evaluation of Optical Time-Wavelength Code-Division Multiple-Access Systems

Elie Inaty

Faculty of Engineering
University of Balamand, Lebanon
elie.inaty@balamand.edu.lb

Abstract. In this paper, we provide an analysis to the performance of optical time-wavelength code-division multiple-access (OTW-CDMA) network when the system is working above the nominal transmission rate limit imposed by the passive encoding-decoding operation. We address the problem of overlapping in such a system and how it can directly affect the bit error rate (BER). A unified mathematical framework is presented under the assumption of one coincidence sequences with non-repeating wavelengths. A closed form expression of the multiple access interference limited BER is provided as a function of different system parameters. Results show that the performance of OTW-CDMA system may be critically affected when working above the nominal limit; an event that may happen when the network operates at high transmission rate. In addition, the impact of the derived error probability on the performance of two newly proposed MAC protocols, the S-ALOHA and the R3T, is also investigated. It is shown that for low transmission rates, the S-ALOHA is better than the R3T; while the R3T is better at very high transmission rates. However, in general it is postulated that the R3T protocol suffers a higher delay mainly because of the presence of additional modes.

Keywords: Optical time-wavelength CDMA, multirate, overlapping coefficient, one coincidence sequences, S-ALOHA, R3T.

1 Introduction

Lately, optical time-wavelength code division multiple access (OTW-CDMA) has received considerable attention as a multiple access scheme for optical local area networks due to its flexibility and diversity [1][4]-[3]. In addition, multi- services supporting multirate transmission using OTW-CDMA, are now feasible due to the rapid evolution of fiber optic technology that offers ultra-wide optical bandwidth capable of handling fast transmission rates. Toward this target, the bit-error-rate (BER) analysis of such a system is a crucial task [4].

OTW-CDMA has been proposed and discussed in numerous works like [2],[9]. In addition, the BER has been derived and studied in detail in [3]. In [2], we have proposed a multirate OTW-CDMA system using fiber Bragg grating and variable PG.

C. Wang (Ed.): AccessNets, LNICST 6, pp. 341–353, 2009.

The idea was to respect the total round trip time for light from a data bit to go through the encoder. One of the key issues that has been emphasized in [2] is the difference between passive optical CDMA and its electrical active counterpart. In fact, it has been argued that in active CDMA systems there is a one-to-one correspondence between the transmitted symbol duration and the processing gain (PG). On the other hand, this one-to-one relation does not exist in passive optical CDMA systems. For instance, decreasing the bit duration will not affect the symbol duration at the output of the optical encoder. Therefore, for a fixed PG, increasing the link transmission rate beyond a given value, known as the nominal rate, leads to bits overlap at the output of the encoder. In [2], the general problem we have considered is by how much we can increase the transmission rates of different classes of traffic beyond the nominal permitted rates so as to optimize performance to meet the quality of service (QoS) requirements. The QoS requirement has been taken to be the signal-to-interference ratio (SIR).

Although the SIR is considered to be a good QoS index, some network managers prefer the BER as a more reliable and exact QoS measure. In [3] and [9], the BER for the OTW-CDMA system has been presented in detail when the system works below the nominal limit. This means that sequences with ideal cross-correlation function of maximum one were assumed. The probability of having one hit between two code sequences was obtained and the BER is derived using the binomial distribution. On the other hand in [1], although the performance analysis of code sequences with arbitrary cross-correlation values is considered, the explicit equation of the probability of having more than one hit between two code sequences was not presented. Only the probability of having one and two hits was shown in [6] where a special family of non-ideal optical orthogonal codes was analyzed.

In this work, we will try to analyze the performance of the OTW-CDMA system when the network is working above the nominal rate limit imposed by the passive encoding-decoding operation. A unified mathematical framework is presented in a way that the probability of having any number of hits between sequences can be obtained. We will focus on the problem of overlapping in such a system and how it can mathematically affect the expression of the BER. Using this expression, the performance of the OTW-CDMA system is investigated in packetized optical networks using two newly proposed MAC protocols, the R^3T [8] and the S-ALOHA [7].

Following the introduction, the paper is structured as follows. Section 2 introduces the system model. The effect of overlapping on frequency hits is discussed in Section 3. Section 4 discusses the hit quantification due to sequence overlap. Section 5 presents the BER analysis assuming multiple access interference (MAI) limited noise effect. Numerical results are covered in Section 6. Finally, the conclusion is presented in Section 7.

2 System Model

Consider an OTW-CDMA system that supports M users, sharing the same optical medium in a star architecture [9]. We will consider that all users are transmitting their data at the same transmission rate and have the same processing gain (PG) G. The encoding-decoding is achieved passively using a sequence of fiber Bragg grating

(FBG). The gratings spectrally and temporary slice the incoming broadband pulse into several components, equally spaced at chip interval T_c. The chip duration and the number of grating G determine the nominal bit duration to be $T_n = GT_c$. The corresponding nominal transmission rate is $R_n = 1/T_n$. Increasing the transmission rate beyond the nominal rate R_n without decreasing G introduces an overlapping coefficient ε_j among the transmitted bits during the same period T_n, as revealed in Fig. 1.

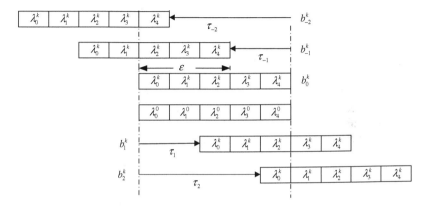

Fig. 1. The concept of overlapping among the bits, showing the effect of the overlapping coefficient ε_j on their transmission rate

In this case, the concept of overlapping is illustrated among six bits of $G = 5$ and the overlapping coefficient is $\varepsilon_j = 3$, which means that there are three chips in each OCDMA-coded bit that overlap with three chips of the other bits in the same class. This, in turn, augments the overall transmission rate of the users involved in this class from three bits after $3T_n$ to six bits. In general, the overlapping coefficient represents the number of overlapped chips among consecutive bits. Accordingly, the new transmission rate of is given by

$$R_j = \frac{G}{G - \varepsilon_j} R_n \qquad (1)$$

where $0 \le \varepsilon_j \le G - 1$. This implies that $R^{(\ell)} \le R_j \le R^{(u)}$ where $R^{(\ell)} = R_n$ and $R^{(u)} = GR_n$ are the lower and the upper data rate common to all users, respectively. Also, we assume that the system is chip-synchronous and of discrete rate variation. Furthermore, all users transmit with the equal power and have the same overlapping coefficient.

From Fig. 1, the optical bit stream can be seen as being serial-to-parallel converted to v optical pulses. Assuming that the desired user is using the *class-s*, which is characterized by a PG $= G$ and an overlapping coefficient ε_s. We define v and τ_v as the index of the overlapping bit and its associated time delay, respectively. The bit $b_X^k \in \{0,1\}$ from the v-bits is delayed by $\tau_X = X\left(G - \varepsilon_s\right)$. Accordingly, the average cross-correlation function between two one-coincidence sequences [10]-[12] has been obtained in [2] and it is given by

$$\bar{R}\left(G, \varepsilon_s\right) = \frac{1}{2F}\left[G + \left(G + \varepsilon_s\right)X - \left(G - \varepsilon_s\right)X^2\right] \qquad (2)$$

where

$$X = \left[\frac{\varepsilon_s}{G - \varepsilon_s}\right] \qquad (3)$$

Although we have been able to study the performance of the multirate OTW-CDMA in [2], the work was based on the average of the cross-correlation function assuming one-coincidence sequences. In this work, we attempt to evaluate the performance of this system probabilistically in a way to obtain a closed form solution of the exact BER analysis of this system.

3   Overlapped Interference Sequences Identification

As it has been shown in [2], increasing the transmission rate will increase the overlapping coefficient, and therefore will induce more interference. Throughout this section we will try to study and quantify the effect of overlapping for one coincidence sequences with non repeating frequencies [11].

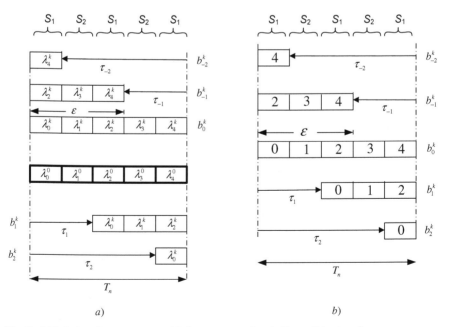

Fig. 2. a) Code interference pattern, b) the corresponding indices of the interference sequences

Consider an interferer user k with (G, ε_j) as the one presented in Fig. 1. During the auto-correlation process, we look only to the nominal period T_n. Therefore, the interfering sequence as seen by the desired user's receiver is shown in Fig. 2. In this figure, we can notice many important aspects. The first one is that at every chip position, there is an interfering pattern that forms a sequence with different elements like $S_1 = \{\lambda_0^k, \lambda_2^k, \lambda_4^k\}$. The second observation is that each interfering sequence is repeated multiple times at different chip positions.

Lemma 1. *In an overlapped optical CDMA system, let an interferer with (G, ε_j). At the desired correlation receiver end, and during the nominal observation time period T_n, the observed interfering sequences are subdivided into two groups. In the first group there are m_1 sequences of length*

$$N_1 = \left\lceil \frac{G}{G - \varepsilon} \right\rceil \tag{4}$$

with

$$m_1 = G - (G - \varepsilon) \left\lceil \frac{\varepsilon}{G - \varepsilon} \right\rceil \tag{5}$$

The remaining

$$m_2 = (G - \varepsilon) \left\lceil \frac{\varepsilon}{G - \varepsilon} \right\rceil - \varepsilon \tag{6}$$

sequences form the second group in which each sequence is of length

$$N_2 = \left\lceil \frac{\varepsilon}{G - \varepsilon} \right\rceil \tag{7}$$

∎

Lemma 1 is very important in the sense that it enables us to quantify the effect of overlapping on the interference patterns at a given receiver.

4   Hits Quantification due to Overlap

By observing Fig. 2, we can notice clearly that there are two different kinds of interfering sequences, $S_1 = \{\lambda_0^k, \lambda_2^k, \lambda_4^k\}$ and $S_2 = \{\lambda_1^k, \lambda_3^k\}$. In addition, S_1 is repeated three times and S_2 is repeated 2 times. Thus, to study the contribution of S_1 on the MAI, we need to compare it with the desired user wavelengths where it is present. Therefore, we need to compare $S_1 = \{\lambda_0^k, \lambda_2^k, \lambda_4^k\}$ with $d_1 = \{\lambda_0^0, \lambda_2^0, \lambda_4^0\}$. The same argument can be applied to the sequence S_2 where we need to compare $S_2 = \left\{ \lambda_1^k, \lambda_3^k \right\}$ to $d_2 = \left\{ \lambda_1^0, \lambda_3^0 \right\}$.

Let's take for example S_1 and d_1. It's clear that there are up to three possible matching events between elements in S_1 and elements in d_1. Thus one element in S_1 can be in d_1, two elements in S_1 can be in d_1, or three elements in S_1 can match with three elements in d_1. Each of those events represents the number of hits the interfering sequence S_1 induces at the desired user's receiver. The probabilities of those events are critical in deriving the BER of this system.

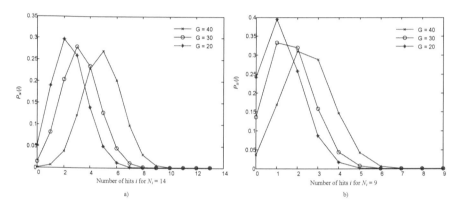

Fig. 3. The probability that the sequence S_i causes i hits in the cross-correlation function

In general, consider an interfering sequence S_i and the desired sequence d_i, both of them with length N_i where N_i can be obtained using Lemma 1. The probability that S_i causes i hits in the cross-correlation function is the probability that exactly i terms in S_i match with i terms in d_i. If we are selecting N_i wavelengths at a time from a set of F possible wavelengths, then the probability of having exactly i wavelengths matching with the sequence d_i of length N_i and $N_i - i$ not matching can be written as

$$P_{S_i}(i) = \frac{\binom{N_i}{i}\binom{F-N_i}{N_i-i}}{\binom{F}{N_i}} \quad \forall \, 0 \leq i \leq N_i < F \tag{8}$$

where $\binom{x}{i}$ is the binomial coefficient. All the permutations of a given combination s_i will result i hits if assuming that there are exactly i wavelengths in s_i that match with i wavelengths in d_i.

An illustration of (8) is shown in Fig. 3 where we plot the probability that the interfering sequence S_i causes i hits versus i for a) $N_i = 14$ and b) $N_i = 9$ and for different values of G. In addition, we assume that $F = 2G$. Notice that as the PG increases, although the probability of having smaller number of hits decreases, the probability of higher number of hits increases. This result is not like we expect as in the case of un-overlapped systems where the length of the interfering sequence is always one and increasing the PG will leads to a decrease in the probability of hits.

5   MAI Limited BER Analysis

Obviously, it is clear that due to the overlapping process, the assumption of one coincidence sequences will not guaranty the upper bound on the number of hits to be one as in the classical non overlapped systems. In fact, the number of hits between two overlapped code sequences is related to the number of interference sequences and the size of each of those sequences. For example, if we return to the case studied and shown in Fig. 2, both interference sequences $S_1 = \{\lambda_0^k, \lambda_2^k, \lambda_4^k\}$ and $S_2 = \{\lambda_1^k, \lambda_3^k\}$ may cause up to five hits with different probability of occurrence. The importance of our work is to highlight those differences and to emphasize their effect on the performance evaluation of the system.

In order to evaluate the performance of the overlapped system, we need to find the probability that two overlapped codes have one, two, or p hits in their cross-correlation function such that $p \le G$. We will proceed by showing the case presented in Fig. 2. The interference pattern of this example can be simplified to two sequences of interference or hits $[H_1, H_2]$ which represent the number of possible hits caused by interference sequences S_1 and S_2, respectively. In our example, H_1 can take four possible values $H_1 = \{0, 1, 2, 3\}$, and H_2 can take three possible values $H_2 = \{0, 1, 2\}$ with different probabilities as revealed in Fig. 4.

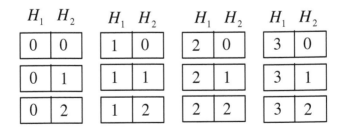

H_1	H_2		H_1	H_2		H_1	H_2		H_1	H_2
0	0		1	0		2	0		3	0
0	1		1	1		2	1		3	1
0	2		1	2		2	2		3	2

Fig. 4. Different possible hit configurations

Different possibilities of hits caused by both sequences are presented in Fig. 4. According to Fig. 4, in order to compute the probability of having j hits from a given interferer, we have to find the probability of having $H_1 + H_2 = s$. For example, the probability of having three hits is obtained as follows;

$$q_3 = \Pr\left\{\begin{array}{l}(H_1 = 3 \cap H_2 = 0) \cup (H_1 = 2 \cap H_2 = 1)\\ \cup (H_1 = 1 \cap H_2 = 2)\end{array}\right\}$$

$$= \frac{1}{(N_1+1)(N_2+1)}\left\{\begin{array}{l}P_{S_1}(3)\cdot P_{S_2}(0) + P_{S_1}(2)\cdot P_{S_2}(1)\\ +P_{S_1}(1)\cdot P_{S_2}(2)\end{array}\right\} \tag{9}$$

$$= \frac{1}{(N_1+1)(N_2+1)}\sum_i \left\{P_{S_1}(j)\cdot P_{S_2}(k)\right\}$$

where $N_1 = 3$ and $N_2 = 2$ are the lengths of the sequences S_1 and S_2, respectively. In addition, the parameters j and k are chosen such that $j+k=3$, $\forall$ $j=\{0,1,2,3\}$ and $k=\{0,1,2\}$. The parameter i represents the number of cases satisfying $j+k=3$.

Lemma 2: *Consider two positive integer numbers* $i=\{0,1,...,N_1\}$ *and* $j=\{0,1,...,N_2\}$ *with* $N_1 < N_2$. *The number of possible couples* (i,j), Λ, *satisfying i+j = s,* $\forall s = \{0,1,...,N_1+N_2\}$, *is given by*

$$\Lambda = \begin{cases}s+1, & \text{if } 0 \le s \le N_1\\ N_1+1, & \text{if } N_1 < s \le N_2\\ N_1+N_2-s+1, & \text{if } N_2 < s \le N_1+N_2\end{cases} \tag{10}$$

■

Using Lemma 2 we can generalize (9) to the case of any number of hits. Therefore, the probability of having s hits is given by

$$q_s = \frac{1}{(N_1+1)(N_2+1)}\sum_{i=a}^{b} P_{S_1}(s-i)\cdot P_{S_2}(i) \tag{11}$$

where

$$(a,b) = \begin{cases}(0,s), & \text{for } 0 \le s \le N_1\\ (0,N_1), & \text{for } N_1 < s \le N_2\\ (s-N_1,N_2), & \text{for } N_2 < s \le N_1+N_2\end{cases} \tag{12}$$

In addition, using Lemma 2, we can generalize the probability of having s hits given in (11) and (12) to any number of interfering sequences. For example, assume that the number of interfering sequences is four. Thus, let $i=\{0,1,...,N_1\}$, $j=\{0,1,...,N_2\}$, $k=\{0,1,...,N_3\}$, and $t=\{0,1,...,N_4\}$ with $N_1 \le N_2 \le N_3 \le N_4$. The distribution of the number of hits is the probability of having s hits, and it is given by

$$q_s = \frac{1}{\prod_{i=1}^{4}(N_i+1)}\sum_{t=0}^{N_4}\sum_{k=0}^{N_3}\sum_{i=a}^{b} P_{S_1}(s-k-t-i)\cdot P_{S_2}(i)\cdot P_{S_3}(k)\cdot P_{S_4}(t) \tag{13}$$

where

$$(a,b) = \begin{cases} (0, s-k-t), & \text{for } 0 \leq s-k-t \leq N_1 \\ (0, N_1), & \text{for } N_1 < s-k-t \leq N_2 \\ (s-k-t-N_1, N_2), & \text{for } N_2 < s-k-t \leq N_1+N_2 \end{cases} \qquad (14)$$

Fig. 5 shows the distribution of the number of hits when $G=15$, $F=18$, and for different values of ε. It is clear that when the system works above the nominal limit, it may induce more then one hit even if the codes used are one coincidence codes. This in turn, will drastically influence the probability of error of the system. Notice that, as we further increase the transmission rate, the probability of having larger number of hits becomes higher, thus increasing the MAI.

Having obtained in (13) the probability of s hits in the cross-correlation function, we can now compute the MAI-limited BER when the system is working above the nominal limit. Let Z, TH, and M denote the cross-correlation value seen by the desired receiver, the decision threshold, and the total number of simultaneous users in the system, respectively. Obviously, an error occurs whenever the transmitted data bit is zero, but the interference at the desired receiver results in $Z > TH$. Thus, the probability of error is given by

$$\begin{aligned} P_e &= \Pr(\text{error} / M \text{ simultaneous users}) \\ &= \frac{1}{2}\Pr(Z \geq TH / M \text{ users and the desired user sent } 0) \end{aligned} \qquad (15)$$

where we have assumed that the data bits zeros and ones are equiprobable.

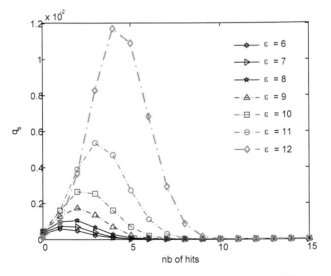

Fig. 5. The Probability mass function of the number of hits for different values of the overlapping coefficient ε

Assuming that S is the total number of interfering pulses in the cross-correlation function and that each interfering user may contribute up to S pulses in it. Let l_j to be the number of interfering users that has a cross-correlation value j. Then, the probability of having $\{l_1, l_2, ..., l_S\}$ interfering users follows a multinomial probability density function [5] and it is given by

$$\Pr(l_1, l_2, ..., l_S) = \frac{(M-1)!}{\left(\prod_{j=1}^{S} l_j!\right)\left(M-1-\sum_{j=1}^{S} l_j\right)!}\left(\prod_{j=1}^{S} q_j^{l_j}\right)\left(1-\sum_{j=1}^{S} q_j\right)^{\left(M-1-\sum_{j=1}^{S} l_j\right)} \tag{16}$$

where q_j is given in (13) and (14). Using (16) in (15) we obtain

$$P_e = \frac{1}{2} - \frac{1}{2}\sum_{l_1=0}^{TH-1}\sum_{l_2=0}^{\left\lfloor\frac{TH-1-l_1}{2}\right\rfloor}\cdots\sum_{l_S=0}^{\left\lfloor\left(TH-1-\sum_{j=1}^{S-1} jl_j\right)/S\right\rfloor}\Pr(l_1, l_2, ..., l_S) \tag{17}$$

6 Numerical Results and Discussion

Throughout this section, we will try to study and discuss the above derived equations using numerical evaluation. In addition, the impact of the exact BER analysis on the performance of two newly proposed MAC protocols, the S-ALOHA and the R3T protocols, is also investigated. For a complete and detailed discussion of both protocols, the reader is invited to refer to [7] and [8]. Throughout this section, we assume that the total number of stations is $M = 15$, and the processing gain is $G = 15$.

In Fig. 6, we show the error probability as a function of the number of users M and for different values of the overlapping coefficient ε when (a) the number of available wavelength is double the code length [11] and when (b) the number of available wavelength is equal to the code length [10]. The error probability increases when increasing M, as expected. In addition, the error probability increases when increasing the transmission rate, therefore; increasing ε. This is due to the increase in the probability of hits. Notice the importance of the number of available frequencies F on the performance of OTW-CDMA by observing that the probability of error shown in Fig. 6(a) for $F = 2G$ is much lower than that presented in Fig. 6(b) where $F = G$. This means that code families that provide a flexibility of choosing F like the one in [11], can offer better performance than that in which $F = G$ [10].

In the following simulation, we assume that the packet length under S-ALOHA protocol is $L = 100$ bits/time slot and the message is one packet. While equivalently, under the R3T protocol the packet length is one bit/time slot and $L = 100$ designates the message length in packets. Note that there is a correspondence between A and P_r. In S-ALOHA, when a terminal enters the backlogged mode, it cannot generate new packets until all the accumulated ones in the system's buffer are retransmitted. Consequently, the offered traffic varies according to the retransmission probability, P_r. Meanwhile, in R3T, the terminal in case of transmission failure retransmits the

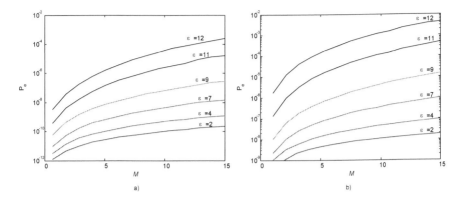

Fig. 6. BER versus the number of users M for different value of ε and when: a) $F = 2G$, b) $F = G$

last unsuccessful t packets with the same transmission probability (user's activity) A whereby which varies the offered traffic. For S-ALOHA, we assume $P_r = 0.6$, whereas for R3T, we assume $A = 0.6$, the time out duration $\tau_o = 1$ time slot and the two-way propagation delay is $t = 2$ time slots.

The throughput of both systems is presented in Fig. 7. In Fig. 7(a) we present the throughput versus the offered traffic using a detection threshold $TH = G/2$, while Fig. 7(b) shows the throughput when using the optimal detection threshold. The impact of the detection threshold is very obvious in the sense that there is a noticeable increase in the network throughput when using the optimal detection threshold.

It is clear that, for high overlapping coefficient, the R3T protocol exhibits higher throughput than the S-ALOHA protocol. While, the throughputs of the S-ALOHA protocol is higher than that of the R3T when ε is relatively small. For the S-ALOHA protocol, when using the optimal detection threshold, the system reaches its maximum throughput of 8 packets per time slot for $\varepsilon < 10$. On the other hand, the R3T protocol reaches its maximum throughput of 7 packets per time slot for $\varepsilon < 10$ as revealed by Fig. 7(b).

As the transmission rate increases, the throughput of the S-ALOHA decreases compared to that of the R3T. This means that the R3T protocol can manage higher-rate users better than the S-ALOHA due to its efficient administration of erroneous packets using the *Round Robin* and the *Go-back-n* protocols.

In Fig. 8 we present the average packet delay versus the system throughput, operating under the two mentioned protocols using the optimal detection threshold as in Fig. 8(b), and a non-optimal detection threshold as in Fig. 8(a), respectively. Here again we remark that the R3T protocol exhibits higher delay at low throughput for relatively small values of ε. On the other hand, the S-ALOHA protocol exhibits higher delay at low throughput for higher values of ε. Notice that when using the optimal detection threshold, the S-ALOHA achieves it maximum throughput with

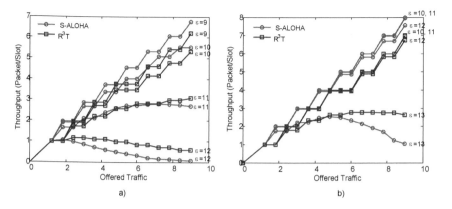

Fig. 7. Throughput versus the offered traffic of the OTW-CDMA system under the two MAC protocols: S-ALOHA and R^3T and using (a) non-optimal detection threshold, (b) optimal detection threshold

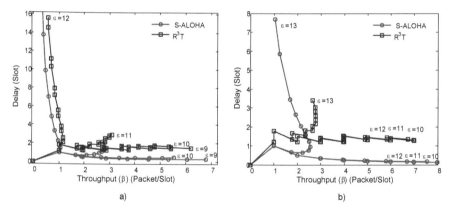

Fig. 8. Average packet delay versus the throughput of the OTW-CDMA system under the two MAC protocols: S-ALOHA and R^3T and using (a) non-optimal detection threshold, (b) optimal detection threshold

virtually not delay when $\varepsilon < 10$, while the R^3T protocol takes around one time slot to achieve its maximum throughput. This is due to the use of the *Go-back-n* protocol.

By comparing the performance of the OTW-CDMA system under both protocols, we notice that for low transmission rates, the S-ALOHA is better than the R3T; while the R3T is better at very high transmission rates.

7 Conclusion

An analysis of the performance of OTW-CDMA network when the system is working above the nominal transmission rate limit has been provided. A unified mathematical framework is presented under the assumption of one coincidence sequences with non-repeating wavelengths. A closed form expression of the BER has been derived. Results show that the performance of OTW-CDMA system may be critically affected when working above the nominal limit. In addition, the impact of the derived error probability on the performance of two newly proposed MAC protocols, the S-ALOHA and the R3T, is also investigated. It is shown that for low transmission rates, the S-ALOHA is better than the R3T; while the R3T is better at very high transmission rates. However, in general, the R3T protocol suffers a higher delay because of the presence of additional modes.

References

[1] Hsu, C.-C., Yang, G.-C., Kwong, W.C.: Performance analysis of 2-D optical codes with arbitrary cross-correlation values under the chip-asynchronous assumption. IEEE Communications Letters 11(2), 170–172 (2007)
[2] Inaty, E., Shalaby, H.M.H., Fortier, P.: On the cutoff rate of a multiclass OFFH-CDMA system. IEEE Trans. on Communications 53, 323–334 (2005)
[3] Bazan, T.M., Harle, D., Andonovic, I.: Performance analysis of 2-D time-wavelength OCDMA systems with coherent light sources: Code design considerations. IEEE J. Lightwave Technology 24, 3583–3589 (2006)
[4] Shalaby, H.M.H.: Complexities, error probabilities, and capacities of optical OOK-CDMA communication systems. IEEE Trans. on Communications 50(12), 2009–2017 (2002)
[5] Azizoglu, M., Salehi, J.A., Li, Y.: Optical CDMA via temporal codes. IEEE Trans. on Communications 40(7), 1162–1170 (2002)
[6] Weng, C.-S., Wu, J.: Optical orthogonal codes with nonideal cross correlation. IEEE J. Lightwave Technology 19, 1856–1863 (2001)
[7] Raad, R., Inaty, E., Fortier, P., Shalaby, H.M.H.: Optical S-ALOHA/CDMA system for multirate applications: architecture, performance evaluation, and system stability. IEEE J. Lightwave Technology 24(5), 1968–1977 (2006)
[8] Shalaby, H.M.H.: Performance analysis of an optical CDMA random access protocol. J. Lightwave Technology 22, 1233–1241 (2004)
[9] Yang, G.-C., Kwong, W.C.: Prime codes with applications to CDMA optical and wireless networks. Artech House inc. (2002)
[10] Wronski, L.D., Hossain, R., Albicki, A.: Extended Hyperbolic Congruencial Frequency Hop Code: Generation and Bounds for Cross- and Auto-Ambiguity Function. IEEE Trans. on Communications 44(3), 301–305 (1996)
[11] Bin, L.: One-Coincidence Sequences with specified Distance Between Adjacent Symbols for Frequency-Hopping Multiple Access. IEEE Trans. on Communications 45(4), 408–410 (1997)
[12] Shaar, A., Davies, P.A.: A survey of one-coincidence sequences for frequency-hopped spread spectrum systems. IEE Proceedings 131(7), 719–724 (1984)

Performance Analysis of Multi-format WDM-RoF Links Based on Low Cost Laser and SOA

Carlos Almeida[1,2], António Teixeira[1,2], and Mário Lima[1,2]

[1] Instituto de Telecomunicações, University of Aveiro, Campus de Santiago,
3810-193 Aveiro, Portugal
[2] Department of Electronics, Telecommunications and Informatics , University of Aveiro,
Campus de Santiago, 3810-193 Aveiro, Portugal
{carlosalmeida,teixeira,mlima}@ua.pt

Abstract. In this paper, we experimentally study the effects of using low cost optical amplifiers and lasers in multi-format multi-wavelength radio over fiber signals. We analyze the propagation of UMTS, WLAN and WiMAX radio signals in a single channel scenario and study the impact of amplifying the referred radio signals together with amplitude modulated ones, which can be ethernet, in WDM scenario.

Keywords: RoF, UMTS, WLAN, WiMAX, SOA.

1 Introduction

Radio waves are nowadays the most popular way to communicate, since they are used in the very front end of every user, as they provide an extremely important facility: mobility. On the other hand, the demand and increase of penetration of data and voice, has pushed the operators into several developments and strategies to enable full time, space and, whenever possible, bandwidth coverage to the users. This attitude leads the operators and their suppliers to find all types of technical solutions that can make the three aforementioned guidelines possible. Some of the challenges are for example to manage bandwidth in highly dense sporadic places, (commercial centers, shows, sport games) or to allow coverage in places where wave propagation is not easy. In some of these cases fiber information distribution can be a solution [1].

Passive Optical Networks (PON) are concurrently being deployed everywhere, in order to allow the operators to arrive with better quality and in a transparent way to the customers' home. Radio distribution over PONs can be seen as a promising technique to overcome many of the radio frequency (RF) spectrum limitations. The signal distribution is also improved with the RF signals being transmitted in their raw form to antennas eliminating some signal processing. Thus, the transmission equipment will be more simplified and by using micro-cells the required power level will be reduced eliminating the need for expensive power amplifiers and frequency multiplexers [2]. However, this can only be a reality if it is proven to be possible to implement in a cost effective way. In Fig. 1 it is presented a possible scenario where one or more services will share the same trunk fiber and can or not share one of the

C. Wang (Ed.): AccessNets, LNICST 6, pp. 354–364, 2009.

arms of the PON, depending on the needs of the location/costumer. The losses of the PON splitting ration need to be compensated by a booster amplifier located at the central office. The presence of several signals can limit their propagation and detection, and this is the topic of this work.

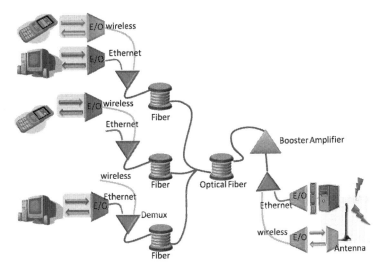

Fig. 1. Block diagram of a possible scenario

In this work we analyze different aspects of such approach. We use low cost optical sources (coarse WDM DFB uncooled lasers, directly modulated) and amplifiers (Semiconductor Optical Amplifiers – SOA) and observe the impact of propagating multi-format multi-wavelength signals through the optical link. We considered three different types of signals of distinct technologies: UMTS, WLAN and WiMAX.

2 UMTS, WLAN and WiMAX Signals

UMTS is a third generation mobile service that uses Code Division Multiple Access (CDMA) in order to guarantee multiple connections. The signal bandwidth available is 3.84 MHz so an increase on the number of accesses will decrease the bandwidth assigned to each user. In a UMTS communication there are two distinct frequency bands: the Uplink band to establish the transmission between the User equipment and the Base Station, and a Downlink band to make the communications in the reverse direction.

A wireless LAN, WLAN, is based on the principle of transmitting simultaneously many narrow-band orthogonal frequencies, provided by Orthogonal Frequency-Division Multiplexing (OFDM). This gives users the mobility to move around within a broad coverage area and still be connected to the network. The 802.11g standard for WLAN offers wireless transmission over relatively short distances at 54 Mbps.

The WiMAX technology uses the same physical layer (OFDM) as WLAN but is a longer range system that allows a growth in the coverage cell area. The communication is established between a Base station and a Subscriber station, and it uses 2 channels: uplink and downlink. WiMAX uses a mechanism based on setting up connections between the Base Station and the user device, guaranteeing a certain quality of service (QoS) for each flow. The 802.16 standard for WiMAX is applied across a wide swath of the RF spectrum that allows if to function on any frequency below 66 GHz, but for higher frequencies the base station range decreases to a few hundred meters in an urban environment.

Some characteristics of these signals are presented on Table 1.

Table 1. Radio signals characteristics

	UMTS - 3G	WLAN	WiMAX
Standard		802.11g	802.16
Physical layer mode	WCDMA-3GPP	OFDM	OFDM
Modulation	QPSK	64 QAM	QPSK ¾
Bit rate (Mbps)	3,84	54	15
Limit for EVM (%)	12	5,62	1,41

The performance metric for signal transmissions is EVM (Error Vector Magnitude) that measures the degradation of the obtained constellation during transmission. In Fig. 2 is expressed the error vector as the difference between the theoretical waveform and a modified version of the measured waveform.

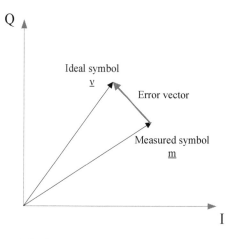

Fig. 2. Error Vector Magnitude (EVM)

3   Semiconductor Optical Amplifier

The SOA gain dynamic is determined by the carrier recombination lifetime (few hundred picoseconds). This means that the amplifier gain will react relatively quickly to changes in the input signal power, producing variations both in power and phase. These variations can cause signal distortion, which will surely be more evident in multichannel systems, where the dynamic gain leads to inter-channel crosstalk. This is in contrast to doped fiber amplifiers, which have recombination lifetimes of the order of milliseconds leading to negligible signal distortion.

SOAs also exhibit nonlinear behavior. These nonlinearities can cause problems such as frequency chirping and generation of inter-modulation products. The main cause for these nonlinearities is the carrier density change. The effects we are interested in within this study are: cross gain modulation (XGM), self gain modulation (SGM), cross phase modulation (XPM) and self-phase modulation (SPM).

When injecting a single channel in the SOA, changes on its optical power may lead to phase shifts creating SPM. If more than one signal is injected into an SOA, there will be cross-phase modulation (XPM) between the signals. XPM can be used to create wavelength converters and other functional devices.

The material gain spectrum of an SOA is homogenously broadened. This means that carrier density changes in the amplifier will affect all of the input signals creating SGM when having only one channel. In the other hand it is possible that a strong signal at one wavelength to affect the gain of a weak signal at another wavelength. This non-linear mechanism is called XGM.

4   Experimental Setup and Results

In Fig. 3 and Fig. 4 are illustrated the setups used. The Radio Frequency (RF) signals are provided through a Rohde & Schwartz vector signal generator that is used to directly modulate a laser, emitting at 1.55 µm. In the WDM scenario the RF signal is on one channel and the AM modulated one (an amplitude modulated ECL laser) 2 nm higher. The optical signal is then pre-amplified in both cases using a SOA with an internal pump laser (1 nm below the RF channel) to control saturation, and transmitted over a standard single mode fiber. At the output the RF signal channel is filtered, detected and applied to a vector signal analyzer to assess performance.

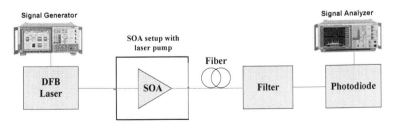

Fig. 3. Single Channel setup

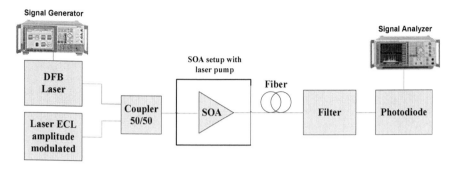

Fig. 4. WDM setup

To study the effects of SOA saturation on the transmission of the RF signals it is important to know the amplifiers gain response. In Fig. 5 are illustrated the curves of the SOA gain response when using different polarizations of the laser pump to saturate it.

For the different biasing currents it is observed the SOA saturation behavior evidenced by its gain decrease and stabilization for the higher currents. Without the pump laser, the gain falls 3 dB when the input signal reaches -11dBm. For the other biasing currents the gain is mainly constant with the increase of the input signal power, showing that the amplifier is already in saturation.

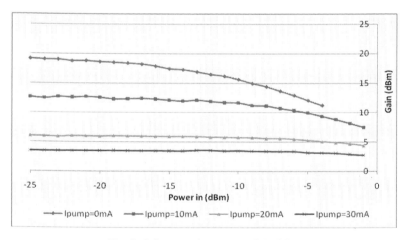

Fig. 5. Gain saturation curves of the SOA

When transmitting UMTS signals (setup of Fig. 3 with L=40 km) the results on Fig. 6 are obtained. The best results for the unsaturated operation (pump laser off) due to higher gain. Biasing the pump laser with 10 mA leads to higher degradation when compared to the other pump biasing currents. This fact can be explained by the observation of the SOA saturation curves, presented in Fig. 5, that show a more linear behavior for higher input powers at the SOA, in the case of 20 and 30 mA. Thus, the gain saturation can be more relevant when pump is biased with 10 mA. When

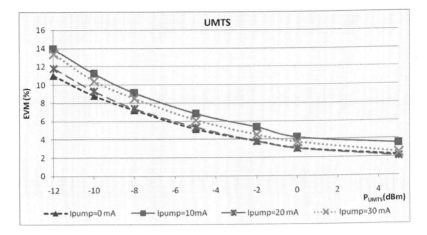

Fig. 6. EVM versus input RF power for SOA with different polarization currents.ves of the SOA

comparing the results for 20 and 30mA, they are similar, but with higher EVM values for 30 mA, due to higher saturation, therefore lower gain.

The results verified for the UMTS are similar to the ones of WiMAX and WLAN therefore not presented here.

Fig. 7 shows the behavior of the signals for two powers of the pump laser and show that indeed the results follow the previously discussed ones, when smaller the saturation the better behavior of the system.

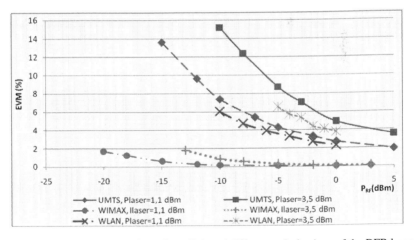

Fig. 7. Single channel setup for a direct link and different polarizations of the DFB laser

To achieve the perception if the distortion effects of the SOA affect propagation transmission over 40 km and 60 km was performed and the results are summarized in Fig. 8.

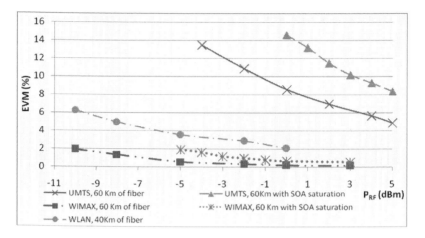

Fig. 8. EVM versus input RF power considering: unsaturated SOA; saturated SOA with a pump laser current of 30mA

From Fig. 8 it can be noticed that with the SOA in saturation the results become worst due to its internal dynamics (SPM and SGM respectively, Self Phase and Self Gain Modulation). Nevertheless for WLAN signals the results get considerably worst and the transmission is only possible for 40 km with unsaturated SOA. This is due to the format used which is based in quite close constellation, where any distortion can induce errors. Constellations can be observed for 40 km of fiber with the SOA in linear operation, in Fig. 9.

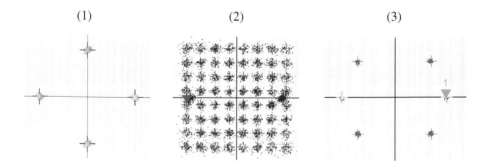

Fig. 9. Constellation of the RF received signals for the single channel setup for 40 km of fiber: (1) UMTS; (2) WLAN; (3) WiMAX

In the described WDM scenario (Fig. 4), when transmitting an Amplitude Modulated (AM) signal together with the referred RF signals, besides SPM and SGM, it will be also present Cross Phase and Cross Gain Modulation (XPM and XGM), caused by phase and gain changes induced by the AM modulated signal. FWM (Four Wave Mixing) effect is mitigated due to the uneven channel separation used. The results are illustrated in Fig. 10 and all EVM values were obtained for a SOA laser

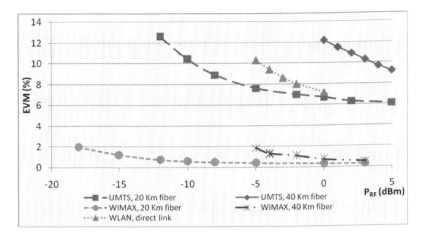

Fig. 10. EVM versus RF signal power for the WDM setup

pump current of 20 mA. The transmission of WLAN signals in this scenario was not possible within the standard values even in a back to back, however for UMTS and WiMAX signals has reached 40 km, however for higher RF powers than in the UMTS case.

In both setups, it can be concluded that the WLAN signals are the ones that require higher RF powers, and the WiMAX case, despite having the smaller EVM limit value, grants transmission with lower levels. The effects of crosstalk can be confirmed observing the constellations of UMTS signals (Fig. 11) obtained for the two setups, single channel and WDM. In the WDM setup, when varying the laser pump current of the SOA, for a fixed power of -5 dBm on the AM laser, we observe the degradation on the results obtained by XGM (Fig. 11 (2) for a pump current of 20 mA and (3) for a pump current of 30 mA).

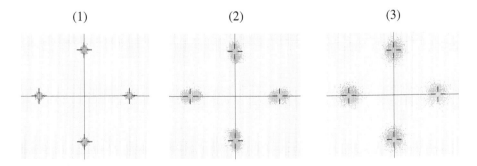

Fig. 11. Constellations of the received UMTS signal: (1) single channel; (2) and (3) WDM with the SOA less (20mA) and more (30mA) saturated by the internal pump

On the next experiment, varying the attenuation of the AM laser output, the modulation index and mean power of this channel will decrease and will result on an improved received RF signal, due to less significant inter-channel crosstalk and lower saturation. This can be observed in Fig. 12, where it is presented the EVM evolution versus AM power considering the SOA's pump laser polarized with 30 mA.

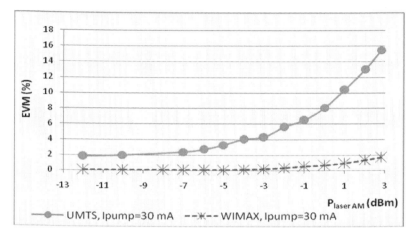

Fig. 12. Varying the power of the AM laser for the WDM setup

With the purpose of measuring the modulation index of the AM channel it was obtained the extinction ratio of the signal by attenuating the laser power and directly connecting it to the PIN followed by an oscilloscope. Considering the PIN photodiode responsivity it was determined the modulation index at the SOA input for a same pump laser biasing. The EVM versus modulation index of the AM laser is presented in Fig. 13.

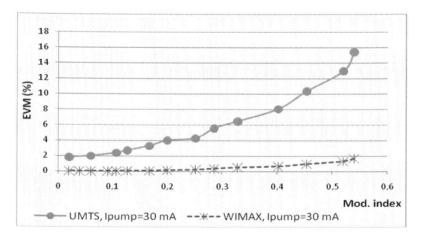

Fig. 13. Varying the modulation index of the AM laser for the WDM setup

Like it was expected the decrease on the modulation index of the AM channel obtained by attenuating the output power of the laser and maintaining the same power on the pump laser to saturate the SOA, showed a system performance increase. This behavior is justified by less interchannel crosstalk effects, thus the results will be less affected by the SOA non-linearities like XPM and XGM.

In Fig. 14 (1) for 3 dBm of the AM laser corresponding to a modulation index of 0.54, are observed besides the amplitude fluctuations, phase changes in the constellation due to the strong saturation and gain dynamics. In (2) and (3) for a modulation index of 0.4 and 0.2 respectively, the crosstalk effects are reduced and the symbols are more concentrated improving the EVM results.

(1)   (2)   (3)

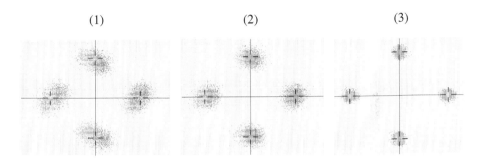

Fig. 14. Constellations of the received UMTS signal: (1)- Mod. index=0.54, (2)- Mod. index=0.4 and (3)- Mod. index=0.2

Table 2 summarizes the obtained results. Two EVM values for each situation were taken: one for the higher power of the RF signal - best transmission conditions, another for the worst condition where transmission was still possible within the standards.

Table 2. Transmission metric EVM values for all setups tested

RF	Single Channel						WDM					
	Direct link		40 km		60 km		Direct link		20 km		40 km	
signal	PRF (dBm)	EVM (%)	PRF (dBm)	EVM (%)	PRF (dBm)	EVM (%)	PRF (dBm)	EVM (%)	PRF (dBm)	EVM (%)	PRF (dBm)	EVM (%)
UMTS	-18	9,6	-12	11	-2	10,9	-15	10	-10	10,4	1	11,5
	5	1,9	5	2,7	5	4,9	5	4,7	5	6,1	5	9,2
WLAN	-10	4,7	-8	5	0	10,5	0	9,4	0	11,4	Not possible	
	0	2,3	0	3,2								
WiMAX	-24	1,26	-15	1,05	-8	1,38	-20	0,93	-15	1,2	-4	1,32
	3	0,026	3	0,063	3	0,19	3	0,15	3	0,29	3	0,52

Analyzing the performance of the RF signals tested in the different setups, the WiMAX was the signal less affected by the nonlinearities providing the transmission within the standard EVM values with the lower RF level. UMTS signals also allowed the transmission over considerable distances but more affected by the nonlinear effects referred producing phase shifts on the received constellations, thus limiting the transmission within the standard. The signal that shown more limited was the WLAN. This fact is related to the modulation used (64-QAM) that, due to the very close constellation used leads to smaller robustness penalizing the EVM and consequently the transmission conditions, not even allowing the transmission with another AM signal.

5 Conclusions

The feasibility of a RoF network, for transporting UMTS, WLAN and WiMAX signals, was experimentally demonstrated. Results demonstrate that the use of a cost effective solution for the optical link, recurring to directly modulated lasers and SOAs, can still provide EVM lower than the standard limits for 60 km on the UMTS and WiMAX cases, and 40 km for the WLAN. It is also shown that a WDM system with SOA, considering a UMTS or WiMAX modulated signal and an AM signal, allows the transmission for 20 km and 40 km. By decreasing the modulation index of the AM laser the results will not be so penalized by the crosstalk effects.

Acknowledgments

The work described in this paper was carried out with the support of the Portuguese FCT project ROFWDM, the NoE ISIS and the BONE-project ("Building the Future Optical Network in Europe"), a Network of Excellence funded by the European Commission through the 7th ICT-Framework Programme.

References

1. Koonen, A., et al.: Perspectives of Radio over Fiber Technologies. In: OFC/NFOEC 2008, San Diego, USA, pp. OThP3
2. Al-Raweshidy, H.: Radio over Fiber Technologies for Mobile Communication Networks

Performance Evaluation of the Cable Bundle Unique Power Back-Off Algorithm

Driton Statovci and Tomas Nordström

Telecommunications Research Center Vienna (ftw.),
Donau-City-Straße 1, A-1220 Vienna, Austria
{statovci,nordstrom}@ftw.at
http://www.ftw.at

Abstract. The latest digital subscriber line (DSL) technology, VDSL2, used for broadband access over twisted-pairs, promises up to 100 Mbit/s for both transmission directions on short loops. Since these systems are designed to operate in a far-end crosstalk (FEXT) limited environment, there is a severe performance degradation when deployed in distributed network scenarios. With power back-off (PBO) the network operators attempt to protect modems deployed on long loops by reducing the transmit power of the short ones. However, currently very little guidance has been given to operators on how to set and optimize the parameters for PBO. In this paper we explore one promising method, the cable bundle unique PBO (CUPBO), which optimizes these parameters according to the actual situation in the cable with regard to noise and network topology. Using real VDSL systems and cables we show that CUPBO algorithm achieves a significant increase in performance compared to the case when one naively takes the PBO values given in the VDSL standard.

Keywords: DSL, VDSL, Power back-off, Optimization, Demonstrator.

1   Introduction

The latest addition to the digital subscriber line (DSL) family is an updated version of very high-speed DSL (VDSL), known as VDSL2 [6]. It can utilize frequencies up to 30 MHz and theoretically deliver up to 100 Mbit/s in both upstream (toward the network) and downstream (toward the customer) directions. Similar to ADSL, VDSL2 is based solely on discrete multi-tone modulation (DMT) and uses frequency division duplex (FDD) in order to avoid near-end crosstalk (NEXT) noise between VDSL systems. However, in contrast to ADSL, VDSL uses the 'Zipper' transmission scheme [4], also known as digital FDD, which allows for greater flexibility in how the frequencies can be divided between the downstream and upstream directions.

VDSL can be deployed from local exchanges/central offices as well as street cabinets. As the bit rate is very much dependent on the line lengths (line attenuations), it is expected that the majority of the VDSL systems will be deployed from cabinets installed in streets or in apartment buildings. In the following we will use the term cabinet to represent the network side.

C. Wang (Ed.): AccessNets, LNICST 6, pp. 365–380, 2009.

A determining factor for the performance of VDSL is crosstalk noise between twisted-pairs in a cable bundle. Since VDSL is using FDD we only need to consider far-end crosstalk (FEXT). Very early in the standardization of VDSL researchers from BT [7] noted that "FEXT is not reciprocal". This means that the FEXT from one line into another might differ significantly compared to the FEXT caused by the latter into the first one. This is particularly pronounced for the so-called near-far problem, as illustrated in Fig. 1, where the modems in the upstream direction that are closer to the cabinet disturb modems located further out in the network.

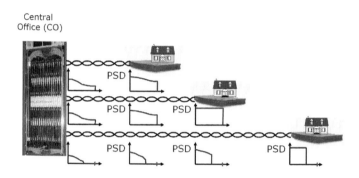

Fig. 1. A distributed DSL scenario which illustrates the near-far problem and a power back-off (PBO) solution in the upstream transmission direction. PSD denotes the power spectral density.

The natural solution to this near-far problem is a reduction of transmit power on the modems closer to the cabinet as shown in Fig. 1, which is known as power back-off (PBO). Many PBO methods were proposed for VDSL, as described by Schelstraete in [3] and the references therein. In the end it was agreed on using the so-called 'reference PBO' method [3]. In this method a desired *received* power spectral density (PSD) is defined as parametrized *reference* PSD for each upstream band. However, the VDSL standard(s) gives little or no guidance to an operator on how to establish 'good' PBO parameters for its particular network and customers. The optimal PBO parameters depend on the topology of the access network, cable characteristics, the mixture of DSL systems, and the type of services (bit rates) that operators want to offer to their customers.

In earlier papers we have identified three *levels* of PBO parameter optimization:

- Regional PBO (RPBO) [2], where the PBO parameters are optimized for a region, e.g. Europe, or a country, e.g. Austria, based on statistical cable models and a predefined set of bit rates;
- Cable bundle unique PBO (CUPBO) [5], where the PBO parameters are optimized for a particular cable bundle; and
- User unique PBO (UUPBO) [1], where the PBO parameters are optimized for each line separately.

For CUPBO and UUPBO the optimization of the PBO parameters depends on the actual situation in a particular cable bundle. We have shown in [1,5] that they give similar performance in comparison to the best schemes proposed for dynamic spectrum management (DSM).

In this paper we will describe our results from implementing CUPBO on real VDSL2 modems connected to a flexible cable plant built for testing distributed network topologies.

The rest of the paper is organized as follows: Section 2 outlines some basic concepts related to standardized PBO for VDSL systems. Section 3 describes the cable bundle unique power back-off (CUPBO) algorithm with the main focus on strategies used to measure (estimate) the parameters required for implementation in practical systems. Then follows a section presenting the developed demonstrator platform used for evaluating the performance of the CUPBO algorithm. In Section 5 we present and evaluate the performance and Section 6 summarizes the major findings of this paper.

2   Standardized Upstream Power Back-Off for VDSL Systems

To solve the near-far problem in DSL access networks many PBO methods have been proposed. For an extensive description of the PBO methods for VDSL systems the reader is referred to [3,8] and the references therein.

The VDSL standards define PBO based on a reference PSD, which is a parametrized function of frequency. Although in principle any shape of PSD could have been selected for the aim of PBO, during the standardization process it has been agreed on using the following reference PSD model:

$$\mathcal{P}_{\mathrm{REF\_dBm}}(f) = -\alpha - \beta\sqrt{f}, \qquad [\mathrm{dBm/Hz}], \qquad (1)$$

where α and β are the PBO parameters to be determined. The frequency f is given in MHz. This shape was selected for ease of implementation and it furthermore simplifies the search for optimal PBO parameters. The VDSL standards allow independent reference PSDs for each upstream band. However, the allowable values of the PBO parameter α range from 40 dBm/Hz to 80.95 dBm/Hz in steps of 0.01 dBm/Hz and of parameter β range from 0 dBm/Hz to 40.95 dBm/Hz in steps of 0.01 dBm/Hz [9]. These ranges have been thought to be sufficient for all potential VDSL2 deployment scenarios.

In addition, modems need also adhere to a maximum allowed transmit PSD, $\mathcal{P}^{\mathrm{max}}$, the so-called PSD mask. Hence, the transmitted PSD of a particular user u in subcarrier n is given by

$$\mathcal{P}_u^n = \min\left\{\frac{\mathcal{P}_{\mathrm{REF}}^n}{\mathcal{H}_{uu}^n}, \mathcal{P}_u^{n,\mathrm{max}}\right\}, \qquad (2)$$

where $\mathcal{H}_{uu}^n$ denotes the squared magnitude of the *direct* channel and $\mathcal{P}_{\mathrm{REF}}^n = \mathcal{P}_{\mathrm{REF}}(f = n\Delta_f)$ with $\Delta_f = 4.3125$ kHz being the subcarrier width. From Eq. (2) we see that $\mathcal{P}_{\mathrm{REF}}$ actually represents the maximum received PSD on any line.

Different optimization strategies have been proposed to determine the optimized values of α and β. The optimization criterion used by Schelstraete in [3] and Statovci *et. al.* in [2] is the minimization of the maximum difference in the loop reach, achieved with collocated modems without PBO and modems using PBO that are distributed in a way to represent the worst-case noise environment. The PBO parameters are usually optimized to protect multiple bit rates (services), which results in not protecting some modems deployed in long loops as illustrated in Fig. 1. Contrarily, the CUPBO algorithm uses the maximization of the minimum bit rate as its optimization criterion [5].

3   Description of the Cable Bundle Unique Power Back-Off Algorithm

One significant feature of the CUPBO algorithm is that it can be implemented in VDSL modems without imposing any changes to the current standards. It finds an optimized set of PBO parameters by taking into account the parameters that characterise the actual network topology, such as line attenuations, noise environment, and FEXT couplings. We denote this set by $\Phi = \{(\alpha_1, \beta_1), \ldots, (\alpha_{SB}, \beta_{SB})\}$, where the subscript SB denotes the number of upstream bands. In the following we describe the methods used to measure the actual noise environment and what we call the *normalized* FEXT couplings. The algorithm also requires the knowledge of the actual line attenuations, but as this is already measured by currently deployed VDSL modems we will not further analyze it here.

3.1   Parameter Estimation for CUPBO

Under the assumption that two-dimensional signal constellations are used, based on Shannon's formula, the bit rate of a particular user u per DMT symbol can be expressed as

$$R_u = \sum_{n \in I} \log_2 \left(1 + \frac{\mathcal{H}_{uu}^n \mathcal{P}_u^n}{\Gamma \mathcal{N}_u^n}\right), \tag{3}$$

where I denotes the set of subcarriers used in the particular transmission direction, in our case upstream; Γ is the gap approximation to Shannon capacity [10]; $\mathcal{P}_u^n$ and $\mathcal{N}_u^n$ are the PSDs of transmitted signal and total noise, respectively, of user u in subcarrier n. All VDSL systems measure the PSD of the total noise; thus, the sum of all noises, since this information is also required for bit-loading. The total noise that is experienced by user u on carrier n consists of background noise, $\mathcal{P}_{u,\text{BGN}}^n$, and FEXT noise, $\mathcal{P}_{u,\text{FEXT}}^n$, originating from the other users sharing the same cable bundle, i.e,

$$\mathcal{N}_u^n = \mathcal{P}_{u,\text{FEXT}}^n + \mathcal{P}_{u,\text{BGN}}^n. \tag{4}$$

Current VDSL systems do not differentiate between various noise sources, but they only consider the total noise. However, we can control the PSD levels of

FEXT noise by controlling the transmit PSDs and, as can be seen in Eq. (3), thereby indirectly also the performance of VDSL systems.

In this paper, we assume that the background noise, $\mathcal{P}^n_{u,\text{BGN}}$, also comprises the alien noise that originates from other non-VDSL modems and the noise from unknown sources, such as impulse noise and radio frequency interference (RFI) for example. The NEXT noise can be neglected, since we are assuming fully synchronized VDSL systems that use the digital FDD transmission scheme.

The FEXT noise of a particular user u is given by

$$\mathcal{P}^n_{u,\text{FEXT}} = \sum_{\substack{v=1 \\ v \neq u}}^{U} \mathcal{H}^n_{uv} \mathcal{P}^n_v, \tag{5}$$

where $\mathcal{H}^n_{uv}$ denotes the squared magnitude of FEXT coupling from user v to user u on subcarrier n.

It is clear that in order to be able to calculate the FEXT noise, the individual FEXT couplings are needed. However, these are not measured by the current VDSL systems. Still, by exploiting some nice properties of standardized PBO it is possible to overcome this problem.

First, we observe that by a suitable selection of $\mathcal{P}_{\text{REF}}$ we can ensure that received PSDs on all lines are the same and equal to the reference PSD. Under this assumption the transmit PSD of user v is given by $\mathcal{P}^n_v = \mathcal{P}^n_{\text{REF}}/\mathcal{H}^n_{vv}$ and the FEXT noise in Eq. (5) can then be written as

$$\mathcal{P}^n_{u,\text{FEXT}} = \sum_{\substack{v=1 \\ v \neq u}}^{U} \frac{\mathcal{H}^n_{uv}}{\mathcal{H}_{vv}} \mathcal{P}^n_{\text{REF}}. \tag{6}$$

By holding $\mathcal{P}_{\text{REF}}$ fixed we can now define the *normalized* FEXT coupling for each user as

$$\mathcal{H}^{n,\text{norm}}_{u,\text{FEXT}} = \sum_{\substack{v=1 \\ v \neq u}}^{U} \frac{\mathcal{H}^n_{uv}}{\mathcal{H}^n_{vv}} = \frac{\mathcal{P}^n_{u,\text{FEXT}}}{\mathcal{P}^n_{\text{REF}}}. \tag{7}$$

Thus, the *normalized* FEXT couplings can easily be estimated by each modem based on a given $\mathcal{P}^n_{\text{REF}}$ and the measured PSDs of the FEXT noise. Rewriting Eq. (4) the FEXT noise can be calculated as

$$\mathcal{P}^n_{u,\text{FEXT}} = \mathcal{N}^n_u - \mathcal{P}^n_{u,\text{BGN}}. \tag{8}$$

After the normalized FEXT couplings are estimated, based on Eq. (6) and (7), the total noise is calculated as

$$\mathcal{N}^n_u = \mathcal{P}^n_{\text{REF}} \mathcal{H}^{n,\text{norm}}_{u,\text{FEXT}} + \mathcal{P}^n_{u,\text{BGN}}. \tag{9}$$

Thus, we take into account the actual FEXT couplings rather than assuming a model for them.

3.2 Optimization Strategies

After experimenting with different optimization strategies for CUPBO algorithm, as described in [5], the maximization of the minimum bit rate (among the modems included in the optimization process) is considered to be the most robust approach. Furthermore, since maximizing the bit rates independently in each band also maximizes their sum, the optimization by CUPBO can independently be done for each transmission band. Thus, the optimization problem for the i-th band can be formulated as

$$\underset{\alpha_i,\beta_i}{\text{maximize}} \left(\min_u \{R_{u,i}\} \right) \tag{10a}$$

subject to:

$$\alpha_{\min} \leq \alpha_i \leq \alpha_{\max} \tag{10b}$$

$$\beta_{\min} \leq \beta_i \leq \beta_{\max}, \tag{10c}$$

where $R_{u,i}$ denotes the bit rate of user u in the i-th upstream band, I_i denotes the set of subcarriers used in that particular band, and $\alpha_{\min}$, $\alpha_{\max}$, $\beta_{\min}$, and $\beta_{\max}$ denote the minimum and maximum values of α and β as specifed in Section 2. Taking the transmit PSD mask constraint into account, the bit rate of a particular user u in the i-th band per DMT symbol during the optimization is approximated by

$$R_{u,i} = \sum_{n \in I_i} \log_2 \left(1 + \frac{\mathcal{H}_{uu}^n \mathcal{P}_u^n}{\Gamma \left(\mathcal{P}_{\text{REF}}^n \mathcal{H}_{u,\text{FEXT}}^{n,\text{norm}} + \mathcal{P}_{u,\text{BGN}}^n \right)} \right), \tag{11}$$

where the transmit PSD, $\mathcal{P}_u^n$, for a give set of PBO parameters is calculated as in Eq. (2).

The above approximation can be interpreted as follows: During the search for the optimal PSD parameters we can not guarantee that $\mathcal{P}_{\text{REF}}$ is not restricted by $\mathcal{P}^{\max}$. If this happens the calculated bit rates will be an underestimate of the real bit rates, since the reference PSD represents the highest possible received PSD and thus the total noise is overestimated. This means that the PBO parameters are optimized towards higher noise levels than the modems in fact are experiencing.

3.3 Optimization Algorithm

The pseudo-code of the CUPBO algorithm, which solves the optimization problem in Eq. (10) is listed as Algorithm 1. The core of the CUPBO is based on the Nelder–Mead simplex search [11], which finds the optimized α and β for each upstream band.

In practice an operator typically wants to offer a predefined minimum bit rate. If this minimum bit rate is not supported, we remove the user with the lowest bit rate and rerun the optimization process. We repeat this step until the minimum predefined bit rate is achieved. Using this procedure, operators will be able to offer a predefined service to the largest number of users possible.

Algorithm 1. Cable bundle unique PBO (CUPBO) algorithm [5]

1: Select suitable $\mathcal{P}_{\mathrm{REF}}$ so that the best estimate of Eq. (7) is achieved
2: Calculate the normalized FEXT couplings for each line using Eq. (7)
3: **for** $i = 1$ *to* SB **do**
4:     $\Phi_i = [\alpha_i, \beta_i]$ {*Starting values*}
5:     **repeat**
6:         $\Phi_i = \mathbf{\mathit{NelderMead}}(@\mathbf{\mathit{RateCalcMin}}, \Phi_i),$
7:     **until** the specified accuracy has been reached
8:     **if** the longest line is not using the current band for transmission **then**
9:         Exclude it from the optimization and go to step 4
10:    **end if**
11: **end for**

12: $\mathbf{\mathit{Function}}\ R^{\mathrm{min}} = \mathbf{\mathit{RateCalcMin}}(\Phi_i)$
13: Calculate $R_{u,i}$ for all lines according to Eq. (11)
14: Calculate $R^{\mathrm{min}} = \min_u \{R_{u,i}\}$

---

4   Description of the Demonstrator Platform

In order to evaluate the performance of our PBO and DSM algorithms in real modems and real cables we have developed a versatile testbed consisting of a VDSL2 DSLAM and modems, four 200 m rolls of 10 pair 0.6 mm cables and a connection board. A photo of the setup is shown in Fig. 2. The cable used is an Austrian 10 pair 'layered' cable based on 5 star-quads and 0.6 mm wires, with model number F-02YHJA2Y. This is the typical cable deployed from cabinets to the customers in Austria. In a distributed scenario like the one considered in this paper the FEXT will vary significantly between different lines. In Fig. 6 and 7 are plotted the actual normalized FEXT couplings as measured by modems during the CUPBO parameter estimation.

With the connection board we can set up many distributed scenarios with modems placed at loop lengths of 200, 400, 600, or 800 m away from the DSLAM. For the experiments described in this paper we connected one modem at 200, one at 400 and one at 600 m, with FEXT coupling lengths of 200 and 400 m.

The VDSL2 systems used for these experiments were provided by Infineon Technologies Austria AG and consist of a line card that acts as a DSLAM and four VDSL2 CPE units. We control the DSLAM using simple object access protocol (SOAP) calls from Matlab running on a separate computer.

4.1   Implementation Details

When implementing CUPBO in real systems there are few practical details worth noting. First, we describe how to select $\mathcal{P}_{\mathrm{REF}}$ and then how to use the total noise measurements to estimate the background noise as well as the normalized FEXT couplings, cf. Eq. (7) and (8).

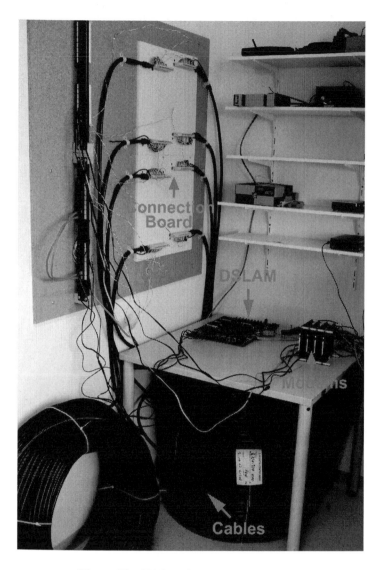

Fig. 2. The VDSL2 demonstrator platform

As mentioned in Section 3, $\mathcal{P}_{REF}$ (independent for each band) should be selected so that the received PSDs on all lines are the same. This selection is crucial for accurate parameter estimation. The suitable $\mathcal{P}_{REF}$ is this that compensates for the highest attenuation on any line while still not violating the maximum transmit PSD mask. At the same time $\mathcal{P}_{REF}$ should be above the PSD of background noise. For short loops both conditions are always satisfied. If we cannot satisfy both criteria, we simply select $\mathcal{P}_{REF}$ to be some dB (e.g. 10 dB) above the PSD of background noise.

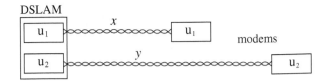

Fig. 3. Network scenario with two users, where x and y denote the loop lengths

The background noise of each user u, $\mathcal{P}^n_{u,\text{BGN}}$, is estimated by initializing the modems in turn; that is, one modem is going into show time while the others are silent. In this case the total noise measured by the modems in fact represents the true background noise. After these steps all modems simultaneously go into the show time with a reference PSD, $\mathcal{P}_{\text{REF}}$, selected as described above. During this phase the measured total noise, $\mathcal{N}^n_u$, is used (after subtraction of the background noise) to estimate the normalized FEXT couplings.

5   Performance Evaluation and Discussions

We will compare the performance of CUPBO against three other configurations: PBO disabled (NoPBO), standardized PBO parameters (StdPBO), and what we call *exhaustive* CUPBO (ExhCUPBO). In the exhaustive CUPBO the optimized PBO parameters are calculated using the modems 'in the loop' during the search. Thus, we use the true bit rates that are achieved by the modems using a particular PBO parameter set in the *Nelder-Mead* simplex search (replacing line 13 in Algorithm 1). It is worth mentioning that exhaustive CUPBO should not be deployed in practical systems, since it is very time consuming and requires a large number of modem restarts for each set of PBO parameters tested. We have implemented it just to prove that our developed strategy for estimating the normalized FEXT couplings and the total noise, cf. Eq. (9), works well in practice.

The performance of the CUPBO algorithm is evaluated in different network scenarios with two and three users. All simulations are performed for the band-plan 998–Annex B–profile 12b (Name 998-M2x-NUS0, Table B-6, [6]), which has two upstream bands. We have selected the standardized PBO parameters for Noise F as defined in the ETSI VDSL standard [12], since they show the best performance in our demonstration platform among all standardized PBO parameters.

5.1   Performance Evaluation for the Two-User Case

The network scenario for the two-user case is shown in Fig. 3. We have evaluated the performance under the following configurations. Scenario A: loop lengths of 200 and 400 m; Scenario B: loop lengths of 400 and 600 m; and Scenario C: loop lengths of 200 and 600 m. The twisted-pairs for the three loops were selected randomly out of the ten twisted-pairs in each section of our cable. The attenuations

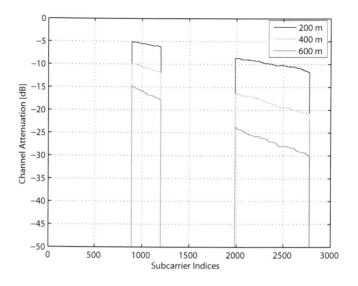

Fig. 4. Channel attenuations for loop lengths of 200, 400, and 600 m

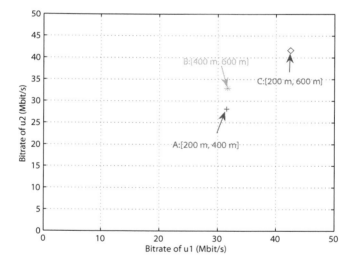

Fig. 5. Bit rates supported by the CUPBO algorithm for three network scenarios with two users shown in Fig. 3. Scenario A: loop lengths of 200 and 400 m; Scenario B: loop lengths of 400 and 600 m; and Scenario C: loop lengths of 200 and 600 m

of these loops as they have been measured by the modems, i.e., including also the attenuation on the analog front-end, are plotted in Fig. 4.

Fig. 5 shows the bit rates supported by the CUPBO algorithm for all three network scenarios. Some results can be considered surprising and counter-intuitive. We are for instance achieving lower bit rates in Scenario A that has shorter

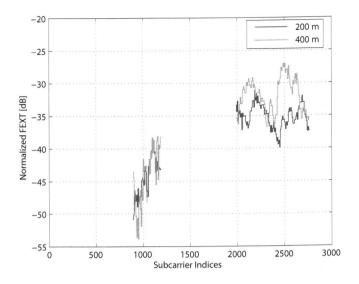

Fig. 6. Normalized FEXT couplings for network Scenario A: Loop lengths of 200 and 400 m

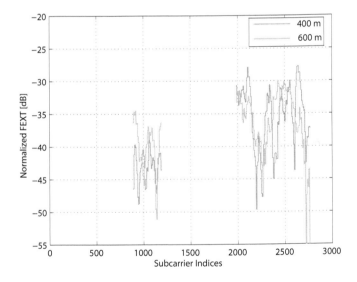

Fig. 7. Normalized FEXT couplings for network Scenario B: Loop lengths of 400 and 600 m

loop lengths (lower attenuations) than in Scenario B and C that have longer loop lengths (higher attenuations). However, based on Eq. (11), we can conclude that the bit rates of users not only depend on the levels of channel attenuations, but also on the levels of normalized FEXT couplings and the PSD levels of background noise.

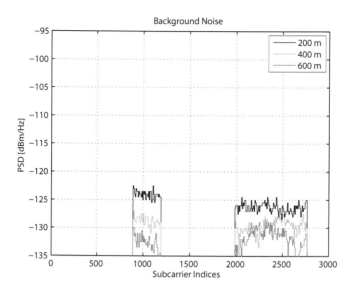

Fig. 8. PSDs of background noise for lines of 200, 400 and 600 m

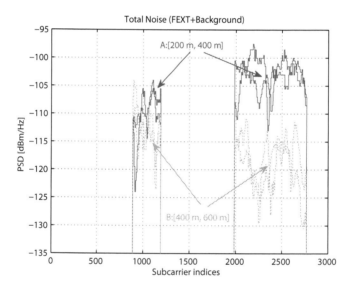

Fig. 9. PSDs of total noise for Scenario A and B after PBO parameter optimization

Fig. 6 and 7 show the normalized FEXT couplings for two out of the three network configurations which, as expected, are different between various lines. Fig. 8 shows the PSDs of background noise for three lines, which surprisingly are *very* different from each other (up to 11.5 dB difference). We can see in the plots in Fig. 6 and 7 that the lines in Scenario A have higher averaged

Table 1. Users' supported bit rates for Scenarios A, B, and C as well as for PBO disabled (NoPBO), standardized PBO (StdPBO), exhaustive CUPBO (ExhCUPBO), and CUPBO

	Users' bit rates in Mbit/s			
	NoPBO	StdPBO	ExhCUPBO	CUPBO
User	Scenario A			
u_1	36.1	19.2	30.7	31.2
u_2	23.1	22.6	28.6	27.8
User	Scenario B			
u_2	41.1	16.0	32.0	31.7
u_3	24.0	22.2	31.9	32.7
User	Scenario C			
u_1	53.9	21.2	42.9	42.7
u_3	27.5	24.2	41.6	41.4

Table 2. CUPBO performance comparison versus NoPBO, StdPBO, and ExhCUPBO

	Bit rate gain/loss(-) in %		
Scenario	NoPBO	StdPBO	ExhCUPBO
A	20.1	45.0	−3.00
B	32.0	98.5	−0.56
C	50.2	95.0	−0.52

normalized FEXT couplings than the lines in Scenario B. Furthermore, PSD-levels of background noise for Scenario A are higher than for Scenario B as can be seen in Fig. 8, which also results in high levels of total noise for Scenario A as shown in the plots in Fig. 9. This also explains why for Scenario A we achieve the worst performance in terms of supported bit rates. With similar analysis we can also justify the bit rates achieved for the other network scenarios.

Table 1 summarizes the achieved bit rates for three network scenarios and various schemes. Table 4, in the appendix, summarizes the PBO parameters as calculated by the CUPBO and ExhCUPBO for the bit rates shown in Table 1. In Table 2 we compare the performance of CUPBO versus NoPBO, StdPBO, and ExhCUPBO. Since we have selected the maximization of minimum bit rate as the optimization criterion, we have also performed the comparisons for the minimum bit rates supported by the modems. The performance improvements of CUPBO compared to NoPBO and StdPBO are in the range from 20% to 98.5%, which are similar to those achieved by simulations in [5]. We see larger improvements over StdPBO than over NoPBO. This is due to the fact that standardized PBO parameters are optimized for a reach of above one kilometer (above three kilofeet) and for twenty VDSL systems, which both are not encountered in our selected network configurations. CUPBO suffers only a loss of 0.5% to 3% compared to ExhCUPBO.

5.2   Performance Evaluation for the Three-User Case

We have also evaluated the performance for a network scenario with three users
with the loop lengths of 200 , 400 , and 600 m, which actually are the same loops
used in the network scenario with two uses. Table 3 summarizes the achieved
bit rates and compare the performance of CUPBO versus NoPBO, StdPBO,
and ExhCUPBO. Table 4, in the appendix, summarizes the PBO parameters as
calculated by the CUPBO and ExhCUPBO for the bit rates shown in Table 3.

CUPBO achieves performance improvements of 28.4% and 36.3% compared
to NoPBO and StdPBO, respectively, which are again similar to those achieved
by simulations in [5]. Furthermore, for this network scenario CUBPO suffers
a loss with respect to the minimum bit rate of less than 0.1% compared to
ExhCUPBO.

Table 3. CUPBO performance comparison versus PBO disabled (NoPBO), standardized PBO (StdPBO), and exhaustive CUPBO (ExhCUPBO)

User	Users' bit rates in Mbit/s			
	NoPBO	StdPBO	ExhCUPBO	CUPBO
u_1	35.7	18.8	25.7	25.7
u_2	22.8	20.5	29.7	29.9
u_3	20.0	22.0	27.9	26.3
Minimum bit rate	20.0	18.8	25.7	25.7
CUBPO gain in %	28.4	36.3	< -0.1	-

5.3   Further Discussions

It should be noted that the methodology and the CUPBO concept in general can
equally well be deployed in the downstream direction. Downstream power back-
off is only necessary when operators mix deployment of VDSL systems from
the local exchange and cabinet in the same cable bundle. This leads to large
performance degradations on all lines; therefore, operators should avoid such
deployments. Due to this we do not expect that downstream power back-off will
in practice be an important issue.

6   Conclusions

In this paper we have evaluated the performance of the cable bundle unique
power back-off (CUPBO) algorithm on real VDSL2 modems and real cables.
The test setup has been connected in four different distributed network scenarios with modems placed at 200, 400, and 600 m. We have found that the CUPBO
algorithm achieves significant improvements in terms of upstream bit rates over
the case when no power back-off (PBO) is used. Compared to the PBO parameters as specified in VDSL standards we have seen even larger performance

improvements. This reduction in performance when using the PBO parameters as suggested by standards stems from the fact that they are very conservative and actually optimized for situations when modems are deployed at much longer loop lengths than encounter in our network configurations. Therefore, we expect that telecom operators will significantly improve the performance of their VDSL systems (i.e., potentially double the upstream bit rates) by using CUPBO.

Acknowledgments

We would like to thank Erwin Wittowetz (Telecommunications Research Center Vienna) for building the demonstration platform and carrying out cable measurements. We furthermore want to thank Infineon Technologies Austria AG for providing the VDSL2 systems and actively supporting us in this work.

This work has been supported in parts by the Austrian Government and the City of Vienna within the competence center program COMET.

References

1. Statovci, D., Nordström, T., Nilsson, R.: Dynamic Spectrum Management for Standardized VDSL. In: IEEE International Conference on Acoustics, Speech and Signal Processing, ICASSP 2007, vol. III, pp. 73–76. IEEE Press, New York (2007)
2. Statovci, D., Nordström, T., Nilsson, R., Oksman, V.: Revised Upstream Power Back-Off for VDSL. In: IEEE International Conference on Acoustics, Speech and Signal Processing, ICASSP 2006, vol. IV, pp. 633–636. IEEE Press, New York (2007)
3. Schelstraete, S.: Defining upstream power backoff for VDSL. IEEE Journal on Selected Areas in Communications, 1064–1074 (2002)
4. Sjöberg, F., Isaksson, M., Nilsson, R., Ödling, P., Wilson, S.K., Börjesson, P.O.: Zipper: a duplex method for VDSL based on DMT. IEEE Transactions on Communications, 1245–1252 (1999)
5. Jakovlević, M., Statovci, D., Nordström, T., Nilsson, R., Zazo, S.: VDSL Power Back-Off parameter Optimization for a Cable Bundle. In: European Signal Processing Conference, EUSIPCO 2007, pp. 350–354 (2007)
6. ITU-T: VDSL2 Very high speed Digital Subscriber Line Trancievers 2. In: ITU-Standard G.993.2 (February 2006)
7. Kirkby, R.: FEXT is not reciprocal. In: ANSI Standardization Contribution, T1E1.4 95-141 (November 1995)
8. Oksman, V.: Optimization of the PSD REF for upstream power back-off in VDSL. In; ANSI Standardization Contribution, T1E1.4 2001-102R1 (February 2001)
9. ITU-T: Physical layer management for digital subscriber line (DSL). In: ITU-T Recommendation G.997.1 (May 2003)
10. Starr, T., Cioffi, J.M., Silverman, P.: Understanding Digital Subscriber Line Technology. Prentice-Hall, Upper Saddle River (1999)
11. Nelder, J.A., Mead, R.: A simplex method for function minimization. Computer Journal 7, 308–313 (1965)
12. ETSI, Transmission and Multiplexing (TM); Access transmission systems on metallic access cables; Very high speed Digital Subscriber Line (VDSL); Part 1: Functional requirements: ETSI, Tech. Rep. TM6 TS 101 270-1, Version 1.3.1 (July 2003)

Appendix

In this appendix we summarize optimized PBO parameters as calculated by the CUPBO and exhaustive CUPBO (ExhCUPBO) for network configurations with two and three users for the bit rates shown in Table 1 and Table 3, respectively.

Table 4. Optimized PBO parameters for the two-user case (Scenarios A, B, and C) as well as the three-user case for CUPBO and ExhCUPBO

Set of PBO parameters in dBm/Hz (c.f. Sections 2 and 3)	
CUPBO	ExhCUPBO
$\{(\alpha_1, \beta_1), (\alpha_2, \beta_2)\}$	$\{(\alpha_1, \beta_1), (\alpha_2, \beta_2)\}$
Scenario A (two-user case)	
$\{(40.00, 11.41), (69.57, 0.39)\}$	$\{(55.20, 5.35), (52.95.5.43)\}$
Scenario B	
$\{(45.48, 12.42), (70.50, 4.16)\}$	$\{(46.15, 12.60), (57.88, 8.56)\}$
Scenario C	
$\{(50.83, 9.45), (40.00, 12.39)\}$	$\{(52.41, 7.36), (40.00, 12.24)\}$
Three-user case	
$\{(45.80, 12.73), (76.85, 0.04)\}$	$\{(45.30, 12.84), (62.84, 4.66)\}$

Estimating Video Quality over ADSL2+
under Impulsive Line Disturbance

Glauco Gonçalves[1], Ramide Dantas[1], André Palhares[1], Judith Kelner[1],
Joseane Fidalgo[1], Djamel Sadok[1], Henrik Almeida[2], Miguel Berg[2],
and Daniel Cederholm[2]

[1] Universidade Federal de Pernambuco, Brazil
{glauco,ramide,andre.vitor,jk,joseane,jamel}@gprt.ufpe.br
[2] Ericsson Research, Sweden
{henrik.almeida,miguel.berg,daniel.cederhom}@ericsson.com

Abstract. QoS Provisioning for 3P over xDSL remains a challenging task due
to the effects of line impairments on such services. Differently from simple
data, video and voice services have strict requirements for loss and delay
tolerance. The accurate assessment of final service quality is part of this
provisioning process, but its direct measurement is yet not practical. In this
paper we explore the possibility of estimating service quality, with focus on
video delivery, by investigating its relationship with performance data available
to xDSL operators and deriving models for estimating quality from this data.
Experiments using a real xDSL platform and different noise types were
conducted. The derived models showed to be accurate enough to estimate video
quality for the scenarios evaluated.

Keywords: Video, QoE, ADSL, performance estimation, noise.

1 Introduction

The provision of triple play (voice, video and data) services over ADSL/2/2+
technology for residential and business customers remains a challenging task when
considering quality assurance. Parasitic effects on the physical layer (L1) of the
access network like non-transient and transient noise, up to now negligible for the
pure best-effort Internet service, are starting to play a damaging role when it comes to
the transport of real-time video content. To meet the quality requirements for the
transportation of these new applications over the network, an end-to-end, real time
quality monitoring architecture must be part of the access infrastructure. Nonetheless,
such architecture remains a long solution ahead for research to pursue.

Existing research into triple play delivery often assumes simple models for packet
loss and delay using well-known statistical distributions. The reality faced on the field
is much more complex than this simplified view. The end-loop is subject to different
types of noise effects and physical impairments that have shown to be hard to capture
and model [12]. In this paper we take a different path for estimating the Quality of
Experience (QoE) in that we study practical scenarios submitted to varying noise

C. Wang (Ed.): AccessNets, LNICST 6, pp. 381–396, 2009.

levels. We show special concern with impulse noise, seen as one of the most harmful noise types, in order to discover and model its impact on video delivery.

Service providers often do not have online access to user feedback nor can they perform deep packet inspection or similar traffic analysis to assess users' QoE. Given the limited applicability of such methods, we opted for a different approach. We investigated how line data provided by DSL equipments is correlated to video streaming quality, thus making it possible to build useful models for video QoE estimation. Operators can embed such models into tools that proactively monitor and adapt line settings for changing scenarios. By doing this, operators can preserve service quality and fulfill customer expectations.

QoE may be seen as a cross cutting concern, depending on physical, network and application layer performance, and therefore we consider metrics on all these layers in our investigation. At the application level, the focus was on the Peak Signal-to-Noise Ratio (PSNR) metric, a well-deployed metric to measure video quality in an objective way [1], [2]. Note that the authors do not claim that this is the most important metric nor that it tells the whole story on its own. At the network level we measured packet loss ratio, which is known to affect video quality strongly [6]. At the physical layer we have collected DSL metrics [10] such as the number of damaged blocks received at a user's modem, line bit rate, actual INP (Impulse Noise Protection), and actual SNR (Signal-to-Noise Ratio) margin, among others. By finding the correlation between those metrics we were able to find models for estimating application and network metrics from physical ones, bridging the gap between these otherwise disjoint figures.

In order to investigate ADSL and video metrics' correlation, a series of experiments were carried out using diverse line settings and environment conditions, such as loop lengths and noise patterns. The data obtained from these experiments was used to feed statistical and mathematical tools to calculate the dependence among metrics and derive models for high-level metric estimation. The models obtained were checked against validation data to verify their accuracy.

The experiments were performed using a test-bed deployment of a commercial ADSL/2/2+ platform and performance data was obtained from actual measurements on this platform. We focused on evaluating SDTV-quality (Standard Television), MPEG-2 video streaming over ADSL2+. An impulsive noise pattern was injected in the ADSL line during video streaming and performance data was collected at both sides of transmission and from DSL equipments.

The rest of this paper is organized as follows. Section 2 describes the experiments setup, including the noise generator we used to inject impulsive noise in the experiments. Section 3 analyses the results obtained from these experiments. The regression models for video quality estimation as well as the methodology used to derive them are presented in Section 4. Section 5 presents some related work and Section 6 draws final remarks and topics for future works.

2 Experiment Configuration

A series of measurements were made in order to acquire performance data of video over ADSL2+. Such experiments were performed using a controlled ADSL2+

network, comprised of equipments such as a DSLAM and a CPE modem, equipments for line emulation and noise generation as well as for video streaming and capture. The experiment procedure is detailed in section 2.1, section 2.2 presents the model used for noise generation, and section 2.3 shows the configuration parameters used.

2.1 Testbed and Experiment Procedure

The ADSL testbed used for the measurements is outlined in Fig. 1. For streaming video content, two Linux boxes were used at the extremes of the DSL line. One behaved as a multimedia client, which receives the video transmitted by the multimedia server. The client is connected to the DSL line through an external DSL modem while the multimedia server is connected to the DSLAM. The VideoLAN Client (VLC) [5] media software was used to stream the video content from server to client sides using UDP as the underlying transport protocol.

The line emulator equipment provided the physical media between the customer premises (CP side) and the central office (CO side), where the DSLAM is placed. An arbitrary wavelength generator (AWG) and a noise injection unit were used in conjunction with the line emulator, allowing various line environments to be tested. While the line emulator provided a wide range of loop length possibilities, the AWG was used to generate different noise patterns into the line.

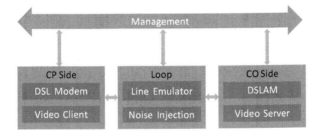

Fig. 1. Test bed scheme

The experiment procedure involves four main steps: 1) configure experiment parameters; 2) activate DSL line and wait for modems synchronization; 3) stream the video from the CO to the CPE side (downstream); and 4) collect the interest metrics at endpoints and DSL equipments. Noise was injected at the CPE side before line synchronization. Therefore, actual line settings could not match exactly configured parameters since the modems try to achieve a better protection level given the line conditions. Injecting noise before synchronization has the advantage of providing more stable experiments when compared to post-synchronization noise injection.

ADSL-related metrics were collected directly from the DSLAM via SNMP. The main metrics collected are presented in Table 1. (more details on these metrics can be found in [10]). Note that these metrics are related to the downstream DSL channel, since the video traffic flows only from the CO side to the CP side. We extracted network-related metrics as packet loss, delay, and jitter from video traffic traces captured at each side of the ADSL line. Moreover, PSNR was calculated afterwards

Table 1. Metrics Collected for Layers 1 and 2

Metric	Description
CRC	Uncorrected FEC Blocks received at CPE
FEC	Corrected FEC Blocks received at CPE
ES	Errored Seconds
SES	Severely Errored Seconds
UAS	Unavailable Seconds
Rate	Synchronized Line Rate
ID_{act}	Actual Channel Interleave Delay
INP_{act}	Actual Impulse Noise Protection
SNR_{act}	Actual SNR margin

using the original encoded video and the transmitted video in order to measure the quality of the video received by the client.

MPEG-2 video streams were used in the experiments. Streams were encoded at bit rate of 4Mbps and 30 frames per second, with image size of 704x480. This choice was made with the goal of characterizing SDTV (Standard Definition Television) video transmission. Two video streams were used: one with 15 seconds of duration and another with about 1 minute. The first video was used to create the regression models and is referred to as "tennis video". The second one was used for validation purpose and is referred to as "bridge video".

2.2 Noise Modeling and Generation

Several types of noises can affect DSL systems, being the Repetitive Electrical Impulse Noise (REIN) one of the most severe of them [12]. REIN is commonly found on the CP side, being its main sources badly shielded household appliances, illumination devices and switching power supplies used in PCs [15]. REIN was chosen for this evaluation given both its severity and common occurrence in DSL installations. REIN is also simpler to model and generate given its more predicable nature compared to random Impulsive Noise. In our study, we generated REIN using an arbitrary wavelength generator based in the model summarized below. We describe the modeling parameters that were used in the experiments in order to shed some light on the physical effect of each model parameter.

A REIN signal $x(t)$ is described as a periodic sequence of bursts as shown in Fig. 2.. The bursts' temporal spacing is denoted by T and defines the periodicity of the noise signal. A burst $x_B(t)$ itself consists of a sequence of N_B base signals $x_S(t)$ with duration T_R. The duration of a burst is denoted by T_B and is clearly given by $T_B=N_BT_R$. The base signal is a sized version of a normalized peak-peak noise shape function $g(t)$ with support $-T_R/2$ to $+T_R/2$. The REIN signal is offset in time by T_0.

The noise shape function $g(t)$ is defined in the time-interval $|t|\leq T_R/2$ with peak-peak value normalized to 1. It can take different forms depending on the desired frequency content. For our experiment we used the sync function ($sin(t)/t$).

When dealing with REIN generation, we focus on these four parameters: 1) the periodicity of the bursts, controlled by the parameter $f = 1/T$; 2) the number of base signals per bursts N_B; 3) the periodicity of the base signal inside a burst, which is

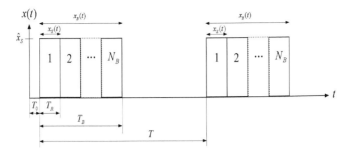

Fig. 2. REIN Signal Composition

controlled by $f_R = 1/T_R$; and 4) the power of the burst, which is given in dBm for 50 Ohms impedance.

2.3 Configuration Parameters

The main problem to deal with real experimentation is the great number of parameters that must be carefully configured to guarantee interesting results. Moreover, parameters configuration has a tradeoff between representative scenarios and viability of experiments in terms of execution time. Considering this tradeoff we varied noise profiles, line protection settings, and loop lengths. The ones we have fixed were noise power level and DSL parameters like maximum interleave delay. Such choice allowed the verification of the video quality under different environment impairments and the effectiveness of the protection mechanisms commonly used by operators.

Table 2. Noise profiles configurations

Profile	Burst Freq. (Hz)	Burst Length (Pulses)	Burst Length (us)	Comments
0Z	-	-	-	No noise
3X	100	25	100	Aggressive
3Y	100	250	1000	Very aggressive

Using the REIN model described in previous section, we can characterize noise by its burst frequency and the number of spikes in each burst (or burst length). Combining these parameters we defined three noise profiles used in the experiments, shown in Table 2. The 0Z profile indicates an environment without noise that is used for reference, while 3X and 3Y indicate aggressive noise profiles. While the former affects one DMT (Discrete Multi-Tone) symbol certainly and can affect up to two consecutive DMT symbols, the latter corrupts four consecutive DMT symbols completely and can affect partially up to 2 additional symbols. Noise power levels of 3X and 3Y profiles were fixed to –24.71 dBm (13 mV), which is compatible with the power range of the impulse noise model presented in [12]. This level determines the amplitude of individual peaks inside each noise burst and does not represent the noise average power, since it depends on burst length and its frequency.

Line protection settings, comprising here Impulse Noise Protection (INP) and SNR margin (SNR_{mar}), were also varied. Values for those parameters are not directly set but provided in terms of a minimum for the INP (INP_{min}) and a target value for the margin ($SNR_{mar,tar}$)[1]. The modems try to configure the line during synchronization so that those constraints are respected. After line synchronization, the line presents actual INP (INP_{act}) and margin ($SNR_{mar,act}$) values which may differ from the configured ones (INP_{min} and $SNR_{mar,tar}$).

SNR margin and INP deal with noise in different ways. Higher SNR margin values prevent the transmitted signal of being corrupted. If such protection is not effective, corrupted data can be recovered using redundancy data sent along with user data. The effectiveness of redundancy can be further improved if various data frames are interleaved, hence spreading the effects of noise bursts across data frames and allowing for better correction. Redundancy and interleaving features are controlled via the INP_{min} parameter. Formula (1) below gives the theoretical definition of INP for a DMT symbol of L bits, FEC (Forward Error Correction) frames of N bytes, being R bytes of redundancy, and D the frame interleave depth [11].

$$INP = D \times \frac{R}{2} \times \frac{1}{L/8} \qquad (1)$$

The SNR margin provides protection against the noise by trying to ensure a signal-to-noise ratio that keeps the BER (bit error rate) below 10^{-7}, what can ultimately decrease the achieved rate. The SNR margin values used in the experiment were 6 dB (a typical value), 12 dB and 18 dB. The values used for INP_{min} were 0, 2 and 4 DMT symbols, which were found to be more applicable in practice. Table 3. Summarizes the experiment parameters.

Table 3. Experiments parameters and values

Parameter	Values
Target SNR margin (dB)	6, 12, 18
Minimum INP (DMT symbols)	0, 2, 4
Noise Profiles	0Z, 3X, 3Y
Loop lengths (m)	1000, 2000, 3000

Each experiment was repeated 10 times providing then 10 samples for each combination of parameters evaluated. This number of samples was determined by previous experiments and provided a good trade-off between statistical quality of the measurements and the time demanded to perform them.

3 Experiment Results Analysis

The graph in Fig. 3 shows the average percentage of lost packets for each experiment configuration. The x-axis presents the combinations of values for noise profile, INP_{min}

---

[1] Minimum ($SNR_{mar,min}$) and maximum ($SNR_{mar,max}$) values for the margin need also to be provided. For all experiments, $SNR_{mar,min} = 0.9* SNR_{mar,tar}$ and $SNR_{mar,max} = 1.1 * SNR_{mar,tar}$.

and $SNR_{mar,tar}$ used in each experiment (10 replications per configuration were made; average loss for each replication is plotted). Each loop length value is represented with a different mark. As expected, in general, more packet loss occurred for low protection scenarios, especially for $INP_{min} = 0$ and $SNR_{mar,tar} = 6$ dB. Loss reached 80% under the most aggressive noise (3Y) and the longer loop (3000m).

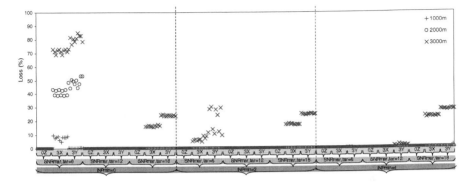

Fig. 3. Packet loss ratio for diverse line and noise configurations grouped by loop length. Each sample represents the average loss ratio over each experiment round.

With higher protection, that is, $INP_{min} = 2$ or 4, no losses were detected for loops of 1000 m and 2000 m. But, for such INP settings, losses between 20% and 30% were found with the 3000 m loop, mostly caused by lack of bit rate, except for the singular case of $INP_{min} = 2$ and $SNR_{mar,tar} = 6dB$ where losses are caused by noise. This lack of bit rate occurs when noise is present during line synchronization and the higher actual INP pushed the line rate lower than the video streaming needs. Higher $SNR_{mar,tar}$ (18 dB) also contributed to decrease the rate and cause more losses. The available bit rate under $SNR_{mar,tar} = 18$ with noise profile 3Y for different loops and INP_{min} values is shown in Table 4. Notice that under these conditions the DSL line rate is below video rate needs for the 3000 m loop, resulting in ordinary packet loss.

The best scenario regarding packet loss was the one with SNR_{margin} set to 12 dB for any INP setting. This configuration provided almost no losses, with the exception of the 3000m loop, 3Y noise, $INP_{min}=4$ case, where losses were lower than 5% and were caused by lack of bit rate.

With respect to the PSNR, the results were mostly influenced by packet loss, with lower PSNR values occurring when losses were detected. The 3000m loop was more affected since it suffered higher loss ratios. An important aspect of PSNR is that little

Table 4. Average line rate in Mbps for diverve INP_{min} and $SNR_{mar,tar} = 18$ dB (3Y noise profile)

INP_{min}	Loop length		
	1000 m	2000 m	3000 m
0	17.57	9.10	3.62
2	15.27	8.75	3.57
4	12.19	7.96	3.46

losses were enough to cause major damage to video quality. Values near 15 dB of PSNR were observed when packet loss exceeded only 3% on noisy and low bit rate scenarios, indicating very low video quality. For lower losses, the PSNR was near or above 30 dB, which means good or very good video. These results were decisive to our modeling as explained in the next sections.

Measurements of delay and jitter had been taken but are not shown in this paper, since their impact on video quality was negligible. However, it must be noticed that this is valid only for the evaluated scenarios. Our experiments used CBR video traffic and no background traffic. Bursty background traffic as Web applications or variable bit rate videos can cause peaks of congestion at the DSL line and would affect the video quality sensibly. Quality models considering delay and delay variation will be approached in future works.

3.1 Metric Correlation

In this section the Pearson's correlation between the most relevant metrics investigated is presented and analyzed. The correlation table with these metrics is shown in Table 5. This table is based on the tennis video data from all the different loops. Some values are highlighted for fast lookup during the explanations.

Initially the correlation coefficient was computed for all data without any data segmentation as presented in the last column of Table 5. The obtained coefficients showed low correlation between metrics, most of them very below 0.9. To improve these results, the data was divided using our previous knowledge on the behavior of video transmission over a noisy ADSL line, as will be explained in Section 4. Right now, it is important to show that with the data segmentation the correlation coefficient increased significantly. For example, the CRC metric that would be the main metric for packet loss correlation showed low correlation considering all data. This occurs because in noisy scenarios with low protection the management data flowing upstream containing the CRC value is corrupted by the noise while querying the DSLAM modem[2]. The segmentation increased CRC correlation for high protection scenarios. Moreover, segmentation increased the correlation coefficient for metrics that compute errored seconds such as ES, SES and UAS.

Table 6 presents the correlation between PSNR and some physical metrics and network metrics. As expected, correlation between packet loss and PSNR is high and inverse. On the one hand, with high losses during transmission, the quality of a video will be affected negatively and the PSNR decrease. On the other hand, transmissions with no loss will result in high PSNR values. Additionally, the correlation between PSNR and packet loss was more significant than the other correlations tested.

An approach for PSNR estimation would be by creating a model directly between PSNR and low-level metrics. However, we opted to estimate packet loss and then use this estimation to obtain a qualitative PSNR model. The main factor behind this choice was our previous knowledge of the behavior of the loss relatively to lower level metrics. Also, it is known that there is a non-linear relation between packet loss and PSNR [6], a result that was in fact verified in our experiments.

---

[2] In these cases, the CRC value retrieved is zero.

Table 5. Correlation coefficients for packet loss ratio and physical metrics for all data and divided in each category

Metric	Packet Loss			All
	Rate < 5 Mbps	Rate ≥ 5 Mbps		
		$INP_{act}<2$	$INP_{act}\geq2$	
CRC	-*	0.330	**0.959**	0.322
Rate	**-0.998**	-0.308	-0.196	-0.254
INP_{act}	-0.186	0.326	-0.173	-0.171
ES	-	0.662	0.795	0.562
SES	-	0.849	0.856	0.671
CRC^2	-	0.328	**0.993**	0.335
$ES*INP_{act}$	-	**0.948**	0.688	0.367
$SES*INP_{act}$	-	**0.978**	0.837	0.457

*The correlation could not be calculated since metrics presented no variation (metrics equal zero in these cases).

Table 6. Correlation coefficients for PSNR and physical metrics for all data

Metric	PSNR
CRC	-0.4289
Rate	0.2997
INP_{act}	0.1177
ES	-0.6696
SES	-0.6356
CRC2	-0.3572
$ES*INP_{act}$	-0.5053
$SES*INP_{act}$	-0.4913
Loss %	-0.7381

4 Video Performance Estimation Models

4.1 Modeling Methodology

Our strategy was to keep models as simple as possible while achieving acceptable accuracy, i.e. coefficient of determination equal or above 0.9. By simple models we mean models relying on only a few variables (or combinations of them). The generated models through the application of regression techniques on all available data presented low coefficients of determination, showing that such simplistic approach should be avoided. Then, we decided to segment data and group variables considering our previous knowledge on DSL and video performance.

The entire data set was separated based on one or more variables to which were applied thresholds, as will be detailed further ahead. With the segmented data, the accuracy of the models increased significantly. For example, data was segmented based on the DSL line rate to separate scenarios where the loss was caused by lack of bit rate of those caused exclusively by noise.

Some predictor variables with similar effects on the response variables were grouped in categories based on this similarity on their semantics. For example, ES, UAS and SES, which all stand for errored seconds were placed together in the same group. It was selected the variable with the greater correlation value in that group, in other words, the one with strongest influence in the response. Some of the variables were combined (by multiplying them) following insights obtained looking at results behavior.

With data segmented and the input variables selected, the next step was to generate the models. At first, models were derived using the multiple linear regression technique and, when a non-linear relation was clearly visible on scatter plots, polynomial regression method was employed. Coefficients whose confidence intervals made them crosscut zero were discarded to simplify the models.

Finally, we validated the models by evaluating the model obtained from the tennis video data with data acquired from the validation video (bridge). At a first moment, the models for each data segment were validated separately. That was reasonable because, when a particular model does not show a representative behavior, it could be fixed separately. In a second moment, we joined all the models estimates and compared them directly with all the validation data. Thus, we could see that the general model is satisfactory.

4.2 Estimating Packet Loss

To build a suitable packet loss model, data was segmented in three categories according to the packet loss behavior. In each category we discovered interesting correlations between the loss and specific metrics or metric combinations. Table 5 shows the most relevant correlations which were used to generate the models for each scenario.

In a first analysis of the data, it was noticed that the data could be divided using the DSL synchronized line rate, since when the line rate is below the needed video bit rate packet loss will occur due to lack of bit rate. Since the tested video bit rate was 4 Mbps, the data was divided into two initial categories at the rate of 5 Mbps. This value was chosen considering header overhead and giving some bit rate for other traffic types in the channel including possible background traffic.

When the rate is lower than 5 Mbps, we observed that the packet loss was strongly correlated with the rate (as highlighted in Table 5.). We generated a linear model using the rate as the explanatory variable. The model obtained is numerically given by the formula (2), where *loss* is the packet loss ratio (ranging between 0 and 1) and *rate* is given in Mbps.

$$loss = -0.2 \times rate + 0.97 \tag{2}$$

When rate is greater than 5 Mbps we observed that the CRC metric presents high correlation when the actual INP (INP_{act}) is greater than or equal to 2, since in this situation line is protected and thus the chance of error in the measured CRC is small. For the other case, when actual INP is less than 2, the SES and ES metrics presented high correlation values. When the INP_{act} is greater than 2, the model obtained is given by:

$$loss = 0.003 \times crc^2 \tag{3}$$

In formula (3), crc is given in thousands of CRC events, which represents the number of corrupted blocks computed at the client side. Please note the non-linear (quadratic) correlation between CRC and packet loss. This model was obtained using polynomial regression with degree 2. As the lower degree coefficients were insignificant, they were removed from the final model.

When INP_{act} is less than 2, we generated a model based on SES, ES, and the actual INP. We observed the following relation:

$$loss \propto (\alpha SES + \beta ES) \times (1 + \gamma INP_{act}) \tag{4}$$

Coefficients α and β in formula (4) are weights of each parameter in the weighted sum between SES and ES. The multiplication by INP_{act} indicates that the damage observed by SES and ES metrics are associated with protection employed, where higher INP values indicate more data loss. One is added to INP_{act} to avoid the relation becoming null when INP is zero. The model obtained for this category is given by:

$$loss = a \times SES + b \times ES + c \times SES \times INP_{act} + d \times ES \times INP_{act} \tag{5}$$

Where $a = 8.1 \times 10^{-4}$; $b = 5.9 \times 10^{-5}$; $c = 9.7 \times 10^{-3}$; $d = -4.8 \times 10^{-3}$.

The weights associated to SES and ES reflect the fact that SES events represent a more harmful condition then ES events, i.e. more packet losses occurred when SES is observed since more CRC events are necessary to trigger a single SES event. Multiplying SES and ES by the actual INP means that, since errors occur (i.e. the protection employed was not effective), higher INP values indicate higher losses. One possible explanation is the fact that higher INP implies deeper interleaving, and since the protection was not able to prevent data corruption, the error tends to be spread across more disperse FEC frames, affecting more packets and leading to a reverse effect than the one expected from the usage of INP.

After generating the models, we evaluated and validated them. Table 7 shows the coefficient of determination obtained for each category in both scenarios: modeling and validation. The table also presents the coefficient of determination for the general model.

The general model was obtained combining all sub-models and, despite the increased complexity by use of three models, the general model implementation does not require more complex operations than comparison and basic arithmetic. Fig. 4 presents the scatter plot between the estimated packet loss and the measured loss for modeling and validation data. These plots show that, despite some imprecision, the generated model is a good approximation for both data sets.

Table 7. Coefficients of determination for each category

Category	Tennis Video (Modeling)	Bridge Video (Validation)
Rate < 5 Mbps	0.997	0.995
Rate $\geq$ 5 Mbps and $INP_{act} < 2$	0.983	0.962
Rate $\geq$ 5 Mbps and $INP_{act} \geq 2$	0.987	0.831
General Model	0.987	0.968

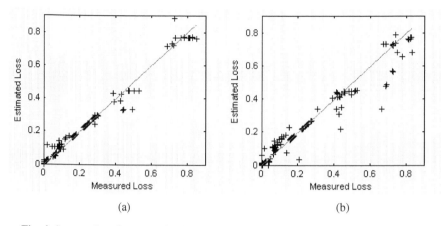

Fig. 4. Scatter plot of measured and estimated loss: (a) modeling data (b) validation data

4.3 Estimating Video Quality

To model the PSNR we chose to use the packet loss, supported by the known relation between these metrics. In [6], it is shown that network layer metrics, as packet loss, have direct impact on application layer metrics such as PSNR. Further, [6] mentions that video quality and packet loss present a non-linear relation. Our results demonstrated this non-linear relationship as showed in Fig. 5. This was the case for both real (measured) and estimated packet loss, where estimated values were generated using the models described previously.

Based on this non-linear behavior, we tried to fit several non-linear functions on the data, but, these fits showed low accuracy. The reasons for this undesirable behavior of the PSNR metric are twofold. First, PSNR does not have a standard upper limit: the best value is achieved when the difference between the received video and the original video is zero leading PSNR to tend to infinite. To avoid this, a 100 dB bound was defined as an arbitrary upper bound. Second, PSNR behaves as a categorical variable.

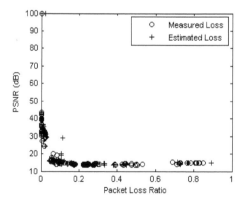

Fig. 5. Scatter plot between the measured loss and the measured PSNR

It is possible to map PSNR values into MOS-based categories, reproducing the human visual perception. Thus, following the relationship between PSNR and MOS presented by [4] we created three categories showed in Table 8.

Table 8. PSNR to Video Quality Mapping

PSNR (dB)	Quality
> 40	Excellent
> 30 and ≤ 40	Good
≤ 30	Poor

We applied these categories to our data to infer thresholds based on the packet loss, obtaining a simple categorical model. By observing the scatter plot between the measured packet loss and PSNR, a packet loss ratio of up to 3% was found to designate *Good* video quality while the threshold of 1% represents *Excellent* video quality. These thresholds revealed accuracy of about 99% in the *Good* video quality and about 98% in the *Excellent* video quality for the modeling video data. This accuracy is calculated as the percentage of correct predictions over the total number of samples.

In practice it is necessary to work with loss prediction since the actual packet loss is not available. Thus, we employed the thresholds using the estimated packet loss. We also verified these thresholds using validation data. All accuracy results were satisfactory as can be verified in Table 9.

Table 9. Accuracy for different scenarios

Data	Video Quality	
	Excellent (Loss < 1%)	Good (Loss < 3%)
Tennis (Measured Loss)	97.8%	99.3%
Tennis (Estimated Loss)	99.3%	99.4%
Bridge (Measured Loss)	100%	100%
Bridge (Estimated Loss)	97.1%	98.7%

Given these good results, we can formalize the model as shown in formula (6), where *loss* is the estimated percentage of lost packets.

$$VideoQuality = \begin{cases} Excellent & if\,(loss < 1\%) \\ Good & if\,(1\% \leq loss < 3\%) \\ Poor & if\,(loss \geq 3\%) \end{cases} \qquad (6)$$

Fig. 6 contains frames taken from the tennis video for different loss conditions, allowing the visualization of the different quality levels. Fig. 6(a) shows the original frame for reference. At Fig. 6(b) we can see the same frame with "excellent quality", as the thresholds in Table 8, whose PSNR is 40.5 dB. Little distortion is perceived, confirming the category. Fig. 6(c) shows a frame with PSNR = 32 dB, meaning a "good quality" video. In this frame we can see some distortion caused by packet loss, although the scene can still be understood. It must be noticed that the PSNR of this frame approaches the lower bound threshold of 30 dB for "poor quality" videos. With PSNR = 21 dB, the video showed in Fig. 6(d) is below this lower bound: its scene cannot be understood properly, although the scene context is still preserved. This phenomenon is caused by the temporal compression employed by MPEG-2 encoders. When there was movement in the scene, packet loss causes loss of information and consequent distortion; scene background was reutilized from previous frames and thus preserved. This last case falls into the "poor video quality" category.

(a)   (b)

(c)   (d)

Fig. 6. Sample frames for different video qualities: original video (a); excellent quality video (b), PSNR=40.5dB; good quality video (c), PSNR=32dB; poor quality video (d), PSNR=21dB

5   Related Work

Various studies of real-time QoE estimation for video applications can be found in the literature. The study developed in [7] uses a simulated network with real video traces to evaluate the impact of packet loss, packet error (caused by noise), delay and jitter on application level quality metrics such as PSNR. The authors conclude that the packet loss is the most degrading event for video quality, but does not discuss how to estimate the video quality based on packet loss as we have done in this work.

In [13], authors develop linear models to estimate a MOS-like subjective quality metric for audio and video transmissions based on application metrics like audio/video synchronization and MSE as well as the video content. Their experiments were run over an Ethernet network with web traffic generating disturbances on video traffic. Results had shown that the proposed approach can estimates video quality with high accuracy. The main difference to our approach is that they used application metrics instead of low-level metrics as we have used.

In [14] was derived analytically a relative PSNR metric, which is a difference between the actual PSNR and a reference PSNR. Besides packet loss effects, the metric considers impact of codec selection, the packetization scheme, and the video content. As pointed by authors, their quality metric underestimates impairments caused by bursty loss events, making it not suitable to environments subject to impulsive noise as xDSL networks.

The studies developed in [8] and [9] are similar to our own. In the former, using a non-reference video quality metric, the authors applied linear regression to estimate the video quality based on layer 3 metrics over a simple emulated network, differently from our environment, which uses real equipment and focuses on the ADSL access network. The latter study modeled the subjective MOS [3] for an interactive game application, based on measurements taken for a real gaming network. The obtained model, interestingly, differently from us, does not consider packet loss, since the experiments conducted by the authors showed that packet losses up to 40% have little impact on their gaming application. Video applications cannot make such assumption, as they are very sensitive to packet losses.

6 Conclusions

This paper presented models for estimating video quality of experience under several noise and line configuration scenarios. It is worth noticing that, unlike most existing works in the literature, our models were built upon experiments on a real DSL test-bed,. Our experiments were by no means exhaustive but we have been able to obtain representative models and important results that we would like to discuss with the community to build further on them.

From a more practical perspective, we believe that the models derived in this work could be directly integrated into a real-time performance monitoring tool to evaluate per-user QoE in an operational xDSL plant. The procedure used to derive such information can be extended, by employing IA techniques or feedback-based approaches, to allow an automatic adjustment of the weights of model variables, allowing for better adequacy to different scenarios.

We are currently working on models for the estimation of other network metrics and their correlation with video quality under noisy conditions. More sophisticated scenarios, including varying background traffic, are going to be investigated.

Furthermore, new experiments can be done by expanding the validation area of our models including the use of other video codecs (e.g. MPEG4). Our goal in this case is to broaden the applicability of our models, as we realize that performing all the possible tests is an unfeasible task. Consequently, building tools for the correct estimation of channel quality especially under noisy conditions is a difficult task, and any real step towards this is encouraging and extremely helpful.

References

1. Fitzek, F., Seeling, P., Reisslein, M.: VideoMeter tool for YUV bitstreams. Technical Report acticom-02-001, Acticom - mobile networks, Germany (2002)
2. Video Quality Experts Group (VQEG), http://www.its.bldrdoc.gov/vqeg/
3. ITU-R: Methodology for the Subjective Assessment of the Quality of Television Pictures. ITU-R Recommendation BT.500-10 (2000)
4. Klaue, J., Rathke, B., Wolisz, A.: EvalVid - A Framework for Video Transmission and Quality Evaluation. In: Computer Performance Evaluation/TOOLS 2003, Illinois, USA, pp. 255–272 (2003)
5. VideoLAN – VLC media player, http://www.videolan.org/
6. Triple-play Services Quality of Experience (QoE) Requirements. Technical Report TR-126, DSL Forum (2006)
7. Venkataraman, M., Sengupta, S., Chatterjee, M., Neogi, R.: Towards a Video QoE Definition in Converged Networks. In: Second International Conference on Digital Telecommunications, p. 16 (2007)
8. Qiu, S., Rui, H., Zhang, L.: No-reference Perceptual Quality Assessment for Streaming Video Based on Simple End-to-end Network Measures. International conference on Networking and Services, p. 53 (2006)
9. Wattimena, F., Kooij, E., van Vugt, J., Ahmed, K.: Predicting the perceived quality of a first person shooter: the Quake IV G-model. In: Proceedings of 5th ACM SIGCOMM Workshop on Network and System Support For Games, Singapore (2006)
10. ITU-T: Physical layer management for digital subscriber line (DSL) transceivers. ITU-T Recommendation G.997.1 (2006)
11. ITU-T: Asymmetric Digital Subscriber Line Transceiver 2 (ADSL2). ITU-T Recommendation G992.3 (2002)
12. Nedev, N.: Analysis of the Impact of Impulse Noise in Digital Subscriber Line Systems. PhD thesis, University of Edinburgh (2003)
13. Tasaka, S., Watanabe, Y.: Real-Time Estimation of User-Level QoS in Audio-Video IP Transmission by Using Temporal and Spatial Quality. In: GLOBECOM, pp. 2661--2666 (2007)
14. Tao, S., Apostolopoulos, J., Guérin, R.: Real-time monitoring of video quality in IP networks. In: NOSSDAV, New York, pp. 129–134 (2005)
15. Moulin, F., Ouzzif, M., Zeddam, A., Gauthier, F.: Discrete-multitone-based ADSL and VDSL systems performance analysis in an impulse noise environment. IEE Science, Measurement and Technology 150(6) (2003)

Wireless Channel Condition Aware Scheduling Algorithm for Hybrid Optical/Wireless Networks

Ying Yan, Hao Yu, and Lars Dittmann

Department of Photonics Engineering
Technical University of Denmark (DTU)
Kgs.Lyngby, Denmark
{Ying.Yan,Hao.Yu,Lars.Dittmann}@fotonik.dtu.dk

Abstract. Recent research activities about hybrid optical wireless networks become attractive. In this paper, we provide an overview on integration of an Ethernet passive optical network (EPON) and a worldwide interoperability for microwave access (WiMAX) network. Gateway node that integrates both optical scheduling and wireless scheduling functions gains most interests. We promote a question: how the scheduler at optical network unit is affected by its wireless connections when ONUs transfer packets to optical line terminal. Scheduling algorithms have been proposed intensively in EPON system. However, the existing scheduling algorithms are only for either pure optical networks or pure wireless networks. Within this paper, we propose to design packet scheduling schemes that take wireless channel condition into account for the hybrid optical wireless networks. Our scheduling scheme is based on a cost function, which considers not only the packet transmission but also the radio link condition.

Keywords: hybrid optical/wireless networks, Ethernet passive optical networks (EPON), WiMAX, resource allocation management, dynamic bandwidth allocation (DBA), cost-function-based scheduling algorithm.

1 Introduction

Recent advances in optical and wireless communications certainly provide ample opportunities of introducing fixed mobile convergence (FMC) network architectures that benefit the broadband access transmission and allow the development of multimedia applications. The wireless access technique has shown rapid growth and future increase as major players of access network. The new-generation broadband wireless access (BWA) technology WiMAX has been, due to its easy deployment and low-cost architecture, considered an economically viable solution to provide last mile access, especially in the hard-to-reach rural area. On the optical domain, EPON has attracted many research attentions for commercial deployment recently. EPON, as a fiber-based access technology, is expected to offer a cheap solution with high bandwidth to the broadband access. The integration of the optical networks and wireless networks offers an attractive and feasible solution to broadband network access.

C. Wang (Ed.): AccessNets, LNICST 6, pp. 397–409, 2009.

Motivations behind the integration are addressed from aspects of low cost of deployment, high bandwidth provision and scalable extension of communication coverage.

- *Cost*: The economic limitation prevents fiber from directly reaching individual customers, especially for those low subscriber density areas and urban areas. In contract, wireless technique with low deployment costs alleviates such difficulty. By replacing fiber with free radio media, the cost of last-mile transmission is reduced in an integrated optical and wireless network.
- *Bandwidth*: Due to the emergence of wavelength division multiplexing (WDM) technologies, the bandwidth of backbone network has increased substantially. In the integrated optical and wireless network, EPON fills in the gap between the subscriber network and the core network. The fiber-based techniques can offer a total 1 Gb/s high bandwidth in both downstream and upstream. If there are 16 WiMAX sub-networks connecting to the EPON system, the shared upstream bandwidth requirement is up to 1.2 Gb/s, which matches the capacity of the fiber transmission.
- *Coverage*: In the integrated optical and wireless network architecture, the high-speed communication is extended by using antenna for wireless distribution. One important good feature in WiMAX technology is its scalability. Without affecting the existing customers, the service provider could install new service areas by adding new base stations as the user demand grows.

The migration requires changes in the media access control (MAC) layer and the network layer that bring services to end-users with compliable users' service level agreement (SLA). A MAC mapping scheme between the optical domain and the wireless domain is necessary to be developed in the gateway node, which is able to translate the communication between two different interfaces. To some extent, the performance of the hybrid network solution relies on the design of the gateway node, which plays an important role in the EPON-WiMAX integration.

Packet scheduling and bandwidth resource allocation are important functions in MAC design. Intensive research of upstream scheduling algorithms for EPON system has been contributed in the literature. In the hybrid optical wireless network, traffic flows arrive at the gateway node from mobile users via wireless upstream links, which are subject to signal attenuation, fading, interference and noise. Thus, these existing algorithms cannot be directly adapted without taking features of wireless links into consideration.

In this paper we first discuss three design issues about the integrated architectures. Then based on the choice of hybrid network architecture, we present a system model with detailed optical upstream scheduler functions. An improved scheduling algorithm for the integrated network is proposed, which jointly considers the packet scheduling and wireless channel conditions.

2 Background and Related Work

Recently, the integration of two greatly developed access technologies, EPON and WiMAX, has gained increasing attention. Some research activities have started to investigate and study system performances and design challenges.

WiMAX is standardized under IEEE 802.16 working group. This technology is designed to provide comparable service to traditional wireline access networks such as xDSL and cable modem networks but with much less installation cost and more rapid deployment. It adopts OFDMA/TDD in multiple access and duplex schemes. WiMAX transmits at a data rate up to 75 Mb/s and with a theoretical coverage radius of 50 km. It can be adopted as the last mile connection to both end-user and business, also a backbone for wireless local area and cellular networks.

EPON has been standardized in the IEEE 802.3ah. A typical EPON system is a tree-based architecture, which consists of one optical line terminal (OLT) functionalized as a central control station, one *1:N* passive optical splitter and multiple (N=16 or 32) optical network users (ONUs). The location of ONU is specified variously, such as inside the home (fiber to the home, FTTH), in the building (FTTB) and at the curb (FTTC). All transmissions in PON are between an OLT and an ONU. The upstream transmission originated from ONUs is in a multipoint-to-point structure, and the downstream transmission originated from an OLT is in a point-to-multipoint structure. Traffic is delivered on two separated wavelengths, typically 1310 nm (for upstream) and 1550 nm (for downstream). A multipoint control protocol (MPCP) is specified in the IEEE 802.3ah standard used as a control and signaling protocol mechanism.

A hybrid wireless-optical broadband-access network (WOBAN) was proposed by *Sarkar et al.* [1]. The integrated architecture is discussed mainly focusing on network setup, network connectivity and fault-tolerant characteristics. Authors also contribute on developing an efficient routing algorithm for the wireless front end of WOBAN [2, 4]. The wireless domain is considered as a multi-hop wireless mesh network. The routing algorithm is designed with minimized delay and reduced packet loss. *Luo et al.* [5, 6] proposed several optical wireless integration scenarios, where the wireless base station is integrated with OLT functions. Authors proposed a centralized admission control in the integrated OLT/BS node, in order to reduce the signaling transmission delay. *Shen et al.* [7] proposed architectures for the integration of EPON and WiMAX. Related control and operation issues are addressed. *Lin et al.* [8] presented an integrated wireless and SONET architecture. An optimal utility based bandwidth allocation scheme is designed for multimedia application. *H. Kim and A. Wolisz*, [9,10] proposed a radio over fiber based network architecture. A centralized MAC layer is designed with discussions on scheduling and resource sharing policy. A dynamic load balancing algorithm is proposed to achieve better resource management in the wireless domain. *K. Ho and J. Mitchell* [11] presented integration between optical networks with IEEE 802.11 wireless local area network (WLAN). The design issues containing PHY layer constraints and MAC layer integration are addressed.

3 Design Issues

In this section we list and look at three significant design issues that affect implementation performances of hybrid optical wireless networks.

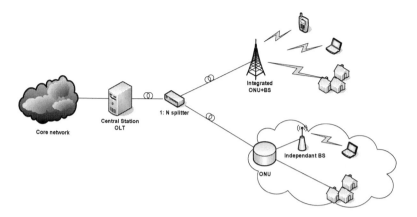

Fig. 1. Independent and hybrid architecture

3.1 Architectures

In the literature, there are several integrated network architectures proposed to the hybrid optical and wireless communication, mainly aimed at augmenting PON system with wireless transmission penetrating to the local area.

- *Independent architectures*: Shown in the lower part of Fig.1, the ONU directly connects the WiMAX base station (BS) via a common standardized interface. There is no direct wireless link between the ONU and the subscribed stations (SS). The main advantage of this architecture is the independent deployment of the two access networks. However, as two domains are separated, communication between ONU and BS, which exchanges information, is unavoidable. Such control signaling messages may suffer a delay and cause traffic overhead.

- *Hybrid architectures*: In the hybrid architecture shown as the upper part of Fig.1, an ONU and a WiMAX BS are integrated in a single device, functionalized as a gateway connecting to both PON and WiMAX access networks. The gateway contains separate buffers for the upstream and downstream traffic. Compared to the independent architecture, this hybrid architecture provides close connection between ONU and BS. Therefore, ONU and BS are aware of the details of network conditions of each other. It enables the integrated bandwidth allocation and packet scheduling scheme to optimize the whole system performance, such as end-to-end service QoS and network throughput.

- *Radio-over-fiber (RoF) architecture:* RoF based wireless access technology has been researched and proposed as a promising alternative to broadband wireless access network. Depicted in Fig.2, the RoF architecture consists of a central head-end and a remote antenna unit connected by an optical fiber link, on which the microwave signals are distributed. The advantages of RoF architecture include its low attenuation loss, immunity to radio frequency interference and reduced power consumption. However, because RoF involves analogue modulation and analogue signal transmission, the signal impairments such as noise and distortion become challenging issues in RoF systems. [7]

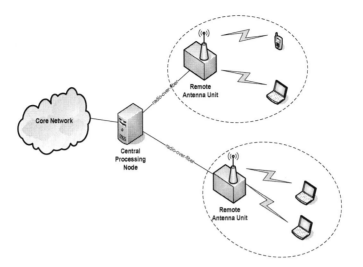

Fig. 2. Radio over fiber architecture

3.2 Topology Management

One major issue is the efficient topology management to minimize network deployment cost without sacrificing the quality of service (QoS) performance for the local and relay connections. In [1] the problem of network setup was solved by finding an optimal deployment of ONUs. Various algorithms are investigated, such as random and deterministic approach, greedy approach, combinational and joint optimization approach.

3.3 Resource Management and QoS Support

In the hybrid optical wireless network, resource management is implemented in centralized architecture, where an intelligent control mechanism in OLT polls and allocates bandwidth to all gateway nodes. There are several methods that can be used to achieve efficient resource management, such as using dynamic bandwidth allocation algorithms and admission control schemes. The resource management functions should be designed with consideration of the end-to-end QoS, such as packet delay, network throughput and so forth. In the hybrid optical wireless network, the resource management is composed of two stages. The first stage is the optical resource allocation among attached gateway nodes in the optical domain. The second one is the radio resource allocation among connected SSs in the wireless domain. Appropriate cooperation and integration of resource allocations in two domains are crucial to investigate in. The node that locates on the common boundary of two domains needs an advanced resource management so as to coordinate the communication between optical and wireless domains.

Current EPON scheduling schemes show favor only to the priority of variant arrival traffic flows. Combined with the hash wireless environment, it is possible that bad channel quality invalidate the theoretical fairness of bandwidth assignment and

QoS support. Thus, it is crucial to import the channel status awareness into the scheduling policy.

4 System Model and Gateway Node Functions

A hybrid optical wireless network with integrated ONU-BS gateway node (GN) is considered. The optical network is configured according to a tree-based EPON structure and a point-to-multipoint (PMP) WiMAX system is deployed in the wireless domain. The service area is partitioned based on the available GNs. For instance, there are N GNs ($GN_{1...N}$) associated with OLT and there are M SSs ($SS_{1...M}$) located in one GN. To ease and simplify our discussion, we assume the coverage of a single WiMAX network is independent and there are no overlaps between two wireless networks.

Concerning resource management, both EPON and PMP WiMAX employ a poll/request/grant mechanism for bandwidth allocation. Differences are that the resource allocation in EPON is per-queue based and in WiMAX is per-connection based.

In the integrated architecture, a central station (i.e. OLT) polls a gateway node. GN responds with requests for bandwidth requests. A grant is permitted by OLT and is sent to GNs with information of the starting time and duration of their upstream transmission. In the upstream direction, multiple GNs share the same optical channel to transmit control and data packets to the OLT. The scheduler mechanism in OLT arbitrates the upstream transmission among the associated GNs without collision.

GN contains two interfaces connecting to both wireless and optical domains. The functions of ONU and BS are both implemented. Thus there are packet schedulers required in both upstream and downstream directions. For GN, the uplink includes transmission from SSs to GN and from GNs to OLT. The downlink transmission is from OLT to GN and from GN to SSs. The scheduling function in a GN can be classified as following:

– *Upstream wireless scheduler*: pools and grants admission among its associated SSs.
– *Upstream optical scheduler*: after receiving assigned bandwidth from OLT, it allocates the aggregated bandwidth to various backlogged traffic queues.
– *Downstream wireless scheduler*: decides the order and capacity of traffic, which are destined to SSs within GN service area.

Our research focuses on the design of the upstream optical scheduler. In the following section, we first give an overview of the upstream optical scheduler in GN. Then, a cost-function based scheduling algorithm with awareness of wireless channel conditions is proposed.

5 Scheduler Design

5.1 Function Overview

The implementation of an upstream optical scheduler in a GN consists of two planes, a data plane and a control plan, shown in Fig.3 The control plane is responsible for call admission control, buffer management, and channel condition monitoring and such functions. The data plane, which is in the path of data flows, focuses on packet classifying, queuing and scheduling, and it is controlled by the components of control plane.

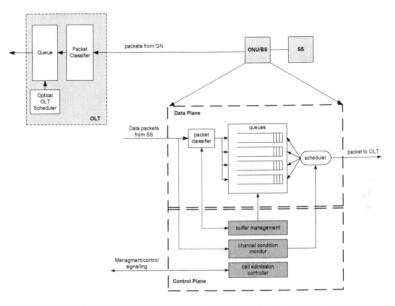

Fig. 3. Resource management functions in hybrid networks

The data plane of the Gateway Node mainly consists of three function modules: packet classifier, queue module and packets scheduler.

- *Packet classifier* is responsible for sorting the incoming packets into different services classes and forwarding them to the corresponding queues. In addition, the packet classifier sends information of the packets to the buffer management module in the control plane and takes the order of dropping or accepting the packets.
- *Queue block* consists of several sub-queues. It is a memory system which is responsible for packet storage and removal. The queue system stores packets according to their service class and creation source. It records the information in a two-dimensioned list and keeps the list up-to-date periodically.
- *Packet scheduler* works as a local server to the packets in the queues, which is discussed in details in next section.

The control plane is basically comprised of three function blocks: buffer management, channel condition monitor and call admission controller.

- *Buffer management* module gathers information from packet classifier and sends commands of dropping or accepting packets to the queue block. Based on the arrival time stamp of each packet, the buffer management module monitors the storage time of each packet. Once the time is longer than the maximum tolerated delay, the packet is supposed to be purged. In addition, the buffer management module should watch the queue size. To avoid increasing the packet delay, buffer manager should begin to reject packet arrivals based on the measurement of queue size or required bandwidth for completing the queuing packets. Thresholds for rejecting and re-accepting packets should be determined so as to eliminate the burst behavior and packet dropping. The threshold can be dynamic according to the statistics of the traffic. However, challenges lie in how the parameter setting of the buffer management module is configured. An appropriate configuration may result in satisfied traffic characteristics.

- *Channel condition monitor* watches the WiMAX wireless channel condition of each user connection. Wireless communication condition can be affected by multi-path fading, inter-channel interference (ICI), and Doppler effects and so on. The data rate of each channel can be examined by the channel condition monitor and the wireless condition can be evaluated. The channel condition monitor reports information of current channel conditions to the packet scheduler based on the results of monitoring. To avoid burst behavior of the channel condition evaluation, the monitor should set up a scanning window that allows a longer period of channel condition tracking instead of using immediate results. Challenges may exist in the response to the changes of channel condition and the efficiency of the reaction.
- *Call admission controller* can be used in resource management. Connection request are examined with its QoS requirements. If the QoS cannot be guaranteed, the connection request will be rejected.

5.2 Problem Statement

In the upstream optical scheduler, traffic flows are received from multiple mobile users (i.e. connections) with diverse QoS requirements and channel quality. In conventional scheduler designed in EPON system, packet and queue information, such as traffic types and queue sizes, are measured to assign priority weights. The limitation of such algorithm is the ignorance of wireless channel quality. Changes of a channel condition could possibly affect the communication, which results in unexpected effects weakening the QoS support. When the quality of a channel drops lower than a threshold value, no traffic can be transmitted. When a connection is detected suffering bad channel condition, the future incoming data rate could be predicted to decrease. Assuming that most of the traffic of a class comes from the "bad" connection, it is viewed as lightly loaded. On the contrary, those traffic classes with "good" connections are viewed as highly loaded.

The basic idea is to increase the throughput of links in good channel condition. In order to avoid that incoming data from "good" connections are dropped due to the queuing overflow, it is reasonable to first serve a highly loaded class, even if the priority is lower than a lightly loaded one. The advantage of channel-condition awared scheduling algorithm compared to priority based one is the QoS assurance of low priority classes with "good" channel condition. That is, the excessive bandwidth of a lightly loaded class is shifted to the highly loaded one to meet the urgent bandwidth demand. However, the disadvantage of such scheduling algorithm is the increase in the delay of high priority traffic class, when it is under a bad channel condition. To overcome this problem, a credit table is used to enforce a minimum delay bound.

5.3 Scheduling Algorithm

As we have stated in previous paragraphs, scheduling algorithms evaluating only traffic class and queue sizes may encounter problems. It is desirable to design a scheduling algorithm reflecting wireless channel condition as well.

Table 1. Scheduling Algorithm: Pseudo-Code for Cost-Function-based Scheduling in GN

```
Initialize: (Invoked when the number of backlogged
packets exceeds the assigned)
 GrantedBW = 0;
 Threshold = SetAppropriate Threshold (AssignedBW);
 SetAllToZero (CF[i, j]);
Loop:
 while (GrantedBW < Threshold)) do
     for (i = 0; i < NumberOfTrafficClasses; i = i +1)
         W[i] = WeightOfTraffic (i);
         for (j = 0; j < NumberOfUserChannels; j = j + 1)
             C[j] = ChannelCondition (j);
             K [i, j] = CreditCondition (i, j);
             CF [i, j] = CF [i, j] + C[j] + K[i, j];
         CF[i, j] = CF[i, j] + W[i];
     SelectedBW = RequiredBW (max(CF[i, j]));
     GrantedBW = GrantedBW + SelectedBW;
 end while
```

We propose a scheduler scheme (shown in Table.1) designed based on the cost function concept, where decisions in complex situations can be evaluated by using a function of relevant features. In our case, channel condition represented by Signal-to-noise ration (SNR) and class priority. The cost function $CF_{i,j}$ is defined in Equation (1), which consists of three phases: weight function, channel function and credit function. [12,13]

$$CF_{i,j}(t) = Func(W_{channel} \cdot C_j, W_{queue} \cdot E_{i,j}, W_{credit} \cdot K_i) \tag{1}$$

where the cost function is calculated for $i\text{-}th$ class with traffic arrival from $j\text{-}th$ connection. C_j represents channel conditions consisting of the packet loss (PL) and channel interference (I_j). $E_{i,j}$ is the size of granted bandwidth in *i-th* class *j-th* connection queue. K_i represents an additional credit value which is specified in system. Three weight parameters, $W_{channel}$, W_{queue} and W_{credit}, are used to select scheduling settings.

- $W_{channel} = 1$ and $W_{queue} = 0$: scheduling algorithm make decisions based on channel conditions of incoming traffic. The fluctuation in channel quality results in a variation of the data rate, R_k, on a channel k with its *PL* and I_k. $R_k(t)$ is the current channel rate at time t, $\overline{R_k}$ is the mean channel rate. The factor $C_k(t) = \dfrac{R_k(t)}{\overline{R_k}}$ represents the mean value of channel quality for channel k. The channel is viewed in good condition when factor $C_k(t)$ is higher than a threshold value. The scheduler distributes bandwidth to queues in an order of starting with the one in the best channel condition.

$$i = \arg\max_k C_k(t),\qquad(2)$$

- $W_{channel} = 0$ and $W_{queue} = 1$: scheduling algorithms are applied to grant bandwidth according to queue information, such as queue priority, queue size and so on. One possibility is that the scheduler distributes available bandwidth to queues with backlogged traffic following a weighted proportionally fair rule, from the highest queue to the lowest queue. The granted bandwidth E_i for queue i can be expressed as:

$$E_i = \alpha_i * B_{granted},\qquad(3)$$

where $B_{granted}$ is the total available bandwidth, which is delivered proportionally according to the weight α_i. The value α_i can be specified statically during system initialization. For instance, based on the traffic priorities, weights are assigned to provide different bandwidth for each queue. The bandwidth guaranteed traffic class is assigned with the highest weight value, while the Best Effort traffic is assigned with the lowest value. This static approach is simple, but it may cause the waste of bandwidth if the granted bandwidth for a queue exceeds its actual requirement. Assigning the value of α_i dynamically, bandwidth is allocated to queues to satisfy QoS requirements. The dynamic assignment method updates $\alpha_i(t)$ at time t. The weight parameter reflects the current queue status, which is adjusted in order to improve system performances, such as delay and throughput.

- $W_{channel} = 1$ and $W_{queue} = 1$: This is our proposed scheduling scheme, where both queue condition and channel condition are taken into account. Considering dynamically assigning the proportional parameter α_i, the scheduling decision is made based on the class priority, queue status and its channel condition. First sort all queues in ascending order of their queue priorities. At the same time, the current channel conditions are calculated based on the gathered PHY information. When a queue associated with bad link conditions, the allocated proportion of bandwidth is reduced to meet other queues' requirements.

- $W_{credit} = 1$: Credit value is a system-specific value, which is set to ensure fair distribution of bandwidth among all queues. The credit K_i is initialized as zero associated with flow $m_{i,j}$ when it becomes backlogged in the system. The credit is increased when the flow is not scheduled. The cost function is increased along with the credit parameter. Thus the non-scheduled packets will be eventually served.

6 Simulation Results

In this section, we provide the simulation results based on the proposed scheduling algorithm. Multiple wireless communication channels are simulated under specific traffic characteristic. We define that the traffic is sorted into four classes, A. B, C and D. Class A is assigned the highest priority and Class D the lowest. Four wireless channels are set up to transmit data to the GN.

We implement both strict priority algorithm and the propose cost-function based scheduling algorithm in two GN separately. To ensure the identical input traffic to the GN nodes, traffic is generated from the same source and is forwarded to both nodes.

We assume that the process capacities of both nodes are the same, 5000 bps, and the queue capacities are both set to 1000 bits. Packet length of each traffic class is 100 bits in total. Thus, the queue can only hold 10 packets and this setting causes a great amount of dropping packets. The traffic source starts to generate packets at t = 0.0 and the two servers of GN nodes begins to serve the backlogged packets at t=1.0 s (simulation time). Packet inter-arrival time is exponential distributed with mean equals to 0.01 second. The assigned bandwidth for each class in strict priority algorithm is set to: Class A 35%, Class B 25%, Class C 25%, and Class D 15%. The channel condition of Channel 2 turns bad during 10s to 60s. To examine the algorithm more clearly, we set the traffic as, 80% of the traffic from Channel 1 and 2 belongs to Class B and 20% belongs to Class A; 80% of the traffic from Channel 3 and 4 is Class C and 20% is Class D.

At t = 10s, the channel condition of Channel 2 becomes infected, thus a considerable amount of Class B traffic is reduced, while Class C and D traffic remain unchanged. The cost-function algorithm intends to re-allocate more bandwidth resource to the lower classes with good channel conditions, i.e. Class C and D in this simulation scenario.

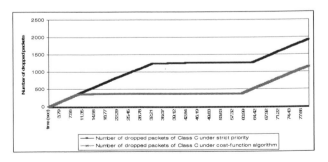

Fig. 4. Number of dropped packets of Class C

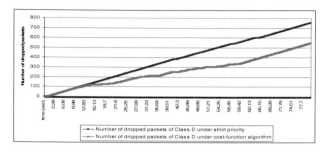

Fig. 5. Number of dropped packets of Class D

Fig.4 and Fig.5 show an increase of accepting packets when the cost-function based algorithm is adopted. Compared to the strict priority, the cost-function based scheduling distributes more fairness among the traffic classes, and the classes with lower priority could utilize more bandwidth. Although the absolute number of dropped packets is very large, it is the relative ratio with total number of transmitted packets that counts. The comparison between two curves shows a trend that more packets are accepted under the cost-function algorithm.

7   Conclusion and Future Work

In this paper, we present an overview of hybrid optical wireless networks. Design issues are addressed in terms of network architecture, topology management and resource management. Efficient use of network resources while supporting QoS for multiple services is significant and challenging. Due to the nature of wireless communication, an integrated scheduler implementation should take the variation of wireless channel condition into account so as to ensure fairness and efficient resource allocation.

We proposed a channel condition aware scheduling algorithm on a cost function basis. The sketchy algorithm is introduced and evaluated by simulation work. The idea of the cost function based scheduling needs more future work on the channel condition measurement and function improvement in order to set up an efficient scheduling system which applies more fairness in the hybrid network.

References

1. Sarkar, S., Dixit, S., Mukherjee, B.: Hybrid Wireless Optical Broadband-Access Network (WOBAN): A Review of Relevant Challenges. Journal of Lightwave Technology 25(11) (November 2007)
2. Sarkar, S., Dixit, S., Mukherjee, B.: Hybrid Wireless Optical Broadband-Access Network (WOBAN): A Review of Relevant Challenges. Journal of Lightwave Technology 25(11) (November 2007)
3. Sarkar, S., Yen, H.-H., Dixit, S., Mukherjee, B.: DARA: Delay-aware routing algorithm in a hybrid Wireless-Optical Broadband Access Network (WOBAN). In: IEEE International Conference on Communications (2007)

4. Sarkar, S., Yen, H.-H., Dixit, S., Mukherjee, B.: RADAR: Risk-and-Delay Aware Routing Algorithm in a Hybrid Wireless-Optical Broadband Access Network (WOBAN). In: Optical Fiber Communication and the National Fiber Optic Engineers Conference (2007)
5. Luo, Y., et al.: Integrating optical and wireless services in the access network. In: Optical Fiber Communication Conference (2006)
6. Luo, Y., et al.: QoS-Aware Scheduling over Hybrid Optical Wireless Networks. In: Optical Fiber Communication Conference (2007)
7. Shen, G., Tucker, R.S., Chae, C.-J.: Fixed Mobile Convergence Architectures for Broadband Access: Integration of EPON and WiMAX. IEEE Communications Magazine, 44–50 (August 2007)
8. Lin, P., et al.: Optimal Utility-Based Bandwidth Allocation Over Integrated Optical And WiMAX Networks. In: Optical Fiber Communication Conference (March 2006)
9. Kim, H.B., Wolisz, A.: A Radio over Fiber Based Wireless Access Network Architecture for Rural Areas. IST Mobile and Wireless Communications Summit (June 2005)
10. Kim, H.B., Wolisz, A.: Load balancing for centralized wireless networks. In: IEEE International Symposium on Personal, Indoor and Mobile Radio Communications, September 2005, vol. 3 (2005)
11. Ho, K.K.L., Mitchell, J.E.: Integration of Hybrid Fibre Radio and IEEE 802.11 WLAN network. In: The London Communication Symposium (2003)
12. Qingwen, L., Xin, W., Giannakis, G.B.: A Cross-Layer Scheduling Algorithm with QoS Support in Wireless Networks. IEEE Trans. Vehic. Tech. 55(3), 839–847 (2006)
13. Iera, A., Molinaro, A., Pizzi, S.: Channel-Aware Scheduling for QoS and Fairness Provisioning in IEEE 802.16/WiMAX Broadband Wireless Access Systems. IEEE Network 21(5), 34–41 (2007)

Planning Multitechnology Access Networks with Performance Constraints

Steven Chamberland

École Polytechnique de Montréal, P.O. Box 6079, Station Centre-Ville, Montréal
(Québec), Canada H3C 3A7
`steven.chamberland@polymtl.ca`

Abstract. Considering the number of access network technologies and
the investment needed for the "last mile" of a solution, in today's highly
competitive markets, planning tools are crucial for the service providers
to optimize the network costs and accelerate the planning process. In this
paper, we propose to tackle the problem of planning access networks composed of four technologies/architectures: the digital subscriber line (xDSL)
technologies deployed directly from the central office (CO), the fiber-to-
the-node (FTTN), the fiber-to-the-micro-node (FTTn) and the fiber-to-
the-premises (FTTP). A mathematical programming model is proposed
for this planning problem that is solved using a commercial implementation of the branch-and-bound algorithm. Next, a detailed access network
planning example is presented followed by a systematic set of experiments
designed to assess the performance of the proposed approach.

Keywords: Access network planning, digital subscriber line (xDSL)
technologies, xDSL from the central office, fiber-to-the-node (FTTN),
fiber-to-the-micro-node (FTTn), fiber-to-the-premises (FTTP), integer
mathematical programming, branch-and-bound algorithm.

1 Introduction

Due to the increasing demand for Internet protocol (IP) based services, the
digital subscriber line (DSL) service providers are investing incessantly in their
access network infrastructure. For instance, with the introduction of the high
definition television (HDTV) over IP (IPTV), new access network architectures
and technologies are currently considered to improve the access rate, principally
in the downstream direction. Typically, a minimum of 25 Mbps downstream is
required per customer for a "triple play" service, i.e., to offer two HDTV signals,
two standard definition TV (SDTV) signals, the telephony over IP (ToIP) service
and a high speed Internet (HSI) access.

It is clear that the best technical solution is to deploy a fiber-to-the-premises
(FTTP) network using, for instance, a passive optical network (PON) as illustrated in Figure 1 (b). The gigabit-capable PON (GPON) technology standardized by the ITU-T G.984.x [7] and the Ethernet PON (EPON) standardized by
the IEEE 802.3ah [4] are currently available. However, those fiber-based access

C. Wang (Ed.): AccessNets, LNICST 6, pp. 410–426, 2009.
© ICST Institute for Computer Sciences, Social-Informatics and Telecommunications Engineering 2009

technologies are still costly and taking into account time-to-market pressures and short-term economic concerns, those technologies cannot be widely deployed today for the majority of the DSL service providers.

The "classical" way of deploying xDSL, e.g., the asymmetric DSL (ADSL, ADSL2 and ADLS2+) (see ITU-T G.992.x [6]) and the very-high-speed DSL (VDSL and VDSL2) (see ITU-T G.993.x [8]), is to install the DSL access multiplexers (DSLAMs) in the COs. With the existing copper infrastructure, the majority of the plain old telephone service (POTS) customers are not qualified for a "triple play" service considering the length of the copper loops and their characteristics such as the number of bridge taps, the number of disturbers per binder, etc. Typically, the maximum loop length for a 25 Mbps service is about 900 meters with VDSL2, one bridge tap and three disturbers per 25-pair binder. As a result, new architectures and technologies have been proposed to improve the performance of the xDSL technologies. The first one, the fiber-to-the-node (FTTN), allows to reduce the copper loop lengths by installing small DSLAMs (i.e., the nodes) at the outside plant interface (OPI) cabinet locations instead of installing them in the COs, as illustrated in Figure 1 (c). Typically, the nodes are supporting both DSL-based FTTN and Ethernet-based FTTN. However, Ethernet-based FTTN is rarely considered as an option for FTTP since important power distribution, batteries, etc. are needed in the outside plant. The second architecture, the fiber-to-the-micro-node (FTTn), allows to install micro-nodes, i.e., small sealed expansion modules, in the outside plant in order to connect the customers far from the cabinets with a good performance (see Figure 1 (c)). An interesting technology is the cable bonding (see ITU-T G.998.1 [9] and G.998.2 [10]). This technology allows the service providers of using two or more copper loops per customer in order to improve the performance of the xDSL technologies for a given loop length and/or to have longer loops for a given performance. Considering that most of POTS customers have two copper loops, this technology is very interesting. Finally, the dynamic spectrum management (DSM) (also called far end crosstalk (FEXT) cancellation), is a promising technology to increase the performance of VDSL2. This technology increases the access rate by adapting the transmit spectra considering the actual time-variable FEXT interference. However, this technology is not standardized yet (see ITU-T temporary document SD-064 [11]).

A viable FTTP deployment scenario consists of using FTTP in the greenfield and to introduce it gradually in the brownfield while considering FTTN. FTTN is then an incremental step to FTTP. Planning a such access network is complex and, in today's highly competitive markets, planning tools are crucial for the service providers to optimize the network costs and accelerate the planning process.

In this paper, we propose to tackle the problem of planning multitechnology access networks considering single-family units (SFUs) and small/medium multi-dwelling units (MDUs) for one or many digital serving areas (DSAs). (For large MDUs and business services, the fiber-to-the-building (FTTB) (point-to-point) architecture can be used, see Figure 1 (a).)

412   S. Chamberland

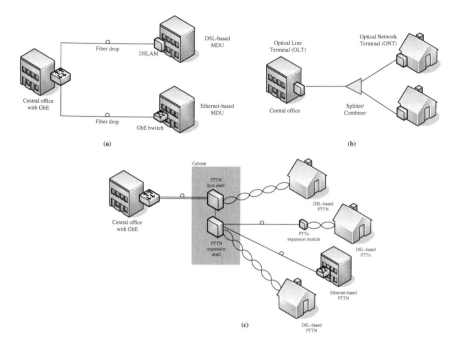

Fig. 1. Access network architectures/technologies: a) Fiber-to-the-building (FTTB) (point-to-point) network; b) Basic passive optical network (PON); c) Fiber-to-the-node (FTTN) network

The planning problem deals with:

- connecting each POTS customer requiring IP services (e.g., IPTV, ToIP, HSI, etc.) with a requested class of service to the network with xDSL technologies (ADSL, ADSL2, ADSL2+ and VDSL2) (with or without bonding) or with GPON;
- connecting each new non-POTS customer to the network with GPON;
- updating, if necessary, the connection of each DSL customer requiring a better class of service;
- locating new DSLAMs in the COs, nodes at the cabinet locations and micro-nodes in the field (at potential sites in the brownfield preselected by the network planner);
- selecting the types of the new DSLAMs, nodes and micro-nodes;
- selecting the number and the types of new line cards to insert in the DSLAMs and in the nodes;
- connecting the new nodes and micro-nodes to the COs with optical links;
- installing, if necessary, new cabinets in the greenfield to install the splitters;
- locating new optical splitters and connecting them while respecting the PON topology selected by the network planner.

The objective is to minimize the total cost for updating the access network.

In the literature, several papers have been published on access network design problems (for "classical" access network design problems, see [1,2] and the references contained therein). The most related papers are by Haidine *et al.* [3] and Zhao *et al.* [17] on the design problem of VDSL access network with reliability and performance constraints. Integer mathematical programming models are proposed as well as heuristic algorithms based on simulated annealing, tabu search and genetic algorithms. Other papers are concentrated on the FTTP network design problem, for instance, see [14,15,16]. In these papers, the authors propose genetic algorithms for the design of passive optical networks with realistic assumptions.

None of the above mentioned references considered the multitechnology access network planning (or design, expansion, update, etc.) problem presented. Moreover, the performance of the xDSL technologies combined with the location of the DSLAMs, nodes and micro-nodes and the possibility of cable bonding has never been considered.

This paper is organized as follows. In Section 2 we present the mathematical notation, the cost functions, a preprocessing algorithm and the integer mathematical programming model for the multitechnology access network planning problem. In Section 3, we present a detailed access network planning example followed by a systematic set of experiments designed to assess the performance of the proposed approach. Conclusions and further works are presented in Section 4.

2   The Modeling Framework

2.1   The Notation

The following notation is used throughout this paper.

Sets

- C, the set of classes of service;
- D, the set of xDSL technologies used in the access network such that $D = \{1,2,3,4\}$ where $d = 1$ for ADSL, $d = 2$ for ADSL2, $d = 3$ for ADSL2+ and $d = 4$ for VDSL2;
- $N = N_J \cup N_O \cup N_P \cup N_M$, the set of positions in the network;
    - $N_J = N_{J1} \cup N_{J2}$, the set of cabinet locations where N_{J1} is the set of OPI cabinets in the brownfield and N_{J2} the set of potential sites to install new cabinets in the greenfield;
        - ξ_j, the maximum number of nodes that can be installed at cabinet location $j \in N_{J1}$;
        - π_j, the maximum number of splitters that can be installed at cabinet location $j \in N_J$;
        - θ_j, the maximum length of a fiber from cabinet location $j \in N_J$ to a point of demand;
        - μ, the maximum number of customers that can be served with a GPON tree to offer the better class of service;

- N_O, the set of COs;
  - κ_o, the maximum number of DSLAMs that can be installed in CO $o \in N_O$;
  - $o(j)$, the associated CO for the cabinet location $j \in N_{J1}$;
- $N_P = N_{P1} \cup N_{P2}$, the set of points of demand where N_{P1} is the set of POTS points of demand (i.e., connected with copper loops) and N_{P2} the set of non-POTS points of demand;
  - α_p^c, the number of customers of class $c \in C$ at the point of demand $p \in N_P$;
  - $\alpha_p = \sum_{c \in C} \alpha_p^c$, the total number of customers at the point of demand $p \in N_P$;
  - β_p^c, a 0-1 constant such that $\beta_p^c = 1$ if and only if $\alpha_p^c > 0$;
  - $o(p)$, the associated CO for the point of demand $p \in N_{P1}$;
  - $j(p)$, the associated cabinet for the point of demand $p \in N_{P1}$;
  - $\gamma_{o(p),p}$, the length of the loops from the CO $o(p) \in N_O$ to the point of demand $p \in N_{P1}$;
  - $\gamma_{j(p),p}$, the length of the loops from the cabinet $j(p) \in N_{J1}$ to the point of demand $p \in N_{P1}$;
  - $\lambda_{o(p),p}$, the number of customers at the point of demand $p \in N_{P1}$ connected to a DSLAM installed in CO $o(p) \in N_O$ necessitating bonding;
  - $\lambda_{j(p),p}$, the number of customers at the point of demand $p \in N_{P1}$ connected to a node installed at the cabinet location $j(p) \in N_{J1}$ necessitating bonding;
  - $\eta_p^{c,d,b}$, the maximum length for the loops (in km) to offer a service of class $c \in C$ to the point of demand $p \in N_{P1}$ with the xDSL technology $d \in D$ and with b bonded loops ($b \in \{1,2\}$);
  - $\rho_{j,p}$, the length of the fiber to install from the cabinet $j \in N_J$ to the point of demand $p \in N_P$;
- N_M, the set of sites to installed the micro-nodes;
  - N_M^p, the set of micro-node sites that can be used for the point of demand $p \in N_{P1}$;
  - $\gamma_{m,p}$, the length of the loops from the site $m \in N_M^p$ to the point of demand $p \in N_{P1}$;
  - $\lambda_{m,p}$, the number of customers at the point of demand $p \in N_{P1}$ connected to a micro-node installed at the site $m \in N_M$ necessitating bonding;
- $T = T_D \cup T_N \cup T_M$, the set of DSLAMs, nodes and micro-nodes types where T_D is the set of DSLAMs types, T_N the set of nodes types and T_M the set of micro-node types;
  - χ^t, the number of slots for a DSLAM of type $t \in T_D$;
  - ν^t, the number of slots for a node of type $t \in T_N$;
  - δ^t, the maximum number of customers that can be connected to a micro-node of type $t \in T_M$;
- L, the set of maximum capacity line cards that can be inserted in the DSLAM and node types;

- $\phi^{\ell(t)}$, the maximum number of customers (without bonding) that can be connected to a line card for a node of type $t \in T_D \cup T_N$.

Variables

- u_o^t, the number of DSLAMs of type $t \in T_D$ installed in CO $o \in N_O$;
- u_j^t, the number of nodes of type $t \in T_N$ installed at cabinet location $j \in N_{J1}$;
- u_m^t, a 0-1 variable such that $u_m^t = 1$ if and only if a micro-nodes of type $t \in T_M$ is installed at site $m \in N_M$;
- v_o^ℓ, the number of line cards of type $\ell \in L$ in the DSLAMs installed in the CO $o \in N_O$;
- v_j^ℓ, the number of line cards of type $\ell \in L$ in the nodes installed at the cabinet location $j \in N_{J1}$;
- w_j, a 0-1 variable such that $w_j = 1$ if and only if a cabinet is installed at site $j \in N_J$;
- $x_{o(p),p}$, a 0-1 variable such that $x_{o(p),p} = 1$ if and only if the point of demand $p \in N_{P1}$ is connected to a DSLAM installed in the CO $o(p) \in N_O$;
- $x_{j(p),p}$, a 0-1 variable such that $x_{j(p),p} = 1$ if and only if the point of demand $p \in N_{P1}$ is connected to a node installed at the cabinet location $j(p) \in N_{J1}$;
- $x_{m,p}$, a 0-1 variable such that $x_{m,p} = 1$ if and only if the point of demand $p \in N_{P1}$ is connected to a micro-node installed at the site $m \in N_M^p$;
- $y_{j,p}$, a 0-1 variable such that $y_{j,p} = 1$ if and only if the point of demand $p \in N_P$ is connected with a fiber to a splitter installed at the cabinet location $j \in N_J$;
- $y_{o(j),j}$, the number of splitters installed at the cabinet location $j \in N_J$ as well as the number of fibers between this cabinet and the CO $o(j) \in N_O$.

In our model, the existing access network is identified by the decision variables overlined. For instance, if the point of demand $p \in N_P$ is connected directly to a DSLAM located in the CO $o \in N_O$ in the existing network, then $\overline{x}_{p,o} = 1$. Similarly, if one DSLAM of type $t \in T_D$ is installed in the CO $o \in N_O$ in the existing network, then $\overline{u}_o^t = 1$.

Cost Parameters

- $a_{o(p),p}$, the minimum cost (in \$) of connecting the point of demand $p \in N_{P1}$ to a DSLAM installed in the CO $o(p) \in N_O$ while respecting the class of service for each customer;
- $A_{o(p),p}$, the cost (in \$) of disconnecting the point of demand $p \in N_{P1}$ from the DSLAM installed in the CO $o(p) \in N_O$;
- $a_{j(p),p}$, the minimum cost (in \$) of connecting the point of demand $p \in N_{P1}$ to a node installed at the cabinet location $j(p) \in N_{J1}$ while respecting the class of service for each customer;
- $A_{j(p),p}$, the cost (in \$) of disconnecting the point of demand $p \in N_{P1}$ from the node installed at the cabinet location $j(p) \in N_{J1}$;
- $a_{m,p}$, the minimum cost (in \$) of connecting the point of demand $p \in N_{P1}$ to a micro-node installed at the site $m \in N_M^p$ while respecting the class of service for each customer;

- $A_{m,p}$, the cost (in \$) of disconnecting the point of demand $p \in N_{P1}$ to a micro-node installed at the site $m \in N_M^p$;
- b_o^t, the cost (in \$) of a DSLAM of type $t \in T_D$ and installing it in CO $o \in N_O$;
- B_o^t, the cost (in \$) of removing a DSLAM of type $t \in T_D$ installed in CO $o \in N_O$;
- b_j^t, the cost (in \$) of a node of type $t \in T_N$ and installing it at cabinet location $j \in N_{J1}$;
- B_j^t, the cost (in \$) of removing a node of type $t \in T_N$ installed at cabinet location $j \in N_{J1}$;
- b_m^t, the cost (in \$) of a micro-node of type $t \in T_M$ and installing it at site $m \in N_M$;
- B_m^t, the cost (in \$) of removing a micro-node of type $t \in T_M$ installed at site $m \in N_M$;
- c^ℓ, the cost (in \$) of a line card of type $\ell \in L$ and installing it;
- C^ℓ, the cost (in \$) of removing a line card of type $\ell \in L$;
- $d_{o(j),j}$, the cost (in \$) of a splitter and installing it at the cabinet location $j \in N_J$ and connecting it to the CO $o(j) \in N_O$;
- $e_{j,p}$, the cost (in \$) of connecting with a fiber the point of demand $p \in N_P$ to a splitter installed at the cabinet location $j \in N_J$;
- f_j, the cost (in \$) of a new cabinet and installing it at site $j \in N_{J2}$;
- g_p, the cost (in \$) of not connecting the customers located at point of demand $p \in N_P$.

2.2   Cost Functions

The total cost function is composed of the cost of the xDSL from the CO network, the cost of the FTTN network, the cost of the FTTn network and the cost of the FTTP network.

The cost of the xDSL from the CO network, denoted Z_{DSL-CO}, given by the following equation, includes the cost of connecting and disconnecting the points of demand, the cost of installing and removing the DSLAMs and the cost of installing and removing line cards.

$$\sum_{p \in N_{P1}} \left(a_{o(p),p} \left(x_{o(p),p} - \overline{x}_{o(p),p} \right)^+ + A_{o(p),p} \left(\overline{x}_{o(p),p} - x_{o(p),p} \right)^+ \right)$$

$$+ \sum_{o \in N_O} \sum_{t \in T_D} \left(b_o^t \left(u_o^t - \overline{u}_o^t \right)^+ + B_o^t \left(\overline{u}_o^t - u_o^t \right)^+ \right)$$

$$+ \sum_{o \in N_O} \sum_{t \in T_D} \left(c_o^{\ell(t)} \left(v_o^{\ell(t)} - \overline{v}_o^{\ell(t)} \right)^+ + C_o^{\ell(t)} \left(\overline{v}_o^{\ell(t)} - v_o^{\ell(t)} \right)^+ \right). \tag{1}$$

The cost of the FTTN network, denoted Z_{FTTN}, given by the following equation, includes the cost of connecting and disconnecting the points of demand, the cost of installing and removing the nodes and the cost of installing and removing line cards.

$$\sum_{p\in N_{P1}} \left(a_{j(p),p} \left(x_{j(p),p} - \overline{x}_{j(p),p} \right)^+ + A_{j(p),p} \left(\overline{x}_{j(p),p} - x_{j(p),p} \right)^+ \right)$$

$$+ \sum_{j\in N_{J1}} \sum_{t\in T_N} \left(b_j^t \left(u_j^t - \overline{u}_j^t \right)^+ + B_j^t \left(\overline{u}_j^t - u_j^t \right)^+ \right)$$

$$+ \sum_{j\in N_{J1}} \sum_{t\in T_N} \left(c_j^{\ell(t)} \left(v_j^{\ell(t)} - \overline{v}_j^{\ell(t)} \right)^+ + C_j^{\ell(t)} \left(\overline{v}_j^{\ell(t)} - v_j^{\ell(t)} \right)^+ \right). \tag{2}$$

The cost of the FTTn network, denoted Z_{FTTn}, given by the following equation, includes the cost of connecting and disconnecting the points of demand and the cost of installing and removing the micro-nodes.

$$\sum_{p\in N_{P1}} \sum_{m\in N_M} \left(a_{m,p} \left(x_{m,p} - \overline{x}_{m,p} \right)^+ + A_{m,p} \left(\overline{x}_{m,p} - x_{m,p} \right)^+ \right)$$

$$+ \sum_{m\in N_M} \sum_{t\in T_M} \left(b_m^t \left(u_m^t - \overline{u}_m^t \right)^+ + B_m^t \left(\overline{u}_m^t - u_m^t \right)^+ \right). \tag{3}$$

The cost of the FTTP network, denoted Z_{FTTP}, given by the following equation, includes the cost of connecting the points of demand, the cost of the splitters and fibers, and the cost of the new cabinets.

$$\sum_{j\in N_J} \left(\sum_{p\in N_P} e_{j,p} \left(y_{j,p} - \overline{y}_{j,p} \right)^+ + d_{o(j),j} \left(y_{o(j),j} - \overline{y}_{o(j),j} \right)^+ \right) + \sum_{j\in N_{J2}} f_j w_j. \tag{4}$$

2.3 Preprocessing

Several variables can be fixed to zero and the number of constraints reduced before solving the model presented in the next subsection. We propose the preprocessing algorithm presented below.

Preprocessing
Step 1: (Initialization)
    1.1 For all $p \in N_{P1}$, set $\lambda_{o(p),p} = 0$ and $\lambda_{j(p),p} = 0$.
    1.2 For all $p \in N_{P1}$ and $m \in N_M^p$, set $\lambda_{m,p} = 0$.
Step 2: (Fixing $x_{o(p),p}$ variables)
    2.1 For all $p \in N_{P1}$ and $c \in C$ do
        If $\beta_p^c = 1$, $\gamma_{o(p),p} > \eta_p^{c,4,1}$ and $\gamma_{o(p),p} \leq \eta_p^{c,4,2}$, set $\lambda_{o(p),p} := \lambda_{o(p),p} + \alpha_p^c$.
    2.2 For all $p \in N_{P1}$ and $c \in C$ do
        If $\beta_p^c = 1$, $\gamma_{o(p),p} > \eta_p^{c,4,2}$, set $x_{o(p),p} := 0$.
Step 3: (Fixing $x_{j(p),p}$ variables)
    3.1 For all $p \in N_{P1}$ and $c \in C$ do
        If $\beta_p^c = 1$, $\gamma_{j(p),p} > \eta_p^{c,4,1}$ and $\gamma_{j(p),p} \leq \eta_p^{c,4,2}$, set $\lambda_{j(p),p} := \lambda_{j(p),p} + \alpha_p^c$.
    3.2 For all $p \in N_{P1}$ and $c \in C$ do
        If $\beta_p^c = 1$, $\gamma_{j(p),p} > \eta_p^{c,4,2}$, set $x_{j(p),p} := 0$.

Step 4: (Fixing $x_{m,p}$ variables)
    4.1 For all $p \in N_{P1}$, $m \in N_M^p$ and $c \in C$ do
        If $\beta_p^c = 1$, $\gamma_{m,p} > \eta_p^{c,4,1}$ and $\gamma_{m,p} \leq \eta_p^{c,4,2}$, set $\lambda_{m,p} := \lambda_{m,p} + \alpha_p^c$.
    4.2 For all $p \in N_{P1}$, $m \in N_M^p$ and $c \in C$ do
        If $\beta_p^c = 1$, $\gamma_{m,p} > \eta_p^{c,4,2}$, set $x_{m,p} := 0$.
Step 5: (Fixing $y_{j,p}$ variables)
    5.1 For all $p \in N_P$ and $j \in N_J$ do
        If $\rho_{j,p} > \theta_j$, set $y_{j,p} := 0$.

2.4   The Model

The model for the multitechnology access network planning problem, denoted P, is presented in Appendix A.

3   Numerical Results

The algorithm was programmed in the C language on a Sun Java workstation under Linux with an AMD Opteron 150 CPU and 2 GB of RAM.

Three classes of service are considered for the tests (5, 15 and 25 Mbps) as well as two xDSL technologies (ADSL2+ and VDSL2). The characteristics of the DSLAMs, nodes and micro-nodes are presented respectively in tables 1, 2 and 3 (note that the costs presented include the installation costs). The maximal loop length per xDSL technology and class of service is presented in Table 4. Moreover, the cost for connecting a node, a micro-node or a splitter to a CO is $1000 plus $2000 per kilometer of fiber. The cost for connecting a customer to a DSLAM or a node is $100 without bonding and $200 with bonding, the cost for connecting a customer to a micro-node is $200 without bonding and $300 with bonding. Finally, the cost of a 1×32 splitter is $1200 and the cost of connecting it to a customer is $500 plus $2000 per kilometer of fiber.

For the tests, the optimal solutions are obtained by using the CPLEX Mixed Integer Optimizer 9.0 (for more information about CPLEX [5]). The algorithm used by CPLEX is the branch-and-bound algorithm. The default settings of CPLEX are used and the branch-and-bound tree memory limit was set to 500 MB and the CPU time limit to 24 hours.

Table 1. Characteristics of the DSLAMs

Maximum number per CO	4
Number of slots	9
Number of ports per card	48
Cost per node [$]	16000
Removing cost per DSLAM [$]	200
Cost per card [$]	3200
Removing cost per card [$]	50

Table 2. Characteristics of the nodes

Maximum number per cabinet	2
Number of slots	4
Number of ports per card	48
Cost per node [$]	9000
Removing cost per node [$]	200
Cost per card [$]	3200
Removing cost per card [$]	50

Table 3. Characteristics of the micro-nodes

Number ports	48
Cost per micro-node [$]	5000
Removing cost per micro-node [$]	200

Table 4. Maximum loop length per xDSL technology and class of service (with one bridge tap and 3 disturbers per 25-pair binder)

ADSL2+		
Class of service	Maximal distance	
	Without bonding	With bonding
	[m]	[m]
5 Mbps	1500	3000
15 Mbps	800	1600
25 Mbps (IPTV)	N/A	1000
VDSL2		
Class of service	Maximal distance	
	Without bonding	With bonding
	[m]	[m]
5 Mbps	2000	4000
15 Mbps	1200	2400
25 Mbps (IPTV)	900	1800

3.1   An Illustrative Example

The example illustrated in Figure 2 has two cabinets (DSAs) and 10 potential sites per DSA to install the micro-nodes. The number of points of demand is 590 (each point of demand represents up to 30 customers). These DSAs are on the Bell Canada's service territory located at the Nuns' Island (officially Ile-des-Sœurs).

In the existing network, the number of POTS customers with a HSI access service is 1098 (358 (5 Mbps); 449 (15 Mbps); 291 (25 Mbps)), the number of non-POTS customers with a HSI access service is 141 (all in the greenfield of DSA #1), the number of nodes is two per cabinet (with seven line cards inserted in the nodes at each cabinet location), the number of splitters installed is 10 at each cabinet location and one micro-node is installed at micro-node site #7 of the DSA #2.

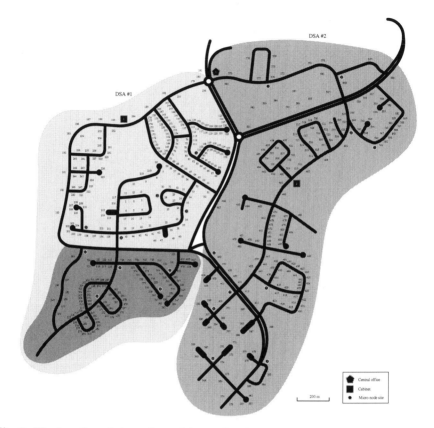

Fig. 2. The location of the points of demand, cabinets and potential micro-node sites for the example

The number of new POTS customers is 956 (345 (5 Mbps); 373 (15 Mbps); 238 (25 Mbps)) and the number of new non-POTS customers is 134. The cost of the solution found by CPLEX is $359 922 and it took 5.0 seconds of CPU time to find it. In the updated network, a new DSLAM with eight line cards is installed in the CO, two additional line cards are inserted in the nodes (one per cabinet location), eight additional splitters are installed in cabinet #1 and seven in cabinet #2 and, finally, a new micro-node is installed at micro-node site #5 of the DSA #2.

An additional network expansion is considered to obtain the final network with 1085 new POTS customers (333 (5 Mbps); 352 (15 Mbps); 400 (25 Mbps)) and 105 new non-POTS customers. The cost of the solution found by the algorithm is $407 664 and it took 9.7 seconds of CPU time to find it. In the updated network, a new DSLAM with nine line cards is installed in the CO, six additional splitters are installed in cabinet #1 and 14 in cabinet #2 and, finally, two new micro-nodes are installed, one at site #2 of the DSA #1 and one at site #7 of the DSA #2.

If all customers requesting the 25 Mbps class of service, in the optimal final network, no DSLAM is installed in the CO. The number of nodes is two per cabinet, the maximum allowed, the number of micro-nodes installed is 13 and the number of splitters is 66. In fact, for this example, when the demand for the 25 Mbps class of service is increasing, the DSL from the CO architecture architecture is less used.

3.2   Performance Evaluation

In this subsection, we use a systematic set of experiments to assess the performance of the proposed approach. Each test problem was generated as follows. First, a starting network is designed and for each starting network, an evolution problem is created by generating the location of the new points of demand in the square of side length 10 km following a uniform distribution. The number of customers at each new point of demand is randomly selected in the interval $[1,5]$ and the class of service of each customer is also selected randomly.

Table 5. Numerical results for $|N_O| = 5$, $|N_{J1}| = 5$, $|N_{J2}| = 5$, $|N_M| = 10|N_{J1}|$ and 150 (100 POTS and 50 non-POTS) points of demand (PoD) already connected

New POTS PoD	New non-POTS PoD	OPT Value [$]	CPU [sec]
100	50	449 000	1.6
100	100	728 236	0.9
100	150	979 678	5.2
100	200	1 224 950	1.8
200	50	629 044	15.1
200	100	748 922	4.4
200	150	1 076 420	4.6
200	200	1 566 314	246.2
300	50	669 892	6560.2
300	100	989 478	71.9
300	150	1 234 862	10.4
300	200	1 577 882	3389.1
400	50	834 846	83.1
400	100	ML(1 101 174)	7771.0
400	150	1 520 588	243.8
400	200	1 688 232	36.4
500	50	942 792	4365.1
500	100	ML(1 248 092)	8951.2
500	150	ML(1 412 823)	8443.5
500	200	2 037042	264.4

Table 6. Numerical results for $|N_O| = 5$, $|N_{J1}| = 10$, $|N_{J2}| = 5$, $|N_M| = 20|N_{J1}|$ and 150 (100 POTS and 50 non-POTS) points of demand (PoD) already connected

New POTS PoD	New non-POTS PoD	OPT Value [$]	CPU [sec]
100	50	371 682	4.5
100	100	650 334	7.5
100	150	911 794	2.6
100	200	1 126 212	4.2
200	50	536 408	6.3
200	100	722 540	53.2
200	150	1 121 910	84.8
200	200	1 399 210	40.3
300	50	609 124	14.5
300	100	934 478	578.7
300	150	1 158 880	513.1
300	200	ML(1 431 036)	319.0
400	50	ML(707 057)	283.6
400	100	ML(1 000 428)	458.0
400	150	ML(1 324 754)	360.0
400	200	1 423 146	414.9
500	50	ML(815 576)	498.9
500	100	ML(1 106 750)	356.9
500	150	ML(1 364 555)	334.4
500	200	ML(1 587 294)	328.5

The numerical results are presented in tables 5 to 7, each one with a different number of COs, cabinets, potential sites to install new cabinets and potential sites to install the micro-nodes per cabinet (i.e., per DSA). In each table, the first column presents the number of new POTS points of demand and column 2 presents the number of new non-POTS points of demand. Column 3 presents the value of the optimal solution or the best solution found by the branch-and-bound algorithm if the memory limit (ML) is reached and column 4, the CPU execution time to find this solution.

From these tables, we note that the CPU execution time of the branch-and-bound algorithm increases dramatically with the number of points of demand and with the number of sites to install the micro-nodes. However, the results show that fair-sized instances can be solved to optimality with 500 MB of memory. 15 out of 60 instances of the problem generated were not solved within this limit. In fact, the proposed approach can be used if the access network planning is done for one or two DSAs (cabinets). Indeed, we have solved instances with up to 5000 customers with two DSAs within 20 sec of CPU times.

Table 7. Numerical results for $|N_O| = 10$, $|N_{J1}| = 10$, $|N_{J2}| = 10$, $|N_M| = 10|N_{J1}|$ and 150 (100 POTS and 50 non-POTS) points of demand (PoD) already connected

New POTS PoD	New non-POTS PoD	OPT Value [$]	CPU [sec]
100	50	466 214	0.8
100	100	618 554	18.4
100	150	871 786	2.3
100	200	1 058 100	4.0
200	50	526 284	3.0
200	100	748 602	78.9
200	150	1 010 164	13.9
200	200	1 238 154	17.6
300	50	620 258	41.7
300	100	812 992	7.0
300	150	1 039 728	820.6
300	200	1 333 576	609.3
400	50	743 552	155.7
400	100	ML(908 958)	492.9
400	150	1 219 824	33.2
400	200	1 394 136	594.0
500	50	850 394	850.2
500	100	ML(1 073 366)	888.7
500	150	ML(1 282 123)	411.2
500	200	ML(1 485 813)	443.2

4   Conclusions and Further Works

In this paper, we have proposed to tackle the multitechnology access network planning problem. Four important access network architectures/technologies are considered: DSL from the CO, FTTN, FTTn and FTTP. The problem has been formulated with an integer mathematical programming model. The numerical results have shown that optimal solutions can generally be found using CPLEX for the size of instances considered.

There are several avenues of research that are open at this point. For instance, in this paper, we considered a model in which the FTTP access network has a star topology. Other topologies are proposed for FTTP [12] and can be included in our model.

Acknowledgements

The completion of this research was made possible thanks to Bell Canada's support through its Bell University Laboratories R&D program.

The author is grateful to Jean Huppé, Lucie Basque, Redouane Zidane and Anthony Di Michele of Bell Canada for having suggested the problem and for enlightening discussions.

References

1. Gavish, B.: Topological Design of Telecommunication Networks — Local Access Design Methods. Annals of Operations Research 33, 17–71 (1991)
2. Girard, A., Sansò, B., Dadjo, L.: A Tabu Search for Access Network Design. Annals of Operations Research 106, 229–262 (2001)
3. Haidine, A., Zhao, R., Domschitz, P., Lehnert, R., Banniza, T.R.: Planning and Optimization of a Hybrid Fibre-VDSL Access Infrastructure. In: International Symposium on Services an Local Access (2004)
4. IEEE: Amendment: Media Access Control Parameters. Physical Layers, and Management Parameters for customer Access Networks. IEEE Standard 802.3ah (2004)
5. ILOG, Inc., Using the CPLEX Callable Library and CPLEX Mixed Integer Library. ILOG, Inc. (2005)
6. ITU-T: Asymmetric Digital Subscriber Line (ADSL) Transceivers. Recommendation G.992.1 (1999)
7. ITU-T: Gigabit-capable Passive Optical Networks (GPON): General Characteristics. Recommendation G.984.1 (2003)
8. ITU-T: Very High Speed Digital Subscriber Line (VDSL) Transceivers, Recommendation G.993.1 (2004)
9. ITU-T: ATM-Based Multi-Pair Bonding, Recommendation G.998.1 (2005)
10. ITU-T: Ethernet-Based Multi-Pair Bonding, Recommendation G.998.2 (2005)
11. ITU-T: Implementation of the "Abuse of Receiver" Method for FEXT. Temporary Document SD-064 (2007)
12. Mayhew, A.J., Page, S.J., Walker, A.M., Fisher, S.I.: Fibre to the Home — Infrastructure Deployment Issues. BT Technology Journal 20, 91–103 (2002)
13. Nemhauser, G.L., Wolsey, L.A.: Integer and Combinatorial Optimization. Wiley, Chichester (1988)
14. Mazzali, C., Whitman, R., Deutsch, B.: Optimization of FTTH Passive Optical Networks Continues. Lightwave Magazine 22 (2005)
15. Poon, K.F., Conway, A., Wardrop, G., Mellis, J.: Successful Application of Genetic Algorithms to Network Design and Planning. BT Technical Journal 18, 32–41 (2000)
16. Poon, K.F., Mortimore, D.B., Mellis, J.: Designing Optimal FTTH and PON Networks Using New Automatic Methods. In: International Conference on Access Technologies 2006, pp. 45–48 (2006)
17. Zhao, R., Götze, S., Lehnert, R.: A Visual Planning Tool for Hybrid Fibre-VDSL Access Networks with Heuristic Algorithms. In: IEEE International Workshop on Design of Reliable Communication Networks, pp. 541–548 (2005)

Appendix A

The model for the multitechnology access network planning problem, denoted P, can now be given. P:

$$\min_{\mathbf{u},\mathbf{v},\mathbf{w},\mathbf{x},\mathbf{y}} Z_{DSL-CO} + Z_{FTTN} + Z_{FTTn} + Z_{FTTP} \qquad (A.1)$$

Subject to
CO and cabinet capacity constraints

$$\sum_{t \in T_D} u_o^t \leq \kappa_o \quad \forall_{o \in N_O} \qquad (A.2)$$

$$\sum_{t \in T_N} u_j^t \leq \xi_j \quad \forall_{j \in N_{J1}} \tag{A.3}$$

Micro-node type uniqueness constraints

$$\sum_{t \in T_M} u_m^t \leq 1 \quad \forall_{m \in N_M} \tag{A.4}$$

DSL loop length constraints

$$x_{o(p),p}\big(\gamma_{o(p),p} - \eta_p^{c,4,2}\big)\beta_p^c \leq 0 \quad \forall_{c \in C,\, p \in N_{P1}} \tag{A.5}$$

$$x_{j(p),p}\big(\gamma_{j(p),p} - \eta_p^{c,4,2}\big)\beta_p^c \leq 0 \quad \forall_{c \in C,\, p \in N_{P1}} \tag{A.6}$$

$$x_{m,p}\left(\gamma_{m,p} - \eta_p^{c,4,2}\right)\beta_p^c \leq 0 \quad \forall_{c \in C,\, p \in N_{P1},\, m \in N_M^p} \tag{A.7}$$

Line card capacity constraints (at the loop level) for the DSLAMs and nodes

$$\sum_{p \in N_{P1}:o=o(p)} (\alpha_p + \lambda_{o,p})\, x_{o,p} \leq \sum_{t \in T_O} \phi^{\ell(t)} v_o^{\ell(t)} \quad \forall_{o \in N_O} \tag{A.8}$$

$$\sum_{p \in N_{P1}:j=j(p)} (\alpha_p + \lambda_{j,p})\, x_{j,p} \leq \sum_{t \in T_N} \phi^{\ell(t)} v_j^{\ell(t)} \quad \forall_{j \in N_{J1}} \tag{A.9}$$

DSLAM and node capacity constraints (at the slot level)

$$v_o^{\ell(t)} \leq \chi^t u_o^t \quad \forall_{o \in N_O,\, t \in T_O} \tag{A.10}$$

$$v_j^{\ell(t)} \leq \nu^t u_j^t \quad \forall_{j \in N_{J1},\, t \in T_N} \tag{A.11}$$

Micro-node capacity constraints (at the loop level)

$$\sum_{p \in N_{P1}:m \in N_M^p} (\alpha_p + \lambda_{m,p})\, x_{m,p} \leq \sum_{t \in T_M} \delta^t u_m^t \quad \forall_{m \in N_M} \tag{A.12}$$

Point of demand maximum assignment constraints

$$x_{o(p),p} + x_{j(p),p} + \sum_{m \in N_M^p} x_{m,p} + \sum_{j \in N_J} y_{j,p} = 1 \quad \forall_{p \in N_{P1}} \tag{A.13}$$

$$\sum_{j \in N_J} y_{j,p} = 1 \quad \forall_{p \in N_{P2}} \tag{A.14}$$

FTTP fiber length constraints

$$y_{j,p}\left(\rho_{j,p} - \theta_j\right) \leq 0 \quad \forall_{p \in N_P,\, j \in N_J} \tag{A.15}$$

Splitter capacity constraints

$$\sum_{p \in N_P} \alpha_p y_{j,p} \leq \mu y_{o(j),j} \quad \forall_{j \in N_J} \tag{A.16}$$

FTTP cabinet constraints

$$y_{o(j),j} \le \pi_j w_j \quad \forall_{j \in N_J} \tag{A.17}$$

Integrality constraints

$$u_o^t \in \mathbb{N}, \ u_j^t \in \mathbb{N}, \ u_m^t \in \mathbb{B},$$
$$v_o^\ell \in \mathbb{N}, \ v_j^\ell \in \mathbb{N}, \ w_j \in \mathbb{B}, \ x_{o(p),p} \in \mathbb{B},$$
$$x_{j(p),p} \in \mathbb{B}, \ x_{m,p} \in \mathbb{B}, \ y_{j,p} \in \mathbb{B}, \ y_{o(j),j} \in \mathbb{N} \tag{A.18}$$

Constraints (A.2) and (A.3) impose the number of DSLAMs (nodes) installed in each CO (at each cabinet location) be less than or equal to the maximum allowed for that CO (cabinet location). Constraints (A.4) are micro-node type uniqueness constraints and they require of installing at most one micro-node type at each site. Constraints (A.5) to (A.7) impose a point of demand connected to a DSLAM, a node or a micro-node to respect the maximum loop length in order to have the specified performance for each class of service. Note that those constraints are not necessary if the proposed preprocessing algorithm is used. Constraints (A.8) and (A.9) are line cards capacity constraints and they require the number of customers (with and without bonding) connected to a DSLAM (node) be less than or equal to the total capacity of the line cards installed in that DSLAM (in that node). Constraints (A.10) and (A.11) impose the number of line cards installed in a DSLAM (node) be less than or equal to its number of slots. Constraints (A.12) are micro-node capacity constraints and they require the number of customers connected to a micro-node be less than or equal to the maximum number of customers that can be connected to it. Constraints (A.13) impose each POTS point of demand to be connected with at most one access link and constraints (A.14) require each non-POTS point of demand to be connected to at most one splitter. Since constraints (A.13) and (A.14) are inequality constraints, a point of demand can be not connected to the network and, in that case, a penalty cost will be considered in the objective function. Constraints (A.15) impose a point of demand connected to the FTTP network to respect the maximum fiber length (power budget). Note that those constraints are not necessary if preprocessing is used. Constraints (A.16) are splitter capacity constraints and constraints (A.17) impose the number of splitters installed at a cabinet location, be less than or equal to the maximum number of splitters that can be installed in that location. Finally, constraints (A.18) are the variable integrality constraints.

It should be pointed out that constraints (A.16) and (A.17) impose the FTTP network to have a star access network topology. Other topologies can be considered by the network planner and the proposed model can be adapted accordingly, for instance, the multiple-tree access topology. In that case, the fibers are installed from the COs to primary optical splitters located at cabinet locations and those splitters are connected to secondary splitters located in the field. Some papers have been published on that problem, for instance, see [14,15,16].

Note that P is NP-hard (transformation from the capacitated facility location problem [13]).

Loop Identification and Capacity Estimation of Digital Subscriber Lines with Single Ended Line Testing

Carine Neus, Wim Foubert, and Leo Van Biesen

Department of Fundamental Electricity and Instrumentation, Vrije Universiteit Brussel,
Pleinlaan 2, 1050 Brussels, Belgium
{cneus,wfoubert,lvbiesen}@vub.ac.be

Abstract. Digital subscriber lines offer the possibility to deliver broadband services over the existing telephone network. Still, beforehand subscriber loops must be tested to see whether they can support high-speed data services, and at what bit rate. From the existing measurement techniques, Single Ended Line Testing is often preferred because all necessary measurements can be performed from the central office. Consequently the capacity cannot be measured directly, but should be calculated through the estimation of the loop make-up. This paper discusses some main difficulties of this identification. Moreover, in contrast to the traditional approach where the data are interpreted in the time domain, this paper presents a new approach by doing most of the processing in the frequency domain.

Keywords: Digital Subscriber Line (DSL), Single Ended Line Testing (SELT), transfer function estimation, channel capacity, loop qualification.

1 Introduction

When offering a digital subscriber line (DSL) subscription to a customer, the operator first needs to check whether this telephone line is physically capable of supporting the offered data rate. This is called 'loop qualification' and is different for each customer since it depends on the subscriber loop, i.e. the twisted pair cables connecting the customer premises to the central office. Many loop make-ups are possible, but typically a subscriber loop consists of a cascade of different cable sections with increasing diameter toward the customer.

The loop capacity could be measured directly with Dual Ended Line Testing (DELT) but this requires equipment at both line extremities. In contrast, with Single Ended Line Testing (SELT) all measurements are performed from the central office. This eliminates the necessity of dispatching a technician to the customer premises if no modem is present and this is the reason why SELT is gaining much attention lately. Unfortunately, the loop capacity cannot be measured directly from SELT data. The make-up of the subscriber loop has to be estimated first and from this, the transfer function can be found, from which we can then calculate the channel capacity estimation through Shannon's formula.

C. Wang (Ed.): AccessNets, LNICST 6, pp. 427–440, 2009.

Discovering information about the loop make-up through single ended line tests is possible with reflectometry. The basic principle is to inject an excitation signal in the subscriber loop under test, at the central office side. The signal propagates along the loop and each time it encounters an impedance discontinuity (gauge change, end of line,…) a part of the signal is reflected and travels back to the measuring instrument. Analyzing these reflections allows identifying the loop make-up. For more information on the kind of discontinuities and the uniqueness of their trace signature, the reader is referred to [1].

Despite the great benefits of single ended loop make-up estimation, there are few papers in literature addressing this problem. Most groups are researching the identification of the loop make-up, with capacity estimation as a possible application. However, an accurate estimate of the loop make-up is also a goal by itself, as it allows updating the loop records database which can be incomplete or inaccurate. Galli et al. [1], [2] use time domain reflectometry (TDR) with a square pulse as excitation signal and consequently the measured reflections are dependent on the shape of the injected pulse. Boets et al. therefore propose to use the one-port scattering parameter, which is the ratio of the reflected to the injected wave, as an indicator of the loop make-up [3],[4]. Here, the excitation signals are discrete multitones (DMT) placed on the ADSL frequency grid. Another measurement technique has been proposed by Dodds et al. [5], by energizing the line with a sinusoid with step-wise increasing frequency. The reflections are then received through coherent detection. Both latter measurement techniques can be catalogued as frequency domain reflectometry (FDR).

Independently of the chosen measurement technique, the collected reflections can be analyzed in the time domain or in the frequency domain. However, till now the identification of the loop make-up has mainly been attempted in the time domain [1]-[4]. In [5], Dodds et al. propose a frequency domain approach to bring out the position of the reflections. Unfortunately this is a non-parametric approach and as such human intervention is still needed to indicate which reflections are significant and to deduce the most probable loop make-up.

The aim of this paper is two-fold. Firstly, it discusses some of the main limitations one encounters when estimating the loop make-up of a subscriber loop and their effects on the existing techniques [1]-[5]. Secondly, it proposes a combination of the techniques mentioned above: the chosen measurement setup uses a DMT excitation as in [3], performs a first non-parametric estimation of the reflections in the frequency domain similar to [5] and finally uses a parametric estimator based on the models described in [4] to compute the most probable loop make-up. From this, the channel capacity can then be estimated.

The remainder of this paper is structured as follows. Section 2 provides the required mathematical background. Section 3 states the main encountered difficulties and physical limitations. Section 4 presents the proposed approach, focusing on the non-parametric estimation of the initial line lengths through frequency domain processing. Finally, Section 5 summarizes the most important conclusions.

2 Theoretical Background

Given that for single ended line measurements only the central office end of the line is accessible, the network should be considered as a one-port. All the information that can be acquired about the network through this port is contained in the one-port scattering parameter $S_{11}(f)$, which is the ratio of the reflected voltage wave b to the incident voltage wave a. The one-port scattering parameter can easily be measured by means of a network analyzer in the frequency domain. If the telephone network consists of a single line, then this transmission line can be modeled as derived in [4].

$$S_{11}(f) = \frac{b}{a} = \frac{-\rho_g + \rho_l e^{-2\gamma L}}{1 - \rho_g \rho_l e^{-2\gamma L}} \qquad (1)$$

L is the unknown length of the line, γ the propagation function of the line, ρ_l the reflection at the line end and ρ_g the reflection at the measurement device, as given by (2) and shown in Fig. 1.

$$\rho_l = \frac{Z_l - Z_c}{Z_l + Z_c}; \quad \rho_g = \frac{Z_g - Z_c}{Z_g + Z_c} \qquad (2)$$

Z_l is the load at the line end, Z_c the characteristic impedance of the line and Z_g the impedance of the measurement device.

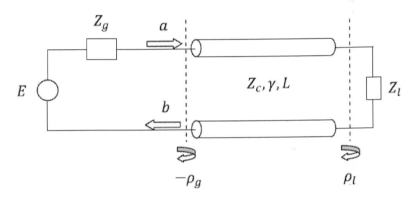

Fig. 1. Reflections for a subscriber loop consisting of a single line

If we linearize formula (1) according to:

$$\frac{1}{1+x} = 1 - x + x^2 - \cdots \qquad \qquad \text{for } |x| < 1$$

we obtain a structure which is straightforward to interpret.

$$S_{11}(f) = -\rho_g + \rho_l\left(1 - \rho_g^2\right)e^{-2\gamma L} + multiples . \qquad (3)$$

The first term represents the reflection at the measurement device, due to the mismatch between the impedance of the measurement device and the characteristic impedance of the line. The second term is the reflection caused by the line end, which is the actual meaningful reflection containing information about the loop make-up. We will also receive multiples of this reflection because the signal bounces (in theory) infinitely back and forth on the line. In practice, however, the attenuation strongly increases with every multiple and as such only a few multiples (if any) will be visible.

We can rewrite (3) with the complex propagation function $\gamma = \alpha + j\beta$ and the following assumptions to keep the example simple without loss of generality: 1) we ignore the multiple reflections, 2) we neglect ρ_g^2 since a good measurement device will be approximately matched to the line under test, leading to a small ρ_g and a negligible ρ_g^2.

$$S_{11}(f) = -\rho_g + \rho_l e^{-2\alpha L} e^{-2j\beta L} \tag{4}$$

In the general case, ρ_g and ρ_l are complex functions. We can write $S_{11}(f)$ in its complex notation:

$$\Re\{S_{11}(f)\} = -\Re\{\rho_g\} + e^{-2\alpha L}[\Re\{\rho_l\}\cos(-2\beta L) - \Im\{\rho_l\}\sin(-2\beta L)] \tag{5}$$

$$\Im\{S_{11}(f)\} = -\Im\{\rho_g\} + e^{-2\alpha L}[\Re\{\rho_l\}\sin(-2\beta L) + \Im\{\rho_l\}\cos(-2\beta L)] . \tag{6}$$

If the line end is open (as is the case for an on-hooked telephone), then $\rho_l = 1$ and the formulas reduce to:

$$\Re\{S_{11}(f)\} = -\Re\{\rho_g\} + e^{-2\alpha L}\cos(-2\beta L) \tag{7}$$

$$\Im\{S_{11}(f)\} = -\Im\{\rho_g\} + e^{-2\alpha L}\sin(-2\beta L) . \tag{8}$$

We will use these quantities in Section 4 to estimate the loop make-up.

Once the loop make-up has been estimated, the transfer function $H(f)$ can easily be calculated using the ABCD parameters [6]:

$$H(f) = \frac{Z_l(f)}{Z_g(f) \cdot [C(f)Z_l(f) + D(f)] + A(f)Z_l(f) + B(f)} . \tag{9}$$

Formula (10) gives the ABCD matrix for a single line [7].

$$\begin{pmatrix} A & B \\ C & D \end{pmatrix} = \begin{pmatrix} cosh(\gamma L) & Z_c sinh(\gamma L) \\ sinh(\gamma L)/Z_c & cosh(\gamma L) \end{pmatrix} . \tag{10}$$

The advantage of the ABCD matrix representation, is that for a cascade, the total ABCD matrix is simply the product of the individual ABCD matrices of the single lines.

The theoretical channel capacity of the subscriber line can then be calculated with Shannon's formula:

$$C = \int_{f_1}^{f_2} log_2\left(1 + \frac{|H(f)|^2 S(f)}{N(f)}\right) df \tag{11}$$

$N(f)$ is the power spectral density (PSD) of the noise, $S(f)$ is the PSD of the transmitted xDSL signal as defined by the standards [8], e.g. -40 dBm/Hz for ADSL downstream, and $[f_1, f_2]$ is the frequency band in which the xDSL service operates.

3   Difficulties

This section discusses some main difficulties one encounters when attempting to estimate the loop make-up of a subscriber loop from single ended line tests. We will illustrate them in the simplest case, namely a single line, with the line length L as the unknown parameter. The described problems are independent of the chosen measurement domain, so they occur with TDR as well as FDR.

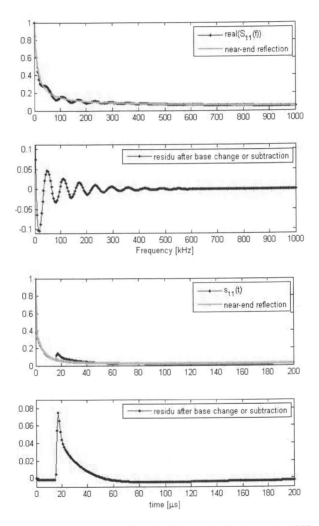

Fig. 2. Near-end reflection partially masking the line end reflection of a 1800 m line; when removing the near-end reflection the end reflection becomes more clearly visible; frequency domain (*top*), time domain (*bottom*)

3.1 Near-End Reflection

The first problem we encounter is the unwanted reflection ρ_g at the measurement device, because the measurement device can never perfectly be matched to the line under test. This impedance mismatch causes a reflection, called the 'near-end' reflection (first term in (7) and (8)), which can partially or totally mask the reflections of interest [1],[3]. Fig. 2 illustrates this problem for a single line of 1800 m.

Several approaches are possible to tackle this problem. In [3] the chosen impedance in which the measured scattering parameter is expressed is changed, as to match the characteristic impedance of the line as well as possible ($Z_{new} \approx Z_c$). This is done through post-processing with (12). This implies that the characteristic impedance of the line needs to be estimated first using a parametric model.

$$S_{11,new} = \frac{Z_g \left(\frac{1 + S_{11}}{1 - S_{11}}\right) - Z_{new}}{Z_g \left(\frac{1 + S_{11}}{1 - S_{11}}\right) + Z_{new}}. \tag{12}$$

In [1] and [5] the near-end reflection ρ_g is estimated by measuring a very long line, in the time and frequency domain respectively. The near-end reflection is then subtracted from the measured data. However, this assumes that a very long line is available. A third possibility is fitting the near-end reflection. In [9] a rational function of second order over first order in the frequency domain was found to give satisfactory results.

In any case, it is important to reduce the near-end reflection as much as possible, to ease the identification of the loop make-up.

3.2 Dispersion

If the near-end reflection can be completely removed, formulas (7) and (8) further simplify to:

$$\Re\{S_{11}(f)\} = e^{-2\alpha(f)L}\cos(-2\beta(f)L) \tag{13}$$

$$\Im\{S_{11}(f)\} = e^{-2\alpha(f)L}\sin(-2\beta(f)L). \tag{14}$$

Note that the frequency dependence has been mentioned explicitly in these expressions. If the phase constant β would be a linear function of the frequency ($\beta = m \cdot f$ with $m \in \mathbb{R}$), an inverse Fourier transform of the sinusoidal term would yield a Dirac pulse at time mL/π. This can then be related to the unknown line length L through the propagation velocity v_p. In practice, β is almost a linear function of frequency and as a consequence we have a lobe around the exact spatial location instead of a Dirac pulse. In the time domain, this phenomenon manifests itself as dispersion due to the fact that the propagation velocity is slightly frequency dependent. The propagation velocity v_p is related to β as follows:

$$v_p(f) = \frac{2\pi f}{\beta(f)}. \tag{15}$$

Moreover, the exponential term will widen the reflection even further. The fact that the attenuation constant α is not a constant, in contrast to what its name suggests, causes supplementary dispersion in the time domain.

As a consequence, in the time domain the reflections show long tails due to the dispersive nature of twisted pairs. This can already be seen in Fig. 2 for a single line. When the loop consists of a cascade of line segments, each k-th reflection r_k will be superimposed on the tail of the preceding reflections $r_{k-1}, r_{k-2},\ldots, r_1$, as such distorting the isolated shape of the individual reflections (see Fig. 3). This complicates the feature extraction and models are needed to take into account the effects of this superposition [10].

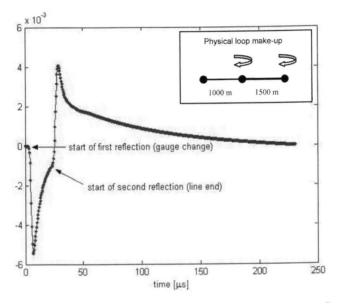

Fig. 3. Due to dispersion, the second reflection is superposed on the tail of the first reflection. This blurs the precise start of the second reflection.

3.3 Spatial Resolution

Fig. 4 shows a typical setup at the central office. The voice signals of the Plain Old Telephony Service (POTS) and the data from the xDSL are separated through a splitter. If the measurement device can be placed between the splitter and the Main Distribution Frame, then the whole frequency band can be measured. However, this is often not possible (e.g. for competitive local exchange carriers) and the measurement device will more probably be placed in the Digital Subscriber Line Access Multiplexer (DSLAM). As a consequence, for test purposes, the low frequencies will be missing or distorted.

Besides the problem of the missing low frequencies, which fixes the minimal usable frequency, in real measurements the maximal frequency is also bounded by practical implementation issues. First of all, the maximal frequency is described in the standards of the considered xDSL technology and sending energy outside this band is

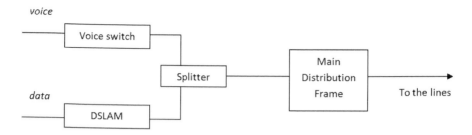

Fig. 4. Splitting of voice and data at the central office

not allowed. Moreover, the signal-to-noise ratio also constrains the maximal usable frequency, as the one-port scattering parameter decreases exponentially. Furthermore, the reliability of some frequencies might be insufficient for other reasons, e.g. distortions due to the nonlinear balun behavior at low frequencies.

As a consequence of these distorted frequencies, the TDR trace will be altered as well. By way of contrast, in the frequency domain only a few data points will be missing or distorted. Therefore, in the frequency domain, the used frequency band can be chosen as to take only the unaffected frequencies into account. This is a main advantage of FDR.

Anyhow, only a part of the measured frequency band will be reliable and should be used for identification. As the spatial precision is inversely proportional to the used frequency band (see 16), a high f_{max} is desired to be able to resolve close discontinuities. On the other hand, (17) illustrates that the maximal resolvable distance is inversely proportional to the frequency grid Δf. For ADSL, the frequency grid consists of multiples of 4312.5 Hz, which leads to a maximal resolvable distance of 11.5 km, which is sufficient for xDSL applications.

$$t_{precision} = \frac{1}{f_{max}-f_{min}} \; ; L_{precision} = \left(\frac{1}{f_{max}-f_{min}}\right)\frac{v_p}{2} \tag{16}$$

$$t_{max} = \frac{1}{2\Delta f} \; ; \qquad L_{max} = \left(\frac{1}{2\Delta f}\right)\frac{v_p}{2} \tag{17}$$

In practical situations, the usable frequency band might be quite small. If, for example the voice band signals are suppressed by the splitter ($f_{min} = 25\ kHz$) and the maximal frequency $f_{max} = 600\ kHz$, this gives a spatial precision of $175\ m$, which is often insufficient. If the maximal frequency cannot be increased any further, then zero padding can be a solution by artificially extending the data sequence with zeroes. Fig. 5 shows a simulation example: a 1200 m 0.4 mm line cascaded with a 400 m 0.5 mm line. When the data record is not extended by increasing f_{max} or by zero padding, then the two reflections cannot be resolved.

A good resolution and peak separation in the time domain are highly desired for good loop make-up estimation and zero padding can help in achieving this goal. However, it must be mentioned that zero padding also introduces small side lobes in the spectrum. Fortunately, the amplitudes of the side lobes are normally small enough not to be mistaken for a reflection.

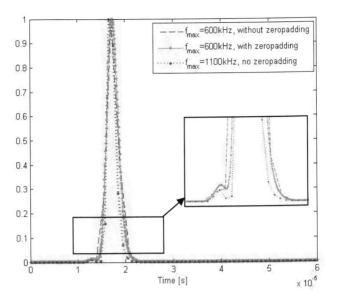

Fig. 5. A 1200 m 0.4 mm line cascaded with a 400 m 0.5 mm line. The time precision can be improved by increasing f_{max} (often not possible in practice) or zero padding.

4 Proposed Approach

As mentioned in the introduction, up till now the processing and identification have mainly been done in the time domain. This has the advantage of being straightforward to understand, as each peak (e.g. Fig. 3) corresponds to the reflection one receives when exciting the line with a pulse. When using TDR as in [1], the reflectogram is measured directly in the time domain. In contrast, in [3] the one-port scattering parameter is measured in the frequency domain and then transformed to the time domain through an ifft. The signal is then processed in the time domain to visualize the reflection information as clearly as possible. This then corresponds to the impulse response of the line, similar to TDR.

We use the same setup as in [3], but instead of transforming the measured one-port scattering parameter into the time domain to analyze it there, we propose to do some processing in the frequency domain first, like in [5]. The main concept is to exploit the information in the periodicity of $S_{11}(f)$ (see Fig. 2.), generated by the standing waves caused by the reflections on the loop. Only after this processing, will the inverse Fourier transform (ifft) be used to return to the time domain, to relate the reflections to line lengths. Finally, a parametric optimization is performed in the frequency domain, based on the models from [4], to obtain the final estimate of the loop make-up.

The one-port scattering parameter is processed in the following way:

- the complex representation is used;
- the near-end reflection is removed;
- the signal is windowed;

- only the reliable frequency band is taken into account;
- the signal is zero padded.

We will now motivate the purpose of each of these processing steps.

4.1 Processing

Complex Representation

A complex quantity, like the one-port scattering parameter is most often expressed in its polar representation. In the case of a single line, the one-port scattering parameter is given by:

$$|S_{11}(f)| = \sqrt{\frac{|\rho_g|^2 + e^{-4\alpha L} -}{2e^{-2\alpha L}\left[\Re\{\rho_g\}\cos(-2\beta L) + \Im\{\rho_g\}\sin(-2\beta L)\right]}} \qquad (18)$$

$$\angle S_{11}(f) = Bgtg\left(\frac{-\Im\{\rho_g\} + e^{-2\alpha L}\sin(-2\beta L)}{-\Re\{\rho_g\} + e^{-2\alpha L}\cos(-2\beta L)}\right). \qquad (19)$$

The magnitude of $S_{11}(f)$, as given by (18) is of the form $\sqrt{A + B\sin(x)}$. Using the series expansion:

$$\sqrt{1+z} = 1 + \frac{1}{2}z - \frac{1}{8}z^2 + \frac{1}{16}z^3 + \cdots$$

results in the following approximation:

$$\sqrt{A + B\sin(x)} = \sqrt{A} + \frac{B}{2\sqrt{A}}\sin(x) - \frac{B^2}{8A\sqrt{A}}\sin^2(x) + \frac{B^3}{16A^2\sqrt{A}}\sin^3(x) + \cdots \qquad (20)$$

The first term is a DC component, the second term is the desired time component at $-2\beta L$ and the following terms give rise to harmonics. In theory the number of harmonics is infinite, however the amplitude quickly decreases. These harmonics are highly undesirable, as they complicate the analysis. In contrast, as one can see from (7) and (8), performing an ifft on the real or imaginary part, will bring out the present periodicities without harmonics. Therefore, we propose to work with the complex representation of $S_{11}(f)$, instead of the more classic polar representation.

The two top rows of Fig. 6 compare $S_{11}(f)$ in polar notation and complex notation for a 0.4 mm cable of 1000 m.

Near-End Reflection

The near-end reflection is removed by fitting it with a rational function of second order over first order [9]. The bottom row of Fig. 6 shows the residue after subtraction of the fit. The one-port scattering parameter $S_{11}(f)$ then reduces to an exponential damped sinusoid as given by (13)-(14).

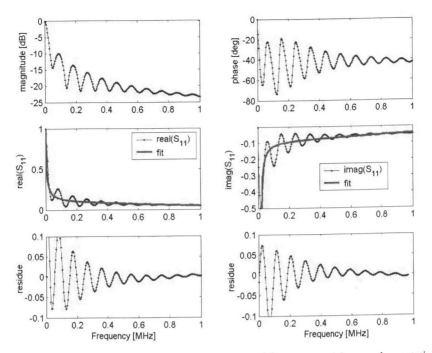

Fig. 6. $S_{11}(f)$ represented in polar notation (*top*), $S_{11}(f)$ represented in complex notation (*middle*) and $S_{11}(f)$ in complex notation after base change or subtraction of fit (*bottom*) for a measured 1000 m segment of 0.4 mm

Windowing

From (13)-(14) we know that the signal is an exponentially damped sine, but the periodicity is unknown. Therefore, before applying the inverse Fourier transform to bring out the periodicities, the signal is windowed in order to avoid leakage. A Hanning window is used for this purpose as it was found to give good results. This windowing will further widen the reflection.

In summary, there are three contributions to the widening of the reflection in the time domain:

a) the propagation speed $v_p(f)$ is not a constant: this means that the sinusoidal function has a slightly changing periodicity;

b) the frequency dependent attenuation $e^{-2\alpha(f)L}$;

c) the use of windowing: if no windowing is used, the reflection would be even wider due to leakage.

Reliable Frequency Band

As explained in section 3.C, the used frequency band should be chosen as large as possible, to have a good spatial resolution. On the other hand, unreliable frequencies

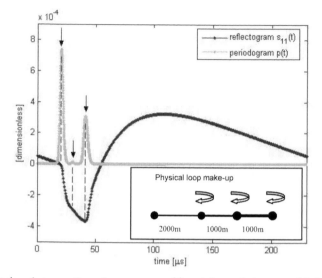

Fig. 7. Comparison between the reflectogram $s_{11}(t)$ and the periodogram $p(t)$ for a simulated cascade of 2000 m (0.4 mm), 1000 m (0.5 mm) and 1000 m (0.6 mm)

should not be taken into account. As such, a trade-off must be found between these two requirements. In the example of Fig. 7, the frequency band $[25,600]kHz$ was used.

Zero padding

In the example of Fig. 7 the reliable frequency band is small and as a consequence the number of remaining measurement points is low. Zero padding is used to improve the spatial resolution, as explained in section III.C. The length of the frequency signal is artificially tripled by adding twice as many zeroes as the length of the data.

4.2 Non-parametric Estimation

After all these operations, the periodogram of the processed signal is calculated:

$$p(t) = |ifft([S_{11}([f_1, f_2]) - fit; 0 \dots 0] \cdot hann)|^2 . \qquad (21)$$

As a consequence, the signal is back in the time domain, but due to the executed manipulations, it has not the physical meaning of the reflectogram (impulse response) anymore. The new signal can be interpreted as a periodogram since it brings out peaks corresponding to each periodicity in $S_{11}(f)$ and each periodicity is generated by a change in the loop make-up. As such, the periodogram will have peaks corresponding to the reflections, just as in the reflectogram. However, due to the performed processing steps, the overlap of the reflections is strongly reduced.

In the case of a single line, there will be a one reflection after a time delay Δt, which can be converted to a line length L by using the propagation speed v_p of the cable:

$$L = \frac{v_p \Delta t}{2} . \qquad (22)$$

Fig. 7 shows a more complicated example: a cascade of 2000 m (0.4 mm), 1000 m (0.5 mm) and 1000 m (0.6 mm). The reflectogram $s_{11}(t)$ and the periodogram $p(t)$ are compared. As one can see, the reflection overlap is strongly reduced with the proposed approach. As indicated by the arrows, the three reflections are now clearly separated in the periodogram, in contrast to the reflectogram where the start of the second reflection is very difficult to detect.

4.3 Parametric Estimation

Next, a reasoning system will analyze the periodogram to determine which reflections are genuine (due to the line end or gauge change) and which ones are multiple reflections or artificial reflections introduced by the processing. It does so by proposing several possible loop make-ups, calculating their periodogram and checking them against the periodogram of the measured subscriber loop.

The genuine reflections can then be translated to line lengths through (22). These lengths are used as initial line lengths for the non-linear optimization. Parametric models for $S_{11}^{mod}(f, \boldsymbol{P})$ are used as described in [4] and the following cost function is minimized:

$$C = \sum_{k=1}^{N} \frac{\left|S_{11}(f_k) - S_{11}^{mod}(f_k, \boldsymbol{P})\right|^2}{\sigma^2(f_k)} . \tag{23}$$

Once the loop make-up has been identified, the transfer function can be calculated with (9). The capacity of the subscriber line can then be estimated for a specific xDSL service with Shannon's formula (11).

5 Conclusions

This paper discussed some difficulties one encounters when identifying the loop make-up from single ended line measurements. Moreover, a new approach for the loop make-up identification by means of single ended line testing was proposed. The main difference with the literature is the domain in which the identification is performed. Till now the identification had mainly been attempted by analysis of the most important features of the reflectogram. This paper proposed a new approach by analyzing the features of another quantity, namely the periodogram of the measured one-port scattering parameter $S_{11}(f)$. The advantage is that the two main drawbacks of the time domain approach, namely dispersion and unreliable frequency bands are tackled. The reduced dispersion eases the loop make-up estimation, which positively affects the results of the estimated channel capacity. Moreover, the new algorithm uses only a chosen frequency band, which makes it unnecessary to by-pass the POTS-filter, which suppresses the voice-band in DSL operation. Once the loop make-up is estimated, the transfer function and the line capacity can be calculated. This is important for telephone companies providing DSL services, in order to have a tool to characterize and evaluate the capability of a subscriber local loop in carrying DSL services.

References

1. Galli, S., Waring, D.L.: Loop Makeup Identification Via Single Ended Testing: Beyond Mere Loop Qualification. IEEE J. Sel. Areas Commun. 20(5), 923–935 (2002)
2. Galli, S., Kerpez, K.J.: Single-Ended Loop Make-Up Identification. IEEE Trans. Instrum. Meas. 55(2), 528–549 (2006)
3. Boets, P., Bostoen, T., Van Biesen, L., Pollet, T.: Pre-Processing of Signals for Single-Ended Subscriber Line Testing. IEEE Trans. Instrum. Meas. 55(5), 1509–1518 (2006)
4. Bostoen, T., Boets, P., Zekri, M., Van Biesen, L., Pollet, T., Rabijns, D.: Estimation of the Transfer Function of a Subscriber Loop by Means of One-Port Scattering Parameter Measurement at the Central Office. IEEE J. Sel. Areas in Commun. 20(5), 936–948 (2002)
5. Celaya, B., Dodds, D.: Single-Ended DSL Line Tester. In: Proc. Canadian Conf. on Electrical and Computer Engineering, pp. 2155–2158 (2004)
6. Chen, W.Y.: DSL: Simulation Techniques and Standards Development for Digital Subscriber Line Systems. MacMillan Technical Publishing, U.S.A (1998)
7. Starr, T., Cioffi, J., Silverman, P.: Understanding Digital Subscriber Line Technology. Prentice Hall, New Jersey (1999)
8. Asymmetric digital subscriber line (ADSL) transceivers. ITU, Recommendation G.992.1 (1999)
9. Neus, C., Boets, P., Van Biesen, L.: Transfer Function Estimation of Digital Subscriber Lines. In: IEEE Proc. Instrum. Meas. Techn. Conf. 1–5 (2007)
10. Vermeiren, T., Bostoen, T., Louage, F., Boets, P., Chehab, X.O.: Subscriber Loop Topology Classification by means of Time Domain Reflectometry. In: Proc. IEEE Int. Conf. Comm, pp. 1998–2002 (2003)

Optical CDMA with Embedded Spectral-Polarization Coding over Double Balanced Differential-Detector

Jen-Fa Huang, Chih-Ta Yen, and Bo-Hau Chen

Institute of Computer and Communications, Department of Electrical Engineering,
National Cheng Kung University, Tainan City, Taiwan, ROC
huajf@ee.ncku.edu.tw

Abstract. A spectral-polarization coding (SPC) optical code-division multiple-access (OCDMA) configuration structured over arrayed-waveguide grating (AWG) router is proposed. The polarization-division double balanced detector is adopted to execute difference detection and enhances system performance. The signal-to-noise ratio (SNR) is derived by taking the effect of PIIN into account. The result indicates that there would be up to 9-dB SNR improvement than the conventional spectral-amplitude coding (SAC) structures with Walsh-Hadamard codes. Mathematical deriving results of the SNR demonstrate the system embedded with the orthogonal state of polarization (SOP) will suppress effectively phase-induced intensity noise (PIIN). In addition, we will analyze the relations about bit error rate (BER) vs. the number of active users under the different encoding schemes and compare them with our proposed scheme. The BER vs. the effective power under the different encoding scheme with the same number of simultaneous active user conditions are also revealed. Finally, the polarization-matched factor and the difference between simulated and experimental values are discussed.

Keywords: spectral polarization coding, optical code-division multiple-access, arrayed-waveguide grating, polarization-division double balanced differential-detector, phase-induced intensity noise, Walsh-Hadamard codes.

1 Introduction

The optical code-division multiple-access (OCDMA) technique in optical communication is gradually noticed in the recent years for requirement of multiple users can access the network asynchronously and simultaneously with high level transmission security [1-3]. The spectral-amplitude coding optical code-division multiple-access (SAC-OCDMA) system was proposed as a means of increasing the maximum permissible number of simultaneous active users by decreasing the codeword length and eliminating the multiple-access interference (MAI) effect [4]-[7]. With regard to spectral-amplitude coding (SAC) technique, it is crucial to identify the maximum number of wavelengths that such dispersive devices could resolve, since this will dictate the length of the code employed for coding. The SAC-OCDMA system not only preserves the ability of MAI cancellation, but also uses cheap sources with reduced complexity. However, in the traditional SAC scheme, the effect of

C. Wang (Ed.): AccessNets, LNICST 6, pp. 441–456, 2009.

polarization is often ignored in the procedure of encoding and decoding. While photodiodes (PDs) are applied to detect in the receiver, the phase-induced intensity noise (PIIN) cannot be suppressed and the signal-to-noise ratio (SNR) of system is degraded. Smith et al. [8] have concluded that the performance of SAC schemes is limited by the presence of beat noise. Hence, the performance is hard to boost enormously even though using the bipolar scheme [9].

A fundamental approach to the PIIN problem is to reduce the number of wavelength collisions in the balanced photo-detector. In the spectral-polarization coding (SPC) scheme proposed in the current study [10], a Walsh-Hadamard code is employed as signature address accomplishing by fiber Bragg gratings (FBGs). This code is characterized by a bipolar property [11] due to orthogonality among states of polarization (SOPs). The spectral efficiency of the proposed complementary bipolar scheme is found to be twice that of the previous unipolar supercodes. Thus, the proposed SPC approach enables a dramatic increase in the permissible number of simultaneous active users for the same optical bandwidth. The other advantage of the proposed system is that the use of two orthogonally polarized chips transmitted at the same wavelength from the same encoder eliminates PIIN.

Since a single-mode fiber (SMF) supports two orthogonal SOPs for the same fundamental mode, a new kind of multiplexing, known as the Polarization-division multiplexing (PDM), in which two orthogonally polarized signals are transmitted simultaneously in a, provides a versatile solution for increasing the utilization of the available bandwidth. In PDM, two channels at the same wavelength are transmitted through the fiber such that their pulse trains are orthogonally polarized at the fiber input. At first glance, such a scheme should not work unless polarization-maintaining fibers (PMFs) are used since the polarization state changes randomly in conventional fibers because of birefringence fluctuations. However, even though the polarization states of each channel does change at the end of the fiber link in an unpredictable manner, their orthogonal nature is preserved, making it possible to isolate each channel through simple optical techniques. Various combinations of PDM with other multiplexing techniques have been proposed [12]-[14]. In [14], the respect to polarization, an arrayed-waveguide grating (AWG) is a linear device, and thus the degree of polarization (DOP) of the AWG-based system should not degrade. Besides, multi-wave optical sources could be used in the PDM transmission systems [15]. However, the PDM demultiplexing technique is rather complex due to the random change of the signal's SOP caused by fluctuations of the fiber birefringence along the fiber's length. This phenomenon induces so-called polarization mode dispersion (PMD). It means that there are two orthogonal polarization modes, which are called principal states of polarization (PSPs) [16], obeying different dispersion relations. Recently, PMD compensation techniques have been applied successfully to enhance the performance of WDM systems as in [17] and [18]. In the general PMD compensation approach, a feedback signal is employed to tune the adaptive polariza-tion controller [19] and delay line [20] in order to adjust the PSPs and the differential group delay (DGD). Such advanced PMD compensation techniques render the proposed SPC scheme feasible for implementation in long-haul networks [21].

The remainder of this paper is organized as follows. Section 2 introduces the proposed system configuration and explains the encoder/decoder (codec) mechanisms. Section 3 describes the encoding/decoding schemes and illustrates the elimination of

MAI by mathematical analyses. Section 4 derives the SNR of the proposed structure and evaluates the system performance in terms of the bit error rate (BER) and the maximum number of permissible simultaneous active users. The analytic results are compared with those of the conventional unipolar and bipolar SAC schemes approach to evaluate the performance improvement. Section 5 compares and discusses some related-curve diagrams of the BER versus effective power under the different number of active users and the different coding schemes with our proposed scheme. Finally, Section 6 provides some concluding remarks.

2 System Configuration

2.1 Encoder Scheme

The OCDMA network coder embedded SPC and polarization-division double balanced differential-detection technique is constructed on the basis of AWGs as shown in Fig. 1. Due to transmitted information data bit for each user is different, the optical polarization modulated module shown at left side in Fig. 1 is independent. In addition, the polarization-division double balanced detector shown at right side in Fig. 1 is also one by one for each user. The encoding procedure includes four steps.

1. A broadband optical source is adopting the modulating source. Then passing through a splitter, it is modulated by desired data and its counterpart, $\overline{data}$, respectively.
2. The modulated optical sources are introduced PBSs to divide mutually orthogonal SOPs. After electric-optical modulator (EOM), a polarization controller (PC) is set to adjust the SOP between an EOM and a PBS. Then two mutually orthogonal SOP optical elements input to the AWG-based OCDMA encoder.
3. According to the wavelength cyclic shifted property of AWGs, two orthogonal SOPs are inputted different input ports of AWG to obtain a set of Walsh-Hadamard code and its complementary code that accompany the mutually orthogonal SOPs. Namely, there will be the spectrum of C_j(H) and $\overline{C}_j$(V) at the upper branch. Note that the sub-index means the codeword is used for user #j; (H) and (V) denote the horizontal and vertical SOP, respectively. Similarly, C_j(V) and $\overline{C}_1$(H) output at the lower branch.
4. Finally, the encoded spectrum for user #j is accomplished by combining two branches.

2.2 Decoder Scheme

The decoding processes can be divided into three steps and explain as following.

1. Taking out the mutually orthogonal SOP components from the encoded spectrum, then input to AWG router to perform OCDMA decoding process.
2. Depend on decoded signature code C_j and its complementary, $\overline{C}_j$ to determine which output port of AWG routers should be coupled each other of star couplers.

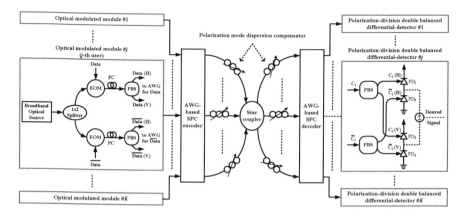

Fig. 1. System structure of proposed SPC scheme with polarization-division double balanced differential-detector

3.   The spectra have the same SOP are executed to realize balanced detection, i.e., the detected electrical signals form the lower branch is subtracted from the correspondence from the upper branch. Finally, the desired data signal for user *#j* can be obtained.

3   Mathematical Analyses

3.1   Codec Scheme over AWG-Based

In Fig. 1, if we consider that K transmitter/receiver pairs are connected to a passive $2K{\times}1$ star coupler. Meanwhile, a set of Walsh-Hadamard code is denoted by C_k and its complementary code $\overline{C}_k$, is assigned to the k-th user. Here we give an example for the number of user equals 7, i.e. $K = 7$, as shown in Fig. 2. The index i of H_i/V_i denotes horizontal/vertical quantity of the i-th user.

By adopting the wavelength cyclic shifted property of AWG routers, we can get the spectra are $C_k(\mathrm{H}) + \overline{C}_k(\mathrm{V})$ and $C_k(\mathrm{V}) + \overline{C}_k(\mathrm{H})$ at the output of the 4x1 star coupler in the upper and the lower branch, respectively. Therefore, the horizontal and vertical quantity spectra are written as

$$E_\mathrm{H} = \sum_{k=1}^{K} b_k\, C_k + \overline{b}_k\, \overline{C}_k \ , \tag{1a}$$

$$E_\mathrm{V} = \sum_{k=1}^{K} b_k\, \overline{C}_k + \overline{b}_k\, C_k \ , \tag{1b}$$

where b_k is the k-th user's data bit ($b_k \in \{0,1\}$), and C_k and $\overline{C}_k$ are respectively the k-th user's direct and complementary codewords in the spectral domain. The summed

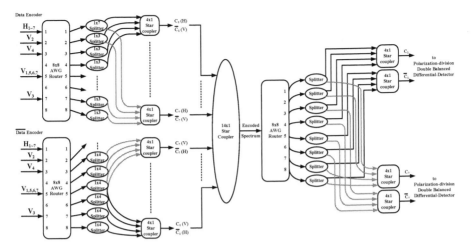

Fig. 2. Structure diagram of AWG-based SPC codec in detail

signal spectrum for all the simultaneous active user, R, is composed of horizontal and vertical states of polarization and is given by

$$R = E_H + E_V .\tag{2}$$

Then the encoded spectrum is sent to the decoder as shown in Fig. 2. After the decoding procedure as described in subsection 2.2 at Section 2, we can obtain the corresponding spectrum for each user's upper branch and lower branch at output of star couplers in the decoder. They are expressed in Eqs. (3a) and (3b), respectively,

$$R \cdot C_k = \sum_{k=1}^{K} b_k\, C_k + \overline{b}_k\, C_k .\tag{3a}$$

$$R \cdot \overline{C}_k = \sum_{k=1}^{K} \overline{b}_k\, \overline{C}_k + b_k\, \overline{C}_k .\tag{3b}$$

In Eqs. (3a) and (3b), the first item belongs to horizontal SOP quantity and the last item belongs to vertical SOP quantity. Moreover, according to the proposed structure, we take out horizontal and vertical components from above two equations to execute the double balanced detection. It is expressed as

$$\sum_{k=1}^{K} [b_k\,(C_k + \overline{C}_k) - \overline{b}_k\,(C_k + \overline{C}_k)]$$

$$= \begin{cases} \displaystyle\sum_{k=1}^{K} (C_k + \overline{C}_k) = \ \ N & \text{for } b_k = 1 , \\[4mm] \displaystyle-\sum_{k=1}^{K} (C_k + \overline{C}_k) = -N & \text{for } b_k = 0 \end{cases}\tag{4}$$

where N is indicated the codeword length.

3.2 MAI Cancellation

The encoded spectrum can be obtained in (2). From (3a), by replacing the external C_k becomes to C_j, the equation is rewritten as

$$R \cdot C_j = [\sum_{k=1}^{K} (b_k\, C_k + \bar{b}_k \overline{C}_k) + \sum_{k=1}^{K} (b_k \overline{C}_k + \bar{b}_k\, C_k)] \cdot C_j. \tag{5a}$$

Similarly, we update (3b) as shown below.

$$R \cdot \overline{C}_j = [\sum_{k=1}^{K} (b_k\, C_k + \bar{b}_k \overline{C}_k) + \sum_{k=1}^{K} (b_k \overline{C}_k + \bar{b}_k\, C_k)] \cdot \overline{C}_j. \tag{5b}$$

In the above equations, the former items in the middle brackets are still represented the horizontal SOP quantity. The latter items are the vertical SOP quantity. According to our polarization-division decoding scheme, we make the parts have the same SOP to execute balanced detection.

$$(5a)_{(H)} - (5b)_{(H)} \Rightarrow$$

$$\sum_{k=1}^{K} [b_k (C_k \cdot C_j - C_k \cdot \overline{C}_j) + \bar{b}_k (\overline{C}_k \cdot C_j - \overline{C}_k \cdot \overline{C}_j)] \tag{6a}$$

$$(5a)_{(V)} - (5b)_{(V)} \Rightarrow$$

$$\sum_{k=1}^{K} [b_k (\overline{C}_k \cdot C_j - \overline{C}_k \cdot \overline{C}_j) + \bar{b}_k (C_k \cdot C_j - C_k \cdot \overline{C}_j)] \tag{6b}$$

By introducing the following Walsh-Hadamard codes correlation properties into Eqs. (6a) and (6b),

$$R_{cc}(k,l) = \sum_{i=1}^{N} C_k(i) C_l(i) = \begin{cases} N/2, & \text{for } k = l \\ N/4, & \text{for } k \neq l \end{cases}, \tag{7a}$$

and

$$R_{c\bar{c}}(k,l) = \sum_{i=1}^{N} C_k(i) \overline{C}_l(i) = \begin{cases} 0, & \text{for } k = l \\ N/4, & \text{for } k \neq l \end{cases}. \tag{7b}$$

We will get an answer of zero when the decoded pattern does not match the coded pattern. Namely, the MAI is eliminated completely in theory for the idea flat spectrum of an incoherent optical source.

Table 1 presents an example of the SPC with polarization-division double balanced differential-detection mechanism for simultaneous active users $K = 3$ and code length $N = 8$. In the illustration, users #1 and #2 transmit logical 1 information bit, and user #3 sends logical 0. We assume the optical source has the ideal flat spectrum and the power unit of each wavelength is equal. Applying our proposed encoding process, the resultant code vectors are $E_H = (2\lambda_1, 2\lambda_2, 3\lambda_3, 1\lambda_4, 1\lambda_5, 1\lambda_6, 2\lambda_7, 0\lambda_8)$ and $E_V = (1\lambda_1, 1\lambda_2, 0\lambda_3, 2\lambda_4, 2\lambda_5, 2\lambda_6, 1\lambda_7, 3\lambda_8)$. When the received signal R pass through the decoder #1, 8 units photocurrent are yielded, which corresponds signature code word, C_1, and horizontal SOP at PD_1 as shown in Fig. 1. In the same method, 4 units photocurrent are obtained for $\overline{C}_1$ with horizontal SOP at PD_2. Moreover, the 4 units and 8 units photocurrent are matched C_1 (V) and $\overline{C}_1$ (V) at PD_3 and PD_4 in the lower arm, respectively. And the numerical values could be calculated by (5a) and (5b). Balanced differential-detection results in $RC_1^{(H)} - R\overline{C}_1^{(H)} = 4$ units power and $RC_1^{(V)} - R\overline{C}_1^{(V)} = -4$ units power. After the second stage differential detecting, 8 units power is obtained and decides that logic "1" is transmitted. Similarly, if substituting decoder #3 for #1, 4, 8, 8, 4 units power photocurrent would be detected at PD_1, PD_2, PD_3, and PD_4, respectively.

Table 1. Simple illustration of polarization-division balanced differential-detection for 3 simultaneous active users

	Data	Spectral Polarization Coding Mechanism																		
		Horizontal SOP										Vertical SOP								
User	bit		λ_1	λ_2	λ_3	λ_4	λ_5	λ_6	λ_7	λ_8		λ_1	λ_2	λ_3	λ_4	λ_5	λ_6	λ_7	λ_8
1	1	C_1	1	1	1	1	0	0	0	0	$\overline{C}_1$	0	0	0	0	1	1	1	1
2	1	C_2	1	0	1	0	1	0	1	0	$\overline{C}_2$	0	1	0	1	0	1	0	1
3	0	$\overline{C}_3$	0	1	1	0	0	1	1	0	C_3	1	0	0	1	1	0	0	1
Received Signal (R)		E_H	2	2	3	1	1	1	2	0	E_V	1	1	0	2	2	2	1	3

Finally, -8 units power will occur in decoder #3 and indicates user #3 sent logic "0". In the decoders of other users, e.g., $C_4 = (1, 1, 0, 0, 0, 0, 1, 1)$, the unit power at each PD is equal. After double balanced differential-detection, it will no power is detected. Hence, MAI from other users with differential detection scheme can be theoretically cancelled.

4 Performance Analysis

4.1 Signal Power Evaluation

Referring to [3] and [10], and applying (2), the detected photo-current coming from K simultaneous active users with a chip length N per user, I_1, from PD_1 shown in Fig. 9, is written as

$$
\begin{aligned}
I_1 &= \Re \int_0^\infty G_1(v)dv \\
&= \frac{\Re P_{sr}}{\sqrt{2}N} \sum_{i=1}^N \sum_{k=1}^K \{b_k[C_k(i) \cdot C_j(i)] + \overline{b}_k[\overline{C}_k(i) \cdot C_j(i)]\}
\end{aligned}
\tag{8a}
$$

where $\Re$ denotes the responsibility of the PD, $G_1(v)$ is the single-sideband power spectral densities (PSDs) of the received signal at PD_1, and P_{sr} is the effective power from a single source at the receiver. The coefficient $\sqrt{2}$ is as a result of adopting PBS. Similarly, the detected photocurrents at photodiode PD_2, PD_3, and PD_4 are written as I_2, I_3, I_4, respectively.

$$I_2 = \Re \int_0^\infty G_2(v)\,dv$$
$$= \frac{\Re P_{sr}}{\sqrt{2}N} \sum_{i=1}^{N} \sum_{k=1}^{K} \{b_k[C_k(i)\cdot\overline{C}_j(i)] + \overline{b}_k[\overline{C}_k(i)\cdot\overline{C}_j(i)]\} . \tag{8b}$$

$$I_3 = \Re \int_0^\infty G_3(v)\,dv$$
$$= \frac{\Re P_{sr}}{\sqrt{2}N} \sum_{i=1}^{N} \sum_{k=1}^{K} \{b_k[\overline{C}_k(i)\cdot C_j(i)] + \overline{b}_k[C_k(i)\cdot C_j(i)]\} . \tag{8c}$$

$$I_4 = \Re \int_0^\infty G_4(v)\,dv$$
$$= \frac{\Re P_{sr}}{\sqrt{2}N} \sum_{i=1}^{N} \sum_{k=1}^{K} \{b_k[\overline{C}_k(i)\cdot\overline{C}_j(i)] + \overline{b}_k[C_k(i)\cdot\overline{C}_j(i)]\} . \tag{8d}$$

The signal from the desired user is given by the difference of the photocurrent outputs. After the second stage balanced detection is expressed as

$$I = (I_1 - I_2) - (I_3 - I_4)$$
$$= \frac{\Re P_{sr}}{\sqrt{2}N} \sum_{i=1}^{N} \sum_{k=1}^{K} \{b_k[C_k(i)\cdot C_j(i) - C_k(i)\cdot\overline{C}_j(i)$$
$$\qquad - \overline{C}_k(i)\cdot C_j(i) + \overline{C}_k(i)\cdot\overline{C}_j(i)] \tag{9}$$
$$\qquad + \overline{b}_k[\overline{C}_k(i)\cdot C_j(i) - \overline{C}_k(i)\cdot\overline{C}_j(i)$$
$$\qquad - C_k(i)\cdot C_j(i) + C_k(i)\cdot\overline{C}_j(i)]\}$$

By introducing the correlation properties of Eqs. (7a) and (7b), Equ. (9) can be simplified to be

$$I = \begin{cases} \Re P_{sr}/\sqrt{2} & \text{for } k = j \text{ and } b_k = 1 \\ -\Re P_{sr}/\sqrt{2} & \text{for } k = j \text{ and } b_k = 0 . \\ 0 & \text{for } k \neq j \end{cases} \tag{10}$$

4.2 PIIN Power Evaluation

Noise that exists in the SAC-OCDMA systems includes PIIN, shot noise and thermal noise. The mathematical description is given by

$$\langle i^2 \rangle = \langle I_{shot}^2 \rangle + \langle I_{PIIN}^2 \rangle + \langle I_{thermal}^2 \rangle$$
$$= 2eIB + I^2 B\tau_c + 4K_b T_n B / R_L \tag{11}$$

where e is the electron's charge, I is the average photocurrent, B is the noise-equivalent electrical bandwidth of the receiver, τ_c is the coherence time of the source, K_b is the Boltzmann's constant, T_n is the absolute receiver noise temperature, and R_L is the receiver load resistor. PIIN is the dominating noise when the received optical power is large enough (more than -10 dBm), we ignore the effect of other noises in large received effective power condition. So, the variance of photocurrent due to the effect of PIIN can be written as

$$\langle i^2 \rangle \cong \langle I^2_{PIIN} \rangle = I^2(1+P^2)B\tau_c , \qquad (12)$$

where P denotes the DOP. Base on the proposed scheme, the parameter P is set to 1. Hence, (12) can be rewritten as

$$\langle I^2_{PIIN} \rangle = 2I^2 B\tau_c$$
$$= 2B\mathfrak{R}^2 \sum_{m=1}^{4} (\int_0^\infty G_m^2(\nu)\, d\nu) \qquad (13)$$

where m is the number of PD are used in our proposing structure. The light source spectrum is assumed to be idea flat with linewidth, $\Delta\nu$. The variance of the photocurrent resulting from the PIIN at PD_1 is expressed as

$$\langle I_1^2 \rangle = \frac{B\mathfrak{R}^2 P_{sr}^2}{2N\Delta\nu} \sum_{i=1}^{N}\sum_{k=1}^{K}\sum_{m=1}^{K} [b_k b_m\, C_k(i)C_m(i)C_j(i)$$
$$+ b_k \overline{b}_m\, C_k(i)\overline{C}_m(i)C_j(i) .$$
$$+ \overline{b}_k b_m\, \overline{C}_k(i)C_m(i)C_j(i)$$
$$+ \overline{b}_k \overline{b}_m\, \overline{C}_k(i)\overline{C}_m(i)C_j(i)] \qquad (14a)$$

In the same way, the variances of the photocurrent are generated by the others PDs (i.e. PD_2, PD_3, and PD_4) can be written as (14b), (14c), and (14d), respectively.

$$\langle I_2^2 \rangle = \frac{B\mathfrak{R}^2 P_{sr}^2}{2N\Delta\nu} \sum_{i=1}^{N}\sum_{k=1}^{K}\sum_{m=1}^{K} [b_k b_m\, C_k(i)C_m(i)\overline{C}_j(i)$$
$$+ b_k \overline{b}_m\, C_k(i)\overline{C}_m(i)\overline{C}_j(i) .$$
$$+ \overline{b}_k b_m\, \overline{C}_k(i)C_m(i)\overline{C}_j(i)$$
$$+ \overline{b}_k \overline{b}_m\, \overline{C}_k(i)\overline{C}_m(i)\overline{C}_j(i)] \qquad (14b)$$

$$\langle I_3^2 \rangle = \frac{B\mathfrak{R}^2 P_{sr}^2}{2N\Delta\nu} \sum_{i=1}^{N}\sum_{k=1}^{K}\sum_{m=1}^{K} [b_k b_m\, \overline{C}_k(i)\overline{C}_m(i)C_j(i)$$
$$+ b_k \overline{b}_m\, \overline{C}_k(i)C_m(i)C_j(i) .$$
$$+ \overline{b}_k b_m\, C_k(i)\overline{C}_m(i)C_j(i)$$
$$+ \overline{b}_k \overline{b}_m\, C_k(i)C_m(i)C_j(i)] \qquad (14c)$$

$$\left\langle I_4^2 \right\rangle = \frac{B\Re^2 P_{sr}^2}{2N\Delta v} \sum_{i=1}^{N} \sum_{k=1}^{K} \sum_{m=1}^{K} [b_k b_m \overline{C}_k(i)\overline{C}_m(i)\overline{C}_j(i)$$

$$+ b_k \overline{b}_m \overline{C}_k(i)C_m(i)\overline{C}_j(i) \qquad (14d)$$

$$+ \overline{b}_k b_m C_k(i)\overline{C}_m(i)\overline{C}_j(i)$$

$$+ \overline{b}_k \overline{b}_m C_k(i)C_m(i)\overline{C}_j(i)]$$

The total variance of the photocurrent resulting from the PIIN involves all four PDs would be gotten. Performing the summation of (14a) to (14d), the total variance of the photocurrent would be gotten.

$$\left\langle I_{PIIN}^2 \right\rangle = \left\langle I_1^2 \right\rangle + \left\langle I_2^2 \right\rangle + \left\langle I_3^2 \right\rangle + \left\langle I_4^2 \right\rangle. \qquad (15)$$

Depending on the relation of $\sum_{i=1}^{N} C_j(i) + \overline{C}_j(i) = N$, and the statement of [20],Equ. (15) could be represented as

$$\left\langle I_{PIIN}^2 \right\rangle = \frac{B\Re^2 P_{sr}^2}{2N\Delta v}[\frac{N}{2}K + \alpha\frac{N}{4}K(K-1)]\times 2$$

$$= \frac{B\Re^2 P_{sr}^2}{4\Delta v}(\alpha K^2 - \alpha K + 2K) \qquad (16)$$

where α denotes the polarization-match factor. It means the SOPs mutually match extent between the encoder and decoder. Depending on [20], if the polarization matches when a differential-detection technique is used, the PIIN can be degraded effectively. So, the cross collision may be eliminated completely in perfect condition.

In addition, the DOP must be considered under real condition. Thus, (16) must be multiplied $(1+P^2)$ then becomes the last result to represent total PIIN in our system.

$$(1 + P^2)\left\langle I_{PIIN}^2 \right\rangle = \frac{B\Re^2 P_{sr}^2}{2\Delta v}(\alpha K^2 - \alpha K + 2K). \qquad (17)$$

4.3 Signal to PIIN Ratio Evaluation

However, on the long-haul transmissions over OCDMA network the DOP effect must be addressed. In the following analyses, we assume an average value, i.e., α is 1/2. Dividing (10) by (17), the SNR due to the effect of PIIN is

$$SNR_{(PIIN)} = \frac{\left\langle I_{b=1} - I_{b=0} \right\rangle^2}{\left\langle I_{PIIN}^2 \right\rangle} = \frac{8\Delta v}{BK(K+3)}. \qquad (18)$$

The relation between SNR and simultaneous active users of conventional unipolar, bipolar, previous SPC scheme over FBG-base [10], and we propose SPC with polarization-division balanced detector embedded OCDMA system as shown in Table 2. Table 2 presents the character comparison for four kinds of techniques base on Walsh-Hadamard code and only PIIN is considered. The SNR$_{(PIIN)}$ of proposed

Table 2. Comparisons of different coding schemes with differential-detector over OCDMA network

Adopted scheme	Code length	User capacity	$SNR_{(PIIN)}$
Unipolar SAC	N	$N-1$	$\dfrac{\Delta v}{BK(K+1)}$
Bipolar SAC	N	$N-1$	$\dfrac{4\Delta v}{BK(K+1)}$
Previous SPC	N	N	$\dfrac{8\Delta v}{BK(K+1)}$
Proposed SPC with polarization division detector	N	N	$\dfrac{8\Delta v}{BK(K+3)}$

SPC with double balanced detector structure would be 9 and 3 dB improvement than the conventional unipolar and bipolar SAC schemes, respectively. However, it would be a little worse than the previous SPC scheme when a compromising position is considered. This is because of our design without using any depolarizer. If the polarization match extent is improved, our system will obtain better performance even than hybrid SPC-SAC scheme [22].

Further, the SNR result is substituting into the following Eq. by using the Gaussian assumption as following

$$BER = \frac{1}{2}\text{erfc}[(\frac{SNR_{(PIIN)}}{8})^{\frac{1}{2}}]. \tag{19}$$

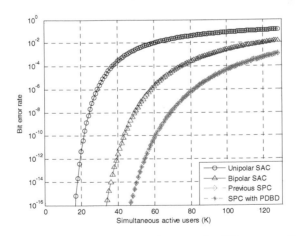

Fig. 3. BER vs. the number of simultaneous active users for different encoding schemes with Walsh-Hadamard code

The relationship between BER and the number of active users for various Hadamard-coded SAC and SPC schemes of OCDMA system is as shown in Fig. 3 based on (19). Transmitting the data bits on two mutually orthogonal SOPs causes some of the PIIN terms to be canceled out. The evaluation results have shown that the use of orthogonal polarizations improves BER. The following parameters: $\Delta v = 6.25$ THz, $B = 80$ MHz, and the center wavelength is working at 1550 nm are used in our analysis.

5 Simulations and Discussions

If we think about the shot noise and thermal noise into total noise power for real noise condition, and (17) is substituted for the middle term of (11). Then (11) is adopted as the variance of photocurrent of noise and rewritten as

$$\langle i^2 \rangle = \langle I_{shot}^2 \rangle + \langle I_{PIIN}^2 \rangle + \langle I_{thermal}^2 \rangle$$

$$= 2e\,I\,B + I^2\,B\tau_c + 4K_b T_n B / R_L \tag{20}$$

$$= 2e\frac{\Re P_{sr}}{\sqrt{2}} B + \frac{B\Re^2 P_{sr}^2}{4\Delta v} K(K+3) + \frac{4K_b T_n B}{R_L}$$

Using the result of (20), the SNR which is involved the shot noise, PIIN, and thermal noise could be represented as

$$SNR_{(total)} = \frac{2\Re^2 P_{sr}^2}{2e\Re P_{sr}B/\sqrt{2} + B\Re^2 P_{sr}^2 K(K+3)/4\Delta v + 4K_b T_n B/R_L}. \tag{21}$$

Hence, we can draw the related curve of the BER and the effective received power under the different number of simultaneous active user, i.e., $K = 55$, 63, and 71, for we proposed system, as shown in Fig. 4. Clearly, when the effective power is smaller than 10^{-7}w, the proposed system appears high BER. When the received effective power is increased, the BER has apparent improvement. After the effective power is greater than 1μw, even if we continue to increase the power level, the BER keeps in constant value.

Following, the same related curve would be shown under the different coding schemes as shown in Fig. 5. We compare the proposed SPC with unipolar and bipolar SACs, previous SPC with $P = 0$ and 1 under the number of simultaneous active user equals 63. In the plenty simultaneous active user situation, the performance of conventional unipolar coding scheme is awful. The bipolar SAC and SPC with $P = 1$ schemes have approach BER. The BER of the system we proposed is slightly worse than SPC with $P = 0$. However, this scheme does not request the DOP equals 1, namely we do not scatter the polarization state in our system. As long as the effective power achieves certain level, the performances of two schemes will be the same.

In (16), we introduce a polarization-match factor to indicate the SOPs mutually match extent between the encoder and the decoder. Above analyses, we take a compromising condition into account and order $\alpha = 1/2$. Certainly, when the polarization states of the system are matched perfectly, the PIIN from cross collision among different wavelengths will be eliminated completely because of α becomes

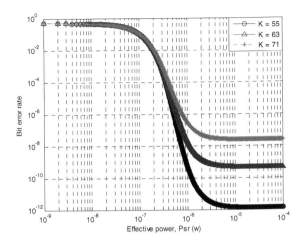

Fig. 4. BER vs. effective power with $\alpha = 0.5$ and considering total noise for different number of simultaneous active user

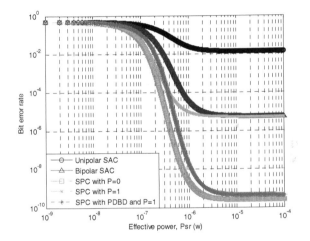

Fig. 5. BER vs. effective power with $\alpha = 0.5$ and considering total noise for different encoding schemes under 63 simultaneous active user

zero. On the other hand, the PIIN is maximum for the proposed mechanism while α equals 1. Figure 6 discusses four different conditions of α to realize them how to affect the performance of the system. Then the BER analysis and comparison under previous SPC, hybrid SPC-SAC, and proposed SPC with three different polarization-match factors is shown in Fig. 7. According to the simulated result, when α achieves 0.25, the performance of our proposed system is near hybrid SPC-SAC scheme.

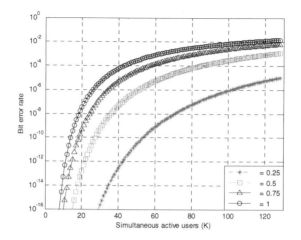

Fig. 6. BER analysis of the proposed system for four different polarization-match factors, i.e., $\alpha = 0.25, 0.5, 0.75,$ and 1

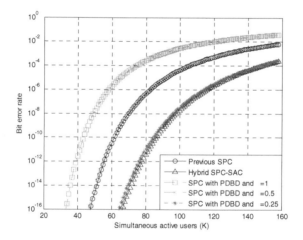

Fig. 7. Performance comparison between the proposed system with three different α and previous SPC scheme

6   Conclusions

In this study, we proposed the modified SPC-OCDMA system structure constructed of hybrid AWG routers and PBSs were implemented over differential photo-detectors. This scheme not only cancels completely the effect of the MAI but also suppresses the PIIN in the multiuser system when the SOPs are controlled. The BER of the OCDMA system has been analyzed numerically for the PIIN limited case. Transmitting the data bits of two users from one encoder on mutually orthogonal SOPs causes some of the PIIN terms to be canceled out. The evaluation results have shown that the use of orthogonal polarizations improves the SNR. However, as the number of active users increase, the number of PIIN terms which vanish is reduced relative to the total number of incoherent beating terms and hence the noise suppression effect is diminished. The SNR of proposed SPC with polarization-division double balanced detection structure setting DOP to 1 (i.e., $P = 1$) would be found 9 and 3 dB better than the conventional unipolar and bipolar SAC schemes when the DOP is set to zero, respectively. And if the polarization of the system could be matched enough, the performance will achieve the same level with hybrid SPC-SAC scheme.

References

[1] Salehi, J.A.: Code division multiple-access techniques in optical fiber network-Part I: Fundamental principles. IEEE Trans. Commun. 37, 824–833 (1989)

[2] Salehi, J.A., Brackett, C.A.: Code division multiple-access Techniques in optical fiber networks-Part II: Systems performance analysis. IEEE Trans. Commun. 37, 834–842 (1989)

[3] Wei, Z., Shalaby, H.M.H., Ghafouri-Shiraz, H.: Modified quadratic congruence codes for fiber bragg-grating-based spectral-amplitude-coding optical CDMA systems. J. Lightwave Technol. 19, 1274–1281 (2001)

[4] Zhou, X., Shalaby, H.M.H., Lu, C., Cheng, T.: Code for spectral amplitude coding optical CDMA systems. Electron. Lett. 36, 728–729 (2000)

[5] Huang, J.F., Yang, C.C.: Reductions of multiple-access interference in fiber-grating-based optical CDMA network. IEEE Trans. Commun. 50, 1680–1687 (2002)

[6] Moslehi, B.: Noise power spectra of optical two-beam interferometers induced by the laser phase noise. J. Lightwave Technol. 4, 1704–1710 (1986)

[7] Smith, E.D.J., Baikie, R.J., Taylor, D.P.: Performance enhancement of spectral-amplitude-coding optical CDMA using pulseposition modulation. IEEE Trans. Commun. 46, 1176–1185 (1998)

[8] Smith, E.D.J., Gough, P.T., Taylor, D.P.: Noise limits of optical spectral-encoding CDMA systems. Electron. Lett. 31, 1469–1470 (1995)

[9] Huang, J.F., Yang, C.C., Tseng, S.P.: Complementary Walsh-Hadamard coded optical CDMA coder/decoders structured over arrayed-waveguide grating routers. Optics Commun. 229, 241–248 (2004)

[10] Chang, Y.T., Huang, J.F.: Complementary bipolar spectral polarization coding over fiber-grating-based differential photodetectors. Optical Engineering 45, 045004 (2006)

[11] Hu, H.W., Chen, H.T., Yang, G.C., Kwong, W.C.: Synchronous walsh-based bipolar-bipolar code for CDMA passive optical networks. J. Lightwave Technol. 25, 1910–1917 (2007)

[12] Sekine, K., Sasaki, S., Kikuchi, N.: 10 Gbit/s four-channel wavelength- and polarisation-division multiplexing transmission over 340 km with 0.5 nm channel spacing. Electron. Lett. 31, 49–50 (1995)

[13] Sotobayashi, H., Chujo, W., Kitayama, K.: 1.6-b/s/Hz 6.4-Tb/s QPSK-OCDM/WDM (4 OCDM × 40 WDM × 40 Gb/s) transmission experiment using optical hard thresholding. IEEE Photon. Technol. Lett. 14, 555–557 (2002)

[14] Tsalamanis, I., Rochat, E., Walker, S., Parker, M., Holburn, D.: Experimental demonstration of cascaded AWG access network featuring bi-directional transmission and polarization multiplexing. Opt. Express 12, 764–769 (2004)

[15] Chraplyvy, A.R., Gnauck, A.H., Tkach, R.W., Zyskind, J.L., Sulhoff, J.W., Lucero, A.J., Sun, Y., Jopson, R.M., Forghieri, F., Derosier, R.M., Wolf, C., McConnick, A.R.: 1-Tb/s Transmission Experiment. IEEE Photonics Technol. Lett. 13, 1370–1372 (2001)
[16] Poole, C.D., Wagner, R.E.: Phenomenological approach to polarization dispersion in long single-mode fibres. Electron. Lett. 22, 1029–1030 (1986)
[17] Khosravni, R., Havstad, S.A., Song, Y.W., Ebrahimi, P., Willner, A.E.: Polarization-mode dispersion compensation in WDM systems. IEEE Photonics Technol. Lett. 13, 1370–1372 (2001)
[18] Willner, A.E., Motaghian Nezam, S.M.R., Yan, L., Pan, Z., Hauer, M.C.: Monitoring and control of polarization-related impairments in optical fiber systems. J. Lightwave Technol. 22, 106–125 (2004)
[19] Heismann, F., Hansen, P.B., Korotky, S.K., Raybon, G., Veselka, J.J., Whalen, M.S.: Automatic polarisation demultiplexer for polarisation-multiplexedtransmission systems. Electron. Lett. 29, 1965–1966 (1986)
[20] Chan, E.H.W., Minasian, R.A.: Suppression of phase-induced intensity noise in optical delay-line signal processors using a differential-detection technique. IEEE Trans. Microw. Theory Tech. 54, 873–879 (2006)
[21] Poole, C.D., Bergano, N.S., Wagner, R.E., Schulte, H.J.: Polarization dispersion and principal states in a 147-km undersea lightwave cable. J. Lightwave Technol. 6, 1185–1190 (1988)
[22] Huang, J.F., Chang, Y.T.: Improved phase noise performance using orthogonal ternary codes over spectral polarization and amplitude coding networks. Opt. Eng. 46, 015005 (2007)

Robust Coverage and Performance Testing for Large-Area Wireless Networks

Caleb Phillips, Russell Senior, Douglas Sicker, and Dirk Grunwald

University of Colorado, Computer Science Department, Boulder, CO, 80303, USA
caleb.phillips@colorado.edu, russell@unwirepdx-watch.org,
{sicker,grunwald}@cs.colorado.edu

Abstract. As large-scale wireless networks continue to proliferate, a reliable way to test coverage and communicate requirements becomes increasingly important. In this paper we discuss concerns and provide guidelines to consider when developing a coverage testing methodology for large-scale wireless networks. We propose a method which complies with these guidelines and apply it to a large municipal mesh network in Portland, Oregon. This approach is at the same time simple, cost-effective, and rigorous. We use commodity hardware to perform both high and low-layer tests at a random sample of points. Our method provides insights into the "expected" performance and coverage of the network. We find that a greater density of nodes is required in Portland to provide the required level of coverage, but that at coverered areas, the performance is within specification. We are able to make these extrapolations with high statistical confidence, on a large network, using only 53 measurement points and a single measurement device which cost less than $200 USD to build.

1 Introduction

Over the past several years more and more cities, townships, and institutions have been deploying large-scale wireless networks. On the largest scale, combination infrastructure and mesh networks are being used in municipalities to cover very large areas [1,2,3]. Many such deployments have been fraught with controversy around deployment motivation, performance expectations, and business model [4]. Our position is that with a robust and rigorous coverage testing methodology, many of these controversies and unfulfilled expectations are mapped into a clear and quantifiable problem and solution space. Indeed, the best way for a municipality to ensure that expectations are met is to be clear about the coverage and performance criterion of the network, and to ensure that this is tested in a thorough way.

To date, most coverage and performance testing of large networks is carried out by contractors (e.g., [5,6]) who use proprietary and sometimes non-rigorous techniques to perform their tests. The authors of this paper devised a testing methodology while doing an independent analysis of the municipal wireless network in Portland, Oregon. This methodology not only comports with Occam's

C. Wang (Ed.): AccessNets, LNICST 6, pp. 457–469, 2009.
© ICST Institute for Computer Sciences, Social-Informatics and Telecommunications Engineering 2009

razor, it is based on low-cost and readily obtainable commodity hardware. Additionally, all techniques are passive, requiring no more access to the network than any casual observer would have. Because the methodology is simple and the hardware inexpensive, it may even be possible for some testing to be carried out by institutions and municipalities themselves. At the very least, simple and well defined approaches to coverage testing will serve to encourage transparency in the testing of contractors, which will go a long way to making results easier to interpret and validate.

Additionally, coverage and performance testing has numerous uses outside of contractual verification. Using the results from tests, network operators can create maps that accurately reflect the *usable coverage* of their network. Moreover, this testing can find gaps and problems in coverage which will help inform the deployment of large and complex networks.

In the next section we give an overview of related work. In section 3 we'll discuss the approach we take and the method we have developed. Section 4 will discuss the application of the method to a large municipal wireless mesh network in Portland and section 5 provides a summary and conclusions.

2   Related Work

To date, large-scale wireless networks have mostly been the domain of commercial vendors. As such, the technical literature contains scarce analysis. The work of Tang et al. in [2] serves as one of the few examples of an academic analysis of a large commercial wireless network. Due to limitations on the dataset, the authors are limited to offering some high-level conclusions about usage patterns.

Some researchers have looked at mapping of access points by using passive sniffing techniques while driving (colloquially called "stumbling" or "wardriving"). In [7], Byers and Kormann provide a good overview of AP mapping and in [8], geography researchers provide their mapping technique for the unplanned networks of Salt Lake City, Utah. Although such information about unplanned networks is compelling ([9] presents a scheme for architecting ubiquitous connectivity using such networks), seldom is completeness, or statistical significance considered.

The vast majority of related work has considered the planning phase of network deployment. Software such as [10,11] have been used successfully by cell network engineers and amateur radio operators. This software makes use of elevation data and RF propagation models (a Longly-Rice model is used in [10]) to make inferences about coverage. While this approach may be effective for long-range radios with high vantages, it simply does not scale down to shorter-range IEEE 802.11x mesh networks in urban environments exhibiting complex fading. It should be noted, however, that technologies such as IEEE 802.16 (WiMax), which are also being considered for municipal wireless applications, might be able to safely make use of this software for coarse-resolution planning.

More examples of work in wireless network planning include [12], where the authors propose an AP-placement algorithm which uses a measured ray-tracing model as input. The derivation of the ray-tracing model is not described in detail, and in any case, this approach is unlikely to scale to large networks – developing a ray-tracing model on the scale of a city is simply infeasable. In [13], Rodrigues et al. plan for an indoor wireless network. They divide the "demand area" into small spots. The spots are then grouped, and measurements are made at each spot-group. The criterion for size, grouping, and alignment of spots is not explained. In [3], Hills discusses the wireless network at CMU and argues for an iterative deployment process where coverage testing feeds back into deployment decisions. However, he uses signal strength alone for coverage mapping, which we will argue is insufficient. Finally, in [14], Dartmouth researchers map one access point using a GPS-enabled PDA, but do not explain how they choose where to make measurements.

3   Method

In this section we will introduce our proposed method for coverage testing of large-scale wireless networks and address concerns about accuracy and appropriateness. Overall, our method is focused on the goal of accurately inferring the usability of the network from the perspective of a typical client.

3.1   Considerations for Radio

The vagaries and complexities of the wireless medium require that measurement strategies are approached carefully. We want to make experimental assumptions that are enlightened with respect to both the properties of RF propagation [15] and of infrastructure wireless networks [14].

Signal Strength Alone Is Not Enough. We argue that neither received signal strength (RSS), nor signal to noise ratio (SNR) are appropriate measures of link quality [16], and hence, form a poor basis for inferring about usable coverage. If one wants to use distance, SNR, or any other variable alone as a single-value indication of link quality, a relationship should be experimentally derived based on the appropriate environment and the equipment. If this is done with acceptable thoroughness, it may produce coverage extrapolations that are acceptable using this value alone.

The rationale behind this reasoning is based on the premise that bidirectional communication in wireless networks requires a symmetric concept of a link: *just because a client device can hear an access point does not guarantee that the access point can hear the client device* [14]. In practice, wireless access points are often much more powerful than wireless clients. A typical outdoor access point may include a 400mW radio connected to a high-gain antenna, resulting in an equivalent isotropically radiated power (EIRP) as high as 4W[1]. In comparison,

---

[1] The Skypilot-brand radios used in Portland, Oregon, for instance, have a transmit power of 400mW and a 7.4dBi omnidirectional antenna, resulting in an EIRP of 2.2W (33.4 dBm).

a common client device might have a 30mW radio attached to a meager antenna (2-5 dBi is common in our experience) providing an EIRP of closer to 17.8 dBm (60.26mW). Although the AP's antenna will provide gain on receive as well as transmit, this cannot make up for the clear asymmetry in power and sensitivity of the two devices, which results in many situations where a client device can see a strong signal from an AP, but is unable to get its communications back to the AP[2].

Environmental Diversity. As discussed in [15], the quality of a wireless signal can vary substantially due to the location and the characteristics of the environment in which it is measured. Due to this, any scheme which purports to quantify the performance or coverage of a wireless network must give careful consideration to where measurements are made so that they do not skew the results in one direction or another. Additionally, it is not safe to use information drawn from one wireless environment to make conclusions about another – any such extrapolations should be treated with extreme skepticism.

Variation in Hardware. Wireless networking hardware varies greatly. Principally, variations in receiver sensitivity, transmit power, and antenna gain are most troublesome. Any equipment used in testing should be convincingly representative and should be carefully calibrated. If non-representative hardware is used, then a normalization procedure should be adopted and independently confirmed. Because normalization is non-trivial, we believe the easiest approach here is to use representative hardware.

Application Layer Testing. Ultimately, we believe the best way to model the usability of the network is to approach problems with the perspective of real use cases. This means that when we do a point-test of network quality we gain the most by doing application layer tests, such as throughput and latency testing in addition to low level tests (such as signal strength and noise level). Ideally, the endpoint for such tests would be very near the endpoint of the network to remove effects from outside the network.

3.2   Sampling Design

For a small network, it may be feasible to measure the entire expected coverage area. However, this quickly becomes intractable for larger networks. Choosing an appropriate statistical sampling design is crucial to draw a useful conclusion from the results. Although there are many approaches to spatial (sometimes called regional) statistical sampling, not all are appropriate for the problem.

Placing Samples. *Simple Random* Sampling (SRS) (see figure 1a) is the classic approach to this type of problem. It is simple, straight-forward, and well understood. It also applies well to spatial sampling problems. In particular, SRS

---

[2] This is especially a concern in the case when a user is indoors and the access point is outdoors, in such cases it may simply be impossible to achieve high quality of service without using a more powerful radio on the client-side.

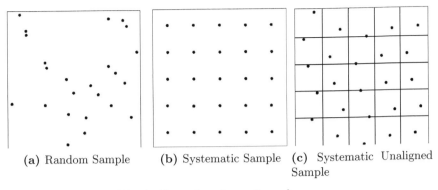

(a) Random Sample   (b) Systematic Sample   (c) Systematic Unaligned
Sample

Fig. 1. Examples of sampling schemes

is convenient in that any consecutive subset of a simple random sample is also a simple random sample itself. This means that one can create a sample of points, and then test them consecutively up until a statistical significance criterion is met. For these reasons, we believe that SRS is an excellent choice for the problem at hand.

Competing sampling schemes might include *systematic, systematic unaligned, or stratified*. Systematic sampling (see figure 1b) can be dangerous because it risks alignment bias. It is admittedly tempting, when measuring coverage, to align samples along an obvious geographic feature of cities - streets. However, we argue that aligning tests along streets has the capacity to highly bias results. Aside from degenerating to a type of one-sided stratified sampling, streets also have the capacity to act as RF wave-guides (sometimes called "street canyons" in the literature). Systematic unaligned sampling (see figure 1c) can be a good comprimise between SRS and systematic as it is more robust to alignment bias, but guarantees an even distribution of sample points among the test area. Stratified sampling is typically used when there are differences and/or differences in variability in different areas. For instance, a municipality may wish to prioritize or set different performance and coverage criterion for different areas of the city.

Dealing with Unreachable Points. It is inevitable that when testing sample points in any well designed spatial sampling scheme, some points will not be reachable. They might, for instance, be in the middle of a free-way, or a river, or on private property. These points should be measured on a best-effort basis as close to the original sample point as possible and the deviation should be carefully documented. Often, an assumption in spatial sampling is that values at geographically close points are similar. While the wireless medium is highly variable, with the exception of extreme shadowing scenarios, it is unlikely two close points will differ substantially in coverage. Hence, making a best-effort measurement in some small set of pathological cases is unlikely to significantly bias results. In the case that it does, careful documentation will be rewarded.

Sample Size. The required sample size for a certain confidence interval is dependent on the variability of the results. If an SRS is used, points can be tested up until the confidence interval narrows to the desired value.

4 Case Study: Portland, Oregon

In September of 2005, the City of Portland, Oregon issued a Request for Proposals to build and operate a "citywide broadband wireless system". In April of 2006, the City chose MetroFi (Mountain View, CA) as the winning bidder, and in the following summer the City and MetroFi signed a Non-exclusive License Agreement. Thereafter, MetroFi began to deploy their network in preparation for a December 2006 launch of a Proof-of-Concept (POC) network, as called for in the agreement. The deal was structured such that the POC network would first be built and afterward an independent third party would test it. When the City was satisfied that the POC network met its performance criteria, it would issue a Certificate of Acceptance.

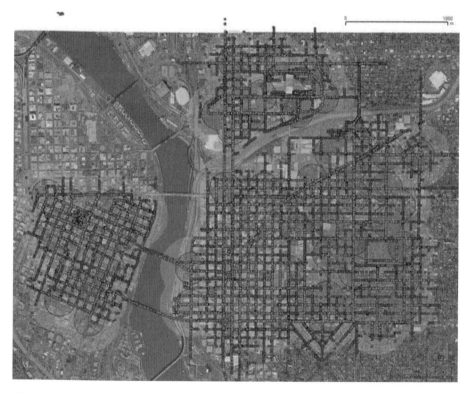

Fig. 2. Signal strength from APs in the Proof-of-Concept area. Lighter dots (green) indicate stronger signal.

Two of the authors of this paper participated in a bid for this testing, but were not selected. Despite this, on January 11, 2007, they chose to do the testing anyway for their own edification and for the benefit of others[3].

4.1   Locating Access Points

Because our tests were carried out without any access to the network infrastructure, our first task was to locate the access points in the POC area. To this end, we drove to every publicly accessible street, collecting signal strength measurements using a battery-powered embedded computer with an external 7 dBi omnidirectional antenna and a GPS device. Figure 2 plots the measured signal strengths. We used this data to triangulate the position of the APs. Not surprisingly, as other researchers have shown that signal strength is poorly correlated with distance [16], we were unable to reach a satisfactory level of precision. To obtain the desired precision, we used triangulation information to locate each AP and then took a reading with a hand-held GPS device directly under the AP.

4.2   Sampling Design

Because it is straight-forward, simple, and incurs little risk of alignment bias, we chose to use a SRS of points. From the list of 72 MetroFi access points that we considered to be in the POC network, we constructed a bounding box in latitude and longitude[4] extending 1000 feet beyond the extremities of the access point locations. Because we expected that many locations in the bounding box would fall outside of the POC areas, and because we were not certain how many locations we would be able to measure, we computed an excessive sample of 1001 locations using a random number generator such that each location in the bounding box had an equal probability of being chosen. Locations not within 1000 feet of an access point were immediately excluded. Each remaining location was plotted against orthoimagery using Google Maps. If the location fell in the Willamette River, was inside a building, or was not practically reachable, it was also excluded.

Ultimately, the first 250 locations in our sample of 1001 were either excluded on the basis of the criteria above or were visited and measured (see Figure 3). We chose to stop at 250 points after finding that this well bypassed our needs in terms of statistical power, both in the POC and overall.

4.3   Test Device and Procedure

To act as a coverage point-tester, we combined a low-cost single-board computer (a Netgear WGT634u router) with a reliable Linux-based firmware (OpenWRT GNU/Linux), a lithium-ion battery, USB GPS receiver, and USB compact-flash

---

[3] All of our data, software, and configuration for the tests is available for public inspection and reuse, as well as our full report, at http://unwirepdx-watch.org

[4] All latitude/longitude coordinates are with respect to the WGS84 ellipsoid, unless otherwise noted.

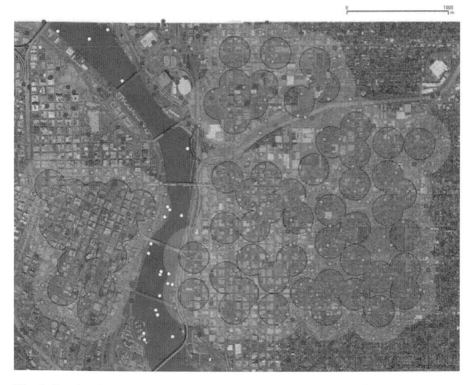

Fig. 3. Random locations and their categorization. Green (light-grey) dots were tested, purple and orange (grey) were points within the POC that were excluded because they were inaccessible, and red (dark-grey) were excluded because they were not within the POC.

storage. Figure 4 shows the device in-situ. In addition to the mandatory components, we also used a USB sound-card and a pair of small speakers to "speak" status updates along with a small bluetooth USB dongle which was used as an "enable key"[5]. All together, this testing apparatus cost less than $200 USD to build. Additionally, the Atheros 5213 802.11b/g radio and attached 2 dBi omni-directional antenna fulfill our requirement that the testing apparatus be representative of a typical client device. The test device was rigged to be free-standing at 6-feet off the ground so that the operators would not interfere with the measurements. When enabled, the test device was programed to carry out a series of tests. The outline of the testing algorithm is in table 1.

We use the standard Unix tools ttcp to test upstream throughput, ICMP ping to test latency and loss, and wget to test downstream throughput. A small script was used to bypass advertisement traps. We also found it necessary to use several watchdog scripts to check for a lost association, GPS issues, and stalled tests (for

[5] We conducted a small test to prove to ourselves that this bluetooth device was not radiating (and thus causing interference with the test device) when used this way.

Fig. 4. Testing apparatus. A battery-powered Netgear WGT634u wireless router outfitted with a GPS device, USB storage, speakers, and an enable key.

example, ttcp has a tendency take a very long time on unstable connections). Depending on the results, a random location test might take anywhere from about 60 seconds (the length of time we would wait for an association) to around 7 minutes. In addition to these steps, we also recorded GPS position and time-stamp throughout the test.

The results of each test were stored on the USB storage device. At the conclusion of the tests we retrieved and analyzed the results. In our analysis we categorized each visited location according the states in table 2. Note that this is essentially a binomially distributed Bernoulli trial - states 1 to 5 indicating failure and state 6 indicating success. Hence, we can use classic binomial hypothesis testing to analyze the results.

4.4   Results

Our first task in analyzing the results from the coverage tests is to infer a coverage percentage and a confidence interval for this inference. Figure 5 shows the P-value for an exact binomial test as the radius of points from the nearest AP changes and the hypothesized coverage percentage changes. Notice that the we reject any area where the P-value is less than $\alpha = 0.05$, which is essentially all of the combinations outside the prominent "ridgeline". In effect, the width of

Table 1. Point-testing procedure

1	Disassociate
2	Try to associate with an access point for 60 seconds
3	Record information about the physical layer (BSSID, Signal, etc.)
4	Try to obtain a DHCP lease by sending up to 10 DHCP requests
5	Attempt to pass traffic to the Internet, if unable, bypass the captive-portal
6	Test latency and loss using ping
7	Test downstream throughput with a 1MB file, and a 5MB file
8	Test upstream throughput using ttcp
9	Store the contents of the ARP table
10	Store some statistics about our test device (memory and CPU utilization, etc.)
11	Perform a traceroute to an internet host to record routing topology

Table 2. Point-test state categorization

1	Could not associate
2	Lost association mid-test
3	Could not get a DHCP lease
4	Could not pass traffic
5	Performance below specified
6	Success

the ridgeline at any radius provides the 95% confidence bounds for the coverage percentage. For instance, we can see that at 150 meters, we have acceptable P-values only between about 50% and 70%. The city of Portland contract required 90% coverage within 500 feet (approximately 150 meters) of each AP. The measured percentage covered was 44.4% overall and 63.46% within the 500-foot radius. The probability of the coverage requirement being satisfied given the overwhelming evidence against it is one in 4,451,872. According to this map, the only radii which can achieve a coverage criterion of 90% are 50 meters or less (where the P-value is near 1).

It should be noted that this value, 44.4%, indicates that less than half of *locations* within the coverage area are expected to be able to acheive a connection at the performance required by the contract. Additionally, if we include poor-performing locations, we can say that at a 95% confidence level, the percentage of locations acheiving *any connection* is between 36.08% and 54.77%. From the perspective of municipalities hoping to deploy a wireless network for the purpose of automated meter reading and other such applications, these numbers are fairly dismal and further serve to highlight the fact that it is essential that requirements are well specified and tested to ensure that both the needs of the network operator, and that of the institution or city are met.

Although the network in Portland does not meet the coverage criterion defined in the contract, we are not sure this coverage criterion was formulated in the best possible way. Instead of defining an arbitrary proof-of-concept area as a certain radius from each AP, we suggest that a more useful metric would be to define a (more conservative) percentage goal for the entire region to be covered.

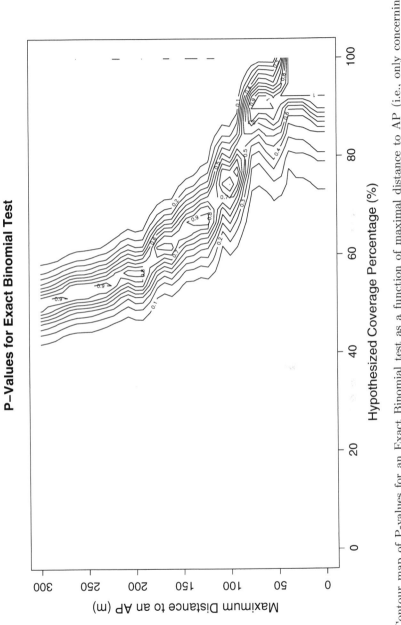

Fig. 5. Contour map of P-values for an Exact Binomial test as a function of maximal distance to AP (i.e., only concerning samples within some radius) and hypothesized coverage percent. P-values below $\alpha = 0.05$ reject the null hypothesis that the hypothesized coverage percent is possible given the observations.

Additionally, the contract should be straight-forward about the way this coverage will be tested in terms of sampling and performance goals. In the case of the network in Portland, at 44.4% it is still very low, indicating that the network operator should seriously consider increasing access-point density. Moreover, since this testing was conducted exclusively outdoors, it can be at best looked at as an extremely liberal estimate of indoor coverage.

Interestingly we find that signal strength is normally distributed among points where we could associate. A Shapiro-Wilkes test gives a p-value of 0.297 - unwilling to reject the null hypothesis that the samples are normal. Overall signal is highly variable among those points where we are successful, providing a mean value of -63.058 dBm and standard deviation of 9.625 dBm. Among those points where we could associate but failed somewhere upstream, the mean signal strength is -77.125 dBm with a standard deviation of 5.793.

State and signal are reasonably linearly correlated, showing a correlation coefficient of 0.47. This correlation is very strong if we assume signal strength -95 dBm (essentially, the noise floor) for those trials that failed to associate (the coefficient is 0.90 in this case). Distance, however, is not linearly correlated well with state or signal (correlation coefficient is -0.36).

For those tests that were successful, we collected information about the performance of the network. Averaging across the random sample allows us to provide an "expected view" of performance for those locations with a usable connection.

5   Conclusion

In this paper we have outlined a simple, but powerful, method for coverage and performance testing of large-scale wireless networks. Our proposed method utilizes a random sample of points within the coverage area to make inferences about *usable coverage* and expected performance. We argue that appropriate spatial sampling design, paired with a testing approach that both considers the perspective of the user and the complexities of the wireless medium is crucial for test results to be meaningful.

We applied this testing method to a large municipal wireless mesh network in Portland, Oregon and presented results from that study. As similar networks continue to proliferate, having a practical and effective method to test them is vital to their success and to achieving a rational way of communicating expectations.

References

1. Kramer, R.D.J., Lopez, A., Koonen, A.M.J.: Municipal broadband access networks in the netherlands - three successful cases, and how new europe may benefit. In: AcessNets 2006: Proceedings of the 1st international conference on Access networks, Athens, Greece, p. 12. ACM Press, New York (2006)
2. Tang, D., Baker, M.: Analysis of a metropolitan-area wireless network. Wireless Networks 8(2-3), 107–120 (2002)

3. Hills, A.: Large-scale wireless lan design. Communications Magazine, IEEE 39(11), 98–107 (2001)
4. Urbina, I.: Hopes for wireless cities fade as internet providers pull out. The New York Times (22) (March 2008)
5. Edx wireless (March 2008), http://www.edx.com/
6. Uptown services (March 2008), http://www.uptownservices.com/
7. Byers, S., Kormann, D.: 802.11b access point mapping. Commun. ACM 46(5), 41–46 (2003)
8. Hsu, J.: Wi-fi cloud hovers over salt lake city. IEEE Spectrum Online (February 2008), http://spectrum.ieee.org/feb08/6025
9. Sastry, N., Crowcroft, J., Sollins, K.: Architecting citywide ubiquitous wi-fi access. In: Hotnets IV (2007)
10. Magliacane, J.A.: Splat! a terrestrial rf path analysis application for linux/unix (March 2008), http://www.qsl.net/kd2bd/splat.html
11. Ericsson, "Planet ev" (March 2008),
http://www.ericsson.com/solutions/tems/network_plan/planetev.shtml
12. Kamenetsky, M., Unbehaun, M.: Coverage planning for outdoor wireless lan systems. Broadband Communications, 2002. Access, Transmission, Networking. 2002 International Zurich Seminar on, pp. 49–1–49–6 (2002)
13. Rodrigues, R., Mateus, G., Loureiro, A.: On the design and capacity planning of a wireless local area network. In: Network Operations and Management Symposium, 2000. NOMS 2000. 2000 IEEE/IFIP, pp. 335–348 (2000)
14. Kotz, D., Newport, C., Elliot, C.: The mistaken axioms of wireless-network research. Dartmouth College of Computer Science, Tech. Rep. (2003)
15. Anderson, J.B., Rappaport, T.S., Yoshida, S.: Propagation measurements and models for wireless communications channels. IEEE Communications Magazine 33, 42–49 (1995)
16. Aguayo, D., Bicket, J., Biswas, S., Judd, G., Morris, R.: Link-level measurements from an 802.11b mesh network. SIGCOMM Comput. Commun. Rev. 34(4), 121–132 (2004)

Author Index